Diversity and Society

Fifth Edition

This book is dedicated to my mother, Alice T. Healey. May she rest in peace.

—Joe

To my friends, family, and colleagues: Your support, wisdom, and humor make my life rich and beautiful. To the undergraduates reading this book: Be open and curious, be critically skeptical, work hard, and have faith. You are our hope for the future.

—Andi

SAGE was founded in 1965 by Sara Miller McCune to support the dissemination of usable knowledge by publishing innovative and high-quality research and teaching content. Today, we publish over 900 journals, including those of more than 400 learned societies, more than 800 new books per year, and a growing range of library products including archives, data, case studies, reports, and video. SAGE remains majority-owned by our founder, and after Sara's lifetime will become owned by a charitable trust that secures our continued independence.

Los Angeles | London | New Delhi | Singapore | Washington DC | Melbourne

Diversity and Society

Race, Ethnicity, and Gender

Fifth Edition

Joseph F. Healey
Christopher Newport University

Andi Stepnick
Belmont University

Los Angeles | London | New Delhi
Singapore | Washington DC | Melbourne

FOR INFORMATION:

SAGE Publications, Inc.
2455 Teller Road
Thousand Oaks, California 91320
E-mail: order@sagepub.com

SAGE Publications Ltd.
1 Oliver's Yard
55 City Road
London EC1Y 1SP
United Kingdom

SAGE Publications India Pvt. Ltd.
B 1/I 1 Mohan Cooperative Industrial Area
Mathura Road, New Delhi 110 044
India

SAGE Publications Asia-Pacific Pte. Ltd.
3 Church Street
#10-04 Samsung Hub
Singapore 049483

Acquisitions Editor: Jeff Lasser
eLearning Editor: Gabrielle Piccininni
Editorial Assistant: Alexandra Croell
Production Editor: Kelly DeRosa
Copy Editor: Cate Huisman
Typesetter: C&M Digitals (P) Ltd.
Proofreader: Theresa Kay
Indexer: Scott Smiley
Cover Designer: Gail Buschman
Marketing Manager: Johanna Swenson

Printed in the United States of America

Library of Congress Cataloging-in-Publication Data

Names: Healey, Joseph F., 1945- | Stepnick, Andi. | Healey, Joseph F., 1945- Race, ethnicity, gender, and class. Adaptation of:

Title: Diversity and society : race, ethnicity, and gender / Joseph F. Healey, Andi Stepnick.

Description: Fifth edition. | Thousand Oaks, CA : SAGE Publications, Inc., [2016] | Includes bibliographical references and index.

Identifiers: LCCN 2015038937 | ISBN 978-1-4522-7574-1 (pbk. : alk. paper)

Subjects: LCSH: Minorities—United States. | Ethnicity—United States. | Racism—United States. | Group identity—United States. | Social conflict—United States. | United States—Race relations. | United States—Ethnic relations. | United States—Social conditions.

Classification: LCC E184.A1 H415 2016 | DDC 305.800973—dc23
LC record available at http://lccn.loc.gov/2015038937

This book is printed on acid-free paper.

SUSTAINABLE FORESTRY INITIATIVE

Certified Chain of Custody
Promoting Sustainable Forestry
www.sfiprogram.org
SFI-01268

SFI label applies to text stock

17 18 19 20 10 9 8 7 6 5 4 3 2

Brief Contents

Detailed Contents

Preface

❖

Of the challenges confronting the United States today, those relating to minority groups continue to be among the most urgent and the most daunting. Discrimination and rejection of "others" are part of our national heritage. Along with equality, freedom, and justice, prejudice, racism, and sexism are among our oldest values. Minority group issues penetrate every aspect of our society, and virtually every item on the national agenda—welfare and health care reform, crime and punishment, safety in the streets, the future of the family, even defense spending, foreign policy, and terrorism—has some connection with dominant–minority relations.

The issues we face will not be resolved easily or quickly. People's feelings are intense, and controversy, indifference, and bitterness often overshadow objective analysis and calm reason. We have little hope of resolving our nation's dilemmas until we address them openly and honestly. They will not disappear, and they will not resolve themselves.

This textbook contributes to this ongoing discussion by presenting information, raising questions, and deeply examining issues. Our intent is to help undergraduate students increase their knowledge, improve their understanding of the issues, and clarify their thinking regarding the inequalities related to race, ethnicity, and gender. We have written for undergraduate students—sociology majors and non-majors alike. We assume little about students' knowledge of history or sociological concepts, and we present the material in an accessible way.

For example, we use a unified set of themes and concepts throughout the text. Our analysis is consistent and continuous, even as we examine multiple perspectives and various points of view. We introduce most of the conceptual framework in the first four chapters. We apply these concepts and analytical themes to a series of case studies of racial and ethnic minority groups. Finally, we review and summarize our main points and bring our analysis to a conclusion in the final chapter, where we also speculate about the future.

The analysis in this text is generally macro and comparative: It is focused on groups and larger social structures—institutions and stratification systems, for example—and systematically compares and contrasts the experiences and situations of America's many minorities. The text is in the tradition of conflict theory, but it is not a comprehensive statement of that tradition. We introduce and apply other perspectives, but we do not attempt to give equal attention to all current sociological paradigms, explain everything, or include all possible analytical points of view. Rather, our goals are (a) to present the sociology of minority group relations in a way that students will find understandable and intellectually challenging and (b) to address the issues (and tell the stories behind the issues) in a way that is highly readable and that demonstrates the power and importance of sociological thinking. Although this textbook presents a unified analytical framework, it offers students a wide variety of perspectives, too.

In every chapter (except the last), we present personal experiences that compellingly and dramatically foreshadow the material that follows. These introductions include the experiences and thoughts of a wide variety of people: immigrants, journalists, racists, and slaves, among others. Also, each chapter (except the last) includes a section called "Focus on Contemporary Issues" that addresses a specific issue in U.S. society that readers will find current and relevant to their lives.

The text focuses on the experiences of minority groups in the United States, but a considerable amount of comparative, cross-national material has also been included. A series of boxed "Comparative Focus" inserts explores group relations in other societies.

Additionally, the text stresses the diversity of experiences within each minority group, especially those due to one's gender, in relation to social beliefs, values, norms, and social structures. We use an intersectional perspective that explores the ways race, ethnicity, social class, gender, and sexual orientation influence one another, creating ever-shifting constellations of dominance and subordination.

Finally, we stress the ways American minority groups are inseparable from the American experience—from the early days of colonial settlements to tomorrow's headlines. The relative success of our society is due no less to the contributions of minority groups than to those of the dominant group. The nature of the minority group experience has changed as society has changed. To understand America's minority groups is to understand some elemental truths about America. To raise the issues of difference and diversity is to ask what it means, and what it has meant, to be an American.

Changes in This Edition

This edition of *Diversity and Society* incorporates notable changes.

New In-Chapter Features

- 112 new "Questions for Reflection" have been added throughout the chapters to help students analyze the material, identify key points, and recognize areas for improvement.
- "Applying Concepts" activities provide students with the opportunity to use key ideas.
- 38 new, approachable "Internet Activities" have been added to Chapters 1, 4, 5, 6, 7, and 8, and five new group activities and discussion questions to Chapter 10.

Other Changes

- Updated research findings and data are incorporated throughout the text and within tables and figures. Like previous editions, this edition relies heavily on the latest information from the U.S. Census Bureau but incorporates a wide range of recent research to make this edition fresh and relevant.

- New opening vignettes in Chapters 2, 3, 4, 5, 6, 7, and 9 foreshadow the chapter content in a personal way to generate student interest.
- Updated and expanded end-of-chapter discussion questions have been added.
- This edition includes an increased emphasis on intersectionality theory, new content on gender, and greater attention to sexual orientation in Chapters 1 and 10. New examples highlight the importance of interlocking social statuses and how they are linked to oppression.
- Updates or additions have been made to the "Comparative Focus" boxed features in Chapters 2, 3, 4, 5, 6, and 8.
- Expanded content throughout the chapters emphasizes current events and applicability of concepts and theories to contemporary social problems (e.g., racial bias in the criminal justice system, immigration issues).
- The "Main Points" chapter summaries have been updated to reflect new material.

Acknowledgments

I thank Professor Andi Stepnick for her contributions to this edition. I am very grateful for the opportunity to work with a coauthor who brings such unflagging professionalism, scholarship, and attention to detail. I also thank professors Edwin H. Rhyne and Charles S. Green, the teacher–scholars who inspired me as a student, and Eileen O'Brien, who has contributed enormously to the development of this project. Finally, I thank my colleagues, past and present, in the Department of Sociology and Anthropology at Christopher Newport University: Stephanie Byrd, Cheri Chambers, Robert Durel, Marcus Griffin, Mai Lan Gustafsson, Jamie Harris, Kai Heidemann, Michael Lewis, Marion Manton, Lea Pellett, Eduardo Perez, Iris Price, Virginia Purtle, Tracey Rausch, Andria Timmer, and Linda Waldron and Ellen Whiting. They have been unflagging in their support of this project, and I thank them for their academic, logistical, and intellectual assistance.

—Joseph F. Healey

I am grateful to Joe Healey for inviting me to participate in this project and for being such a thoughtful partner. He gave me new insights into the process of scholarship, generously offered help and encouragement along the way, and inspired me with his passion for sociology and social justice. Additionally, I am indebted to my family, friends, colleagues, and former teachers for their support, wisdom, and humor. They are too numerous to acknowledge, but I owe special thanks to Courtney Bright, Catherine Bush, Kris De Welde, Jennifer Hackett, Jennifer James, Shelby Longard, Wendy Marsh, Patricia Y. Martin, Irene Padavic, Erin Pryor, Anna Randolph, Ken Spring, Shari Stepnick, Jennifer Thomas, Ashley Virgin, the "Wild Women," and my parents. Their faith in my skill as a teacher and as a scholar has buoyed me throughout the years and on this project, specifically. Lastly, I am grateful for my students, who remind me why I do this work.

—Andi Stepnick

We both thank Nathan Davidson and Jeff Lasser of SAGE Publications for their invaluable assistance in the preparation of this manuscript, and Dave Repetto, Ben Penner, and Steve Rutter, formerly of SAGE Publications, for their help in the development of this project. Also, we thank Alex Croell and Cate Huisman for their editorial assistance.

This text has benefited in innumerable ways from reviewers who offered valuable insights about the subject matter and about the challenges of college teaching. We thank them for their expertise and for their comments, which led to significant improvements in the scholarship and clarity of this textbook. We are responsible for the shortcomings that remain.

Fifth Edition Reviewers

Ronald Huskin, Del Mar College

Roblyn Rawlins, The College of New Rochelle

Fiona Hennah, Coleg y Cymoedd

Kate D'Arcy, University of Bedfordshire

Wen Wang, California State University, Northridge

Only when lions have historians will hunters cease to be heroes.

—African Proverb

Not everything that is faced can be changed, but nothing can be changed until it is faced.

—James Baldwin

PART I

An Introduction to the Study of Minority Groups in the United States

The United States is a nation of groups as well as individuals. These groups vary in many ways, including their size, wealth, education, race, ethnicity, culture, religion, and language. Some groups have been part of U.S. society since colonial days while others have formed fairly recently.

Questions of unity and diversity are among the most pressing to face the United States today. How should these groups relate to one another? Who should be considered American? Should we preserve the many cultural heritages and languages that currently exist and stress our diversity? Should we encourage everyone to adopt Anglo

American culture and strive to become more similar? Or, should we celebrate our differences? Is it possible to do both?

We begin to address these questions and other related issues in chapters 1 and 2. Our goal is to help you develop a broader, more informed understanding of the past and present forces that have created and sustained the groups that make up U.S. society. We will sustain this focus throughout the text.

Diversity in the United States: Questions and Concepts

Who am I?... Where do I fit into American society?... For most of my 47 years, I have struggled to find answers to these questions. I am an American of multiracial descent and culture [Native American, African American, Italian American, and Puerto Rican]. In this aspect, I am not very different from many Americans [but] I have always felt an urge to feel and live the intermingling of blood that runs through my veins. American society has a way of forcing multiracial and biracial people to choose one race over the other. I personally feel this pressure every time I have to complete an application form with instructions to check just one box for race category.

—Butch, a 47-year-old man[1]

Actually, I don't feel comfortable being around Asians except for my family... I couldn't relate to... other Asians [because] they grew up in [wealthier neighborhoods]. I couldn't relate to the whole "I live in a mansion" [attitude]. This summer, I worked in a media company and it was kind of hard to relate to them [other Asians] because we all grew up in a different place... the look I would get when I say "Yeah, I'm from [a less affluent neighborhood]" they're like, "Oh, Oh" like, "That's unfortunate for your parents, I'm sorry they didn't make it."

—Rebecca, a 19-year-old Macanese-Chinese-Portuguese woman[2]

Yeah, my people came from all over—Italy, Ireland, Poland, and others too. I don't really know when they got here or why they came and, really, it doesn't matter much to me. I mean, I'm just an American.... I'm from everywhere... I'm from here!

—Jennifer, a 25-year-old white American woman[3]

What do these people have in common? How do they differ? They think about their place in U.S. society in very different ways. All are connected to a multitude of groups and traditions but not all find this fact interesting or important. One feels alienated from the more affluent members of her group, one seeks to embrace his multiple memberships, and one dismisses the issue of ancestry as irrelevant and is comfortable and at ease being "just an American."

Today, the United States is growing more diverse in culture, race, religion, and language. The number of people who can connect themselves to different cultural traditions is increasing, as is the number of Americans of mixed race. Where will this lead us? Will increasing diversity lead to greater tolerance and respect for one another? Can we overcome the legacies of racism and inequality that stretch back to colonial days? Will we fragment along these lines of difference and dissolve into warring ethnic enclaves (the fate of more than one modern, apparently unified nation)?

This text raises a multitude of questions about the past, present, and future of group relationships in U.S. society. What historical, social, political, and economic forces shaped those relationships in the past? How do racial and ethnic groups relate to each other today? What issues and problems can we expect in the years to come? Why do some people struggle with their identity? What is an American?

The United States is a nation of immigrants and groups; we have been arguing, often passionately, about what this means, about inclusion and exclusion, and about unity and diversity, since the infancy of this society. Every member of our society is in some sense an immigrant or the descendant of immigrants. Even American Indians migrated to this continent, albeit thousands of years ago. We are all from someplace else, with roots in another part of the globe. Some came here in chains; others came on ocean liners, on jet planes, or on foot. Some arrived last week and others have had family here for centuries. Each wave of newcomers has altered the social landscape of the United States. As many have observed, our society is continually becoming, permanently unfinished.

Today, the United States is remaking itself yet again. Large numbers of immigrants are arriving from all over the world, and their presence has raised questions about who belongs, what it means to be a U.S. citizen, and how much diversity we can tolerate. Even as we debate the implications of immigration, other long-standing issues of belonging, fairness, and justice remain unresolved. American Indians and African Americans have been a part of this society since its inception, but they have existed largely as "others," slaves and outsiders, servants and laborers—groups outside the mainstream, not accepted as "true Americans" or full citizens. The legacies of racism and exclusion continue to affect these groups today and, as we shall see in chapters to come, they and other American minority groups continue to suffer from inequality, discrimination, and marginalization.

Today, the definition of "American" seems up for grabs. After all, we have twice elected a black man to the most powerful position in our society (and, arguably, the world). To some, President Barack Obama's victories prove that the United States has finally become what it so often claimed to be: a truly open society and the last, best hope for all humanity.

Yet, even a casual glance at our schools, courts, neighborhoods, churches, corporate board rooms—indeed, at any nook or cranny of our society—reveals pervasive patterns of inequality, different opportunities, injustice, and unfairness. Which is the real America: the land of tolerance and opportunity, or the one of narrow-mindedness and inequity?

We may be at a crossroads in this era of growing diversity. We have an opportunity to reexamine the fundamental questions of citizenship and inclusion in this society: What is an American? How can we incorporate all groups while avoiding fragmentation and disunity? Should we celebrate our diversity or stress the need for similarity? What can hold us together?

The groups to which we belong affect our understanding of these issues and our answers to these questions. Some of us feel intensely connected to people with similar backgrounds and identify closely with our heritage(s). Others are uncertain about who they are exactly, where they fit in the social landscape. Others feel no particular connection with any tradition, group, or homeland. Still, these elements of our identity influence our lives and perceptions. They help to shape who we are and how we relate to the larger society. They affect the ways others perceive us, the opportunities available to us, the way we think about ourselves, and our view of U.S. society and what it means to be American. Finally, they impact our view of the world.

Minority Groups: Trends and Questions

The group memberships discussed in the previous section can shape the choices we make in the voting booth and in other areas of social life. Also, we need to be aware that members of different groups will evaluate these decisions in different ways. The issues will be filtered through the screens of our divergent experiences, group histories, and present situations. The debates over which direction our society should take are unlikely to be meaningful or even mutually understandable without some comprehension of the variety of ways of being American.

Increasing Diversity

The choices about the future of our society are especially urgent because the diversity of U.S. society is increasing dramatically, largely due to high rates of immigration. Since the 1960s, the number of immigrants arriving in the United States each year has tripled and includes groups, literally, from all over the globe (U.S. Department of Homeland Security, 2013b). Can our society deal successfully with this diversity of cultures, languages, and races? Concerns about increasing diversity are compounded by other long-standing minority issues and grievances that remain unresolved. For example, charts and graphs in Part 3 of this text document continuing gaps in income, poverty rates, and other measures of affluence and equality between minority groups and national norms. In fact, in many ways the problems of African Americans, American Indians, Hispanic Americans, and Asian Americans today are just as formidable as they were a generation ago.

As one way of gauging the dimensions of diversity in our nation, consider the changing makeup of U.S. society. Figure 1.1 presents the percentage of the total U.S. population in each of five groups. First, we will consider this information "on its face" and analyze some of its implications. Then, we will consider (and question) the framing of this information.

The figure reports the actual relative sizes of the groups for 1980 through 2010 and the projected relative sizes through 2060. Note how the increasing diversity of U.S. society is reflected in the declining numerical predominance of non-Hispanic whites. As recently as 1980, more than 8 out of 10 Americans were members of this group but, by the middle of this century, non-Hispanic whites will become a numerical minority.

Figure 1.1   The U.S. Population by Race and Ethnicity, 1980–2060 (Projected)

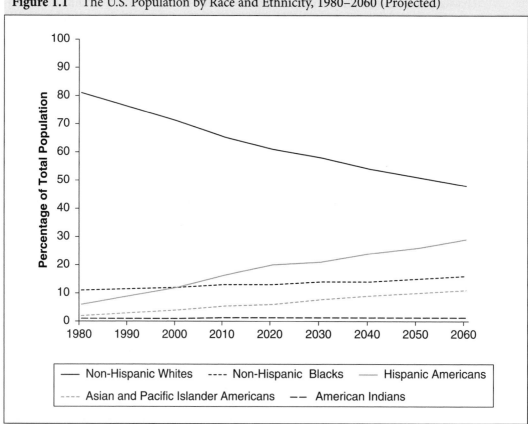

Source: U.S. Census Bureau (2012b).

Note: "Hispanics" may be of any race.

Several states (Texas, California, Hawaii, and New Mexico) are already "majority-minority," and for the first time in history, most of the babies in the United States (50.4%) are members of minority groups (U.S. Census Bureau, 2012a).

African Americans and American Indians will grow in absolute numbers but are projected to remain stable in their relative size. Hispanic American, Asian American, and Pacific Islander populations, on the other hand, will grow dramatically. Asian American and Pacific Islander groups together constituted only 2% of the population in 1980, but that figure will grow to 10% by midcentury. The most dramatic growth, however, will be among Hispanic Americans. This group became the largest minority group in 2002, surpassing blacks, and will grow to about 30% of the population by 2060.

The projections into the future are just educated guesses, of course, but they forecast profound change for the United States. As this century unfolds, our society will grow more diverse racially, culturally, and linguistically. The United States will become less white, less European, and more like the world as a whole. Some people see these changes as threats to "traditional" white middle-class American values and lifestyles. Others see them as an opportunity for other equally legitimate value systems and lifestyles to emerge.

What's in a Name?

Let's take a moment to reflect on the categories in Figure 1.1. The group names we used are arbitrary, and none of these groups has clear or definite boundaries. We use these terms because they are convenient, familiar, and consistent with the labels found in census reports, much of the sociological research literature, and other sources of information. This does not mean that the labels are "real" in any absolute sense or equally useful in all circumstances. In fact, these group names have some serious shortcomings, several of which we note here. These names are social conventions whose meanings change from time to time and place to place. To underscore the social construction of racial and ethnic groups, we use group names interchangeably (e.g., blacks and African Americans; Hispanic Americans and Latinos).

First, the people within these groups may have very little in common with each other. Any two people in one of these categories might be as different from each other as any two people selected from different categories. They may share some general, superficial physical or cultural traits, but they will also vary by social class, religion, and gender, and in thousands of other ways. People in the "Asian American and Pacific Islander" group, for example, represent scores of different national and linguistic backgrounds (Japanese, Pakistanis, Samoans, Vietnamese, and so forth), and the category "American Indian or Alaska Native" includes people from hundreds of different tribal groups.

Second, people do not necessarily use these labels when they think about their identity or who they are. In this sense, the labels are not "real" or important for all of the people in these categories. For example, many whites in the United States (like Jennifer, quoted in the opening of this chapter) think of themselves as "just an American." A Hispanic American may think of herself more in national terms, as a Mexican or a Cuban, or, even more specifically, she may identify with a particular region or village in her homeland. Gay or lesbian members of any of these five groups may identify themselves more in terms of their sexual orientation than their race or ethnicity. Still others identify most with their class. Thus, the labels do not always reflect the ways people think about themselves, their families, or where they come from. The categories are statistical classifications created by researchers and census takers to help them organize information and clarify their analyses. They do not grow out of or always reflect the everyday realities of the people who happen to be in them.

Third, even though the categories in Figure 1.1 are broad, they provide no place for a number of groups. For example, where should we place Arab Americans and recent immigrants from Africa? These groups are relatively small in size (about 1 million people each), but there is no clear place for them in these categories. Should Arab Americans be classified as "Asian"? Should recent immigrants from Africa be placed in the same category as African Americans? Of course, we don't need to have a category for every person, but we should recognize that classification schemes like the one used in Figure 1.1 (and in many other contexts) have boundaries that can be fuzzy and ambiguous.

A related problem with this classification scheme will become increasingly apparent in the years to come: there is no category for the growing number of people who (like Butch, quoted in the opening of this chapter) are members of more than one racial or ethnic group. The number of "mixed-group" Americans is relatively small today, slightly less than 3% of the total population. However, the number of people who chose more than one racial or ethnic category to describe themselves increased by 32% (from 2.4% to 2.9% of the total population) between 2000 and 2010 (Jones & Bullock, 2012) and is likely to continue to increase rapidly because of the growing number of marriages across group lines.

To illustrate, Figure 1.2 shows dramatic increases in the percentage of "new" marriages (couples that got married in the year prior to the survey date) and all marriages that unite members of different racial or ethnic groups (Wang, 2012, p. 5). Obviously, the greater the number of mixed (racial or ethnic) marriages, the greater the number of mixed Americans. One study estimates that 21% of the population will claim membership in this category by 2050 (Smith & Edmonston, 1997, p. 119).

Finally, we should note that these categories and group names are **social constructions**, created in particular historical circumstances and reflective of particular power relationships.[4] For example, the group we call "American Indians" today didn't exist prior to the European exploration and colonization of North America. Before the arrival of Europeans, hundreds of separate societies spread across the North American continent, each with its own language and culture. American Indians thought of themselves primarily in terms of their tribe and had no sense of a common identity with the other peoples that inhabited North America. However, European conquerors stressed similarities among tribes and constructed them as one group: the enemy. The fact that American Indians are often defined as a single group today reflects their historical defeat and subordination and their status as a minority group: They became the "others" in contrast to white European colonists.

Figure 1.2   Interracial and Interethnic Marriages in the United States 1980–2011

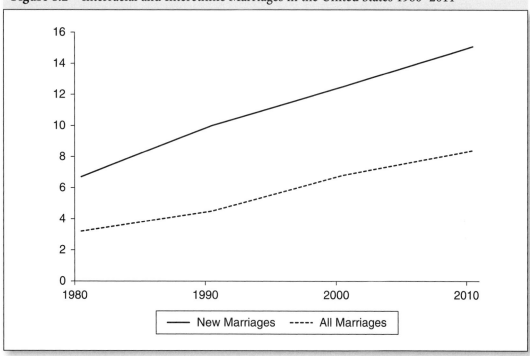

Source: Wang, Wendy. February 16, 2012. "The Rise of Intermarriage: Rates, Characteristics Vary by Race and Gender." Reprinted with permission of Pew Research Center.

In the same way (although through different processes), African, Hispanic, and Asian Americans came to be seen as separate groups not by their own choices, but as one outcome of an unequal interaction with white Americans. These groups have become "real," and much of this text is organized around a consideration of each of them (e.g., see the chapter titles in Part 3). Nonetheless, we use the terms and labels to facilitate our discussion of complex topics, not as a reflection of some unchangeable reality. These groups are real because they are seen as real from a particular perspective—that of the dominant group in this society: white Americans.

QUESTIONS FOR REFLECTION

1. If you were asked for your group membership, which of the groups listed in Figure 1.1 (if any) would you select? Do you feel that you belong to one and only one group? Are these groups part of your self-image, or are they just statistical categories? Do you think they affect your view of the world or shape your circle of friends? How?

(Continued)

(Continued)

2. Over the past 5 to 10 years, what signs of increasing diversity have you seen in your home community or high school? How has increasing diversity enriched everyday life in these areas? What problems or issues have arisen from rising diversity?

Questions About the Future, Sociology, and the Plan of This Book

Even though the labels used in Figure 1.1 are arbitrary, the trends displayed have important implications for the future of the United States. What kind of society are we becoming? What should it mean to be American? In the past, opportunity and success have been far more available to white Anglo-Saxon Protestant men than to members of other groups. Most of us, even the most favored, would agree that this definition of American is far too narrow, but how inclusive should the definition be? Should we stress unity or celebrate diversity? How wide can the limits be stretched before societal cohesion is threatened? How narrowly can they be defined before the desire to preserve cultural and linguistic diversity is unjustly and unnecessarily stifled?

We've raised a lot of question in these first few pages. The purpose of this book is to help you develop some answers and some thoughtful, informed positions on these issues. You should be aware that these questions are complex and that the answers are not obvious or easy. Indeed, there is no guarantee that we, as a society, will be able or willing to resolve all the problems of intergroup relations in the United States. However, we will never make progress unless we confront the issues honestly and with an accurate base of knowledge and understanding. Certainly, these issues will not resolve themselves or disappear if they are ignored.

In the course of our inquiry, we will rely on sociology and other social sciences for concepts, theory, and information that will help us gain a greater understanding of the issues. The first two chapters introduce and define many of the ideas that will guide our investigation. Part 2 explores how relations between the dominant group and minority groups have evolved in American society. Part 3 analyzes the current situation of U.S. racial and ethnic minority groups. In Part 4, the final section of the book, we explore many of the challenges and issues facing our society (and the world) and see what conclusions we can glean from our investigations and how they might shape the future.

What Is a Minority Group?

Before we can begin to sort out the issues, we need common definitions and a common vocabulary for discussion. We begin with the term **minority group**. Taken literally, the mathematical connotation of this term is a bit misleading because it implies that minority groups are small. In reality, a minority group can be quite large and can even be a numerical majority of the population. Women, for example, are sometimes considered to be a separate minority group, even though they are a numerical majority of the U.S. population. In South Africa, as in many nations created by European colonization, whites are a numerical minority (less than 10% of the population), but they have been the most powerful and affluent group by far and, despite recent changes, they retain their advantages in many ways.

Minority status has more to do with the distribution of resources and power than with simple numbers. We use the definition of minority group based on Wagley and Harris (1958). According to this definition, a minority group has five characteristics:

1. The members of the group experience a pattern of *disadvantage or inequality*.

2. The members of the group share a *visible trait or characteristic* that differentiates them from other groups.

3. Minority groups are *self-conscious social units*.

4. Membership in the group is usually *determined at birth*.

5. Members tend to *form intimate relationships* (close friendships, dating partnerships, and marriages) *within the group*.

We will examine each of these defining characteristics and, a bit later, we will examine the first two—inequality and visibility—in greater detail because they are the most important characteristics of minority groups.

1. Inequality. The first and most important defining characteristic of a minority group is *inequality*—that is, some pattern of disability and disadvantage. The nature of the disability and the degree of disadvantage are variable and can range from exploitation, slavery, and **genocide** to slight irritants such as a lack of desks for left-handed students or a policy of racial or religious exclusion at an expensive country club. (Note, however, that you might not agree that the irritant is slight if you are a left-handed student awkwardly taking notes at a right-handed desk or if you are a golf aficionado who happens to be African American or Jewish American.)

Whatever its scope or severity, whether it extends to wealth, jobs, housing, political power, police protection, or health care, the pattern of disadvantage is the key characteristic of a minority group. Because the group has less of what is valued by society, the term *subordinate group* is sometimes used instead of *minority group*.

The pattern of disadvantage is the result of the actions of another group, often in the distant past, that benefits from and tries to sustain the unequal arrangement. This group can be called the core group or the **dominant group**. The latter term is used most frequently in this book because it reflects the patterns of inequality and the power realities of minority group status.

2. Visibility. The second defining characteristic of a minority group is some *visible trait* or characteristic that sets members of the group apart and that the dominant group holds in low esteem. The trait can be cultural (language, religion, speech patterns, or dress styles), physical (skin color, stature, or facial features), or both. Groups that are defined primarily by their cultural characteristics are called **ethnic minority groups**. Examples of such groups are Irish Americans and Jewish Americans. Groups defined primarily by their physical characteristics are **racial minority groups**, such as African Americans or American Indians, for example. Note that these categories overlap. So-called ethnic groups may have (or may be thought to have) distinguishing physical characteristics (for example, the stereotypical Irish red hair or "Jewish nose"), and racial groups commonly have (or are thought to have) cultural traits that differ from those of the dominant group (e.g., differences in dialect, religious values, or cuisine).

These distinguishing traits set boundaries and separate people into distinct groups. The traits are outward signs that identify minority group members and help to maintain the patterns of disadvantage. That is, the dominant group has (or at one time had) sufficient power to create the distinction between groups and thus solidify a higher position for itself. These markers of group membership are crucial. Without visible signs, it would be difficult or impossible to identify who was in which group, and the system of minority group oppression would soon collapse. (We discuss a partial exception to this generalization, the Burakumin of Japan, in Chapter 8.)

It is important to realize that the characteristics that mark the boundaries between groups usually are not significant in and of themselves. They are selected for their visibility and convenience, and, objectively, they may be quite trivial and unimportant. For example, scientists have concluded that skin color and other so-called racial traits have little scientific, evolutionary, medical, or biological importance. As we shall see, skin color is an important marker of group membership in our society because it was selected during a complex and lengthy historical process, not because it has any inherent significance. These markers are social constructions that become important because we attribute significance to them.

3. Awareness. A third characteristic of minority groups is that they are *self-conscious social units*, aware of their differentiation from the dominant group, their shared disabilities, and their common fate. This shared social status can provide the basis for strong intragroup bonds and a sense of solidarity, and can lead to views of the world that are markedly different from those of the dominant group and other minority groups. Minority and dominant groups can live in different cultural worlds. For example, public opinion polls frequently show sizeable differences between dominant and minority groups in their views of the seriousness and extent of discrimination in American society. Figure 1.3 shows persistent and sizeable gaps in the percentage of nationally representative samples of whites and blacks who agree that blacks and whites have equal job opportunities. As would be expected, given their different histories, experiences, and locations in the social structure, blacks have much more negative views of racial equality, even though both groups have become somewhat more optimistic over the years. Even after the election of President Barack Obama in 2008, the percentage of black Americans who perceived that racial opportunity was equal was about half the corresponding percentage of white Americans.

Figure 1.3   Percentage of Whites and Blacks Who Believe That There Is Equal Opportunity in Their Community, 1963–2011

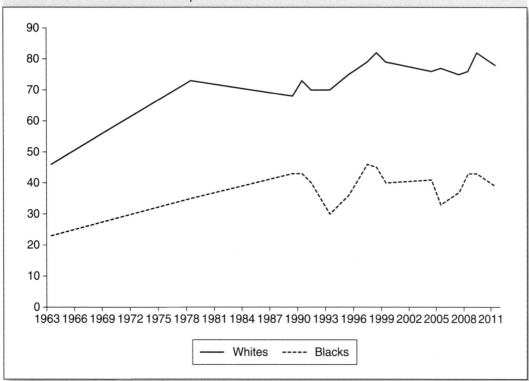

Source: Gallup Polls (2013).

4. Ascription. A fourth characteristic of minority groups is that, in general, membership is an **ascribed status**, or one determined at birth. The traits that identify minority group membership are typically not easy to change, and minority group status is usually involuntary and for life.

5. Intimate Relationships. Finally, group members tend to *form emotionally close bonds with people like themselves.* That is, members tend to choose each other as close friends, dating partners, and spouses (legal and cohabitational). (Members of the dominant group do this, too.)

This pattern is often shaped by the pervasive racial and ethnic segregation of U.S. neighborhoods, schools, and other areas of social life that influence who one meets or spends time with on a regular basis. It can be voluntary, but it can also be dictated by the dominant group. For example, interracial marriages were illegal in many states, and laws against **miscegenation** were declared unconstitutional by the U.S. Supreme Court less than 50 years ago, in the late 1960s (Bell, 1992).

This inclusive, multipart definition of minority groups encompasses "traditional" minority groups such as African Americans and American Indians, but it could be applied to other groups, also. For instance, women as a group fit the first four criteria and can be analyzed with many of the same concepts and ideas that will guide our analysis of other minority groups. Also, Americans who are gay, lesbian, bisexual, and transgender; Americans who are differently abled; Americans who are left-handed; Americans who are aged; and Americans who are very short, very tall, or very obese could fit the definition of minority group without much difficulty. In short, it is important to note that the analyses developed in this book can be applied more generally than you might realize at first. We hope that leads you to some fresh insights about a wide variety of groups and people.

QUESTIONS FOR REFLECTION

3. Do gay and lesbian Americans fit all five parts of this definition of minority groups? From some perspectives, gays and lesbians are seen as sinners, deviants, or mentally ill. Are all these views valid? Why or why not?

Patterns of Inequality

As mentioned earlier, the most important defining characteristic of minority group status is inequality. As is documented in later chapters, minority group membership can affect access to jobs, education, wealth, health care, and housing. It is associated with a lower (often much lower) proportional share of goods and services and more limited (often much more limited) opportunities for upward mobility.

Stratification, or the unequal distribution of valued goods and services, is a feature of U.S. society. Every human society, except perhaps the simplest hunter–gatherer societies, is stratified to some degree. That is, the resources of the society are distributed so that some people get more while others get less of whatever is valued. Societies are divided into horizontal layers (or strata), often called **social classes**, that differ from one another by the amount of resources they command. Figure 1.4 shows one view of the American social class system. Many criteria (such as education, age, gender, and talent) may affect a person's social class position and his or her access to goods and services. Minority group membership is one of these criteria, and it has a powerful impact on the distribution of resources in the United States and in many other societies.

The next section considers different theories about the nature and dimensions of stratification. Then, it focuses on how minority group status relates to stratification.

Theoretical Perspectives

Sociology and the other social sciences have been concerned with stratification and human inequality since the formation of the discipline in the 19th century; we highlight

Figure 1.4 Class in the United States (Gilbert-Kahn Model)

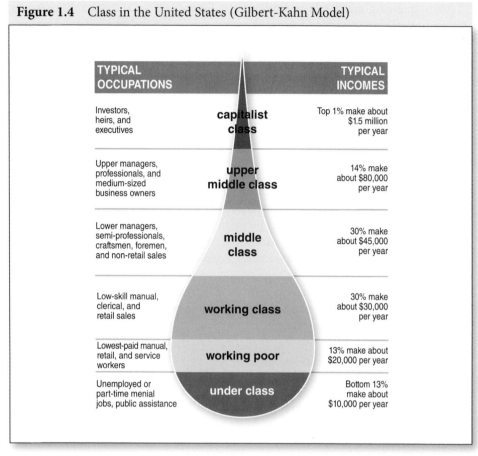

Source: Gilbert, D.L. (2011). *The American Class Structure in an Age of Growing Inequality*. Thousand Oaks, CA: Pine Forge Press.

the work of four significant thinkers in this section. An early and important contributor to our understanding of the nature and significance of social inequality was Karl Marx, the noted social philosopher and revolutionary. Half a century later, a sociologist named Max Weber, a central figure in the development of sociology, critiqued and elaborated on Marx's view of inequality. Gerhard Lenski is a contemporary sociologist whose ideas about the influence of economic and technological development on social stratification have considerable relevance for comparing societies and understanding the evolution of intergroup relations. We close with a consideration of the views of another contemporary sociologist, Patricia Hill-Collins, who argues that we need to view class, racial, gender, and other inequalities holistically and as a single, interlocking pattern.

Karl Marx. Although best known as the father of modern Communism, Karl Marx was also the primary architect of a political, economic, and social philosophy that has played a major role in world affairs for more than 150 years. Marxism is a complex theory of history and social change in which inequality is a central concern.

Marx argued that the most important source of inequality in society was the system of economic production. More specifically, he focused on the **means of production**, or the materials, tools, resources, and social relationships by which the society produces and distributes goods and services. In an agricultural society, the means of production include land, draft animals, and plows. In an industrial society, the means of production include factories, commercial enterprises, banks, and transportation systems, such as railroads.

In Marx's view, all societies include two main social classes that struggle over the means of production. One class, the **bourgeoisie** or capitalist class, owns or controls the means of production. The other, the **proletariat** or working class, is exploited and oppressed by the dominant class, whose members benefit from that arrangement. Marx believed that conflict between these classes was inevitable and that, ultimately, the working class would successfully revolt against the bourgeoisie and create a utopian society without exploitation, coercion, or inequality. In other words, they would create a classless society.

Marxism has been extensively critiqued and modified over the past century and a half. Still, modern social science owes a great deal to Marx's views on inequality and his insights on class struggle and social conflict. As you will see, Marxism remains an important body of work and a rich source of insight into group relations in industrial society (Marx & Engels, 1848/1967).

Max Weber. One of Marx's major critics was Max Weber, a German sociologist who did most of his work around the turn of the 20th century. Weber thought that Marx's view of inequality was too narrow. Marx saw social class as a matter of economic position or relationship to the means of production, but Weber argued that inequality was more complex and included dimensions other than just the economic. Individuals could be members of the elite in some ways but not in others. For example, an aristocratic family that has fallen on hard financial times might belong to the elite in terms of family lineage but not in terms of wealth. To use a more contemporary example, a major figure in the illegal drug trade could enjoy substantial wealth but be held in low esteem.

Weber expanded on Marx's view of inequality by identifying three separate stratification systems. First, economic inequality is based on ownership or control of property, wealth, and income. This is similar to Marx's concept of class, and Weber used the term *class* to identify this form of inequality.

A second system of stratification revolves around differences in **prestige**, or the amount of honor, esteem, or respect given to us by others. Class position is one factor that affects the amount of prestige a person enjoys. Other factors might include family lineage, athletic ability, and physical appearance. In the United States and other societies, the groups to which people belong affect prestige. Members of minority groups typically have less prestige than members of the dominant group. Thus, a wealthy minority group member might be ranked high on class or control of property, wealth, and income, but low on status or prestige.

Weber's third stratification system is **power**, or the ability to influence others, impact the decision-making process of society, and pursue and protect one's self-interest and achieve one's goals. One source of power is a person's standing in politically active organizations, such as labor unions or pressure groups, that lobby state and federal legislatures. Some politically active groups have access to great wealth and can use their riches to promote their causes. Other groups may rely more on their size and their ability to mobilize large demonstrations to achieve their goals. Political groups and the people they represent vary in their abilities to affect the political process and control decision making. That is, they vary in the amount of power they can mobilize.

Typically, these three dimensions of stratification go together: wealthy, prestigious groups will be more powerful (more likely to achieve their goals or protect their self-interest) than low-income groups or groups with little prestige. However, power is a separate dimension: even very impoverished groups have sometimes found ways to express their concerns and pursue their goals.

Gerhard Lenski. Gerhard Lenski is a contemporary sociologist who expands on Weber's ideas by analyzing stratification in the context of societal evolution or the **level of development** of a society (Nolan & Lenski, 2004). He argues that the nature of inequality (the degree of inequality or the specific criteria affecting a group's position) is closely related to **subsistence technology**, the means by which the society satisfies basic needs such as hunger and thirst. A preindustrial agricultural society relies on human and animal labor to generate the calories necessary to sustain life. Inequality in this type of society centers on control of land and labor because they are the most important means of production at that level of development.

In a modern industrial society, however, land ownership is not as crucial as control of financial, manufacturing, and commercial enterprises. At the industrial level of development, control of capital is more important than control of land, and the nature of inequality will change accordingly.

The United States and other societies have entered another stage of development, often referred to as **postindustrial society**. In this type of society, economic growth is powered by developments in new technology, computer-related fields, information processing, and scientific research. In the postindustrial era, economic success will be closely related to specialized knowledge, familiarity with new technologies, and education in general (Chirot, 1994, p. 88; see also Bell, 1973).

These changes in subsistence technology, from agriculture to industrialization to the "information society," alter the stratification system. As the sources of wealth, success, and power change, so do the relationships between minority and dominant groups. For example, the shift to an information-based, "hi-tech," postindustrial society means that the advantages conferred by higher levels of education will be magnified and that groups that have less access to schooling are likely to rank low on all dimensions of stratification.

Patricia Hill Collins. Sociologist Patricia Hill Collins (2000) calls for an approach to the study of inequality and group relations that recognizes the multiplicity of systems of inequality and privilege that operate in society. Some systems are based on social class, while others divide people by gender, race, ethnicity, sexuality, age, disability, and multiple other criteria. Almost everyone holds a mixed set of statuses, some more privileged and some less. For example, consider a college-educated man who holds a professional job. All of these statuses rank high in the United States. But, what if this individual is also Mexican American and gay? These statuses put him at a disadvantage in a society where whiteness and heterosexuality are more valued.

Collins stresses **intersectionality**, a view that acknowledges that everyone has multiple group memberships and that these crisscross and create very different realities for people with varying combinations of statuses. The realities faced by gay, white-collar, Mexican American men are different from those faced by heterosexual, blue-collar Puerto Rican women, even though both would be counted as "Hispanic" in Figure 1.1. There is no singular or uniform Hispanic American (or African American or Asian American) experience, and we need to recognize how gender, class, sexual orientation, and other factors intersect with and reinforce one another.

In part, Collins and other intersectionality theorists are reacting against the tendency to see inequality in terms of separate dichotomous systems, based on class (blue collar vs. white collar), race (black vs. white), gender (women vs. men), or some other criterion. An intersectional approach analyzes how these statuses link together and form a "matrix of domination." For example, white Americans are not simply the "dominant group," undifferentiated and homogenous. Some segments of this group, such as women or poor whites, may occupy a privileged status in terms of their race but be subordinate in other ways, as defined by their gender or economic status. In the same way, minority groups are internally differentiated along lines of class and gender, and members of some segments are more privileged than others. Who is the oppressed and who is the oppressor changes across social contexts, and people can occupy both statuses simultaneously.

Everyone experiences some relative degree of advantage and disadvantage, and the separate systems of domination and subordination crosscut and overlap one another. Opportunity and individual experience are shaped by this matrix of domination. For example, as we shall see in later chapters, race and gender interact with each other and create especially disadvantaged positions for people who rank lower on both dimensions simultaneously (e.g., see Figure 5.5, which shows that black women consistently fall below black men and white men and women in terms of income).

Likewise, stereotypes and other elements of prejudice are gendered. That is, they are attached to men or women, not to the entire group. For example, some stereotypical traits might be applied to all African Americans (such as laziness), but others are reserved for women (e.g., the "welfare queen" or "mammy") or men (e.g., the "thug" or "buffoon").

An intersectionality approach stresses the multiplicity of the systems of inequality and probes the links among them. Groups are seen as differentiated and complex, not uniform. In this text, one of our main concerns will be to explore how minority-group experience is mediated by class and gender using an intersectional lens. However, you can apply this approach to other dimensions of power and inequality, including disability, sexual orientation, and religion.

Minority Group Status and Stratification

The theoretical perspectives we have just reviewed raise three important points about the connections between minority group status and stratification. First, as already noted, minority group status affects access to wealth and income, prestige, and power. A society in which minority groups systematically receive less of these valued goods is stratified, at least partly, by race and ethnicity. In the United States, minority group status has been and continues to be one of the most important and powerful determinants of one's life chances, or opportunities for health, wealth, and success (e.g., education). We explore these complex patterns of inequality in Part 3, but even observation of U.S. society will reveal that minority groups control proportionately fewer resources and that minority group status and stratification are intimately and complexly intertwined.

Second, although social classes and minority groups are correlated, they are separate social realities. The degree to which one is dependent on the other varies from group to group. Some groups, such as Irish or Italian Americans, enjoy considerable **social mobility**, or easy access to opportunity even though they faced considerable discrimination in the past. Furthermore, as stressed by the intersectional approach, degrees of domination and subordination are variable and all groups are subdivided by crosscutting lines of differentiation.

Social class and minority group status are different dimensions of inequality and they vary independently. Some members of a minority group can be successful economically, wield great political power, or enjoy high prestige even though the vast majority of their group languishes in poverty and powerlessness. Each minority group is internally divided by systems of inequality based on class, status, or power, and in the same way, members of the same social class may be separated by ethnic or racial differences.

The third point concerning the connections between stratification and minority groups brings us back to group conflict. Dominant–minority group relationships are created by struggle over the control of valued goods and services. Minority group structures (such as slavery) emerge so that the dominant group can control commodities such as land or labor, maintain its position in the stratification system, or eliminate a perceived threat to its well-being. Struggles over property, wealth, prestige, and power lie at the heart of every dominant–minority relationship. Karl Marx believed that all aspects of society and culture were shaped to benefit the elite or ruling class and sustain the economic system that underlies its privileged position. The treatment of minority groups throughout American history provides a good deal of evidence to support Marx's point.

Visible Distinguishing Traits: Race and Gender

In this section, we focus on the second defining characteristic of minority groups: the visible traits that represent membership. The boundaries between dominant and minority groups have been established along a wide variety of lines, including religion, language, and occupation. Specifically, we consider race and gender, two of the more physical and stable—and thus more socially visible—markers of group membership.

Race

In the past, race has been widely misunderstood, but the false ideas and exaggerated importance attached to race have not just been errors of logic, subject to debate. In various times and places, they have been associated with some of the greatest tragedies in human history: massive exploitation and mistreatment, slavery, and genocide. Myths about race continue in the present though in diluted form. It is important to cultivate accurate understandings about race to decrease the likelihood of further tragedies.

Thanks to advances in the sciences of genetics, biology, and physical anthropology, we know more about what race is and, more importantly, what race it is not. We cannot address all of the confusion in these few pages, but we can establish a basic framework and use the latest scientific research to dispel some of the myths.

Race and Human Evolution. Our species first appeared in East Africa about 100,000 years ago. Our ancient ancestors were hunters and gatherers who gradually wandered away from their ancestral region in search of food and other resources. Over the millennia, our ancestors traveled across the entire globe, first to what is now the Middle East and then to Asia, Europe, Australia, and North and South America.

Human "racial" differences evolved during this period of dispersion, as our ancestors adapted, physically as well as culturally, to different environments and ecological conditions. For example, consider skin color, the most visible "racial" characteristic. Skin color is derived from a pigment called melanin. In areas with intense sunlight, at or near the equator, melanin screens out the ultraviolet rays of the sun that cause sunburn and, more significantly, protects against skin cancer. Higher levels of melanin and, thus, darker skin colors are found in peoples who are adapted to equatorial locations.

In peoples adapted to areas with less intense sunlight, the amount of melanin is lower, and, thus, their skin color is lighter. The lower concentration of melanin may also be an adaptation to a particular ecology, because it maximizes the synthesis of vitamin D, which is important for the absorption of calcium and protection against disorders such as rickets. In other words, the skin color of any group reflects the melanin in their skin that helps them balance the need for vitamin D against the need to protect their skin from ultraviolet rays.

Peoples with darker skin are generally found closer to the equator, whereas peoples with lighter skin are found primarily in the northern hemisphere, in locales distant from tropical sunlight. Our oldest ancestors were adapted to the equatorial sun of Africa. This almost certainly means that they were dark skinned (had a high concentration of melanin) and that lighter skin colors are the more recent adaptation.

The period of dispersion and differentiation, depicted in Figure 1.5, began to end about 10,000 years ago, when some of our hunting and gathering ancestors developed a new subsistence technology and settled down in permanent agricultural villages.

Figure 1.5 The Migration of Anatomically Modern Humans

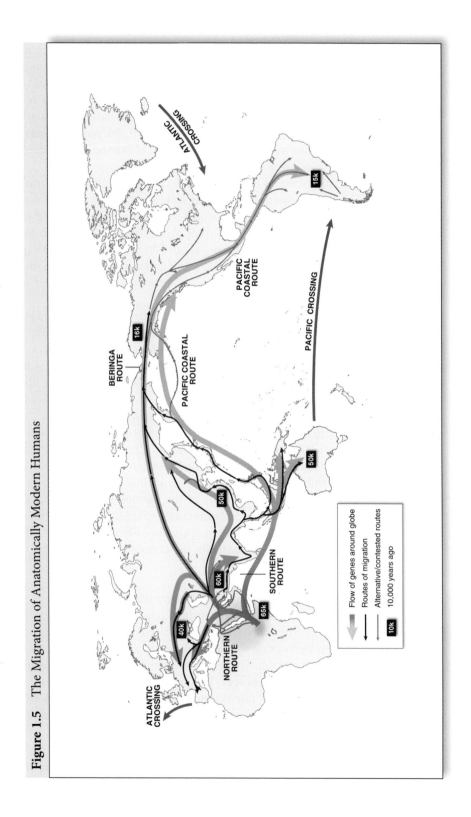

Over the centuries, some of these settlements grew into larger societies, kingdoms, and empires that conquered and absorbed neighboring societies, some of which differed culturally, linguistically, and racially from each other. The great agricultural empires of the past—Roman, Egyptian, Chinese, Aztec—united different peoples, reversed the process of dispersion and differentiation, and began a phase of consolidation and merging of human cultures and genetics. Over the 10,000 years following the first settlements, human genes were intermixed and spread around the globe, eliminating any "pure" races (if such ever existed).

The differentiation created during the period of global dispersion was swamped by the consolidation that continues in the present. In our society, consolidation manifests itself in the increasing numbers of people of mixed-race descent, and similar patterns are common across the globe and throughout more recent human history. The consolidation phase accelerated beginning about 500 years ago with the expansion of European power that resulted in the exploration and conquest of much of the rest of the world.

Race and Western Traditions. Aided by breakthroughs in navigation and ship design, the people of Western Europe began to travel to Africa, Asia, and eventually North and South America in the 1400s. Europeans had been long aware of racial variation, but their concern with race increased as they came into continuous contact with the peoples of these continents and became more aware of and curious about the physical differences they saw.

Europeans also conquered, colonized, and sometimes destroyed the peoples and cultures they encountered. From the beginning, the European awareness of the differences between the races was linked to notions of inferior and superior (conquered versus conquering) peoples. For centuries, the European tradition has been to see race in this political and military context and to intermix biological and physical variation with judgments about the relative merits of the various races. Racist thinking has been used to justify military conquest, genocide, exploitation, and slavery. The toxic form of racism that bloomed during the expansion of European power continues to haunt the world today and was the basis for the concept of race that took root in the United States.

Race and Biology. While Europeans generally used race primarily to denigrate, reject, and exclude non-whites, some attempted to apply the principles of scientific research to the concept. These investigations focused on the construction of typologies or taxonomies, systems of classification that were intended to provide a category for every race and every person. Some of these typologies were quite elaborate and included scores of races and subraces. For example, the Caucasian race was often subdivided into Nordics (blond, fair-skinned Northern Europeans), Mediterraneans (dark-haired Southern Europeans), and Alpines (people falling between the first two categories).

One major limitation of these systems of classification was that the dividing lines between the so-called racial groups are arbitrary and blurred. There is no clear or definite point where, for example, "black" skin color stops and "white" skin color begins. The characteristics used to define race blend imperceptibly into each other, and one racial trait (skin color) can be blended with others (e.g., hair texture) in an infinite variety of ways. A given individual might have a skin color that is associated with one race, the hair texture of a second, the nasal shape of a third, and so forth.

Even the most elaborate racial typologies could not handle the fact that many individuals fit into more than one category or none at all. Although people undeniably vary in their physical appearance, these differences do not sort themselves out in a way that permits us to divide people up as we do species of animals. The differences between the so-called human races are not at all like the differences between elephants and butterflies. The ambiguous and continuous nature of racial characteristics makes it impossible to establish categories that have clear, nonarbitrary boundaries.

Over the past several decades, rapid advances in genetics have provided additional information and new insights into race that continue to refute many racial myths and further undermine the validity of racial typologies. Perhaps the most important single finding of modern research is that genetic variation *within* the "traditional" racial groups is greater than the variation *among* those groups (American Sociological Association, 2003). In other words, any two randomly selected members of, say, the "black" race are likely to vary genetically from each other at least as much as they do from a randomly selected member of the "white" race. No single finding could be more destructive of traditional racial categories that are, after all, intended to group people into homogenous categories. Just as certainly, the traditional American perception of race based primarily on skin color has no scientific validity.

The Social Construction of Race. Despite its limited scientific usefulness, race continues to animate intergroup relations in the United States and around the world. It continues to be socially important and a significant way of differentiating among people. Race, along with gender, is one of the first things people notice about one another. In the United States, we still tend to see race as a simple, unambiguous matter of skin color alone and to judge everyone as belonging to one and only one group, ignoring the realities of multiple ancestry and ambiguous classification.

How can the concept retain its relevance? Because of the way they developed, Western concepts of race have a social as well as a biological or scientific dimension. To sociologists, race is a social construction, and its meaning has been created and sustained not by science but by historical, social, economic, and political processes (see Omi & Winant, 1986; Smedley, 2007). For example, in Chapter 3 we will analyze the role of race in the creation of American slavery and will see that the physical differences between blacks and whites became important *as a result of* the creation of that system of inequality. The elites of colonial society needed to justify their unequal treatment of Africans and seized on the obvious differences in skin color, elevated it to a matter of supreme importance, and used it to justify the enslavement of blacks. In other words, the importance of race was socially constructed as the result of a particular historical conflict, and it remains important not because of objective realities, but because of the widespread, shared social perception that it is important.

Gender

You have already seen that minority groups can be internally divided by social class and other factors. An additional source of differentiation is gender. Like race, gender has both a biological and a social component and can be a highly visible and convenient way of judging and sorting people. From birth, the biological differences between the sexes form the basis for different **gender roles**, or societal expectations about proper behavior, attitudes, and personality traits. In the contemporary United States, nurturance, interpersonal skills, and "emotion work" (Hochschild, 1979) tend to be stressed for girls, while boys are expected to learn to be assertive and independent.

Gender roles and relationships vary across time and from one society to another, but gender and inequality have usually been closely related. Typically, men possess more property, prestige, and power. Figure 1.6 provides some perspective on the variation in gender inequality across the globe. The map shows the distribution of a statistic called the Gender Inequality Index, which measures the amount of inequality between men and women across a range of variables including education, health, and political representation. As you can see, gender equality is generally highest in the more developed, industrialized nations of North America and Western Europe and lowest in the less developed, more agricultural nations of sub-Saharan Africa.

Part of the problem is that all societies, including Western Europe and North America, have strong traditions of **patriarchy**, or men's dominance. Parallel to the various forms of racism that sought to justify and continue racial inequality, women have been subjected to **sexism**, or belief systems that "explained" inequality based on gender. Women, for example, were sometimes seen in traditional cultures as "delicate flowers," too emotional and physically weak for the harsh demands of "manly" occupations outside the home. (Note that, in the American tradition, this view has a racial component and has been applied to white women only. The same men who placed white women on a pedestal did not hesitate to send women of color into the fields to perform the most difficult, physically demanding, "unfeminine" tasks.)

Even in the most progressive societies, women continue to possess many characteristics of a minority group (namely, a pattern of disadvantage based on group membership marked by a physical characteristic). Thus, women could be, and in many ways should be, treated as a separate minority group, but throughout the text, we will address the divergent experiences of men and women within each minority group. We will consider how the interests and experiences of women of different groups and classes coincide with and diverge from one another and from those of the men in their groups. For example, on some issues African American women might have interests identical to those of white women and opposed to those of African American men, and on other issues the constellations of interests might be reversed. As stressed in the intersectionality approach, the experience of minority group membership varies by gender (along with other criteria), and the way gender is experienced is not the same for every group.

History generally has been and is written from the standpoint of the "winners"—that is, those in power. The voices of minority groups have generally been repressed, ignored, forgotten, or trivialized. Much of the history of slavery in America, for

Figure 1.6   Gender Inequality Worldwide (2012)

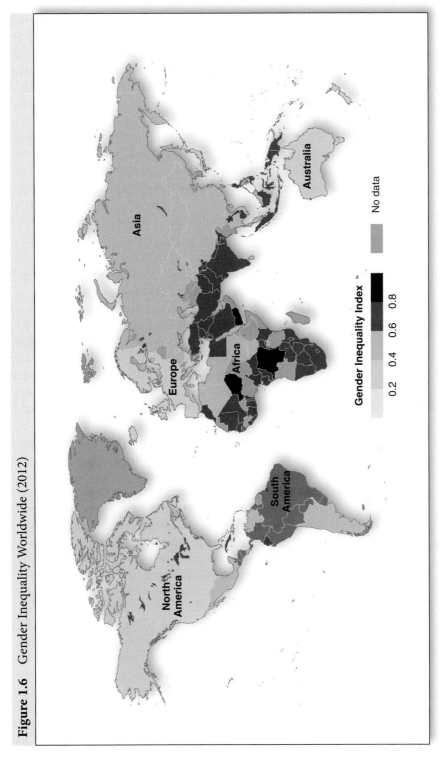

Source: Florida (2012). From "The Geography of Women's Economic Opportunities" by Richard Florida. The Atlantic Cities. January 11, 2012. Map by Zara Matheson of the Martin Prosperity Institute. Reprinted with permission.

instance, has been told from the viewpoint of the slave owners. Slaves were kept illiterate by law and had few mechanisms for recording their thoughts or experiences. A more balanced and accurate picture of slavery began to emerge only in the past few decades, when scholars began to dig beneath the written records and memoirs of the slave owners and reconstruct the experiences of African Americans from nonwritten materials such as oral traditions and the physical artifacts left by the slaves.

However, our understanding of the experiences of minority groups is often based almost entirely on the experiences of minority group men. The experiences of women minorities are much less well known and documented. If the voices of minority groups have been hushed, those of woman minority group members have been virtually silenced. One of the important trends in contemporary scholarship is to adjust this skewed focus and systematically incorporate gender as a factor that is vital to our understanding of minority group experiences (Baca Zinn & Thornton Dill, 1994; Espiritu, 1996).

The Social Construction of Gender. Social scientists see race as a social construction formulated in certain historical circumstances (such as the era of European colonialism) when it was needed to help justify the unequal treatment of non-white groups. What about gender? Is it also merely a social creation designed to rationalize the higher status of men and their easier access to power, prestige, and property? Figure 1.6 shows that all contemporary nations have some degree of gender inequality. Is this because—as many people believe—boys and men are "naturally" more aggressive and independent, and girls and women are more emotional and expressive? What is the basis of these distinctions? What connection, if any, do they have with biology and genetics?

First, the traits commonly seen as "typical" of men or women—aggressiveness or emotional expressiveness, for example—are not disconnected, separate categories. Every person has these qualities to some degree. To the extent that gender differences exist at all, they are manifested not in absolutes but in averages, tendencies, and probabilities. Many people consider aggressiveness to be a masculine characteristic, but many women are more aggressive than many men. Likewise, emotionality tends to be associated with women but many men are more expressive and emotional than many women. As with racial differences, research shows that there is more variation *within* gender categories than among them—a finding that seriously undermines the view that gender differences are genetic or biological (Basow, as cited in Rosenblum & Travis, 2002).

Second, that gender is a social construction is illustrated by the fact that what is thought to be "appropriate" gender behavior varies from time to time and from society to society. The behavior expected of a woman in Victorian England would be thoroughly out of place in 21st century America, and the typical behavior of a contemporary man would be regarded as outrageously scandalous in Puritan America. This variability makes it difficult to argue that the differences between the genders are "hardwired" in the genetic code; if they were, the variations over time and place would be nonexistent.

Third, the essentially social nature of gender roles is further illustrated by the relationship between subsistence technology and gender inequality. As we noted previously, our species evolved in East Africa and relied on hunting and gathering to satisfy their need for food. Our distant ancestors lived in small, nomadic bands that relied on cooperation and sharing for survival. Societies at this level of development typically divide adult labor roles by gender (with men hunting and women gathering) and, although they may tend toward patriarchy, women and women's work are highly valued and gender inequality is minimal. The subordination of women is more closely associated with settled agricultural communities, the first of which appeared about 10,000 years ago in what is now the Middle East. Survival in preindustrial farming societies requires the combined efforts of many people; thus, large families are valued as a cheap labor force. Women are consigned to household and domestic duties, with a strong emphasis on producing and raising children. Since the infant mortality rate in these societies is high (approximately 50% or more), women spend much of their lives confined and secluded, pregnant or nursing young children, far removed from the possibility of contending for leadership roles in their communities.

Industrialization and urbanization, linked processes that began in the mid-1700s in Great Britain, changed the cost–benefit ratios for childbearing. The expenses associated with having children rose in the city, and the nature of industrial work increasingly required education and literacy—qualities and abilities available to both genders. Thus, gender inequality probably reached its peak in preindustrial agrarian societies and has tended to decline as societies industrialized. It is no accident of timing that the push for gender equality and the women's liberation movement is associated with industrial societies and that gender equality is highest today in industrial and postindustrial societies (see Figure 1.6).

Biology may shape one's personality to some degree, and researchers continue to explore the links between genetics and gender roles (e.g., see Hopcroft, 2009; Huber, 2007; Udry, 2000) as well as the interaction between them. However, at its core, gender is social and experiential, not biological (Booth, Granger, Mazur, & Kivligham, 2006, pp. 167–191; see also Ridgeway, 2011, pp. 18–23). Gender, like race, is a social construction, especially when the supposed differences between men and women are treated as categorical, "natural," and fixed, and then used to deny opportunity and equality to women.

QUESTIONS FOR REFLECTION

4. Are both gender and race *merely* social constructions? Aren't they *real* in some ways? In what ways do they exist apart from people's perception of them? Are they both social constructions in the same way? Are they *equally* matters of perception?

Key Concepts in Dominant–Minority Relations

Whenever sensitive issues such as dominant–minority group relations are raised, the discussion often turns to matters of prejudice and discrimination. We need to clarify what we mean by these terms. This section introduces and defines four concepts that will help you understand dominant–minority relations in the United States.

This book addresses how individuals from different groups interact, as well as how groups interact with each other. Thus, we need to distinguish between what is true for individuals (the more psychological level of analysis) and what is true for groups or society as a whole (the more sociological level of analysis). Beyond that, we must attempt to trace the connections between these two levels of analysis.

At the individual level, what people think and feel about other groups may differ from how they actually behave toward members of another group. A person might express negative feelings about other groups in private but deal fairly with members of the group in face-to-face interactions. Groups and entire societies may display this same kind of inconsistency. A society may express support for equality in its official documents or formal codes of law and simultaneously treat minority groups in unfair and destructive ways. An example of this kind of inconsistency is the contrast between the commitment to equality stated in the Declaration of Independence ("All men are created equal") and the actual treatment of black slaves, Anglo American women, and American Indians at that time.

At the individual level, social scientists refer to the "thinking/feeling" part of this dichotomy as prejudice and the "doing" part as discrimination. At the group level, the term **ideological racism** describes the "thinking/feeling" dimension and **institutional discrimination** describes the "doing" dimension. Table 1.1 depicts the differences among these four concepts.

Prejudice

Prejudice is the tendency of an individual to think about other groups in negative ways, to attach negative emotions to those groups, and to prejudge individuals on the basis of their group memberships. Individual prejudice has two aspects: **cognitive prejudice**, or the thinking aspect, and **affective prejudice**, or the feeling part. A prejudiced person thinks about other groups in terms of **stereotypes** (cognitive prejudice), generalizations that he or she thinks apply to group members. Examples of familiar stereotypes include notions such as "women are emotional," "Jews are stingy," "blacks

Table 1.1 Four Concepts in Dominant-Minority Relations

	Level of Analysis	
Dimension	*Individual*	*Group or Societal*
Thinking/feeling	Prejudice	Ideological racism
Doing	Discrimination	Institutional discrimination

are lazy," "the Irish are drunks," and "Germans are authoritarian." A prejudiced person also experiences negative emotional responses to other groups (affective prejudice), including contempt, disgust, arrogance, and hatred.

People vary in their levels of prejudice, and levels of prejudice vary in the same person from one time to another and from one group to another. We can say that people are prejudiced to the extent that they use stereotypes in their thinking about other groups or have negative emotional reactions to other groups.

Generally, the two dimensions of prejudice are highly correlated with each other; however, they are distinct and separate aspects of prejudice that can vary independently. One person may think entirely in stereotypes but feel no particular negative emotional response to any group. Another person may feel a very strong aversion toward a group but be unable to articulate a clear or detailed stereotype of that group.

We should note here that individual prejudice, like all aspects of society, evolves and changes. In the past, American prejudice was strongly felt, baldly expressed, and laced with clear, detailed stereotypes. In modern societies in which there is a strong emphasis on mutual respect and tolerance, prejudice tends to be expressed in subtle, indirect ways. For example, it might be manifested in code words, as when people disparage "welfare cheats" or associate criminality with certain minority groups. We will explore the modern forms of prejudice further, but we need to be clear that the relative absence of blatant stereotyping or expressions of strong public emotions against minority groups in modern society does not mean that we have eliminated individual prejudice in the United States.

Causes of Prejudice

American social scientists have made prejudice a primary concern of their research and have produced thousands of articles and books on the topic, asking a wide array of different questions from a variety of theoretical perspectives. One firm conclusion is that prejudice is not a single, unitary phenomenon. It has a variety of possible causes (some more psychological and individual, others more sociological and cultural) and can present itself in a variety of forms (some blatant and vicious, others subtle and indirect). No single theory has emerged that can explain prejudice in all its complexity. In keeping with the macro sociological approach of this text, we will focus primarily on the theories related to culture, social structure, and group relationships.

Competition Between Groups and the Origins of Prejudice. Every form of prejudice—even the most ancient—started at some specific point in history. If we go back far enough in time, we can find a moment that predates anti-black prejudice, anti-Semitism, negative stereotypes about American Indians or Hispanic Americans, or antipathy against Asian Americans. What sorts of conditions create prejudice?

The most important single factor in the origin of prejudice is competition between groups: prejudice originates in the heat of that competition and is used to justify and rationalize the privileged status of the winning group. If we go back far enough, we can always find some instance in which one group successfully dominates, takes resources from, or eliminates a perceived threat by another group. The successful group becomes the dominant group, and the other becomes the minority group.

Why is group competition associated with the emergence of prejudice? Typically, prejudice is more the result of the competition rather than a reason for it. Its role is to help mobilize emotional energy for the conflict, justify rejection and attack, and rationalize the structures of domination, like slavery or segregation, that result from the competition. Groups react to the competition and to the threat presented by other groups with antipathy and stereotypes about the "enemy" group. Prejudice emerges from the high levels of emotion but then can solidify and persist for years (even centuries) after the end of the conflict.

The relationship between prejudice and competition has been demonstrated in a variety of settings and situations ranging from labor strikes to international war to social psychology labs. In the chapters to come, we will examine the role of prejudice during the creation of slavery in North America, as a reaction to periods of high immigration, and as an accompaniment to myriad forms of group competition. Here, to illustrate our central point about group competition and prejudice, we will examine a classic experiment from the sociological literature. The experiment was conducted in the 1950s at a summer camp for 11- and 12-year-old boys known as Robber's Cave.

The camp director, social psychologist Muzafer Sherif, divided the campers into two groups, the Rattlers and the Eagles (Sherif, Harvey, White, Hood, & Sherif, 1961). The groups lived in different cabins and were continually pitted against each other in a wide range of activities. Games, sports, and even housekeeping chores were set up on a competitive basis. The boys in each group developed and expressed negative feelings (prejudice) against the other group. Competition and prejudicial feelings grew quite intense and were manifested in episodes of name calling and raids on the "enemy" group.

Sherif attempted to reduce the harsh feelings he had created by bringing the campers together in various pleasant situations featuring food, movies, and other treats. But the rival groups only used these opportunities to express their hostility. Sherif then came up with some activities that required the members of the rival groups to work cooperatively with each other. For example, the researchers deliberately sabotaged some plumbing to create an emergency that required the efforts of everyone to resolve. As a result of these cooperative activities, intergroup "prejudice" was observed to decline, and, eventually, friendships formed across groups.

In the Robber's Cave experiment, as in many actual group relationships, prejudice (negative feelings and stereotypes about other campers) arose to help mobilize feelings and to justify rejection and attacks, both verbal and physical, against the out-group. When group competition was reduced, the levels of prejudice abated and eventually disappeared, again demonstrating that competition causes prejudice, and not the other way around.

Although the Robber's Cave experiment illustrates our central point, we must be cautious in generalizing from these results. The experiment was conducted in an artificial environment with young boys (all white) who had no previous acquaintance with each other and no history of grievances or animosity. Thus, these results may be only partially generalizable to group conflicts in the "real world." Nonetheless, Robber's Cave illustrates a fundamental connection between group competition and prejudice that we will observe repeatedly in the chapters to come. Competition and the desire to protect resources and status and to defend against threats—perceived or real—from other groups are the primary motivations for the creation of prejudice and structures of inequality that benefit the dominant group.

QUESTIONS FOR REFLECTION

5. How are the ideas presented in this section sociological? How do they differ from more psychological theories of prejudice and discrimination?

Culture, Socialization, and the Persistence of Prejudice. Prejudice originates in group competition but often outlives the conditions of its creation. It can persist, full-blown and intense, long after the episode that sparked its creation has faded from memory. How does prejudice persist through time?

In his classic analysis of American race relations, *An American Dilemma* ([1944] 1962), Swedish economist Gunnar Myrdal proposed the idea that prejudice is perpetuated through time by a self-fulfilling prophecy or a **vicious cycle of prejudice**, as illustrated in Figure 1.7. The dominant group uses its power to force the minority group into an inferior status, such as slavery, as shown in the diagram in Area 1. Partly to motivate the construction of a system of racial stratification and partly to justify its existence, individual prejudice and racist belief systems are invented and accepted by the dominant group, as shown in Area 2. Individual prejudices are reinforced by the everyday observation of the inferior status of the minority group. The fact that the minority group is in fact impoverished, enslaved, or otherwise exploited, confirms and strengthens the attribution of inferiority. The belief in inferiority motivates further discrimination and unequal treatment, as shown in Area 3 of the diagram, which reinforces the inferior status, which validates the prejudice and racism, which justifies further discrimination, and so on. Over a few generations, a stable, internally reinforced system of racial inferiority and an elaborate, widespread set of prejudiced beliefs and feelings can become an integral, unremarkable, and (at least for the dominant group) accepted part of everyday life.

Culture is slow to change, and, once created, prejudice will be sustained over time just like any set of attitudes, values, and beliefs. Future generations will learn prejudice in the same way and for the same reasons that they learn any other aspect of their culture. Thus, prejudice and racism come to us through our cultural heritage as a package of stereotypes, emotions, and ideas. We learn which groups are "good" and which are "bad" in the same way we learn table manners and religious beliefs (Pettigrew, 1958, 1971, p. 137; Simpson & Yinger, 1985, pp. 107, 108). When prejudice is part of the cultural heritage, individuals learn to think and feel negatively toward other groups

Figure 1.7 Myrdal's Vicious Cycle

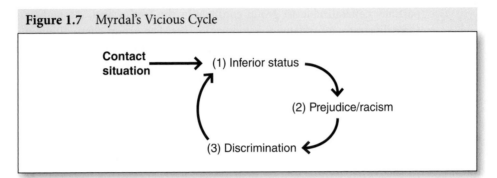

Source: Myrdal (1944/1962).

as a routine part of socialization. Much of the prejudice expressed by Americans—and the people of many other societies—is the normal result of a typical socialization in families, communities, and societies that are, to some degree, racist. Given our long history of intense racial and ethnic exploitation, it is not surprising that Americans continue to manifest antipathy toward and stereotypical ideas about other groups.

The Development of Prejudice in Children. The idea that prejudice is learned during socialization is reinforced by studies of the development of prejudice in children. Research generally shows that children become aware of group differences (e.g., black vs. white) at a very early age, perhaps as early as six months (Katz, 2003, p. 898). By age three or younger, they recognize the significance and the permanence of racial groups and can accurately classify people on the basis of skin color and other cues (Brown, 1995, pp. 121–136; Katz, 1976, p. 126). Once the racial or group categories are mentally established, the child begins the process of learning the "proper" attitudes and stereotypes to associate with the various groups; both affective and cognitive prejudice begin to grow at an early age.

It is important to note that children can acquire prejudice even when parents and other caregivers do not teach it overtly or directly. Adults control the socialization process and valuable resources (food, shelter, praise), and children are motivated to seek their approval and conform to their expectations (at least in the early years). There are strong pressures on the child to learn and internalize the perceptions of the older generation, and even a casual comment or an overheard remark can establish or reinforce negative beliefs or feelings about members of other groups (Ashmore & DelBoca, 1976). Children need not be directly instructed about presumed minority group characteristics; it is often said that racial attitudes are "caught and not taught."

Additionally, research shows that children are actively engaged in their learning and that their levels of prejudice reflect their changing intellectual capabilities. Children as young as five to six months old can make some simple distinctions (e.g., by gender or race) between categories of people. The fact that this capability emerges so early in life suggests that it is not simply a response to adult teaching. "Adults use categories to simplify and make sense of their environment; apparently children do the same" (Brown, 1995, p. 126). Gross, simplistic distinctions between people may help very young children organize and understand the world around them. The need for such primitive categorizations may decline as the child becomes more experienced in life and more sophisticated in his or her thinking. Doyle and Aboud (1995), for example, found that prejudice was highest for younger children and actually decreased between kindergarten and the third grade. The decline was related to increased awareness of racial similarities (as well as differences) and diverse perspectives on race (see also Black-Gutman & Hickson, 1996; Bronson & Merryman, 2009; Brown, 1995, pp. 149–159; Cristol & Gimbert, 2008; Powlishta, Serbin, Doyle, & White, 1994; Van Ausdale & Feagin, 2001). Thus, changing levels of prejudice in children may reflect an interaction between children's changing mental capacities and their environment rather than a simple or straightforward learning of racist cultural beliefs or values.

Social Distance Scales. Further evidence for the cultural nature of prejudice is provided by research on the concept of **social distance**, which is related to prejudice but is not quite the same thing. Social distance is the degree of intimacy that a person is willing to accept in his or her relations with members of other groups. On this scale, the most intimate relationship would be close kinship, and the most distant relationship would be exclusion from the country. The inventor of the social distance scale was Emory Bogardus (1933), who specified a total of seven degrees of social distance:

1. To close kinship by marriage

2. To my club as personal chums

3. To my street as neighbors

4. To employment in my occupation

5. To citizenship in my country

6. As visitors only to my country

7. Would exclude from my country

Research using social distance scales demonstrates that Americans rank other groups in similar ways across time and space. The consistency indicates a common frame of reference or set of perceptions, a continuity of vision possible only if perceptions have been standardized by socialization in a common culture.

Table 1.2 presents some results of seven administrations of the scale to samples of Americans from 1926 to 2011. The groups are listed by the rank order of their scores for 1926. In that year, the sample expressed the least social distance from the English and the most distance from Asian Indians. While the average social distance score for the English was 1.02, indicating virtually no sense of distance, the average score for Indians was 3.91, indicating a distance between "to my street as neighbors" to "to employment in my occupation."

APPLYING CONCEPTS

Do you have a sense of social distance from different groups? Has it changed over the past 10 years? Use the seven degrees of social distance to indicate the level of intimacy you would feel comfortable sharing with members of each of the groups listed. Also, estimate the degree of social distance you would have felt for each group 10 years ago.

How did you acquire your sense of social distance? Was it from your family or community, or is it based on actual experience with members of these groups? Do you think it was "caught and not taught"? Why has it changed over the past 10 years (if it has)?

Group	Your Social Distance Score Today	Your Social Distance Score 10 Years Ago
White Americans		
Irish		
Russians		
Italians		
American Indians		
Jews		
Mexicans		
African Americans		
Chinese		
Muslims		

TURN TO TABLE 1.2 ON THE NEXT PAGE TO SEE THE RANKINGS OF THESE GROUPS OVER THE YEARS.

First, as you inspect Table 1.2, note the stability in the rankings. The actual *scores* (not shown) generally decrease from decade to decade, indicating less social distance and presumably a decline in prejudice over the years. The group rankings, however, tend to be the same year after year. Considering the changes that society has experienced between 1926 and 2011 (the Great Depression; World War II, the Korean War, and other wars; the Cold War with the former Soviet Union; the civil rights movement; the resumption of large-scale immigration, etc.), this overall continuity in group rankings is remarkable.

Second, note the nature of the ranking: groups with origins in Northern and Western Europe are ranked highest, followed by groups from Southern and Eastern Europe, with racial minorities near the bottom. These preferences reflect the relative

Table 1.2   Social Distance Scores of Selected Groups (Ranks for Each Year)

Group	1926	1946	1977	2011
English (British)	1	3	2	4
Americans (white)	2	1	1	1
Canadians	3	2	3	3
Irish	5	4	7	5
Germans	7	10	11	8
Russians	13	13	29	20
Italians	14	16	5	2
Poles	15	14	18	14
American Indians	18	20	10	12
Jews	19	19	15	11
Mexicans	21	24	26	25
Japanese	22	30	25	22
Filipinos	23	23	24	16
African Americans	24	29	17	9
Turks	25	25	28	—
Chinese	26	21	23	17
Koreans	27	27	30	24
Asian Indians	28	28	27	26
Vietnamese	—	—	—	28
Muslims	—	—	—	29
Arabs	—	—	—	30
Mean (all scores)	2.14	2.12	1.93	1.68
Range	2.85	2.57	1.38	1.08

Sources: 1926 to 1977, Smith & Dempsey (1983, p. 588); 2011, Parrillo & Donoghue (2013).

Note: Values in the table are ranks for that year. To conserve space, some groups and ranks have been eliminated. Scores are the group's rank for the year in question. For example, the Irish were ranked fifth of 28 groups in 1926, rose to fourth of 30 in 1946, and so forth. To conserve space, some groups and ranks have been eliminated.

status of these groups in the U.S. hierarchy of racial and ethnic groups. The rankings also reflect the relative amount of exploitation and prejudice directed at each group over the course of U.S. history.

Although these patterns of social distance scores support the general point that prejudice is cultural, this body of research has some important limitations. The respondents were generally college students from a variety of campuses, not representative samples of the population, and the differences in scores from group to group are sometimes very small.

Still, the stability of the patterns cannot be ignored: the top two or three groups are always Northern European, Poles and Jews are always ranked in the middle third of the groups, and Koreans and Japanese always fall in the bottom third. African Americans and American Indians were ranked toward the bottom until the most recent rankings.

Finally, note how the relative positions of some groups change with international and domestic relations. For example, both Japanese and Germans fell in the rankings at the end of World War II (1946). Comparing 1966 with 1946, Russians fell and Japanese rose, reflecting changing patterns of alliance and enmity in the global system of societies. The dramatic rise of African Americans in 2011 may reflect declining levels of overt prejudice in American society, and the low ranking of Arabs reflects the negative feelings generated by the terrorist attacks on September 11, 2001.

How do we explain the fact that group rankings generally remain stable from the 1920s to 2011? The stability strongly suggests that Americans view the various groups through the same culturally shaped lens. A sense of social distance, a perception of some groups as "higher" or "better" than others, is part of the cultural package of intergroup prejudices we acquire from socialization into American society. The social distance patterns illustrate the power of culture to shape individual perceptions and preferences and attest to the deep streak of prejudice and racism built into American culture.

Modern Racism: The New Face of Prejudice? A large and growing body of research demonstrates that prejudice evolves as group relations and cultural beliefs and information change. The harsh, blatant forms of prejudice that typified U.S. society in its first several centuries have become muted in recent decades, leading some people to conclude that individual prejudice is no longer a significant problem in American life. However, while some celebrate the decline in harsh, overt prejudice, many social scientists argue strongly that prejudice has *not* declined but, rather, has evolved into a more subtle, less obvious, but just as consequential form. This new form of prejudice has been called a number of things, including **modern racism**, symbolic racism, and color-blind racism, and there is considerable debate over its exact shape, extent, and—indeed—existence. However, even while the issues continue to be debated and researched, the evidence that prejudice, even in its more subtle and disguised forms, remains a potent force in American society continues to accumulate.

People who are prejudiced in these ways typically reject "old-fashioned" blatant prejudice and the traditional view that racial inferiority is innate or biological. They often proclaim their allegiance to the ideals of equality of opportunity and treatment for all. Analysis of their thinking, however, reveals prejudice lurking just beneath the surface of these egalitarian sentiments, powerfully influencing their views of racial issues.

Sociologist Eduardo Bonilla-Silva (2006, pg. 28), one of the leading researchers in this area, argues that the new form of prejudice is often expressed in seemingly neutral language or "objective" terms. For example, the modern racist might attribute the underrepresentation of people of color in high-status positions to cultural rather than biological factors ("*they* don't emphasize education enough") or explain continuing residential and school segregation by the "natural" choices people make ("*they* would rather be with their own kind"). This kind of thinking rationalizes the status quo and permits dominant group members to live in segregated neighborhoods and send their children to segregated schools without guilt or hesitation. It obscures the myriad, not-so-subtle social forces that created segregated schools, neighborhoods, and other manifestations of racial inequality in the first place and maintains them in the present (e.g., see Satter, 2009). The naturalization framework permits people to ignore the social, political, and economic realities that actually create and sustain racial inequality and, by this **selective perception,** to support a kind of racism without appearing to be a racist. We will return to the subject of modern racism frequently, and especially in Chapter 5.

The Sociology of Individual Prejudice. The sociological approach to prejudice in this text stresses several points. Prejudice is created as a result of competition between groups. It is created to help mobilize feelings and emotional energy for competition and to rationalize the creation of minority group status. Then it becomes a part of the cultural heritage passed on to later generations as part of their "taken-for-granted" world, where it helps to shape their perceptions and reinforce group inferiority that created it in the first place. Although it has evolved into a more subtle form, prejudice remains an important force in U.S. society and will continue as long as there are patterns of inequality and systems of group privilege and disadvantage that require justification by the dominant group.

Discrimination

Discrimination is the unequal treatment of a person or persons based on group membership. An example of discrimination is an employer who decides not to hire an individual because he or she is African American (or Puerto Rican, Jewish, Chinese, etc.). If the unequal treatment is based on the group membership of the individual, the act is discriminatory.

Just as the cognitive and affective aspects of prejudice can be independent, discrimination and prejudice do not necessarily occur together. Even highly prejudiced individuals may not act on their negative thoughts or feelings. In social settings regulated by strong egalitarian codes or laws (for example, restaurants and other public facilities), people who are highly bigoted in their private thoughts and feelings may follow the codes in their public roles.

On the other hand, social situations in which prejudice is strongly approved and supported might evoke discrimination in otherwise unprejudiced individuals. In the southern United States during the height of segregation, and in South Africa during the period of state-sanctioned racial inequality called apartheid, it was usual and customary for whites to treat blacks in discriminatory ways. Regardless of individuals' actual levels of prejudice, they faced strong social pressure to conform to the official patterns of racial superiority and participate in acts of discrimination.

QUESTIONS FOR REFLECTION

6. Like most Americans, you are probably familiar with the stereotypes commonly attached to various groups. Does this mean you are prejudiced against those groups? Does it mean you have negative emotions about those groups and are likely to discriminate against them? Explain.

Ideological Racism

Ideological racism, a belief system that asserts that a particular group is inferior, is the group or societal equivalent of individual prejudice. Members of the dominant group use these ideas and beliefs to legitimize or rationalize the inferior status of minority groups. These ideas become incorporated into the culture of a society and are passed on from generation to generation through the process of socialization.

Because it is a part of the cultural heritage, ideological racism exists apart from the individuals who inhabit the society at a specific time (Andersen, 1993, p. 75; See & Wilson, 1988, p. 227). An example of a racist ideology is the elaborate system of beliefs and ideas that attempted to justify slavery in the American South. The exploitation of slaves was "explained" in terms of the innate racial inferiority of blacks and the superiority of whites.

Distinguishing between individual prejudice and societal racist ideologies naturally leads to a consideration of the relationship between these two phenomena. We will explore this relationship in later chapters, but for now we can make what is probably an obvious point: people socialized into societies with strong racist ideologies are likely to absorb racist ideas and be highly prejudiced. It should not surprise us that a high level of personal prejudice existed among whites in the antebellum American South or in other highly racist societies, such as in South Africa. At the same time, we need to remember that ideological racism and individual prejudice are different phenomena with different causes and different locations in the society. Racism is not a prerequisite for prejudice; prejudice may exist even in the absence of an ideology of racism.

Institutional Discrimination

Institutional discrimination is the societal equivalent of individual discrimination and refers to a pattern of unequal treatment based on group membership that is built into the daily operations of society, whether or not it is consciously intended. Public schools, the criminal justice system, and political and economic institutions can operate in ways that put members of some groups at a disadvantage.

Institutional discrimination can be obvious and overt. For many years following the Civil War, African Americans in the American South were prevented from voting by practices such as poll taxes and rigged literacy tests designed to ensure that they would fail. For nearly a century, well into the 1960s, elections and elected offices in the South were restricted to whites only. The purpose of this blatant pattern of institutional discrimination was widely understood by African American and white Southerners alike: it existed to disenfranchise the African American community and keep it politically powerless.

At other times, institutional discrimination may operate more subtly and without conscious intent. If public schools use aptitude tests that are biased in favor of the dominant group, decisions about who does and who does not take college preparatory courses may be made on racist grounds, even if everyone involved sincerely believes that they are merely applying objective criteria in a rational way. If a decision-making process has unequal consequences for dominant and minority groups, institutional discrimination may well be at work.

Note that although a particular discriminatory policy may be implemented and enforced by individuals, the policy is more appropriately thought of as an aspect of the operation of the institution as a whole. Election officials in the South during segregation did not and public school administrators today do not have to be personally prejudiced themselves to implement these discriminatory policies.

However, a major thesis of this book is that both racist ideologies and institutional discrimination are created to sustain the positions of dominant and minority groups in the stratification system. The relative advantage of the dominant group is maintained from day to day by widespread institutional discrimination. Members of the dominant group who are socialized into communities with strong racist ideologies and a great deal of institutional discrimination are likely to be personally prejudiced and to routinely engage in acts of individual discrimination. The respective positions of dominant and minority groups are preserved over time through the mutually reinforcing patterns of prejudice, racism, and discrimination on both the individual and the institutional levels. Institutional discrimination is but one way that members of a minority group can be denied access to valued goods and services, opportunities, and rights (such as voting). That is, institutional discrimination helps to sustain and reinforce the unequal positions of racial and ethnic groups in the stratification system.

A Global Perspective

In the chapters that follow, we will focus on developing a number of concepts and theories and applying those ideas to the minority groups of the United States. However, it is important to expand our perspective beyond the experiences of just a single nation and consider the experiences and histories of other peoples and places. Thus, we will take time throughout this text to apply our ideas to other societies and non-American minority groups. If the ideas and concepts developed in this text can help us make sense of these situations, we will have some assurance that they have some general applicability and that the dynamics of intergroup relations in the United States are not unique.

On another level, we must also take account of the ways in which group relations in the United States are shaped by economic, social, and political forces beyond our borders. As we will see, the experiences of this society cannot be understood in isolation. The United States is part of the global system of societies and now, more than ever, we must systematically take account of the complex interconnections between the domestic and the international, particularly with respect to issues related to immigration. The world is indeed growing smaller, and we must see our society as one part of a larger system. The next section explores one connection between the global and the local.

FOCUS ON CONTEMPORARY ISSUES:
Immigration and Globalization

Immigration is a major concern in our society today, and we will address this issue in the pages to come. Here, we will point out that immigration is a global phenomenon that affects virtually every nation in the world. About 214 million people—a little more than 3% of the world's population—live outside their countries of birth, and the number of migrants has increased steadily over the past several decades (United Nations Department of Economic and Social Affairs, Population Division, 2013). Figure 1.8 depicts the major population movements from 1990 to 2000 and clearly demonstrates the global nature of immigration. Note that Western Europe is a major destination for immigrants, as is the United States.

What has caused this massive population movement? One very important underlying cause is globalization, or the increasing interconnectedness of people, groups, organizations, and nations. This process is complex and multidimensional, but perhaps the most powerful dimension of globalization—especially for understanding contemporary immigration—is economic, and the movement of jobs and opportunity from place to place. People flow from areas of lower opportunity to areas with greater opportunity.

To illustrate, consider the southern border of the United States. For the past several decades, there has been an influx of people into the United States from Mexico and Central America, and the presence of these newcomers has generated a great deal of emotional and political heat, especially since many of these migrants are undocumented.

Some Americans see these newcomers as threats to American culture and the English language, and others associate them with crime, violence, and drug smuggling. Others see them simply as people trying to survive as best they can, desperate to support themselves and their families. Few, however, see these immigrants as the human consequences of the economic globalization of the world.

Figure 1.8 Major Global Migration Flows, 1990–2000

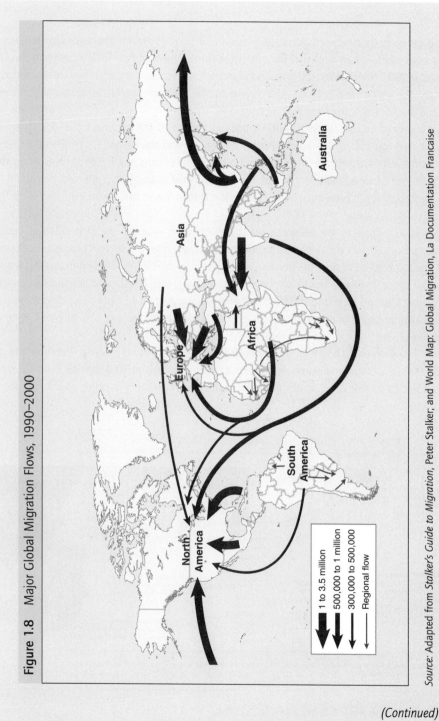

Legend:
- 1 to 3.5 million
- 500,000 to 1 million
- 300,000 to 500,000
- Regional flow

Source: Adapted from Stalker's Guide to Migration, Peter Stalker; and World Map: Global Migration, La Documentation Francaise

(Continued)

(Continued)

What is the connection between globalization and this immigrant stream? The population pressure on the U.S. southern border is in large part a result of the North American Free Trade Agreement (NAFTA), implemented in 1994. NAFTA united the three North American nations into a single trading bloc—economically "globalizing" the region—and permitted goods and capital (but not people) to move freely between Canada, the United States, and Mexico.

Among many other consequences, NAFTA opened Mexico to the importation of food products produced at very low cost by the agribusinesses of Canada and the United States. This cheap food (corn, in particular) destroyed the livelihoods of many rural Mexicans and forced them to leave their villages in search of work. Millions pursued the only survival strategy that seemed even remotely sensible: migration north. Even the meanest job in the United States can pay many times more than the average Mexican wage.

Even as NAFTA changed the economic landscape of North America, the United States became increasingly concerned with the security of its borders (especially after the terrorist attacks of September 11, 2001) and attempted to stem the flow of people, partly by building fences and increasing the size of the Border Patrol. The easier border crossings were quickly sealed, but this did not stop the pressure from the south. Migrants moved to more difficult and dangerous crossing routes, including the deadly, forbidding Sonoran Desert in southern Arizona, resulting in an untold number of deaths on the border since the mid-1990s.

Figure 1.9 displays one estimate of recent deaths along the southern U.S. border, but these are only the bodies that were discovered. Some estimates put the true number at 10 deaths for every recovered corpse, suggesting thousands of deaths along the border between the mid-1990s and the present.

Figure 1.9 Immigrant Deaths on the Southern Border, 2000–2010

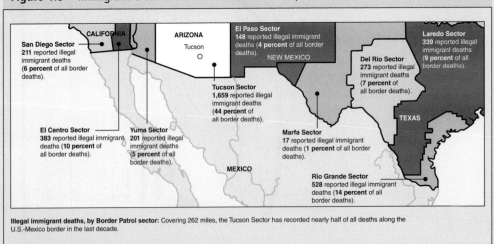

San Diego Sector 211 reported illegal immigrant deaths (**6 percent** of all border deaths).

El Centro Sector 383 reported illegal immigrant deaths (**10 percent** of all border deaths).

Yuma Sector 201 reported illegal immigrant deaths (**5 percent** of all border deaths).

Tucson Sector 1,659 reported illegal immigrant deaths (**44 percent** of all border deaths).

El Paso Sector 148 reported illegal immigrant deaths (**4 percent** of all border deaths).

Del Rio Sector 273 reported illegal immigrant deaths (**7 percent** of all border deaths).

Laredo Sector 339 reported illegal immigrant deaths (**9 percent** of all border deaths).

Marfa Sector 17 reported illegal immigrant deaths (**1 percent** of all border deaths).

Rio Grande Sector 528 reported illegal immigrant deaths (**14 percent** of all border deaths).

Illegal immigrant deaths, by Border Patrol sector: Covering 262 miles, the Tucson Sector has recorded nearly half of all deaths along the U.S.-Mexico border in the last decade.

Source: Arizona Daily Star and U.S. Border Patrol, 8/22/2010.

The relationship between NAFTA and immigration to the United States is just one aspect of a complex, global relationship. Around the globe, people are moving in huge numbers from less developed nations to more developed, more affluent economies. The wealthy nations of Western Europe, including Germany, Ireland, France, and the Netherlands, are also receiving large numbers of immigrants, and the citizens of these nations are concerned about their jobs, communities, housing, and language—as well as the integrity of their national cultures—in much the same ways as Americans. The world is changing, and contemporary immigration must be understood in terms of changes that affect many nations and, indeed, the entire global system of societies.

Conclusion

This chapter raises a lot of questions. Our intent is not so much to provide answers as to apply the sociological perspective. With the concepts, theories, and body of research developed over the years, we can illuminate and clarify the issues. In many cases, we can identify approaches and ideas that are simply wrong and others that hold promise. Sociology can't answer all questions, but it does supply research tools and ideas that can help us think more clearly and with greater depth and nuance about the issues facing our society.

Notes

1. Schwartzbaum, S. E., and A. J. Thomas. 2008. *Dimensions of Multicultural Counseling.* Thousand Oaks, CA: SAGE, p. 92.

2. O'Brien, E. 2008. *The Racial Middle: Latinos and Asian Americans Living Beyond the Racial Divide.* New York: New York University Press, p. 45.

3. Personal communication, June 2009.

4. Boldface terms in the text are defined in the glossary at the end of the book.

Main Points

- The United States faces enormous problems in dominant–minority relationships. Although many historic grievances of minority groups remain unresolved, our society is becoming increasingly diverse.
- The United States is a nation of immigrants, and many different groups and cultures are represented in its population.
- A minority group has five defining characteristics: a pattern of disadvantage, identification by some visible trait, awareness of its minority status, a membership determined at birth, and a tendency to marry within the group.
- A stratification system has three different dimensions (class, prestige, and power), and the nature of inequality in a society varies by its level of development. Minority groups and social class are correlated in complex ways.
- Race is a criterion widely used to identify minority group members. Scientists have largely discredited race as a biological concept. However, as a social category, race powerfully influences the way we think about one another as well as how we organize society.

- Minority groups are internally differentiated by social class, age, region of residence, and many other variables. Four crucial concepts for analyzing dominant–minority relations are prejudice, discrimination, ideological racism, and institutional discrimination.

Review Questions

1. What is the significance of Figure 1.1? What are some of the limitations and problems with the group names used in this graph? Are the group names "social constructions"? How? What kind of society should the United States strive to become? In your view, does the increasing diversity of American society represent a threat or an opportunity? Should we acknowledge and celebrate our differences, or should we strive for more similarity? What possible dangers and opportunities are inherent in increasing diversity? What are the advantages and disadvantages of stressing unity and conformity?

2. What groups should be considered "minorities"? The five-part definition presented in this chapter was developed with racial and ethnic minorities in mind. Does it apply to gay and lesbian Americans? How? How about people who are left-handed or people who are very overweight? Explain and justify your answers.

3. What does it mean to say that something is a social construction? As social constructions, how are race and gender the same and how do they differ? What does it mean to say, "Gender becomes a social construction—like race—when it is treated as an unchanging, fixed difference and then used to deny opportunity and equality to women"?

4. Define and explain each of the terms in Table 1.1. Cite an example of each from your own experiences. How does ideological racism differ from prejudice?

Internet Activities

1. In this chapter we discussed race—arguably the most consequential concept in the history of this nation (and the globe). To extend the discussion, we can use resources on the Internet, including a website created to accompany a fascinating documentary, "Race: The Power of an Illusion," at www.pbs.org/race/000_General/000_00-Home.htm. The single major point of the website parallels that of this text: specifically, that race is a social construction, a cultural and political perception invented during particular historical eras, largely to justify and rationalize the differential treatment of others. Once established and passed from generation to generation, race becomes hugely consequential in the lives of all U.S. citizens—it becomes its own reality, shaping and controlling peoples' lives. We encourage you to explore all six subsections of the website. Prepare answers to each of the questions below and use this information along with ideas from this chapter to discuss the concept of race with others.

    1. In what ways should race be considered a "modern" idea?
    2. In what ways is race *not* a biological concept?
    3. How have ideas about race evolved and changed since ancient times?
    4. What are some U.S. examples of how public policy has treated people differently based on race? What are some of the consequences?
    5. How have definitions of black and white changed over the years? How have U.S. Census Bureau definitions of race changed? Why?

6. Try the "Sorting People" exercise and record your number of "correct" classifications here: _____. What does this exercise make you think about race as a concept? Can you accurately tell someone's race by looking at her or him? If not, what does this say about the concept of race?

7. Take the quiz under the "Human Diversity" tab and record the number of correct answers here: _____. Was your information accurate? Where did you get this information?

8. Click on the "Explore Diversity" button under "Human Diversity" and explore the activities. Does this information support the idea that "race isn't biological"? How?

2. In this chapter, we treated prejudice as a set of attitudes, opinions, stereotypes, and emotions that people express in their everyday conversations and that can be measured by surveys like the social distance scale. A group of psychologists has developed a very different approach to the topic: They believe that people have a largely unconscious and unspoken set of attitudes toward other groups that affects their thinking, feelings, and actions (Greenwald et al., 2002; Greenwald & Banaji, 1995). These implicit or hidden prejudices are acquired during socialization and shape our relationships with other groups, even when we are not aware of it. This form of prejudice can exist even in people who have no conscious prejudice and who behave in nondiscriminatory ways. Do you have an implicit negative reaction to other groups? You can find out by taking the Implicit Association Test (IAT) at the Project Implicit website. To complete this test, follow these instructions:

a. Go to the IAT website at https://implicit.harvard.edu/implicit/. Alternately, you can search for "Implicit Association Test" using your search engine.

b. Find the box on the left labeled "Project Implicit Social Attitudes." You may want to proceed as a guest user rather than registering, so click "GO!" in the lower panel of the box, next to the U.S. English window.

c. Read the information and disclaimer on the next window. Then, click "I wish to proceed." Take several of the tests, including the Race IAT.

d. Learn more about the IAT by clicking the "Education" button on the top of the window after you finish the tests and then clicking "About the IAT." Browse the rest of the site and, especially, read the "Frequently Asked Questions."

3. After taking the tests and gathering some perspective on the IAT, consider these questions:

a. What is an "implicit" attitude? How does implicit prejudice differ from affective prejudice, stereotypes, social distance, and modern racism?

b. If test shows you have a preference for one group over another, does this mean that you are prejudiced against the less preferred group? Do you feel that the test accurately reflects your feelings and ideas? Why or why not? (Remember that your implicit attitudes can be quite different from your explicit or conscious attitudes.)

4. Research using the IAT reveals that many white Americans have a preference for whites over blacks. Why do you think this is so? What aspects of American culture might create and sustain this preference?

5. Which of the situations listed below would be most and least affected by a person's implicit attitudes? Why?

a. Friendship choices in a multigroup elementary school classroom.

b. Friendship choices in a multigroup high school or university.

c. Reactions to hearing that a friend is dating a member of a different racial or ethnic group.

d. Reactions to a news story that a minority group man has raped and killed a dominant group woman.

e. Reactions to a news story that a dominant group man raped and killed a minority group woman.

    f. Choices between political candidates who are from different racial or ethnic groups.

    g. Support for policies such as affirmative action that can be controversial.

    h. Hiring decisions involving applicants from a variety of groups.

    i. Choices about which neighborhoods to live in.

    j. Choices in a "shoot / don't shoot" situation involving a white police officer and a *possibly* armed black man suspect. How about if the suspect were a white woman?

5. If the IAT shows that you have a group preference you would rather *not* have, what are some things you could do to change yourself?

Group Discussion

For Activity 1, select three questions to discuss. For Activity 2, select three of the questions from #4 above to discuss with classmates. To aid the discussion, bring a summary of what you learned about yourself to class. What was the most important thing you learned each of these activities?

Note: Individual students may prefer *not* to reveal their IAT scores during these discussions. Group members should respect that.

Learning Resources on the Web

$SAGE edge™

edge.sagepub.com/healeyds5e

SAGE edge offers a robust online environment featuring an impressive array of free tools and resources for review, study, and further exploration, keeping both instructors and students on the cutting edge of teaching and learning.

SAGE edge for Students provides a personalized approach to help you accomplish your course-work goals in an easy-to-use learning environment.

Assimilation and Pluralism: From Immigrants to White Ethnics

> *We have room for but one flag, the American flag.... We have room for but one language and that is the English language ... and we have room for but one loyalty and that is a loyalty to the American people.*
>
> —Theodore Roosevelt, 26th president of the United States, 1907

> *If we lose our language [Ojibwa] ..., I think, something more will be lost.... We will lose something personal.... We will lose our sense of ourselves and our culture.... We will lose beauty—the beauty of the particular, the beauty of the past and the intricacies of a language tailored for our space in the world. That Native American cultures are imperiled is important and not just to Indians.... When we lose cultures, we lose American plurality—the productive and lovely discomfort that true difference brings.*
>
> —David Treuer (2012, pp. 304–305)

> *Welcome to America. Now, speak English.*
>
> —Bumper sticker, 2013

More than 300 different languages are spoken in the United States today, including more than 150 different American Indian languages. Most are spoken by relatively few people, but the sheer number of languages suggests the dimensions of contemporary American diversity.

Does this multiplicity of languages and cultures bring confusion and inefficiency? Does it enrich everyday life and spark creativity? Does it really matter if a language disappears and we lose the "lovely discomfort" of difference?

These are some of the questions Americans (and the citizens of many other nations) must ask as we confront the issues of inclusion and diversity. Should we encourage groups to retain their unique cultural heritage, including their language, or should we stress unity and conformity? How have these issues been addressed in the past? How should we approach them in the future?

This chapter continues to look at the ways in which ethnic and racial groups in the United States relate to each other. Two concepts, assimilation and pluralism, are at the core of the discussion. Each includes a variety of possible group relations and pathways along which group relations might develop.

Assimilation is a process in which formerly distinct and separate groups come to share a common culture and merge together socially. As a society undergoes assimilation, differences among groups decrease. **Pluralism**, on the other hand, exists when groups maintain their individual identities. In a pluralistic society, groups remain separate, and their cultural and social differences persist over time.

In some ways, assimilation and pluralism are contrary processes, but they are not mutually exclusive. They may occur together in a variety of combinations within a particular society or group. Some groups in a society may be assimilating while others are maintaining (or even increasing) their differences. As we shall see in Part 3, virtually every minority group in the United States has, at any given time, some members who are assimilating and others who are preserving or reviving traditional cultures. Some Native Americans, for example, are pluralistic. They live on or near reservations, are strongly connected to their heritage, practice the old ways as much as they can, and speak their native language. Other Native Americans are mostly assimilated into the dominant society: They live in urban areas, speak English only, and know relatively little about their traditional cultures. Both assimilation and pluralism are important forces in the everyday lives of Native Americans and most other minority group members.

Over the past century, American sociologists have been very concerned with these processes, especially assimilation. This concern was stimulated by the massive migration from Europe to the United States that occurred between the 1820s and the 1920s. More than 31 million people crossed the Atlantic during this time, and a great deal of energy has been devoted to documenting, describing, and understanding the experiences of these immigrants and their descendants. These efforts have resulted in the development of a rich and complex literature that we will refer to as the "traditional" perspective on how newcomers are incorporated into U.S. society.

This chapter begins with a consideration of the "traditional" perspective on both assimilation and pluralism and a brief examination of several other possible group relationships. Then, we apply concepts and theories of the traditional perspective to

European immigrants and their descendants, and we develop a model of American assimilation based on these experiences. We will use this model in our analysis of other minority groups throughout the text and especially in Part 3.

Since the 1960s, the United States has been experiencing a second mass immigration, and a particularly important issue now is whether the theories, concepts, and models based on the first mass immigration to the United States (from the 1820s to the 1920s) apply to this wave. The newest arrivals differ in many ways from those who came earlier, and ideas and theories based on the earlier experiences will not necessarily apply to the present. We will briefly note some of the issues in this chapter and explore them in more detail in the case study chapters in Part 3.

Finally, at the end of this chapter, we briefly consider the implications of these first two chapters for the exploration of intergroup relations throughout this text. By the end of this chapter, you will be familiar with many of the concepts that will guide us as we examine the variety of possible dominant–minority group situations and the directions our society (and the groups within it) can take.

Assimilation

We begin with assimilation because the emphasis in U.S. group relations has historically been on this goal rather than on pluralism. This section presents some of the most important sociological theories and concepts that have been used to describe and analyze the assimilation of the 19th century immigrants from Europe.

Types of Assimilation

Assimilation is a general term for a process that can follow a number of different pathways. One form of assimilation is expressed in the metaphor of the **melting pot**, a process in which different groups come together and contribute in roughly equal amounts to create a common culture and a new, unique society. People often think of the American experience of assimilation in terms of the melting pot. This view stresses the ways in which diverse peoples helped to construct U.S. society and made contributions to American culture. The melting-pot metaphor sees assimilation as benign and egalitarian, a process that emphasizes sharing and inclusion.

Although it is a powerful image in our society, the melting pot is not an accurate description of how assimilation actually proceeded for American minority groups (Abrahamson, 1980, pp. 152–154). Some groups—especially the racial minority groups—have been largely excluded from the "melting" process. Furthermore, the melting-pot brew has had a distinctly Anglocentric flavor: "For better or worse, the white Anglo-Saxon Protestant tradition was for two centuries—and in crucial respects still is—the dominant influence on American culture and society" (Schlesinger, 1992, p. 28).

Contrary to the melting-pot image, assimilation in the United States generally has been a largely one-sided process better described by the terms **Americanization** or **Anglo-conformity**. Rather than an equal sharing of elements and a gradual blending of diverse peoples, assimilation in the United States was designed to maintain the predominance of the English language and the British-type institutional patterns created during the early years of American society.

The stress on Anglo-conformity is clearly reflected in the quote from President Roosevelt that opens this chapter. Many Americans today agree with Roosevelt: 77% of respondents in a recent survey—the overwhelming majority—agreed that "the United States should require immigrants to be proficient in English as a condition of remaining in the U.S." Interestingly, about 60% of Hispanic Americans (versus 80% of non-Hispanic whites and 76% of blacks) also agreed with this statement (Carroll, 2007). We should note that the apparent agreement between Hispanic and white Americans for learning English may flow from different orientations and motivations. For some whites, the response may mix prejudice and contempt with support for Americanization, while the Hispanic responses may be based on direct experiences with the difficulties of negotiating the monolingual institutions of American society.

Under Anglo-conformity, immigrant and minority groups are expected to adapt to Anglo-American culture as a precondition for acceptance and access to better jobs, education, and other opportunities. Assimilation has meant that minority groups have had to give up their traditions and adopt Anglo-American culture. To be sure, many groups and individuals were (and continue to be) eager to undergo Anglo-conformity, even if it meant losing much or all of their heritage. For other groups, Americanization created conflict, anxiety, demoralization, and resentment. We assess these varied reactions in our examination of America's minority groups in Part 3.

The "Traditional" Perspective on Assimilation: Theories and Concepts

American sociologists have developed a rich body of theories and concepts based on their studies of the immigrants who came from Europe between the 1820s and 1920s. We shall refer to this body of work as the traditional perspective on assimilation. As you will see, the scholars working in this tradition have made invaluable contributions, and their thinking is impressively complex and comprehensive. This does not mean, of course, that they have exhausted the possibilities or answered (or asked) all the questions. Theorists working in the pluralist tradition and contemporary scholars studying the experiences of more recent immigrants have questioned many aspects of traditional assimilation theory and have made a number of important contributions of their own.

Robert Park. Many theories of assimilation are grounded in the work of Robert Park. He was one of a group of scholars who had a major hand in establishing sociology as a discipline in the United States in the 1920s and 1930s. Park believed that intergroup relations go through a predictable set of phases that he called a **race relations cycle**. When groups first come into contact (through immigration, conquest, etc.), relations are conflictual and competitive. Eventually, however, the process, or cycle, moves toward assimilation, or the "interpenetration and fusion" of groups (Park & Burgess, 1924, p. 735).

Park argued further that assimilation is inevitable in a democratic and industrial society. In a political system based on democracy, fairness, and impartial justice, all groups will eventually secure equal treatment under the law. In an industrial economy, people tend to be judged on rational grounds—that is, on the basis of their abilities and talents—and not by ethnicity or race. Park believed that as American society continued to modernize, urbanize, and industrialize, ethnic and racial groups would gradually lose their importance. The boundaries between groups would eventually dissolve, and a more "rational" and unified society would emerge (see also Geschwender, 1978, pp. 19–32; Hirschman, 1983).

Social scientists have examined, analyzed, and criticized Park's conclusions for decades. One frequently voiced criticism is that he did not specify a time frame for the completion of assimilation, and therefore his idea that assimilation is "inevitable" cannot be tested. Until the exact point in time when assimilation is deemed complete, we will not know whether the theory is wrong or whether we just have not waited long enough. What do you think about this criticism?

An additional criticism of Park's theory is that he does not describe the nature of the assimilation process in much detail. How would assimilation proceed? How would everyday life change? Which aspects of the group would change first?

Milton Gordon. To clarify some of the issues Park left unresolved, we turn to the works of sociologist Milton Gordon who made a major contribution to theories of assimilation in his book *Assimilation in American Life* (1964). Gordon broke down the overall process of assimilation into seven subprocesses; we will focus on the first three. Before considering these phases of assimilation, we need to consider some new concepts.

Gordon makes a distinction between the cultural and the structural components of society. **Culture** encompasses all aspects of the way of life associated with a group of people. It includes language, religious and other beliefs, customs and rules of etiquette, and the values and ideas people use to organize their lives and interpret their existence. The **social structure**, or structural components of a society, includes networks of social relationships, groups, organizations, stratification systems, communities, and families. The social structure organizes the work of the society and connects individuals to one another and to the larger society.

It is common in sociology to separate the social structure into primary and secondary sectors. The **primary sector** includes interpersonal relationships that are intimate and personal, such as families and groups of friends. Groups in the primary sector are small. The **secondary sector** consists of groups and organizations that are more public, task oriented, and impersonal. Organizations in the secondary sector often are very large and include businesses, factories, schools and colleges, and bureaucracies.

Now we can examine Gordon's earliest stages of assimilation, which are summarized in Table 2.1.

1. **Acculturation** or **cultural assimilation.** Members of the minority group learn the culture of the dominant group. For groups that immigrate to the United States, acculturation to the dominant Anglo-American culture may include changes both great and small, including learning the English language, changing eating habits, adopting new value systems and gender roles, and altering the spelling of the family surname.

2. **Integration** or **structural assimilation.** The minority group enters the social structure of the larger society. Integration typically begins in the secondary sector and gradually moves into the primary sector. That is, before people can form friendships with members of other groups (integration into the primary sector), they must first become acquaintances. The initial contact between groups often occurs in public institutions such as schools and workplaces (integration into the secondary sector). The greater their integration into the secondary sector, the more equal the minority group will be to the dominant group in income, education, and occupational prestige. Once a group has entered the institutions and public sectors of the larger society, according to Gordon, integration into the primary sector and the other stages of assimilation will follow inevitably (although not necessarily quickly). Measures of integration into the primary sector include the extent to which people have acquaintances, close friends, or neighbors from other groups.

3. **Intermarriage** or **marital assimilation.** When integration into the primary sector becomes substantial, the basis for Gordon's third stage of assimilation is established. People are most likely to select spouses from among their primary relations. Thus, in Gordon's view, primary structural integration typically comes before intermarriage.

Gordon argued that acculturation was a prerequisite for integration. Given the stress on Anglo-conformity, a member of an immigrant or minority group would not be able to compete for jobs or other opportunities in the secondary sector of the social structure until he or she had learned the dominant group's culture. Gordon recognized, however, that successful acculturation does not automatically ensure that a group will begin the integration phase. The dominant group may still exclude the minority group from its institutions and limit the opportunities available to the group. Gordon argued that "acculturation without integration" (or Americanization without equality) is a common situation in the United States for many minority groups, especially for racial minority groups.

Table 2.1 Gordon's Stages of Assimilation

Stage	Process
1. Acculturation	The group learns the culture of the dominant group, including language and values.
2. Integration (structural assimilation)	
a. At the secondary level	Members of the group enter the public institutions and organizations of the dominant society.
b. At the primary level	Members of the group enter the cliques, clubs, and friendship groups of the dominant society.
3. Intermarriage (marital assimilation)	Members of the group marry with members of the dominant society on a large scale.

Source: Adapted from Gordon (1964, p. 71).

In Gordon's theory, movement from acculturation to integration is the crucial step in the assimilation process. Once that step is taken, all the other subprocesses will occur inevitably, although movement through the stages can be very slow. Gordon's idea that assimilation runs a certain course in a certain order echoes Park's conclusion regarding the inevitability of the process.

More than 50 years after Gordon published his analysis of assimilation, some of his conclusions about American assimilation have been called into question. For example, the individual subprocesses of assimilation that Gordon saw as linked in a certain order are often found to occur independently of one another (Yinger, 1985, p. 154). A group may integrate before acculturating or combine the subprocesses in other ways. Also, many researchers no longer think of the process of assimilation as necessarily linear or one-way (Greeley, 1974). Groups (or segments thereof) may "reverse direction" and become less assimilated over time, revive their traditional cultures, relearn their old language, or revitalize ethnic organizations or associations.

Nonetheless, Gordon's overall model continues to guide our understanding of the process of assimilation, to the point that a large part of the research agenda for contemporary studies of immigrants involves assessment of the extent to which their experiences can be described in Gordon's terms (Alba & Nee, 1997). In fact, Gordon's model will provide a major organizational framework for the case study chapters presented in Part 3 of this text.

Human Capital Theory. Why did some European immigrant groups acculturate and integrate more rapidly than others? Although not a theory of assimilation per se, **human capital theory** offers one possible answer to this question. This theory argues that status attainment, or the level of success achieved by an individual in society, is a direct result of educational levels, personal values and skills, and other individual characteristics and abilities. Education is seen as an investment in human capital, not unlike the investment a business might make in machinery or new technology. The greater the investment in a person's human capital, the higher the probability of success. Blau and Duncan (1967), in their pioneering statement of status attainment theory, found that even the relative advantage conferred by having a high-status father is largely mediated through education. In other words, high levels of affluence and occupational prestige are not so much a result of being born into a privileged status as they are the result of the superior education that affluence makes possible.

Why did some immigrant groups achieve upward mobility more rapidly than others? Human capital theory answers questions such as these in terms of the resources and cultural characteristics of the members of the groups, especially their levels of education and familiarity with English. Success is seen as a direct result of individual effort and the wise investment of personal resources. From this perspective, people or groups who fail have not tried hard enough, have not made the right kinds of educational investments, or have values or habits that limit their ability to compete with others.

Human capital theory is quite consistent with traditional American ideals. Both tend to see success as an individual phenomenon, a reward for hard work, sustained effort, and good character. Both tend to assume that success is equally available to all and that the larger society is open and neutral in its distribution of rewards and opportunity. Both tend to see assimilation as a highly desirable, benign process that blends diverse peoples and cultures into a strong, unified society. Thus, people or groups that resist Americanization or question its benefits are seen as threatening or illegitimate.

On one level, human capital theory is an important theory of success and upward mobility, and we will use it on occasion to analyze the experiences of minority and immigrant groups. However, because it resonates with American "common-sense" views of success and failure, we may tend to use it uncritically, ignoring flaws in the theory.

A final judgment on the validity of the theory will be more appropriately made at the end of the text, but you should be aware of the major limitations of the theory from the beginning. First, as an explanation of minority group experience, human capital theory is incomplete. It does not take account of all the factors that affect mobility and assimilation. Second, as we shall see, its assumption that U.S. society is equally open and fair to all groups is simply incorrect. We will point out other strengths and limitations of this perspective as we move through the text.

QUESTIONS FOR REFLECTION

1. What are the limitations of the melting-pot view of assimilation?

2. Why does Gordon place acculturation as the first step in the process of assimilation? Could one of the other stages occur first? Why or why not?

3. What does human capital theory leave out? In what ways is it consistent with American values?

Pluralism

Sociological discussions of pluralism often begin with a consideration of the work of Horace Kallen. In articles published in *The Nation* magazine in 1915, Kallen argued that people should not have to surrender their culture and traditions to become full participants in American society. He rejected the Anglo-conformist, assimilationist model and contended that the existence of separate ethnic groups, even with separate cultures, religions, and languages, was consistent with democracy and other core American values. In Gordon's terms, Kallen believed that integration and equality were possible without extensive acculturation and that American society could be a federation of diverse groups, a mosaic of harmonious and interdependent cultures and peoples (Kallen, 1915a, 1915b; see also Abrahamson, 1980; Gleason, 1980).

Assimilation has been such a powerful theme in U.S. history that in the decades following the publication of Kallen's analysis, support for pluralism remained somewhat marginalized. In recent decades, however, interest in pluralism and ethnic diversity has increased, in part because the assimilation predicted by Park (that many Americans assumed would happen) has not occurred. Perhaps we have not waited long enough, but as the 21st century unfolds, social distinctions among the racial minority groups in our society show few signs of disappearing. In fact, some members of these groups question whether assimilation is desirable or not. Also, more surprising perhaps, white ethnicity has not disappeared, although it has changed in form and grown weaker.

An additional reason for the growing interest in pluralism, no doubt, is the everyday reality of the increasing diversity of U.S. society, as seen in Figure 1.1 from the first chapter. Controversies over issues such as "English Only" language policies, bilingual education, and welfare rights for immigrants are common and often bitter. Many Americans believe that diversity or pluralism has exceeded acceptable limits and that the unity of the nation is at risk.

Finally, interest in pluralism and ethnicity in general has been stimulated by developments around the globe. Several nation-states have disintegrated into smaller units based on language, culture, race, and ethnicity. Recent events in India, the Middle East, former Yugoslavia, the former USSR, Canada, and Africa, just to mention a few, have provided dramatic and often tragic evidence of how ethnic identities and enmities can persist across decades or even centuries of submergence and suppression in larger national units.

In contemporary debates, discussions of diversity and pluralism are often couched in the language of **multiculturalism**, a general term for a variety of programs and ideas that stress mutual respect for all groups and for the multiple heritages that have shaped the United States. Some aspects of multiculturalism are controversial and have evoked strong opposition. In many ways, however, these debates merely echo a recurring argument about the character of American society, a debate that will be revisited throughout this text.

Types of Pluralism

We can distinguish various types of pluralism by using some of the concepts introduced in the discussion of assimilation. **Cultural pluralism** exists when groups have not acculturated and each maintains its own identity. The groups might speak different languages, practice different religions, and have different value systems. The groups are part of the same society and might even live in adjacent areas, but in some ways they live in different worlds. Many Native Americans are culturally pluralistic and maintain traditional languages and cultures and live on isolated reservations. The Amish, a religious community sometimes called the Pennsylvania Dutch, are a culturally pluralistic group, also. They are committed to a way of life organized around farming, and they maintain a culture and an institutional life that is separate from the dominant culture (see Hostetler, 1980; Kephart & Zellner, 1994; and Kraybill & Bowman, 2001).

Following Gordon's subprocesses, a second type of pluralism exists when a group has acculturated but not integrated. That is, the group has adopted the Anglo-American culture but does not have full and equal access to the institutions of the larger society. In this situation, called **structural pluralism**, cultural differences are minimal, but the groups occupy different locations in the social structure. The groups may speak with the same accent, eat the same food, pursue the same goals, and subscribe to the same values, but they may also maintain separate organizational systems, including different churches, clubs, schools, and neighborhoods.

Under structural pluralism, groups practice a common culture but do so in different places and with minimal interaction across group boundaries. An example of structural pluralism can be found on any Sunday morning in the Christian churches of the United States, where local congregations are often identified with specific ethnic groups or races. What happens in the various churches—the rituals, expressions of faith, statements of core values and beliefs—is similar and expresses a common, shared culture. Structurally, however, this common culture is expressed in separate buildings and by separate congregations.

A third type of pluralism reverses the order of Gordon's first two phases: integration without acculturation. This situation is exemplified by a group that has had some material success (measured by wealth or income, for example) but has not become Americanized (become fluent in English, adopted uniquely American values and norms, etc.). Some immigrant groups have found niches in U.S. society in which they can survive and occasionally prosper economically without acculturating much.

Two different situations can be used to illustrate this pattern. An **enclave minority group** establishes its own neighborhood and relies on a set of interconnected businesses, each of which is usually small in scope, for its economic survival. Some of these businesses serve the group, whereas others serve the larger society. The Cuban American community in South Florida and Chinatowns in many larger American cities are examples of ethnic enclaves.

A similar pattern of adjustment, the **middleman minority group**, also relies on small shops and retail firms, but the businesses are more dispersed throughout a large area rather than concentrated in a specific locale. Some Chinese American communities fit this second pattern, as do Korean American grocery stores and Indian American–owned motels (Portes & Manning, 1986). We discuss these types of minority groups further in Part 3.

The economic success of enclave and middleman minorities is partly due to the strong ties of cooperation and mutual aid within their groups. The ties are based, in turn, on cultural bonds that would weaken if acculturation took place. In contrast with Gordon's idea that acculturation is a prerequisite to integration, whatever success these groups enjoy is due in part to the fact that they have *not* Americanized. At various times and places, Jewish, Chinese, Japanese, Korean, and Cuban Americans have been enclave or middleman minorities (see Bonacich & Modell, 1980; Kitano & Daniels, 2001).

The situation of enclave and middleman minorities, integration without acculturation, can be considered either a type of pluralism (emphasizing the absence of acculturation) or a type of assimilation (emphasizing the relatively high level of economic equality). Keep in mind that assimilation and pluralism are not opposites but can occur in a variety of combinations. It is best to think of acculturation, integration, and the other stages of assimilation (or pluralism) as independent processes.

QUESTIONS FOR REFLECTION

4. Is the United States becoming more pluralistic? Explain. What are some of the costs and some of the benefits of increasing pluralism?

5. What are the differences between middleman and enclave minority groups? Do these groups challenge the idea that assimilation moves step-by-step in a certain order?

FOCUS ON CONTEMPORARY ISSUES:
Language and Assimilation

The bumper sticker mentioned at the start of the chapter expresses a common sentiment: "Welcome to America. Now, speak English." Many Americans are concerned about the increase in the number of non-English speakers in their communities, and the bumper sticker succinctly—if crudely—expresses the opinion that newcomers should learn English as a condition for acceptance. In Gordon's terms, the slogan expresses support for Anglo-conformity, the model that guided the assimilation of immigrants in the past.

The bumper sticker also reflects a common concern: How well can we manage a multi-lingual society? Americans from all walks of life and political persuasions wonder about the difficulties of everyday communication and the problems created when people speak multiple languages. Also, people wonder if increasing language diversity will weaken social solidarity and the sense of unity that every society requires in order to function effectively. In 2013, about 300 different languages were spoken in the United States, and about 21% of the population spoke a language other than English at home (U.S. Census Bureau, 2015c). Of course, most of these languages, except Spanish, have few speakers. Still, people wonder if this multiplicity of tongues threatens unity and efficiency. What does sociological research reveal about language acculturation for today's immigrants?

First, for the first great wave of immigrants to the United States—those who came from Europe between the 1820s and the 1920s—language acculturation happened by generation. The first generation largely lived and died speaking their native language. Their children learned English in school and often served as bilingual go-betweens for their parents and the larger society. However, they largely failed to pass on the lan-guage of their parents to their children, and the third generation tended to grow up in nonethnic settings and speak English as their first and only language. Thus, by the third

(Continued)

(Continued)

(or fourth) generation, English had replaced the old language, especially after immigration from Europe ended in the 1920s and 1930s and few newcomers arrived to keep the old ways alive.

Today, more than 90 years since the end of the first mass wave of immigration, the importance of language is not lost on immigrants, and language acculturation appears to be following, more or less, a similar generational pattern. As in the past, "The immigrant generation makes some progress but remains dominant in their native tongue, the second generation is bilingual, and the third generation speaks English only" (Waters & Jimenez, 2005, p. 110).

For many Americans, the finding that language acculturation is occurring now much as it did in the past will seem counterintuitive. Their everyday experience in their communities tells them that the use of non-English languages (particularly Spanish) is *not* waning over the years, but is growing more common.

The persistence of the "old" language reflects the continuing high rate of immigration. Even as the children and grandchildren of immigrants learn English, knowledge of the old language is replenished by newcomers. In other words, assimilation and pluralism are occurring simultaneously in the United States today: the movement of the second and third generations toward speaking English is counterbalanced by continuing immigration. The assimilation of European immigrant groups was sharply reinforced by the cessation of immigration after the 1920s. Language diversity today is sustained by the continuing flow of new immigrants. This is an important difference in the assimilation experience of the two waves and we will explore it more in chapters to come. For now, we can say that immigration today will continue, newcomers will keep the "old" language alive, and language diversity will continue to be perceived as a problem and, for some, as a threat.

Given these trends, it seems likely that language will continue to be an important political issue in the years ahead. Although Americans espouse a variety of opinions on the issue, one widely supported proposal is to make English the official language of the United States (much as suggested by the bumper sticker slogan). Generally, English Only laws require that the official business of the society (including election ballots, court proceedings, public school assemblies, and street signs) be conducted in *only* English.

Some questions come to mind about these laws. First, are these laws necessary? Would such laws speed up the acquisition of English in the first generation? This seems unlikely, since a large percentage of immigrants arrive with little formal education and low levels of literacy in their native language, as we will see in chapters to come. Furthermore, the laws would have little impact on the second and third generation, since they are already learning English at the "normal," generational pace.

Second, is there something behind the support for these laws besides concern for language diversity? Is support for English Only laws an expression of prejudice? Recall the concept of modern racism (disguised ways of expressing disdain for other groups without appearing to be racist) from Chapter 1. Support for English Only laws provides a perfect cover for "nonracist racism." It permits people to express their fears and act on their stereotypes in language that is neutral and that even seems patriotic. Does the English Only movement hide a deeper, more exclusionist agenda? Is it a way of sustaining the dominance of Anglo culture, a manifestation of the ideological racism we discussed in Chapter 1?

Of course, not all supporters of English Only laws are racist or prejudiced. Our point is that some (many?) of those feelings and ideas are prejudicial. We must carefully sort out the real challenges created by immigration, assimilation, and language diversity from the more hysterical and racist concerns.

Other Group Relationships

This book concentrates on assimilation and pluralism, but there are, of course, other possible group relationships and goals. Two commonly noted goals for minority groups are separatism and revolution (Wirth, 1945). The goal of **separatism** is for the group to sever all ties (political, cultural, and geographic) with the larger society. Thus, separatism goes well beyond pluralism. Some Native Americans have expressed separatist and pluralist goals. Separatism has also been pursued by some African American organizations, such as the Black Muslims (also known as the Nation of Islam). Separatist movements exist among groups in French Canada, Scotland, Chechnya, Cyprus, southern Mexico, Hawaii, and scores of other places, too.

A minority group promoting **revolution** seeks to switch places with the dominant group and become the ruling elite or create a new social order, perhaps in alliance with members of the dominant group. Although revolutionary activity can be found among some American minority groups (e.g., the Black Panthers), this goal has been relatively rare for minority groups in the United States. Revolutionary minority groups are more commonly found in situations such as those in colonial Africa, in which one nation conquered and controlled another racially or culturally different nation.

Additionally, the dominant group may pursue goals other than assimilation and pluralism, including forced migration or expulsion, extermination or genocide, and continued subjugation of the minority group. Chinese immigrants were the victims of a policy of expulsion, beginning in the 1880s, when the Chinese Exclusion Act (1882) closed the door on further immigration and concerted efforts were made to encourage Chinese people to leave the United States (see Chapter 8). Native Americans have been the victims of expulsion, too. In 1830, all tribes living east of the Mississippi were forced to migrate to a new territory in the West (see Chapter 3). The most infamous example of genocide is the Holocaust in Nazi Germany, during which 6 million Jews and millions of other minority group members (such as the Roma, or gypsies, and gay people) were murdered. Tragically, many other examples exist (see Figure 2.1). The dominant

Figure 2.1   Select Genocides Around the World, 1914 to Present

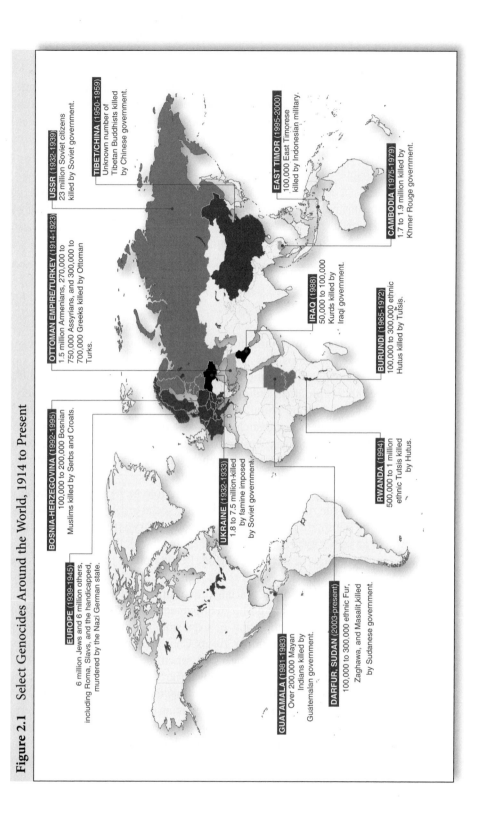

EUROPE (1939–1945)
6 million Jews and 6 million others, including Roma, Slavs, and the handicapped, murdered by the Nazi German state.

BOSNIA-HERZEGOVINA (1992–1995)
100,000 to 200,000 Bosnian Muslims killed by Serbs and Croats.

OTTOMAN EMPIRE/TURKEY (1914–1923)
1.5 million Armenians, 270,000 to 750,000 Assyrians, and 300,000 to 700,000 Greeks killed by Ottoman Turks.

USSR (1932–1939)
23 million Soviet citizens killed by Soviet government.

TIBET/CHINA (1950–1959)
Unknown number of Tibetan Buddhists killed by Chinese government.

EAST TIMOR (1995–2000)
100,000 East Timorese killed by Indonesian military.

CAMBODIA (1975–1979)
1.7 to 1.9 million killed by Khmer Rouge government.

IRAQ (1988)
50,000 to 100,000 Kurds killed by Iraqi government.

BURUNDI (1965–1972)
100,000 to 300,000 ethnic Hutus killed by Tutsis.

UKRAINE (1932–1933)
1.8 to 7.5 million killed by famine imposed by Soviet government.

RWANDA (1994)
500,000 to 1 million ethnic Tutsis killed by Hutus.

GUATAMALA (1981–1983)
Over 200,000 Mayan Indians killed by Guatemalan government.

DARFUR, SUDAN (2003–present)
100,000 to 300,000 ethnic Fur, Zaghawa, and Masalit killed by Sudanese government.

group pursues "continued subjugation" when, as with slavery in the antebellum South, it attempts to maintain the powerless and exploited position for the minority group. A dominant group may simultaneously pursue different policies with different minority groups and may, of course, change policies over time.

From Immigrants to White Ethnics

In this section, we will explore the experiences of the minority groups that stimulated the development of what we are calling the traditional perspective on assimilation. A massive immigration from Europe began in the 1820s, and over the next century millions of people made the journey from the Old World to the New. They came from every corner of the continent: Germany, Greece, Ireland, Italy, Poland, Portugal,

Figure 2.2 European Immigration to the United States, 1820–1920

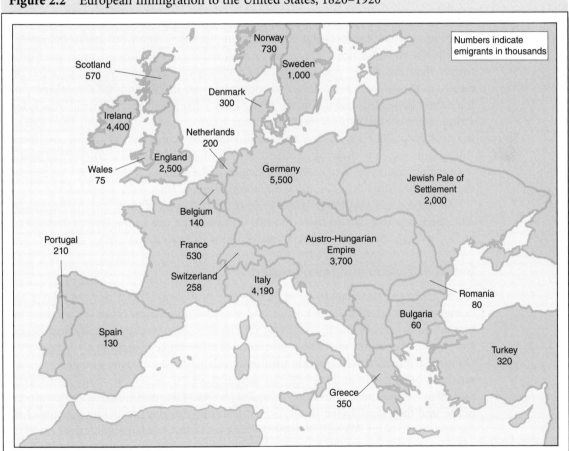

Source: Adapted from Immigration in America.

Russia, Ukraine, and scores of other nations and provinces. They came as young men and women seeking jobs, as families fleeing religious persecution, as political radicals fleeing the police, as farmers seeking land and a fresh start, and as paupers barely able to scrape together the cost of the passage. They came as immigrants, became minority groups upon their arrival, experienced discrimination and prejudice in all its forms, went through all the varieties and stages of assimilation and pluralism, and eventually merged into the society that had rejected them so viciously. Figure 2.2 shows the major European sending nations.

This first mass wave of immigrants shaped the United States in countless ways. When the immigration started in the 1820s, the United States was an agricultural nation clustered along the East Coast, not yet 50 years old. The nation was just coming into contact with Mexicans in the Southwest, immigration from China had not yet begun, slavery was flourishing in the South, and conflict with Native Americans was intense and brutal. When the immigration ended in the 1920s, the population of the United States had increased from fewer than 10 million to more than 100 million, and the society had industrialized, become a world power, and stretched from coast to coast, with colonies in the Pacific and the Caribbean.

It was no coincidence that European immigration, American industrialization, and the rise to global prominence occurred simultaneously. These changes were intimately interlinked, the mutual causes and effects of one another. Industrialization fueled the growth of U.S. military and political power, and the industrial machinery of the nation depended heavily on the flow of labor from Europe. By World War I, for example, 25% of the nation's total labor force was foreign born, and more than half of the workforce in New York, Detroit, and Chicago consisted of immigrant men. Immigrants were the majority of the workers in many important sectors of the economy, including coal mining, steel manufacturing, the garment industry, and meatpacking (Martin & Midgley, 1999, p. 15; Steinberg, 1981, p. 36).

In the sections that follow, we explore the experiences of these groups, beginning with the forces that caused them to leave Europe and come to the United States, and ending with an assessment of their present status in American society.

Industrialization and Immigration

What forces stimulated this mass movement of people? Like any complex phenomenon, immigration from Europe had a multitude of causes, but underlying the process was a massive and fundamental shift in subsistence technology: the **Industrial Revolution**. We mentioned the importance of subsistence technology in Chapter 1. Dominant–minority relations are intimately related to the system a society uses to satisfy its basic needs, and they change as that system changes. The immigrants were pushed out of Europe as industrial technology wrecked the traditional agricultural way of life, and they were drawn to the United States by the jobs created by the spread of the same technology. We will consider the impact of this fundamental transformation of social structure and culture in some detail.

Industrialization began in England in the mid-1700s, spread to other parts of Northern and Western Europe and then, in the 1800s, to Eastern and Southern Europe.

As it rolled across the continent, the Industrial Revolution replaced people and animal power with machines and new forms of energy (steam, coal, and eventually oil and gas), causing an exponential increase in the productive capacity of society.

At the dawn of the Industrial Revolution, most Europeans lived in small, rural villages and survived by traditional farming practices that had changed very little over the centuries (see Figure 2.3). The work of production was **labor-intensive** or done by hand or with the aid of draft animals. Productivity was low, and the tasks of food production and survival required the efforts of virtually the entire family working ceaselessly throughout the year.

Industrialization destroyed this traditional way of life as it introduced new technology, machines, and new sources of energy to the tasks of production. The new technology was **capital-intensive** or dependent on machine power, and it reduced the need for human labor in rural areas as it modernized agriculture. Also, farmland was consolidated into larger and larger tracts for the sake of efficiency, further decreasing the need for human laborers. At the same time, even as survival in the rapidly changing rural economy became more difficult, the rural population began to grow.

In response, peasants began to leave their home villages and move toward urban areas. Factories were being built in or near the cities, opening up opportunities for employment. The urban population tended to increase faster than the job supply, however, and many migrants were unable to find work and had to move on. Many of these former peasants responded to opportunities available in the New World, especially in the United States, where the abundance of farmland on the frontier kept people moving out of the cities and away from the East Coast, thereby sustaining a fairly constant demand for labor in the areas that were easiest for Europeans to reach. As industrialization took hold on both continents, the population movement to European cities and then to North America eventually grew to become one of the largest in human history.

The timing of immigration from Europe followed the timing of industrialization. The first waves of immigrants, often called the **Old Immigration**, came from Northern and Western Europe starting in the 1820s. A second wave, the **New Immigration**, began arriving from Southern and Eastern Europe in the 1880s. Figure 2.4 shows both waves and the rates of legal immigration up to 2010. Note that the New Immigration was much more voluminous than the Old Immigration, and that the number of immigrants declined drastically after the 1920s. We will explore the reasons for this decline later in this chapter and discuss in detail in Chapters 7 through 9 the more recent (post-1965) increase in immigration.

European Origins and Conditions of Entry

The immigrants from Europe varied in innumerable ways. They followed a variety of pathways into the United States, and their experiences were shaped by their cultural and class characteristics, their countries of origin, and the timing of their arrival. Some groups encountered much more resistance than others, and different groups played different roles in the industrialization and urbanization of America. To discuss these diverse patterns systematically, we distinguish three subgroups of European immigrants: Protestants from Northern and Western Europe, the largely Catholic

Figure 2.3 Timeline of the Industrial Revolution, 1712–1903

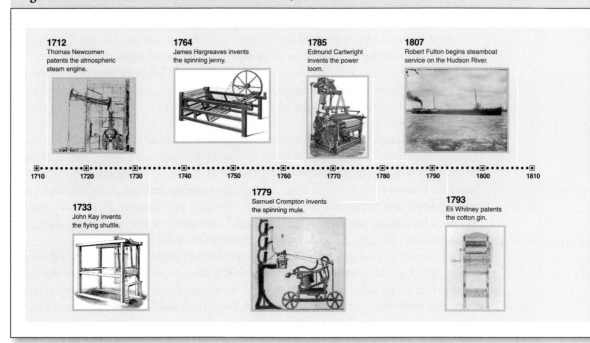

Source: Adapted from Industrial Revolution: Timeline, Facts, and Resources. Research by B. Sobey, TheFreeResource.com

immigrant laborers from Ireland and from Southern and Eastern Europe, and Jewish immigrants from Eastern Europe. We look at these subgroups roughly in the order of their arrival. In later sections, we will consider other sociological variables such as social class and gender that further differentiated these groups.

Northern and Western Protestant Europeans

Northern and Western European immigrants included Danes, Dutch, English, French, Germans, Norwegians, Swedes, and Welsh. These groups were similar to the dominant group in their racial and religious characteristics and also shared many cultural values with the host society, including the Protestant ethic—which stressed hard work, success, and individualism—and support for the principles of democratic government. These similarities eased their acceptance into a society that was highly intolerant of religious and racial differences until well into the 20th century, and these immigrant groups generally experienced a lower degree of ethnocentric rejection and racist disparagement than did the Irish and the immigrants from Southern and Eastern Europe.

Northern and Western European immigrants came from nations that were just as developed as the United States. Thus, these immigrants tended to be more skilled and educated than other immigrant groups, and often brought money and other resources

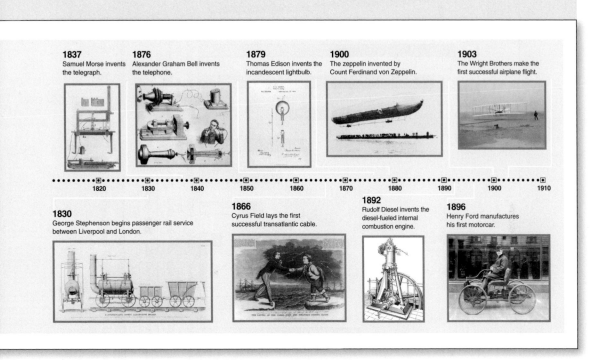

1837
Samuel Morse invents the telegraph.

1876
Alexander Graham Bell invents the telephone.

1879
Thomas Edison invents the incandescent lightbulb.

1900
The zeppelin invented by Count Ferdinand von Zeppelin.

1903
The Wright Brothers make the first successful airplane flight.

1820   1830   1840   1850   1860   1870   1880   1890   1900   1910

1830
George Stephenson begins passenger rail service between Liverpool and London.

1866
Cyrus Field lays the first successful transatlantic cable.

1892
Rudolf Diesel invents the diesel-fueled internal combustion engine.

1896
Henry Ford manufactures his first motorcar.

with which to secure a comfortable place for themselves in their new society. Many settled in the sparsely populated Midwest and in other frontier areas, where they farmed the fertile land that had become available after the conquest and removal of American Indians and Mexican Americans (see Chapter 3). By dispersing throughout the midsection of the country, they lowered their visibility and their degree of competition with dominant group members. Two brief case studies, first of Norwegians and then of Germans, outline the experiences of these groups.

Immigrants From Norway. Norway had a small population base, and immigration from this Scandinavian nation to the United States was never large in absolute numbers. However, "America fever" struck here as it did elsewhere in Europe, and on a per capita basis, Norway sent more immigrants to the United States before 1890 than did any other European nation except Ireland (Chan, 1990, p. 41).

The first Norwegian immigrants were moderately prosperous farmers searching for cheap land. They found abundant acreage in upper-Midwest states, such as Minnesota and Wisconsin, and then found that the local labor supply was too small to effectively cultivate the available land. Many turned to their homeland for assistance and used their relatives and friends to create networks and recruit a labor force. Thus, chains of communication and migration linking Norway to the Northern Plains were

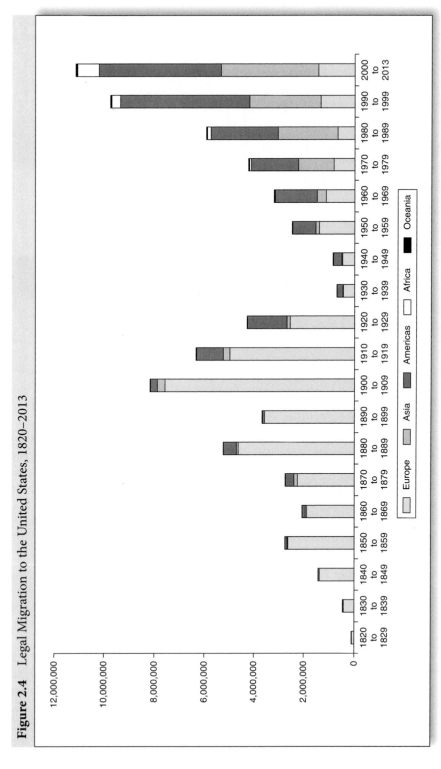

Figure 2.4 Legal Migration to the United States, 1820–2013

Source: Data from Table 2, Persons Obtaining Legal Permanent Status by Region and Selected Country of Last Residence: Fiscal Years 1920 to 2012. *Yearbook of Immigration Statistics: 2012 Legal Permanent Residents.* U.S. Department of Homeland Security.

established, supplying immigrants to these areas for decades (Chan, 1990, p. 41). Today, a strong Scandinavian heritage is still evident in the farms, towns, and cities of the upper Midwest.

Immigrants From Germany. The stream of immigration from Germany was much larger than that from Norway, and German Americans left their mark on the economy, political structure, and cultural life of their new land. In the latter half of the 19th century, at least 25% of the immigrants each year were German (Conzen, 1980, p. 406), and today more Americans (about 15%) trace their ancestries to Germany than to any other country (Brittingham & de la Cruz, 2003).

The German immigrants who arrived earlier in the 1800s moved into the newly opened farmland and the rapidly growing cities of the Midwest, as had many Scandinavians. By 1850, large German communities could be found in Milwaukee, St. Louis, and other midwestern cities (Conzen, 1980, p. 413). Some German immigrants followed the trans-Atlantic route of the cotton trade between Europe and the southern United States, and entered through the port of New Orleans, moving from there to the Midwest and Southwest.

German immigrants arriving later in the century were more likely to settle in urban areas, in part because fertile land was less available. Many of the city-bound German immigrants were skilled workers and artisans, and others found work as laborers in the rapidly expanding industrial sector. The double penetration of German immigrants into the rural economy and the higher sectors of the urban economy is reflected by the fact that by 1870 most employed German Americans were involved in skilled labor (37%) or farming (25%) (Conzen, 1980, p. 413).

German immigrants took relatively high occupational positions in the U.S. labor force, and their sons and daughters were able to translate that relative affluence into economic mobility. By the dawn of the 20th century, large numbers of second-generation German Americans were finding their way into white-collar and professional careers. Within a few generations, German Americans had achieved parity with national norms in education, income, and occupational prestige.

Assimilation Patterns. By and large, assimilation for Norwegian, German, and other Protestant immigrants from Northern and Western Europe was consistent with the traditional model discussed earlier in this chapter. Although members of these groups felt the sting of rejection, prejudice, and discrimination, their movement from acculturation to integration and equality was relatively smooth, especially when compared with the experiences of racial minority groups. Their relative success and high degree of assimilation is suggested in Table 2.3, presented later in this chapter.

Immigrant Laborers From Ireland and Southern and Eastern Europe

The relative ease of assimilation for Northern and Western Europeans contrasts sharply with the experiences of non-Protestant, less-educated, and less-skilled immigrants. These "immigrant laborers" came in two waves. The Irish were part of the Old Immigration that began in the 1820s, but the bulk of this group—Bulgarians, Greeks,

Hungarians, Italians, Poles, Russians, Serbs, Slovaks, Ukrainians, and scores of other Southern and Eastern European groups—made up the New Immigration that began in the 1880s.

Peasant Origins. Most of the immigrants in these nationality groups (like many recent immigrants to the United States) were peasants or unskilled laborers, with few resources other than their willingness to work. They came from rural, village-oriented cultures in which family and kin took precedence over individual needs or desires. Family life for them tended to be autocratic; men dominated and children were expected to subordinate their personal desires and to work for the good of the family as a whole. Arranged marriages were common. This cultural background was less consistent with the industrializing, capitalistic, individualistic, Protestant, Anglo-American culture of the United States and was a major reason that these immigrant laborers experienced a higher level of rejection and discrimination than the immigrants from Northern and Western Europe.

The immigrant laborers were much less likely to enter the rural economy than were the Northern and Western European immigrants. Much of the better frontier land had already been claimed by the time these new immigrant groups began to arrive, and a large number of them had been permanently soured on farming by the oppressive and exploitative agrarian economies from which they were trying to escape.

Regional and Occupational Patterns. They settled in the cities of the industrializing Northeast and found work in plants, mills, mines, and factories. They supplied the armies of laborers needed to power the Industrial Revolution in the United States, although their view of this process was generally from the bottom looking up. They arrived during the decades in which the American industrial and urban infrastructure was being constructed. They built roads, canals, and railroads, as well as the buildings that housed the machinery of industrialization. For example, the first tunnels of the New York City subway system were dug, largely by hand, by laborers from Italy. Other immigrants found work in the coalfields of Pennsylvania and West Virginia and the steel mills of Pittsburgh, and they flocked by the millions to the factories of the Northeast.

Like other low-skilled immigrant groups, these newcomers took jobs in which strength and stamina were more important than literacy or skilled labor. In fact, the minimum level of skills required for employment actually declined as industrialization proceeded through its early phases. To keep wages low and take advantage of what seemed like an inexhaustible supply of cheap labor, industrialists and factory owners developed technologies and machines that required few skills and little knowledge of English to operate. As mechanization proceeded, unskilled workers replaced skilled workers in the workforce. Not infrequently, women and children replaced men because they could be hired for lower wages (Steinberg, 1981, p. 35).

Assimilation Patterns. Eventually, as the generations passed, the prejudice, systematic discrimination, and other barriers to upward mobility for the immigrant laborer groups weakened, and their descendants began to rise out of the working class. Although the first and second generations of these groups were largely limited to jobs at the unskilled or semiskilled level, the third and later generations rose in the American social class system. As Table 2.3 shows (later in this chapter), the descendants of the immigrant laborers achieved parity with national norms by the latter half of the 20th century.

Eastern European Jewish Immigrants and the Ethnic Enclave

Jewish immigrants from Russia and other parts of Eastern Europe followed a third pathway into U.S. society. These immigrants were a part of the New Immigration and began arriving in the 1880s. Unlike the immigrant laborer groups, who were generally economic refugees and included many young, single men, Eastern European Jews were fleeing religious persecution and arrived as family units intending to settle permanently and become citizens. They settled in the urban areas of the Northeast and Midwest. New York City was the most common destination, and the Lower East Side became the best-known Jewish American neighborhood. By 1920, about 60% of all Jewish Americans lived in the urban areas between Boston and Philadelphia, with almost 50% living in New York City alone. Another 30% lived in the urban areas of the Midwest, particularly in Chicago (Goren, 1980, p. 581).

Urban Origins. In Russia and other parts of Eastern Europe, Jews had been barred from agrarian occupations and had come to rely on the urban economy for their livelihoods. When they immigrated to the United States, they brought these urban skills and job experiences with them. For example, almost two thirds of the immigrant Jewish men had been tailors and other skilled laborers in Eastern Europe (Goren, 1980, p. 581). In the rapidly industrializing U.S. economy of the early 20th century, they were able to use these skills to find work.

Other Jewish immigrants joined the urban working class and took manual labor and unskilled jobs in the industrial sector (Morawska, 1990, p. 202). The garment industry in particular became the lifeblood of the Jewish community and provided jobs to about one third of all Eastern European Jews residing in the major cities (Goren, 1980, p. 582). Women as well as men were involved in the garment industry. Jewish women, like the women of more recent immigrant laborer groups, found ways to combine their jobs and their domestic responsibilities. As young girls, they worked in factories and sweatshops, and after marriage, they did the same work at home, sewing precut garments together or doing other piecework such as wrapping cigars or making artificial flowers, often assisted by their children (Amott & Matthaei, 1991, p. 115).

An Enclave Economy. Unlike most European immigrant groups, Jewish Americans became heavily involved in commerce and often found ways to start their own businesses and become self-employed. Drawing on their experience in the "old country," many started businesses and small independent enterprises and developed an enclave economy. Jewish neighborhoods were densely populated and provided a ready market for all kinds of services such as bakeries, butcher and candy shops, and other retail enterprises.

Capitalizing on their residential concentration and close proximity, Jewish immigrants created dense networks of commercial, financial, and social cooperation. The Jewish American enclave survived because of the cohesiveness of the group; the willingness of wives, children, and other relatives to work for little or no monetary compensation; and the commercial savvy of the early immigrants. Also, a large pool of cheap labor and sources of credit and other financial services were available within the community. The Jewish American enclave grew and provided a livelihood for many of the children and grandchildren of the immigrants (Portes & Manning, 1986, pp. 51–52). As has been the case with other enclave groups that we will discuss in future chapters, including Chinese Americans and Cuban Americans, economic advancement preceded extensive acculturation, and Jewish Americans made significant strides toward economic equality before they became fluent in English or were otherwise Americanized.

Americanized Generations. One obvious way in which an enclave immigrant group can improve its position is to develop an educated and acculturated second generation. The Americanized, English-speaking children of the immigrants used their greater familiarity with the dominant society and their language facility to help preserve and expand the family enterprise. Furthermore, as the second generation appeared, the American public school system was expanding, and education through the college level was free or inexpensive in New York City and other cities (Steinberg, 1981, pp. 128–138). There was also a strong push for the second and third generations to enter professions, and as Jewish Americans excelled in school, resistance to and discrimination against them increased. By the 1920s, many elite colleges and universities, such as Dartmouth, had established quotas that limited the number of Jewish students they would admit (Dinnerstein, 1977, p. 228). These quotas were not abolished until after World War II.

Assimilation Patterns. The enclave economy and the Jewish neighborhoods established by the immigrants proved to be an effective base from which to integrate into American society. The descendants of the Eastern European Jewish immigrants moved out of the ethnic neighborhoods years ago, and their positions in the economy—their pushcarts, stores, and jobs in the garment industry—have been taken over by more recent immigrants. When they left the enclave economy, many second- and third-generation Eastern European Jews did not enter the mainstream occupational structure at the bottom, as the immigrant laborer groups tended to do. They used the resources generated by the entrepreneurship of the early generations to gain access to prestigious and advantaged social class positions (Portes & Manning, 1986, p. 53). Studies show that Jewish Americans today, as a group, surpass national averages in income, levels of education, and occupational prestige (Sklare, 1971, pp. 60–69; see also Cohen, 1985; Massarik & Chenkin, 1973). The relatively higher status of Russian Americans shown in Table 2.3 (later in this chapter) is due in part to the fact that many Jewish Americans are of Russian descent.

Chains of Immigration

All immigrant groups tend to follow "chains" established and maintained by the members of their groups. Some versions of the traditional assimilation perspective (especially human capital theory) treat immigration and status attainment as purely the result of individual effort. To the contrary, scholars have demonstrated that immigration to the United States was in large measure a group (sociological) phenomenon. Immigrant chains stretched across the oceans, held together by the ties of kinship, language, religion, culture, and a sense of common peoplehood (Bodnar, 1985; Tilly, 1990). The networks supplied information, money for passage, family news, and job offers.

Here is how chain immigration worked (and, although modified by modern technology, continues to work today): Someone from a village in, for instance, Poland, would make it to the United States. The successful immigrant would send word to the home village, perhaps by hiring a letter writer. Along with news and stories of his adventures, he would send his address. Within months, another immigrant from the village, perhaps a relative, would show up at the address of the original immigrant. After months of experience in the new society, the original immigrant could lend assistance, provide a place to sleep, help with job hunting, and orient the newcomer to the area.

Before long, others would arrive from the village in need of the same sort of introduction to the mysteries of America. The compatriots would tend to settle close to one another, in the same building or on the same block. Soon, entire neighborhoods were filled with people from a certain village, province, or region. In these ethnic enclaves, people spoke the old language and observed the old ways. They started businesses, founded churches or synagogues, had families, and began mutual aid societies and other organizations. There was safety in numbers and comfort and security in a familiar, if transplanted, set of traditions and customs.

Immigrants often responded to U.S. society by attempting to re-create as much of their old world as possible. Partly to avoid the harsher forms of rejection and discrimination and partly to band together for solidarity and mutual support, immigrants created their own miniature social worlds within the bustling metropolises of the industrializing Northeast and the West Coast. These Little Italys, Little Warsaws, Little Irelands, Greektowns, Chinatowns, and Little Tokyos were safe havens that insulated the immigrants from the larger society and allowed them to establish bonds with one another, organize a group life, pursue their own group interests, and have some control over the pace of their adjustment to American culture. For some groups and in some areas, the ethnic subcommunity was a short-lived phenomenon. For others (the Jewish enclave discussed earlier, for example), the neighborhood became the dominant structure of their lives, and the networks continued to function long after the arrival of group members in the United States.

The Campaign Against Immigration: Prejudice, Racism, and Discrimination

Today, it may be hard to conceive of the bitterness and intensity of the prejudice that greeted the Irish, Italians, Jews, Poles, and other new immigrant groups. Even as they were becoming an indispensable segment of the American workforce, they were castigated, ridiculed, attacked, and disparaged. The Irish were the first immigrant laborers to arrive; thus, they were the first to feel this intense prejudice and discrimination. White Americans waged campaigns against immigrants; mobs attacked Irish neighborhoods and burned Roman Catholic churches and convents. Some employers blatantly refused to hire the Irish, often advertising their ethnic preferences with signs that read "No Irish Need Apply." Until later arriving groups pushed them up, the Irish were mired at the bottom of the job market. Indeed, at one time they were referred to as the "niggers of Boston" (Blessing, 1980; Potter, 1973; Shannon, 1964).

Other groups felt the same sting of rejection as they arrived. Italian immigrants were particularly likely to be the victims of violent attacks, one of the most vicious of which took place in New Orleans in 1891. The city's police chief was assassinated, and rumors of Italian involvement in the murder were rampant. Hundreds of Italians were arrested, and nine were brought to trial. All were acquitted. Anti-Italian sentiment was running so high, however, that a mob lynched 11 Italians while police and city officials did nothing (Higham, 1963).

Anti-Catholicism. Much of the prejudice against the Irish and the new immigrants was expressed as anti-Catholicism. Prior to the mid-19th century, Anglo-American society had been almost exclusively Protestant. Catholicism, with its celibate clergy, Latin masses, and cloistered nuns, seemed alien, exotic, and threatening. The growth of Catholicism, especially because it was associated with non-Anglo immigrants, raised fears that the Protestant religions would lose status. There were even rumors that the Pope was planning to move the Vatican to America and organize a takeover of the U.S. government.

Although Catholics were often stereotyped as single groups, they varied along a number of dimensions. For example, the Catholic faith as practiced in Ireland differed significantly from that practiced in Italy, Poland, and other countries. Catholic immigrant groups often established their own parishes, with priests who could speak the old language. These cultural and national differences often separated Catholic groups, despite their common faith (Herberg, 1960).

Anti-Semitism. Jews from Russia and Eastern Europe faced intense prejudice and racism (or **anti-Semitism**) as they began arriving in large numbers in the 1880s. Biased sentiments and negative stereotypes about Jews have been a part of Western tradition for centuries. In fact, they have been stronger and more vicious in Europe than in the United States. For nearly two millennia, Christians chastised and persecuted European Jews as the "killers of Christ" and stereotyped them as materialistic moneylenders and crafty business owners.

The stereotype that links Jews and money lending has its origins in the fact that in premodern Europe, the Church forbade Catholics to engage in usury (charging interest for loans). Jews were under no such restriction, and they filled the gap within the economy. The most dreadful episode in the long history of European anti-Semitism was, of course, the Nazi Holocaust, in which 6 million Jews died. European anti-Semitism did not end with the demise of the Nazi regime, and it remains a prominent concern throughout Europe and Russia today.

Before the mass immigration of Eastern European Jews began in the late 1800s, anti-Semitism in the United States was relatively mild, perhaps because the group was so small. As the immigration continued, anti-Semitism increased in intensity and viciousness, fostering the view of Jews as cunning but dishonest merchants. In the late 19th century, whites began to ban Jews from social clubs and the boardrooms of businesses and other organizations. Summer resorts began posting notices such as, "We prefer not to entertain Hebrews" (Goren, 1980, p. 585).

By the 1920s and 1930s, anti-Semitism had become quite prominent among American prejudices and was being preached by the Ku Klux Klan and other extreme racist groups. Also, because many political radicals and labor leaders of the time were Jewish immigrants, anti-Semitism became fused with a fear of Communism and other anti-capitalist doctrines. Some prominent Americans espoused anti-Semitic views, including Henry Ford, the founder of Ford Motor Company; Charles Lindbergh, the aviator who was the first to fly solo across the Atlantic; and Father Charles Coughlin, a Catholic priest with a popular radio show (Selzer, 1972).

Anti-Semitism reached a peak before World War II and tapered off in the decades following the war, but it remains part of U.S. society (Anti-Defamation League, 2000). Anti-Semitism also has a prominent place in the ideologies of a variety of extremist groups that have emerged in recent years, including "skinheads" and various contemporary incarnations of the Ku Klux Klan. Some of this targeting of Jews seems to increase during economic recession and may be related to the stereotypical view of Jewish Americans as extremely prosperous and materialistic.

A Successful Exclusion. The prejudice and racism directed against the immigrants also found expression in organized, widespread efforts to stop the flow of immigration. A variety of anti-immigrant organizations appeared almost as soon as the mass European immigration started in the 1820s. The strength of these campaigns waxed and waned, largely in harmony with the strength of the economy and the size of the job supply. Anti-immigrant sentiment intensified, and the strength of its organized expressions increased during hard times and depressions and tended to soften when the economy improved.

The campaign ultimately triumphed with the passage of the National Origins Act in 1924, which established a quota system limiting the number of immigrants that would be accepted each year from each sending nation, a system that was openly racist. For example, the size of the quota for European nations was based on the proportional representation of each nationality in the United States as of 1890. This year was chosen because it predated the bulk of the New Immigration and gave the most generous quotas to northern and western European nations.

The quota system allocated nearly 70% of the available immigration slots to the nations of Northern and Western Europe, despite the fact that immigration from those areas had largely ended by the 1920s. Immigration from western hemisphere nations was not directly affected by this legislation, but immigration from Asian nations was

banned altogether. At this time, almost all parts of Africa were still the colonial possessions of various European nations and received no separate quotas. In other words, the
quota for immigrants from Africa was zero.

The National Origins Act drastically reduced the overall number of immigrants
that would be admitted each year. The effectiveness of the numerical restrictions is
clearly apparent in Figure 2.3. By the time the Great Depression took hold of the
American economy in the 1930s, immigration had dropped to the lowest level in a
century. The National Origins Act remained in effect until 1965.

QUESTIONS FOR REFLECTION

6. What forces motivated people to leave Europe and come to North America? How did
    these motives change from time to time and from place to place?

7. What motivated the forces of resistance and discrimination in the United States? How
    did the "exclusionists" finally triumph? What roles did class play in these processes?

Patterns of Assimilation

In this section, we will explore some of the common patterns in the process of
assimilation followed by European immigrants and their descendants. These patterns
have been well established by research conducted in the traditional perspective and are
consistent with the model of assimilation developed by Gordon. They include assimilation by generation, ethnic succession, and structural mobility. We discuss each separately in this section.

The Importance of Generations

People today—social scientists, politicians, and ordinary citizens—often fail to
recognize the time and effort it takes for a group to become completely Americanized.
For most European immigrant groups, the process took generations, and it was the
grandchildren or the great-grandchildren (or even great-great-grandchildren) of the
immigrants who finally completed acculturation and integration. Mass immigration
from Europe ended in the 1920s, but the assimilation of some European ethnic groups
was not completed until late in the 20th century.

Here is a rough summary of how assimilation proceeded for these European immigrants: The first generation, the actual immigrants, settled in ethnic neighborhoods,
such as Little Italy in New York City, and made only limited movement toward acculturation and integration. They focused their energies on the network of family and
social relationships encompassed within their own groups. Of course, many of them—
most often the men—had to leave their neighborhoods for work and for other reasons,
and these excursions required some familiarity with the larger society. Some English
had to be learned, and taking a job outside the neighborhood is, almost by definition,

a form of integration. Nonetheless, the first generation lived and died largely within the context of the old country, which had been re-created within the new.

The second generation, or the children of the immigrants, found themselves in a position of psychological or social marginality: They were partly ethnic and partly American but full members of neither group. They were born in America but in households and neighborhoods that were ethnic, not American. They learned the old language first and were socialized in the old ways. As they entered childhood, however, they entered the public schools, where they were socialized into the Anglo-American culture.

Often, the world the second generation learned about at school conflicted with the world they inhabited at home. For example, the old country family values often expected children to subordinate their self-interests to the interests of their elders and of the family as a whole. Parents arranged marriages, or at least they heavily influenced them; marriages were subject to parents' approval. Needless to say, these customs conflicted sharply with American ideas about individualism and romantic love. Differences of this sort often caused painful conflict between the ethnic first generation and their Americanized children.

As the second generation progressed toward adulthood, they tended to move out of the old neighborhoods. Their geographic mobility was often motivated by desires for social mobility. They were much more acculturated than their parents, spoke English fluently, and enjoyed a wider range of occupational choices and opportunities. Discriminatory policies in education, housing, and the job market sometimes limited them, but they were upwardly mobile, and in their pursuit of jobs and careers, they left behind their ethnic communities and many of their parents' customs.

The members of the third generation, or the grandchildren of the immigrants, were typically born and raised in nonethnic settings. English was their first (and often their only) language, and their values and perceptions were thoroughly American. Although family and kinship ties with grandparents and the old neighborhood often remained strong, ethnicity for this generation was a relatively minor part of their daily realities and their self-images. Visits on weekends and holidays and family rituals revolving around the cycles of birth, marriage, and death—these activities might have connected the third generation to the world of their ancestors, but in terms of their everyday lives, they were American, not ethnic.

The pattern of assimilation by generation progressed as follows:

- The first generation began the process and was at least slightly acculturated and integrated.
- The second generation was quite acculturated and highly integrated (at least into the secondary sectors of the society).
- The third generation finished the acculturation process and enjoyed high levels of integration at both the secondary and primary levels.

Table 2.2 illustrates these patterns in terms of the structural assimilation of Italian Americans. The educational and occupational characteristics of this group converge with those of white Anglo-Saxon Protestants (WASPs) as the generations change. For example, the percentage of Italian Americans with some college shows a gap of more than 20 points between the first and second generations and WASPs. Italians of the third and fourth generations, though, are virtually identical to WASPs on this measure of integration in the secondary sector. The other differences between Italians and WASPs shrink in a similar fashion from generation to generation.

The first five measures of educational and occupational attainment in Table 2.2 illustrate the generational patterns of integration (or structural assimilation). The sixth measures marital assimilation, or intermarriage. It displays the percentage of men of "unmixed," or 100%, Italian heritage who married women outside the Italian community. Note once more the tendency for integration, now at the primary level, to increase across the generations. The huge majority of first-generation men married within their group (only 21.9% married non-Italians). By the third generation, 67.3% of the men were marrying non-Italians.

Of course, this model of step-by-step, linear assimilation by generation fits some groups better than others. For example, immigrants from Northern and Western Europe (with the exception of the Irish) were generally more similar, racially and culturally, to the dominant group and tended to be more educated and skilled. They experienced relatively easier acceptance and tended to complete the assimilation process in three generations or less.

In contrast, immigrants from Ireland and from Southern and Eastern Europe were mostly uneducated, unskilled peasants who were more likely to join the huge army of industrial labor that manned the factories, mines, and mills. These groups were more

Table 2.2   Some Comparisons Between Italians and WASPs

	Indicators:	WASPs*	Generation		
			First	*Second*	*Third and Fourth*
1	Percentage with some college	42.4%	19.0%	19.4%	41.7%
2	Average years of education	12.6	9.0	11.1	13.4
3	Percentage white collar	34.7%	20.0%	22.5%	28.8%
4	Percentage blue collar	37.9%	65.0%	53.9%	39.0%
5	Average occupational prestige	42.5	34.3	36.8	42.5
6	Percentage of "unmixed" Italian men marrying non-Italian women		21.9%	51.4%	67.3%

Source: Adapted from Alba (1985, Tab. 5-3, 5-4, 6-2). Data are originally from the NORC General Social Surveys (1975–1980) and the Current Population Survey (1979). Copyright ©1985 Richard D. Alba.

Note: *White Anglo-Saxon Protestants (WASPs) were not separated by generation, and some of the differences between groups may be the result of factors such as age. That is, older WASPs may have levels of education more comparable to those of first-generation Italian Americans than to those of WASPs as a whole.

likely to remain at the bottom of the American class structure for generations and to have risen to middle-class prosperity only in the recent past. As mentioned earlier, Eastern European Jews formed an enclave and followed a distinctly different pathway of assimilation, using the enclave as a springboard to launch the second and third generations into the larger society (although their movements were circumscribed by widespread anti-Semitic sentiments and policies).

It is important to keep this generational pattern in mind when examining immigration to the United States today. It is common for contemporary newcomers (especially Hispanics) to be criticized for their "slow" pace of assimilation, but this process should be seen in the light of the generational time frame for assimilation of European immigrants. Modern forms of transportation allow immigration to happen quickly. Assimilation, on the other hand, is slow by nature.

Ethnic Succession

A second factor that shaped the assimilation experience is captured in the concept of **ethnic succession**, or the myriad ways in which European ethnic groups unintentionally affected each other's positions in the social class structure of the larger society. The overall pattern was that each European immigrant group tended to be pushed to higher social class levels and more favorable economic situations by the groups that arrived after it. As more experienced groups became upwardly mobile and began to move out of the neighborhoods that served as their "ports of entry," new groups of immigrants replaced them and began the process all over again. Some neighborhoods in the cities of the Northeast served as the ethnic neighborhood—the first safe haven in the new society—for a variety of successive groups. Some neighborhoods continue to fill this role today.

This process can be understood in terms of the second stage of Gordon's model: integration at the secondary level (see Table 2.1) or entry into the public institutions and organizations of the larger society. Three pathways of integration tended to be most important for European immigrants: politics, labor unions, and the church. We will cover each in turn, illustrating with the Irish, the first immigrant laborers to arrive in large numbers, but the general patterns apply to all white ethnic groups.

Politics. The Irish tended to follow the Northern and Western Europeans in the job market and social class structure and were, in turn, followed by the wave of new immigrants. In many urban areas of the Northeast, they moved into the neighborhoods and took jobs left behind by German laborers. After a period of acculturation and adjustment, the Irish began to create their own connections with the mainstream society and to improve their economic and social positions. They were replaced in their neighborhoods and at the bottom of the occupational structure by Italians, Poles, and other immigrant groups arriving after them.

As the years passed and the Irish gained more experience, they began to forge more links to the larger society; in particular, they allied themselves with the Democratic Party and helped construct the political machines that came to dominate many city governments in the 19th and 20th centuries. Machine politicians were often corrupt and even criminal, regularly subverting the election process, bribing city and state officials, using city budgets to fill the pockets of the political bosses and their cronies, and passing out public jobs as payoffs for favors and faithful service. Although not exactly models of good government, the political machines performed a number of valuable social services for their constituents and loyal followers. Machine politicians, such as Boss Tweed of Tammany Hall in New York City, could find jobs, provide food and clothing for the destitute, aid victims of fires and other calamities, and intervene in the criminal and civil courts.

Much of the power of the urban political machines derived from their control of the city payroll. The leaders of the machines used municipal jobs and the city budget as part of a "spoils" system (as in "to the victor go the spoils") and as rewards for their supporters and allies. The faithful Irish party worker might be rewarded for service to "the machine" with a job in the police department (thus the stereotypical Irish cop) or some other agency. Private businesspeople might be rewarded with lucrative contracts to supply services or perform other city business.

The political machines served as engines of economic opportunity and linked Irish Americans to a central and important institution of the dominant society. Using the resources controlled by local government as a power base, the Irish (and other immigrant groups after them) began to integrate themselves into the larger society and carve out a place in the mainstream structures of American society.

Labor Unions. The labor movement provided a second link between the Irish, other European immigrant groups, and the larger society. Although virtually all white ethnic groups had a hand in the creation and eventual success of the movement, many of the founders and early leaders were Irish. For example, Terence Powderly, an Irish Catholic, founded one of the first U.S. labor unions, and in the early years of the 20th century, about one third of union leaders were Irish, and more than 50 national unions had Irish presidents (Bodnar, 1985, p. 111; Brody, 1980, p. 615).

As the labor movement grew in strength and gradually acquired legitimacy, the leaders of the movement also gained status, power, and other resources, while the rank-and-file membership gained job security, increased wages, and improved fringe benefits. The labor movement provided another channel through which resources, power, status, and jobs flowed to the white ethnic groups.

Because of the way in which jobs were organized in industrializing America, union work typically required communication and cooperation across ethnic lines. The American workforce at the turn of the 20th century was multiethnic and multilingual, and union leaders had to coordinate and mobilize the efforts of many different language and cultural groups to represent the interest of the workers as a social class. Thus, labor union leaders became important intermediaries between the larger society and European immigrant groups.

Women were also heavily involved in the labor movement. Immigrant women were among the most exploited segments of the labor force, and they were involved in some of the most significant events in American labor history. For example, one of the first victories of the union movement occurred in New York City in 1909. The Uprising of the 20,000 was a massive strike of mostly Jewish and Italian girls and women (many in their teens) against the garment industry. The strike lasted four months, despite attacks by thugs hired by the bosses and abuses by the police and the courts. The strikers eventually won recognition of the union from many employers, a reversal of a wage decrease, and a reduction in the 56- to 59-hour week they were expected to work (Goren, 1980, p. 584).

One of the great tragedies in the history of labor relations in the United States also involved European immigrant women. In 1911, a fire swept through the Triangle Shirtwaist Company, a garment industry shop located on the 10th floor of a building in New York City. The fire spread rapidly, and the few escape routes were quickly cut off. About 140 young immigrant women died; many chose to leap to their deaths rather than be killed by the flames. The disaster outraged the public, and more than a quarter of a million people attended the victims' funerals. The incident fueled a drive for reform and improvement of work conditions and safety regulations (Amott & Matthaei, 1991, pp. 114–116; see also Schoener, 1967).

European immigrant women also filled leadership roles in the labor movement and served as presidents and in other offices, although usually in women-dominated unions. One of the most significant union activists was Mother Jones, an Irish immigrant who worked tirelessly to organize miners:

> Until she was nearly one hundred years old, Mother Jones was where the danger was greatest—crossing militia lines, spending weeks in damp prisons, incurring the wrath of governors, presidents, and coal operators—she helped to organize the United Mine Workers with the only tools she felt she needed: "convictions and a voice." (Forner, 1980, p. 281)

Women workers often faced opposition from men as well as from employers. The major unions were not only racially discriminatory, but also hostile to organizing women. For example, companies required women laundry workers in San Francisco at the start of the 20th century to live in dormitories and work from 6 a.m. until midnight. When they applied to the international laundry workers union for a charter, men union members blocked them. The women eventually went on strike and won the right to an eight-hour workday in 1912 (Amott & Matthaei, 1991, p. 117).

Religion. Religious institutions provided a third avenue of mobility for the Irish and other white ethnic groups. The Irish were the first large group of Catholic immigrants, and therefore were eventually in a favorable position to dominate the church's administrative structure. The Catholic priesthood became largely Irish and, as these priests were promoted through the hierarchy, they eventually became bishops and cardinals. The Catholic faith was practiced in different ways in different nations. As other Catholic immigrant groups began to arrive, conflict within the Irish-dominated church increased. Both Italian and Polish Catholic immigrants demanded their own parishes in which they could speak their own languages and celebrate their own customs and festivals. Dissatisfaction was so intense that some Polish Catholics broke with Rome and formed a separate Polish National Catholic Church (Lopata, 1976, p. 49).

The other Catholic immigrant groups eventually began to supply priests and other religious functionaries and to occupy leadership positions within the church. Although the church continued to be disproportionately influenced by the Irish, other white ethnic groups also used the Catholic Church as part of their power base for gaining acceptance and integration into the larger society.

Other Pathways. Besides party politics, the union movement, and religion, European immigrant groups forged other not-so-legitimate pathways of upward mobility. One alternative to legitimate success was offered by crime, a pathway that has been used by every ethnic group to some extent. Crime became particularly lucrative and attractive when Prohibition, the attempt to eliminate all alcohol use in the United States, went into effect in the 1920s. The criminalization of liquor failed to lower the demand, and Prohibition created a golden economic opportunity for those willing to take the risks involved in manufacturing and supplying alcohol to the American public.

Italian Americans headed many of the criminal organizations that took advantage of Prohibition. Criminal leaders and organizations with roots in Sicily, a region with a long history of secret antiestablishment societies, were especially important (Alba, 1985, pp. 62–64). The connection between organized crime, Prohibition, and Italian Americans is well known, but it is not widely recognized that ethnic succession operated in organized crime just as it did within legitimate opportunity structures. The Irish and Germans had been involved in organized crime for decades before the 1920s. The Italians competed with these established gangsters, and with Jewish crime syndicates, for control of bootlegging and other criminal enterprises. The pattern of ethnic succession continued after the repeal of Prohibition in 1933, and members of groups newer to urban areas, including African Americans, Jamaicans, and Hispanic Americans, have recently challenged the Italian-dominated criminal "families."

Ethnic succession can be observed in the institution of sports, also. Since the beginning of the 20th century, sports have offered a pathway to success and affluence that has attracted countless millions of young men and women. Success in many sports requires little in the way of formal credentials, education, or English fluency, and sports have been particularly appealing to the young men in minority groups that have few other resources or opportunities.

For example, at the turn of the century the Irish dominated the sport of boxing, but boxers from the Italian American community and other new immigrant groups eventually replaced them. Each successive wave of boxers reflected the concentration of a particular ethnic group at the bottom of the class structure. The succession of minority groups continues to this day, with boxing now dominated by African American and Latino fighters (Rader, 1983, pp. 87–106). A similar progression, or "layering," of ethnic and racial groups can be observed in other sports and in the entertainment industry.

Continuing Industrialization and Structural Mobility

We have already mentioned that dominant–minority relations tend to change along with changes in subsistence technology, and we can find an example of this relationship in the history of the European immigrant groups across the 20th century.

Industrialization is a continuous process. As it proceeded, the nature of work in America evolved and changed and created opportunities for upward mobility for white ethnic groups. One important form of upward mobility throughout the 20th century, called **structural mobility**, resulted more from changes in the structure of the economy and the labor market than from any individual effort or desire to "get ahead."

Structural mobility is the result of the continuing mechanization and automation of the workplace. As machines replaced people in the workforce, the supply of manual, blue-collar jobs that had provided employment for so many first- and second-generation European immigrant laborers dwindled. At the same time, the supply of white-collar jobs increased, but access to the better jobs depended heavily on educational credentials. For white ethnic groups, a high school education became much more available in the 1930s, and college and university programs began to expand rapidly in the late 1940s, spurred in large part by the educational benefits made available to World War II veterans. Each generation of white ethnics, especially those born after 1925, was significantly more educated than the previous generation, and many were able to translate their increased human capital into upward mobility in the mainstream job market (Morawska, 1990, pp. 212–213).

The descendants of European immigrants became upwardly mobile not only because of their individual ambitions and efforts but also because of the changing location of jobs and the progressively greater opportunities for education available to them. Of course, the pace and timing of this upward movement was highly variable from group to group and place to place. Ethnic succession continued to operate, and the descendants of the most recent immigrants from Europe (Italians and Poles, for example) tended to be the last to benefit from the general upgrading in education and the job market.

Still, structural mobility is one of the keys to the eventual successful integration of all white ethnic groups that is displayed in Table 2.3 (later in this chapter). During these same years, racial minority groups, particularly African Americans, were excluded from the dominant group's educational system and, therefore, from the opportunity to compete for better jobs.

QUESTIONS FOR REFLECTION

8. Why is generation important for understanding assimilation?

9. What were the major institutional pathways through which European immigrants adapted to U.S. society? Can you cite evidence from your home community of similar patterns for immigrant groups today?

Variations in Assimilation

In the previous section, we discussed patterns that were common to European immigrants and their descendants. Now we address some of the sources of variation and diversity in assimilation, a complex process that is never exactly the same for any two groups. Sociologists have paid particular attention to the way that degree of similarity, religion, social class, and gender shaped the overall assimilation of the descendants of the mass European immigration. They have also investigated the way in which immigrants' reasons for coming to this country have affected the experiences of different groups.

Degree of Similarity

Since the dominant group consisted largely of Protestants with ethnic origins in Northern and Western Europe, especially in England, it is not surprising to learn that the degree of resistance, prejudice, and discrimination encountered by the different European immigrant groups varied, in part, by the degree to which they differed from these dominant groups. The most significant differences included religion, language, cultural values, and, for some groups, physical characteristics (which were often seen as "racial"). Thus, Protestant immigrants from Northern and Western Europe experienced less resistance than the English-speaking Catholic Irish, who in turn were accepted more readily than the new immigrants, who were both non–English speaking and overwhelmingly non-Protestant.

The preferences of the dominant group correspond roughly to the arrival times of the immigrants. The most similar groups immigrated earliest, and the least similar tended to be the last to arrive. Because of this coincidence, resistance to any one group of immigrants tended to fade as new groups arrived. For example, anti-German prejudice and discrimination never became particularly vicious or widespread (except during the heat of the World Wars) because the Irish began arriving in large numbers at about the same time. Concerns about the German immigrants were swamped by fears that the Catholic Irish could never be assimilated. Then, as the 19th century drew to a close, immigrants from Southern and Eastern Europe—even more different from the dominant group—began to arrive and made concerns about the Irish seem trivial.

In addition, the New Immigration was far larger than the Old Immigration (see Figure 2.3). Southern and Eastern Europeans arrived in record numbers in the early 20th century. The sheer volume of the immigration raised fears that American cities and institutions would be swamped by hordes of what were seen as racially inferior, inassimilable immigrants, a fear that resonates today in our debates about modern immigrants.

Thus, a preference hierarchy was formed in American culture that privileged Northern and Western Europeans over Southern and Eastern Europeans, and Protestants over Catholics and Jews. These rankings reflect the ease with which the groups have been assimilated and have made their way into the larger society. This hierarchy of ethnic preference is still a part of American prejudice, as we saw in the social distance scores displayed in Table 1.2 (in Chapter 1) although it is much more muted today than in the heyday of immigration.

Religion

A major differentiating factor in the experiences of the European immigrant groups, recognized by Gordon and other students of American assimilation, was religion. Protestant, Catholic, and Jewish immigrants lived in different neighborhoods, occupied different niches in the workforce, formed separate networks of affiliation and groups, and chose their marriage partners from different pools of people.

One important study that documented the importance of religion for European immigrants and their descendants (and also reinforced the importance of generations) was conducted by sociologist Ruby Jo Kennedy (1944). She studied intermarriage patterns in New Haven, Connecticut, over a 70-year period ending in the 1940s and found that the immigrants generally chose marriage partners from a pool whose boundaries were marked by ethnicity and religion. For example, Irish Catholics married other Irish Catholics, Italian Catholics married Italian Catholics, Irish Protestants married Irish Protestants, and so forth across all the ethnic and religious divisions she studied.

The pool of marriage partners for the children and grandchildren of the immigrants continued to be bounded by religion but not as much by ethnicity. Thus, later generations of Irish Catholics continued to marry other Catholics but were less likely to marry other Irish. As assimilation proceeded, ethnic group boundaries faded (or "melted"), but religious boundaries did not. Kennedy described this phenomenon as a **triple melting pot**: a pattern of structural assimilation within each of the three religious denominations (Kennedy, 1944, 1952).

Will Herberg (1960), another important student of American assimilation, also explored the connection between religion and ethnicity. Writing in the 1950s, he noted that the pressures of acculturation did not affect all aspects of ethnicity equally. European immigrants and their descendants were strongly encouraged to learn English, but they were not as pressured to change their religious beliefs. Very often, their religious faith was the strongest connection between later generations and their immigrant ancestors. The American tradition of religious tolerance allowed the descendants of the European immigrants to preserve this tie to their roots without being seen as "un-American." As a result, the Protestant, Catholic, and Jewish faiths eventually came to occupy roughly equal degrees of legitimacy in American society.

Thus, for the descendants of the European immigrants, religion became a vehicle through which their ethnicity could be expressed. For many members of this group, religion and ethnicity were fused, and ethnic traditions and identities came to have a religious expression.

Social Class

Social class is a central feature of social structure, and it is not surprising that it affected the European immigrant groups in a number of ways. First, social class combined with religion to shape the social world of the descendants of the European immigrants. In fact, Gordon (1964) concluded that U.S. society in the 1960s actually incorporated not three, but four melting pots (one for each of the major ethnic or religious groups and one for black Americans), each of which was internally subdivided by social class. In his view, the most significant structural unit within American society was the **ethclass**, defined by the intersection of the religious, ethnic, and social class boundaries (e.g., working-class Catholic, upper-class Protestant.). Thus, people were not "simply American," but tended to identify with, associate with, and choose their spouses from within their ethclasses.

Second, social class affected structural integration. The huge majority of the post-1880s European immigrants were working class, and because they "entered U.S. society at the bottom of the economic ladder, and . . . stayed close to that level for the next half century, ethnic history has been essentially working class history" (Morawska, 1990, p. 215; see also Bodnar, 1985). For generations, many groups of Eastern and Southern European immigrants did not acculturate to middle-class American culture, but to an urban working-class, blue-collar set of lifestyles and values. Even today, ethnicity for many groups remains interconnected with social class factors, and a familiar stereotype of white ethnicity is the hard-hat construction worker.

Gender

Anyone who wants to learn about the experience of immigration will find a huge body of literature incorporating every imaginable discipline and genre. The great bulk of this material, however, concerns the immigrant experience in general or focuses specifically on men immigrants. The experiences of women immigrants have been much less recorded and are hence far less accessible. Many immigrant women came from cultures with strong patriarchal traditions. Thus, they had much less access to leadership roles, education, and prestigious, high-paying occupations. As is the case with women of virtually all minority groups, the voices of immigrant women have been muted. The research that has been done, however, documents that immigrant women played multiple roles both during immigration and during the assimilation process. As would be expected in patriarchal societies, the roles of wife and mother were central, but immigrant women were involved in myriad other activities as well.

In general, men immigrants tended to precede women, and it was common for the men to send for the women only after they had secured lodging, jobs, and a certain level of stability. However, women immigrants' experiences were quite varied, often depending on the economic situation and cultural traditions of their home societies. In some cases, women not only were prominent among the "first wave" of immigrants, but also began the process of acculturation and integration. During the 19th century, for example, a high percentage of Irish immigrants were young, single women. They came to the United States seeking jobs and often wound up employed in domestic work, a role that permitted them to live "respectably" in a family setting. In 1850, about 75% of all employed Irish immigrant women in New York City worked as servants; the rest were employed in textile mills and factories. As late as 1920, 81% of employed Irish-born women in the United States worked as domestics. Factory work was the second most prevalent form of employment (Blessing, 1980; see also Steinberg, 1981).

Because the economic situation of immigrant families was typically precarious, it was common for women to be involved in wage labor. The type and location of the work varied from group to group. Whereas Irish women were concentrated in domestic work and factories and mills, it was rare for Italian women to work outside the home. Italian culture had strong patriarchal norms, and "one of the culture's strongest prohibitions was directed against contact between women and male strangers" (Alba, 1985, p. 53). Thus, acceptable work situations for Italian women were likely to involve tasks that could be done at home: doing laundry, taking in boarders, and doing piece-work for the garment industry. Italian women who worked outside the home were likely to find themselves in single-sex settings among other immigrant women. Thus, women immigrants from Italy tended to be far less acculturated and integrated than those from Ireland.

Eastern European Jewish women represent still another pattern of assimilation. They were refugees from religious persecution, and most came with their husbands and children in intact family units. According to Steinberg (1981), "few were inde-pendent bread-winners, and when they did work, they usually found employment in the . . . garment industry. Often they worked in small shops with other family members" (p. 161).

Generally, immigrant women, like working-class women in general, were expected to work until they married, after which time it was expected that their husbands would support them and their children. In many cases, however, immigrant men could not earn enough to support their families, and their wives and children were required by necessity to contribute to the family budget. Immigrant wives sometimes continued to work outside the home, or they found other ways to make money. They took in board-ers, did laundry or sewing, tended gardens, and were involved in myriad other activi-ties that permitted them to contribute to the family budget and still stay home and attend to family and child-rearing responsibilities.

A 1911 report on Southern and Eastern European households found that about half kept lodgers and that the income from this activity amounted to about 25% of the husbands' wages. Children contributed to the family income by taking afterschool and summertime jobs, too (Morawska, 1990, pp. 211–212). Compared with the men, immigrant women were more closely connected to home and family, less likely to learn to read or speak English or otherwise acculturate, and significantly more influential in preserving the heritage of their groups.

When they sought employment outside the home, they found opportunities in the industrial sector and in clerical and sales work, occupations that were quickly stereo-typed as "women's work." Women were seen as working only to supplement the family treasury, and this assumption was used to justify a lower wage scale. Evans (1989) reports that in the late 1800s, "Whether in factories, offices, or private homes . . . wom-en's wages were about half of those of men" (p. 135).

Finally, in addition to the myriad other roles they played, women tended to func-tion as the primary keepers of cultural traditions from the old country, also. Husbands were often more involved in the larger society and had greater familiarity with Anglo culture and the English language. Women, even when they were employed, tended to be more oriented to home, children, family, and the neighborhood, and more likely to maintain the traditional diet and dress, speak to their children in the old language, and observe the time-honored holidays and religious practices. Thus, in addition to their economic roles, the women of the immigrant groups performed crucial cultural and socialization functions and tended to be more culturally conservative and more resistant to Anglo values and practices than were the men. These gender role patterns are common in immigrant groups today, not only in the United States but also in Western Europe.

Sojourners

Some versions of the traditional perspective and the taken-for-granted views of many Americans assume that assimilation is desirable and therefore desired. However, immigrant groups from Europe were highly variable in their interest in Americanization, a factor that greatly shaped their experiences.

Some groups were very committed to Americanization. Eastern European Jews, for example, came to America because of religious persecution and planned to make America their home from the beginning. They left their homeland in fear for their lives and had no plans and no possibility of returning. They intended to stay, for they had nowhere else to go. (The nation of Israel was not founded until 1948.) These immigrants committed themselves to learning English, becoming citizens, and familiarizing themselves with their new society as quickly as possible.

Other immigrants had no intention of becoming American citizens and therefore had little interest in Americanization. These **sojourners**, or "birds of passage," were oriented to the old country and intended to return once they had accumulated enough capital to be successful in their home villages or provinces. Because immigration records are not very detailed, it is difficult to assess the exact numbers of immigrants who returned to the old country (see Wyman, 1993). We do know, for example, that a large percentage of Italian immigrants were sojourners. Although 3.8 million Italians landed in the United States between 1899 and 1924, around 2.1 million departed during the same interval (Nelli, 1980, p. 547).

QUESTIONS FOR REFLECTION

10. What are some of the most important variations in the ways European immigrants adjusted to U.S. society?

11. What was the "triple melting pot," and how did it function?

12. What important gender role differences existed in European immigrant groups? Would you guess that men or women would be more likely to be sojourners? Why?

The Descendants of the Immigrants Today

Geographic Distribution

Figure 2.5 shows the geographical distribution of 15 racial and ethnic groups across the United States. The map displays the single largest group in each state. There

Figure 2.5   Ancestry With Largest Population in Each State, 2000

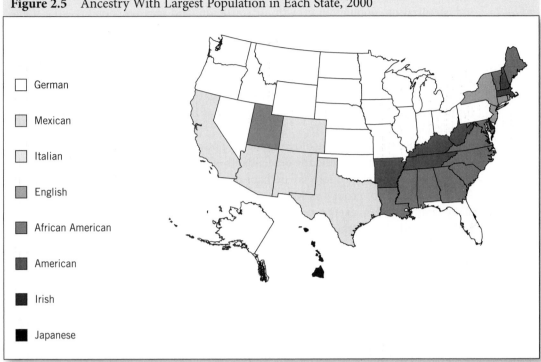

☐ German

▨ Mexican

☐ Italian

▨ English

▨ African American

▨ American

▨ Irish

▨ Japanese

Source: U.S. Census Bureau (2004).

is a lot of detail in the map, but for our purposes, we will focus on some of the groups mentioned in this chapter, including Norwegian, German, Irish, and Italian Americans. (The Jewish population is too small to appear on this map.)

First, the single largest ancestry group is German American, and this is reflected by the predominance of yellow from Pennsylvania to the west coast. Note also how the map reflects the original settlement areas for this group, especially in the Midwest. Although the map does not show it, Norwegian Americans (and Swedish Americans) are numerically dominant in some sections of the upper Midwest (e.g., northwestern Minnesota and northern North Dakota). Irish Americans and Italian Americans are also concentrated in their original areas of settlement, with the Irish more concentrated in Massachusetts and Italians more concentrated around New York City.

Thus, almost a century after the end of mass immigration from Europe, many of the descendants of the immigrants have not wandered far from their ancestral locales. Of course, the map shows that the same point could be made for other groups, including blacks (concentrated in the "black belt" across the states of the old Confederacy), Mexican Americans (concentrated along the southern border from Texas to California), and Native Americans (their concentration in the upper Midwest, eastern Oklahoma, and the Southwest reflects the locations of the reservations into which they were forced after the end of the Indian wars).

Given all that has changed in American society over the past century—industrialization, population growth, urbanization, and massive mobility—the stable location of white ethnics (and other ethnic and racial groups) seems remarkable. Why aren't people distributed more randomly across the nation's landscape?

The stability is somewhat easier to explain for some groups. African Americans, Mexican Americans, and American Indians have been limited in their geographic as well as their social mobility by institutionalized discrimination, racism, and limited resources. We will examine the power of these constraints in detail in later chapters.

For white ethnics, on the other hand, the power of exclusion and rejection waned as the generations passed and the descendants of the immigrants assimilated and integrated. Their current locations are perhaps more a reflection of the fact that the United States is a nation of groups as well as of individuals. Our group memberships, especially family and kin, exert a powerful influence on our decisions about where to live and work and, despite the transience and mobility of modern American life, can keep people connected to their relatives, the old neighborhood, their ethnic roots, and the sites of their ancestors' struggles.

Integration and Equality

Perhaps the most important point, for our purposes, about white ethnic groups (the descendants of the European immigrants) is that they are on the verge of being completely assimilated. Even the groups that were the most despised and rejected in earlier years are acculturated, integrated, and thoroughly intermarried.

To illustrate this point, consider Table 2.3, which illustrates the degree to which a variety of white ethnic groups had been integrated as far back as 1990. The table displays data for nine of the more than 60 white ethnic groups that people mentioned when asked to define their ancestries. The groups include the two largest white ethnic groups (German and Irish Americans) and seven more chosen to represent a range of geographic regions of origin and times of immigration (U.S. Census Bureau, 2008).

The table shows that by 1990, all nine of the groups selected were at or above national norms ("all persons") for all measures of equality. There is some variation among the groups, of course, but all exceeded the national averages for both high school and college education and had dramatically lower poverty rates, usually less than half the national average. All nine groups exceed the national average for median household income, some—Russians, for example, many of whom are Jewish—by a considerable margin.

In other areas, the evidence for assimilation and equality is persuasive. For example, the distinct ethnic neighborhoods that these groups created in American cities (Little Italy, Greektown, Little Warsaw, etc.) have faded away or been taken over by other groups, and the rate of intermarriage between members of different white ethnic groups is quite high. For example, based on data from the 1990 census, about 56% of all married whites have spouses whose ethnic backgrounds do not match their own (Alba, 1995, pp. 13–14).

Table 2.3 Median Household Income, Percent of Families Living in Poverty, and Educational Attainment for Selected White Ethnic Groups, 1990

	Median Household Income	Percentage of Families Living in Poverty	Percentage Who Completed High School or More	Percentage Who Received an Undergraduate Degree or More
All Persons	**$30,056**	**10%**	**75.2%**	**20.3%**
Russian	$45,778	3.6%	90.8%	49%
Italian	$36,060	4.9%	77.3%	21%
Polish	$34,763	4.3%	78.5%	23.1%
Ukrainian	$34,474	4%	77.5%	28.3%
Swedish	$33,881	4.5%	87.3%	27.4%
German	$32,730	5.5%	82.7%	22%
Slovak	$32,352	3.8%	78.2%	21.6%
Norwegian	$32,207	5.1%	85.9%	26%
Irish	$31,845	6.5%	79.6%	21.2%

Source: U.S. Census Bureau (2008).

The Evolution of White Ethnicity

Absorption into the American mainstream was neither linear nor continuous for the descendants of European immigrants. Over the generations, white ethnic identity sporadically reasserted itself in many ways, two of which are especially notable. First, there was a tendency for later generations to be more interested in their ancestry and ethnicity than were earlier generations. Marcus Hansen (1952) captured this phenomenon in his **principle of third-generation interest**: "What the second generation tries to forget, the third generation tries to remember" (p. 495). Hansen observed that the children of immigrants tended to minimize or deemphasize ("forget") their ethnicity to avoid the prejudice and intolerance of the larger society and compete on more favorable terms for jobs and other opportunities. As they became adults and started families of their own, the second generation tended to raise their children in nonethnic settings, with English as their first and only language.

By the time the third generation reached adulthood, especially in the New Immigrant groups that arrived last, the larger society had become more tolerant of white ethnicity and diversity. Having little to risk, the third generation tried to reconnect with its grandparents and roots. These descendants wanted to remember their ethnic heritage and understand it as part of their personal identities, their sense of who they were and where they belonged in the larger society. Thus, interest in the "old ways" and the strength of the identification with the ancestral group was often stronger in the more Americanized third generation than in the more ethnic second. Ironically, of course, the grandchildren of the immigrants could not recover much of the richness and detail of their heritage because their parents had spent their lives trying to forget it. Nonetheless, the desire of the third generation to reconnect with its ancestry and recover its ethnicity shows that assimilation is not a simple, one-dimensional, or linear process.

In addition to this generational pattern, the strength of white ethnic identity also responded to the changing context of American society and the activities of other groups. For example, in the late 1960s and early 1970s, there was a notable increase in the visibility of and interest in white ethnic heritage, an upsurge often referred to as the **ethnic revival**. The revival manifested itself in a variety of ways. Some people became more interested in their families' genealogical roots, and others increased their participation in ethnic festivals, traditions, and organizations. The "white ethnic vote" became a factor in local, state, and national politics, and appearances at the churches, meeting halls, and neighborhoods associated with white ethnic groups became almost mandatory for candidates for office. Demonstrations and festivals celebrating white ethnic heritages were organized, and buttons and bumper stickers proclaiming the ancestry of everyone from Irish to Italians were widely displayed. Politicians, editorialists, and intellectuals endorsed the revival (e.g., see Novak, 1973), reinforcing the movement and giving it additional legitimacy.

The ethnic revival may have been partly fueled, à la Hansen's principle, by the desire to reconnect with ancestral roots, even though most groups were well beyond their third generations by the 1960s. More likely, the revival was a reaction to the increase in pluralistic sentiment in the society in general and the pluralistic, even separatist assertions of other groups. In the 1960s and 1970s, virtually every minority group generated a protest movement (Black Power, Red Power, Chicanismo, etc.) and proclaimed a recommitment to its own heritage and to the authenticity of its own culture and experience. The visibility of these movements for cultural pluralism among racial minority groups helped make it more acceptable for European Americans to express their own ethnicity and heritage.

Besides the general tenor of the times, the resurgence of white ethnicity had some political and economic dimensions that bring us back to issues of inequality and competition for resources. In the 1960s, a white ethnic urban working class made up largely of Irish and Southern and Eastern European groups still remained in the neighborhoods of the industrial Northeast and Midwest and continued to breathe life into the old networks and traditions (see Glazer & Moynihan, 1970; Greeley, 1974). At the same time that cultural pluralism was becoming seen as more legitimate, this ethnic working class was feeling increasingly threatened by minority groups of color. In the industrial cities, it was not unusual for white ethnic neighborhoods to adjoin black and Hispanic neighborhoods, putting these groups in direct competition for housing, jobs, and other resources.

Many members of the white ethnic working class saw racial minority groups as inferior and perceived the advances being made by these groups as unfair, unjust, and threatening. Additionally, they reacted to what they saw as special treatment and attention being accorded on the basis of race, such as school busing and affirmative action. They had problems of their own (the declining number of good, unionized jobs; inadequate schooling; and declining city services) and believed that their problems were being given lower priority and less legitimacy because they were white. The revived sense of ethnicity in the urban working-class neighborhoods was in large part a way of resisting racial reform and expressing resentment for the racial minority groups. Thus, among its many other causes and forms, the revival of white ethnicity that began in the 1960s was fueled by competition for resources and opportunities. As we will see throughout this text, such competition commonly leads to increased prejudice and a heightened sense of cohesion among group members.

The Twilight of White Ethnicity?[1]

As the conflicts of the 1960s and 1970s faded and white ethnic groups continued to leave the old neighborhoods and rise in the class structure, the strength of white ethnic identity resumed its slow demise. Today, several more generations removed from the tumultuous 1960s, white ethnic identity has become increasingly nebulous and largely voluntary. It is often described as **symbolic ethnicity** or as an aspect of self-identity that symbolizes one's roots in the "old country" but is otherwise minor. The descendants of the European immigrants feel vaguely connected to their ancestors, but this part of their identities does not affect their lifestyles, circles of friends and neighbors, job prospects, eating habits, or other everyday routines (Gans, 1979; Lieberson & Waters, 1988). For the descendants of the European immigrants today, ethnicity is an increasingly minor part of their identities that is expressed only occasionally or sporadically. For example, they might join in ethnic or religious festivals (e.g., St. Patrick's Day for Irish Americans, Columbus Day for Italian Americans), but these activities are seasonal or otherwise peripheral to their lives and self-images. The descendants of the European immigrants have choices, in stark contrast to their ancestors, members of racial minority groups, and recent immigrants: they can stress their ethnicity, ignore it completely, or maintain any degree of ethnic identity they choose. Many people have ancestors in more than one ethnic group and may change their sense of affiliation over time, sometimes emphasizing one group's traditions and sometimes another's (Waters, 1990).

In fact, white ethnic identity has become so ephemeral that it may be on the verge of disappearing. For example, based on a series of in-depth interviews with white Americans from various regions of the nation, Gallagher (2001) found a sense of ethnicity so weak that it did not even rise to the level of "symbolic." His respondents were the products of ancestral lines so thoroughly intermixed and intermarried that any trace of a unique heritage from a particular group was completely lost. They had virtually no knowledge of the experiences of their immigrant ancestors or of the life and cultures of the ethnic communities they had inhabited, and for many, their ethnic ancestries were no more meaningful to them than their states of birth. Their lack of interest in and information about their ethnic heritage was so complete that it led Gallagher (2001) to propose an addendum to Hansen's principle: "What the grandson wished to remember, the great-granddaughter has never been told."

At the same time that more specific white ethnic identities are disappearing, they are also evolving into new shapes and forms. In the view of many analysts, a new identity is developing that merges the various "hyphenated" ethnic identities (German-American, Polish-American, etc.) into a single, generalized "European American" identity based on race and a common history of immigration and assimilation. This new identity reinforces the racial lines of separation that run through contemporary society, but it does more than simply mark group boundaries. Embedded in this emerging identity is an understanding, often deeply flawed, of how the white immigrant groups succeeded and assimilated in the past and a view, often deeply ideological, of how the racial minority groups should behave in the present. These understandings are encapsulated in "immigrant tales": legends that stress heroic individual effort and grim determination as key ingredients leading to success in the old days. These tales feature impoverished, victimized immigrant ancestors who survived and made a place for themselves and their children by working hard, saving their money, and otherwise exemplifying the virtues of the Protestant Ethic and American individualism. They stress the idea that past generations became successful despite the brutal hostility of the dominant group and with no government intervention, and they equate the historical difficulties faced by immigrants from Europe with those suffered by racial minority groups (slavery, segregation, attempted genocide, etc.). They strongly imply—and sometimes blatantly assert—that the latter groups could succeed in America by simply following the example set by the former (Alba, 1990; Gallagher, 2001).

These accounts mix versions of human capital theory and traditional views of assimilation with prejudice and racism. Without denying or trivializing the resolve and fortitude of European immigrants, equating their experiences and levels of disadvantage with those of African Americans, Native Americans, and Mexican Americans is widely off the mark, as we shall see in the remainder of this text. These views support an attitude of disdain and lack of sympathy for the multiple dilemmas faced today by the racial minority groups and by many contemporary immigrants. They permit a more subtle expression of prejudice and racism and allow whites to use these highly distorted views of their immigrant ancestors as a rhetorical device to express a host of race-based grievances without appearing racist (Gallagher, 2001).

Alba (1990) concludes as follows:

> The thrust of the [emerging] European American identity is to defend the individualistic view of the American system, because it portrays the system as open to those who are willing to work hard and pull themselves out of poverty and discrimination. Recent research suggests that it is precisely this individualism that prevents many whites from sympathizing with the need for African Americans and other minorities to receive affirmative action in order to overcome institutional barriers to their advancement. (p. 317)

What can we conclude? The generations-long journey from immigrant to white ethnic to European American seems to be drawing to a close. The separate ethnic identities are merging into a larger sense of "whiteness" that unites descendants of the immigrants with the dominant group and provides a rhetorical device for expressing disdain for other groups, especially African Americans and undocumented immigrants.

QUESTIONS FOR REFLECTION

13. In what concrete ways are the descendants of the European immigrants successful?

14. What is Hansen's principle, and why is it significant? What is Gallagher's addendum to this principle, and why is it important?

15. Does white ethnic identity have a future? Why or why not?

Contemporary Immigrants: Does the Traditional Perspective Apply?

Does the traditional perspective—based as it is on the experiences of European immigrants and their descendants—apply to more recent immigrants to the United States? Will contemporary immigrants duplicate the experiences of earlier groups? Will they acculturate before they integrate? Will religion, social class, and race be important forces in their lives? Will they take three generations to assimilate? More than three? Fewer? What will their patterns of intermarriage look like? Will they achieve socioeconomic parity with the dominant group? When? How?

Sociologists (as well as the general public and policymakers) are split in their answers to these questions. Some social scientists believe that the "traditional" perspective on assimilation does not apply and that the experiences of contemporary immigrant groups will differ greatly from those of European immigrants. They believe that assimilation today is fragmented or **segmented** and will have a number of different outcomes. Although some contemporary immigrant groups may integrate into the middle-class mainstream, others will find themselves permanently mired in the impoverished, alienated, and marginalized segments of racial minority groups. Still others may form close-knit enclaves based on their traditional cultures and become successful in the United States by resisting the forces of acculturation (Portes & Rumbaut, 2001, p. 45).

In stark contrast, other theorists believe that the traditional perspective on assimilation is still relevant and that contemporary immigrant groups will follow the established pathways of mobility and assimilation. Of course, the process will be variable from group to group and from place to place, but even the groups that are today the most impoverished and marginalized will, in time, move into mainstream society.

How will the debate be resolved? We cannot say at the moment, but we can point out that this debate is reminiscent of the critique of Park's theory of assimilation. In both cases, the argument is partly about time: even the most impoverished and segmented groups may find their way into the economic mainstream eventually, at some unspecified time in the future. Other levels of meaning in the debate exist, however, related to one's perception of the nature of modern U.S. society. Is U.S. society today growing more tolerant of diversity, more open and equal? If so, this would seem to favor the traditionalist perspective. If not, this trend would clearly favor the segmented-assimilation hypothesis.

Although we will not resolve this debate in this text, we will consider the traditional and segmented views on assimilation as a useful framework to understand the experiences of these groups (see Chapters 8, 9, and 10).

QUESTIONS FOR REFLECTION

16. What is segmented assimilation, and why is this an important concept? How would social class and gender relate to the debate over whether contemporary assimilation is segmented?

Implications for Examining Dominant–Minority Relations

Chapters 1 and 2 have introduced many of the terms, concepts, and themes that form the core of the rest of this text. Although the connections between the concepts are not simple, some key points can be made to summarize these chapters and anticipate the material to come.

First, minority group status has much more to do with power and the distribution of resources than with simple numbers or the percentage of the population in any particular category. We saw this notion expressed in Chapter 1 in the definition of a minority group and in our exploration of inequality. The themes of inequality and differentials in status were also covered in our discussion of prejudice, racism, and discrimination. To understand minority relations, we must examine some basic realities of human society: inequalities in wealth, prestige, and the distribution of power. To discuss changes in minority group status, we must be prepared to discuss changes in the way society does business, makes decisions, and distributes income, jobs, health care, and opportunities.

A second area that we will focus on in the rest of the book is the question of how our society should develop. Assimilation and pluralism, with all their variations, define two broad directions. Each has been extensively examined and discussed by social scientists, by leaders and decision makers in American society, and by ordinary people from all groups and walks of life. The analysis and evaluation of these two broad directions is a thread running throughout this book.

COMPARATIVE FOCUS:
Immigration and Ireland

Just as the United States has been a major receiver of immigrants for the past 200 years, Ireland has been a major supplier. Mass emigration from Ireland began with the potato famines of the 1840s and continued through the end of the 20th century, motivated by continuing hard times, political unrest, and unemployment. This mass out-migration—combined with the death toll of the famines—cut the 1840 Irish population of 7 million in half, and the population today is still only about 4.5 million.

History rarely runs in straight lines, however. In the 1990s and into the 21st century, after nearly 200 years of supplying immigrants, Ireland (along with other nations of Northern and Western Europe) became a consumer. As Figure 2.6 shows, the number of newcomers entering Ireland soared between 1987 and 2007, and the number of people leaving decreased. Starting in about 2007, however, the trend reversed: The number of newcomers plummeted, and the historic pattern of out-migration reappeared.

What explains these patterns? Answers are not hard to find. The influx of immigrants starting in the late 1980s was largely a response to rapid economic growth. The Irish economy—the so-called Celtic Tiger—had entered a boom phase, spurred by investments from multinational corporations and the benefits of joining the European Economic Union. Irish nationals who had left seeking work abroad returned home in large numbers, and people from Europe and other parts of the globe also began to arrive. In

Figure 2.6   Migration Into and Out of Ireland, 1987–2014

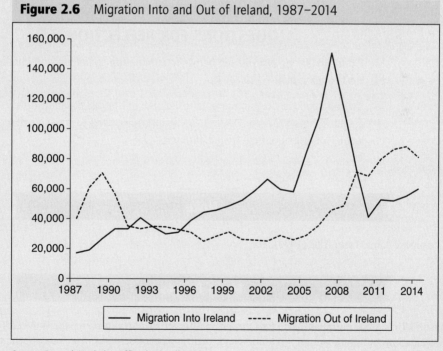

Source: Central Statistics Office [Ireland] (2014).

(Continued)

(Continued)

addition, Ireland began to receive refugees and people seeking asylum from Africa, the Middle East, and other trouble spots.

The changes that started in 2007 have an equally obvious cause. The global economy faltered badly in that year, and the Irish economy followed suit: Banks failed, companies went bankrupt, the housing market collapsed, and jobs disappeared. The Irish returned to their historic role as a supplier of immigrants to other economies around the world.

Although the era of in-migration lasted only a few decades, it may have created some permanent changes in Irish society. For example, the number of Irish of African and Asian descent has increased by a factor of 8 since 1996 (although both groups are less than 2% of the total population). Over the centuries, many different groups (e.g., Vikings, Spanish, and Anglo-Normans) have become part of Ireland, but, for the first time in their history, the Irish are dealing with issues of racial diversity.

QUESTIONS FOR REFLECTION

17. What similarities can you see between immigration to Ireland and immigration to the United States?

18. Do you suppose that immigrants to Ireland will be assimilated in the same way as immigrants to the United States? If you could travel to Ireland, what questions would you ask about the assimilation process?

Note

1. The phrase comes from Alba (1990).

Main Points

- Assimilation and pluralism are two broad pathways of development for intergroup relations. Assimilation and pluralism are, in some ways, contrary processes. But, they can appear together in a variety of combinations.
- Two types of assimilation are the melting pot and Anglo-conformity. The latter has historically been the dominant value in the United States.
- Gordon theorized that assimilation occurs through a series of stages, with integration being the crucial stage. In his view, it is common for American minority groups, especially racial minority groups, to be

acculturated but not integrated. Once a group has begun to integrate, all other stages will follow in order.

- In the past few decades, people's interest in pluralism has increased. Three types of pluralistic situations exist: cultural, or full, pluralism; structural pluralism; and enclave, or middleman, minority groups.
- According to many scholars, white ethnic groups survived decades of assimilation, though in different forms. New ethnic (and racial) minority groups continue to appear, and old ones change as society changes. As the 21st century unfolds, white ethnicity may be less relevant for most people, except perhaps as a context for criticizing other groups.
- In the United States today, assimilation may be segmented and have outcomes other than equality with and acceptance into the middle class.

APPLYING CONCEPTS

Imagine you are interviewing the grandchildren (third generation) and great-grandchildren (fourth generation) of immigrants from Europe about their families' assimilation experiences. Some of the questions you might ask are listed below. Identify the stage of Gordon's model of assimilation that each question is testing.

A. What language did you speak at home when you were growing up?

B. What was your total household income last year?

C. (If married) Does your spouse share your religious faith?

D. (If married) Does your spouse share your ethnic background?

E. Did your parents have the same ethnic background? How about your grandparents?

F. Did you vote in the most recent presidential election?

G. What percentage of your friends share your ethnic background?

H. What percentage of your friends share your religious faith?

I. What is the highest level of education you have achieved?

J. Has your family name been changed or "Americanized"?

Stage	Items
Acculturation	
Integration (secondary level)	
Integration (primary level)	
Marital assimilation	

TURN TO THE END OF THIS SECTION TO FIND OUR ANSWERS.

Review Questions

1. Summarize Gordon's model of assimilation. Identify and explain each stage and how the stages are linked together. Explain Table 2.2 in terms of Gordon's model.

2. "Human capital theory is not so much wrong as it is incomplete." Explain this statement. What does the theory leave out? What are the strengths of the theory? What questionable assumptions does it make?

3. What are the major dimensions along which the experience of assimilation varies? Explain how and why the experience of assimilation can vary.

4. Define pluralism and explain the ways in which it differs from assimilation. Why has interest in pluralism increased? Explain the difference between structural and cultural pluralism and cite examples of each. Describe enclave minority groups in terms of pluralism and in terms of Gordon's model of assimilation. How have contemporary theorists added to the concept of pluralism?

5. Define and explain segmented assimilation and explain how it differs from Gordon's model. What evidence is there that assimilation for recent immigrants is not segmented? What is the significance of this debate for the future of U.S. society? For other minority groups (e.g., African Americans)? For the immigrants themselves?

6. Do American theories and understandings of assimilation apply to Ireland? Do you suppose that immigrants to Ireland will assimilate in the same way as immigrants to the United States? If you could travel to Ireland, what questions would you ask about the assimilation process?

Group Discussion

Bring your answers to class. Compare your results with those of four to six other people. Consider the issues raised in the questions above and in the chapter, and develop some ideas about why various groups are where they are relative to each other and to the total population.

ANSWERS TO APPLYING CONCEPTS

Stage	Items
Acculturation	A, J
Integration (secondary level)	B, F, I
Integration (primary level)	G, H
Marital assimilation	C, D, E

Learning Resources on the Web

⑤SAGE edge™

edge.sagepub.com/healeyds5e

SAGE edge offers a robust online environment featuring an impressive array of free tools and resources for review, study, and further exploration, keeping both instructors and students on the cutting edge of teaching and learning.

SAGE edge for Students provides a personalized approach to help you accomplish your coursework goals in an easy-to-use learning environment.

PART 2

The Evolution of Dominant-Minority Relations in the United States

❧ ❧

❧ ❧

The chapters in Part 2 explore several questions: Why do some groups become minorities? How and why do dominant–minority relations change over time? These questions are more than casual or merely academic. Understanding the dynamics that created and sustained prejudice, racism, discrimination, and inequality in the past will build understanding about group relations in the present and future. This knowledge is crucial if we are ever to deal effectively with these problems. By understanding these dynamics, you can help be a part of social change.

Both chapters in Part 2 use African Americans as the primary case study. Chapter 3 focuses on the preindustrial United States and the creation of slavery but also considers the fate of American Indians and Mexican Americans during the same period. Chapter 4 analyzes the changes in group relations that were caused by the Industrial Revolution and focuses on the shift from slavery to segregation for African Americans and their migration out of the South. Throughout the 20th century, industrial technology continued to evolve and shape American society and group relationships. We begin to explore the consequences of these changes in Chapter 4, and we continue the investigation in the case studies of contemporary minority groups in Part 3.

The concepts that you learned in Part 1 will be used throughout the next two chapters. And, we'll introduce you to some important new concepts and theories. By the end of Part 2, you will be familiar with virtually the entire conceptual framework that will guide us through the remainder of this text.

A Note on the Morality and the History of Minority Relations in America: Guilt, Blame, Understanding, and Communication

Very often, when people confront the kind of material presented in the next few chapters, they react on a personal level. Some might feel a sense of guilt for America's less-than-wholesome history of group relations. Others might respond with anger about the injustice and unfairness that remains in American society. Still others might respond with denial or indifference and might argue that the events discussed in Chapters 3 and 4 are so distant in time that they have no importance or meaning today.

These reactions—denial, guilt, anger, and indifference—are common, and we ask you to think about them as you read these chapters. First, the awful things we will discuss did happen, and they were done largely by members of a particular racial and ethnic group: white Europeans and their descendants in America. No amount of denial, distancing, or disassociation can make these facts go away. African Americans, American Indians, Mexican Americans, and other groups were victims, and they paid a terrible price for the early growth and success of white American society.

Second, the successful domination and exploitation of these groups was made easier by the cooperation of members of each of the minority groups. The slave trade relied on black African slavers and agents, some American Indians aided the cause of white society, and some Mexicans cheated other Mexicans. There is plenty of guilt to go around, and European Americans do not have a monopoly on greed, bigotry, or viciousness. Indeed, some white Southerners opposed slavery and fought for the abolition of the "peculiar institution." Many of the ideas and values on which the United States was founded (justice, equality, liberty) had their origins in European intellectual traditions. Minority group protest has often involved little more than insisting that the nation live up to these ideals. Segments of the white community were appalled at the treatment of American Indians and Mexicans and attempted to stop it. Some members of the dominant group devoted (and sometimes gave) their lives to end the oppression, bigotry, and racial stratification.

Our point is to urge you to avoid, insofar as is possible, a "good guy/bad guy" approach to this subject matter. Guilt, anger, denial, and indifference are common reactions to this material, but these emotions do little to advance our understanding, and often they inhibit communication between members of different groups. We believe that an understanding of America's racial past is vitally important for understanding the present. Historical background provides a perspective for viewing the present and allows us to identify important concepts and principles that we can use to disentangle the intergroup complexities surrounding us.

The goal of these chapters is not to make you feel any particular emotion. We will try to present the often ugly facts neutrally and without extraneous editorializing. As scholars, your goal should be to absorb the material, understand the principles, and apply them to your own life and the society around you—not to indulge yourself in elaborate moral denunciations of American society, develop apologies for the past, or deny the realities of what happened. By dealing objectively with this material, we can begin to liberate our perspectives and build an understanding of the realities of American society and American minority groups.

The Development of Dominant-Minority Group Relations in Preindustrial America: The Origins of Slavery

The year was 1781, and the *Zong*, with its cargo of 471 African slaves, had been sailing for nearly three months. The ship was approaching its destination in the New World, but water was running short and disease had broken out. To deal with the dilemma, the captain ordered 54 of the sickest slaves to be chained together and thrown overboard, reasoning that they would die soon anyway. In the next two days, another 78 slaves were cast over the sides of the ship and drowned. The captain knew that the ship's insurance policy would cover losses due to drowning but not those due to "natural causes."*

The slave trade that brought Africans to North America was a business, subject to the calculation of profit and loss and covered by the same insurance companies that backed farmers, bankers, and merchants. To the captain and owners of the *Zong,* and to others involved in the slave trade, the 132 unfortunates who were thrown over the rails were just cargo, cyphers in a ledger book.

*This account is based on materials from a PBS documentary, *Africans in America*. See www.pbs.org/wgbh/aia/part1/1h280.html.

What lay behind this cold, businesslike approach to trafficking in human beings? Was the same calculating eye for profit and efficiency behind the decision to use Africa as a source for slaves? How did the slave trade get linked to the British colonies that became the United States? How could a nation that, from its earliest days, valued liberty and freedom be founded on slavery?

From the first settlements in the 1600s until the 19th century, most people living in what was to become the United States relied directly on farming for food, shelter, and other necessities of life. In an agricultural society, land and labor are central concerns, and the struggle to control these resources led directly to the creation of minority group status for three groups: African Americans, American Indians, and Mexican Americans. Why did the colonists create slavery? Why were Africans enslaved but not American Indians or Europeans? Why did American Indians lose their land and most of their population by the 1890s? How did the Mexican population in the Southwest become "Mexican Americans"? How did the experience of becoming a subordinated minority group vary by gender?

In this chapter, we'll use the concepts introduced in Part 1 to answer these questions. We'll introduce some new ideas and theories, and by the end of the chapter we will have developed a theoretical model of the process that leads to the creation of a minority group. The establishment of black slavery in colonial America, arguably the single most significant event in the early years of this nation, will be used to illustrate the process of minority group creation. We will also consider the subordination of American Indians and Mexican Americans—two more historical events of great significance—as additional case studies. We will follow the experiences of African Americans through the days of segregation (Chapter 4) and into the contemporary era (Chapter 5). The story of the development of minority group status for American Indians and Mexican Americans will be picked up again in Chapters 6 and 7, respectively.

Two broad themes underlie this chapter and, indeed, the remainder of the text:

1. The nature of dominant–minority group relations at any point in time is largely a function of the characteristics of the society as a whole. The situation of a minority group will reflect the realities of everyday social life and particularly the subsistence technology (the means by which the society satisfies basic needs such as food and shelter). As explained by Gerhard Lenski (see Chapter 1), the subsistence technology of a society acts as a foundation, shaping and affecting every other aspect of the social structure, including minority group relations.

2. The contact situation—the conditions under which groups first come together—is the single most significant factor in the creation of minority group status. The nature of the contact situation has long-lasting consequences for the minority group and the extent of racial or ethnic stratification, the levels of racism and prejudice, the possibilities for assimilation and pluralism, and virtually every other aspect of the dominant–minority relationship.

The Origins of Slavery in America

By the early 1600s, Spanish explorers had conquered much of Central and South America, and the influx of gold, silver, and other riches from the New World had made Spain a powerful nation. Following Spain's lead, England proceeded to establish its presence in the western hemisphere, but its efforts at colonization were more modest than those of Spain. By the early 1600s, the English had established only two small colonies: Plymouth, settled by pious Protestant families, and Jamestown, populated primarily by men seeking their fortunes.

By 1619, the British colony at Jamestown, Virginia, had survived for more than a decade. The residents of the settlement had fought with the local natives and struggled continuously to eke out a living from the land. Starvation, disease, and death were frequent visitors, and the future of the enterprise continued to be in doubt.

In August of that year, a Dutch ship arrived. The master of the ship needed provisions and offered to trade his only cargo: about 20 black Africans. Many of the details of this transaction have been lost, and we probably will never know exactly how these people came to be chained in the hold of a ship. Regardless, this brief episode was a landmark event in the formation of what would become the United States. In combination with the strained relations between the English settlers and American Indians, the presence of these first few Africans raised an issue that has never been fully resolved: How should different groups in this society relate to each other?

The colonists at Jamestown had no ready answer. In 1619, England and its colonies did not practice slavery, so these first Africans were probably incorporated into colonial society as **indentured servants**, contract laborers who are obligated to serve a master for a specific number of years. At the end of the indenture, or contract, the servant became a free citizen. The colonies depended heavily on indentured servants from the British Isles for labor, and this status provided a convenient way of defining the newcomers from Africa, who, after all, had been treated as commodities and exchanged for food and water (see Figure 3.1).

The position of African indentured servants in the colonies remained ambiguous for several decades. American slavery evolved gradually and in small steps; in fact, there was little demand for African labor during the years following 1619. By 1625, there were still only 23 black people in Virginia, and that number had increased to perhaps 300 by midcentury (Franklin & Moss, 1994, p. 57). In the decades before the dawn of slavery, we know that some African indentured servants did become free citizens. Some became successful farmers and landowners and, like their white neighbors, purchased African and white indentured servants themselves (Smedley, 2007, p. 104). By the 1650s, however, many African Americans (and their offspring) were being treated as the property of others, or in other words, as slaves (Morgan, 1975, p. 154).

It was not until the 1660s that the first laws defining slavery were enacted. In the century that followed, hundreds of additional laws were passed to clarify and formalize the status of Africans in colonial America. By the 1750s, slavery had been clearly defined in law and in custom, and the idea that a person could own another

Figure 3.1 Slave Trade Routes, 1518–1850

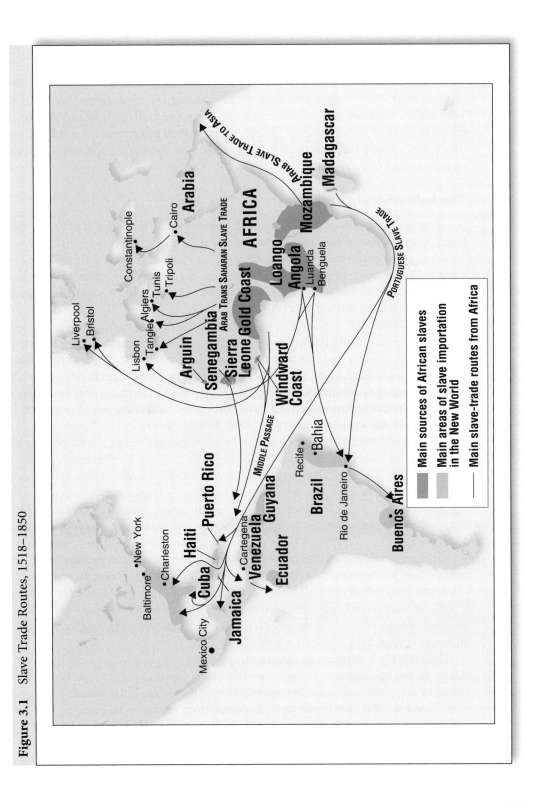

Main sources of African slaves

Main areas of slave importation in the New World

Main slave-trade routes from Africa

person—not just the labor or the energy or the work of a person, but also the actual person—had been thoroughly institutionalized.

What caused slavery? The gradual evolution of and low demand for indentured servants from Africa suggest that slavery was not somehow inevitable or preordained. Why did the colonists deliberately create this repressive system? Why did they reach out all the way to Africa for their slaves? If they wanted to create a slave system, why didn't they enslave the American Indians nearby or the white indentured servants already present in the colonies?

The Labor Supply Problem

American colonists of the 1600s saw slavery as a solution to several problems they faced. The business of the colonies was agriculture, and farm work at this time was labor-intensive, performed almost entirely by hand. The Industrial Revolution (see Chapter 2) was two centuries in the future, and there were few machines or labor-saving devices available to ease the everyday burden of work. A successful harvest depended largely on human effort.

As colonial society grew and developed, a specific form of agricultural production began to emerge. The **plantation system** was based on cultivating and exporting crops such as sugar, tobacco, and rice on large tracts of land using a large, cheap labor force. Profit margins tended to be small, so planters sought to stabilize their incomes by keeping the costs of production as low as possible. Profits in the labor-intensive plantation system could be maximized if a large, disciplined, and cheap workforce could be maintained by the landowners (Curtin, 1990; Morgan, 1975).

At about the same time the plantation system began to emerge, the supply of white indentured servants from the British Isles began to dwindle. Furthermore, the white indentured servants who did come to the colonies had to be released from their indenture every few years. Land was available, and these newly freed citizens tended to strike out on their own. Thus, landowners who relied on white indentured servants had to deal with high turnover rates in their workforces and faced a continually uncertain supply of labor.

Attempts to solve the labor supply problem by using American Indians failed. The tribes closest to the colonies were sometimes exploited for manpower. By the time the plantation system had evolved, however, the local tribes had dwindled in numbers as a result of warfare and, especially, disease. Other Indian nations across the continent retained enough power to resist enslavement, and it was relatively easy for American Indians to escape back to their kinfolk.

This left black Africans as a potential source of manpower. The slave trade from Africa to the Spanish and Portuguese colonies of South America had been established in the 1500s and could be expanded to fill the needs of the British colonies as well. The colonists came to see slaves imported from Africa as the most logical, cost-effective way to solve their vexing shortage of labor. The colonists created slavery to cultivate their lands and generate profits, status, and success. The paradox at the core of U.S. society had been established: the construction of a social system devoted to freedom and individual liberty in the New World "was made possible only by the revival of an institution of naked tyranny foresworn for centuries in the Old" (Lacy, 1972, p. 22).

The Contact Situation

The conditions under which groups first come into contact determine the immediate fate of the minority group and shape intergroup relations for years to come. We discussed the role of group competition in creating prejudice in Chapter 1. Here, we expand on some of these ideas by introducing two theories that will serve as analytical guides for understanding the contact situation.

The Noel Hypothesis. Sociologist Donald Noel (1968) identified three features of the contact situation that in combination lead to some form of inequality between groups. The Noel hypothesis states, *"If two or more groups come together in a contact situation characterized by ethnocentrism, competition, and a differential in power, then some form of racial or ethnic stratification will result"* (p. 163). If the contact situation has all three characteristics, some dominant–minority group structure will be created.

Noel's first characteristic, **ethnocentrism**, is the tendency to judge other groups, societies, or lifestyles by the standards of one's own culture. Ethnocentrism is probably a universal component of human society, and some degree of ethnocentrism is essential to the maintenance of social solidarity and cohesion. Without some minimal level of pride in and loyalty to one's own society and cultural traditions, there would be no particular reason to observe the norms and laws, honor the sacred symbols, or cooperate with others in doing the daily work of society.

Regardless of its importance, ethnocentrism can have negative consequences. At its worst, it can lead to the view that other cultures and peoples are not just different but inferior. At the very least, ethnocentrism creates a social boundary line that members of the groups involved will recognize and observe. When ethnocentrism exists in any degree, people will tend to sort themselves out along group lines and identify characteristics that differentiate "us" from "them."

Noel's second factor, **competition,** is a struggle over a scarce commodity. As we saw in Chapter 1, competition between groups often leads to harsh negative feelings (prejudice) and hostile actions (discrimination). In competitive contact situations, the victorious group becomes the dominant group, and the losers become the minority group. The competition may center on land, labor, jobs, housing, educational opportunities, political office, or anything else that is mutually desired by both groups or that one group has and the other group wants.

Competition provides the eventual dominant group with the motivation to establish superiority. The dominant group serves its own interests by ending the competition and exploiting, controlling, eliminating, or otherwise dominating the minority group.

The third feature of the contact situation is a **differential in power** between the groups. Power, as you recall from Chapter 1, is the ability of a group to achieve its goals even in the face of opposition from other groups. The amount of power commanded by a group is a function of three factors:

- First, the size of the group can make a difference, and all other things being equal, larger groups are more powerful.
- Second, the degree of organization, discipline, and quality of group leadership can make a difference in a group's ability to pursue its goals.
- The third component of power is resources: anything that can be used to help the group achieve its goals. Depending on the context, resources might include anything from land to information to money. The greater the number and variety of resources at the group's disposal, the greater that group's potential ability to dominate other groups.

Thus, a larger, better-organized group with more resources at its disposal will generally be able to impose its will on smaller, less-well-organized groups with fewer resources. The Noel hypothesis is diagrammed in Table 3.1.

Note the respective functions of each of the three factors in shaping the contact situation and the emergence of inequality. If ethnocentrism is present, the groups will recognize their differences and maintain their boundaries. If competition is also present, the group that eventually dominates will attempt to maximize its share of scarce commodities by controlling or subordinating the group that eventually becomes the "minority" group. The differential in power allows the dominant group to succeed in establishing a superior position. Ethnocentrism tells the dominant group *whom* to dominate, competition tells the dominant group *why* it should establish a structure of dominance, and power is *how* the dominant group imposes its will on the minority group.

The Noel hypothesis can be applied to the creation of minority groups in a variety of situations. We will also use the model to analyze changes in dominant–minority structures over time.

The Blauner Hypothesis. Sociologist Robert Blauner also analyzed the contact situation in his book *Racial Oppression in America* (1972). Blauner identifies two different

Table 3.1 The Noel Hypothesis: A Model of the Establishment of Minority Group Status

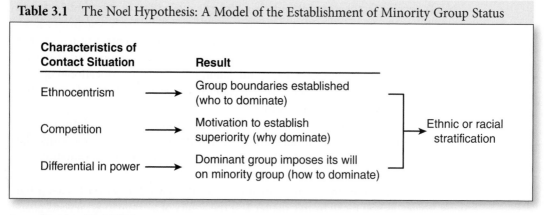

Source: Based on Noel (1968).

initial relationships: colonization and immigration. His analysis is complex and nuanced but, for our purposes, we can summarize his thinking in terms of what we will call the **Blauner hypothesis**: *Minority groups created by colonization will experience more intense prejudice, racism, and discrimination than those created by immigration. Furthermore, the disadvantaged status of colonized groups will persist longer and be more difficult to overcome than the disadvantaged status faced by groups created by immigration* (Blauner, 1972, pp. 52–75).

Colonized minority groups, such as African Americans, are forced into minority status by the superior military and political power of the dominant group. At the time of contact with the dominant group, colonized groups are subjected to massive inequalities and attacks on their cultures. They are assigned to positions, such as slave status, from which any form of assimilation is extremely difficult and perhaps even forbidden by the dominant group. Frequently, members of the minority group are identified by highly visible racial or physical characteristics that maintain and reinforce the oppressive system. Thus, minority groups created by colonization experience harsher and more persistent rejection and oppression than do groups created by immigration.

Immigrant minority groups are at least in part voluntary participants in the host society. That is, although the decision to immigrate may be motivated by extreme pressures, such as famine or political persecution, immigrant groups have at least some control over their destinations and their positions in the host society. As a result, they do not occupy positions that are as markedly inferior as those of colonized groups. They retain enough internal organization and resources to pursue their own self-interests, and they commonly experience more rapid acceptance and easier movement to equality. The boundaries between groups are not so rigidly maintained, especially when the groups are racially similar. In discussing European immigrant groups, for example, Blauner (1972) states that entering into American society

> involved a degree of choice and self-direction that was for the most part denied to people of color. Voluntary immigration made it more likely that . . . European . . . ethnic groups would identify with America and see the host culture as a positive opportunity. (p. 56)

Acculturation and, particularly, integration were significantly more possible for European immigrant groups than for the groups formed under conquest or colonization.

Blauner (1972) stresses that the initial differences between colonized and immigrant minority groups have consequences that persist long after the original contact. For example, based on measures of equality—or integration into the secondary sector, the second step in Gordon's model of assimilation (see Chapter 2)—such as average income, years of education, and unemployment rate, descendants of European immigrants are equal with national norms today (see Chapter 2 for specific data). In contrast, descendants of colonized and conquered groups (e.g., African Americans) are, on the average, below the national norms on virtually all measures of equality and integration (see Chapters 5–8 for specific data).

We should think of Blauner's two types of minority groups as opposite ends of a continuum, with intermediate positions between the extremes. One such intermediate position is held by enclave and middleman minorities (see Chapter 2). These groups often originate as immigrant groups who bring some resources and, thus, have more opportunities than do colonized minority groups. However, they are usually racially distinct from Anglos, and certain kinds of opportunities are closed to them.

For instance, U.S. citizenship was expressly forbidden to immigrants from China until World War II. Federal laws restricted the entrance of Chinese immigrants, and state and local laws restricted their opportunities for education, jobs, and housing. For these and other reasons, the Asian immigrant experience cannot be equated with European immigrant patterns (Blauner, 1972, p. 55). Because they combine characteristics of both the colonized and the immigrant minority group experience, we can predict that in terms of equality, enclave and middleman minority groups will occupy an intermediate status between the more assimilated white ethnic groups and the colonized racial minorities.

Blauner's typology has proven to be an extremely useful conceptual tool for the analysis of U.S. dominant–minority relations, and it is used extensively throughout this text. In fact, the case studies that compose Part 3 of this text are arranged in approximate order from groups created by colonization to those created by immigration. Of course, it is difficult to measure objectively or precisely such a thing as the extent of colonization, and the exact order of the groups is somewhat arbitrary.

The Creation of Slavery in the United States

The Noel hypothesis helps explain why colonists enslaved black Africans instead of white indentured servants or American Indians. First, all three groups were the objects of ethnocentric feelings on the part of the elite groups that dominated colonial society. Black Africans and American Indians were perceived as being different on religious as well as racial grounds. Many white indentured servants were Irish Catholics, criminals, or paupers. They not only occupied a lowly status in society, but also were perceived as different from the British Protestants who dominated colonial society.

Second, competition of some sort existed between the colonists and all three groups. The competition with American Indians was direct and focused on control of land. Competition with indentured servants, white and black, was more indirect; these groups were the labor force that the landowners needed to work on their plantations and to become successful in the New World.

Noel's third variable, differential in power, is the key variable that explains why Africans were enslaved instead of the other groups. During the first several decades of colonial history, the balance of power between the colonists and American Indians was relatively even. In fact, it often favored American Indians (Lurie, 1982, pp. 131–133). The colonists were outnumbered, and their muskets and cannons were only marginally more effective than bows and spears. The American Indian tribes were well-organized social units capable of sustaining resistance to and mounting reprisals against the colonists, and it took centuries for the nascent United States to finally defeat American Indians militarily.

White indentured servants, on the one hand, had the advantage of being preferred over black indentured servants (Noel, 1968, p. 168). Their greater desirability gave them bargaining power and the ability to negotiate better treatment and more lenient terms than could black indentured servants. If the planters had attempted to enslave white indentured servants, this source of labor would have dwindled even more rapidly.

Africans, on the other hand, had become indentured servants by force and coercion. In Blauner's terms, they were a colonized group that did not freely choose to enter the British colonies. Thus, they had no bargaining power. Unlike American Indians, they had no nearby relatives, no knowledge of the countryside, and no safe havens to which to escape. Table 3.2 summarizes the impact of these three factors on the three potential sources of labor in colonial America.

Table 3.2   The Noel Hypothesis Applied to the Origins of Slavery

	Three Causal Factors		
Potential Sources of Labor	*Ethnocentrism*	*Competition*	*Differential in Power*
White indentured servants	Yes	Yes	No
American Indians	Yes	Yes	No
Black indentured servants	Yes	Yes	Yes

Source: From "A Theory of the Origin of Ethnic Stratification" by Donald Noel in *Social Problems,* vol. 16, no. 2, Autumn 1968, copyright © 1968. Reprinted by permission of The University of California Press, via the Copyright Clearance Center.

QUESTIONS FOR REFLECTION

1. How do the concepts of subsistence technology and contact situation help clarify the origins of slavery in colonial America?

2. How do the three concepts in the Noel hypothesis apply to the decision to create slavery?

3. Blauner identifies two types of minority groups. How does this distinction apply to Africans in colonial America?

4. Why were African indentured servants—not white indentured servants or American Indians—selected as the labor supply for slavery?

Paternalistic Relations

Recall the first theme stated at the beginning of this chapter: the nature of inter-group relationships will reflect the characteristics of the larger society. The most important and profitable unit of economic production in the colonial South was the plantation, and the region was dominated by a small group of wealthy landowners. A society with a small elite class and a plantation-based economy will often develop a form of minority relations called **paternalism** (van den Berghe, 1967; Wilson, 1973).

The key features of paternalism are vast power differentials and huge inequalities between dominant and minority groups, elaborate and repressive systems of control over the minority group, caste-like barriers between groups, elaborate and highly stylized codes of behavior and communication between groups, and low rates of overt conflict.

Chattel Slavery. As slavery evolved in the colonies, the dominant group shaped the system to fit its needs. To solidify control of the labor of their slaves, the plantation elite designed and enacted an elaborate system of laws and customs that gave masters nearly total legal power over slaves. In these laws, slaves were defined as **chattel**, or personal property, rather than as persons, and they were accorded no civil or political rights. Slaves could not own property, sign contracts, bring lawsuits, or even testify in court (except against another slave). The masters were given the legal authority to determine almost every aspect of a slave's life, including work schedules, living arrangements, diets, and even names (Elkins, 1959; Franklin & Moss, 1994; Genovese, 1974; Jordan, 1968; Stampp, 1956).

The law permitted the master to determine the type and severity of punishment for misbehavior. Slaves were forbidden by law to read or write, and marriages between slaves were not legally recognized. Masters could separate husbands from wives and parents from children if it suited them. In short, slaves had little control over their lives or the lives of their loved ones.

A Closed System. In colonial America, slavery became synonymous with race. Race, slavery, inferiority, and powerlessness became intertwined in ways that still affect the ways black and white Americans think about each other (Hacker, 1992). Slavery was a **caste system**, or closed stratification system. In a caste system, there is no mobility between social positions, and the social class you are born into (your ascribed status) is permanent. Slave status was for life and was passed on to any children a slave might have. Whites, no matter what they did, could not become slaves.

Interaction between members of the dominant and minority groups in a paternalistic system is governed by a rigid, strictly enforced code of etiquette. Whites expected slaves to show deference and humility and to visibly display their lower status when interacting with them. These rigid behavioral codes made it possible for blacks and whites to work together, sometimes intimately, sometimes for their entire lives, without threatening the power and status differentials inherent in the system. Plantation and farm work required close and frequent contact between blacks and whites, and status differentials were maintained socially rather than by geographical separation.

Pseudotolerance. The frequent but unequal interactions allowed the elites to maintain a pseudotolerance, an attitude of benevolent despotism, toward their slaves. Their prejudice and racism were often expressed as positive emotions of affection for their black slaves. The attitude of the planters toward their slaves was often paternalistic and even genteel (Wilson, 1973, pp. 52–55). For their part, black slaves often could not hate their owners as much as they hated the system that constrained them. The system defined slaves as pieces of property owned by their masters—yet they were, undeniably, human beings. Thus, slavery was founded, at its heart, on a contradiction.

> The master learned to treat his slaves both as property and as men and women, the slaves learned to express and affirm their humanity even while they were constrained in much of their lives to accept their status as chattel. (Parish, 1989, p. 1)

Powerlessness and Resistance. The powerlessness of slaves made it difficult for them to openly reject or resist the system. Slaves had few ways to directly challenge the institution of slavery or their position in it, because open defiance was ineffective and could result in punishment, including death. In general, masters would not be prosecuted for physically abusing their slaves.

One of the few slave revolts that occurred in the United States illustrates both the futility of overt challenge and the degree of repression built into the system. In 1831, in Southampton County, Virginia, a slave named Nat Turner led an uprising during which 57 whites were killed. The revolt was starting to spread when the state militia met the growing slave army in battle. More than 100 slaves died in the armed encounter, and Nat Turner and 13 others were later executed.

Slave owners and white Southerners, in general, were greatly alarmed by the uprising. Consequently, they tightened the system of control over slaves, making it even more repressive (Franklin & Moss, 1994, p. 147). Ironically, the result of Nat Turner's attempt to lead slaves to freedom was greater oppression and control by the dominant group.

Others were more successful in resisting the system. Runaway slaves were a constant problem for slave owners, especially in the states bordering the free states of the North. The difficulty of escape and the low likelihood of successfully reaching the North did not deter thousands from attempting the feat, some of them repeatedly. Many runaway slaves received help from the Underground Railroad, an informal network of safe houses supported by African Americans and whites involved in **abolitionism**, the movement to abolish slavery. These escapes created colorful legends and heroic figures, including Frederick Douglass, Sojourner Truth, and Harriet Tubman.

Besides running away and open rebellion, slaves used the forms of resistance most readily available to them: sabotage, intentional carelessness, dragging their feet, and work slowdowns. As historian Peter Parish (1989) points out, it is difficult to separate "a natural desire to avoid hard work [from a] conscious decision to protest or resist" (p. 73), and much of this behavior may fall more into the category of noncooperation than of deliberate political rebellion. Nonetheless, these behaviors were widespread and document the rejection of the system by its victims.

An African American Culture. On an everyday basis, slaves managed their lives as best they could. Most slaves were neither docile victims nor unyielding rebels. As the institution of slavery developed, a distinct African American experience accumulated, and traditions of resistance and accommodation developed. Most slaves worked to create a world for themselves within the confines and restraints of the plantation system, avoiding the more vicious repression as much as possible while attending to their own needs and those of their families. African American culture was forged in response to the realities of slavery and was manifested in folklore, music, religion, family and kinship structures, and other aspects of everyday life (Blassingame, 1972; Genovese, 1974; Gutman, 1976).

QUESTIONS FOR REFLECTION

5. How did the plantation system shape slavery in colonial America?

6. Define *chattel slavery* and *caste system*. Explain how they apply to the American system of slavery. Does the United States still have a racial caste system? Explain.

7. How did slaves resist their oppression? What were the risks associated with resistance?

The Dimensions of Minority Group Status

The situation of African Americans under slavery can be understood more completely by applying some of the concepts you learned in Part 1.

Power, Inequality, and Institutional Discrimination. The key concepts for understanding the creation of slavery are power, inequality, and institutional discrimination. The plantation elite used its greater power resources to consign black Africans to an inferior status. The system of racial inequality was implemented and reinforced by institutionalized discrimination and became a central aspect of everyday life in the antebellum South. The legal and political institutions of colonial society were shaped to benefit the landowners and give them almost total control over their slaves.

Prejudice and Racism. What about the attitudes and feelings of the people involved? What was the role of personal prejudice? How and why did the ideology of anti-black racism start? As we discussed in Chapter 1, individual prejudice and ideological racism are not as important as causes of the creation of minority group status, but are more the results of systems of racial inequality (Jordan, 1968, p. 80; Smedley, 2007, pp. 100–104). Colonists did not enslave black indentured servants because they were prejudiced or because they disliked blacks or thought them inferior. They did it to resolve a labor supply problem. The primary roles of prejudice and racism in the creation of minority group status are to rationalize and "explain" the emerging system of racial and ethnic advantage (Wilson, 1973, pp. 76–78).

Prejudice and racism helped mobilize support for the creation of minority group status and helped stabilize the system as it emerged. Prejudice and racism can provide convenient and convincing justifications for exploitation. They can help insulate a system such as slavery from questioning and criticism and make it appear reasonable and even desirable. Thus, the intensity, strength, and popularity of anti-black Southern racism actually reached its height almost 200 years after slavery began to emerge. During the early 1800s, the American abolitionist movement brought slavery under heavy attack, and in response the ideology of anti-black racism was strengthened (Wilson, 1973, p. 79). The greater the opposition to a system of racial stratification or the greater the magnitude of the exploitation, the greater the need of the beneficiaries and their apologists to justify, rationalize, and explain.

Once created, dominant group prejudice and racism become widespread and common ways of thinking about the minority group. In the case of colonial slavery, anti-black beliefs and feelings became part of the standard package of knowledge, understanding, and truths shared by members of the dominant group. As the decades wore on and the institution of slavery solidified, prejudice and racism were passed on from generation to generation. For succeeding generations, anti-black prejudice became just another piece of information and perspective on the world learned during socialization. Anti-black prejudice and racism began as part of an attempt to control the labor of black indentured servants, became embedded in early American culture, and were established as integral parts of the socialization process for future generations (see Myrdal's "vicious cycle" in Chapter 1).

We show these conceptual relationships in Figure 3.2. Racial inequality arises from the contact situation, as specified earlier in the Noel hypothesis. As the dominant–minority relationship begins to take shape, prejudice and racism develop as rationalizations. Over time, a vicious cycle develops as prejudice and racism reinforce the pattern of inequality between groups, which was the cause of prejudice and racism in the first place. Thus, the Blauner hypothesis states, the subordination of colonized minority groups is perpetuated through time.

Assimilation. There is an enormous literature on American slavery, and research on the nature and meaning of the system continues to this day. Many issues remain

Figure 3.2   A Model for the Creation of Prejudice and Racism

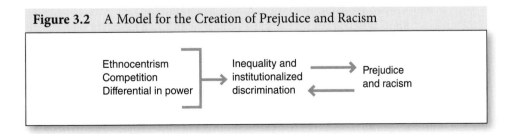

unsettled, however, and one of the more controversial, consequential, and interesting of these concerns the effect of slavery on the slaves.

Apologists for the system of slavery and some historians of the South writing early in the 20th century accepted the rationalizations inherent in anti-black prejudice and argued that slavery was actually beneficial for black Africans. According to this view, British American slavery operated as a "school for civilization" (Phillips, 1918) that rescued savages from the jungles of Africa and exposed them to Christianity and Western civilization. Some argued that slavery was benevolent because it protected slaves from the evils and exploitation of the factory system of the industrial North. These racist views were most popular a century ago, early in the development of the social sciences. Since that time, scholars have established a number of facts (e.g., Western Africa, the area from which most slaves came, had been the site of a number of powerful, advanced civilizations) that make this view untenable by anyone but the most dedicated racist thinkers.

At the opposite extreme, slavery has been compared with Nazi concentration camps and likened to a "perverted patriarchy" that brainwashed, emasculated, and dehumanized slaves, stripping them of their heritage and culture. Historian Stanley Elkins (1959) provocatively argued this interpretation, now widely regarded as over-stated, in his book *Slavery: A Problem in American Institutional and Intellectual Life.* Although his conclusions might be overdrawn, Elkins's argument and evidence are important for any exploration of the nature of American slavery. In fact, much of the scholarship on slavery since the publication of Elkins's book has been an attempt to refute or at least modify the points he made.

Still a third view of the impact of slavery maintains that through all the horror and abuse of enslavement, slaves retained a sense of self and a firm anchor in their African traditions. This point of view stresses the importance of kinship, religion, and culture in helping African Americans cope; it has been presented most poignantly in Alex Haley's (1976) semifictional family history *Roots*, but it is also represented in the schol-arly literature on slavery since Elkins (see Blassingame, 1972; Genovese, 1974).

The debate over the impact of slavery continues, and we cannot hope to resolve the issues here. However, it is clear that African Americans, in Blauner's (1972) terms, were a "colonized" minority group who were extensively—and coercively—accultur-ated. Language acculturation began on the slave ships, where different tribal and lan-guage groups were mixed together to inhibit communication and lower the potential for resistance and revolt (Mannix, 1962).

The plantation elite and their agents needed to communicate with their workforce and insisted on using English. Within a generation or two, African language use died out. Some scholars argue that some African words and language patterns persist to the present day, but even if this is true, the significance of this survival is trivial compared with the coerced adoption of English. To the extent that culture depends on language, Africans under slavery experienced massive acculturation.

Acculturation through slavery was clearly a process that was forced on African Americans. Because they were a colonized minority group and unwilling participants in the system, they had little choice but to adjust to the conditions established by the plantation elite as best they could. Their traditional culture was suppressed, and their choices for adjustment to the system were sharply constrained. Black slaves developed new cultural forms and social relationships, but they did so in a situation with few options or choices (Blauner, 1972, p. 66). Some African cultural elements may have survived the institution of slavery, but, given the power differentials inherent in the system, African Americans had few choices regarding their manner of adjustment.

Gender Relations. Southern agrarian society developed into a complex social system stratified by race and gender as well as class. The plantation elite, small in number but wealthy and politically powerful, were at the top of the structure. Most whites in the South were small farmers, and relatively few of them owned slaves. In 1860, for example, only 25% of all Southern whites owned slaves (Franklin & Moss, 1994, p. 123).

The principal line of differentiation in the antebellum South was, of course, race, which was largely synonymous with slave versus nonslave status. Each of the racial groups was, in turn, stratified by gender. White women were subordinate to the men of the plantation elite, and the slave community echoed the patriarchal pattern of Southern society, except that the degree of gender inequality among blacks was sharply truncated by the fact that slaves had little autonomy and few resources.

At the bottom of the system were African American women slaves. Minority women are generally in double jeopardy, oppressed through their gender as well as their race. For black women slaves, the constraints were triple: "Black in a white society, slave in a free society, women in a society ruled by men, female slaves had the least formal power and were perhaps the most vulnerable group of antebellum America" (White, 1985, p. 15).

The race and gender roles of the day idealized Southern white women and placed them on a pedestal. A romanticized conception of femininity was quite inconsistent with the roles women slaves were required to play. Besides domestic roles, women slaves also worked in the fields and did their share of the hardest, most physically demanding, and least "feminine" farm work. Southern ideas about feminine fragility and daintiness were quickly abandoned when they interfered with work and the profit to be made from slave labor (Amott & Matthaei, 1991, p. 146).

Reflecting their vulnerability and powerlessness, women slaves were sometimes used to breed more slaves to sell. They were raped and otherwise abused by the men of the dominant group. John Blassingame (1972) expresses their vulnerability to sexual victimization:

> Many white men considered every slave cabin a house of ill-fame. Often through "gifts" but usually by force, white overseers and planters obtained the sexual favors of black women. Generally speaking, the women were literally forced to offer themselves "willingly" and receive a trinket for their compliance rather than a flogging for their refusal (p. 83).

Note the power relationships implicit in this passage: women slaves had little choice but to feign willing submission to their white owners.

The routines of work and everyday life differed for men and women slaves. Although they sometimes worked with the men, especially during harvest time, women more often worked in sex-segregated groups organized around domestic as well as farm chores. In addition to working in the fields, they attended the births and cared for the children of both races, cooked and cleaned, wove cloth and sewed clothes, and did the laundry. The women often worked longer hours than the men, doing housework and other chores long after the men had retired for the night (Robertson, 1996, p. 21; White, 1985, p. 122).

The group-oriented nature of their tasks gave women slaves an opportunity to develop bonds and relationships with other slave women. Women cooperated in their chores, in caring for their children, in the maintenance of their quarters, and in myriad other domestic and family chores. These networks and interpersonal bonds could be used to resist the system. For example, slave women sometimes induced abortions rather than bring more children into bondage. They often controlled the role of midwife and were able to effectively deceive slave owners and disguise the abortions as miscarriages (White, 1985, pp. 125–126). The networks of relationships among the women slaves provided mutual aid and support for everyday problems, solace and companionship during the travails of a vulnerable and exploited existence, and some ability to buffer and resist the influence and power of the slave owners (Andersen, 1993, pp. 164–165).

Slaves in the American system were brutally repressed and exploited, but women were even more subordinated than men. Also, their oppression and exclusion sharply differentiated women slaves from white women. The white "Southern belle," chaste, untouchable, and unremittingly virtuous, had little in common with African American women under slavery.

QUESTIONS FOR REFLECTION

8. The key concepts for understanding American slavery are power and inequality, not prejudice or racism. Explain and evaluate this statement.

9. Were American slaves acculturated? Were they integrated? Under what conditions? How do these concepts relate to Blauner's distinction between immigrant and colonized minorities?

10. What, if anything, did black and white women have in common under slavery? How were their gender roles similar? How were they different?

FOCUS ON CONTEMPORARY ISSUES:
Slavery and Indentured Servitude Today

You might think of slavery as a distant piece of history, remote and bizarre. The idea that a person could be owned by another person, and bought and sold like livestock, might seem alien, especially in a culture so devoted to individual happiness and personal well-being. Yet, the ancient institution of slavery is not as rare as it might seem. In fact, slavery exists around the world and in advanced industrial nations, including in the United States.[1] The Internet Research Project at the end of this chapter will introduce you to the realities of modern slavery. Here, we will provide a general overview.

It is impossible to know the extent of modern slavery, but it is estimated that 30 million or more people are enslaved today. Contemporary slavery takes a variety of forms, but all feature dynamics similar to those in the Noel hypothesis: the motivation is a desire for profits, and the populations from which slaves are taken are relatively powerless and lack the resources to defend themselves. Furthermore, ethnocentrism factors in as slaves and owners are frequently from different cultures or racial or religious groups.

Many modern-day slaves are laborers living within their country of birth. They are forced into bondage by various means, including debt bondage. In this system, individuals are not owned outright, but work for little or no wages until some debt is paid off. However, their unfree status is maintained by high interest rates that prevent them from paying off their debts. For example, Skinner (2008) reports the case of a man in India working to pay off a debt of $0.62 cents incurred by his great-grandfather in 1958. With interest rates of 100% per year, he is forced to work in a quarry for no pay, three generations after the debt was originally incurred.

Most forced labor slaves are in Southeast Asia, especially India and China, but others are part of an international trafficking system that is aided by globalization, instantaneous communication, and rapid, cheap travel. A large part of this trafficking is connected to commercial sexual enterprises such as prostitution and pornography. Sex trafficking involves children as well as women. Traffickers find their victims in less-developed nations where many people have been displaced from their village communities and are no longer protected by their traditional familial, religious, or political institutions. Traffickers trick women into believing that they are being hired for legitimate jobs such as domestic work or childcare in a more-developed nation. When workers arrive at their destination, the traffickers take their travel documents and force them into sex work. Workers are isolated and kept powerless by their lack of documents, their illegal status, and their inability to speak the language of their new country. Their situation reflects the huge power differentials between slaves and masters that we saw under American slavery, such as is the masters' ability to treat their slaves however they please.

The United States is a prime destination for victims of sex trafficking and for other workers who are held captive by forms of debt bondage. Some modern slaves provide the unskilled labor that keeps enclaves like Chinatowns functioning, while others work in agriculture, the seafood industry, landscaping, construction, and other areas. Many workers enter the United States legally as "guest workers." However, once they are in the country, there is little federal or state oversight of their situation. According to one report,

(Continued)

(Continued)

these workers are often abused, forced to live and work in horrible conditions, and cheated of their wages by the brokers that brought them into the country (Bauer, 2008).

While similar in many ways to the system of American slavery, modern forms of involuntary servitude are different, too. Modern slaves can be shipped around the globe in hours or days instead of traveling for months from Africa. Instead of cotton plantations, contemporary slaves work in factories and brothels. Like all forms of slavery, however, the modern versions are involuntary, coercive, and maintained by violence and force.

The Creation of Minority Status for American Indians and Mexican Americans

Two other groups became minorities during the preindustrial period. In this section, we will review the dynamics of these processes and make some comparisons with African Americans. As you will see, both the Noel and Blauner hypotheses provide extremely useful insights for understanding these experiences.

American Indians

As Europeans entered the New World, they encountered hundreds of societies that had lived on this land for thousands of years. American Indian societies were highly variable in culture, language, size, and subsistence technology. Some were small, nomadic hunter–gatherer bands, whereas others were more developed societies in which people lived in settled villages and tended large gardens. Regardless of their exact nature, the relentless advance of white society eventually devastated them all. Contact began in the East and established a pattern of conflict and defeat for American Indians that continued until the last of the tribes were finally defeated in the late 1800s. The continual expansion of white society into the West allowed many settlers to fulfill their dreams of economic self-sufficiency, but American Indians, who lost not only their lives and their land but also much of their traditional way of life, paid an incalculable price.

An important and widely unrecognized point about American Indians is that there is no such thing as *the* American Indian. Rather, there were—and are—hundreds of different tribes or nations, each with its own language, culture, home territory, and unique history. There are, of course, similarities from tribe to tribe, but there are also vast differences between, for example, the forest-dwelling tribes of Virginia, who lived in long-houses and cultivated gardens, and the nomadic Plains tribes, who relied on hunting to satisfy their needs. Each tribe was and remains a unique blend of language, values, and social structure. Because of space constraints, we will not always be able to consider all these differences. Nonetheless, it is important to be aware of that diversity and to be sensitive to the variety of peoples and histories within the category of "American Indian."

A second important point is that many American Indian tribes no longer exist or are vastly diminished in size. When Jamestown was established in 1607, it is estimated that there were anywhere from several million to 10 million or more American Indians living in what became the United States. By 1890, when the Indian wars finally ended, the number of American Indians had fallen to fewer than 250,000. By the end of the nearly 300-year-long "contact situation," American Indian populations had declined by at least 75%, perhaps as much as 95% (Mann, 2011; Wax, 1971, p. 17; see also McNickle, 1973).

Very little of this population loss was due directly to warfare and battle casualties. The greatest part was caused by European diseases brought over by the colonists and by the destruction of the food supplies on which American Indian societies relied. American Indians died by the thousands from measles, influenza, smallpox, cholera, tuberculosis, and a variety of other infectious diseases (Wax, 1971, p. 17; see also Oswalt & Neely, 1996; Snipp, 1989). Expanding American society took over traditional hunting grounds and garden plots, and slaughtered game such as the buffalo to the point of extinction. The result of the contact situation for American Indians came close to genocide.

American Indians and the Noel and Blauner Hypotheses. We have already used the Noel hypothesis to analyze why American Indians were not enslaved during the colonial era. Their competition with whites centered on land, not labor, and the Indian nations were often successful in resisting domination (at least temporarily). As American society spread to the West, competition over land continued, and the growing power, superior technology, and greater resource base of the dominant group gradually pushed American Indians to near extinction.

Various attempts were made to control the persistent warfare, the most important of which occurred before independence from Great Britain. In 1763, the British Crown ruled that the various tribes were to be considered "sovereign nations with inalienable rights to their land" (see Lurie, 1982; McNickle, 1973; Wax, 1971). In other words, each tribe was to be treated as a nation-state, like France or Russia, and the colonists could not simply expropriate tribal lands. Rather, negotiations had to take place, and treaties of agreement had to be signed by all affected parties. The tribes had to be compensated for any loss of land.

After the American Revolution, the newborn federal government often ignored this policy. The principle of sovereignty is important because it established a unique relationship between the federal government and American Indians. Because white society ignored the policy and regularly broke the treaties, American Indians have legal claims against the federal government that are unique.

East of the Mississippi River, the period of open conflict was brought to a close by the Indian Removal Act of 1830, a policy of forced emigration. The law required all tribes in the East to move to lands west of the Mississippi. Some of the affected tribes went without resistance, others fought, while some fled to Canada rather than move to the new territory. Regardless, the Indian Removal Act "solved" the perceived Indian problem in the East. Today, we continue to see the impact of this law in the relative scarcity of American Indians in the eastern United States and the majority of American Indians living in the western two thirds of the nation.

In the West, the grim story of competition for land accompanied by rising hostility and aggression repeated itself. Wars were fought, buffalo were killed, territory was expropriated, atrocities were committed on both sides, and the fate of the tribes became more and more certain. By 1890, the greater power and resources of white society had defeated the Indian nations. All of the great warrior chiefs were dead or in prison, and almost all American Indians were living on reservations controlled by agencies of the federal government. The reservations consisted of land set aside for the tribes by the government during treaty negotiations. Often, these lands were not the traditional homelands and were hundreds or even thousands of miles away from what the tribe considered to be "home." It is not surprising that the reservations were usually on undesirable, often worthless, land.

The 1890s mark a low point in American Indian history, a time of great demoralization and sadness. The tribes had to find a way to adapt to reservation life and new forms of subordination to the federal government. Although elements of the tribal way of life have survived, the tribes were impoverished and without resources and had little ability to pursue their own interests.

American Indians, in Blauner's terms, were a colonized minority group who faced high levels of prejudice, racism, and discrimination. Like African Americans, they were controlled by paternalistic systems (the reservations) and, in a variety of ways, were coercively acculturated. Furthermore, according to Blauner, the negative consequences of colonized minority-group status will persist long after the contact situation has been resolved. As we will see in Chapter 6, the experiences of this group after the 1890s provide a great deal of evidence to support Blauner's prediction.

Gender Relations. In the centuries before contact with Europeans, American Indian societies distributed resources and power in a wide variety of ways. At one extreme, some American Indian societies were highly stratified, and many practiced various forms of slavery. Others stressed equality, sharing of resources, and respect for the autonomy and dignity of each individual, including women and children (Amott & Matthaei, 1991, p. 33). American Indian societies were generally patriarchal and followed a strict gender-based division of labor, but this did not necessarily mean that women were subordinate. In many tribes, women held positions of great responsibility and controlled the wealth. For example, among the Iroquois (a large and powerful federation of tribes located in the Northeast), women controlled the land and the harvest, arranged marriages, supervised the children, and were responsible for the appointment of tribal leaders and decisions about peace and war (Oswalt & Neely, 1996, pp. 404–405). It was not unusual for women in many tribes to play key roles in religion, politics, warfare, and the economy. Some women even became highly respected warriors and chiefs (Amott & Matthaei, 1991, p. 36).

Gender relations were affected in a variety of ways during the prolonged contact period. In some cases, the relative status and power of women rose. For example, the women of the Navajo tribe (located mainly in what is now Arizona and New Mexico) were traditionally responsible for the care of herd animals and livestock. When the Spanish introduced sheep and goats into the region, the importance of this sector of the subsistence economy increased, and the power and status of women grew along with it.

In other cases, women were affected adversely. The women of the tribes of the Great Plains, for example, suffered a dramatic loss following the contact period. The gendered division of labor in these tribes meant that women were responsible for gardening while men hunted. When horses were introduced from Europe, the productivity of the men hunters greatly increased. As their economic importance increased, men became more dominant and women lost status and power.

Women in the Cherokee nation—a large tribe whose original homelands were in the Southeast—similarly lost considerable status and power under the pressure to assimilate. Traditionally, Cherokee land was cultivated, controlled, and passed down from generation to generation by the women. This matrilineal pattern was abandoned in favor of the European pattern of men's ownership when the Cherokee attempted (futilely, as it turned out) to acculturate and avoid relocation under the Indian Removal Act of 1830 (Evans, 1989, pp. 12–18).

Summary. By the end of the contact period, the surviving American Indian tribes were impoverished, powerless, and clearly subordinate to white society and the federal government. Like African Americans, American Indians were sharply differentiated from the dominant group by race, and, in many cases, the tribes were internally stratified by gender. As was the case with African American slaves, the degree of gender inequality within the tribes was limited by their overall lack of autonomy and resources.

QUESTIONS FOR REFLECTION

11. What was the nature of the competition between British colonists and American Indians? How did this differ from the competition between Anglos and blacks? What were the consequences of these differences?

12. In Blauner's terms, were American Indians a colonized minority group? Explain.

13. How did gender relations vary from tribe to tribe? How were these relationships affected by contact with Anglo society?

COMPARATIVE FOCUS:
Hawaii

In 1788, while American Indians and whites continued their centuries-long struggle, white Europeans first made contact with the indigenous people of Hawaii (see map on the back inside cover). The contact situation and the system of group relations that

(Continued)

(Continued)

evolved on the island nation provide an interesting and instructive contrast with the history of American Indians.

Hawaii first came into contact with Europeans in 1788, but conquest and colonization did not follow the initial contact. Early relations between Hawaiian islanders and Europeans were organized around trade and commerce—not agriculture, as was the case in the United States, South Africa, Northern Ireland, and so many other places. Thus, the contact situation did not immediately lead to competition over the control of land or labor.

Also, the indigenous Hawaiian society was highly developed, and had sufficient military strength to protect itself from the relatively few Europeans who first came to the islands. Thus, two of the three conditions stated in the Noel hypothesis for the emergence of a dominant–minority situation, competition and a power differential, were not present in the early days of European–Hawaiian contact. Anglo dominance did not emerge until decades after first contact.

Contact with Europeans brought other consequences, including smallpox and other diseases to which native Hawaiians had no immunity. Death rates rose, and the population of native Hawaiians, which numbered about 300,000 in 1788, fell to less than 60,000 a century later (Kitano & Daniels, 1995, p. 137).

As relations between the islands and Europeans developed, the land was gradually turned to commercial agriculture. By the mid-1800s white planters had established large sugar plantations; these enterprises are extremely labor-intensive, and have often been associated with systems of enforced labor and slavery (Curtin, 1990). By that time, however, there were not enough native Hawaiians to fill the demand for labor, and the planters began to recruit abroad, mostly in China, Portugal, Japan, Korea, Puerto Rico, and the Philippines. Thus, the original immigrants of the Asian American groups that we will discuss (in Chapter 8) came first to the Hawaiian Islands, not the mainland.

The white plantation owners began to dominate the island economy and political structure. Other groups, however, were not excluded from secondary structural assimilation. Laws banning entire groups from public institutions or practices such as school segregation are nonexistent in Hawaiian history. Americans of Japanese ancestry, for example, are very powerful in politics and have produced many of the leading Hawaiian politicians. (In contrast to Japanese Americans on the mainland, Japanese Americans living in Hawaii were not interned in camps during World War II.) Most other groups have taken advantage of the relative openness of Hawaiian society and carved out niches for themselves in the institutional structure.

In terms of primary structural assimilation, rates of intermarriage among the various groups have been much higher than on the mainland, reflecting the openness to intimacy across group lines that characterized Hawaii since first contact. From 2008 through 2010, about 42% of all marriages in Hawaii crossed group lines; this rate is much higher rate than that of any other state. In particular, Native Hawaiians have intermarried freely with other groups (Kitano & Daniels, 1995, pp. 138–139).

> Although Hawaii has no history of the most blatant and oppressive forms of group discrimination, all is not perfect in the reputed racial paradise. Ethnic and racial stratification exist, as do prejudice and discrimination. Native Hawaiians, like Native Americans and other colonized groups, have developed organizations to pursue compensation for lands illegally taken and to resolve other grievances. There have been reports of attacks on whites by Native Hawaiians, incidents that some are calling hate crimes (Kasindorf, 2012). However, the traditions of tolerance and acceptance remain strong in the island state, even though it is not the paradise of mutual respect sometimes imagined.

Mexican Americans

As the population of the United States increased and spread across the continent, contact with Mexicans inevitably occurred. Spanish explorers and settlers had lived in what is now the southwestern United States long before the wave of American settlers broke across this region. For example, Santa Fe, New Mexico, was founded in 1598, nearly a decade before Jamestown. As late as the 1820s, Mexicans and American Indians were almost the sole residents of the region.

In the early 1800s, four areas of Mexican settlement had developed, roughly corresponding with what would become Texas, California, New Mexico, and Arizona. These areas were sparsely settled, and most Mexicans lived in what was to become New Mexico (Cortes, 1980, p. 701). The economy of the regions was based on farming and herding. Most people lived in villages and small towns or on ranches and farms. Social and political life was organized around family and the Catholic Church, and tended to be dominated by an elite class of wealthy landowners.

Texas. Some of the first effects of U.S. expansion to the West were felt in Texas early in the 1800s. Mexico was no military match for its neighbor to the north, and the farmland of East Texas was a tempting resource for the cotton-growing interests in the American South. Anglo-Americans began to immigrate to Texas in sizable numbers in the 1820s, and by 1835, they outnumbered Mexicans 6 to 1. The attempts by the Mexican government to control these immigrants were clumsy and ineffective and eventually precipitated a successful revolution by the Anglo-Americans, with some Mexicans also joining the rebels. At this point in time, competition between Anglos and Texans of Mexican descent (called Tejanos) was muted by the abundance of land and opportunity in the area. Population density was low, fertile land was readily available for all, and the "general tone of the time was that of intercultural cooperation" (Alvarez, 1973, p. 922).

Competition between Anglo-Texans and Tejanos became increasingly intense. When the United States annexed Texas in the 1840s, full-scale war broke out, and Mexico was defeated. Under the Treaty of Guadalupe Hidalgo in 1848, Mexico ceded much of the Southwest to the United States. In the Gadsden Purchase of 1853, the United States acquired the remainder of the territory that now composes the southwestern United States. As a result of these treaties, the Mexican population of this

QUESTIONS FOR REFLECTION

17. What were the key differences in the contact situations in New Spain, New France, and the British colonies? How do the concepts of competition and power apply?

18. What are some contemporary differences between Mexico, the United States, and Canada that might be traced to the contact situation?

Notes

1. For a powerful account of how a form of slavery in the United States survived the Civil War, see Blackmon (2008).

2. This section is largely based on Russell (1994).

Main Points

- Dominant–minority relations are shaped by the characteristics of society. In particular, the nature of the subsistence technology will affect group relations, culture, family structure, and virtually all aspects of social life. The single most important factor in the development of dominant–minority relations is the contact situation; it will have long-term consequences.
- The Noel hypothesis states that ethnic or racial stratification will result when a contact situation is characterized by ethnocentrism, competition, and a differential in power. American colonists enslaved Africans instead of white indentured servants or American Indians because only the Africans fit all three conditions. American slavery was a paternalistic system.
- The Blauner hypothesis states that minority groups created by colonization will experience greater, more long-lasting disadvantages than minority groups created by immigration.
- Prejudice and racism are more the results of systems of racial and ethnic inequality than they are the causes. They serve to rationalize, "explain," and stabilize these systems.
- The colonists' competition with American Indians centered on control of the land. American Indian tribes were conquered and pressed into a paternalistic relationship with white society. American Indians became a colonized minority group subjected to forced acculturation.
- Mexican Americans were the third minority group created during the preindustrial era. Mexican Americans competed with white settlers over land and labor. Like Africans and American Indians, Mexican Americans were a colonized minority group subjected to forced acculturation.
- Conquest and colonization affected men and women differently. Women's roles changed, sometimes becoming less constrained by patriarchal traditions. These changes were always in the context of increasing powerlessness and poverty for the group as a whole. Minority women have been doubly oppressed by their gender and their minority group status in comparison to white women and minority men.

Review Questions

1. State and explain the two themes from the beginning of the chapter. Apply each to the contact situations between white European colonists, African Americans, American Indians, and Mexican Americans. Identify and explain the key differences and similarities among the three situations.

2. Explain what a plantation system is and why this system of production is important for understanding the origins of slavery in colonial America. Why are plantation systems usually characterized by (a) paternalism, (b) huge inequalities between groups, (c) repressive systems of control, (d) rigid codes of behavior, and (e) low rates of overt conflict?

3. Explain the Noel and Blauner hypotheses and how they apply to the contact situations covered in this chapter. Explain each of the following key terms: *ethnocentrism, competition, power, colonized minority group,* and *immigrant minority group.* How did group conflict vary when competition was over land instead of labor?

4. Explain the role of prejudice and racism in the creation of minority group status. Do prejudice and racism help cause minority group status, or are they caused by minority group status? Explain.

5. Compare and contrast gender relations in each of the contact situations discussed in this chapter. Why do the relationships vary?

6. What does it mean to say that, under slavery, acculturation for African Americans was coerced? What are the implications for assimilation, inequality, and African American culture given this type of acculturation?

7. Compare and contrast the contact situations of Native Hawaiians with those of American Indians. What were the key differences in the contact situations? How are these differences reflected in the groups' current situations?

8. Compare and contrast the contact situations in colonial America, Canada, and Mexico. What groups were involved in each situation? What was the nature of the competition, and what were the consequences?

Internet Activity

Americans today might look at slavery as a distant relic of history, remote and bizarre. The idea that a person could be owned by another person, defined as a piece of property, and bought and sold like livestock probably seems hopelessly alien to people who live in a culture devoted to individual happiness and personal well-being. Yet, slavery still exists around the world, on every continent, in advanced industrial societies, including in the United States.

This activity will provide you with an opportunity to take what you've learned so far and apply it to modern slavery. You will explore the volume and scope of modern slavery, collect case studies or personal examples, compare modern slavery to American slavery of the past, and learn what is being done to combat it.

Because the internet is notorious for spreading incomplete, deeply biased, or false information, you should possess healthy skepticism about the information, ideas, and arguments that you find. Also, recognize that the facts you gather (e.g., the number of people currently enslaved) will be approximations and, in some cases, guesswork. Just do the best you can.

Websites for This Project

1. http://www.freetheslaves.net/Page.aspx?pid=584

   Home page of "Free the Slaves" that explains the state of modern slavery around the world, the organization's efforts to combat it, and ideas about how you can become involved.

2. http://www.ijm.org/?gclid=CJ__pezm56YCFVln5QodCTD_0w

Home Page for the International Justice Mission, a Christian advocacy and activist group dedicated to combating slavery.

3. http://www.state.gov/j/tip/rls/tiprpt/2014/

U.S. Department of State's most recent Trafficking in Persons report, which includes victims' stories, global law enforcement data, helpful Fact Sheets, and more.

Questions to Explore

1. Scope and Volume
   a. Approximately how many people are currently enslaved or in a condition of involuntary servitude? (*Note: You might want to cite both high and low estimates.*)
   b. Describe this population in terms of gender, age, race, and nationality in terms of their numbers or percentages.
   c. Where are modern slaves most numerous in the world?
   d. What are the major sending areas or nations? What are the most important destination areas and nations?

2. Experiences
   a. Describe the mechanisms and practices by which slave status is enforced. What is the role of debt bondage in modern slavery or involuntary servitude? How often are coercion and violence used? How do these practices vary across different types of slavery (e.g., sex trafficking versus involuntary labor)?
   b. Find at least three to five case studies of people who have been victimized by modern slavery. Briefly summarize each case in a sentence or two and include the Internet links you found.
   c. What important social characteristics do the people in your case studies share (e.g., age, gender, social class, race, and ethnicity)?

3. Dynamics and Causes
   a. American slavery was shaped by the level of development and labor-intensive subsistence technology of the colonial era. Do similar factors shape modern slavery? Explain. What other factors are relevant?
   b. What elements of the Noel hypothesis apply to modern slavery? How does ethnocentrism, prejudice, or sexism play a role? What resources and abilities do modern slaves have that make them the objects of competition? What role does power play in shaping and maintaining modern slavery?

4. Markets: Supply and Demand
   a. What jobs do modern slaves hold? What economic niches are being filled by slaves? Identify two or three types of people or groups that profit from slavery. Describe the minority–dominant group situations you found.

5. Enforcement Efforts, Legal Considerations, Human Rights
   a. Where is slavery illegal? By what authority? Outside of legality, identify three to five specific human rights or ethical issues related to modern slavery.
   b. Find at least three national and international programs aimed at stopping modern slavery and describe what they are doing. Which seems most effective to you and why?

Group Discussion

Bring your findings to class and discuss them with your classmates. Focus on comparing and contrasting modern and colonial American slavery, especially the roles of ethnocentrism and power, subsistence technology, demand and supply, human rights, and enforcement efforts. What surprised you the most about what you learned? If you're interested in the issue of slavery, what skills or talents do you have that might help decrease or end modern slavery? (Think broadly.)

Learning Resources on the Web

⑤SAGE edge™

edge.sagepub.com/healeyds5e

SAGE edge offers a robust online environment featuring an impressive array of free tools and resources for review, study, and further exploration, keeping both instructors and students on the cutting edge of teaching and learning.

SAGE edge for Students provides a personalized approach to help you accomplish your coursework goals in an easy-to-use learning environment.

Industrialization and Dominant–Minority Relations: From Slavery to Segregation and the Coming of Postindustrial Society

A war sets up in our emotions: one part of our feelings tells us it is good to be in the city, that we have a chance at life here, that we need but turn a corner to become a stranger, that we need no longer bow and dodge at the sight of the Lords of the Land. Another part of our feelings tells us that, in terms of worry and strain, the cost of living in the kitchenettes is too high, that the city heaps too much responsibility on us and gives too little security in return . . .

The kitchenette, with its filth and foul air, with its one toilet for thirty or more tenants, kills our black babies so fast that in many cities twice as many of them die as white babies . . .

The kitchenette scatters death so widely among us that our death rate exceeds our birth rate, and if it were not for the trains and autos bringing us daily into the city from the plantations, we black folk who dwell in northern cities would die out entirely over the course of a few years . . .

The kitchenette throws desperate and unhappy people into an unbearable closeness of association, thereby increasing latent friction, giving birth to never-ending quarrels of recrimination, accusation, and vindictiveness, producing warped personalities.

The kitchenette injects pressure and tension into our individual personalities, making many of us give up the struggle, walk off and leave wives, husbands, and even children behind to shift for themselves...

The kitchenette reaches out with fingers of golden bribes to the officials of the city, persuading them to allow old firetraps to remain standing and occupied long after they should have been torn down.

The kitchenette is the funnel through which our pulverized lives flow to ruin and death on the city pavement, at a profit.

—Richard Wright[1]

Richard Wright (1908–1960), one of the most powerful writers of the 20th century, lived through and wrote about many of the social changes discussed in this chapter. He grew up in the South during the height of the Jim Crow system, and his passionate hatred for segregation and bigotry is expressed in his major works, *Native Son* (1940) and the autobiographical *Black Boy* (1945). In 1941, Wright helped to produce *Twelve Million Black Voices*, a folk history of African Americans. A combination of photos and brief essays, the work is a powerful commentary on three centuries of oppression.

The selection above is adapted from "Death on the City Pavement," which expresses Wright's view of the African-American migration out of the South that began in the early 1900s as a reaction to Jim Crow segregation. Wright himself moved from the South to the North, a bittersweet journey that often traded harsh, rural repression for overcrowded, anonymous ghettos. Housing discrimination, both overt and covert, confined African American migrants to the least desirable, most overcrowded areas of the city—in many cases, the neighborhoods that had first housed immigrants from Europe. Unscrupulous landlords subdivided buildings into the tiniest possible apartments ("kitchenettes"), and as impoverished newcomers who could afford no better, African American migrants were forced to cope with overpriced, substandard housing as best they could.

One theme stated at the beginning of Chapter 3 was that a society's subsistence technology shapes dominant–minority group relations, specifically, that dominant–minority relations in the formative years of the United States were profoundly shaped by agrarian technology and the desire to control land and labor. The agrarian era ended in the 1800s, and the United States has experienced two major transformations in subsistence technology since that time, each of which has transformed dominant–minority relations and required the creation of new structures and processes to maintain racial stratification and white privilege. In this chapter, we'll explore a corollary of this theme: *dominant–minority group relations change as the subsistence technology changes.*

The first transformation, the Industrial Revolution, began in the early 19th century when machine-based technologies began to develop, especially in the North. In the agrarian era, work was labor-intensive, done by hand or with the aid of draft animals. During industrialization, work became capital-intensive (see Chapter 2), and machines replaced people and animals.

The new industrial technology rapidly increased the productivity and efficiency of the U.S. economy and quickly began to change all other aspects of society, including the nature of work, politics, communication, transportation, family life, birth rates and death rates, the system of education, and, of course, dominant–minority relations. The groups that had become minorities during the agrarian era (African Americans, American Indians, and Mexican Americans) faced new possibilities and new dangers, but industrialization also created new minority groups, new forms of exploitation and oppression and, for some, new opportunities to rise in the social structure and succeed in America. In this chapter, we will explore this transformation and illustrate its effects on the status of African Americans, focusing primarily on the construction of Jim Crow segregation in the South. The impact of industrialization on other minority groups will be considered in the case studies presented in Part 3.

The second transformation in subsistence technology brings us to more recent times. In the mid-20th century, the United States (and other advanced industrial societies) entered the postindustrial era, also called **deindustrialization**. This shift in subsistence technology was marked by (1) a decline in the manufacturing sector of the economy and a decrease in the supply of secure, well-paid, blue-collar, manual-labor jobs, and (2) an expansion in the service and information-based sectors of the economy and an increase in the relative proportion of white-collar and "high-tech" jobs.

Like the 19th century Industrial Revolution, these changes have profound implications for every aspect of modern society, not just for dominant–minority relations. Indeed, every characteristic of American society—work, family, politics, popular culture—is being transformed as the subsistence technology continues to evolve. In the latter part of this chapter, we examine this most recent transformation in general terms and point out some of its implications for minority groups. We will examine some new concepts—especially modern institutional discrimination—to help us understand group relations in this new era. And, we will establish some important groundwork for the case studies in Part 3, in which we will consider in detail the implication of postindustrial society for America's minority groups.

Table 4.1 summarizes the characteristics of the three major subsistence technologies considered in this text. As U.S. society has moved through these stages, group relations and the nature of racial stratification have continuously changed.

Industrialization and the Shift From Paternalistic to Rigid Competitive Group Relations

As we noted in Chapter 2, the Industrial Revolution began in England in the mid-1700s and spread to the rest of Europe, to the United States, and eventually to the rest of the world. The key innovations associated with this change in subsistence technology were

Table 4.1 Three Subsistence Technologies and the United States

Technology	Key Trends and Characteristics	Dates
Agrarian	Labor-intensive agriculture. Control of land and labor are central.	1607 to early 1800s
Industrial	Capital-intensive manufacturing. Machines replace animal and human labor.	Early 1800s to mid-1900s
Postindustrial	Shift away from manufacturing to a service economy. The "information society."	Mid-1900s to the present

the application of machine power to production and the harnessing of inanimate sources of energy, such as steam and coal, to fuel the machines. As machines replaced humans and animals, work became many times more productive, the economy grew, and the volume and variety of goods produced increased dramatically.

In an industrial economy, the close, paternalistic control of minority groups found in agrarian societies becomes irrelevant. Paternalistic relationships such as slavery are found in societies with labor-intensive technologies and are designed to organize and control a large, involuntary, geographically immobile labor force. An industrial economy, in contrast, requires a workforce that is geographically and socially mobile, skilled, and literate. Furthermore, with industrialization comes urbanization, and close, paternalistic controls are difficult to maintain in a city.

Thus, as industrialization progresses, agrarian paternalism tends to give way to **rigid competitive group** relations (see Table 4.2). Under this system, minority group members are freer to compete with dominant group members, especially those in the lower-class segments, for jobs and other valued commodities. As competition increases, the threatened members of the dominant group become more hostile, and attacks on the minority groups tend to increase.

Whereas paternalistic systems were designed to directly dominate and control the minority group (and its labor), rigid competitive systems are more defensive in nature. The threatened segments of the dominant group seek to minimize or eliminate minority group encroachment on jobs, housing, or other valuable goods or services (van den Berghe, 1967; Wilson, 1973).

Paternalistic systems such as slavery required members of the minority group to be active, if involuntary, participants. In contrast, in rigid competitive systems, the dominant group seeks to handicap the minority group's ability to compete effectively or, in some cases, eliminate competition from the minority group altogether.

We have already considered an example of a dominant group attempt to protect itself from a threat. As you recall, the National Origins Act was passed in the 1920s to stop the flow of cheaper labor from Europe and protect jobs and wages (see Chapter 2). In this chapter, we consider dominant group attempts to keep African Americans powerless and impoverished—to maintain black–white racial stratification—as society shifted from an agricultural to an industrial base.

The Impact of Industrialization on the Racial Stratification of African Americans: From Slavery to Segregation

Industrial technology began to transform American society in the early 1800s, but its effects were not felt equally in all regions. The northern states industrialized first, while the plantation system and agricultural production continued to dominate the South. This economic diversity was one of the underlying causes of the regional conflict that led to the Civil War. Because of its more productive technology, the North had more resources and defeated the Confederacy in a bloody war of attrition. Slavery was abolished, and black–white relations in the South entered a new era when the Civil War ended in April 1865.

The southern system of race relations that ultimately emerged after the Civil War was designed in part to continue the control of African American labor that was institutionalized under slavery. It was intended, also, to eliminate any political or economic threat from the African American community.

This rigid competitive system grew to be highly elaborate and inflexible, partly because of the high racial visibility and long history of inferior status and powerlessness of African Americans in the South, and partly because of the particular needs of southern agriculture. In this section, we look at black–white relations from the end of the Civil War through the ascendance of segregation in the South and the mass migration of African Americans to the cities of the industrializing North.

Reconstruction

The period of **Reconstruction**, from 1865 to the 1880s, was a brief respite in the long history of oppression and exploitation of African Americans. The Union Army and other agencies of the federal government, such as the Freedman's Bureau, were used to enforce racial freedom in the defeated Confederacy. Black Southerners took advantage of the Fifteenth Amendment to the Constitution, passed in 1870, which states that the right to vote cannot be denied on the grounds of "race, color, or previous condition of servitude." They registered to vote in large numbers and turned out on Election Day, and some were elected to high political office. Schools for the former slaves were opened, and African Americans purchased land and houses and founded businesses.

The era of freedom was short, however, and Reconstruction began to end when the federal government demobilized its armies of occupation and turned its attention to other matters. By the 1880s, the federal government had withdrawn from the South, Reconstruction was over, and black Southerners began to fall rapidly into a new system of exploitation and inequality.

Reconstruction was too brief to change two of the most important legacies of slavery. First, the centuries of bondage left black Southerners impoverished, largely illiterate and uneducated, and with few power resources. When new threats of racial oppression appeared, African Americans found it difficult to defend their group interests. These developments are consistent with the Blauner hypothesis: colonized minority groups face greater difficulties in improving their disadvantaged status because they confront greater inequalities and have fewer resources at their disposal.

Second, slavery left a strong tradition of racism in the white community. Anti-black prejudice and racism originated as rationalizations for slavery but had taken on lives of their own over the generations. After two centuries of slavery, the heritage of prejudice and racism was thoroughly ingrained in Southern culture. White Southerners were predisposed by this cultural legacy to see racial inequality and exploitation of African Americans as normal and desirable. They were able to construct a social system based on the assumption of racial inferiority after Reconstruction ended and the federal government withdrew.

De Jure Segregation

The system of race relations that replaced slavery in the South was **de jure segregation**, sometimes referred to as the **Jim Crow system**. Under segregation, the minority group is physically and socially separated from the dominant group and consigned to an inferior position in virtually every area of social life. The term *de jure* ("by law") means that the system is sanctioned and reinforced by the legal code; the inferior status of African Americans was actually mandated or required by state and local laws. For example, Southern cities during this era had laws requiring African Americans to ride at the back of the bus. If an African American refused to comply with this seating arrangement, he or she could be arrested.

De jure segregation came to encompass all aspects of southern social life. Neighborhoods, jobs, stores, restaurants, and parks were segregated. When new social forms, such as movie theaters, sports stadiums, and interstate buses appeared in the South, they, too, were quickly segregated.

The logic of segregation created a vicious cycle. The more African Americans were excluded from the mainstream of society, the greater their objective poverty and powerlessness became. The more inferior their status and the greater their powerlessness, the easier it was to mandate more inequality. High levels of inequality reinforced racial prejudice and made it easy to use racism to justify further separation. The system kept turning on itself, finding new social niches to segregate and reinforcing the inequality that was its starting point. For example, at the height of the Jim Crow era, the system had evolved to the point that some courtrooms maintained separate Bibles for African American witnesses to swear on. Also, in Birmingham, Alabama, it was against the law for blacks and whites to play checkers or dominoes together (Woodward, 1974, p. 118).

What were the causes of this massive separation of the races? Once again, the concepts of the Noel hypothesis prove useful. Because strong anti-black prejudice was already in existence when segregation began, we do not need to account for ethnocentrism. The post-Reconstruction competition between the racial groups was reminiscent of the origins of slavery, in that black Southerners had something that white Southerners wanted: labor. In addition, a free black electorate threatened the political and economic dominance of the elite segments of the white community. Finally, after the withdrawal of federal troops and the end of Reconstruction, white Southerners had sufficient power resources to end the competition on their own terms and construct repressive systems of control for black Southerners.

The Origins of De Jure Segregation. Although the South lost the Civil War, its basic class structure and agrarian economy remained intact. The plantation elite remained the dominant class, and they were able to use their power to build a system of racial stratification to replace slavery.

Control of Black Labor. The plantation elite retained ownership of huge tracts of land, and cotton remained the primary cash crop in the South. As was the case before the Civil War, the landowners needed a workforce to farm the land. Because of the depredations and economic disruptions of the war, the old plantation elite were short on cash and liquid capital and could not always hire workers for wages. In fact, almost as soon as the war ended, southern legislatures attempted to force African Americans back into involuntary servitude by passing a series of laws known as the "Black Codes." Only the beginning of Reconstruction and the active intervention of the federal government halted the implementation of this legislation (Geschwender, 1978, p. 158; Wilson, 1973, p. 99).

The plantation elite solved their manpower problem this time by developing a system of **sharecropping**, or tenant farming. The sharecroppers worked the land, which was actually owned by the planters, in return for payment in shares of the profit when the crop was taken to market. The landowner would supply a place to live and food and clothing on credit. After the harvest, tenant and landowner would split the profits (sometimes very unequally), and tenants' debts would be deducted from their share. The accounts were kept by the landowner, who could cheat and take advantage of the tenants with great impunity. With few or no political and civil rights, black sharecroppers found it difficult to keep unscrupulous white landowners honest. Landowners could inflate the indebtedness of sharecroppers and claim that they were still owed money even after profits had been split. Under this system, sharecroppers had few opportunities to improve their situations and could be bound to the land until their "debts" were paid off (Geschwender, 1978, p. 163).

By 1910, more than half of all employed African Americans worked in agriculture, and more than half of the remainder (25% of the total) worked in domestic occupations, such as maid or janitor (Geschwender, 1978, p. 169). The labor shortage in Southern agriculture was solved, and the African American community once again found itself in a subservient status. At the same time, the white Southern working class was protected from direct job competition with African Americans. As the South began to industrialize, white workers were able to exclude black workers and reserve the better-paying jobs using a combination of whites-only labor unions and strong anti-black laws and customs. White workers took advantage of the new jobs created by industrialization, while black Southerners remained a rural peasantry, excluded from participation in the modernizing job structure.

In some sectors of the changing southern economy, the status of African Americans actually fell lower than it had been during slavery. For example, in 1865, 83% of the artisans, or skilled craftsmen, in the South were African Americans; by 1900, this percentage had fallen to 5% (Geschwender, 1978, p. 170). The Jim Crow system confined African Americans to the agrarian and domestic sectors of the labor force, denied them the opportunity for a decent education, and excluded them from politics. The system was reinforced by still more laws and customs that drastically limited the options and life opportunities available to black Southerners.

Political and Civil Rights Under Jim Crow. A final force behind the creation of de jure segregation was political. As the 19th century drew to a close, a wave of agrarian radicalism known as populism spread across the country. This anti-elitist movement was a reaction to changes in agriculture caused by industrialization. The movement attempted to unite poor whites and blacks in the rural South against the traditional elite classes.

The economic elite were frightened by the possibility of a loss of power and split the incipient coalition between whites and blacks by fanning the flames of racial hatred. The strategy of "divide and conquer" proved to be effective (as it often has both before and since this time), and the white elite classes in states throughout the South eliminated the possibility of future threats by depriving African Americans of the right to vote (Woodward, 1974).

The disenfranchisement of the black community was accomplished by measures such as literacy tests, poll taxes, and property requirements. The literacy tests were officially justified as promoting a better-informed electorate but were shamelessly rigged to favor white voters. The requirement that voters pay a tax or prove ownership of a certain amount of property could also disenfranchise poor whites, but again, the implementation of these policies was racially biased.

The policies were extremely effective, and by the early 20th century, the political power of the southern black community was virtually nonexistent. For example, as late as 1896 in Louisiana there had been more than 100,000 registered African American voters, and they were a majority in 26 parishes (counties). In 1898, the state adopted a new constitution containing stiff educational and property requirements for voting unless the voter's father or grandfather had been eligible to vote as of January 1, 1867. At that time, the Fourteenth and Fifteenth Amendments, which guaranteed suffrage for black men, had not yet been passed.

Such "grandfather clauses" made it easy for white men to register while disenfranchising blacks. By 1900, only about 5,000 African Americans were registered to vote in Louisiana, and African American voters were not a majority in any parish. A similar decline occurred in Alabama, where an electorate of more than 180,000 African American men was reduced to 3,000 by provision of a new state constitution. This story repeated itself throughout the South, and African American political powerlessness was a reality by 1905 (Franklin & Moss, 1994, p. 261).

This system of legally mandated racial privilege was approved by the U.S. Supreme Court, which ruled in the case of *Plessy v. Ferguson* (1896) that it was constitutional for states to require separate facilities (schools, parks, etc.) for African Americans as long as the separate facilities were fully equal. The southern states paid close attention to "separate" but ignored "equal."

Reinforcing the System. Under de jure segregation, as under slavery, the subordination of the African American community was reinforced and supplemented by an elaborate system of racial etiquette. Everyday interactions between blacks and whites proceeded according to highly stylized and rigidly followed codes of conduct intended to underscore the inferior status of the African American community. Whites were addressed as "mister" or "ma'am," whereas African Americans were called by their first names or, perhaps, by an honorific title such as "aunt," "uncle," or "professor." Blacks were expected to assume a humble and deferential manner, remove their hats, cast their eyes downward, and enact the role of the subordinate in all interactions with whites. If an African American had reason to call on anyone in the white community, he or she was expected to go to the back door.

These expectations and "good manners" for black Southerners were systematically enforced. Anyone who ignored them ran the risk of reprisal, physical attacks, and even death by lynching. During the decades in which the Jim Crow system was being imposed, there were thousands of lynchings in the South. From 1884 until the end of the century, lynchings averaged almost one every other day (Franklin & Moss, 1994, p. 312). The bulk of this violent terrorism was racial and intended to reinforce the system of racial advantage more than to punish real or imagined transgressors. Also, various secret organizations, such as the Ku Klux Klan, engaged in terrorist attacks against the African American community and anyone else who failed to conform to the dictates of the white supremacist system.

COMPARATIVE FOCUS:
Jim Crow Segregation and South African Apartheid

Systems of legalized, state-sponsored racial segregation like Jim Crow can be found in many nations, but perhaps the most infamous system was apartheid, as practiced in South Africa. Here, we will note some of the many similarities apartheid shared with Jim Crow segregation.

First, and most important, both apartheid and American de jure segregation were deliberately constructed by the dominant group (whites) to control and exploit the minority group (blacks) and to keep them powerless. In both systems, segregation was comprehensive and encompassed virtually every area of life, including neighborhoods, schools, movie theaters, parks, public buildings, buses, and water fountains.

In both systems, whites benefited from a cheap, powerless labor supply in agriculture and in business. Domestically, even white families of modest means could afford servants, gardeners, and nannies.

Blacks in both systems were politically disenfranchised and closely controlled by police and other agencies of the state. Their low status was reinforced by violence and force, sometimes administered by the police, sometimes by extralegal vigilante and terrorist groups.

Elaborate rituals and customs governed interaction between the races: All were intended to overtly display and reinforce the power differential between the groups. Under both apartheid and Jim Crow segregation, blacks generally lived in abject poverty, with incomes a tiny fraction of those of the white community.

In both cases, protest movements formed in the black community and helped end the systems of racial segregation. The protests were met with extreme violence and repression from the state, and the ensuing struggles created heroes such as Martin Luther King Jr. and Nelson Mandela, among others. Also, in both cases, state-sponsored racial oppression ended only after prolonged, intense conflict. Apartheid was dismantled in the early 1990s.

Apartheid was more repressive than Jim Crow segregation and more viciously defended by the white dominant group. Why? Part of the reason is simple arithmetic. Whites in South Africa were a numerical minority (no more than 10% of the total population) and felt that their privileged status was under extreme threat from the black majority. White South Africans had a "fortress mentality" and feared that they would be swamped by the black majority if they allowed even the slightest lapse in the defense of their racial privilege.

Today, South Africa continues to deal with the legacies of racial segregation, as does the United States. In both nations, racial divisions run deep, and neither has been able to completely resolve its myriad issues of fairness, justice, and equality.

QUESTIONS FOR REFLECTION

1. Why did whites in South Africa and the American South respond so violently to black protest movements? What was at stake, as they saw it?

2. What other differences, besides the numerical one, can you identify between the two situations? For example, is it important that one system was regional and the other national? What are the implications of this difference?

Increases in Prejudice and Racism. As the system of racial advantage formed and solidified, levels of prejudice and racism increased (Wilson, 1973, p. 101). The new system needed justification and rationalization, just as slavery did, and anti-black sentiment, stereotypes, and ideologies of racial inferiority grew stronger. At the start of the 20th century, the United States in general—not just the South—was a very racist and intolerant society. This spirit of rejection and scorn for all out-groups coalesced with the need for justification of the Jim Crow system and created an especially negative brand of racism in the South.

QUESTIONS FOR REFLECTION

3. How does the concept of subsistence technology clarify the shift from a paternalistic to a rigid competitive system of race relations?

4. How do the concepts of competition and differential in power in the Noel hypothesis apply to the creation of the Jim Crow system of segregation?

5. From a sociological point of view, what were the most important features of de jure segregation?

The Great Migration

Although African Americans lacked the power resources to withstand the resurrection of southern racism and oppression, they did have one option that had not been available under slavery: freedom of movement. African Americans were no longer legally tied to a specific master or to a certain plot of land. In the early 20th century, a massive population movement, often called the Great Migration, began out of the South. Slowly at first, African Americans began to move to other regions of the nation and from the countryside to the city. The movement increased when hard times hit Southern agriculture and slowed down during better times. In discussing the Great Migration, it has been said that African Americans voted against Southern segregation with their feet.

As Figure 4.1 shows, the black population was highly concentrated in the South as recently as 1910, a little more than a century ago. By 1990, African Americans had become much more evenly distributed across the nation, spreading to the Northeast and the upper Midwest. Since 1990, the distribution of the black population has remained roughly the same, although there has been some movement back to the South.

Figure 4.2 shows that, in addition to movement away from the South, the Great Migration was also a movement from the countryside to the city. A century ago, blacks were overwhelmingly rural, but today more than 90% are urban.

Thus, an urban black population living outside of the South is a 20th century phenomenon. The significance of this population redistribution is manifold. Most important, perhaps, was the fact that by moving out of the South and into urban areas, African Americans moved from areas of great resistance to racial change to areas of lower resistance. In the northern cities, for example, it was far easier to register and vote. Black political power began to grow and eventually provided many of the crucial resources that fueled the civil rights movement of the 1950s and 1960s.

Life in the North

What did African American migrants find when they got to the industrializing cities of the North? There is no doubt that life in the North was better for the vast majority of them. The growing Northern African American communities relished the absence of Jim Crow laws and oppressive racial etiquette, the relative freedom to

Figure 4.1 Distribution of the African American Population in the United States, 1790–1990

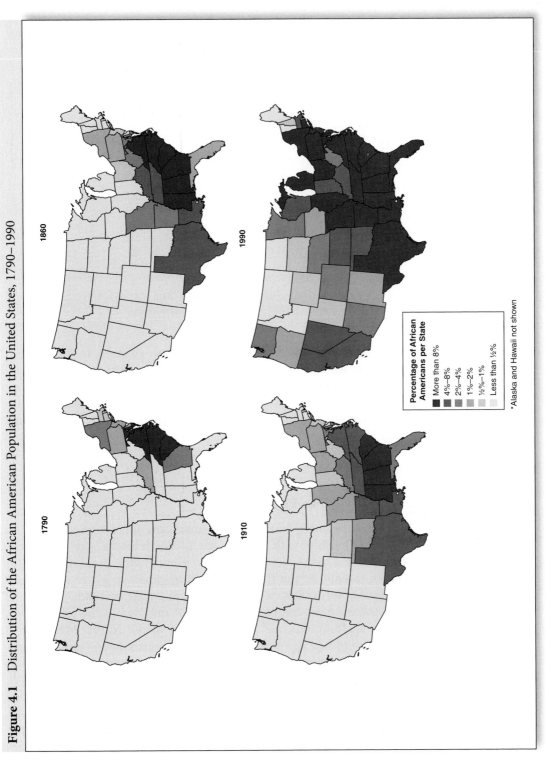

1790

1860

1910

1990

Percentage of African Americans per State

- More than 8%
- 4%–8%
- 2%–4%
- 1%–2%
- ½%–1%
- Less than ½%

*Alaska and Hawaii not shown

Figure 4.2   Percentage of African Americans Living in Urban Areas, 1890–2010

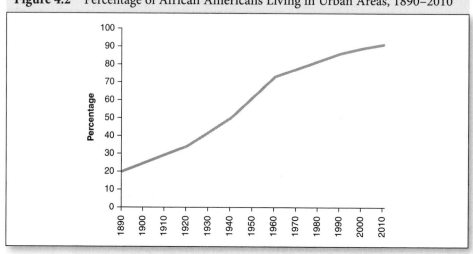

Sources: For data for 1890 to 1960, Geschwender (1978); for 1970, 1980, and 1990, Pollard and O'Hare (1999); for 2000, U.S. Census Bureau (2000b); for 2010, U.S. Census Bureau (2013f).

pursue jobs, and the greater opportunities to educate their children. Inevitably, however, life in the North fell far short of utopia. Many aspects of African American culture—literature, poetry, music—flourished in the heady new atmosphere of freedom, but on other fronts Northern African American communities faced massive discrimination in housing, schools, and the job market. Along with freedom and such cultural flowerings as the Harlem Renaissance came black ghettos and new forms of oppression and exploitation. In Chapter 5, we will explore these events and the workings of de facto segregation.

Competition With White Ethnic Groups

It is useful to see the movement of African Americans out of the South in terms of their resultant relationships with other groups. Southern blacks began to move to the North at about the same time as the New Immigration from Europe (see Chapter 1) began to end. By the time substantial numbers of black Southerners began arriving in the North, European immigrants and their descendants had had years, decades, and even generations to establish themselves in the job markets, political systems, labor unions, and neighborhoods of the North. Many of the European ethnic groups had also been the victims of discrimination and rejection. And, as we discussed in Chapter 1, their hold on economic security and status was tenuous for much of the 20th century. Frequently, they saw the newly arriving black migrants as a threat to their status, a perception that was reinforced by the fact that industrialists and factory owners often used African Americans as strikebreakers and scabs during strikes. White ethnic groups responded by developing defensive strategies to limit the dangers presented by these migrants from the South. They tried to exclude African Americans from their labor unions and other associations and limit their impact on the political system. Often they successfully attempted to maintain segregated neighborhoods and schools (although the legal system outside the South did not sanction overt de jure segregation).

This competition led to hostile relations between black southern migrants and white ethnic groups, especially the lower- and working-class segments of those groups. Ironically, however, in another chapter of the ethnic succession discussed in Chapter 1, the newly arriving African Americans actually helped white ethnic groups become upwardly mobile. Dominant group whites became less contemptuous of white ethnic groups as their alarm over the presence of African Americans increased. The greater antipathy of the white community toward African Americans made the immigrants more desirable and, thus, hastened their admission into the institutions of the larger society. For many white ethnic groups, the increased tolerance of the larger society coincided happily with the coming of age of the more educated and skilled descendants of the original immigrants, further abetting the rise of these groups in the U.S. social class structure (Lieberson, 1980).

For more than a century, each new European immigrant group had helped to push previous groups up the ladder of socioeconomic success and out of the old, ghettoized neighborhoods. Black Southerners got to the cities after immigration from Europe had been curtailed, and no newly arrived immigrants appeared to continue the pattern of succession for northern African Americans. Instead, American cities developed concentrations of low-income blacks that were economically vulnerable and politically weak and whose position was further solidified by anti-black prejudice and discrimination (Wilson, 1987, p. 34).

The Origins of Black Protest

As mentioned earlier, African Americans have always resisted their oppression and protested their situation. Under slavery, however, the inequalities they faced were so great and their resources so meager that their protest was ineffective. With the increased freedom that followed slavery, a national African American leadership developed, and spoke out against oppression and founded organizations that eventually helped to lead the fight for freedom and equality. Even at its birth, the black protest movement was diverse and incorporated a variety of viewpoints and leaders.

Booker T. Washington was the most prominent African American leader prior to World War I. Washington had been born in slavery and was the founder and president of Tuskegee Institute, a college in Alabama dedicated to educating African Americans. His public advice to African Americans in the South was to be patient, to accommodate the Jim Crow system for the time being, to raise their levels of education and job skills, and to take full advantage of whatever opportunities became available. This nonconfrontational stance earned Washington praise and support from the white community and widespread popularity in the nation. Privately, he worked behind the scenes to end discrimination and implement full racial integration and equality (Franklin & Moss, 1994, pp. 272–274; Hawkins, 1962; Washington, 1965).

Washington's most vocal opponent was W. E. B. Du Bois, an intellectual and activist who was born in the North and educated at some of the leading universities of the day. Among his many other accomplishments, Du Bois was part of a coalition of blacks and white liberals who founded the National Association for the Advancement of Colored People (NAACP) in 1909. Du Bois rejected Washington's accommodationist stance and advocated immediate pursuit of racial equality and a direct assault on de jure segregation. Almost from the beginning of its existence, the NAACP filed lawsuits that challenged the legal foundations of Jim Crow segregation (Du Bois, 1961). As we shall see in Chapter 5, this legal strategy was eventually successful and led to the demise of the Jim Crow system.

Washington and Du Bois may have differed on matters of strategy and tactics, but they agreed that the only acceptable goal for African Americans was an integrated, racially equal United States. A third leader emerged early in the 20th century and called for a very different approach to the problems of U.S. race relations. Marcus Garvey was born in Jamaica and immigrated to the United States during World War I. He argued that the white-dominated U.S. society was hopelessly racist and would never truly support integration and racial equality. He advocated separatist goals, including a return to Africa. Garvey founded the Universal Negro Improvement Association in 1914 in his native Jamaica and founded the first U.S. branch in 1916. Garvey's organization was very popular for a time in African American communities outside the South, and he helped to establish some of the themes and ideas of black nationalism and pride in African heritage that would become prominent again in the pluralistic 1960s (Essien-Udom, 1962; Garvey, 1969, 1977; Vincent, 1976).

These early leaders and organizations established some of the foundations for later protest movements, but prior to the mid-20th century they made few actual improvements in the situation of African Americans in the North or South. Jim Crow was a formidable opponent, and the African American community lacked the resources to successfully challenge the status quo until the century was well along and some basic structural features of American society had changed.

The Dimensions of Minority–Group Status

Acculturation and Integration

During this era of Southern segregation and migration to the North, assimilation was not a major factor in the African American experience. Rather, the black–white relations of the time are better described as a system of structural pluralism combined with great inequality. Excluded from the mainstream but freed from the limitations of slavery, African Americans constructed a separate subsociety and subculture. In all regions of the nation, African Americans developed their own institutions and organizations, including separate neighborhoods, churches, businesses, and schools. Like immigrants from Europe in the same era, they organized their communities to cater to their own needs and problems and pursue their agenda as a group.

During segregation, a small African American middle class emerged based on leadership roles in the church, education, and business. A network of black colleges and universities was constructed to educate the children of the growing middle class, as well as other classes. Through this infrastructure, African Americans began to develop the resources and leadership that in the decades ahead would attack, head on, the structures of racial inequality.

Gender and Race

For African American men and women, the changes wrought by industrialization and the population movement to the North created new possibilities and new roles. However, as African Americans continued to be the victims of exploitation and exclusion in both the North and the South, African American women continued to be among the most vulnerable groups in society.

Following emancipation, there was a flurry of marriages and weddings among African Americans, as they were finally able to legitimate their family relationships (Staples, 1988, p. 306). African American women continued to have primary responsibility for home and children. Historian Herbert Gutman (1976) reports that it was common for married women to drop out of the labor force and attend solely to household and family duties, because a working wife was too reminiscent of a slave role. This pattern became so widespread that it created serious labor shortages in many areas (Gutman, 1976; see also Staples, 1988, p. 307).

The former slaves were hardly affluent, however, and as sharecropping and segregation began to shape race relations in the South, women often had to return to the fields or to domestic work for the family to survive. One former slave woman noted that women "do double duty, a man's share in the field and a woman's part at home" (Evans, 1989, p. 121). During the bleak decades following the end of Reconstruction, Southern black families and black women in particular lived "close to the bone" (Evans, 1989, p. 121).

In the cities and in the growing African American neighborhoods in the North, African American women played a role that in some ways paralleled the role of immigrant women from Europe. The men often moved north first and sent for the women after they had attained some level of financial stability or after the pain of separation became too great (Almquist, 1979, p. 434). In other cases, African American women by the thousands left the South to work as domestic servants; they often replaced European immigrant women, who had moved up in the job structure (Amott & Matthaei, 1991, p. 168).

In the North, discrimination and racism created constant problems of unemployment for the men, and families often relied on the income supplied by the women to make ends meet. It was comparatively easy for women to find employment, but only in the low-paying, less-desirable areas, such as domestic work. In both the South and the North, African American women worked outside the home in larger proportions than did white women. For example, in 1900 41% of African American women were employed, compared with only 16% of white women (Staples, 1988, p. 307).

In 1890, more than a generation after the end of slavery, 85% of all African American men and 96% of African American women were employed in just two occupational categories: agriculture and domestic or personal service. By 1930, 90% of employed African American women were still in these same two categories, whereas the corresponding percentage for employed African American men had dropped to 54% (although nearly all of the remaining 46% were unskilled workers) (Steinberg, 1981, pp. 206–207). Since the inception of segregation, African American women have had consistently higher unemployment rates and lower incomes than African American men and white women (Almquist, 1979, p. 437). These gaps, as we shall see in Chapter 5, persist to the present day.

During the years following emancipation, some issues did split men and women, within both the African American community and the larger society. Prominent among these was suffrage, or the right to vote, which was still limited to men only. The abolitionist movement, which had been so instrumental in ending slavery, also supported universal suffrage. Efforts to enfranchise women, though, were abandoned by the Republican Party and large parts of the abolitionist movement to concentrate on efforts to secure the vote for African American men in the South. Ratification of the Fifteenth Amendment in 1870 extended the vote, in principle, to African American men, but the Nineteenth Amendment enfranchising women would not be passed for another 50 years (Almquist, 1979, pp. 433–434; Evans, 1989, pp. 121–124).

QUESTIONS FOR REFLECTION

6. Why did African Americans begin to migrate to the North in the early 20th century? Did this move improve their situation? Explain.

7. What African American strategies for protest were developed early in the 20th century? How were these strategies shaped by the overall situation of the group?

8. Did African Americans become more or less acculturated and integrated during the Jim Crow era? Explain.

9. How was the experience of African Americans shaped by gender during this time period?

Industrialization, the Shift to Postindustrial Society, and Dominant–Minority Group Relations: General Trends

The processes of industrialization that began in the 19th century continued to shape the larger society and dominant–minority relations throughout the 20th century. Today, the United States bears little resemblance to the society it was a century ago. The population has more than tripled in size and has urbanized even more rapidly than it has grown. New organizational forms (bureaucracies, corporations, multinational businesses) and new technologies (computers, the Internet, cell phones) dominate everyday life. Levels of education have risen, and the public schools have produced one of the most literate populations and best-trained workforces in the history of the world.

Minority groups grew in size during this period, and most became even more urbanized than the general population. Minority group members have come to participate in an increasing array of occupations, and their average levels of education have risen, too.

Despite these real improvements, however, virtually all U.S. minority groups continue to face racism, poverty, discrimination, and exclusion. As industrialization proceeded, the mechanisms for maintaining racial stratification also evolved, morphing into forms that are subtle and indirect, but, in their way, as formidable as Jim Crow segregation.

In this section, we outline the social processes that began in the industrial era and continue to shape the postindustrial stage. We note the ways in which these processes have changed American society and examine some of the general implications for minority groups. We then summarize these changes in terms of a transition from the rigid competitive Jim Crow era to a new stage of group relations called *fluid competitive* relations. The treatment here is broad and intended to establish a general framework for the examination of the impacts of industrialization and deindustrialization on group relations in the case studies that make up Part 3 of this text.

Urbanization

We have already noted that urbanization made close, paternalistic controls of minority groups irrelevant. For example, the racial etiquette required by southern de jure segregation, such as African Americans deferring to whites on crowded sidewalks, tended to disappear in the chaos of an urban rush hour.

Besides weakening dominant group controls, urbanization also created the potential for minority groups to mobilize and organize large numbers of people. As stated in Chapter 1, the sheer size of a group is a source of power. Without the freedom to organize, however, size means little, and urbanization increased both the concentration of populations and the freedom to organize.

Occupational Specialization

One of the first and most important results of industrialization, even in its earliest days, was an increase in occupational specialization and the variety of jobs available in the workforce. The growing needs of an urbanizing population increased the number of jobs available in the production, transport, and sale of goods and services. Occupational specialization was also stimulated by the very nature of industrial production. Complex manufacturing processes could be performed more efficiently if they were broken down into the narrower component tasks. It was easier and more efficient to train the workforce in the simpler, specialized jobs. Assembly lines were invented, work was subdivided, the division of labor became increasingly complex, and the number of different occupations continued to grow.

The sheer complexity of the industrial job structure made it difficult to maintain rigid, caste-like divisions of labor between dominant and minority groups. Rigid competitive forms of group relations, such as Jim Crow segregation, became less viable as the job market became more diversified and changeable. Simple, clear rules about which groups could do which jobs disappeared.

As the more repressive systems of control weakened, job opportunities for minority group members sometimes increased. However, conflict between groups also increased as the relationships between group memberships and positions in the job market became more blurred. For example, as we have noted, African Americans moving from the South often found themselves in competition for jobs with members of white ethnic groups, labor unions, and other elements of the dominant group.

Bureaucracy and Rationality

As industrialization continued, privately owned corporations and businesses came to have workforces numbering in the hundreds of thousands. Gigantic factories employing thousands of workers became common. To coordinate the efforts of these huge workforces, bureaucracy became the dominant form of organization in the economy and, indeed, throughout the society.

Bureaucracies are large, impersonal, formal organizations that run "by the book." They are governed by rules and regulations (i.e., "red tape") and are "rational" in that they attempt to find the most efficient ways to accomplish their tasks. Although they typically fail to attain the ideal of fully rational efficiency, bureaucracies tend to recruit, reward, and promote employees on the basis of competence and performance (Gerth & Mills, 1946).

The stress on rationality and objectivity can counteract the more blatant forms of racism and increase the array of opportunities available to members of minority groups. Although they are often nullified by other forces (see Blumer, 1965), these antiprejudicial tendencies do not exist at all or are much weaker in preindustrial economies.

The history of the concept of race illustrates the impact of rationality and scientific ways of thinking. Today, virtually the entire scientific community rejects the traditional idea that race is an important determinant of intelligence or personality traits such as dependability or competence. These conclusions are based on decades of research. These scientific findings undermined and contributed to the destruction of the formal systems of privilege based solely on race (e.g., segregated school systems) and traditional prejudice, which is based on the assumption that race is a crucial personal characteristic.

Growth of White-Collar Jobs and the Service Sector

Industrialization changed the composition of the labor force. As work became more complex and specialized, the need to coordinate and regulate the production process increased, and as a result bureaucracies and other organizations grew larger still. Within these organizations, white-collar occupations—those that coordinate, manage, and deal with the flow of paperwork—continued to expand throughout much of the century. As industrialization progressed, mechanization and automation reduced the number of manual or blue-collar workers, and white-collar occupations became the dominant sector of the job market in the United States.

The changing nature of the workforce can be illustrated by looking at the proportional representation of three different types of jobs:

1. **Extractive (or primary) occupations** are those that produce raw materials, such as food and agricultural products, minerals, and timber. The jobs in this sector often involve unskilled manual labor, require little formal education, and are generally low paying.

2. **Manufacturing (or secondary) occupations** transform raw materials into finished products ready for sale in the marketplace. Like jobs in the extractive sector, these blue-collar jobs involve manual labor, but they tend to require higher levels of skill and are more highly rewarded. Examples of occupations in this sector include the assembly line jobs that transform steel, rubber, plastic, and other materials into finished automobiles.

3. **Service (or tertiary) occupations** do not produce "things"; rather, they provide services. As urbanization increased and self-sufficiency decreased, opportunities for work in this sector grew. Examples of tertiary occupations include police officer, clerk, waiter, teacher, nurse, doctor, and cabdriver.

The course of industrialization is traced in the changing structure of the labor market depicted in Figure 4.3. In 1840, when industrialization was just beginning in the United States, most of the workforce (70%) was in the extractive sector, with agriculture being the dominant occupation. As industrialization progressed, the manufacturing, or secondary, sector grew, reaching a peak after World War II. Today, in the postindustrial era, the large majority of U.S. jobs are in the service, or tertiary, sector.

This shift away from blue-collar jobs and manufacturing since the 1960s is sometimes referred to as *deindustrialization* or the shift to a *postindustrial* subsistence technology. The U.S. economy has lost millions of unionized, high-paying factory jobs since the 1960s, and the downward trend continues. The industrial jobs that sustained so many generations of American workers have moved to other nations where wages are considerably lower than in the United States. Additionally, jobs have been eliminated by robots or other automated manufacturing processes (see Rifkin, 1996).

The changing structure of the job market helps to clarify the nature of intergroup competition and the sources of wealth and power in society. Job growth in the United States today is largely in the service sector, and these occupations are highly variable. At one end are low-paying jobs with few, if any, benefits or chances for advancement (e.g., washing dishes in a restaurant). At the other end are high-prestige, lucrative positions, such as Supreme Court justice, scientist, and financial analyst.

The new service sector jobs are either highly desirable technical, professional, or administrative jobs with demanding entry requirements (e.g., physician or nurse)

Figure 4.3   The Changing U.S. Workforce: The Distribution of Jobs From
1840 to 2010

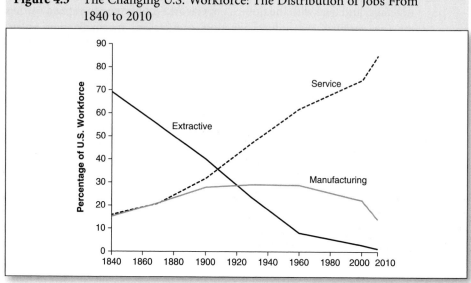

Sources: For data for 1840 and 1990, adapted from Lenski, Nolan, & Lenski (1995); for 2000, calculated from U.S. Census Bureau (2005, pp. 385–388); for 2010, calculated from U.S. Census Bureau (2012b, pp. 393–396).

or low-paying, low-skilled jobs with few benefits and little security (e.g., receptionist, nurse's aide). For the past half century, job growth in the United States has been either in areas in which educationally deprived minority group members find it difficult to compete or in areas that offer little compensation, upward mobility, or security. As we will see in Part 3, the economic situation of contemporary minority groups reflects these fundamental trends.

The Growing Importance of Education

Education has been an increasingly important prerequisite for employability in the United States and in other advanced industrial societies. A high school or, increasingly, a college degree has become the minimum entry-level requirement for employment. However, opportunities for high-quality education are not distributed equally across the population. Some minority groups, especially those created by colonization, have been systematically excluded from the schools of the dominant society, and today they are less likely to have the educational backgrounds needed to compete for better jobs.

Access to education is a key issue for all U.S. minority groups, and the average educational levels of these groups have been rising since World War II. Still, minority children continue to be much more likely to attend segregated, under-funded, deteriorated schools and to receive inferior educations (see Orfield & Lee, 2007).

A Dual Labor Market

The changing composition of the labor force and increasing importance of educational credentials has split the U.S. labor market into two segments or types of jobs. The **primary labor market** includes jobs usually located in large, bureaucratic organizations. These positions offer higher pay; more security; better opportunities for advancement, health and retirement benefits; and other amenities. Entry requirements include college degrees, even when people with fewer years of schooling could competently perform the work.

The **secondary labor market**, sometimes called the competitive market, includes low-paying, low-skilled, insecure jobs. Many of these jobs are in the service sector. They do not represent a career, per se, and offer little opportunity for promotion or upward mobility. Very often, they do not offer health or retirement benefits, have high rates of turnover, and are part time, seasonal, or temporary.

Many American minority groups are concentrated in the secondary job market. Their exclusion from better jobs is perpetuated not so much by direct or overt discrimination as by their lack of access to the educational and other credentials required to enter the primary sector. The differential distribution of educational opportunities, in the past as well as in the present, effectively protects workers in the primary sector from competition from minority groups.

Globalization

Over the past century, the United States became an economic, political, and military world power with interests around the globe. These worldwide ties have created new minority groups through population movement and have changed the status of others. Immigration to this country has been considerable for the past three decades. The American economy is one of the most productive in the world, and jobs, even those in the low-paying secondary sector, are the primary goals for millions of newcomers. For other immigrants, this country continues to play its historic role as a refuge from political and religious persecution.

Many of the wars, conflicts, and other disputes in which the United States has been involved have had consequences for American minority groups. For example, both Puerto Ricans and Cuban Americans became U.S. minority groups as the result of processes set in motion during the Spanish-American War of 1898. Both World War I and World War II created new job opportunities for many minority groups, including African Americans and Mexican Americans. After the Korean War in the early 1950s, international ties were forged between the United States and South Korea, and this led to an increase in immigration from that nation. In the 1960s and 1970s, the military involvement of the United States in Southeast Asia led to the arrival of Vietnamese, Cambodians, Hmong, and other immigrant and refugee groups. The most recent war in Iraq has also produced new communities of immigrants and refugees.

Dominant–minority relations in the United States have been increasingly played out on an international stage, as the world has effectively "shrunk" and become more interconnected by international organizations, such as the United Nations; by ties of trade and commerce; and by modern means of transportation and communication. In a world in which two thirds of the population is non-white and many important nations (such as China, India, and Nigeria) are composed of peoples of color, the treatment of racial minorities by the U.S. dominant group has come under increased scrutiny. It is difficult to preach principles of fairness, equality, and justice—which the United States claims as its own—when domestic realities suggest an embarrassing failure to fully implement these standards. Part of the incentive for the United States to end blatant systems of discrimination such as de jure segregation came from the desire to maintain a leading position in the world.

Postindustrial Society and the Shift From Rigid to Fluid Competitive Relationships

The coming of postindustrial society brought changes so fundamental and profound that they are often described in terms of a revolution: from an industrial society, based on manufacturing, to a postindustrial society, based on information processing and computer-related or other new technologies. As the subsistence technology evolved, so did American dominant–minority relations. The rigid competitive systems (such as Jim Crow) associated with earlier phases of industrialization gave way to **fluid competitive systems** of group relations.

In fluid competitive relations, formal or legal barriers to competition—such as Jim Crow laws or South African apartheid—no longer exist. Both geographic and social mobility are greater in the newer system, and the limitations imposed by minority group status are less restrictive and burdensome. Rigid caste systems of stratification, in which group membership determines opportunities, adult statuses, and jobs, are replaced by more open class systems, in which the relationships between group membership and wealth, prestige, and power are weaker. Because fluid competitive systems are more open and the position of the minority group is less fixed, the fear of competition from minority groups becomes more widespread for the dominant group, and intergroup conflict increases. Table 4.2 compares the characteristics of the three systems of group relations.

Compared with previous systems, the fluid competitive system is closer to the American ideal of an open, fair system of stratification in which effort and competence are rewarded and race, ethnicity, gender, religion, and other "birthmarks" are irrelevant. However, as we will see in chapters to come, race and ethnicity continue to affect life chances and limit opportunities for minority group members even in fluid competitive systems. As suggested by the Noel hypothesis, people continue to identify themselves with particular groups (ethnocentrism), and competition for resources continues to play out along group lines. Consistent with the Blauner hypothesis, the minority groups that were formed by colonization remain at a disadvantage in the pursuit of opportunities, education, prestige, and other resources.

Table 4.2 Characteristics of Three Systems of Group Relationships

	Systems of Group Relations		
		Competitive	
	Paternalistic	*Rigid*	*Fluid*
Subsistence technology	**Agrarian**	**Industrial**	**Postindustrial**
Stratification	**Caste**. Group determines status.	**Mixed**. Elements of caste and class. Status largely determined by group.	**Variable**. Status strongly affected by group. Inequality varies within groups.
Division of labor	**Simple**. Determined by group.	**More complex**. Job largely determined by group, but some sharing of jobs by different groups.	**Most complex**. Group and job are less closely related. Complex specialization and great variation within groups.
Contact between groups	**Common**, but statuses unequal.	**Less common**, and mostly unequal.	**More common**. Highest rates of equal status contact.
Overt intergroup conflict	**Rare**.	**More common**.	**Common**.
Power differential	**Maximum**. Minority groups have little ability to pursue self-interests.	**Less**. Minority groups have some ability to pursue self-interests.	**Least**. Minority groups have more ability to pursue self-interests.

Source: Based on Farley (2000, p. 109).

QUESTIONS FOR REFLECTION

10. Why did black–white relations shift from a rigid to a fluid competitive system? What was the role of subsistence technology in the shift?

11. What are the key changes in the shift to postindustrial subsistence technology? What are the implications of these changes for American minority groups?

Gender Inequality in a Globalizing, Postindustrial World

Deindustrialization and globalization transformed gender relations along with relations among racial and ethnic groups. Everywhere, even in the most patriarchal societies, women have been moving away from their traditional wife and mother roles, taking on new responsibilities, and facing new challenges. In the United States, the transition to a postindustrial society has changed gender relations and the status of women on a number of levels.

Women and men are now equal in terms of education levels (U.S. Census Bureau, 2012c, p. 151), and the shift to fluid competitive group relations has weakened the barriers to gender equality, along with those to racial equality, although formidable obstacles remain. The changing role of women is also shaped by other characteristics of a modern society: smaller families, higher divorce rates, and rising numbers of single mothers who must work to support their children as well as themselves.

One of the most fundamental changes in U.S. gender relations has been the increasing participation of women in the paid labor force, a change related to both demographic trends (e.g., lower birthrates) and changing aspirations. Women are now employed at almost the same levels as men. In 2010, for example, 63% of single women (vs. about 67% of single men) and about 61% of married women (vs. about 76% of married men) had jobs outside the home (U.S. Census Bureau, 2012c, p. 384). Furthermore, between 1970 and 2009, the workforce participation of married women with children increased from a little less than 40% to almost 70% (p. 385).

One reflection of changing aspirations is that U.S. women are entering a wider variety of careers. In the past, women were largely concentrated in a relatively narrow range of women-dominated jobs such as nurse and elementary school teacher. Figure 4.4 focuses on four pairs of careers and illustrates both the traditional pattern and recent changes. Each pair includes an occupation dominated by women and a comparable but higher-status, more lucrative, occupation traditionally dominated by men. While the "women's" jobs remain largely done by women, the percentage of women in the higher-status occupations has increased dramatically (even though, except for university professor, the more lucrative careers remain disproportionately filled by men).

QUESTIONS FOR REFLECTION

12. Is the glass half empty or half full for women today? Consider how the comparison group we choose—women of the past versus men of the present—might influence our answer to that question.

13. Consider how race, class, sexual orientation, and religion might have affected the gender advances and restrictions described in this section. For example, are men of every class, race, and background excelling over comparable women? Are all women able to take advantage of educational and occupational opportunities, regardless of religion, sexual orientation, and other characteristics? Explain.

Figure 4.4   Percentage of Women in Selected Occupations for Selected Years

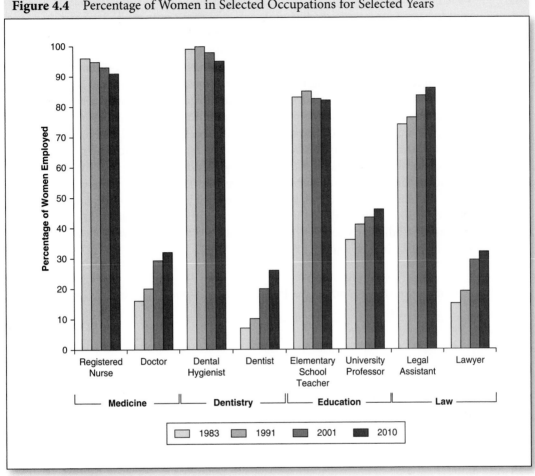

Sources: For figures for 1983 and 1991, calculated from U.S. Census Bureau (1993, pp. 392–393); for 2001, calculated from U.S. Census Bureau (2002, pp. 587–588); for 2010, calculated from U.S. Census Bureau (2012c, pp. 393–394).

Jobs and Income. As is the case with many other minority groups, the economic status of women has improved over the past few decades but has stopped well short of equality. For example, as displayed in Figure 4.5, there is a persistent, although decreasing, gender gap in income. Notice the median incomes (in 2013 dollars to control for inflation) for both men and women (read from the left vertical axis) and the percentage of men's incomes that women earn (read from the right vertical axis). Note that only full-time, year-round workers are included in the graph.

On the average, women workers today earn about 79% of what men earn, up from about 65% in 1955. The relative increase in women's income is due to a variety of factors, including the movement of women into more lucrative careers, as reflected in Figure 4.4. Another cause of women's rising income is that some of the occupations in which women are highly concentrated have benefited from deindustrialization and the shift to a service economy. For example, job opportunities in the FIRE (finance, insurance, and real estate) sector of the job market have expanded rapidly since the 1960s, and since a high percentage of the workers in this sector are women, this has tended to elevate average salaries for women in general (Farley, 1996, pp. 95–101).

A third reason for the narrowing gender income gap has more to do with men's wages than women's. Before deindustrialization began to transform U.S. society, men monopolized the more desirable, higher-paid, unionized jobs in the manufacturing sector. For much of the 20th century, these blue-collar jobs paid well enough to subsidize a comfortable lifestyle, a house in the suburbs, and vacations, with enough left over to save for a rainy day or the kids' college education. However, with deindustrialization, many of these desirable jobs were lost to automation and cheaper labor forces outside the United States, and were replaced, if at all, by low-paying jobs in the service sector. The result, reflected in Figure 4.5, is that while women's wages increased steadily between the 1950s and about 2000, men's wages have remained virtually level since the early 1970s.

Figure 4.5 Median Income for Full-Time, Year-Round Workers by Gender, 1955–2013

Source: U.S. Bureau of the Census, 2014.

These large-scale, macrolevel forces have tended to raise the status of women and narrow the income gap, but they have not equalized gender relations. Far from it! For example, although women and men are now equal in terms of education, women tend to get lower returns on their investment in human capital. Figure 4.6 compares men and women full-time workers in 2013. Notice the wage gap at every level of education. Wages rise as education rises for both genders but the wage gap persists.

Figure 4.6 Mean Annual Income for Full-Time, Year-Round Workers Ages 25–64 by Gender and Educational Attainment, 2013

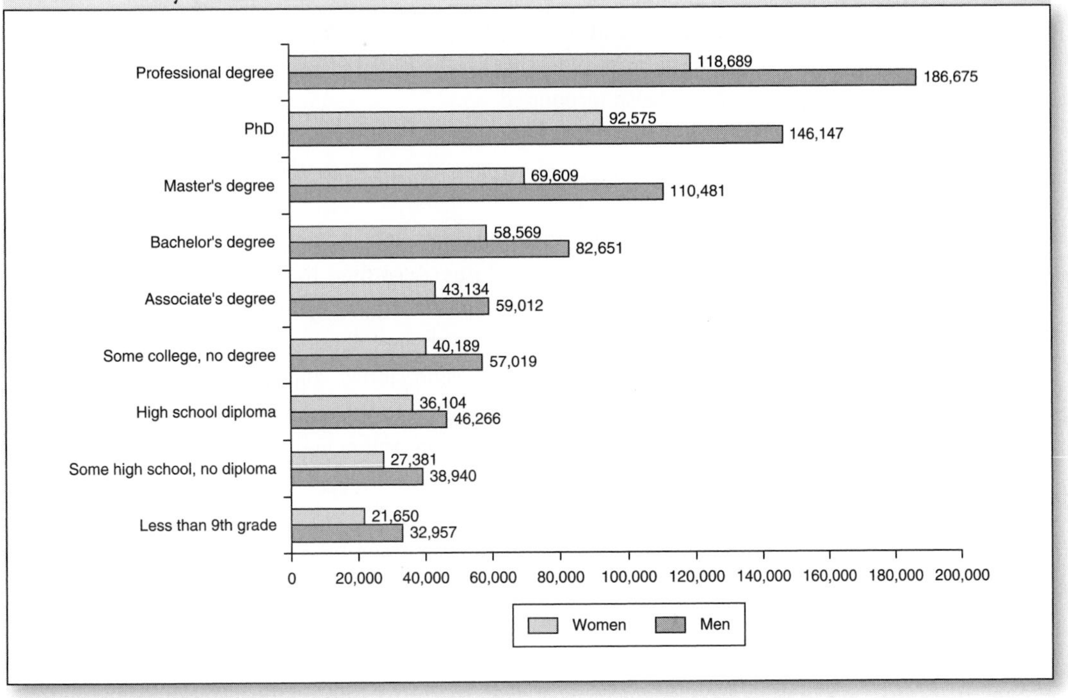

Source: U.S. Bureau of the Census, 2013b.

COMPARATIVE FOCUS:
Women's Status in Global Perspective

On October 9, 2012, in the Swat region of Pakistan, an armed assailant attacked 15-year-old Malala Yousafzai while she was riding a bus to school. Her attacker sought her out and even asked for her by name. He shot at her three times, one bullet passing through her left eye and out her shoulder.

The reason for the attack? Malala wanted an education and was an outspoken advocate for schooling for girls. The gunman was sent by the Taliban to punish Malala because she flaunted, publicly and repeatedly, the organization's ideas regarding the proper place of women.

Malala survived the attack and was transported to the United Kingdom, where she underwent a lengthy and painful recovery. Far from being intimidated, she resumed her advocacy for education and was frequently featured by the mass media in Western

(Continued)

(Continued)

Europe, the United States, and around the globe. In recognition of her courage, eloquence, and passion, she was nominated for the Nobel Peace Prize in 2013, becoming the youngest person to be so recognized.

Why was Malala willing to risk her life? How oppressed are women in Pakistan? How does the status of Pakistani women compare to that of women in other nations?

In Pakistan and around the globe, women are moving out of their traditional and often highly controlled and repressed status. According to United Nations (United Nations Department of Economic and Social Affairs, Population Division, 2013) statistics, rates of early marriage and childbirth are falling, and education levels and participation in the paid labor force are rising. Today, almost 50% of all women worldwide are in the paid labor force (vs. 72% of all men), although they still tend to be concentrated in lower-status, less-lucrative, and more-insecure jobs everywhere (pp. 8, 20–22).

The women of Pakistan are not as repressed as women in many other nations, including Saudi Arabia, where women are not allowed to drive and won the right to vote only in 2015. Some simple statistics will illustrate the range of possibilities. Table 4.3 provides information on women's status in four nations representing various levels of development, locations, and religious backgrounds.

As we have noted, the status of women is partly a function of subsistence technology. Mali is the most agricultural of these four nations (with 80% of its workforce in farming), and the women there have more children, earlier in life, and are far more likely to die in childbirth. They are also much less educated than the women of other nations and the men of their own nation.

Pakistan is less agricultural than Mali, and the status of women is relatively higher, although they are indeed much less likely than men to be educated. Note, also, that the statistics suggest that Pakistani women are still largely focused on producing and maintaining large families.

Women's status generally rises as industrialization and urbanization proceed, as indicated by the profiles of Chile and Sweden. Sweden is more industrialized than Chile, and Swedish women have fewer children, later in life, and are just as educated as men in their nation.

Why does the status of women generally improve as societies move away from agricultural subsistence technology? One reason, no doubt, is the changing economies of childbearing: Large families are useful in the labor-intensive economies of agrarian nations, but children become increasingly expensive in modern urban-industrial economies. Also, consistent with Malala's point, more-educated women tend to make different choices about career and family and about their own life goals.

Table 4.3 Status of Women in Select Nations, 2013

Variables	Nation			
	Mali	Pakistan	Chile	Sweden
Percentage of labor force in agriculture	80	45.1	13.2	1.1
Mother's mean age at first birth	18.6	22.7	23.7	28.6
Maternal mortality rate (deaths of mothers per 100,000 live births)	540	260	25	4
Total fertility rate (average number of children per woman, lifetime)	6.25	2.96	1.85	1.67
Percentage literate				
Men	43	68	99	99
Women	25	40	99	99

Source: Central Intelligence Agency (2013).

QUESTIONS FOR REFLECTION

14. From the statistics presented in Table 4.3, what can you infer about the lives of women in Mali? Would they live in the city or countryside? Would they attend school at all? What power would they have regarding decisions about family size? What kinds of activities would they pursue during the day? What dreams would they have for their daughters? For their sons? How would their lives compare with those of women in Sweden?

15. How important is Malala's cause? What effect would higher levels of education have on women in less-developed nations? Why?

Modern Institutional Discrimination

In general, American minority groups continue to lag behind national averages in income, employment, and other measures of equality, despite the greater fluidity of group relations, the end of legal barriers such as Jim Crow laws, the dramatic declines in overt prejudice, and the introduction of numerous laws designed to ensure that all people are treated without regard to race, gender, or ethnicity. After all this change, shouldn't there be less minority group inequality and racial stratification?

As we will discuss in Chapter 5, many Americans attribute the persisting patterns of inequality to a lack of willpower or motivation to get ahead on the part of minority group members. In the remaining chapters of this text, however, we argue that the major barriers facing minority groups in postindustrial, post–Jim Crow America are pervasive, subtle, but still powerful forms of discrimination that together can be called **modern institutional discrimination.**

As you read in Chapter 1, institutional discrimination is built into the everyday operation of the social structure of society. The routine procedures and policies of institutions and organizations are arranged so that minority group members are automatically put at a disadvantage. In the Jim Crow era in the South, for example, African Americans were deprived of the right to vote by overt institutional discrimination and could acquire little in the way of political power.

The forms of institutional discrimination that persist in the present are more subtle and difficult to document than the blatant, overt customs and laws of the Jim Crow system. In fact, they are sometimes unintentional or unconscious and are manifested more in the results for minority groups than in the intentions or prejudices of dominant group members. Modern institutional discrimination is not necessarily linked to prejudice, and the decision makers who implement it may sincerely think of themselves as behaving rationally and in the best interests of their organizations.

The Continuing Power of the Past

Many forces conspire to maintain racial stratification in the present. Some are the legacies of past discriminatory practices. Consider, for example, **past-in-present institutional discrimination**, which involves practices in the present that have discriminatory consequences because of some pattern of discrimination or exclusion in the past (Feagin & Feagin, 1986, p. 32).

One form of this discrimination is found in workforces organized around the principle of seniority. In these systems, which are quite common, workers who have been on the job longer have higher incomes, more privileges, and other benefits, such as longer vacations. The "old-timers" often have more job security and are designated in official, written policy as the last to be fired or laid off in the event of hard times. Workers and employers alike may think of the privileges of seniority as just rewards for long years of service, familiarity with the job, and so forth.

Personnel policies based on seniority may seem perfectly reasonable, neutral, and fair; however, they can have discriminatory results in the present because in the past members of minority groups and women were excluded from specific occupations by racist or sexist labor unions, discriminatory employers, or both. As a result, minority group workers and white women may have fewer years of experience than dominant group workers and men, and may be the first to go when layoffs are necessary. The adage "last hired, first fired" describes the situation of minority group and woman employees who are more vulnerable not because of some overtly racist or sexist policy in the present, but because of the routine operation of the seemingly neutral principle of seniority.

Racial differences in home ownership provide a second example of the myriad ways in which the past shapes the present and maintains the moving target of racial stratification. Today, about 72% of non-Hispanic whites own their own homes, and these houses have a median value of $179,000. In contrast, only 44% of non-Hispanic blacks are homeowners, and the median value of their homes is $125,900 (U.S. Census Bureau, 2013a). Homeownership is an important source of family wealth because home equity can be used to establish credit, to finance businesses and other purchases and investments, and to fund education and other sources of human capital for the next generation. What is the origin of these huge differences in family wealth?

Part of answer lies in events that date back 80 years. As you know, President Franklin D. Roosevelt's administration responded to the Great Depression of the 1930s, in part, by instituting the New Deal: a variety of programs that provided assistance to distressed Americans. What is not as widely known is that these programs were racially discriminatory and provided few or no benefits to African Americans (Massey, 2007, p. 60; see also Katznelson, 2005; Lieberson, 1998).

One of the New Deal programs was administered by the Federal Housing Administration (FHA): the agency offered low-interest mortgages and made home ownership possible for millions of families. However, the FHA sanctioned racially restrictive covenants that forbade whites to sell to blacks and helped to institutionalize the practice of "redlining" black neighborhoods, which prevented banks from making home loans in these areas. Together, these and other discriminatory practices effectively excluded black Americans from home ownership (Massey, 2007, pp. 60–61; Massey & Denton, 1993, pp. 53–54). Thus, another racial divide was created that, over the generations, has helped countless white families develop wealth and credit but made it impossible for black families to qualify for home ownership, the "great engine of wealth creation" (Massey, 2007, p. 61).

More broadly, racial residential segregation—which is arguably the key factor in preserving racial stratification in the present—provides another illustration of modern institutional discrimination. The overt, Jim Crow–era laws and customs that created racially segregated neighborhoods and towns in the past were abolished decades ago, and racial discrimination in selling and renting houses has been illegal since the passage of the Fair Housing Act in 1968. However, blacks continue to be concentrated in all- or mostly-black neighborhoods (see, e.g., Figure 4.7), many of which are also characterized by inadequate services and high levels of poverty and crime. How is racial residential segregation maintained in an era of fair housing laws?

Some of the practices that preserve racial residential segregation have been documented by audit studies. In this technique, black and white (and sometimes Latino and Asian) individuals with carefully matched background credentials (education, employment and credit histories, and finances) and sent to test the market for racial fairness. Characteristically, the black customer is steered away from white neighborhoods, required to furnish larger down payments or deposits, charged higher interest rates, or otherwise discouraged from a successful sale or rental. Sometimes, the black customer may be told that a unit is already sold or rented, or otherwise given false or misleading information (see Pager & Shepherd, 2008, for a review).

The result is that blacks are discouraged from breaking the housing color line, but not directly, blatantly, or in ways that clearly violate the fair housing laws. The gatekeepers (e.g., real estate agents, landlords, mortgage bankers) base their behavior not on race

Figure 4.7 Concentration of Whites, Blacks, and Hispanics in Chicago, 2008

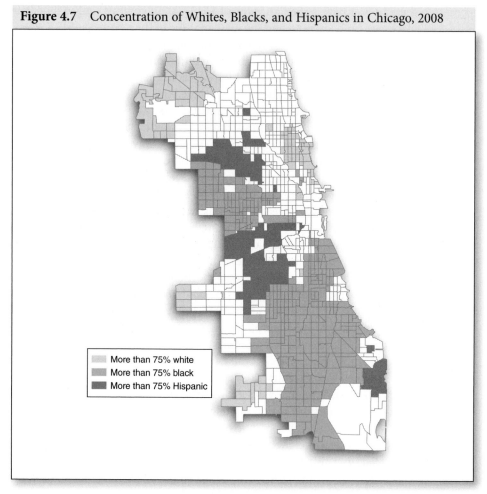

More than 75% white
More than 75% black
More than 75% Hispanic

Source: Center for Governmental Studies, Northern Illinois University.

per se but on characteristics associated with race—accent, dialect, home address, and so forth—to make decisions about what levels of service and responsiveness to provide to customers. Sociologist Douglas Massey (2000, p. 4) has even demonstrated racially biased treatment based on the use of "Black English" in telephone contacts.

Audit studies have also documented racial discrimination in the job market (e.g., see Bertrand & Mullainathan, 2004). Other forms of modern institutional discrimination include the use of racially and culturally biased standardized tests in school systems, the pattern of drug arrests that sends disproportionate numbers of black teenage boys and young men to jail and prison (see Chapter 5 for more on this trend), and decisions by businesspeople to move their operations away from center-city neighborhoods. Part of what makes modern institutional discrimination so challenging to document is that race, ethnicity, or gender may not be a conscious or overt part of these decision-making processes. Still, the results are that blacks and other minorities—in the present as in the past—are filtered away from opportunities and resources, and racial stratification is maintained, even in the new age of a supposedly color-blind society.

Modern institutional discrimination routinely places black Americans in less desirable statuses in education, residence and home ownership, jobs, the criminal justice system—indeed, across the entire expanse of the socioeconomic system. The result is racial stratification maintained not by monolithic Jim Crow segregation or slavery, but by a subtle and indirect system that is the "new configuration of inequality" (Katz & Stern, 2008, p. 100). We will apply the concept of modern institutional discrimination throughout the case study chapters in Part 3 of this text.

Affirmative Action

Modern institutional discrimination is difficult to identify, measure, and eliminate, and some of the most heated disputes in recent group relations have concerned public policy and law in this area. Among the most controversial issues is **affirmative action**, a group of programs that attempt to reduce the effects of past discrimination or increase diversity in the workplace or in schools. In the 1970s and 1980s, the Supreme Court found that programs designed to favor minority employees as a strategy for overcoming past discrimination were constitutional (e.g., *Firefighters Local Union No. 1784 v. Stotts,* 1984; *Sheet Metal Workers v. EEOC,* 1986; *United Steelworkers of America, AFL-CIO-CLC v. Weber,* 1979).

Virtually all these early decisions concerned blatant policies of discrimination, which are becoming increasingly rare as we move farther away from the days of Jim Crow. Even so, the decisions were based on narrow margins (votes of five to four) and featured acrimonious and bitter debates. More recently, the Supreme Court narrowed the grounds on which such past grievances could be redressed (e.g., *Adarand Constructors Inc. v. Peña,* 1995).

A Case of Discrimination? A recent case involving affirmative action programs in the workplace is *Ricci v. DeStefano,* 2009, involving firefighters in New Haven, Connecticut. In 2003, the city administered a test for promotion in the city's fire department. More than 100 people took the test but no African American scored high enough to qualify for promotion. The city decided to throw out the test results on the grounds that its dramatically unequal racial results strongly suggested that it was biased against African Americans.

This decision is consistent with the legal concept of *disparate impact.* That is, if a practice has unequal results, federal policy and court precedents tend to assume that the practice is racially biased. The city feared that using these possibly "tainted" test scores might result in lawsuits by black and other minority firefighters. Instead, a lawsuit was filed by several white and Hispanic firefighters who *had* qualified for promotion, claiming that invalidating the test results amounted to reverse racial discrimination. In 2009, the Supreme Court ruled in favor of the white and Hispanic plaintiffs in a five to four ruling.

This case illustrates some of the difficult issues that accompany attempts to address modern institutional discrimination. The issue in *Ricci v. Stefano* is not overt, Jim Crow discrimination, but rather a test that might be discriminatory in its results, although not in its intent. New Haven was attempting to avoid racial discrimination. How far do employers need to go to ensure racial fairness? Should policies and procedures be judged by the outcomes or their intents? What does "fairness" and "equal treatment" mean in a society in which minority groups have only recently won formal equality and still have lower access to quality schooling and jobs in the mainstream economy? Did the city of New Haven go too far in its attempt to avoid discrimination? (Five of the Supreme Court Justices thought so.) Can there be a truly fair, race-neutral policy for employment and promotion in the present when opportunities and resources in the past were so long allocated on the basis of race? If the problem is color-coded, can the solution be color-neutral?

Higher Education and Affirmative Action. Colleges and universities have been another prominent battleground for affirmative action programs. Since the 1960s, many institutions of higher education have implemented programs to increase the number of minority students on campus at both the undergraduate and graduate levels, sometimes admitting minority students who had lower grade point averages (GPAs) or test scores than dominant group students who were turned away. In general, advocates of these programs have justified them in terms of redressing the discriminatory practices of the past or increasing diversity on campus and making the student body a more accurate representation of the surrounding society. To say the least, these programs have been highly controversial and the targets of frequent lawsuits, some of which have found their way to the highest courts in the land.

Recent decisions by the U.S. Supreme Court have limited the application of affirmative action to colleges and universities. In two lawsuits involving the University of Michigan in 2003 (*Grutter v. Bollinger* and *Gratz v. Bollinger*), the Supreme Court held that the university's law school *could* use race as one criterion in deciding admissions but that undergraduate admissions *could not* award an automatic advantage to minority applicants. In other words, universities could take account of an applicant's race but only in a limited way, as one factor among many.

In more recent cases involving affirmative action in higher education, the Supreme Court further narrowed the ability of universities to consider race in admissions decisions. One case, decided in June 2013, was *Fisher v. University of Texas at Austin*. The University of Texas (UT) had been using a unique admissions system according to which the top 10% of the student body in each high school in Texas were automatically admitted. Because of the residential segregation in towns and cities across the state, the student body at many high schools is disproportionately black, white, or Hispanic, and the 10% rule guarantees substantial diversity in the UT student body. Some 80% of the students are selected by this method. The remaining 20% are selected using a variety of criteria, including race and ethnicity. It is common for selective institutions such as UT to use many criteria—not just test scores—to diversify their student body.

The case was brought by Amy Fisher, a white student who was not admitted to UT. She argued that some of the admitted minority students had lower GPAs and test scores than she did. The university argued that the educational benefit of a diverse student body justifies its partial and limited use of race as one admission criterion among many.

The Supreme Court sent the case back to the federal appeals court with instructions to apply a strict standard: Race could be used as an admission criterion only if there were no workable race-neutral alternatives that would result in a diverse student body. The decision was not a death blow to affirmative action, but it appeared to continue the trend of limiting the circumstances under which affirmative action policies could be applied.

In a second recent decision (*Schuette v. BAMN*), decided in April 2014, the Supreme Court upheld an amendment to the state constitution of Michigan that banned the use of race as a factor in admissions and hiring decisions in all state agencies. This decision effectively ended affirmative action, in any form, in Michigan and in several other states with similar laws. Combined with the 2013 *Fisher* decision, it seems that the role of affirmative action in higher education has been severely curtailed.

The Future of Affirmative Action. What lies ahead for affirmative action? On the one hand, there is a clear trend in court decisions to narrow the scope and applicability of these programs. Also, there is very little public support for affirmative action, especially for programs that are perceived as providing specific numerical quotas for minority groups in jobs or university admissions. For example, in 2012, a representative sample of Americans was asked in a survey if they supported "preferential hiring and promotion of blacks." Only 15% of white respondents expressed support. Somewhat surprisingly, less than half (43%) of black respondents supported preferential hiring (National Opinion Research Council, 1972–2012).

On the other hand, although white (and many minority group) Americans object to fixed quotas, people support programs that expand the opportunities available to minority groups, including enhanced job training, education, and recruitment in minority communities (Wilson, 2009, p. 139). Programs of this sort are more consistent with traditional ideologies and value systems that stress individual initiative, personal responsibility, and equality of opportunity.

Many businesses and universities are committed to the broad principles of affirmative action and see the need to address past injustices and the usefulness and desirability of creating diversity in workplaces and colleges. Thus, they are likely to sustain their programs to the extent allowed by court decisions and legislation into the future. By and large, it seems that affirmative action programs, especially those that stress equality of opportunity, will continue in some limited form into the foreseeable future.

QUESTIONS FOR REFLECTION

16. What is *modern* institutional discrimination, and how does it differ from *traditional* or blatant institutional discrimination? What are some of the common forms of modern institutional discrimination?

17. What is affirmative action, and what are some of the ways it has been used to combat modern institutional discrimination?

FOCUS ON CONTEMPORARY ISSUES:
Hate Crimes

Hate crimes are attacks or other acts of intimidation motivated by the group membership of the victim or victims. Victims can be chosen randomly and are often strangers to their assailants. They are chosen because they are taken as representatives of a group, not because of who they are as individuals. These crimes are expressions of hatred or disdain, strong prejudice, and blatant racism, and are not committed for profit or gain. In recent years, they have included homicides—such as the seven murders committed in 2015 by Dylann Roof in a black church in Charleston, South Carolina—and assaults, arson against black churches, vandalism of Jewish synagogues, cross burnings, nooses prominently tied to office doors of black university professors, and other acts of intimidation and harassment. Furthermore, a number of violent, openly racist extremist groups—skinheads, the Ku Klux Klan (KKK), White Aryan Resistance (WAR), the Minutemen, and Aryan Nations—have achieved widespread notoriety and have a prominent presence not only in some local communities but also on the Internet.

As we will see in chapters to come, racial violence, hate crimes, and extremist racist groups are hardly new to the United States. Violence between whites and non-whites began in the earliest days of this society (e.g., conflicts with American Indians, the kidnapping and enslavement of Africans) and has continued, in one form or another, to the present. Contemporary racist attacks and hate crimes, in all their manifestations, have deep roots in the American past.

Are hate crimes increasing or decreasing? It's difficult to answer this question, though the FBI (Federal Bureau of Investigation) has been collecting and compiling information on hate crimes since 1996. Not all localities report these incidents or classify them in the same way, and perhaps more important, not all hate crimes are reported. Thus, the actual volume of hate crimes may be many times greater than the "official" rate compiled by the FBI. (For a recent analysis, see Fears, 2007.)

Keeping these sharp limitations in mind, here is some of what is known. Figure 4.8 reports the breakdown of hate crimes in 2013 and shows that most incidents were

Figure 4.8   Breakdown of 5,922 Single-Bias Hate Crimes in 2013

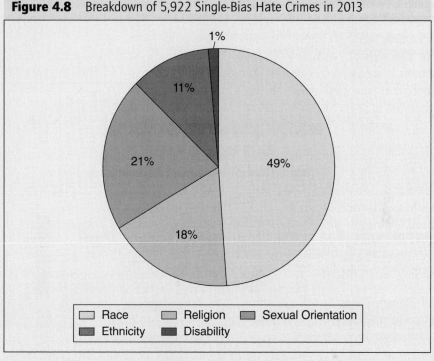

Race   Religion   Sexual Orientation
Ethnicity   Disability

Source: FBI (2014).

motivated by race. In the great majority (70%) of these racial cases, the victims were black Americans. Most of the religious incidents (67%) involved Jewish victims, and most of the anti-ethnic attacks were against Hispanics (67%). The majority (57%) of the attacks motivated by the sexual orientation of the victims were directed against male homosexuals (FBI, 2013).

Hate crimes and hate groups are not limited to a particular region. The Southern Poverty Law Center (SPLC) tracks hate groups and hate crimes around the nation and estimates that there were 1,002 hate groups (defined as groups that "have beliefs or practices that attack or malign an entire class of people, typically for their immutable characteristics") active in the United States in 2010 (Potok, 2013).

These groups include the KKK, various skinhead and white power groups, and black groups such as the Nation of Islam. The SPLC maintains a map at its website showing the locations of the known hate groups (see Figure 4.9). The map shows that although the greatest concentration is in the Southeast, Texas, and California, hate groups are spread across the nation and can be found in all states.

What causes hate crimes? One possible explanation for at least some hate crimes is that they are fueled by frustration and fear. Some white Americans believe that

(Continued)

Figure 4.9 Active Hate Groups in the United States, 2012

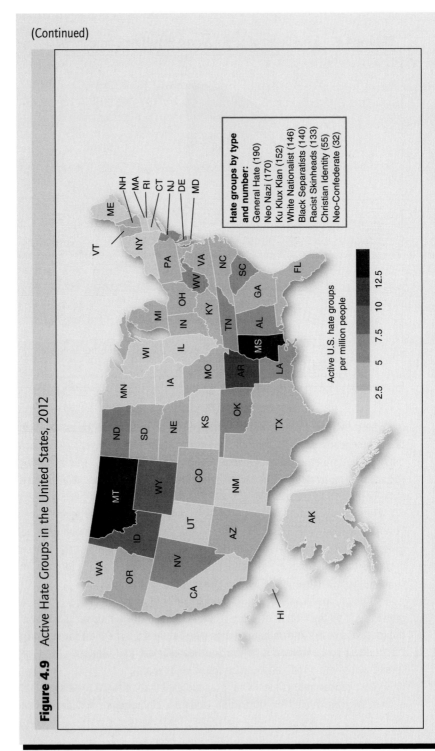

Hate groups by type
and number:
General Hate (190)
Neo Nazi (170)
Ku Klux Klan (152)
White Nationalist (146)
Black Separatists (140)
Racist Skinheads (133)
Christian Identity (55)
Neo-Confederate (32)

Active U.S. hate groups
per million people

2.5 5 7.5 10 12.5

Source: Reprinted with permission; originally appeared in *The Atlantic:* "The Geography of Hate" by Richard Florida, May 2011. Map by Zara Matheson, Martin Prosperity Institute. Data source: www. Splcenter.org/get-information/hate-map.

minority groups are threatening their position in society and making unfair progress at their expense. They feel threatened by what they perceive to be an undeserved rise in the status of minority groups and fear that they may lose their jobs, incomes, neighborhoods, and schools to what they see as "inferior" groups.

Given the nature of American history, it is logical to suppose that the white Americans who feel most threatened and angriest are those toward the bottom of the stratification system: lower-class and working-class whites. There is evidence that men from these classes commit the bulk of hate crimes and are the primary sources of membership for the extremist racist groups (Schafer & Navarro, 2004). In the eyes of the perpetrators, attacks on minorities may represent attempts to preserve status and privilege.

The connection between social class and hate crimes might also reflect some broad structural changes in the economy, especially the shift from an industrial, manufacturing economy to a postindustrial, information-processing economy. This change has meant a decline in the supply of secure, well-paying, blue-collar jobs. Many manufacturing jobs have been lost to other nations with cheaper workforces; others have been lost to automation and mechanization. The tensions resulting from the decline in desirable employment opportunities for people with lower levels of education have been exacerbated by industry downsizing, increasing inequality in the class structure, and rising costs of living. These economic forces have squeezed the middle and lower ranges of the dominant group's class system, creating considerable pressure and frustration, some of which may be directed at immigrants and minority groups.

Several studies support these ideas. One study found that at the state level, the rate of hate crimes increased as unemployment rose and as the percentage of the population between 15 and 19 years old increased. Also, the rate fell as average wages rose (Medoff, 1999, p. 970; see also Jacobs & Wood, 1999). Another study, based on county-level data gathered in South Carolina, found a correlation between white-on-black hate crimes and economic competition (D'Alessio, Stolzenberg, & Eitle, 2002). Finally, Arab Americans have been victimized by a rash of violent attacks since September 11, 2001 (Ibish, 2003). These patterns are exactly what one would expect if the perpetrators of hate crimes tended to be young men motivated by a sense of threat and economic distress.

Social Change and Minority Group Activism

This chapter has focused on the continuing Industrial Revolution and its impact on minority groups in general and black–white relations in particular. For the most part, changes in group relations have been presented as the results of the fundamental transformation of the U.S. economy from agrarian to industrial to postindustrial. However, the changes in the situation of African Americans and other minority groups did not "just happen" as society modernized. Although the opportunity to pursue favorable change was the result of broad structural changes in American society, the realization of these opportunities came from the efforts of the many who gave their time, their voices, their resources, and sometimes their lives in pursuit of racial justice in America. Since World War II, African Americans have often been in the vanguard of protest activity, and we focus on the contemporary situation of this group in the next chapter.

Note

1. From Twelve Million Black Voices by Richard Wright. Copyright 1941 by Richard Wright. Published by Thunder's Mouth Press, an imprint of Avalon Publishing Group Incorporated.

Main Points

- Group relations change as the subsistence technology and the level of development of the larger society change. As nations industrialize and urbanize, dominant–minority relations change from paternalistic to rigid competitive forms.
- In the South, slavery was replaced by de jure segregation, a system that combined racial separation with great inequality. The Jim Crow system was intended to control the labor of African Americans and eliminate their political power.
- Black Southerners responded to segregation, in part, by moving to urban areas outside the South, particularly in the Northeast and Midwest. The African American population enjoyed greater freedom and developed some political and economic resources away from the South, but a large concentration of low-income, relatively powerless African Americans developed in ghetto neighborhoods. The resources and relative freedom of blacks living outside the South became an important foundation for the various movements that dramatically changed American race relations, starting in the middle of the 20th century.
- The African American community developed a separate institutional life centered on family, church, and community. An African American middle class emerged, as well as a protest movement. Combining work with family roles, African American women were employed mostly in agriculture and domestic service during the era of segregation and were one of the most exploited groups.
- Urbanization, specialization, bureaucratization, the changing structure of the occupational sector, the growing importance of education, and other trends have changed the shape of race relations. The shifts in subsistence technology created more opportunity and freedom for all minority groups but also increased the intensity of struggle and conflict.
- Paternalistic systems are associated with an agrarian subsistence technology and the desire to control a large, powerless labor force. Under industrialization, group relationships feature more competition for jobs and status, and lower levels of contact between groups. As a postindustrial society began to emerge, group relations in the United States shifted from rigid to fluid competitive. The postindustrial subsistence technology is associated with the highest levels of openness and opportunity for minorities, along with continuing power differentials between groups.

- Modern institutional discrimination consists of subtle, indirect, difficult-to-document forms of discrimination that are built into society's daily operation, including past-in-present discrimination and other policies, such as the use of racially biased school aptitude tests and drug laws, that are more punitive for minority groups. Affirmative action policies are intended, in part, to combat these forms of discrimination.

APPLYING CONCEPTS

How have the trends discussed in this section affected you and your family? If the United States had not industrialized, where would your family live? What kind of career would your parents and grand-parents have had? Would you have had the opportunity for a college education?

You can get some insight on the answers to these questions by researching your family history over the past several generations and completing the table below. You may not have all the information requested, but that might be a good reason to give your parents or grandparents a call! If you know nothing at all about your family history and have no way to get the information, ask a roommate or friend for information about his or her family history instead.

To complete the table, pick *one* ancestor from each generation, perhaps the one about which you know the most. To get you started and provide a comparison, one of the authors has completed the table. When you get to the bottom row of the right hand side of the table, fill in the blanks in terms of your desires or plans. Would you rather live in the city, suburbs, or country? What is your ideal job or the career for which you are preparing? What degree are you pursuing?

	Healey			You		
Generations	Residence	Education	Occupation	Residence	Education	Occupation
Great-grandparent	City	Unknown	Coal miner			
Grandparent	City	Eighth grade (?)	Clerk, bar owner			
Parent	City	High school, some college	Agent for the Internal Revenue Service			
Healey	Suburbs	PhD	College professor			

TURN TO THE END OF THIS SECTION TO FIND OUR OBSERVATIONS ABOUT TRENDS IN ANSWERS TO APPLYING CONCEPTS.

Review Questions

1. The opening paragraph of this chapter offers a corollary to two themes from Chapter 3: *dominant–minority group relations change as the subsistence technology changes.* How does the material in this chapter illustrate the usefulness of that idea?

2. Explain paternalistic and rigid competitive relations and link them to industrialization. How does the shift from slavery to de jure segregation illustrate the dynamics of these two systems?

3. What was the Great Migration to the North? How did it change American race relations?

4. Explain the transition from rigid competitive to fluid competitive relations and explain how this transition is related to the coming of postindustrial society. Explain the roles of urbanization, bureaucracy, the service sector of the job market, and education in this transition.

5. What is modern institutional discrimination? How does it differ from "traditional" institutional discrimination? Explain the role of affirmative action in combating each.

6. Explain the impact of industrialization and globalization on gender relations. Compare and contrast these changes with the changes that occurred for racial and ethnic minority groups.

7. What efforts have been made on your campus to combat modern institutional discrimination? How effective have these efforts been?

Internet Activities

1. Watch this 2-minute video of Billie Holiday singing her iconic song "Strange Fruit": https://www.you tube.com/watch?v=h4ZyuULy9zs. It has inspired books, an opera, a documentary, and more. Why do you think this song resonates with so many people? What "strange fruit" did she sing about? What's your reaction to this song? How do the lyrics illustrate ideas from the chapter? To find out more about protest music, including music about slavery, visit http://www.pbs.org/independentlens/strangefruit/protest.html.

2. Go to the Jim Crow Stories link http://www.pbs.org/wnet/jimcrow/stories.html. Listen to at least three of the narratives. What do these oral histories teach you that you didn't know before? How do they relate to the textbook?

3. Check out Jacob Lawrence's famous Great Migration series at http://www.moma.org/interactives/exhibitions/2015/onewayticket/. You may wish to read a review of the exhibit first, such as this article in the *New Yorker*: http://www.newyorker.com/magazine/2015/04/20/telling-the-whole-story. Read the text for Panel 1, which includes information about key Northern cities, including Harlem in New York City. Read through "One-Way Ticket" and "Bound No'th Blues" (1926) by poet Langston Hughes. (If you click on his name, you'll find a list of key figures to learn more about.) Listen to Maggie Jones singing "Northbound Blues," an early song about the Great Migration (1925). What are the key themes in these poems and song? How do they illustrate ideas from the chapter? Click on two more panels of your choosing. You may wish to look at those relating to the book (e.g., panels 10–11 on poverty, panels 14–16 and 22 on violence). What relevant or new ideas do you learn there? How do they relate to what you've learned so far? For an article that links Lawrence's work to modern racialized violence, see

"Black Bodies in Motion and in Pain" at http://www.newyorker.com/culture/cultural-comment/black-bodies-in-motion-and-in-pain. What do you think of the connections the author makes?

4. Consider visiting the Virtual Jim Crow Museum of Racist Memorabilia created by sociologist David Pilgrim at www.ferris.edu/news/jimcrow/index.htm. This video gives an overview of the museum: https://www.youtube.com/watch?v=yf7jAF2Tk40.

Group Discussion

With some classmates, discuss what you learned from this chapter and from the websites you visited for the Internet Activities. Before you start the discussion, write a brief reaction to both the chapter and the online content. Consider the following questions in your essay and during the discussion:

1. Why did de jure segregation happen? What was at stake? Who gained and who lost? Be sure to discuss class and gender differences in connection with these issues.

2. How was the Jim Crow system sustained across time? What was the role of prejudice and racism? Subsistence technology? Law and custom? How was violence used to enforce the system? What organizations were involved in the creation and persistence of segregation?

3. What does it mean to call this system "rigid competitive"? How did it differ from the paternalistic system of slavery?

4. How did the black community react to segregation? What means of resistance and escape were available? Were they effective? Why or why not?

5. Why did de jure segregation end? What macro-level changes in subsistence technology made segregation untenable? Why?

ANSWERS TO APPLYING CONCEPTS

Based on the trends discussed in this chapter, and as partially illustrated by Healey's family history, it is likely that you will see these trends in your family history:

1. Movement from rural to urban residence

2. Decrease in jobs in the primary sector (extractive jobs such as farmer or coal miner) and secondary sector (manufacturing jobs)

3. Increase in service-sector jobs

4. Increase in education

Of course, each family is unique, and it is entirely possible that your history will not follow any of these trends. Nonetheless, given the pressures created by these macro-level changes, the bulk of families should conform to most of these tendencies. Did your family follow or buck the trends?

Learning Resources on the Web

⑤SAGE edge™

edge.sagepub.com/healeyds5e

SAGE edge offers a robust online environment featuring an impressive array of free tools and resources for review, study, and further exploration, keeping both instructors and students on the cutting edge of teaching and learning.

SAGE edge for Students provides a personalized approach to help you accomplish your coursework goals in an easy-to-use learning environment.

PART 3

Understanding Dominant-Minority Relations in the United States Today

ଚ୍ଚ ଓ

ଚ୍ଚ ଓ

In Part 3, we turn to contemporary intergroup relations. The emphasis is on the present situation of American racial and ethnic minority groups, but the recent past is also investigated to see how present situations developed. We explore the ways minority and dominant groups respond to a changing American society and to each other and

to constrain and limit their lives and, as far into the future as they could see, the lives of their children. The pluralistic Black Power ideology was a response to the failure to go beyond the repeal of Jim Crow laws and fully implement the promises of integration and equality.

Black Nationalism, however, was and remains more than simply a reaction to a failed dream. It was also a different way of defining what it means to be black in America. In the context of black–white relations in the 1960s, the Black Power movement served a variety of purposes. First, along with the civil rights movement, it helped carve out a new identity for African Americans. The cultural stereotypes of black Americans (see Chapter 1) stressed laziness, irresponsibility, and inferiority. This image needed to be refuted, rejected, and buried. The black protest movements supplied a view of African Americans that emphasized power, assertiveness, seriousness of purpose, intelligence, and courage.

Second, Black Power served as a new rallying cry for solidarity and unified action. Following the success of the civil rights movement, these new themes and ideas helped to focus attention on "unfinished business": the black–white inequalities that remained in U.S. society.

Finally, the ideology provided an analysis of the problems of American race relations in the 1960s. The civil rights movement, of course, had analyzed race relations in terms of integration, equality of opportunity, and an end to exclusion. After the demise of Jim Crow, that analysis became less relevant. A new language was needed to describe and analyze the continuation of racial inequality. Black Power argued that the continuing problems of U.S. race relations were structural and institutional, not individual or legal. Taking the next steps toward actualizing racial equality and justice would require a fundamental and far-reaching restructuring of the society. Ultimately, white Americans, as the beneficiaries of the system, would not support restructuring. The necessary energy and commitment had to come from African Americans pursuing their own self-interests.

The nationalistic and pluralistic demands of the Black Power movement evoked defensiveness and a sense of threat in white society. By questioning the value of assimilation and celebrating a separate African heritage equal in legitimacy with white European heritage, the Black Power movement questioned the legitimacy and worth of Anglo American values. In fact, many Black Power spokespersons condemned Anglo American values fiercely and openly and implicated them in the creation and maintenance of a centuries-long system of racial repression. Today, almost 50 years after the success of the civil rights movement, assertive and critical demands by the African American community continue to be perceived as threatening.

Gender and Black Protest

Both the civil rights movement and the Black Power movement tended to be dominated by men. African American women were often viewed as supporters of men rather than as equal partners in liberation. Although African American women were heavily involved in the struggle, they were often denied leadership roles or decision-making positions in favor of men. In fact, the women in one organization, the Student

Nonviolent Coordinating Committee, wrote position papers to protest their relegation to lowly clerical positions and the frequent references to them as "girls" (Andersen, 1993, p. 284). The Nation of Islam emphasized girls' and women's subservience, imposing a strict code of behavior and dress for women and separating the people by gender in many temple and community activities. Thus, the battle against racism and the battle against sexism were separate struggles with separate and often contradictory agendas, as the black protest movements continued to subordinate women (Amott & Matthaei, 1991, p. 177).

When the protest movements began, however, African American women were already heavily involved in community and church work, and they often used their organizational skills and energy to further the cause of black liberation. Many people view African American women as the backbone of the movement, even if they were often relegated to less glamorous but vital organizational work (Evans, 1979).

Fannie Lou Hamer of Mississippi, an African American who became a prominent leader in the black liberation movement, illustrates the importance of the role played by women. Born in 1917 to sharecropper parents, Hamer's life was so circumscribed that until she attended her first rally at the beginning of the civil rights movement she was unaware that blacks could—even theoretically—register to vote. The day after the rally, she quickly volunteered to register:

> I guess if I'd had any sense I'd a-been a little scared, but what was the point of being scared? The only thing they could do to me was kill me and it seemed like they'd been trying to do that a little bit at a time ever since I could remember. (Evans, 1989, p. 271)

As a result of her activism, Hamer lost her job, was evicted from her house, and was jailed and beaten on a number of occasions. She devoted herself entirely to the civil rights movement and founded the Freedom Party, which successfully challenged the racially segregated Democratic Party and the all-white political structure of the State of Mississippi (Evans, 1979; Hamer, 1967).

Much of the energy that motivated black protest was forged in the depths of segregation and exclusion, a system of oppression that affected all African Americans. Not all segments of the community had the same experience; the realities faced by the black community, as always, were differentiated by class as well as gender.

QUESTIONS FOR REFLECTION

5. How did de facto segregation differ from de jure segregation? Were the differences merely cosmetic? Why or why not?

6. How and why did the Black Power movement differ from the civil rights movement?

7. Did the Black Power movement succeed? Explain.

8. What were some of the important gender dimensions of black protest movements?

Black–White Relations Since the 1960s: Issues and Trends

Black–white relations have changed over the past five decades, of course, but the basic outlines of black inequality and white dominance have persisted. To be sure, improvements have been made in integrating society and eliminating racial inequality. Obama's election—unimaginable just a few decades ago (and maybe a few years ago)—stands as one unmistakable symbol of racial progress, a breakthrough so stunning it has led many to conclude that America is now "postracial" and that people's fates are no longer connected to the color of their skin, an argument that is easily refuted by a consideration of the trends and statistics presented in this chapter.

Without denying the signs of progress, the situation of the African American community today has stagnated in many dimensions, and the problems that remain are deep rooted and inextricably mixed with the structure and functioning of modern American society. As was the case in earlier eras, racism and racial inequality today cannot be addressed apart from the trends of change in the larger society, especially changes in subsistence technology. This section examines the racial separation that continues to characterize so many areas of U.S. society and applies many of the concepts from previous chapters to present-day black–white relations.

COMPARATIVE FOCUS:
Race in Another America

One of the key characteristics of traditional U.S. anti-black prejudice is a simple "two-race" view: Everyone belongs to one and only one race, and a person is either black or white. This perception is a legacy of the assumption of black inferiority that was at the heart of both U.S. slavery and Jim Crow segregation in the South. The southern states formalized the racial dichotomy in law as well as custom with the "one-drop rule": Any trace of black ancestry, even "one drop" of African blood, meant that a person was legally black and subject to all the limitations of extreme racial inequality.

The U.S. perception of race contrasts sharply with the racial sensibilities in many other nations. Throughout Central and South America, for example, race is perceived as a continuum of possibilities and combinations, not as a simple split between white and black. This does not mean that these societies are egalitarian, racially open utopias. To the contrary, they incorporate a strong sense of status and position and clear notions of who is higher and who is lower. However, other factors, especially social class, are considered more important than race as criteria for judging and ranking other people. In fact, social class can affect perceptions of skin color to the extent that people of higher status can be seen as "whiter" than those of lower status, regardless of actual skin color.

One interesting comparison is between the United States and Brazil, the largest nation in South America. The racial histories of Brazil and the United States run parallel in many ways, and prejudice, discrimination, and racial inequality are very much a part of Brazilian society, past and present. Like other Central and South Americans, however, Brazilians recognize many gradations of skin color and the different blends that are possible in people of mixed-race heritage. Commonly used terms in Brazil include *branco* (white), *moreno* (brown), *moreno claro* (light brown), *claro* (light), *pardo* (mixed race), and *negro* and *preto* (black). Some reports count scores of Brazilian racial categories, but Telles (2004, p. 82) reports that fewer than 10 are in common use. Still, this system is vastly more complex than the traditional U.S. perception of race.

Why does Brazil have a more open-ended, less rigid system than the United States? Let's consider several important points:

- The foundation for the Brazilian racial perception was laid in the distant past. The Portuguese, the colonial conquerors of Brazil, were mostly single men, and they intermarried with other racial groups, thus producing a large class of mixed-race people.
- Slavery was not so thoroughly equated with race in Brazil as it was in North America and did not carry the same presumption of racial inferiority as in North America, where slavery, blackness, and inferiority were tightly linked in the dominant ideology, an equation with powerful echoes in the present.
- After slavery ended, Brazil did not go through a period of legalized racial segregation like the Jim Crow system in the U.S. South or apartheid in South Africa. Thus, there was less need politically, socially, or economically to divide people into rigid groups in Brazil.

We should stress that Brazil is not a racial utopia, as is sometimes claimed. Prejudice is an everyday reality, the legacy of slavery is strong, and there is a high correlation between skin color and social status. Black Brazilians have much higher illiteracy, unemployment, and poverty rates, and are much less likely to have access to a university education. Whites dominate the more prestigious and lucrative occupations and the leadership positions in the economy and in politics, while blacks are concentrated at the bottom of the class system, with mixed-race people in between (Haan & Thorat, 2012; Kuperman, 2001, p. 25; Marteleto, 2012).

It would be difficult to argue that race prejudice in Brazil is less intense than in the United States. On the other hand, given the vastly different perceptions of race in the two societies, we can conclude that Brazilian prejudice has a different content and emotional texture and reflects a different contact situation and national history (Mikulak, 2011).

QUESTIONS FOR REFLECTION

9. Compare and contrast the understandings of race in the United States and Brazil. Why do these differences exist?

10. What is the role of the contact situation in shaping contemporary race relations in these two societies?

Continuing Separation

More than 45 years ago, a presidential commission charged with investigating black urban unrest warned that the United States was "moving towards two societies, one black, one white, separate and unequal" (National Advisory Commission, 1968, p. 1). We could object to the commission's use of the phrase "moving towards," with its suggestion that U.S. society was at one time racially unified, but the warning still seems prophetic.

While race relations are clearly better today, African Americans and white Americans, in many ways, continue to live in separate worlds. The separation is especially complete when race is compounded with class and residence: The black urban poor lead lives that barely intersect with the lives of the more affluent whites of suburbia.

Each group has committed violence and hate crimes against the other, but the power differentials and the patterns of inequality that are the legacy of our racist past guarantee that African Americans will more often be seen as "invaders" pushing into areas where they do not belong and are not wanted. Sometimes the reactions to these perceived intrusions are immediate and bloody, but other, subtler attempts to maintain the exclusion of African Americans continue to be part of everyday life, even at the highest levels of society. For example, in a lawsuit reminiscent of Jim Crow days, a national restaurant chain was accused of discriminating against African American customers by systematically providing poor service. In 2004, the company agreed to pay $8.7 million to settle the lawsuit (McDowell, 2004).

Many African Americans mirror the hostility of whites, and as the goals of full racial equality and integration continue to seem remote, frustration and anger continue to run high. While Obama's election stirred strong optimism and positive attitudes toward the future in the black community, the more typical mood is pessimistic. (Recall our discussion of public opinion poll results and the differences in black and white perceptions of U.S. race relations from Chapter 1.)

The discontent and frustration have been manifested in violence and riots; the most widely publicized example was the racial violence that began with the 1991 arrest and beating of Rodney King by police officers in Los Angeles. The attack on King was videotaped and shown repeatedly on national and international news, and contrary to the expectations of most who saw the videotape, the police officers were acquitted of almost all charges in April 1992. On hearing word of the acquittals, African American communities in several cities erupted in violence. The worst disturbance occurred in the Watts section of Los Angeles, where 58 people lost their lives and millions of dollars' worth of property was damaged or destroyed (Wilkens, 1992).

This aftermath of the beating of Rodney King illustrates several of the common ingredients that have sparked black collective violence and protest since the 1960s: the behavior of the police and the ubiquity of recording devices. An additional example occurred in 2009 in Oakland, California. Oscar Grant, a 23-year-old black man, was returning from New Year's Eve celebrations in San Francisco when he was caught up in an altercation at a subway station. Police had Grant down on the ground when Officer Johannes Mehserle shot him in the back. Grant was not handcuffed, and Mehserle claimed that Grant was reaching for his waistband—possibly for a weapon— when he fired the fatal shot. In fact, Grant was unarmed. These events were recorded on multiple cameras and cell phones, and quickly went viral on the Internet. To many, Grant's death appeared to be an intentional, unprovoked execution.

The black community responded with both peaceful protests and violent rioting. Mehserle was eventually convicted of involuntary manslaughter and sentenced to a two-year prison term. The punishment seemed a mere slap on the wrist to many and provoked further protest, both peaceful and violent (Bulwa, 2010; Egelko, 2009). These types of incidents continue. The deaths of Michael Brown, Eric Garner, Freddie Gray, and others in 2014 and 2015 have sparked protests such as those in Ferguson, Missouri, as well as other forms of activism (like #BlackLivesMatter) across the United States.

In some ways, these events were similar to the 1960s riots. The protests and mass violence were spontaneous and expressed diffuse but bitter discontent with the racial status quo. They signaled the continuing racial inequality, urban poverty and despair, and reality of separate communities, unequal and hostile.

The Criminal Justice System and African Americans

As illustrated by the shooting of Grant, Garner, Brown, and Gray, no area of race relations is more volatile and controversial than the relationship between the black community and the criminal justice system. There is considerable mistrust and resentment of the police among African Americans, and the perception that the entire criminal justice system is stacked against them is common.

A Biased Criminal Justice System? The perception of bias is not without justification: The police and other elements of the criminal justice system have a long tradition of abuse, harassment, and mistreatment of black citizens, who, in turn, commonly see the police as the enemy and the entire criminal justice system as an occupying force. For example, a 2013 nationally representative poll found that 68% of black respondents— two thirds of the sample—thought the American justice system was racially biased. Only 25% of whites agreed (Newport, 2013a). We should note that this poll was conducted shortly after George Zimmerman was acquitted of murder and manslaughter charges in the shooting death of Trayvon Martin. We would generally expect such incidents to intensify the perception of bias. On the other hand, the percentage of black respondents who perceived bias was essentially unchanged from two previous polls, one in 2008 and the other in 1993.

The great majority of social science research has documented the continuing bias of the criminal justice system, at all levels, against African Americans (and other minorities). In a comprehensive summary of this research, Rosich (2007) concluded that, while blatant and overt discrimination has diminished over the past few decades, the biases that remain have powerful consequences for the black community, even though they often are more subtle and harder to tease out. Even slight acts of discrimination can have a cumulative effect throughout the stages of processing in the criminal justice system and result in large differences in racial outcomes (Rosich, 2007).

The magnitude of these racial differences is documented by a report that found that, while African Americans make up 16% of all young people, they account for 28% of juvenile arrests, 34% of youths formally processed by the courts, and 58% of youths sent to adult prison (National Council on Crime and Delinquency, 2007, p. 37; see also Mauer, 2011). Civil rights advocates and other spokespersons for the black community charge that there is a dual justice system in the United States and that blacks, adults as well as juveniles, are likely to receive harsher treatment than are whites charged with similar crimes.

The greater vulnerability of the African American community to the criminal justice system is further documented in two recent studies. The first (Pettit & Western, 2004) focused on men born between 1965 and 1969 and found that 20% of blacks, compared with 3% of whites, had been imprisoned by the time they were 30 years old. Also, the study found that education was a key variable affecting the probability of imprisonment: Nearly 60% of African American men in this cohort who had not completed high school went to prison. The second study (Pew Charitable Trust, 2008) found that black men were imprisoned at far higher rates than white men: While less than 1% of all white men were in prison, the rate for black men was 7%. Furthermore, 11% of black men aged 20 to 34 were imprisoned.

The War on Drugs. Perhaps the most important reason for these racial differences is that, since the 1980s, black men have been much more likely than white men to get caught up in the national "get tough" policy on drugs, especially crack cocaine. Crack cocaine is a cheap form of the drug, and the street-level dealers who have felt the brunt of the national antidrug campaign disproportionately have been young African American men from less affluent areas.

Some see the "war on drugs" as a not-so-subtle form of racial discrimination. For example, until 2010, federal law required a mandatory prison term of 5 years for possession of five grams of crack cocaine, a drug much more likely to be dealt by poor blacks. In contrast, comparable levels of sentencing for dealing powder cocaine— the more expensive form of the drug—are not reached until the accused possesses a minimum of 500 grams (Rosich, 2007).

In 2010, the sentencing disparity was reduced by congressional action, and the mandatory 5-year prison term for simple possession of crack cocaine was eliminated (Eckholm, 2010), but Figure 5.1 illustrates the much higher drug arrest rate for black juveniles since the early 1980s. Notice that the arrest rate for blacks spiked in the late 1980s, when the war on drugs began.

Another recent study focused on marijuana arrests and found huge racial disparities in the nation as a whole, in every state except Hawaii, and in the great majority of counties (American Civil Liberties Union, 2013). Nationally, in 2010, blacks were arrested at a rate of about 700 per 100,000 population, while the white arrest rate was slightly less than 200 per 100,000 population. Thus, blacks were roughly 3.5 times more likely to be arrested for this crime. Is this because black Americans use the drug more than do white Americans? Decidedly not. There was virtually no difference in the rate of use for blacks and whites either in the populations as a whole or among younger people.

If there is no racial difference in use of marijuana, what accounts for the huge racial disparity in arrests? Like Brent Staples, whose essay opened this chapter, blacks are more likely to be policed, watched, stopped and frisked, and profiled than are whites. Their greater vulnerability to arrest for this relatively minor offense is echoed in patterns throughout the criminal justice system and reflects the continuing "otherness" of African Americans in U.S. society.

Racial Profiling. The racial differences in vulnerability to arrest are captured by the concept of racial profiling: the police use of race as an indicator when calculating

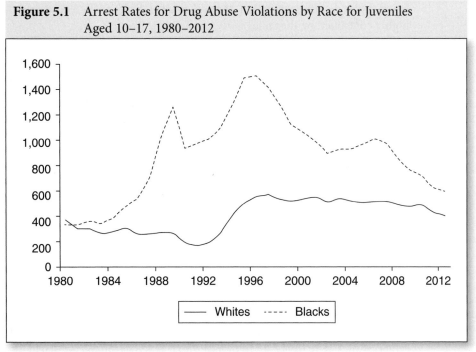

Figure 5.1 Arrest Rates for Drug Abuse Violations by Race for Juveniles Aged 10–17, 1980–2012

Source: National Center for Health Statistics (2010).

whether a person is suspicious or dangerous (Kennedy, 2001, p. 3). The tendency to focus more on blacks and disproportionately to stop, question, and follow them is a form of discrimination that generates resentment and increases the distrust (and fear) many African Americans feel toward their local police forces.

According to some, humiliating encounters with police (e.g., being stopped and questioned for "driving while black") are virtually a rite of passage for black men (Kennedy, 2001, p. 7). According to one national survey, 17% of young black men felt that they had been "treated unfairly" in dealings with the police within the previous 30 days (Newport, 2013b).

The charges of racial profiling and discrimination in the war on drugs can be controversial, but these patterns sustain the ancient perceptions of African Americans as dangerous outsiders, and in the African American community they feed the tradition of resentment and anger toward the police.

The New Jim Crow? Many of the themes and ideas in this section are presented in a provocative and important book that argues that the racial differentials in the war on drugs amount to a new racial control system that has halted the advances made during the civil rights era (Alexander, 2012). The millions of black men who have been convicted under the racially biased drug laws are not only sent to prison; they also carry the stigma of a felony conviction for their entire lives. Their prospects for legitimate employment are miniscule, they lose the right to vote, and they are ineligible for many government programs, including student loans for college. Like the entire black population under de jure segregation, they are marginalized, excluded, second-class citizens highly controlled by the state.

Increasing Class Inequality

As black Americans moved out of the rural South and as the repressive force of de jure segregation receded, social class inequality within the African American population increased. Since the 1960s, the black middle class has grown, but black poverty continues to be a serious problem.

The Black Middle Class. A small African American middle class, based largely on occupations and businesses serving only the African American community, had been in existence since before the Civil War (Frazier, 1957). Has this more affluent segment benefited from increasing tolerance in the larger society, civil rights legislation, and affirmative action programs? Does Obama's election and reelection signal the continuing rise of the black middle class?

The answer to these questions appears to be no. Any progress that might have been made since the civil rights era seems to have been wiped out by the downturn in the American economy that began in 2007.

In actuality, it seems that the size and prosperity of the black middle class was always less than is sometimes assumed. Two studies illustrate this point. Kochhar (2004) found that between 1996 and 2002, the percentage of blacks that could be considered middle and upper class never exceeded 25% of the black population. The comparable figure for whites was almost 60%. Thus, according to this study, the black middle and upper classes were less than half the size of the white middle and upper classes.

The other study (Oliver & Shapiro, 2006) indicates that, prior to the 2007 economic disruption, the African American middle class was not only smaller than the white middle class, but also much less affluent. The researchers studied racial differences in wealth, which includes not only income but all other financial assets: the value of houses, cars, savings, other property, and so forth.

Figure 5.2 compares the wealth of blacks and whites, using two different definitions of middle class and two different measures of wealth. Middle-class status is defined, first, in terms of level of education, with a college education indicating middle-class status and, second, in terms of occupation, with a white-collar occupation indicating middle-class status.

Wealth is defined first in terms of net worth, which includes all assets (houses, cars, and so forth) minus debt. The second measure, net financial assets, is the same as net worth but excludes the value of a person's investments in home and cars. This second measure is a better indicator of the resources that are available to invest in educating the next generation or financing new businesses (Oliver & Shapiro, 2006, pp. 60–62).

Figure 5.2 Wealth by Definition of Middle Class by Race

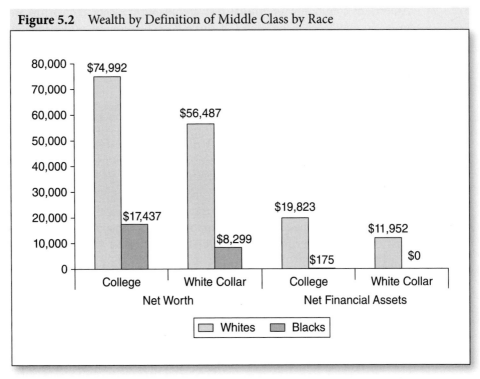

Source: Based on Oliver & Shapiro (2006, p. 96).

By either definition, the black middle class was at a distinct disadvantage. There are huge differentials in net worth between blacks and whites, and even greater differences in net financial assets. Note, in fact, that the figure for net financial assets of blacks in white-collar occupations is exactly zero. Once their equity in houses and cars is subtracted out, they are left with no wealth at all, a statistic that strongly underscores the greater precariousness of middle-class standing for blacks.

While the bad economic times that began in 2007 have affected virtually all Americans, they appear to have had a disproportionately harsh effect on African Americans in general and the African American middle class in particular. One study found that, while both blacks and whites lost wealth after 2007, the median wealth for black families was only 10% of that for white families in 2009 (Shapiro, Meschede, & Osoro, 2013, p. 2; see also Kochhar, Fry, & Taylor, 2011).

These economic differences are due partly to discrimination in the present and partly to the racial gaps in income, wealth, and economic opportunity inherited from past generations. As we mentioned in Chapter 4, racial differences in homeownership are a key component of the racial gap in wealth (Shapiro et al., 2013, p. 4). The greater economic marginality of the African American middle class today is a form of past-in-present institutional discrimination (see Chapter 4). It reflects the greater ability of white parents (and grandparents), in large part rooted in higher rates of homeownership, to finance higher education and subsidize business ventures and home mortgages (Oliver & Shapiro, 2006).

Not only is their economic position more marginal, but middle-class African Americans commonly report that they are unable to escape the narrow straitjacket of race. No matter what their level of success, occupation, or professional accomplishments, race continues to be seen as their primary defining characteristic (Benjamin, 2005; Cose, 1993; Hughes & Thomas, 1998). Without denying the advances of some, many analysts argue that the stigma of race continues to set sharp limits on the life chances of African Americans.

There is also a concern that greater class differentiation may decrease solidarity and cohesion within the African American community. There is greater income inequality among African Americans than ever before, with the urban poor at one extreme and some of the wealthiest, most recognized figures in the world—millionaires, celebrities, business moguls, politicians, and sports and movie stars—at the other. Will the more affluent segment of the African American community disassociate itself from the plight of the less fortunate and move away from the urban neighborhoods, taking with it its affluence, articulateness, and leadership skills? If this happens, it would reinforce the class division and further seal the fate of impoverished African Americans, who are largely concentrated in urban areas.

Urban Poverty. African Americans have become an urban minority group, and the fate of the group is inextricably bound to the fate of America's cities. The issues of black–white relations cannot be successfully addressed without dealing with urban issues, and vice versa.

As we saw in Chapter 4, automation and mechanization in the workplace have eliminated many of the manual labor jobs that sustained city dwellers in earlier decades (Kasarda, 1989). The manufacturing, or secondary, segment of the labor force has declined in size, and the service sector has continued to expand. The more desirable jobs in the service sector have more and more demanding educational prerequisites. The service-sector jobs available to people with lower educational credentials pay low wages, often less than the minimum necessary for the basics, including food and shelter, and offer little in the way of benefits, little security, and few links to more rewarding occupations. This form of past-in-present institutional discrimination constitutes a powerful handicap for colonized groups such as African Americans, who have been excluded from educational opportunities for centuries.

Furthermore, many of the blue-collar jobs that have escaped automation have migrated away from the cities. Industrialists have been moving their businesses to areas where labor is cheaper, unions have less power, and taxes are lower. This movement to the suburbs, to the Sunbelt, and offshore has been devastating for the inner city. Poor transportation systems, the absence of affordable housing outside the center city, and outright housing discrimination have combined to keep urban poor people of color confined to center-city neighborhoods, distant from opportunities for jobs and economic improvement (Feagin, 2001, pp. 159–160; Kasarda, 1989; Massey & Denton, 1993).

Sociologist Rogelio Saenz (2005) recently analyzed the situation of blacks in the 15 largest metropolitan areas in the nation and found that they are much more likely than whites to be living in highly impoverished neighborhoods, cut off from the "economic opportunities, services, and institutions that families need to succeed" (para 2). Saenz found that the greater vulnerability and social and geographical isolation of blacks is pervasive, however, and includes not only higher rates of poverty and unemployment, but also large differences in access to cars and even phones, amenities taken for granted in the rest of society. In the areas studied by Saenz, blacks were as much as three times more likely not to have a car (and, thus, no means to get to jobs outside center-city areas) and as much as eight times more likely not to have a telephone.

Some of these industrial and economic forces affect all poor urbanites, not just minority groups or African Americans in particular. The dilemma facing many African Americans is not only due to racism or discrimination; the impersonal forces of evolving industrialization and social class structures contribute in some part as well. However, when immutable racial stigmas and centuries of prejudice (even disguised as modern racism) are added to these economic and urban developments, the forces limiting and constraining many African Americans become extremely formidable.

For the past 60 years, the African American poor have been increasingly concentrated in narrowly delimited urban areas ("the ghetto") in which the scourge of poverty has been compounded and reinforced by a host of other problems, including joblessness, high rates of school dropout, crime, drug use, teenage pregnancy, and welfare dependency. These increasingly isolated neighborhoods are fertile grounds for the development of oppositional cultures, which reject or invert the values of the larger society. The black urban counterculture may be most visible in music, fashion, speech, and other forms of popular culture, but it is also manifest in widespread lack of trust in the larger society, and whites in particular. An **urban underclass**, barred from the

Figure 5.3 Annual Average Unemployment Rate by Race, 1972–2014

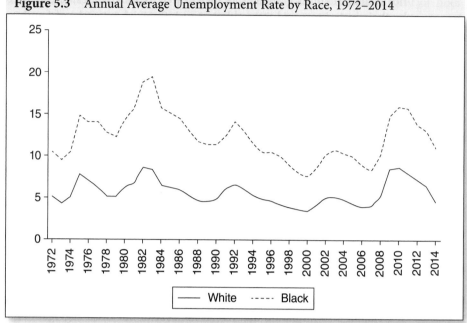

Source: U.S. Bureau of Labor, 2014.

Not surprisingly, black Americans have suffered more in this area, as they have in unemployment. A recent report (Oliver & Shapiro, 2008) found that black Americans and other minority groups of color, compared with whites, were more than three times as likely to be victimized by toxic "subprime" home loans and more than twice as likely to suffer foreclosure as a result. Subprime home loans were new financial instruments that enabled many previously ineligible people to qualify for home mortgages. Predatory lenders marketed the loans especially to more vulnerable populations, and the deals had hidden costs, higher interest rates, and other features that made keeping up with payments difficult. One result of the housing market's collapse was "the greatest loss of financial wealth" in the African American community (Oliver & Shapiro, 2008, p. A11).

Thus, a group that was already more vulnerable and economically marginal suffered the greatest proportional loss—an economic collapse that will take years to recover from. Societal disasters such as the recent recession are not shared equally by everyone, but are especially severe for the groups that are the most vulnerable and have the most tenuous connections with prosperity and affluence. Thus, racial inequality persists decades after the end of blatant, direct, state-supported segregation.

The Family Institution and the Culture of Poverty

The state of African American families as a social institution has been a continuing source of concern and controversy. On one hand, some analysts see the African

American family as structurally weak, a cause of continuing poverty and a variety of other problems. No doubt the most famous study in this tradition was the Moynihan (1965) report, which focused on the higher rates of divorce, separation, desertion, and illegitimacy among African American families and the fact that black families were far more likely to be woman headed than were white families. Moynihan concluded that the fundamental barrier facing African Americans was a family structure that he saw as crumbling, a condition that would perpetuate the cycle of poverty entrapping African Americans (p. iii). Today, many of the differences between black and white families identified by Moynihan are even more pronounced. Figure 5.4, for example, compares the percentage of households headed by women (black and white) with the percentage of households headed by married couples. (Note that the trends seem to have stabilized since the mid-1990s.)

The line of analysis implicit in the Moynihan (1965) report locates the problem of urban poverty in the characteristics of the African American community, particularly in the African American family. These structures are "broken" in important ways and need to be "fixed." This argument is consistent with the **culture of poverty theory**, which argues that poverty is perpetuated by the particular characteristics of the poor. Specifically, poverty is said to encourage **fatalism** (the sense that one's destiny is beyond one's control) and an orientation to the present rather than the future. The desire for instant gratification is a central trait of the culture of poverty, as opposed to the ability to defer gratification, which is thought to be essential for middle-class success. Other characteristics include violence, school failure, authoritarianism, and high rates of alcoholism and family desertion by men (Lewis, 1959, 1965, 1966; for a recent

Figure 5.4   Characteristics of Family Households in the United States, 1970–2014

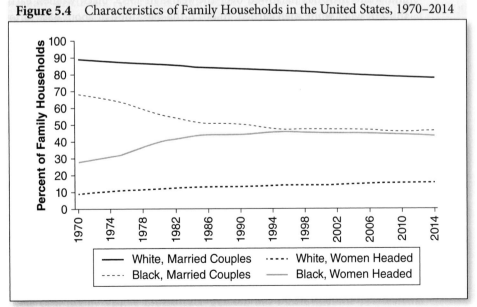

Sources: U.S. Census Bureau (1978, p. 43; 2007, p. 56; 2012c, p. 56; 2015b).

A fourth explanation, consistent with modern racism, attributes racial inequality to a lack of effort by African Americans ("the differences are because most blacks just don't have the motivation or willpower to pull themselves up out of poverty"). Of the white respondents, 49% chose this explanation, the most popular of the four. Thus, modern racism—the view that the root of the problem of continuing racial inequality lies in the black community, not in society as a whole—has a great deal of support among white Americans.

What makes this view an expression of prejudice? Besides blaming the victim, it deflects attention away from centuries of oppression and continuing inequality and discrimination in modern society. It stereotypes African Americans and encourages the expression of negative feelings against them (but without invoking the traditional image of innate inferiority).

Researchers consistently have found that modern racism is correlated with opposition to policies and programs intended to reduce racial inequality (Bobo, 2001, p. 292; Quillian, 2006). In the survey summarized earlier, for example, respondents who blamed continuing racial inequality on the lack of motivation or willpower of blacks—the "modern racists"—were the least likely to support affirmative action and were comparable to traditional racists (those who choose the "inborn ability" explanation for racial inequality) in their opposition to government help for African Americans (see Figure 5.7).

In the view of many researchers, modern racism has taken the place of traditional or overt prejudice. If this view is correct, the "report card" on progress in the reduction

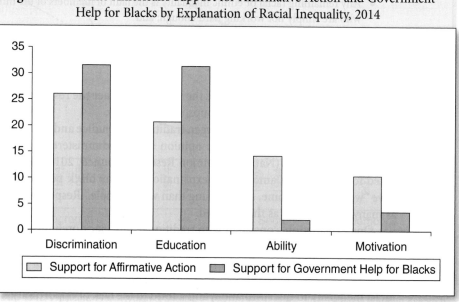

Figure 5.7 White American's Support for Affirmative Action and Government Help for Blacks by Explanation of Racial Inequality, 2014

Source: National Opinion Research Council (1972–2014).

of racial hostility in the United States must be rather mixed. On one hand, we should not understate the importance of the fading of blatant, overt prejudice. On the other hand, we cannot ignore the evidence that anti-black prejudice has changed in form rather than declined in degree. Subtle and diffuse prejudice is probably preferable to the blunt and vicious variety, but it should not be mistaken for its demise.

How can the pervasive problems of racial inequality be addressed in the present atmosphere of modern racism, low levels of sympathy for the urban poor, and subtle but powerful institutional discrimination? Many people advocate a color-blind approach to the problems of racial inequality: The legal and political systems should simply ignore skin color and treat everyone the same. This approach seems sensible to many people because, after all, the legal and overt barriers of Jim Crow discrimination are long gone and, at least at first glance, there are no obvious limits to the life chances of blacks.

In the eyes of others, however, a color-blind approach is doomed to failure. To end racial inequality and deal with the legacy of racism, society must follow race-conscious programs that explicitly address the problems of race and racism. Color-blind strategies amount to inaction. All we need to do to perpetuate (or widen) the present racial gap is nothing.

QUESTIONS FOR REFLECTION

14. What are the key differences between modern racism and traditional prejudice? Which is the more challenging to identify and measure? Why?

Assimilation and Pluralism

In this section, we will use the major concepts of the Gordon model of assimilation to assess the status of African Americans. Of course, we will not be able to address all aspects of these patterns or go into much depth, so these sections should be regarded as overviews and suggestions for further research.

Acculturation

The Blauner hypothesis states that the culture of groups created by colonization will be attacked, denigrated, and, if possible, eliminated, and this assertion seems well validated by the experiences of African Americans. African cultures and languages were largely eradicated under slavery. As a powerless, colonized minority group, slaves had few opportunities to preserve their heritage even though traces of African homelands have been found in black language patterns, kinship systems, music, folk tales, and family legends (see Levine, 1977; Stuckey, 1987).

Cultural domination continued under the Jim Crow system, albeit through a different structural arrangement. Under slavery, slaves and their owners worked together,

Primary Structural Assimilation

Interracial contact in the more public areas of society, such as schools or the workplace, is certainly more common today. As Gordon's model of assimilation predicts, this has led to increases in more intimate contacts across racial lines. To illustrate, one study looked at changing intimate relationships among Americans by asking a nationally representative sample about the people with whom they discuss "important matters." Although the study did not focus on black–white relations per se, the researchers did find that the percentage of whites that included African Americans as intimate contacts increased from 9% to more than 15% between 1984 and 2004 (McPherson, Smith-Lovin, & Brashears, 2006). While this increase would be heartening to those committed to a more integrated, racially unified society, these low percentages could also be seen as discouraging because they suggest that about 85% of white Americans maintain racially exclusive interpersonal networks of friends and acquaintances.

Another interesting study (Fisher, 2008) looked at interracial friendships on a sample of 27 college campuses across the nation. First-year students were interviewed at the end of their second semester and asked about the group membership of their 10 closest friends on campus. The study found that cross-group friendships were common but that white students had the least diverse circles of friends. For whites, 76% of their friends were also white, a much higher percentage of in-group exclusiveness than Asian students (51%), Hispanic students (56%), and black students (27%).

Obviously, these percentages reflect the racial composition of the campuses (all were majority white), but it is significant that cross-group choices were positively related to more tolerant attitudes and a history of having a friend from another group in high school. Most interesting, perhaps, was that cross-group choices were positively related to greater diversity on campus. This finding supports the contact hypothesis and Gordon's assertion that integration at the secondary level leads to integration at the primary level.

Consistent with the decline in traditional, overt prejudice, Americans are much less opposed to interracial dating and marriage today. One national poll, for example, reports that 83% of a nationally representative sample approve of black–white dating (up from 48% in 1987) and 66% approve of black–white marriage (Wang, 2012, pp. 35–36). Approval of interracial dating and marriage appears to be especially high among younger people: In a 2009 poll, 88% of Americans in the 18 to 29 age range approved of interracial marriage, as opposed to 36% of those aged 65 and older (p. 38).

Behavior appears to be following attitudes as the rates of interracial dating and marriage are increasing. A number of studies find that interracial dating is increasingly common (see Wellner, 2007), and marriages between blacks and whites are also increasing in number, although they are still a tiny percentage of all marriages. According to the U.S. Census Bureau, there were 65,000 black–white married couples in 1970 (including persons of Hispanic origin), about 0.10% of all married couples. By 2010, the number of black–white married couples had increased by a factor of 8.5, to 558,000, but this is still less than 1% (or 0.9%) of all married couples (U.S. Census Bureau, 2012b, p. 54).

Finally, a study comparing intermarriage based on the 1980 and 2008 censuses found a slight trend toward decreasing in-marriage, particularly for black men. The results are summarized in Table 5.1. Most black men who married outside their race were married to whites (14.4%) and Hispanics (4.8%). Black women who married outside their group showed a similar pattern: 6.5% were married to whites and 2.3% to Hispanics.

Table 5.1 Percentage Married to a Person of the Same Race, 1980 and 2008

	Whites		*Blacks*	
Year	*Men*	*Women*	*Men*	*Women*
1980	96%	95%	93%	97%
2008	93%	92%	77%	88%

Source: Qian and Lichter (2011, p. 1072). Copyright © 2011 National Council on Family Relations. Reprinted with permission.

QUESTIONS FOR REFLECTION

15. This section examines a variety of dimensions of acculturation and integration for African Americans. Which is most important? Why?

16. In which of these areas has there been the most progress over the past 50 years? Explain.

17. What evidence can you cite for the claim that "black–white relations are the best they've ever been"? What evidence can you cite against this claim?

FOCUS ON CONTEMPORARY ISSUES: Does the Election of President Obama Mean That America Is Postracial?

The election of President Barack Obama in 2008 led many people to conclude that the United States had finally and decisively rejected racism and had become "postracial," or a society in which race was irrelevant. Others warned that reports of the death of racism were vastly exaggerated and that the triumph of one person—even one as significant as

(Continued)

(Continued)

the president—had little relevance for the situation of black Americans in general or for other minority groups.

Which view is more sensible? We won't be able to fully address the issue in these few paragraphs, but consider a few important points that suggest that American society is far from being postracial.

First, race figured prominently in the presidential campaign, although its effects tended to be below the surface. The Obama campaign knew that they had to avoid the third rail of American racism if their candidate was to be successful. They deemphasized his racial identity and presented him as a serious candidate who happened to be black, not as "the black candidate." Obama avoided racially charged issues (e.g., civil rights, affirmative action, or the war on drugs), and stressed issues that were of broad concern (e.g., the economy, the wars in Iraq and Afghanistan, and health care). His strategy was to discuss race "only in the context of other issues" (Ifill, 2009, p. 53).

This strategy, of course, could not defuse all of the concerns, fears, and anxieties triggered by Obama's race. Given the traditional stereotypes about whites and blacks, the mixed-race Obama had to be seen as "more white" and the negativity associated with his blackness had to be contained. The most potentially disastrous racial episode during the campaign linked Obama with the flamboyant Pastor Jeremiah Wright, the minister of a Chicago church that Obama had attended. A YouTube video, in which Wright strongly condemned the United States for its treatment of blacks and other people of color (http://www.youtube.com/watch?v=9hPR5jnjtLo), surfaced and threatened to sink Obama's candidacy by associating him with the angry, militant rhetoric of the African American outsider. Forced to confront American racism openly, Obama crafted an elegant speech in which he acknowledged racism past and present but rejected Reverend Wright's views as distorted, saying that Wright elevated "what is wrong with America above all that we know is right with America" (Obama, 2008). The speech successfully defused the immediate issue, but race continued to lurk in the background of the campaign. There was a persistent tendency to see Obama as something other than a "true American"—as a Muslim, a Kenyan, an outsider, a terrorist, a revolutionary, or just an angry black man. His campaign was ultimately successful because it was able to portray him as "white-assimilated, acceptable, mixed-race, and thus less black (or not really black)" (Wingfield & Feagin, 2010, p. 219). The first president of color in American history owed his success to the perception of many that he wasn't "really" black.

Second, support for Obama on Election Day was highly racialized. The candidate built a broad coalition of supporters that included the young, first-time voters, low-income voters, liberals, Democrats, and women. However, his staunchest support came from the black community. Obama actually lost among white voters by a considerable margin (55% voted for McCain, the Republican candidate) but attracted 95% of black voters.

> Furthermore, since his election, the perceptions of Obama's effectiveness have been highly racialized. Weekly surveys show that the percentage of whites who approve the job the president is doing varies between 30% and 40%, while the percentage of approval among blacks runs between 80% and 90% and sometimes exceeds 90% (Gallup, 2012). Thus, his support in the black community is roughly two to three times his support in the white community.
>
> Finally, and most detrimental to the argument that the United States is postracial, the racial gaps that existed when Obama took office have persisted, and may have grown larger (see the figures in this chapter); racial issues regularly animate public discourse. U.S. race relations are arguably the best they have ever been but, given a history that features slavery and segregation, they are far from "postracial."

Is the Glass Half Empty or Half Full?

The contemporary situation of African Americans is perhaps what might be expected for a group so recently "released" from exclusion and subordination. The average situation of African Americans improved vastly during the latter half of the 20th century in virtually every area of social life. As demonstrated by the data presented in this chapter, however, racial progress has stopped well short of equality.

In assessing the present situation, one might stress the improved situation of the group (the glass is half full) or the challenges that remain before full racial equality and justice are achieved (the glass is half empty). While African Americans can now be found at the highest level of the society (including the Oval Office and the Supreme Court), a large percentage of the African American population has merely traded rural peasantry for urban poverty and faces an array of formidable and deep-rooted problems.

The situation of African Americans is intimately intermixed with the plight of our cities and the changing nature of the labor force. It is the consequence of nearly 400 years of prejudice, racism, and discrimination, but it also reflects broader social forces, such as urbanization and industrialization. Consistent with their origin as a colonized minority group, relative poverty and powerlessness has persisted for African Americans long after other groups (e.g., the descendants of the European immigrants who arrived between the 1820s and the 1920s) have achieved equality and acceptance. African Americans were enslaved to meet the labor demands of an agrarian economy, became rural peasants under Jim Crow segregation, were excluded from the opportunities created by early industrialization, and remain largely excluded from the better jobs in the emerging postindustrial economy.

Progress toward racial equality has slowed since the heady days of the 1960s, and in many areas, earlier advances seem hopelessly stagnated. Public opinion polls indicate that there is little support or sympathy for the cause of African Americans. Traditional prejudice has declined, only to be replaced by modern racism. In the court of public opinion, African Americans are often held responsible for their own plight. Biological racism has been replaced with indifference to racial issues or with blaming the victims.

Of course, real improvements have been made in the lives of African Americans. Compared with their counterparts in the days of Jim Crow, African Americans today on average are more prosperous and more politically powerful, and some are among the most revered of current popular heroes (the glass is half full). However, the increases in average income and education and the glittering success of the few obscure a tangle of problems for the many, problems that may well grow worse. Poverty, unemployment, a failing educational system, residential segregation, subtle racism, and continuing discrimination continue to be inescapable realities for millions of African Americans. In many African American neighborhoods, crime, drugs, violence, poor health care, malnutrition, and a host of other factors compound these problems (the glass is half empty).

Given this gloomy situation, it should not be surprising to find in the African American community significant strength in pluralistic, nationalistic thinking, as well as resentment and anger. Black Nationalism and Black Power remain powerful ideas, but their goals of development and autonomy for the African American community remain largely rhetorical sloganeering without the resources to bring them to actualization.

The situation of the African American community in the early 21st century might be characterized as a combination of partial assimilation, structural pluralism, and inequality—a depiction that reflects the continuing effects, in the present, of a colonized origin. The problems that remain are less visible (or perhaps just better hidden from the average white middle-class American) than those of previous eras. Responsibility is more diffused; the moral certainties of opposition to slavery or to Jim Crow laws are long gone. Contemporary racial issues must be articulated and debated in an environment of subtle prejudice and low levels of sympathy for the grievances of African Americans. Urban poverty, modern institutional discrimination, and modern racism are less dramatic and more difficult to measure than an overseer's whip, a lynch mob, or a sign that says "Whites Only," but they can be just as real and just as deadly in their consequences.

Main Points

- At the beginning of the 20th century, the racial oppression of African Americans took the form of a rigid competitive system of group relations and de jure segregation. This system ended because of changing economic and political conditions, changing legal precedents, and a mass protest movement initiated by African Americans.
- The U.S. Supreme Court decision in *Brown v. Board of Education of Topeka* (1954) was the single most powerful blow struck against legalized segregation. A nonviolent direct action campaign was launched in the South to challenge and defeat segregation. The U.S. Congress delivered the final blows to de jure segregation in the 1964 Civil Rights Act and the 1965 Voting Rights Act.
- Outside the South, the concerns of the African American community had centered on access to schooling, jobs, housing, health care, and other opportunities. African Americans' frustration and anger were expressed in the urban riots of the 1960s. The Black Power movement addressed the massive problems of racial inequality remaining after the victories of the civil rights movement.
- Black–white relations since the 1960s have been characterized by continuing inequality, separation, and hostility, along with substantial improvements in status for some African Americans. Class differentiation within the African American community is greater than ever before.

- The African American family has been perceived as weak, unstable, and a cause of continuing poverty. Culture of poverty theory attributes poverty to certain characteristics of the poor. An alternative view sees problems such as high rates of family desertion by men as the result of poverty, rather than the cause.
- Anti-black prejudice and discrimination are manifested in more subtle, covert forms (modern racism and institutional discrimination) in contemporary society.
- African Americans are largely acculturated, but centuries of separate development have created a unique black experience in American society.
- There have been real improvements for many African Americans, but, the overall secondary structural assimilation of African Americans remains low. Evidence of racial inequalities in residence, schooling, politics, jobs, income, unemployment, and poverty is massive and underlines the realities of the urban underclass.
- In the area of primary structural assimilation, interracial interaction and friendships are rising. Interracial marriages are increasing, although they remain a tiny percentage of all marriages.
- Compared with their situation at the start of the 20th century, African Americans have made considerable improvements in quality of life but the distance to true racial equality remains enormous.

APPLYING CONCEPTS

The table below lists 10 metropolitan areas from across the nation in alphabetical order. Based on what you have learned in this chapter and Chapter 4, which ones do you think have the highest levels of racial residential segregation? Cities in the South? Cities in the Northeast or the West? Cities with a higher or lower black population?

What's your best guess? Rank order the cities from 1 (most segregated) to 10 (least segregated).

	City	Region	Percentage Black, 2010*	Rank
1	Atlanta, Georgia	South	32%	
2	Baltimore, Maryland	Border	29%	
3	Boston, Massachusetts	Northeast	7%	
4	Dallas–Fort Worth, Texas	Southwest	15%	
5	Kansas City, Kansas	Midwest	13%	
6	Pittsburgh, Pennsylvania	Northeast	8%	
7	Richmond, Virginia	South	38%	
8	San Diego, California	West	5%	
9	San Francisco, California	West	8%	
10	Washington, DC	South/border	26%	

*Percentage in entire metropolitan area, including suburbs. Data from U.S. Census Bureau (2012c, p. 31).

TURN THE LAST PAGE OF THIS CHAPTER TO SEE THE ACTUAL RANKS AND SCORES.

Review Questions

1. What forces led to the end of de jure segregation? To what extent was this change a result of broad social forces (e.g., industrialization), and to what extent was it the result of the actions of African Americans acting against the system (e.g., the Southern civil rights movement)? By the 1960s and 1970s, how had the movement for racial change succeeded, and what issues were left unresolved? What issues remain unresolved today?

2. Describe the differences between the Southern civil rights movement and the Black Power movement. Why did these differences exist? How are the differences related to the nature of de jure versus de facto segregation? To what degree do these movements remain relevant today? How?

3. How does gender affect contemporary black–white relations and the African American protest movement? Is it true that African American women are a "minority group within a minority group"? Explain.

4. According to an old folk saying, "When America catches a cold, African Americans get pneumonia." Evaluate this idea using the information, data, and analysis presented in this chapter. Is it true? Exaggerated? Untrue? What other kinds of information would be needed for a fuller assessment of the quote? How could you get this information?

5. What are the implications of increasing class differentials among African Americans? Does the greater affluence of middle-class blacks mean that they are no longer a part of a minority group? Will future protests by African Americans be confined only to working-class and lower-class blacks?

6. Regarding contemporary black–white relations, is the glass half empty or half full? Considering the totality of evidence presented in this chapter, which of the following statements would you agree with? Why? (1) American race relations are the best they've ever been; racial equality has been essentially achieved (even though some problems remain); or (2) American race relations have a long way to go before society achieves true racial equality.

ANSWERS TO APPLYING CONCEPTS

Here are the 10 metro areas listed from most to least segregated. Many American cities are more segregated than Pittsburgh; some are less segregated than San Diego. These 10 cities were selected to represent a variety of regions and race relations histories, and are not, of course, representative of the society as a whole.

	City	Score (Dissimilarity Index)
1	Pittsburgh, Pennsylvania	64.9
2	Baltimore, Maryland	62.2
3	Kansas City, Kansas	57.7
4	Boston, Massachusetts	57.6

	City	Score (Dissimilarity Index)
5	Washington, D.C.	56.1
6	Atlanta, Georgia	54.1
7	San Francisco, California	50.5
8	Richmond, Virginia	49.6
9	Dallas–Fort Worth, Texas	47.5
10	San Diego, California	38.6

Source: Data from Glaeser and Vigdor (2012).

Group Discussion

In groups of four to six people, compare your ranking of the cities with those of others. Explain the rationale for your ranking. How well did everyone do? What lessons can you take away from this activity?

Internet Activities

Listen to or watch the following. Take notes on what's interesting or useful to you. Note ideas that relate to what you've learned in this (or other) chapters.

1. Watch the six-minute clip "The House We Lived In" from the excellent documentary *Race: The Power of an Illusion* at https://www.youtube.com/watch?v=mW764dXEI_8. It explains how the post–World War II housing boom, funded by government support, made houses a mass, affordable good. However, lending and purchasing practices excluded families of color. How does this clip relate to ideas from this or other chapters? For example, how does this practice relate to institutional discrimination? Additionally, given that home ownership is the major source of wealth for most families, to what degree do you think these historic practices influence African American families today? Think about issues of inheritance, tax deductions for mortgage interest, the impact on children's school districts, and the ability to take out college (or other) loans using one's house as collateral.

2. For a modern look at discrimination in housing, listen to "House Rules" from the podcast *This American Life* at http://www.thisamericanlife.org/radio-archives/episode/512/house-rules?act=0#play. Much of the story features Nikole Hannah-Jones, a reporter whose series on fair housing laws can be found at http://www.propublica.org/series/segregation-now. What was most interesting or relevant to you from this episode? What did you learn that was new that builds on ideas from this and prior chapters? What needs clarifying?

3. Watch this short TED Talk about race and incarceration featuring Bryan Stevenson, award-winning human rights lawyer and founder and director of the Equal Justice Initiative (EJI): at http://www.eji.org/

TED. You may wish to look around the EJI website, too, and watch the interesting video at http://www
.eji.org/slaveryevolved, which offers information about slavery in the United States. It argues that the
social construction of race, specifically the idea of real racial difference between whites and blacks,
allowed for the creation and maintenance of slavery. Further, it argues that these ideas have merely
changed and that vestiges of these ideas are embedded in our criminal justice system and contribute to
disproportionate arrest and sentencing of African Americans, especially boys and men.

4. For a more in-depth view of racial inequality in the criminal justice system, watch this talk by Bryan
Stevenson based on his book best-selling book, *Just Mercy: A Story of Justice and Redemption:* https://
www.youtube.com/watch?v=lQHe6AxX1zo. This talk by Michelle Alexander, a civil rights lawyer and
associate professor of law at Ohio State University, is based on her groundbreaking book, *The New Jim
Crow: Mass Incarceration in the Age of Colorblindness*: https://www.youtube.com/watch?v=Gln1JwDUI64.

Learning Resources on the Web

ⓈSAGE edge™

edge.sagepub.com/healeyds5e

SAGE edge offers a robust online environment featuring an impressive array of free tools and
resources for review, study, and further exploration, keeping both instructors and students on the
cutting edge of teaching and learning.

SAGE edge for Students provides a personalized approach to help you accomplish your coursework goals in an easy-to-use learning environment.

American Indians: From Conquest to Tribal Survival in a Postindustrial Society

Lorinda announced that the [Blessing Way ceremony for Lynette's unborn child] was about to start . . . [so we] walked into the hoghan. A single light bulb lit the room dimly. Couches, futon mattresses, and large pillows were set against the walls for the night's sing. A coffee-maker, microwave, and crock-pot sat on a folding table against the northern wall for the midnight eating. This was the same Navajo adaptation I'd grown up seeing, the age-old ritual with modern technology.

The hataałii sat against the western wall. . . . He wore thick silver bracelets and a silk bandana across his brow, the knot tied off at his right temple in traditional style. A basket of tádídíín (sacred corn pollen) sat at his left.

[There were] gifts: . . . a stethoscope, that the baby would have good health and might be a healer; . . . a pair of running shoes, that the child would be a strong runner; dollar bills . . . to wish the child a wealthy life; cowboy boots and work gloves so that the child would be a hard worker. . . .

The hataałii spoke in quiet Navajo as he passed the basket of tádídíín to Dennis, who sprinkled the yellow pollen at each corner of the hoghan, first East, South, West, then North. Then he passed the basket around the room in a clockwise order; when it came to me, I did what the others had done: I placed a pinch inside my lower lip, pressed a second pinch to my forehead, then spread the pollen in the air above in a small arch to resemble the rainbow that promises life and beauty.

The hataałii began the sing. Brandon and the two burly men entered the chant with accenting rhythms as articulate as wind chimes, but with the resonance of distant thunder. . . .

Lorinda leaned forward and rocked slowly, speaking her own prayer: I heard the word hózhó sung many times. There is no English equivalent, but mostly it means "beautiful harmony." Christians might call it grace.

—Jim Kristofic (2011, pp. 183–184)

At the end of first grade, Jim Kristofic found himself moving from western Pennsylvania to the Navajo reservation in Arizona, where his mother had taken a job as a nurse. At first rejected and bullied by the Navajo kids, he eventually developed a deep respect for and understanding of the "rez," the people, and the Navajo way of life. In this passage, he gives us a glimpse of a Navajo ceremony that has been practiced for centuries. Can ancient traditions such as this—and the tribes that practice them—survive?

We discussed the contact period for American Indians in Chapter 3. As you recall, this period began in the earliest colonial days and lasted nearly 300 years, ending only with the final battles of the Indian wars in the late 1800s. The Indian nations fought for their land and to preserve their cultures and ways of life. The tribes had enough power to win many battles, but they eventually lost all the wars. The superior resources of the burgeoning white society made the eventual defeat of American Indians inevitable, and by 1890 the last of the tribes had been conquered, their leaders had been killed or were in custody, and their people were living on U.S. government–controlled reservations.

By the start of the 20th century, American Indians were, in Blauner's (1972) terms, a conquered and colonized minority group. Like the slave plantations, the reservations were paternalistic systems that controlled American Indians with federally mandated regulations and government-appointed Indian agents. For most of the past 100 years, as Jim Crow segregation, Supreme Court decisions, industrialization, and urbanization shaped the status of other minority groups, American Indians subsisted on the fringes of development and change, marginalized, relatively powerless, and isolated. Their links to the larger society were weaker and, compared with African Americans, white ethnic groups, and other minorities, they were less affected by the forces of social and political evolution. While other minority groups maintained a regular presence in national headlines, American Indians have been generally ignored and unnoticed, except perhaps as mascots for sports teams, including the Washington Redskins, Atlanta Braves, and Cleveland Indians.

The last decades of the 20th century witnessed some improvement in the status of American Indians in general, and some tribes, especially those with casinos and other gaming establishments, made notable progress toward parity with national standards. Also, the tribes are now more in control of their own affairs, and many have effectively used their increased autonomy and independence to address problems in education, health, joblessness, and other areas. Despite this progress, however, large gaps remain between American Indians' norms and national norms in virtually every area of social and economic life. American Indians living on reservations are among the poorest groups in U.S. society.

In this chapter, we will bring the history of American Indians up to the present and explore both recent progress and persisting problems. Some of the questions we address include: What accounts for the lowly position of this group for much of the past century? How can we explain the improvements in the most recent decades? Now, early in the 21st century, what problems remain, and how does the situation of American Indians compare with that of other colonized and conquered minority groups? What are the most promising strategies for closing the remaining gaps between American Indians and the larger society?

Size of the Group

How many Native Americans are there? This question has several different answers, partly because of the way census information is collected and partly because of the social and subjective nature of race and group membership. The most current answers come from the 2010 U.S. census.

The task of determining the size of the group is also complicated by the way the census collects information on race. As you recall, beginning with the 2000 census, people were allowed to claim membership in more than one racial category. If we define American Indians as consisting of people who identify themselves as *only* American Indian, we will get one estimate of the size of the group. If we use a broader definition and include people who claim mixed racial ancestry (listed under "Alone or in Combination" in Table 6.1), our estimate of group size will be much larger.

At any rate, Table 6.1 shows that there were more than 5 million people who claimed at least some American Indian or Alaska Native ancestry but only about half that number if we confine the group to people who select one race only. By either count, the group is a tiny minority (about 1%) of the total population of the United States. Table 6.1 presents information for American Indians and Alaska Natives separately, for the ten largest tribal groupings of American Indians, and for the four largest tribal groupings of Alaska Natives.

The American Indian population has grown rapidly over the past several decades, but this fact needs to be seen in the full context of history. As we mentioned in Chapter 3, in 1492 there were anywhere from several million to 10 million or more American Indians living in what is now the continental ("Lower 48") United States (Mann, 2011, pp. 105–109). Losses suffered during the contact period reduced the population to fewer than 250,000 by 1900, a loss of at least 75%, possibly much larger.

Recent population growth has been quite rapid, especially in recent decades (see Figure 6.1). This more recent growth is largely the result of changing definitions of race in the larger society and people's much greater willingness to claim Indian ancestry, a pattern that again underscores the basically social nature of race.

Table 6.1 American Indians and Alaska Natives, 2010

	Alone	*Alone or in combination (2 or more groups)*
ALL AMERICAN INDIANS AND ALASKA NATIVES	2,932,248	5,220,579
AMERICAN INDIANS	2,042,825	3,831,740
ALASKA NATIVES	113,902	162,504
Ten Largest Tribal Groupings for American Indians		
Cherokee	284,247	819,858
Navajo	286,731	332,129
Choctaw	103,910	195,764
Chippewa	112,757	170,742
Sioux	112,176	170,110
Apache	63,193	118,810
Blackfeet	27,279	105,304
Pueblo	72,270	91,242
Creek	48,352	88,332
Iroquois	40,570	40,432
Largest Tribal Groupings for Alaska Natives		
Yupik	27,329	30,868
Inupiat	20,941	25,687
Tlingit-Haida	8,547	13,486
Alaskan Athabascan	12,318	16,665

Source: Norris, Vines, & Hoeffel (2012).

American Indian Cultures

The dynamics of American Indian and Anglo American relationships have been shaped by the vast differences in culture, values, and norms between the two groups. These differences have hampered communication in the past and continue to do so in the present. A comprehensive analysis of American Indian cultures is well beyond the scope of this text, but the past experiences and present goals of the group can be appreciated only with some understanding of their views of the world.

We must note here, as we did in Chapter 3, that there were (and are) hundreds of different tribes in what is now the United States, each with its own language and heritage, and that a complete analysis of American Indian culture would have to take this diversity into account. However, some patterns and cultural characteristics are widely shared across the tribes, and we will concentrate on these similarities.

Figure 6.1 American Indian and Alaska Native Population, 1900–2010

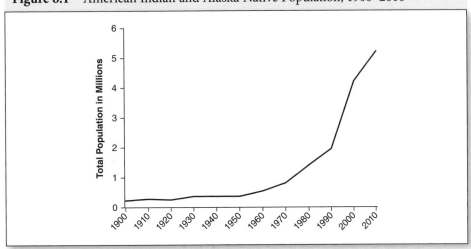

Sources: For data for 1900 to 1990, Thornton (2001, p. 142); 2000 and 2010, U.S. Census Bureau (2007, p. 14; 2010) and Norris et al. (2012).

Before exploring the content of their culture, we should note that most Native American tribes that existed in what is now the United States relied on hunting and gathering to satisfy their basic needs, although some cultivated gardens as well. This is important because, as noted by Gerhard Lenski (see Chapter 1), societies are profoundly shaped by their subsistence technology.

Hunting-and-gathering societies often survive on the thin edge of hunger and want. They endure because they stress cultural values such as sharing and cooperation, and maintain strong bonds of cohesion and solidarity. As you will see, American Indian societies are no exception to this fundamental survival strategy.

The relatively lower level of development of American Indians is reflected in what is perhaps their most obvious difference with Western cultures: their ideas about the relationship between human beings and the natural world. In the traditional view of many American Indian cultures, the universe is a unity. Humans are simply a part of a larger reality, no different from or more important than other animals, plants, trees, and the earth itself. The goal of many American Indian tribes was to live in harmony with the natural world, not "improve" it, or use it for their own selfish purposes, views that differ sharply from Western concepts of development, commercial farming, and bending the natural world to the service of humans. The gap between the two worldviews is evident in the reaction of one American Indian to the idea that his people should become farmers: "You ask me to plow the ground. . . . Shall I take a knife and tear my mother's bosom? You ask me to cut grass and make hay . . . but how dare I cut my mother's hair?" (Brown, 1970, p. 273).

The concept of private property, or the ownership of things, was not prominent in American Indian cultures and was, from the Anglo American perspective, most notably absent in conceptions of land ownership. The land simply existed, and the notion of owning, selling, or buying it was foreign to American Indians. In the words of Tecumseh, a chief of the Shawnee, a man could no more sell the land than the "sea or the air he breathed" (Josephy, 1968, p. 283).

As is typical at the hunting-and-gathering level of development, American Indian cultures and societies also tended to be more oriented toward groups (e.g., the extended family, clan, or tribe) than toward individuals. The interests of the self were subordinated to those of the group, and child-rearing practices strongly encouraged group loyalty (Parke & Buriel, 2002). Cooperative, group activities were stressed over those of a competitive, individualistic nature. The bond to the group was (and is) so strong that "students go hungry rather than ask their parents for lunch money, for in asking they would be putting their needs in front of the group's needs" (Locust, 1990, p. 231).

Many American Indian tribes were organized around egalitarian values that stressed the dignity and worth of every man, woman, and child. Virtually all tribes had a division of labor based on gender, but women's work was valued, and women often occupied far more important positions in tribal society than was typical for women in Anglo American society. In many of the American Indian societies that practiced gardening, women controlled the land. In other tribes, women wielded considerable power and held the most important political and religious offices. Among the Iroquois, for example, a council of older women appointed the chief of the tribe and made decisions about when to wage war (Amott & Matthaei, 1991, pp. 34–35).

These differences in values, compounded by the power differentials that emerged, often placed American Indians at a disadvantage when dealing with the dominant group. The American Indians' conception of land ownership and their lack of experience with deeds, titles, contracts, and other Western legal concepts often made it difficult for them to defend their resources from Anglo Americans. At other times, cultural differences led to disruptions of traditional practices, further weakening American Indian societies. For example, Christian missionaries and government representatives tried to reverse the traditional American Indian division of labor, in which women were responsible for the gardening. In the Western view, only men did farm work. Also, the military and political representatives of the dominant society usually ignored women tribal leaders and imposed Western notions of patriarchy and men leadership on the tribes (Amott & Matthaei, 1991, p. 39).

QUESTIONS FOR REFLECTION

1. Why are there different estimates for the size of the American Indian and Alaska Native population? How do these differences support the idea that race is a social construction?

2. What are the key characteristics of Native American cultures? How do these vary from Anglo culture? How did these differences shape Anglo–Indian relations?

Relations With the Federal Government After the 1890s

By the end of the Indian Wars in 1890, Americans Indians had few resources with which to defend their self-interests. In addition to being confined to reservations, most

Figure 6.2   American Indian Reservations in the United States

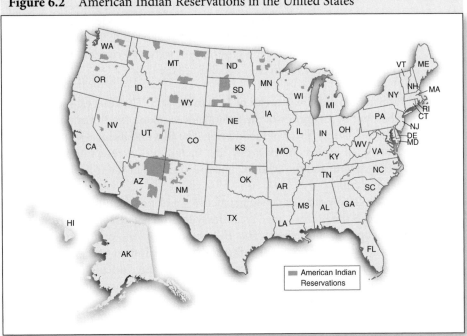

Source: National Park Service (2014).

American Indian groups were scattered throughout the western two thirds of the United States and split by cultural and linguistic differences. Politically, the power of the group was further limited by the facts that the huge majority of American Indians were not U.S. citizens and that most tribes lacked a cultural basis for understanding representative democracy as practiced in the larger society.

Economically, American Indians were among the most impoverished groups in society. Reservation lands were generally of poor quality, traditional food sources such as buffalo and other game had been destroyed, and traditional hunting grounds and gardening plots had been lost to white farmers and ranchers. The tribes had few means of satisfying even their most basic needs. Many became totally dependent on the federal government for food, shelter, clothing, and other necessities.

Prospects for improvement seemed slim. Most reservations were in remote areas, far from sites of industrialization and modernization (see Figure 6.2), and American Indians had few of the skills (knowledge of English, familiarity with Western work habits and routines) that would have enabled them to compete for a place in the increasingly urban and industrial American society of the early 20th century. Off the reservations, racial prejudice and strong intolerance limited them. On the reservations, they were subjected to policies designed either to maintain their powerlessness and poverty or to force them to Americanize. Either way, the future of American Indians was in serious jeopardy, and their destructive relations with white society continued in peace as they had in war.

Reservation Life

As would be expected for a conquered and still hostile group, the reservations were intended to closely supervise American Indians and maintain their powerlessness. Relationships with the federal government were paternalistic and featured a variety of policies designed to coercively acculturate the tribes.

Paternalism and the Bureau of Indian Affairs. The reservations were run not by the tribes, but by an agency of the federal government: the Bureau of Indian Affairs (BIA) of the U.S. Department of the Interior. The BIA and its local superintendent controlled virtually all aspects of everyday life, including the reservation budget, the criminal justice system, and the schools. The BIA (again, not the tribes) even determined tribal membership.

The traditional leadership structures and political institutions of the tribes were ignored as the BIA executed its duties with little regard for, and virtually no input from, the people it supervised. The BIA superintendent of the reservations "ordinarily became the most powerful influence on local Indian affairs, even though he was a government employee, not responsible to the Indians but to his superiors in Washington" (Spicer, 1980, p. 117). The superintendent controlled the food supply and communications to the world outside the reservation. This control was used to reward tribal members who cooperated and to punish those who did not.

Coercive Acculturation: The Dawes Act and Boarding Schools. Consistent with the Blauner hypothesis, American Indians on the reservations were subjected to coercive acculturation or forced Americanization. Their culture was attacked, their languages and religions were forbidden, and their institutions circumvented and undermined. The centerpiece of U.S. Indian policy was the Dawes Allotment Act of 1887, a deeply flawed attempt to impose white definitions of land ownership and to transform American Indians into independent farmers by dividing their land among the families of each tribe. The intention of the act was to give each Indian family the means to survive like their white neighbors.

Although the law might seem benevolent in intent (certainly thousands of immigrant families would have been thrilled to own land), it was flawed by a gross lack of understanding of American Indian cultures and needs, and in many ways it was a direct attack on those cultures. Most American Indian tribes did not have a strong agrarian tradition, and little or nothing was done to prepare them for their transition to peasant yeomanry. More important, American Indians had little or no concept of land as private property, and it was relatively easy for settlers, land speculators, and others to separate Indian families from the land allocated to them by this legislation. By allotting land to families and individuals, the legislation sought to destroy the broader kinship, clan, and tribal social structures and replace them with Western systems that featured individualism and the profit motive (Cornell, 1988, p. 80).

About 140 million acres were allocated to the tribes in 1887. By the 1930s, nearly 90 million of those acres—almost 65%—had been lost. Most of the remaining land was desert or otherwise nonproductive (Wax, 1971, p. 55). From the standpoint of the

Indian nations, the Dawes Allotment Act was a disaster and a further erosion of their already paltry store of resources. (For more details, see Josephy, 1968; Lurie, 1982; McNickle, 1973; Wax, 1971.)

Additionally, coercive acculturation operated through a variety of other avenues. Whenever possible, the BIA sent American Indian children to boarding schools, sometimes hundreds of miles away from parents and other kin, where they were required to speak English, go by European names, convert to Christianity, and become educated in the ways of Western civilization such as dressing in western style clothing. Consistent with the Blauner (1972) hypothesis, tribal languages, dress, and religion were forbidden, and to the extent that native cultures were mentioned at all, they were attacked and ridiculed. Children of different tribes were mixed together as roommates to speed the acquisition of English. When school was not in session, children were often boarded with local white families, usually as unpaid domestic helpers or farmhands, and prevented from visiting their families and revitalizing their tribal ties (Hoxie, 1984; Spicer, 1980; Wax, 1971).

American Indians were virtually powerless to change the reservation system or avoid the campaign of acculturation. Nonetheless, they resented and resisted coerced Americanization, and many languages and cultural elements survived the early reservation period, although often in altered form. For example, the traditional tribal religions remained vital through the period, despite the fact that by the 1930s the great majority of Indians had affiliated with one Christian faith or another. Furthermore, many new religions were founded, some combining Christian and traditional elements (Spicer, 1980, p. 118).

The Indian Reorganization Act

By the 1930s, the failure of the reservation system and the policy of forced assimilation had become obvious to all who cared to observe. The quality of life for American Indians had not improved, and there was little economic development and fewer job opportunities on the reservations. Health care was woefully inadequate, and education levels lagged far behind national standards.

The plight of American Indians eventually found a sympathetic ear in the administration of Franklin D. Roosevelt, who was elected president in 1932, and John Collier, the man he appointed to run the BIA. Collier was knowledgeable about American Indian issues and concerns, and was instrumental in securing the passage of the **Indian Reorganization Act (IRA)** in 1934.

This landmark legislation contained a number of significant provisions for American Indians and broke sharply with the federal policies of the past. In particular, the IRA rescinded the Dawes Act of 1887 and the policy of individualizing tribal lands. It also provided means by which the tribes could expand their landholdings. Many of the mechanisms of coercive Americanization in the school system and elsewhere were dismantled. Financial aid in various forms and expertise were made available for the economic development of the reservations. In perhaps the most significant departure from earlier policy, the IRA proposed an increase in American Indian self-governance and a reduction of the paternalistic role of the BIA and other federal agencies.

Although sympathetic to American Indians, the IRA had its limits and shortcomings. Many of its intentions were never realized, and the empowerment of the tribes was not unqualified. The move to self-governance generally took place on the dominant group's terms and in conformity with the values and practices of white society. For example, the proposed increase in the decision-making power of the tribes was contingent on their adoption of Anglo American political forms, including secret ballots, majority rule, and written constitutions. These were alien concepts to those tribes that selected leaders by procedures other than popular election (e.g., leaders might be chosen by councils of elders) or that made decisions by open discussion and consensus building (i.e., decisions required the agreement of everyone with a voice in the process, not a simple majority). The incorporation of these Western forms illustrates the basically assimilationist intent of the IRA.

The IRA had variable effects on American Indian women. In tribes that were dominated by men, the IRA gave women new rights to participate in elections, run for office, and hold leadership roles. In other cases, new political structures replaced traditional forms, some of which, as in the Iroquois culture, had accorded women considerable power. Although the political effects were variable, the programs funded by the IRA provided opportunities for women on many reservations to receive education and training for the first time. Many of these opportunities were oriented toward domestic tasks and other roles traditionally done by Western women, but some prepared American Indian women for jobs outside the family and off the reservation, such as clerical work and nursing (Evans, 1989, pp. 208–209).

In summary, the IRA of 1934 was a significant improvement over prior federal Indian policy, but was bolder and more sympathetic to American Indians in intent than in execution. On the one hand, not all tribes were capable of taking advantage of the opportunities provided by the legislation, and some ended up being further victimized. For example, in the Hopi tribe, located in the Southwest, the Act allowed a Westernized group of American Indians to be elected to leadership roles, with the result that dominant group firms were allowed to have access to the mineral resources, farmland, and water rights controlled by the tribe. The resultant development generated wealth for the white firms and their Hopi allies, but most of the tribe continued to languish in poverty (Churchill, 1985, pp. 112–113). On the other hand, some tribes prospered (at least comparatively speaking) under the IRA. One impoverished, landless group of Cherokee in Oklahoma acquired land, equipment, and expert advice through the IRA, and between 1937 and 1949 they developed a prosperous, largely debt-free farming community (Debo, 1970, pp. 294–300). Many tribes remained suspicious of the IRA, and by 1948 fewer than 100 tribes had voted to accept its provisions.

The Termination Policy

The IRA's stress on the legitimacy of tribal identity seemed "un-American" to many. There was constant pressure on the federal government to return to an individualistic policy that encouraged (or required) Americanization. Some viewed the tribal structures and communal property-holding patterns as relics of an earlier era and as impediments to modernization and development. Not so incidentally, some elements of dominant society still coveted the remaining Indian lands and resources, which could be more easily exploited if property ownership were individualized.

In 1953, the assimilationist forces won a victory when Congress passed a resolution calling for an end to the reservation system and to the special relationships between the tribes and the federal government. The proposed policy, called **termination**, was intended to get the federal government "out of the Indian business." It rejected the IRA and proposed a return to the system of private land ownership imposed on the tribes by the Dawes Act. Horrified at the notion of termination, the tribes opposed the policy strongly and vociferously. Under this policy, all special relationships—including treaty obligations—between the federal government and the tribes would end. Tribes would no longer exist as legally recognized entities, and tribal lands and other resources would be placed in private hands (Josephy, 1968, pp. 353–355).

About 100 tribes, most of them small, were terminated. In virtually all cases, the termination process was administered hastily, and fraud, misuse of funds, and other injustices were common. The Menominee of Wisconsin and the Klamath on the West Coast were the two largest tribes to be terminated. Both suffered devastating economic losses and precipitous declines in quality of life. Neither tribe had the business or tax base needed to finance the services (e.g., health care and schooling) formerly provided by the federal government, and both were forced to sell land, timber, and other scarce resources to maintain minimal standards of living. Many poor American Indian families were forced to turn to local and state agencies, which placed a severe strain on welfare budgets. The experience of the Menominee was so disastrous that at the concerted request of the tribe, reservation status was restored in 1973; for the Klamath it was restored in 1986 (Raymer, 1974; Snipp, 1996, p. 394).

Relocation and Urbanization

At about the same time the termination policy came into being, various programs were established to encourage American Indians to move to urban areas. The movement to the city had already begun in the 1940s, spurred by the availability of factory jobs during World War II. In the 1950s, the movement was further encouraged with programs of assistance and by the declining government support for economic development on the reservation, the most dramatic example of which was the policy of termination (Green, 1999, p. 265). Centers for American Indians were established in many cities, and various services (e.g., job training, housing assistance, English instruction) were offered to assist in the adjustment to urban life.

The urbanization of the American Indian population is displayed in Figure 6.3. Note the rapid increase in the movement to the city that began in the 1950s. Over 70% of all American Indians are now urbanized, and since 1950 Indians have urbanized faster than the general population. Nevertheless, American Indians are still the least urbanized minority group. The population as a whole is about 80% urbanized; in contrast, African Americans (see Figure 4.2) are about 90% urbanized.

Figure 6.3 Urbanization of American Indians, 1900–2010

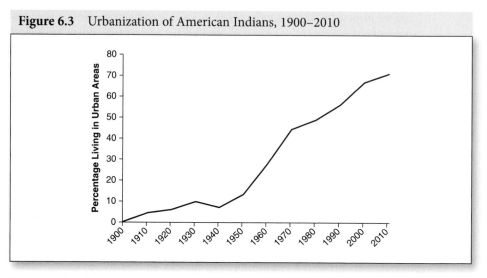

Sources: For data for 1900 through 1990, Thornton (2001, p. 142); 2000 and 2010, U.S. Census Bureau (2012d, Table PCT2).

Like African Americans, American Indians arrived in the cities after the mainstream economy had begun to deemphasize blue-collar or manufacturing jobs. Because of their relatively low average levels of educational attainment and their racial and cultural differences, American Indians in the city tended to encounter the same problems experienced by African Americans and other minority groups of color: high rates of unemployment, inadequate housing, and all the other travails of the urban underclass.

American Indian women also migrated to the city in considerable numbers. The discrimination, unemployment, and poverty of the urban environment often made it difficult for the men of the group to fulfill the role of breadwinner, thus the burden of supporting the family tended to fall on the women. The difficulties inherent in combining child rearing and a job outside the home were compounded by isolation from the support networks provided by extended family and clan back on the reservations. Nevertheless, one study found that American Indian women in the city continued to practice their traditional cultures and maintain the tribal identity of their children (Joe & Miller, 1994, p. 186).

American Indians living in the city are, on average, better off than those living on reservations, where unemployment can reach 80% or even 90%. The improvement is relative, however. Although many individual Indians prosper in the urban environment, income figures for urban Indians as a whole are comparable to those for African Americans and well below those for whites. American Indian unemployment rates run much higher than the national average. For example, in the first half of 2010 unemployment for all American Indians was about 15%, comparable to the figure for African Americans (see Figure 5.3) and 67% higher than that for whites (Austin, 2010).

Thus, a move to the city often means trading rural poverty for the urban variety, with little net improvement in life chances.

American Indians will probably remain more rural than other minority groups for years to come. Despite the poverty and lack of opportunities for schooling and jobs, the reservation offers some advantages in services and lifestyle. On the reservation, there may be opportunities for political participation and leadership roles that are not available in the cities, where American Indians are a tiny minority. Reservations also offer kinfolk, friends, religious services, and tribal celebrations (Snipp, 1989, p. 84). Lower levels of education, work experience, and financial resources combine with the prejudice, discrimination, and racism of the larger society to lower the chances of success in the city, and will probably sustain a continuing return to the reservations.

Although the economic benefits of urbanization have been slim for the group as whole, other advantages have accrued from life in the city. It was much easier to establish networks of friendship and affiliation across tribal lines in the cities, and urban Indians have been one of the sources of strength and personnel for a movement of protest that began early in the 20th century. Virtually all the organizational vehicles of American Indian protest have had urban roots.

Self-Determination

The termination policy aroused so much opposition from American Indians and was such an obvious disaster that the pressure to push tribes to termination faded in the late 1950s, although the act itself was not repealed until 1975. Since the 1960s, federal Indian policy has generally returned to the tradition set by the IRA. Termination and forced assimilation continue to be officially rejected, and, within limits, the tribes have been granted more freedom to find their own way, at their own pace, of relating to the larger society.

Several federal programs and laws have benefited the tribes during the past few decades, including the antipoverty and "Great Society" campaigns launched in the 1960s. In 1970, President Richard Nixon affirmed the government's commitment to fulfilling treaty obligations and the right of the tribes to self-governance. The Indian Self-Determination and Education Assistance Act was passed in 1975. This legislation increased aid to reservation schools and American Indian students and increased tribal control over the administration of the reservations, from police forces to schools to road maintenance.

The Self-Determination Act primarily benefited the larger tribes and those that had well-established administrative and governing structures. Smaller and less well-organized tribes have continued to rely heavily on the federal government (Snipp, 1996, p. 394). Nonetheless, in many cases this new phase of federal policy has allowed American Indian tribes to plot their own courses free of paternalistic regulation, and, just as important, it has given them the tools and resources to address their problems and improve their situations. Decision making was returned to local authorities, who were "held more accountable to local needs, conditions, and cultures than outsiders" (Taylor & Kalt, 2005, p. xi).

In the view of many, self-determination is a key reason for the recent improvements in the status of American Indians, and we will look at some of these developments after examining the American Indian protest movement.

Protest and Resistance

Early Efforts

As BIA-administered reservations and coercive Americanization came to dominate tribal life in the early 20th century, new forms of Indian activism appeared. The modern protest movement was tiny at first and, with few exceptions, achieved a measure of success only in recent decades. In fact, the American Indian protest movement in the past was not so much unsuccessful as simply ignored. The movement has focused on several complementary goals: protecting American Indian resources and treaty rights, striking a balance between assimilation and pluralism, and finding a relationship with the dominant group that would permit a broader array of life chances without sacrificing tribal identity and heritage.

Formally organized American Indian protest organizations have existed since the 1910s, but the modern phase of the protest movement began during World War II. Many American Indians served in the military or moved to the city to take jobs in aid of the war effort and were thereby exposed to the world beyond the reservation. Also, political activism on reservations, which had been stimulated by the IRA, continued through the war years, as the recognition of growing problems that were shared across tribal lines.

These trends helped stimulate the founding of the National Congress of American Indians (NCAI) in 1944. This organization was pan-tribal (i.e., included members from many different tribes); its first convention was attended by representatives of 50 different tribes and reservations (Cornell, 1988, p. 119). The leadership consisted largely of American Indians educated and experienced in the white world. However, the NCAI's program stressed the importance of preserving the old ways and tribal institutions as well as protecting Indian welfare. An early victory for the NCAI and its allies came in 1946 when an Indian Claims Commission was created by the federal government. This body was authorized to hear claims brought by the tribes with regard to treaty violations. The commission has settled hundreds of claims, resulting in awards of millions of dollars to the tribes, and it continues its work today (Weeks, 1988, pp. 261–262).

In the 1950s and 1960s, the protest movement was further stimulated by the threat of termination and by the increasing number of American Indians living in the cities who developed friendships across tribal lines. Awareness of common problems, rising levels of education, and the examples set by the successful protests of other minority groups also increased readiness for collective action.

Red Power

By the 1960s and 1970s, American Indian protest groups were finding ways to express their grievances and problems to the nation. The Red Power movement, like the Black Power movement (see Chapter 5), encompassed a coalition of groups, many considerably more assertive than the NCAI, and a varied collection of ideas, most of which stressed self-determination and pride in race and cultural heritage. Red Power protests included a "fish-in" in Washington State in 1965, an episode that also illustrates the nature of American Indian demands. The State of Washington had tried to limit the fishing rights of several different tribes on the grounds that the supply of fish was diminishing and needed to be protected. The tribes depended on fishing for subsistence and survival, and they argued that their right to fish had been guaranteed by treaties signed in the 1850s, and it was the pollution and commercial fishing of the dominant society that had depleted the supply of fish. They organized a "fish-in" in violation of the state's policy and were met by a contingent of police officers and other law officials. Violent confrontations and mass arrests ensued. Three years later, after a lengthy and expensive court battle, the tribes were vindicated, and the U.S. Supreme Court confirmed their treaty rights to fish the rivers of Washington State (Nabakov, 1999, pp. 362–363).

Another widely publicized episode took place in 1969, when American Indians from various tribes occupied Alcatraz Island in San Francisco Bay, the site of a closed federal prison. The protesters were acting on a law that granted American Indians the right to reclaim abandoned federal land. The occupation of Alcatraz was organized in part by the American Indian Movement (AIM), founded in 1968. More militant and radical than the previously established protest groups, AIM aggressively confronted the BIA, the police, and other forces that were seen as repressive. With the backing of AIM and other groups, Alcatraz was occupied for nearly 4 years and generated a great deal of publicity for the Red Power movement and the plight of American Indians.

In 1972, AIM helped organize a march on Washington, DC, called the "Trail of Broken Treaties." Marchers came from many tribes and represented both urban and reservation Indians. The intent of the marchers was to dramatize the problems of the tribes. The leaders demanded the abolition of the BIA, the return of illegally taken land, and increased self-governance for the tribes, among other things. When they reached Washington, some of the marchers forcibly occupied the BIA offices. Property was damaged (by which side is disputed), and records and papers were destroyed. The marchers eventually surrendered, and none of their demands was met. The following year, AIM occupied the village of Wounded Knee in South Dakota to protest the violation of treaty rights. Wounded Knee was the site of the last armed confrontation between Indians and whites, in 1890, and was selected by AIM for its deep symbolic significance. The occupation lasted more than two months and involved several armed confrontations with federal authorities. Again, the protest ended without the federal government meeting any of the demands made by the Indian leadership (Olson & Wilson, 1984, pp. 172–175). Since then, lawsuits and court cases have predominated over dramatic, direct confrontations.

Ironically, the struggle for Red Power encouraged assimilation as well as pluralism. The movement linked members of different tribes and forced Indians of diverse heritages to find common ground, often in the form of a generic American Indian culture. Inevitably, the protests were conducted in English, and the grievances were expressed in ways that were understandable to white society, thus increasing the pressure to acculturate even while arguing for the survival of the tribes. Furthermore, successful protest required that American Indians be fluent in English, trained in the law and other professions, skilled in dealing with bureaucracies, and knowledgeable about the formulation and execution of public policy. American Indians who became proficient in these areas thereby took on the characteristics of their adversaries (Hraba, 1979, p. 235).

As the pan-tribal protest movement forged ties between members of diverse tribes, the successes of the movement and changing federal policy and public opinion encouraged a rebirth of commitment to tribalism and "Indianness." American Indians were simultaneously stimulated to assimilate (by stressing their common characteristics and creating organizational forms that united the tribes) and to retain a pluralistic relationship with the larger society (by working for self-determination and enhanced tribal power and authority). Thus, part of the significance of the Red Power movement was that it encouraged both pan-tribal unity and a continuation of tribal diversity (Olson & Wilson, 1984, p. 206). Today, American Indians continue to seek a way of existing in the larger society that merges assimilation with pluralism.

Table 6.2 summarizes this discussion of federal policy and Indian protest. The four major policy phases since the end of overt hostilities in 1890 are listed on the left. The thrust of the government's economic and political policies are listed in the next two columns, followed by a brief characterization of tribal response. The last column shows the changing bases for federal policy, sometimes aimed at weakening tribal structures and individualizing American Indians, and sometimes (including most recently) aimed at working with and preserving tribal structures.

QUESTIONS FOR REFLECTION

3. What are the major phases in Indian–white relations since the 1890s? What laws and federal policies shaped these changes? How did Indians respond?

4. Compare and contrast the Red Power movement with the Black Power movement discussed in Chapter 5.

5. How were the similarities and differences shaped by the groups' situations?

Table 6.2 Federal Indian Policy and Indian Response

Period	Economic Impact	Political Impact	Indian Response	Government Approach
Reservation late 1800s–1930s	Land loss (Dawes Act) and welfare dependency	Government control of reservation and coerced acculturation	Some resistance; growth of religious movements	Individualistic; creation of self-sufficient farmers

Period	Economic Impact	Political Impact	Indian Response	Government Approach
Reorganization (IRA) 1930s and 1940s	Stabilized land base and supported some development of reservation	Establish federally sponsored tribal governments	Increased political participation in many tribes; some pan-tribal activity	Incorporated tribes as groups; creation of self-sufficient "Americanized" communities
Termination and relocation late 1940s–early 1960s	Withdrawal of government support for reservations; promotion of urbanization	New assault on tribes, new forms of coercive acculturation	Increased pan-tribalism; widespread and intense opposition to termination	Individualistic; dissolved tribal ties and promoted incorporation into the modern, urban labor market
Self-determination 1960s to present	Developed reservation economies; increased integration of Indian labor force	Support for tribal governments	Greatly increased political activity	Incorporated tribes as self-sufficient communities with access to federal programs of support and welfare

Source: Based on Cornell, Kalt, Krepps, and Taylor (1998, p. 5).

FOCUS ON CONTEMPORARY ISSUES:
Were American Indians the Victims of Genocide?

By 1900, American Indians had lost at least 75% of their population base and numbered fewer than 250,000 people. There is no question that American Indians suffered untold horrors during the contact period (and inflicted horrors of their own), but should this be classified as genocide? Was there a deliberate attempt to destroy American Indians and their culture, or was the population loss simply a sad, unavoidable result of a clash of civilizations?

We should begin by defining what *genocide* means. According to a resolution adopted by the United Nations in 1948, genocide consists of acts "committed with the intent to destroy, in whole or in part, a national, ethnic, racial, or religious group" (United Nations, 1948). It includes actions other than outright killing, such as inflicting serious bodily or mental harm or creating conditions of life designed to cause the destruction of the group.

(Continued)

(Continued)

The core concepts you've been reading about in this text apply to the discussion of genocide, since genocide almost always involves a dominant–minority group situation, in which the dominant group regards the minority group with contempt, racism, and extreme prejudice. Also, power, one of the concepts in the Noel hypothesis, is a key element in genocide. The dominant group must have sufficient power resources to attempt the mass extermination of the minority group.

Before addressing American Indians, let's briefly consider some well-known historical examples of genocide to provide some comparison and context. Unfortunately, there are many instances from which to draw.

The most infamous example of genocide was the effort of German Nazis to exterminate Jews, Slavs, Gypsies, and other "inferior" groups before and during World War II. Millions of people, including 6 million Jews, were systematically slaughtered in Nazi death camps. This massive, highly bureaucratized, and rationally organized genocide was motivated and "justified" by deep racism and anti-Semitism. Nazi ideology demonized Jews and pictured them as a separate, lower, contemptible race that had to be destroyed for the good of all "proper" Germans and for the health of the Third Reich.

A more recent episode of genocide occurred in the tiny African nation of Rwanda in the early 1990s. The two main Rwandan ethnic groups, Hutus and Tutsis, had a long history of mutual enmity that had been exacerbated by their German and Belgian colonial rulers' policy of "divide and conquer." The colonizers had given the Hutus a privileged status, and their greater power continued after Rwanda became independent in 1962. The sporadic clashes between the tribal groups blossomed into full-blown genocide in 1994, occasioned by a Tutsi-led rebellion and the death of the Hutu president of Rwanda in a plane crash that was thought to have been the result of sabotage and Tutsi treachery.

The slaughter that ensued resulted in the deaths of perhaps 800,000 Tutsis, perhaps many more. No one was spared—not even pregnant women, children, and old people—and much of the killing was done by neighbors and acquaintances with bare hands or machetes. The killing was encouraged by Hutu-controlled radio, which characterized the Tutsi as "cockroaches" and worse (see Gourevitch, 1999). Insults such as these express the prejudice and contempt of the dominant group, but they also abet the slaughter by minimizing the humanity of the victimized group and maximizing their perceived lower status and "otherness."

How does the history of American Indians compare? First, note that international law specifies that acts of genocide must be intentional (United Nations, 1948). The Nazis clearly and openly intended to carry out their "final solution" and exterminate the Jewish people, and the Hutus that led the Rwandan genocide meant to annihilate their Tutsi neighbors. What was the intent of whites with regard to Indians? To be classified as genocide, there must be an intention to exterminate the group as a whole (as opposed to killing enemy combatants in battle).

It is not difficult to find statements that show that some whites clearly wanted to eliminate American Indians. For example, in 1864, troops under the command of Colonel John Chivington attacked a Cheyenne village near Sand Creek, Colorado, and killed several hundred Indians, most of them women, children, and old men. The incident is sometimes called the Massacre at Sand Creek, but what makes it a candidate for genocide is Chivington's motivation as revealed in his statement: "My intention is to kill all Indians I come across," including babies and infants, because "nits make lice" (Churchill, 1985, p. 229).

However, it is also easy to find white expressions of sympathy for the plight of the Indians and outrage over incidents such as Sand Creek (Lewy, 2004). As many have noted, sympathy for American Indians in the 19th century tended to be most intense in the areas farthest removed from actual battle. Nevertheless, there is no reason to suspect its sincerity (although, as in the case of the Dawes Act, sympathy unaccompanied by understanding of Indian culture could have harmful consequences). While it is abundantly clear that some— perhaps most—whites wanted to exterminate all Indians, that sentiment was not universal or unanimous.

Also, we must take account of the reasons for the population loss. Recall that much of the population decline was caused by the diseases imported by European colonists, not by deliberate attacks. While there were a few instances of "biological warfare" in which Indians were deliberately infected with smallpox, for the most part the diseases simply took their toll unguided by intention or deliberate plan (Lewy, 2004).

Some people argue that the intent to exterminate was implicit in the coercive, one-sided assimilation that was the centerpiece of policies such as the Dawes Act and institutions such as Indian boarding schools. If these policies had succeeded, the American Indian way of life would have been completely destroyed, even though individual descendants of the tribes might have survived. Also, the deliberate attempts to destroy the Indian food base (e.g., by slaughtering buffalo herds on the Great Plains) and to move Indian tribes from their homelands, and the poor support for reservations could be seen as attempts to create living conditions so desperate and impoverished that they would result in massive loss of life and the disappearance of the group. The intention to exterminate does not have to be overtly stated to be effective or to have that result.

We want to be careful in applying a term like *genocide* and not dilute its power by overuse. We also want to be clear about what actually happened to Indians and not minimize the horror or loss. Was this genocide? Certainly, it looks like genocide, and various authors, scholars, and activists have made that case (see, for example, Churchill, 1997; Stannard, 1992). Others acknowledge the enormous suffering but argue that the case for genocide is weakened by the fact that most of the population loss was caused by the impersonal spread of disease, not by direct violence or physical assaults (Lewy, 2004).

(Continued)

(Continued)

Did American Indians nearly disappear as a group? Yes. Was there intent to exterminate this group? Yes, at least among many members of the dominant group. Did the U.S. government create conditions for the conquered tribes that were so desperate that they resulted—directly or indirectly—in widespread loss of life? Yes, in many instances and for many years. The story of American Indians doesn't feature state-sponsored slaughter like the Nazi Holocaust or the bloody person-to-person violence of Hutus killing Tutsis. Perhaps this was not an instance of genocide by the literal letter of the law. The results for this conquered and colonized group, however, are the same.

Contemporary American Indian–White Relations

Conflicts between American Indians and the larger society are far from over. Although the days of deadly battle are (with occasional exceptions) long gone, the issues that remain are serious, difficult to resolve, and, in their way, just as much matters of life and death. American Indians face enormous challenges in their struggle to improve their status, but, largely as a result of their greater freedom from stifling federal control since the 1970s, they also have some resources, some opportunities, and a leadership that is both talented and resourceful (Bordewich, 1996, p. 11).

Natural Resources

Ironically, land allotted to American Indian tribes in the 19th century sometimes turned out to be rich in resources that became valuable in the 20th century. These resources include oil, natural gas, coal, and uranium, basic sources of energy in the larger society. In addition (and despite the devastation wreaked by the Dawes Act of 1887), some tribes hold title to water rights, fishing rights, woodlands that could sustain a timber industry, and wilderness areas that could be developed for camping, hunting, and other forms of recreation. These resources are likely to become more valuable as the earth's natural resources and undeveloped areas are further depleted in the future.

The challenge faced by American Indians is to retain control of these resources and to develop them for their own benefit. Threats to the remaining tribal lands and assets are common. Mining and energy companies continue to cast envious eyes on American Indian land, and other tribal assets are coveted by real estate developers, fishers (recreational as well as commercial), backpackers and campers, and cities facing water shortages (Harjo, 1996).

Some tribes have succeeded in developing their resources for their own benefit, in part because of their increased autonomy and independence since the passage of the 1975 Indian Self-Determination Act. For example, the White Mountain Apaches of Arizona own a variety of enterprises, including a major ski resort and a casino (see

Cornell & Kalt, 1998, pp. 3–4). On many other reservations, however, even rich stores of resources lie dormant, awaiting the right combination of tribal leadership, expertise, and development capital.

On a broader level, tribes are banding together to share expertise and negotiate more effectively with the larger society. For example, 25 tribes founded the Council of Energy Resource Tribes in 1975 to coordinate and control the development of the mineral resources on reservation lands. Since its founding, the council has successfully negotiated a number of agreements with dominant group firms, increasing the flow of income to the tribes and raising their quality of life (Cornell, 1988; Snipp, 1989). The council now encompasses more than 50 tribes and several Canadian First Nations (Council of Energy Resource Tribes, n.d.).

COMPARATIVE FOCUS:
Australian Aborigines and American Indians

Many indigenous societies around the globe—not just American Indians—have been conquered and colonized by European societies, and similar dynamics have been at play in these episodes, even though each has its own unique history. To illustrate, we will compare the impact of European domination on Australian Aborigines and on the indigenous peoples of North America.

Australia came under European domination in the late 1700s, nearly two centuries after the beginning of Anglo–American Indian relations. In spite of the time difference, however, the two contact situations shared many features. In both cases, the colonial power was Great Britain, first contact occurred in the preindustrial era, both indigenous groups were thinly spread across vast areas, and both were greatly inferior to the British in their technological development.

The Aboriginal peoples had lived in Australia for 50,000 years by the time the British arrived. They were organized into small, nomadic hunting-and-gathering bands and lacked the population base, social organization, and resources that would have permitted sustained resistance to the invasion of their land. There was plenty of violence in the contact situation, but unlike the situation in North America, there were no sustained military campaigns pitting large armies against each other.

The initial thrust of colonization was motivated by Great Britain's need for a place to send convicts; so the European population grew slowly at first and consisted mostly of prisoners. The early economic enterprises were subsistence farming and sheepherding, not large-scale operations that required forced labor.

Early relations between the English and the Aborigines centered on competition for land. The invaders pushed the Aborigines aside or killed them if they resisted. As in the Americas, European diseases took their toll, and the indigenous population

(Continued)

(Continued)

declined rapidly. Because they were not desired as laborers, they were pushed away from the areas of white settlement into the fringes of development, where they and their grievances could be ignored. Like the Indians in North America, they were seen as "savages": a culture that would wither away and soon disappear.

The contemporary situation of Australian Aborigines has many parallels to that of American Indians. The group is largely rural and continues to live on land that is less desirable. After the initial—and dramatic—declines, their numbers have been increasing of late, partly because of higher birthrates and partly because of changing perceptions, growing sympathy for their plight, and increased willingness of people to claim their Aboriginal heritage. The population fell to a low of fewer than 100,000 at the start of the 20th century but is now put at 517,000, or about 2.5% of the total population (Australian Bureau of Statistics, 2012).

Just as in North America, there are huge differences between the indigenous population's norms and national norms. Life expectancy for Aborigines is as much as 12 years lower than that of the general population. They have less access to health care, and Aboriginal communities are much more afflicted with alcoholism, suicide, and malnutrition than the general population. Unemployment rates are triple that of the general population, Aboriginal housing is typically overcrowded and in poor repair, and only about 22% had completed Grade 12 in 2008 (up from 18% in 2002) (Australian Bureau of Statistics, 2012).

The issues animating Aboriginal affairs should have a familiar ring to anyone acquainted with the challenges faced by American Indians. They include concerns for the preservation of Aboriginal culture, language, and identity; self-determination and autonomy; the return of lands illegally taken by the Anglo invaders; and an end to discrimination and unequal treatment.

The Aboriginal peoples of Australia, like American Indians, face many—often overwhelming—challenges to securing a better future for themselves and their children. Their history and their present situation clearly validate both the Blauner and Noel hypotheses: They are a colonized minority group, victims of European domination, with all the consequences that status implies.

QUESTIONS FOR REFLECTION

6. Compare and contrast the contact situations of American Indians and Australian Aborigines. In what ways were both colonized minorities?

7. Compare and contrast the contemporary situations of the groups. Why do these differences exist?

Attracting Industry to the Reservation

Many efforts to develop the reservations have focused on creating jobs by attracting industry through such incentives as low taxes, low rents, and a low-wage pool of labor—not unlike the package of benefits offered to employers by less-developed nations in Asia, South America, and Africa. With some notable exceptions, these efforts have not been particularly successful (for a review, see Cornell, 2006; Vinje, 1996). Reservations are often so geographically isolated that transportation costs become prohibitive. The jobs that have materialized are typically low wage and have few benefits; usually, non-Indians fill the more lucrative managerial positions. Thus, the opportunities for building economic power or improving the standard of living from these jobs are sharply limited. These new jobs may transform "the welfare poor into the working poor" (Snipp, 1996, p. 398), but their potential for raising economic vitality is low.

To illustrate the problems of developing reservations by attracting industry, consider the Navajo, the second-largest American Indian group. The Navajo reservation spreads across Arizona, New Mexico, and Utah, and encompasses about 20 million acres, an area a little smaller than either Indiana or Maine (see Figure 6.2 above). The reservation seems huge on a map, but much of the land is desert and not suitable for farming or other uses. As they have for the past several centuries, the Navajo today rely heavily on the cultivation of corn and sheepherding for sustenance.

Most wage-earning jobs on the reservation are with the agencies of the federal government (e.g., the BIA) or with the tribal government. Tourism is a large industry, but the jobs are typically low wage and seasonal. There are reserves of coal, uranium, and oil on the reservation, but these resources have not generated many jobs. In some cases, the Navajo have resisted the damage to the environment that would be caused by mines and oil wells because of their traditional values and respect for the land. When exploitation of these resources has been permitted, the companies involved often use highly automated technologies that generate few jobs (Oswalt & Neely, 1996, pp. 317–351).

Figures 6.4 and 6.5 contrast Navajo income, poverty, and education with those of the total U.S. population. The poverty rate for the Navajo is almost three times greater than the national norm, and they are below national standards in terms of education, especially in terms of college education. Educational achievement is even lower for members of the tribe living on the reservation, where only about 64% have finished high school (versus 73% of all Navajo) (U.S. Census Bureau, 2013b). Also, median household income for the Navajo is less than 60% of household income for non-Hispanic whites, and their per capita income is only 43% of the national norm.

On the other hand, some tribes have managed to achieve relative prosperity by bringing jobs to their people. The Choctaw Nation of Mississippi, for example, is one of the 10 largest employers in the state. Tribal leaders have been able to attract companies such as McDonald's and Ford Motor Company by promising (and delivering) high-quality labor for relatively low wages. The tribe runs a variety of business enterprises, including two casinos. Incomes have risen; unemployment is relatively low; the

Figure 6.4 Poverty Rates and Educational Attainment for the Total Population, American Indians and Alaska Natives (AIAN), Navajo, and Choctaw, 2013

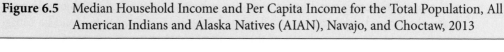

Source: Ogunwole (2006).

Figure 6.5 Median Household Income and Per Capita Income for the Total Population, All American Indians and Alaska Natives (AIAN), Navajo, and Choctaw, 2013

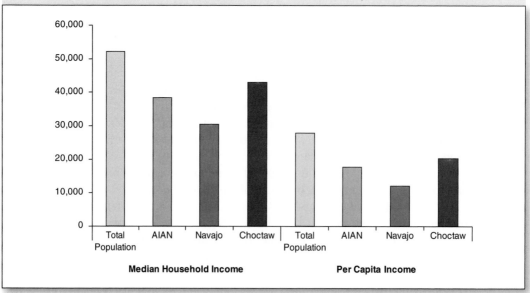

Source: Ogunwole (2006).

tribe has built schools, hospitals, and a television station; and it administers numerous other services for its members (Mississippi Band of Choctaw Indians, 2011).

The poverty rate for the Choctaw is about half that for the Navajo (although still higher than the national norm), and their educational levels are higher than the national standard for high school education and much closer to the national standard for college education than are those of the Navajo or American Indians in general. Median household income for the Choctaw is about 80% of the national norm and more than $12,000 greater than the median income for the Navajo.

The Choctaw are not the most affluent tribe, and the Navajo are far from being the most destitute. They illustrate the mixture of partial successes and failures that typify efforts to bring prosperity to the reservations; together, these two cases suggest that attracting industry and jobs to the reservations is a possible—but difficult and uncertain—strategy for economic development.

It is worth repeating that self-determination, the ability of tribes to control development on the reservation, seems to be one of the important keys to success. Tribes such as the Choctaw are, in a sense, developing ethnic enclaves (see Chapter 2) in which they can capitalize on local networks of interpersonal relationships. As with other groups that have followed this strategy, success in the enclave depends on solidarity and group cohesion, not Americanization and integration (see Cornell, 2006).

Broken Treaties

For many tribes, the treaties signed with the federal government in the 19th century offer another potential resource. These treaties were often violated by white settlers, the military, state and local governments, the BIA, and other elements and agencies of the dominant group, and many tribes are pursuing this trail of broken treaties and seeking compensation for the wrongs of the past. For example, in 1972 the Passamaquoddy and Penobscot tribes filed a lawsuit demanding the return of 12.5 million acres of land—an area more than half the state of Maine—and $25 billion in damages. The tribes argued that this land had been illegally taken from them more than 150 years earlier. After eight years of litigation, the tribes settled for a $25 million trust fund and 300,000 acres of land. Although far less than their original demand, the award gave the tribes control over resources that could be used for economic development, job creation, upgrading educational programs, and developing other programs that would enhance human and financial capital (Worsnop, 1992, p. 391).

Virtually every tribe has similar grievances, and if pursued successfully, the long-dead treaty relationship between the Indian nations and the government could be a significant fount of economic and political resources. Of course, lawsuits require considerable (and expensive) legal expertise and years of effort before they bear fruit. Because there are no guarantees of success, this avenue has some sharp limitations and risks.

Gaming and Other Development Possibilities

Another resource for American Indians is the gambling industry, the development of which was made possible by federal legislation passed in 1988. There are currently more than 400 tribally owned gaming establishments (National Indian Gaming Commission, 2014), and the industry has grown many times over, from almost $5 million in revenues in 1995 to almost $28 billion in 2012 (National Indian Gaming Commission, 2014). Figure 6.6 charts the growth of revenues from gaming on American Indian reservations from 1995 to 2013.

Most operations are relatively small in scale. The 21 largest Indian casinos—about 5% of all Indian casinos—generate almost 40% of the total income from gaming, and the 74 smallest operations—about 17% of all Indian casinos—account for less than 1% of the income (National Indian Gaming Commission, 2011).

The single most profitable Indian gambling operation is the Foxwoods Casino in Connecticut, operated by the Pequot tribe. This casino is one of the largest in the world and generates more revenue than all the casinos of Atlantic City. The profits from the casino are used to benefit tribal members in a variety of ways, including the repurchase of tribal lands, housing assistance, medical benefits, educational scholarships, and public services, such as a tribal police force (Bordewich, 1996, p. 110). Other tribes have used gambling profits to purchase restaurants and marinas and to finance the development of outlet malls, manufacturing plants, and a wide variety of other businesses and enterprises (Spilde, 2001).

The power of gaming to benefit the tribes is suggested by the information displayed in Table 6.3, which shows that on a number of indicators, both gaming and nongaming reservations enjoyed significant improvements in their quality of life in the

Figure 6.6   Gaming Revenues From American Indian Casinos, 1995–2013

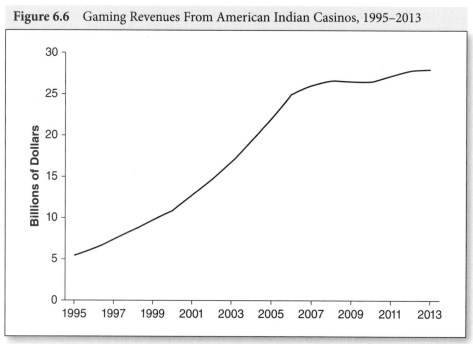

Source: National Indian Gaming Commission.

Table 6.3 Various Indicators of Improvement on Gaming vs. Nongaming Reservations and Total United States, 1990–2000

Indicator	Nongaming	Gaming	Total United States
Per capita income	+21%	+36%	+11%
Family poverty	−7%	−12%	−1%
Unemployment	−2%	−5%	−1%
High school graduates	−1%	+2%	−1%
College graduates	+2%	+3%	+4%

Source: Adapted from "Changes on Reservations Other Than Navajo," p. xi in *American Indians on Reservations: A Databook of Socioeconomic Change between the 1990 and 2000 Censuses* by Jonathan A. Taylor and Joseph P. Kalt. Copyright © 2005 The Harvard Project on American Indian Economic Development.

last decade of the 20th century, but the gaming reservations improved more rapidly. For example, all reservations increased their per capita income faster than the nation as a whole (+11%), but gaming reservations improved faster (+36%) than nongaming reservations (+21%).

Various tribes have sought other ways to capitalize on their freedom from state regulation and taxes. Some have established small but profitable businesses selling cigarettes tax free. Also, because they are not subject to state and federal environmental regulations, some reservations are exploring the possibility of housing nuclear waste and other refuse of industrialization—a somewhat ironic and not altogether attractive use of the remaining Indian lands.

Clearly, the combination of increased autonomy, treaty rights, natural resources, and gambling means that American Indians today have an opportunity to dramatically raise their standards of living and creatively take control of their own destinies. Some tribes have enjoyed enormous benefits, but for others, these assets remain a potential that is waiting to be actualized. Without denying the success stories or the improvements in recent years, the lives of many American Indians continue to be limited by poverty and powerlessness, prejudice, and discrimination. We document these patterns in the next section.

Prejudice and Discrimination

Anti-Indian prejudice has been a part of American society since first contact. Historically, negative feelings such as hatred and contempt have been widespread and strong, particularly during the heat of war, and various stereotypes of Indians have been common. One stereotype, especially strong during periods of conflict, depicts Indians as bloodthirsty, ferocious, cruel savages capable of any atrocity. The other image of American Indians is that of "the noble Red Man" who lives in complete harmony with nature and symbolizes goodwill and pristine simplicity (Bordewich, 1996,

p. 34). Although the first stereotype tended to fade away as hostilities drew to a close, the latter image retains a good deal of strength in modern views of Indians found in popular culture and among environmentalist and "new age" spiritual organizations.

A variety of studies have documented continued stereotyping of American Indians in the popular press, textbooks, the media, cartoons, and various other places (see Aleiss, 2005; Bird, 1999; Meek, 2006; Rouse & Hanson, 1991). In the tradition of "the noble Red Man," American Indians are often portrayed as bucks and squaws, complete with headdresses, bows, tepees, and other such generic Indian artifacts. These simplified portrayals obliterate the diversity of American Indian culture and lifestyles.

American Indians are often referred to in the past tense, as if their present situation were of no importance or, worse, as if they no longer existed. Many history books continue to begin the study of American history in Europe or with the "discovery" of America, omitting the millennia of civilization prior to the arrival of European explorers and colonizers. Contemporary portrayals of American Indians, such as in the movie *Dances with Wolves* (Costner, 1990), are more sympathetic but still treat the tribes as part of a bucolic past forever lost, not as peoples with real problems in the present.

The persistence of stereotypes and the extent to which they have become enmeshed in modern culture is illustrated by continuing controversies surrounding nicknames for athletic teams (e.g., the Washington Redskins, the Cleveland Indians, and the Atlanta Braves) and the use of American Indian mascots, tomahawk "chops," and other practices offensive to many American Indians. Protests have been held at athletic events to increase awareness of these derogatory depictions, but as was the case so often in the past, the protests have been attacked, ridiculed, or simply ignored.

Relatively few studies of anti-Indian prejudice exist within the social science literature. Therefore, it is difficult to fully understand the changes that may have occurred over the past several decades. We do not know whether there has been a shift to more symbolic or "modern" forms of anti-Indian racism, as there has been for anti-black prejudice, or whether the stereotypes of American Indians have declined in strength or changed in content.

One of the few records of national anti-Indian prejudice over time is that of social distance scale results (see Table 1.2). When the scales were first administered in 1926, American Indians were ranked in the middle third of all groups (18th out of 28), at about the same level as southern and eastern Europeans and slightly above Mexicans, another colonized group. The ranking of American Indians remained stable until 1977, when there was a noticeable rise in their position relative to other groups. In the most recent polls, the rankings of American Indians have remained stable, at about the same level as Jews and Poles but below African Americans. These shifts may reflect a decline in levels of prejudice, a change from more overt forms to more subtle modern racism, or both. Remember, however, that the samples for the social distance research were college students, for the most part, and the results do not necessarily reflect trends in the general population (see also Hanson & Rouse, 1987; Smith & Dempsey, 1983).

Additionally, research is unclear about the severity or extent of discrimination against American Indians. Certainly, the group's lower average levels of education limit their opportunities for upward mobility, choice of occupations, and range of income. This is a form of institutional discrimination in the sense that the opportunities to develop human capital are much less available to American Indians than to much of the rest of the population.

In terms of individual discrimination or more overt forms of exclusion, there is simply too little evidence to sustain clear conclusions (Snipp, 1992, p. 363). The situation of American Indian women is also under-researched, but Snipp reports that, like their counterparts in other minority groups and the dominant group, they "are systematically paid less than their men counterparts in similar circumstances" (p. 363).

The very limited evidence available from social distance scales suggests that overt anti-Indian prejudice has declined, perhaps in parallel with anti-black prejudice. A great deal of stereotyping remains, however, and demeaning, condescending, or negative portrayals of American Indians are common throughout the dominant culture. Institutional discrimination is a major barrier for American Indians, who have not had access to opportunities for education and employment.

QUESTIONS FOR REFLECTION

8. This section examined a number of issues in contemporary Indian–white relations. In your opinion, which of these is most important? Why?

9. Thinking about the concepts developed in this text, what is the single most important force shaping the situation of American Indians over the past century? Why?

10. Compare and contrast anti-black prejudice with anti-Indian prejudice. How and why are the two forms of prejudice different?

Assimilation and Pluralism

In this section, we continue to assess the situation of American Indians today using the same conceptual framework used in Chapter 5. Once again, please regard this material as an overview and as starting points for further research.

Compared with other groups, information about American Indians is scant. Nonetheless, a relatively clear picture emerges. The portrait stresses a mixed picture: improvements for some combined with continued colonization, marginalization, and impoverishment for others. Like African Americans, Native Americans can be found at every status and income level in the United States, but Indians living on reservations continue as one of the most impoverished, marginalized groups in society. American Indians as a group face ongoing discrimination and exclusion, and continue the search for a meaningful course between assimilation and pluralism.

Acculturation

Despite more than a century of coercive Americanization, many tribes have been able to preserve at least a portion of their traditional cultures. For example, many tribal languages continue to be spoken on a daily basis. Approximately 20% of American Indians and Alaska Natives speak a language other than English at home, about the same percentage as the total population. Figure 6.7 suggests the extent of language preservation. For 7 of the 10 largest tribes, less than 10% of their members speak the tribal language at home. Some tribes, however, continue to speak their native language, including about 25% of Apache and half of Navajo.

While some American Indian languages have survived, even the most widely spoken of these languages is endangered. One study (Krauss, 1996) estimates that only about 11% of the surviving 200 languages are being taught by parents to their children in the traditional way and that most languages are spoken on a daily basis only by the older generation. Few, if any, people are left who speak only a tribal language. One authority (A. Treuer, 2012, p. 80) reports that only 20 tribal languages in the United States and Canada are spoken by children in significant numbers. If this pattern persists, American Indian languages will disappear as the generations change. A number of tribes have instituted programs to try to renew and preserve their language, along with other elements of their culture, but the success of these efforts is uncertain (Schmid, 2001, p. 25; see also D. Treuer, 2012, pp. 300–305).

Figure 6.7   Percentage of Total Population, All American Indians and Alaska Natives (AIAN), and 10 Largest Tribes That Speak a Language Other Than English at Home, 2012

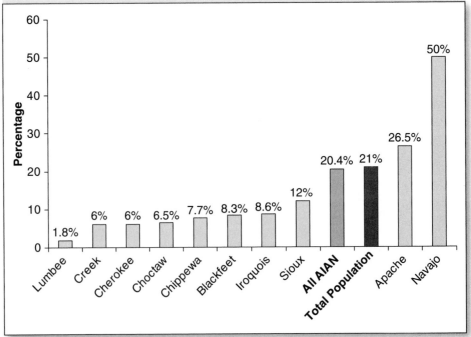

Source: U.S. Census Bureau (2013g).

Traditional culture is retained in other forms besides language. Religions and value systems, political and economic structures, and recreational patterns have all survived the military conquest and the depredations of reservation life, but each pattern has been altered by contact with the dominant group. Cornell (1987), for example, argues that the strong orientation to the group rather than the individual is being significantly affected by the "American dream" of personal material success.

The tendency to filter the impact of the larger society through continuing vital American Indian culture is also illustrated by the Native American Church. The Native American Church is an important American Indian religion, with more than 100 congregations across the nation.

This religion combines elements from both cultures, and church services freely mix Christian imagery and the Bible with attempts to seek personal visions by using peyote, a hallucinogenic drug. The latter practice is consistent with the spiritual and religious traditions of many tribes but clashes sharply with the laws and norms of the larger society. The difference in traditions has generated many skirmishes with the courts, and as recently as 2004 the right of the Native American Church to use peyote was upheld by the Supreme Court of Utah ("Utah Supreme Court Rules," 2004).

American Indians have been more successful than African Americans in preserving their traditional cultures, a pattern that is partly explained by the differences in the relationship between each minority group and the dominant group. African Americans were exploited for labor, whereas the competition with American Indians involved land. African cultures could not easily survive because the social structures that transmitted the cultures and gave them meaning were destroyed by slavery and sacrificed to the exigencies of the plantation economy.

In contrast, American Indians confronted the dominant group as tribal units, intact and whole. The tribes maintained integrity throughout the wars and throughout the reservation period. Tribal culture was attacked and denigrated during the reservation era, but the basic social unit that sustained the culture survived, albeit in altered form. The fact that American Indians were placed on separate reservations, isolated from one another and the "contaminating" effects of everyday contact with the larger society, also supported the preservation of traditional languages and culture (Cornell, 1990).

The vitality of Indian cultures may have increased in the current atmosphere of greater tolerance and support for pluralism in the larger society, combined with increased autonomy and lower government regulation on the reservations. However, a number of social forces are working against pluralism and the continuing survival of tribal cultures. Pan-tribalism may threaten the integrity of individual tribal cultures as it represents American Indian grievances and concerns to the larger society. Opportunities for jobs, education, and higher incomes draw American Indians to more developed urban areas and will continue to do so as long as the reservations are underdeveloped. Many aspects of the tribal cultures can be fully expressed and practiced only with other tribal members on the reservations. Thus, many American Indians must make a choice between "Indian-ness" on the reservation and "success" in the city. The younger, more educated American Indians will be most likely to confront this choice, and the future vitality of traditional American Indian cultures and languages will hinge on which option they choose.

Secondary Structural Assimilation

This section assesses the degree of integration of American Indians into the various institutions of public life, following the general outlines of the parallel section in Chapter 5.

Residential Patterns. Since the Indian Removal Act of 1830 (see Chapter 3), American Indians have been concentrated in the western two thirds of the nation, as illustrated in Figure 6.8, although some pockets of population still can be found in the East. The states with the largest concentrations of American Indians—California, Oklahoma, and Arizona—together include about 30% of all American Indians. As Figure 6.8 illustrates, most U.S. counties have few American Indian residents. The population is concentrated in eastern Oklahoma, the upper Midwest, and the Southwest (Norris et al., 2012, p. 8).

Since American Indians are such a small, rural group, it is difficult to assess the overall level of residential segregation. An earlier study using 2000 census data found that they were less segregated than African Americans and that the levels of residential segregation had declined since 1980 (Iceland, Weinberg, & Steinmetz, 2002, p. 23). More detailed data from the 2000 census for the 10 metropolitan areas with the highest numbers of Native American residents show that residential segregation was "extremely high" (dissimilarity index at or above 60) in four of the cities (New York, Phoenix, Albuquerque, and Chicago) but lower than the levels of black–white segregation. Also, a couple of the cities (Oklahoma City and Tulsa) had low scores, or a dissimilarity index at or below 30 (Social Science Data Analysis Network, n.d.).

What can we conclude? It seems that residential segregation for American Indians is lower than it is for African Americans. However, it is difficult to come to firm conclusions because of the small size of the group and the fact that 30% of American Indians live on rural reservations, where the levels of isolation and racial segregation are quite high.

School Integration and Educational Attainment. As a result of the combined efforts of missionaries and federal agencies, American Indians have had a long but not necessarily productive acquaintance with Western education. Until the past few decades, schools for American Indians were primarily focused on "Westernizing" children, not so much on educating them.

For many tribes, the percentage of high school graduates has increased in the recent past, but American Indians' graduation rates as a whole are still somewhat below national rates and the rates of non-Hispanic whites, as shown in Figure 6.9. The differences in schooling are especially important because the lower levels of educational attainment limit mobility and job opportunities in the postindustrial job market.

One positive development for the education of American Indians is the rapid increase in tribally controlled colleges. There are now 37 tribal colleges: All offer 2-year

Figure 6.8 Percentage of County Population Self-Identifying as American Indian or Alaska Native (AIAN), Alone or in Combination, 2010

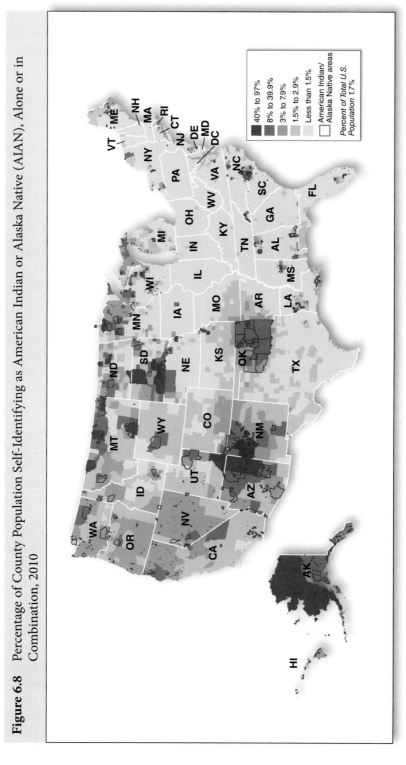

40% to 97%
8% to 39.9%
3% to 7.9%
1.5% to 2.9%
Less than 1.5%
American Indian/
Alaska Native areas
*Percent of Total U.S.
Population 1.7%*

Sources: Primary source: U.S. Census Bureau, 2010 Census Redistricting Data (Public Law 94-171) Summary File, Table P1. Secondary source: Norris, Vines, and Hoeffel, 2012.

Figure 6.9 Educational Attainment for Non-Hispanic Whites, All American Indians (AIAN), and 10 Largest Tribes, 2012

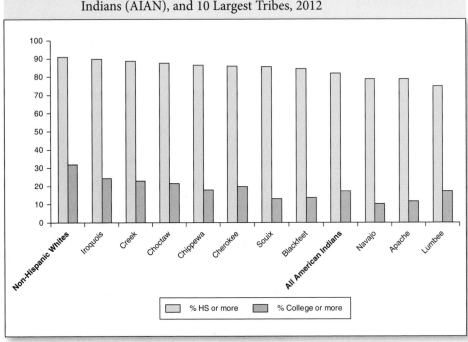

Source: U.S. Census Bureau (2013a).

degrees, six offer 4-year degrees, and two offer master's degrees. These institutions are located on or near reservations; some have been constructed with funds generated in the gaming industry. They are designed to be more sensitive to the educational and cultural needs of the group, and tribal college graduates who transfer to 4-year colleges are more likely to graduate than are other American Indian students (Pego, 1998; see also His Horse Is Thunder, Anderson, & Miller, 2013).

An earlier study found that American Indian school children were less segregated than African American school children in the 2005–2006 school year, but that the levels of racial isolation might be increasing (Fry, 2007). Again, it is difficult to assess trends because of the small size of the group and their concentration in rural areas.

Political Power. The ability of American Indians to exert power as a voting bloc or to otherwise directly affect the political structure is very limited by group size; they are a tiny percentage of the electorate. Furthermore, their political power is limited by their lower average levels of education, language differences, lack of economic resources, and small differences within and between tribes and reservations. The number of American Indians holding elected office is minuscule, far less than 1% (Pollard & O'Hare, 1999). In 1992, however, Ben Nighthorse Campbell, of Colorado, a member of the Northern Cheyenne tribe, was elected to the U.S. Senate and served until 2005.

Jobs and Income. Some of the most severe challenges facing American Indians relate to work and income. The problems are especially evident on the reservations, where jobs traditionally have been scarce and affluence rare. As mentioned previously, the overall unemployment rate for all American Indians is about double the rate for whites. For Indians living on or near reservations, however, the rate is much higher, sometimes rising to 70% to 80% on the smaller, more-isolated reservations (U.S. Census Bureau, 2010).

Nationally, American Indians are underrepresented in the higher-status, more lucrative professions and overrepresented in unskilled labor and service jobs (U.S. Census Bureau, 2010). Like African Americans, American Indians who hold white-collar jobs are more likely than whites to work in lower-income occupations, such as typist or retail salesperson (Ogunwole, 2006, p. 10).

The data in Figure 6.10 show median household income in 2012 for non-Hispanic whites, all American Indians and Alaska Natives, and the 10 largest tribes. Median household income for American Indians and Alaska Natives is about 66% of that of non-Hispanic whites. There is a good deal of variability among the 10 largest tribes, but again, none approach the incomes of non-Hispanic whites.

These income statistics reflect lower levels of education as well as the interlocking forces of past discrimination and lack of development on many reservations. The rural isolation of much of the population and their distance from the more urbanized centers of economic growth limit possibilities for improvement and raise the likelihood that many reservations will remain the rural counterparts to urban underclass ghettos.

Figure 6.11 supplements the information in Figure 6.10 by displaying the distribution of income for American Indians and Alaska Natives (AIAN) compared with that of non-Hispanic whites. This type of graph was introduced in the chapter on African Americans and its format is similar to the format of Figure 5.14. In both graphs, the pattern of income inequality is immediately obvious. Starting at the bottom, we see that American Indians and Alaska Natives are overrepresented in the lowest income groups, as were African Americans. For example, about 12% of American Indians and Alaska Natives have incomes less than $10,000—this is double the percentage for whites (6%) in this range.

Moving up the figure through the lower- and middle-income brackets, we see that American Indian and Alaska Native households continue to be overrepresented. There is a notable clustering of both groups in the $50,000 to $100,000 categories, but it is whites who are overrepresented at these higher-income levels: almost a third of white households compared with only 26% of AIAN households are in these categories. The income differences between the groups are especially obvious at the top of the figure. More than 22% of white households versus 12% of American Indian and Alaska Native households are in the top three income categories. Figure 6.11 also shows the median household income for both groups in 2010, and the difference of more than $16,000 further illustrates the lower socioeconomic level of American Indians.

Finally, Figure 6.12 shows the poverty levels for non-Hispanic whites, all American Indians, and the 10 largest tribes. The poverty rate for all American Indian families is almost triple the rate for non-Hispanic whites, and 6 of the 10 largest tribes have an even higher percentage of families living in poverty. The poverty rates for children show

Figure 6.10   Median Household Income for Non-Hispanic Whites, All American Indians (AIAN), and 10 Largest Tribes, 2012

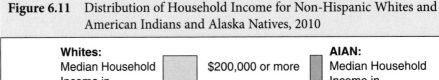

Source: U.S. Census Bureau (2013a).

Figure 6.11   Distribution of Household Income for Non-Hispanic Whites and American Indians and Alaska Natives, 2010

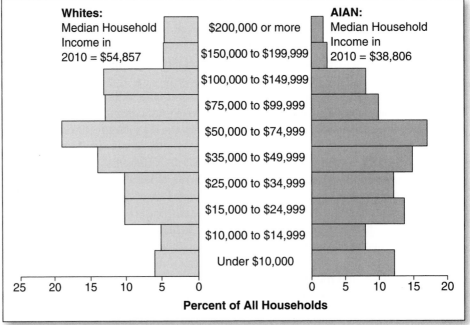

Source: U.S. Census Bureau (2013g).

Figure 6.12   Families and Children in Poverty for Non-Hispanic Whites, American Indians and Alaska Natives (AIAN), and 10 Largest Tribes, 2012

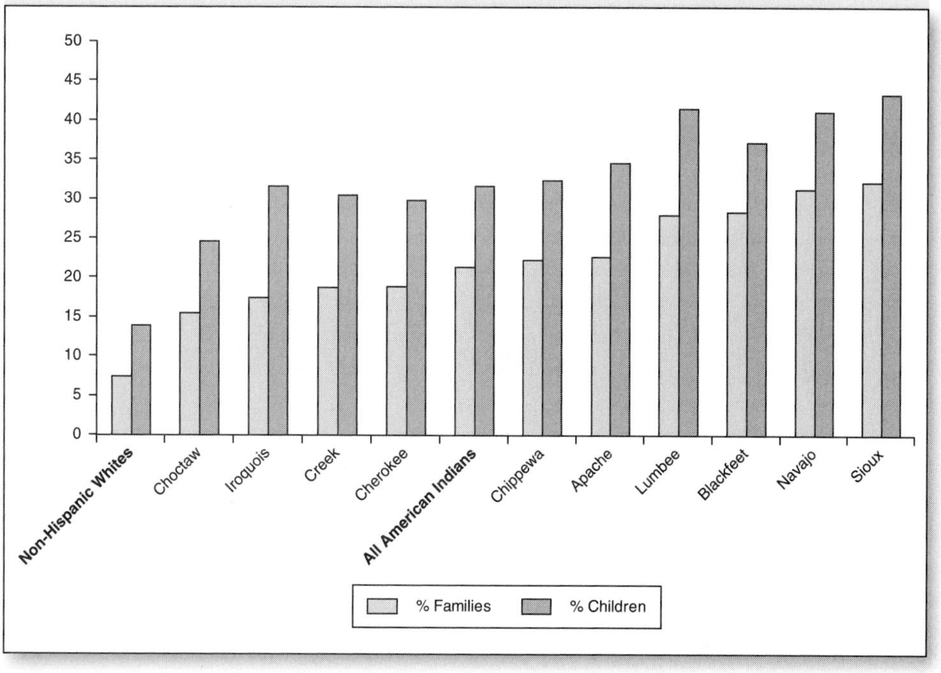

Source: U.S. Census Bureau (2013a).

a similar pattern, with very high rates for the Lumbee, Navajo, and Sioux. As a whole, this information on income and poverty shows that despite the progress American Indians have made over the past several decades, a sizable socioeconomic gap persists.

Primary Structural Assimilation

Rates of out-marriage for American Indians are quite high compared with those of other groups, as displayed in Table 6.4. While the overwhelming majority of whites were married to other whites in both years, a little more than 40% of American Indians had marriage partners within the group. This pattern is partly the result of the small size of the group. As less than 1% of the total population, American Indians are numerically unlikely to find dating and marriage partners within their own group, especially in those regions of the country and urban areas where the group is small in size. For example, an earlier study found that in New England, which has the lowest relative percentage of American Indians of any region, more than 90% of Indian marriages were to partners outside the group. But even in the mountain states, which have a greater number of American Indians who are also highly concentrated on reservations, only about 40% of Indian marriages involved partners outside the group (Snipp, 1989, pp. 156–159). Also, the social and legal barriers to Indian–white intermarriages have been comparatively weak (Qian & Lichter, 2011).

Table 6.4 Percentage Married to a Person of the Same Race, 1980 and 2008

Year	Whites		Native Americans	
	Men	Women	Men	Women
1980	96%	95%	41%	43%
2008	93%	92%	43%	42%

Source: Qian, Zhenchao and Lichter, Daniel. "Changing Patterns of Interracial Marriage in a Multiracial Society." *Journal of Marriage and Family*, 75:1065–1084. Copyright © 2011 National Council on Family Relations. Reprinted with permission.

QUESTIONS FOR REFLECTION

11. This section examined a variety of dimensions of acculturation and integration for American Indians. Which is most important? Why?

12. In which of these areas has there been the most progress over the past 50 years? Explain.

Comparing Minority Groups

Comparing the experiences of American Indians with those of other groups will further our understanding of the complexities of dominant–minority relationships and permit us to test the explanatory power of the concepts and theories that are central to this text. No two minority groups have had the same experiences, and our concepts and theories should help us understand the differences and the similarities. We will make it a point to compare groups in each of the chapters in this part of the text. We begin by comparing American Indians with African Americans.

First, note the differences in the stereotypes attached to the two groups during the early years of European colonization. While Indians were seen as cruel savages, African Americans under slavery were seen as lazy, irresponsible, and in need of constant supervision. The two stereotypes are consistent with the outcomes of the contact period. The supposed irresponsibility of blacks under slavery helped justify their subordinate, highly controlled status, and the alleged savagery of American Indians helped to justify their near extermination by white society.

Second, both American Indians and African Americans were colonized minority groups, but their contact situations were governed by very different dynamics (competition for labor vs. land) and a very different dominant group agenda (the capture and control of a large, powerless workforce vs. the elimination of a military threat). These differing contact situations shaped subsequent relationships with the dominant group and the place of the groups in the larger society.

For example, consider the situations of the two groups a century ago. At that time, the most visible enemy for African Americans was de jure segregation, the elaborate system of repression in the South that controlled them politically, economically, and socially (see Chapters 4 and 5). In particular, the southern system of agriculture needed the black population—but only as a powerless, cheap workforce. The goals of African Americans centered on assimilation, equality, and dismantling this oppressive system.

American Indians, in contrast, were not viewed as a source of labor and, after their military defeat, were far too few in number and too dispersed geographically to constitute a political threat. Thus, there was little need to control them in the same way African Americans were controlled. The primary enemies of the tribes were the reservation system, various agencies of the federal government (especially the BIA), rural isolation, and the continuing attacks on their traditional cultures and lifestyles, which are typical for a colonized minority group. American Indians had a different set of problems, different resources at their disposal, and different goals in mind. They always have been more oriented toward a pluralistic relationship with the larger society and toward preserving what they could of their autonomy, their institutions, and their heritage. African Americans spent much of the 20th century struggling for inclusion and equality; American Indians were fighting to maintain or recover their traditional cultures and social structures. This difference in goals reflects the different histories of the two groups and the different circumstances surrounding their colonization.

Progress and Challenges

What does the future hold for American Indians? Their situation has certainly changed over the past 100 years, but is it "better" or just "different," as is the case for large segments of the African American community? The answer seems to be a little of both, as the group grows in size and improves its status. To reach some conclusions, we will look at several aspects of the situation of American Indians and assess the usefulness of our theoretical models and concepts.

Since the 1960s, the decline of intolerance in society, the growth of pride in ancestry in many groups (e.g., Black Power), and the shift in federal government policy to encourage self-determination have all helped spark a reaffirmation of commitment to tribal cultures and traditions. Like the Black Power movement, the Red Power movement asserted a distinct and positive Indian identity, a claim for the validity of American Indian cultures within the broad framework of the larger society. During the same period, the favorable settlements of treaty claims, the growth in job opportunities, and the growth of the gambling industry have enhanced the flow of resources and benefits to some reservations. In popular culture, American Indians have enjoyed a strong upsurge of popularity and sympathetic depictions. This enhanced popularity accounts for much of the growth in population size as people of mixed ancestry resurrect and reconstruct their Indian ancestors and their own ethnic identities.

Linear or simplistic views of assimilation do not fit the current situation or the past experiences of American Indians very well. Some American Indians are intermarrying with whites and integrating into the larger society; others strive to retain a tribal culture in the midst of an urbanized, industrialized society; and still others labor to use the profits from gaming and other enterprises for the benefit of the tribe as a whole. Members of the group can be found at every degree of acculturation and integration, and the group seems to be moving toward assimilation in some ways and away from it in others.

From the standpoint of the Noel and Blauner hypotheses, we can see that American Indians have struggled with conquest and colonization, experiences made more difficult by the loss of so much of their land and other resources and by the concerted, unrelenting attacks on their culture and language. The legacy of conquest and colonization was poor health and housing, an inadequate and misdirected education system, and slow (or nonexistent) economic development. For most of the 20th century, American Indians were left to survive as best they could on the margins of the larger society, too powerless to establish meaningful pluralism and too colonized to pursue equality.

Today, one key to further progress for some members of this group is economic development on reservation lands and the further strengthening of the tribes as functioning social units. Some tribes do have assets—natural resources, treaty rights, and the gambling industry—that could fuel development. However, they often do not have the expertise or the capital to finance the exploitation of these resources. They must rely, in whole or in part, on non-Indian expertise and white-owned companies and businesses. Thus, non-Indians, rather than the tribes, may be the primary beneficiaries of some forms of development. (This would, of course, be quite consistent with American history.) For those reservations for which gambling is not an option and for those without natural resources, investments in human capital (primarily education) may offer the most compelling direction for future development.

Urban Indians confront the same patterns of discrimination and racism that confront other minority groups of color. Members of the group with lower levels of education and job skills face the prospect of becoming a part of a permanent urban underclass. More educated and more skilled American Indians share with African Americans the prospect of a middle-class lifestyle that is more tenuous compared with comparable segments of the dominant group.

The situation of American Indians today is vastly superior to the status of the group a century ago, and this chapter has documented the notable improvements that have occurred since 1990. Given the depressed and desperate conditions of the reservations in the early 20th century, however, it would not take much to show an improvement. American Indians are growing rapidly in numbers and are increasingly diversified by residence, education, and degree of assimilation. Some tribes have made dramatic progress over the past several decades, but enormous problems remain, both on and off the reservations. The challenge for the future, as it was in the past, is to find a course between pluralism and assimilation, pan-tribalism and traditional lifestyles that will balance the issues of quality of life against the importance of retaining an Indian identity.

Main Points

- American Indian and Anglo American cultures are vastly different. These differences have hampered communication and understanding, usually in ways that harmed American Indians or weakened the integrity of their tribal structures.
- At the beginning of the 20th century, American Indians faced the paternalistic reservation system, poverty and powerlessness, rural isolation and marginalization, and the Bureau of Indian Affairs. American Indians began to urbanize rapidly in the 1950s but are still less urbanized than is the population as a whole. They are the least urbanized American minority group.
- The Red Power movement rose to prominence in the 1960s and had some successes but was often simply ignored. The Red Power movement was partly assimilationist even though it pursued pluralistic goals and greater autonomy for the tribes.
- Current conflicts between American Indians and the dominant group center on control of natural resources, preservation of treaty rights, and treaties that have been broken in the past. The gaming industry offers another possible source of development (and conflict).
- Anti-Indian prejudice seems to have shifted to more modern forms. Institutional discrimination and access to education and employment remain major problems confronting American Indians.
- American Indians have preserved much of their traditional culture, although in altered form. The secondary structural assimilation of American Indians remains relatively low, despite recent improvements in quality of life for many tribes. Primary structural assimilation is comparatively high.
- Over the course of the past 100 years, American Indians have struggled from a position of powerlessness and isolation. Today, the group faces an array of problems similar to those faced by all American colonized minority groups of color, as Indians try to find ways to raise their quality of life and continue their commitment to their tribes and to an Indian identity.

APPLYING CONCEPTS

How much do you and Americans in general know about Native Americans? Here is a true/false quiz that tests your knowledge. Some items can be answered from information presented in this chapter, but others test your knowledge in general. How well do you think most Americans would do on this quiz? Why?

1. Native Americans have their college expenses paid for by their tribe.
2. Pocahontas was a real American Indian princess.
3. Native Americans scalped their enemies.
4. The term *powwow* is a derogatory, stereotypical term used to describe negotiating sessions between Indians and whites.
5. Native Americans practiced slavery.
6. Native Americans use the drug peyote in religious ceremonies.
7. American Indians are getting rich from casinos.
8. Anyone with an American Indian ancestor is automatically a member of that ancestor's tribe.
9. American Indians were always considered U.S. citizens.
10. American Indian tribes are sovereign nations.

SEE THE ANSWERS AT THE END OF THIS SECTION.

Review Questions

1. What were the most important cultural differences between American Indian tribes and the dominant society? How did these affect relations between the two groups?

2. Compare and contrast the effects of paternalism and coercive acculturation on American Indians after the end of the contact period with those of African Americans under slavery. What similarities and differences existed in the two situations? Which system was more oppressive and controlling? How? How did these different situations shape the futures of the groups?

3. How did federal Indian policy change over the course of the 20th century? What effects did these changes have on the tribes? Which were more beneficial? Why? What was the role of the Indian protest movement in shaping these policies?

4. What options do American Indians have for improving their position in the larger society and developing their reservations? Which strategies seem to have the most promise? Which seem less effective? Why?

5. Compare and contrast the contact situations of American Indians, African Americans, and Australian Aborigines. What are the most crucial differences in the situations? What implications did these differences have for the development of each group's situation after the initial contact situation?

6. Characterize the present situation of American Indians in terms of acculturation and integration. How do they compare with African Americans? What factors in the experiences of the two groups might help explain contemporary differences?

7. How does gender impact the experiences of American Indians? How do these compare with the gendered experiences of African Americans?

8. Given the ideas presented in this chapter, speculate about the future of American Indians. How likely are American Indian cultures and languages to survive? What are the prospects for achieving equality? Explain both fully.

9. Given their small population size and marginal status, recognition of their situations and problems continues to be a central struggle for American Indians. What are some ways that the group can build a more realistic, informed, and empathetic relationship with the larger society, the federal government, and other authorities? Are there lessons in the experiences of other groups or in the various protest strategies followed in the Red Power movement? What could dominant group members do to facilitate this process?

Internet Activities

1. Watch this TED Talk featuring photographer Aaron Hughey: http://www.ted.com/talks/aaron_huey?language=en. Then answer the following questions as completely as possible:

   - What did you find most interesting or useful about this TED Talk? Would you recommend this talk to your friends? Why or why not? How would you describe it to them?
   - Hughey says that he is *wasichu*, a Lakota word for "non-Indian." Another interpretation means "the one who takes the best meat for himself." Why do you think he mentions this early in the talk? Does this latter interpretation seem fitting? Identify three examples from the talk, the chapter, or other resources to support your answer.

- Hughey asks: "How should you feel about the statistics of today? What is the connection between these images of suffering and the history that I just read to you? And how much of this history do you need to own, even? Is any of this your responsibility today?" How would you answer him?
- Prior to hearing this talk or reading this book, what did you know about Native American history, AIM (the American Indian Movement), Russell Means, Leonard Peltier, the stand-off at Oglala, the mass execution of the Santee Sioux in Minnesota, Wounded Knee, poverty on Native reservations, or any of the other information Hughey presents? What do you make of this awareness (or lack thereof)? What questions does the film raise for you? That is, what do want to know? How can you begin to find it out?
- Hughey ends his talk saying, "The United States continues on a daily basis to violate the terms of the 1851 and 1868 Fort Laramie treaties with the Lakota. The call to action I offer . . . is this: Honor the treaties. Give back the Black Hills." Should the U.S. government give back the Black Hills? Why or why not? What other issues complicate this matter? Find two websites that discuss the issue and use them to further inform your opinion.
- To what degree does prior treatment of Native peoples (including the contact situation) impact their current experiences?
- Find one organization taking action on behalf of Native peoples. What are they doing and how would you evaluate their efforts?

2. Mount Rushmore is a massive carving of four U.S. presidents built on sacred Native land that was taken by the U.S. Government and, eventually, developed into Badlands National Park. Read more about it at http://www.pbs.org/wgbh/americanexperience/films/rushmore/player/. How does it relate to this chapter? Now, read about the making of the Crazy Horse monument at http://www.cnn.com/videos/us/2015/01/08/crazy-horse-memorial-elam-orig.cnn or at other websites. What do you think about this endeavor? What does it represent to you? Why might it be important to build this monument?

3. Watch this (2-minute) video by the National Congress of American Indians (NCAI): http://www.ncai.org/proudtobe. Then, watch this short, satirical clip from *The Daily Show* about the controversy surrounding the name of the Washington Redskins football team: https://www.youtube.com/watch?v=loK2DRBnk24, taking notes about the key points and any connections to this chapter or this book. Then, answer the following questions:

- Are team mascot names (like "Redskins") a "real" issue, or should offended people "just get over it"? What harm is done in using these names? Do such names "impair, disable, and disenfranchise" the Native population and are they "a racial slur," as Stewart's guests suggest? Or, do the names (and images) "honor" Native Americans? If so, what is being honored?
- How might these images reinforce or perpetuate stereotypical images? Based on what you've learned so far, why might that be problematic?
- Who "owns" these images? Who should decide if they are offensive? Team supporters or owners? Politicians? The people being depicted? Who gets to say what is offensive? Why?
- If it's wrong for the Washington DC NFL team to use "Redskins" as their name, is it OK for the University of Notre Dame to use "Fighting Irish"? Why or why not?
- What gender dimensions can you identify in this debate? Is it okay for universities to refer to women's sports teams as "Lady ___"? Why or why not? What does the term *lady* suggest?
- What other mascot names might be problematic and why?

4. For more in-depth understanding of American Indian stereotypes in sport mascots, watch this talk by Smithsonian Indian Museum Director Kevin Gover: http://www.c-span.org/video/?323984-1/american-indian-stereotypes-sports.

5. Use the Internet to learn more about American Indian boarding schools. For example, see http://www .twofrog.com/rezsch.html which has many useful links. Consider looking at photos such as those from http://www.english.illinois.edu/maps/poets/a_f/erdrich/boarding/gallery.htm. What's relevant for you? How do these sites expand on what you've learned in this chapter?

6. Explore at least two of the sections from the exhibit "The Plains Indians: Artists of Earth and Sky" at http://www.metmuseum.org/exhibitions/listings/2015/plains-indians-artists-of-earth-and-sky/about-the-exhibition. Identify three objects or paintings that strike you as relevant or interesting, or that contribute most to your understanding of Native peoples. In a short paragraph for each, explain why they are meaningful to you. If you wish, search the National Museum of the American Indian (http://www.nmai .si.edu/searchcollections/home.aspx) to find objects of interest. Note that you can search for specific artifacts and regions. What objects came from where you live?

7. Use the Internet to find photographs that build on what you've learned. For example, you could research American Indian life during a certain time frame, particular Native American leaders, or current challenges facing Native Americans such as poverty, unemployment, and mountain top removal at sacred sites. One place to start is http://proof.nationalgeographic.com/2014/12/09/in-1867-alexander-gardner-captured-a-native-life-now-lost/. What did you find at this site, how does it relate to the chapter, and why is it relevant or important?

8. Learn about Native American code talkers who were crucial to the U.S. victory in World War I and, especially, in World War II. Go to http://nmai.si.edu/education/codetalkers/ and, if possible, use the Flash version with audio on. Start with the introduction and scroll through the links such as "Protecting the Homelands." Take notes as you go. Then, examine the Boarding School section. What do you make of the irony regarding the United States and its stance on language at different times? Visit other sections of relevance. Be sure to visit the Resource section for its many useful links. You may also wish to watch interviews with code talkers at http://navajocodetalkers.org/. What had you learned about code talkers before now? What do you make of that? What other Native contributions have been important to the United States? Use the Internet to do some research that expands your knowledge and understanding. Write a few paragraphs about what you learned through this activity.

ANSWERS TO APPLYING CONCEPTS

1. False. Many tribes offer scholarships to enrolled members with strong academic qualifications, but the urban legend that all American Indians get a free ride to college is not true.

2. True. Pocahontas was indeed a real person and may have saved the life of English colonist John Smith, as legend has it. She was the daughter of the premier chief of a large confederation of tribes, although the title of "princess" may overstate her status.

3. True, although the custom may have been introduced by Europeans.

4. False. Today, powwows are festivals celebrating American Indian culture and traditions. They are held across the nation.

5. True. Various forms of slavery were widespread, but none in the territory that became the United States involved exploiting a large, powerless workforce, as was true of African American slavery. Also, many runaway slaves escaped to Indian tribes.

6. True. For example, the Native American Church uses peyote as part of its rituals, as explained in this chapter.

7. False. See the relevant sections of this chapter.

8. False. Tribes have specific rules about membership eligibility, and an Indian ancestor is no guarantee of acceptance.

9. False. American Indians were granted citizenship in 1924.

10. False, but tribes have considerable autonomy and the power to govern their own affairs under a variety of laws.

Note: These and many other ideas about American Indians are explored in A. Treuer (2012).

Learning Resources on the Web

⑤SAGE edge™

edge.sagepub.com/healeyds5e

SAGE edge offers a robust online environment featuring an impressive array of free tools and resources for review, study, and further exploration, keeping both instructors and students on the cutting edge of teaching and learning.

SAGE edge for Students provides a personalized approach to help you accomplish your coursework goals in an easy-to-use learning environment.

7

Hispanic Americans: Colonization, Immigration, and Ethnic Enclaves

Graham Avenue in [Brooklyn] was the broadest street I'd ever seen.... Most of these stores were ... run by Jewish people [and there were special restaurants called delis where Jewish people ate].... We didn't go into the delis because, Mami said, they didn't like Puerto Ricans in there. Instead, she took me to eat pizza.

"It's Italian," she said.

"Do Italians like Puerto Ricans?" I asked as I bit into hot cheese and tomato sauce that burned the tip of my tongue.

"They're more like us than Jewish people are," she said, which wasn't an answer.

In Puerto Rico the only foreigners I'd been aware of were Americanos. In two days in Brooklyn I had already encountered Jewish people, and now Italians. There was another group of people Mami had pointed out to me. Morenos [African Americans]. But they weren't foreigners, because they were American. They were black, but they didn't look like Puerto Rican negros. They dressed like Americanos but walked with a jaunty hop that made them look as if they were dancing down the street, only their hips were not as loose as Puerto Rican men's were. According to Mami, they too lived in their own neighborhoods, frequented their own restaurants, and didn't like Puerto Ricans.

"How come?" I wondered, since in Puerto Rico, all of the people I'd ever met were either black or had a black relative somewhere in their family. I would have thought morenos would like us, since so many of us looked like them.

"They think we're taking their jobs."

"Are we?"

"There's enough work in the United States for everybody," Mami said.

—Esmeralda Santiago (1993)

Esmeralda Santiago moved from Puerto Rico to Brooklyn the summer before she began eighth grade. It was the 1950s, well before the surge of newcomers to the United States and New York City that began after the change in immigration policy in 1965. Still, she was overwhelmed with the variety of groups and cultures, cuisines, and languages she had to navigate. Like many Puerto Ricans who move to the mainland, she also had to deal with different ideas about the meaning of race and the importance of skin color.

Puerto Ricans have been U.S. citizens since 1917, but they live in a different cultural world. Just as Santiago was changed by contact with U.S. culture, so Puerto Rican and other Hispanic cultures were influenced. Now, as we shall see in this chapter, a variety of fast-growing and diverse Hispanic American groups are changing and altering Anglo lifestyles. What will American society look like a few decades from now?

Hispanic Americans are more than 16.6% of the total U.S. population, which makes them the nation's largest minority group. (African Americans are about 13% of the population.) The group is concentrated in the West and South (particularly in California, Texas, and Florida) where there have been large Hispanic Americans communities for many years. But, it is also growing rapidly in every region and state (Ennis, Rio-Vargas, & Albert, 2011, p. 6). Communities throughout the nation are, for the first time, hearing Spanish on their streets and finding "exotic" foods—tortillas, salsa, and refried beans—in their grocery stores. America is, as discussed in earlier chapters, being reshaped and remade.

Of course, not all Hispanic American groups are newcomers. Some groups were in North America before the Declaration of Independence was signed, before slavery began, and before European colonists founded Jamestown. Also, Hispanic American groups are diverse and distinct from one another in many ways. These groups connect themselves to a variety of traditions; like the larger society, they are dynamic and changeable, unfinished and evolving. Hispanic Americans share a language and some cultural traits but do not generally think of themselves as a single social entity. Many identify with their national origin groups (e.g., Mexican American) rather than broader, more encompassing labels.

Table 7.1 Size and Growth of All Hispanic Americans and 10 Largest Groups 1990–2010

Country of Origin	1990	2000	2010	Growth (Number of times larger, 1990–2010)	Percentage of Total Population, 2009
Mexico	13,496,000	20,640,711	31,798,258	2.4	10.3%
Puerto Rico*	2,728,000	3,406,178	4,623,716	1.7	1.5%
Cuba	1,044,000	1,241,685	1,785,547	1.7	< 1%
Dominican Republic	520,521	764,945	1,414,703	2.7	< 1%
El Salvador	565,081	655,165	1,648,968	2.9	< 1%
Guatemala	268,779	372,487	1,044,209	3.9	< 1%
Colombia	378,726	470,684	908,734	2.4	< 1%
Honduras	131,066	217,569	633,401	4.8	< 1%
Ecuador	191,198	260,559	564,631	3.0	< 1%
Nicaragua	202,658	177,684	348,202	1.7	< 1%
Total Hispanic	22,355,990	35,305,818	50,477,594	2.3	16.4%
Percentage of U.S. population	9.0%	12.6%	16.4%	—	—
Total U.S. population	248,710,000	281,421,906	308,745,538	1.2	—

Sources: For data for 1990, U.S. Census Bureau (1990); for 2000, U.S. Census Bureau (2000a); for 2010, Ennis, Ríos-Vargas, & Albert (2011, p. 3).

Note: *Living on mainland only.

In this chapter, we look at the development of Hispanic American groups over the past century, examine their contemporary relations with the larger society, and assess their current status. We focus on the three largest Hispanic groups: Mexican Americans, Puerto Ricans, and Cuban Americans. (In Chapter 9, we will cover other, smaller groups in more detail.)

Table 7.1 displays some information on the size and growth of Hispanic Americans and the 10 largest Latino groups from 1990 to 2010. Mexican Americans, the largest single group, are over 10% of the total U.S. population (and almost two thirds of all Hispanic Americans), but the other groups are small. The relative sizes of the 10 largest Latino groups in the United States are displayed in Figure 7.1.

Latino groups are growing rapidly, partly because of their relatively high birth-rates, but mainly because of immigration. The number of Mexican Americans more than doubled between 1990 and 2012, and the Hispanic American population in general is growing almost twice as fast as the national average. This growth is projected to continue well into the century, and Hispanic Americans will become an increasingly important part of life in the United States. Today, 16.4 out of every 100 Americans are Hispanic, but by 2050 this ratio is projected to almost double to more than 30 out of every 100 (see Figure 1.1). One result of these high rates of immigration is that the majority—in some cases the great majority—of many Hispanic groups are first generation or foreign-born as displayed in Figure 7.2.

It is appropriate to discuss Hispanic Americans at this point in the book because they include both colonized and immigrant groups, and in that sense they combine elements of the polar extremes of Blauner's typology of minority groups. We would expect that Hispanic groups that were more colonized in the past to have much in

Figure 7.1 Relative Size of Hispanic American Groups by Origin, 2012

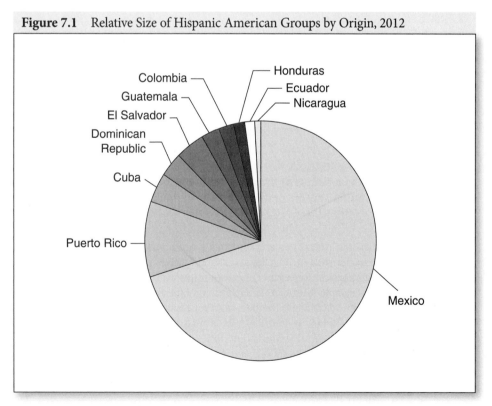

Source: U.S. Census Bureau (2013a).

Figure 7.2 Percentage Foreign Born for Total Population, All Hispanic Americans, and Ten Largest Hispanic American Groups, 2012

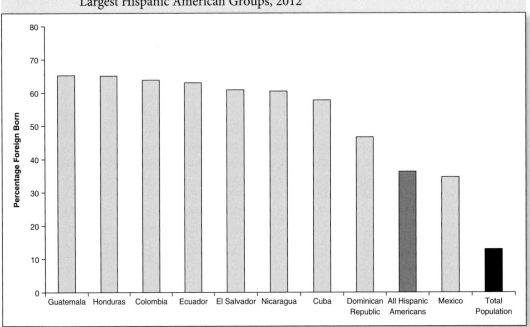

Source: U.S. Census Bureau (2013a).

common with African Americans and Native American today and Hispanic groups whose experiences lie closer to the "immigrant" end of the continuum to have different characteristics and follow different pathways of adaptation. We test these ideas by reviewing the histories of the groups and by analyzing their current status and degree of acculturation and integration.

Two additional introductory comments can be made about Hispanic Americans:

- Hispanic Americans are partly an ethnic minority group (i.e., identified by cultural characteristics such as language) and partly a racial minority group (i.e., identified by their physical appearance). Latinos bring a variety of racial backgrounds to U.S. society. For example, Mexican Americans combine European and Native American ancestries and are identifiable by their physical traits as well as by their culture and language. Puerto Ricans, in contrast, have a mixture of white and black ancestry. The original inhabitants of the island of Puerto Rico, the Arawak and Caribe tribes, were decimated by the Spanish conquest, and the proportion of Native American ancestry is much smaller there than it is in Mexico. Africans were originally brought to the island as slaves, and there has been considerable intermarriage between whites and blacks. The Puerto Rican population today varies greatly in its racial characteristics, combining every conceivable combination of European and African ancestry. Hispanic Americans are often the victims of racial discrimination in the United States. Racial differences often (but not always) overlap with cultural distinctions and reinforce the separation of Hispanic Americans from Anglo American society. Even members of the group who are completely acculturated may still experience discrimination based on their physical appearance.

- As is the case with all American minority groups, labels and group names are important. The term *Hispanic American* is widely applied to this group and might seem neutral and inoffensive to non-Hispanics. In fact, a recent survey shows that only about 25% of Hispanic Americans use *Hispanic* or *Latino* to describe themselves. Most (51%) identify themselves by their family's country of origin and 21% think of themselves simply as "American" (Taylor, Lopez, Martinez, & Velasco, 2012, p. 9). Further, the preferred identity varies widely by primary language, generation, and education of the respondent. For example, almost two thirds of Spanish speakers and first-generation (foreign-born) Latinos prefer to identify themselves in terms of their countries of origin, whereas the "American" designation is most popular with the college educated, the third and higher generations, and English speakers (Taylor et al., 2012, pp. 12–13). At any rate, both the *Hispanic* and *Latino* labels are similar to the term *American Indian,* in that they were invented and applied by the dominant group and may reinforce the mistaken perception that all Spanish-speaking peoples are the same. Also, the term *Hispanic* highlights Spanish heritage and language but does not acknowledge the roots of these groups in African and Native American civilizations. On the other hand, the *Latino* label stresses the common origins of these groups in Latin America and the fact that each culture is a unique blend of diverse traditions. Further, both labels are sometimes mistakenly applied to immigrant groups that bring French, Portuguese, or English traditions (e.g., Haitians, Brazilians, and Jamaicans, respectively). In this chapter, we use the terms *Latino* and *Hispanic* interchangeably.

Mexican Americans

In Chapter 3, we applied the Noel and Blauner hypotheses to this group. Mexicans were conquered and colonized in the 19th century and used as a cheap labor force in agriculture, ranching, mining, railroad construction, and other areas of the dominant group economy in the Southwest. In the competition for control of land and labor, they became a minority group, and the contact situation left them with few power resources with which to pursue their self-interests.

By the dawn of the 20th century, the situation of Mexican Americans resembled that of American Indians in some ways. Both groups were small, numbering about 0.5% of the total population (Cortes, 1980, p. 702). Both differed from the dominant group in culture and language, and both were impoverished, relatively powerless, and isolated in rural areas distant from the centers of industrialization and modernization.

In other ways, Mexican Americans resembled African Americans in the South: They, too, supplied much of the labor power for the agricultural economy of their region and were limited to low-paying occupations and subordinate status in the social structure. All three groups were colonized by Europeans and, at least in the early decades of the 20th century, lacked the resources to end their exploitation and protect their cultural heritages from continual attack by the dominant society (Mirandé, 1985, p. 32).

Some important differences exist between the historic situation of Mexican Americans and those of the other two colonized minority groups. Perhaps the most crucial difference was the proximity of the sovereign nation of Mexico. Population movement across the border was constant, and Mexican culture and the Spanish language were continually rejuvenated, even as they were attacked and disparaged by Anglo American society.

Cultural Patterns

Besides language differences, Mexican American and Anglo American cultures differ in many ways. Whereas the dominant society is largely Protestant, the overwhelming majority of Mexican Americans are Catholic, and the church remains one of the most important institutions in any Mexican American community. Religious practices also vary: Mexican Americans (especially men) are relatively inactive in church attendance, preferring to express their spiritual concerns in more spontaneous, less-routinized ways.

In the past, everyday life among Mexican Americans was often described in terms of the "culture of poverty" (see Chapter 5), an idea originally based on research in several different Hispanic communities (see Lewis, 1959, 1965, 1966). This perspective asserts that Mexican Americans suffer from an unhealthy value system that includes a weak work ethic, fatalism, and other negative attitudes. Today, this characterization is widely regarded as exaggerated or simply mistaken. More recent research shows that the traits associated with the culture of poverty tend to characterize people who are poor and uneducated, rather than any particular racial or ethnic group. In fact, a number of studies show that there is little difference between the value systems of Mexican Americans and other Americans with similar length of residence in the United States, social class, and educational background (e.g., see Buriel, 1993; Moore & Pinderhughes, 1993; Pew Hispanic Center, 2005, p. 20; Valentine & Mosley, 2000).

A recent survey illustrates the similarity in values systems. The survey found that Hispanic Americans were *more* supportive of "hard work" as a recipe for getting ahead—perhaps the central value in the American creed—than was the population in general. About 75% of Hispanic Americans—versus only 58% of the general population—agreed that most people can "get ahead with hard work" (Taylor et al., 2012, pp. 18–19).

Another area of cultural difference involves **machismo**, a value system that stresses men's dominance, honor, virility, and violence. The stereotypes of the dominant group exaggerate the negative aspects of machismo and often fail to recognize that it can also be expressed through being a good provider and a respected father, as well as in other positive ways. In fact, the concern for men's dignity is not unique to Hispanics and can be found in many cultures, including Anglo American cultures, in varying ways (Moore & Pachon, 1985). Compared with Anglo Americans, Mexican Americans tend to place more value on family relations and obligations. Strong family ties can be the basis for support networks and cooperative efforts but can also conflict with the emphasis on individualism and individual success in the dominant culture. For example, strong family ties may inhibit geographical mobility and people's willingness to pursue educational and occupational opportunities distant from their home communities (Moore, 1970, p. 127).

These cultural and language differences have inhibited communication with the dominant group and have served as the basis for excluding Mexican Americans from the larger society. However, they have provided a basis for group cohesion and unity that has sustained common action and protest activity.

Immigration

Although Mexican Americans originated as a colonized minority group, their situation since the early 1900s (and especially since the 1960s) has been largely shaped by immigration. The numbers of legal Mexican immigrants to the United States are shown in Figure 7.3. The fluctuations in the rate of immigration can be explained by conditions in Mexico; the varying demand for labor in the low-paying, unskilled sector of the U.S. economy; broad changes in North America and the world; and changing federal immigration policy. As you will see, competition, one of the key variables in

Figure 7.3 Legal Immigration From Mexico, 1905–2013

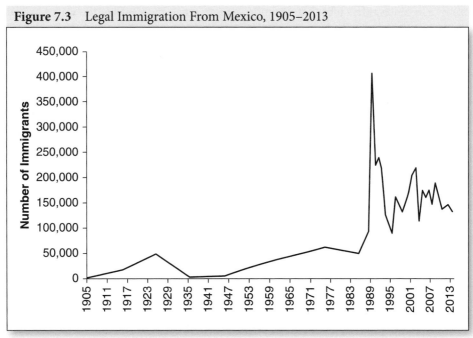

Source: U.S. Department of Homeland Security (2013c).

Notes:

1. The very high number of "immigrants" in the late 1980s and early 1990s was the result of people already in the United States legalizing their status under the provisions of the Immigration Reform and Control Act (IRCA).

2. Values are averages per year during each decade until 1989.

Noel's hypothesis, has shaped the relationships between Mexican immigrants and the larger American society.

Push and Pull. Like the massive wave of immigrants from Europe that arrived between the 1820s and 1920s (see Chapter 2), Mexicans have been pushed from their homeland and toward the United States by a variety of sweeping changes both domestic and global. European immigration was propelled by industrialization, urbanization, and rapid population growth. Mexican immigrants have been motivated by similar broad forces, including continuing industrialization and globalization.

At the heart of the immigration lies a simple fact: the almost 2,000-mile-long border between Mexico and the United States is the longest continuous point of contact between a less developed nation and a more developed nation in the world. For the past century, the United States has developed faster than Mexico, moving from an industrial to a postindustrial society and sustaining a substantially higher standard of living. The continuing wage gap between the two nations has made even menial work in the North attractive to millions of Mexicans (and other Central and South Americans). Mexico has a large number of people who need work, and the United States offers jobs that pay more—often much more—than the wages available south of the border. Today, roughly 10% of the Mexican population lives in the United States. Just as the air flows from high to low pressure, people move from areas of lower to higher economic opportunities. The flow is not continuous, however, and has been affected by conditions in both the sending and receiving nations.

Conditions in Mexico, Fluctuating Demand for Labor, and Federal Immigration Policy. Generally, for the past 100 years, Mexico has served as a reserve pool of cheap labor for the benefit of U.S. businesses, agricultural interests, and other groups, and the volume of immigration largely reflects changing economic conditions in the United States. Immigration increases with good times in the United States and decreases when times are bad, a pattern reinforced by the policies and actions of the federal government. The most important events in the complex history of Mexican immigration to the United States are presented in Table 7.2, along with some comments regarding the nature of each event and its effects.

Prior to the early 1900s, the volume of immigration was generally low and largely unregulated. People crossed the border—in both directions—as the need arose, informally and without restriction. The volume of immigration and concern over controlling the border began to rise with the increase of political and economic turmoil in Mexico in the early decades of the 20th century, but still remained a comparative trickle.

Immigration increased in the 1920s, when federal legislation curtailed the flow of cheap labor from Europe, and then decreased in the 1930s, when hard times came to the United States (and the world) during the Great Depression. Many Mexicans in the United States returned home during that decade, sometimes voluntarily, often by force. As competition for jobs increased, efforts began to expel Mexican laborers, just as the Noel hypothesis would predict.

Table 7.2   Significant Dates in Mexican Immigration

Dates	Event	Result	Effect on Immigration from Mexico
1910	Mexican Revolution	Political turmoil and unrest in Mexico.	Increased.
Early 20th century	Mexican industrialization	Many groups (especially rural peasants) displaced.	Increased.
1920s	Passage of National Origins Act of 1924	Decreased immigration from Europe.	Increased.
1930s	Great Depression	Decreased demand for labor and increased competition for jobs leads to repatriation campaign.	Decreased, many return to Mexico.
1940s	World War II	Increased demand for labor leads to Bracero Guest Worker Program.	Increased.
1950s	Concern over illegal immigrants	Operation Wetback.	Decreased, many return to Mexico.
1965	Repeal of National Origins Act	New immigration policy gives high priority to close family of citizens.	Increased.
1986	IRCA	Illegal immigrants given opportunity to legalize status.	Many undocumented immigrants gain legal status.
1994	NAFTA	Many groups in Mexico (especially rural peasants) displaced.	Increased.
2007	Recession in the United States	Widespread unemployment in the United States, job supply shrinks.	Decreased.

The federal government instituted a **repatriation** campaign aimed specifically at deporting illegal Mexican immigrants. In many localities, repatriation was pursued with great zeal, and the campaign intimidated many legal immigrants and native-born Mexican Americans into moving to Mexico. The result was that the Mexican American population of the United States declined by an estimated 40% during the 1930s (Cortes, 1980, p. 711).

When the Depression ended and U.S. society began to mobilize for World War II, federal policy about immigrants from Mexico changed once more as employers again turned to Mexico for workers. In 1942, the Bracero Program was initiated to permit contract laborers, usually employed in agriculture and other areas requiring unskilled labor, to work in the United States for a limited time. When their contracts expired, the workers were required to return to Mexico.

The Bracero Program continued for several decades after the war and was a crucial source of labor for the American economy. In 1960 alone, **braceros** supplied 26% of the nation's seasonal farm labor (Cortes, 1980, p. 703). The program generated millions of dollars of profit for growers and other employers, because they were paying braceros much less than they would have paid American workers (Amott & Matthaei, 1991, pp. 79–80).

At the same time that the Bracero Program permitted immigration from Mexico, other programs and agencies worked to deport undocumented (or illegal) immigrants, large numbers of whom entered the United States with the braceros. Government efforts reached a peak in the early 1950s with **Operation Wetback**, a program under which federal authorities deported almost 4 million Mexicans (Grebler, Moore, & Guzman, 1970, p. 521). During Operation Wetback, raids on Mexican American homes and businesses were common, and authorities often ignored their civil and legal rights. In an untold number of cases, U.S. citizens of Mexican descent were deported along with illegal immigrants. These violations of civil and legal rights have been a continuing grievance of Mexican Americans (and other Latinos) for decades (Mirandé, 1985, pp. 70–90).

In 1965, the overtly racist national immigration policy incorporated in the 1924 National Origins Act (see Chapter 2) was replaced by a new policy that gave a high priority to immigrants who were family and kin of U.S. citizens. The immediate family (parents, spouses, and children) of U.S. citizens could enter without numerical restriction. Some numerical restrictions were placed on the number of immigrants from each sending country, but about 80% of these restricted visas were reserved for other close relatives of citizens. The remaining 20% of the visas went to people who had skills needed in the labor force (Bouvier & Gardner, 1986, pp. 13–15, 41; Rumbaut, 1991, p. 215).

Immigrants have always tended to move along chains of kinship and other social relationships, and the new policy reinforced those tendencies. The social networks connecting Latin America with the United States expanded, and the rate of immigration from Mexico increased sharply after 1965 (see Figure 7.3) as immigrants became citizens and sent for family members.

Most of the Mexican immigrants, legal as well as undocumented, who have arrived since 1965 continue the pattern of seeking work in the low-wage, unskilled sectors of the labor market in the cities and fields of the Southwest. For many, work is seasonal or temporary. When the work ends, they often return to Mexico, commuting across the border as they have done for decades.

In 1986, Congress attempted to deal with illegal immigrants, most of whom were thought to be Mexican, by passing the Immigration Reform and Control Act. This legislation allowed illegal immigrants who had been in the country continuously since 1982 to legalize their status. According to the U.S. Immigration and Naturalization Service (1993, p. 17), about 3 million people—75% of them Mexican— took advantage of this provision, but the program did not slow the volume of illegal immigration. In 1988, at the end of the amnesty application period, there were still almost 3 million undocumented immigrants in the United States. In 2011, the number of undocumented immigrants was estimated at 11.1 million, down from a high of 12 million in 2007 (Pew Hispanic Center, 2013, p. 2).

Recent Immigration From Mexico. Mexican immigration to the United States continues to reflect the difference in level of development and standard of living between the two societies. Mexico remains a more agricultural nation and continues to have a lower standard of living, as measured by average wages, housing quality, health care, or any number of other criteria. To illustrate, the gross national income per capita for Mexico in 2012 was $9,600, 70% higher than in 2002 but still only about a fifth of the comparable figure for the United States. About half of the Mexican population lives in poverty (World Bank, 2013). Opportunities for work are scarce, and many Mexicans are drawn to the opportunities of their affluent northern neighbor. Since the average length of schooling in their homeland is only about 8.5 years, Mexican immigrants have much lower levels of job skills than U.S. citizens and compete for work in the lower levels of the U.S. job structure (United Nations Development Programme, 2013).

The impetus to immigrate was reinforced by the globalization of the Mexican economy. In the past, the Mexican government insulated its economy from foreign competition with a variety of tariffs and barriers. These protections have been abandoned over the past several decades, and Mexico, like many less developed nations, has opened its doors to the world economy. The result has been a flood into Mexico of foreign agricultural products (cheap corn, in particular), manufactured goods, and capital, which, while helpful in some parts of the economy, has disrupted social life and forced many Mexicans, especially the poor and rural dwellers, out of their traditional way of life.

The most significant changes to Mexican society have probably come from the 1994 North American Free Trade Agreement, or NAFTA. As discussed in Chapter 1, this policy united the three nations of North America into a single trading zone. U.S. companies began to move their manufacturing operations to Mexico, attracted by lower wages, less-stringent environmental regulations, and weak labor unions. They built factories (called *maquiladoras*) along the border and brought many new jobs to the Mexican economy. However, other jobs—no longer protected from global competition—were lost, more than offsetting these gains. Mexican wages actually declined after the implementation of NAFTA, increasing the already large number of Mexicans living in poverty. One analyst estimates that more than 2.5 million families have been driven out of the rural economy because they cannot compete with U.S. and Canadian agribusinesses (Faux, 2004).

Thus, globalization in general and NAFTA in particular have reinforced the long-term relationship between the two nations. Mexico, like other nations of the less developed "South," continues to produce a supply of unskilled, less educated workers, while the United States, like other nations of the more developed and industrialized "North", provides a seemingly insatiable demand for cheap labor. Compared with what is available at home, the wages in *el Norte* are quite attractive, even when the jobs are at the margins of the mainstream economy or in the irregular, underground economy (e.g., day laborers paid off the books, illegal sweatshops in the garment industry, and sex work) and even when the journey requires Mexican immigrants to break American laws, pay large sums of money to "coyotes" to guide them across the border, and live in constant fear of raids by *la Migra* (the Border Patrol or other immigration authorities).

The movement of people from Mexico that began in the 1960s and accelerated in the 1990s was the largest immigration from a single nation to the United States in history (Passel, Cohn, & Gonzalez-Barrera, 2012, p. 6). Some 12 million people, about 51% unauthorized, crossed the border in this period.

More recently, the historic trend has reversed. As Figure 7.4 shows, immigration from Mexico has declined dramatically since 2005. The decline is due to multiple factors, including enhanced border enforcement efforts, the growing dangers of crossing illegally, and Mexico's declining birthrate (Passel, Cohn, & Gonzalez-Barrera, 2013, p. 6). Perhaps most central to the declining numbers is the U.S. economic recession and the weak job market. The pull that attracted immigrants in the past has weakened considerably, particularly after the collapse of the housing market in 2007. This relationship suggests that immigration may resume as the U.S. economy recovers.

The Continuing Debate Over Immigration Policy. Immigration has once again become a hotly debated issue in the United States. How many immigrants should be admitted? From which nations? With what skills? Should the relatives of U.S. citizens continue to receive a high priority? And, perhaps the issue that generates the most

Figure 7.4 Number of Legal and Unauthorized Immigrants Arriving Each Year From Mexico, 1991–2010

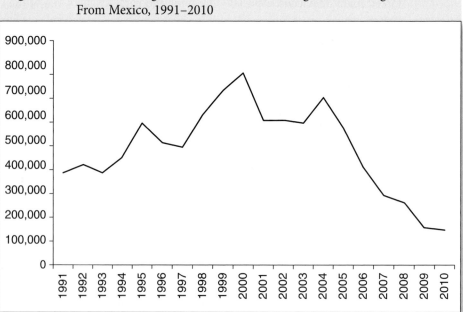

Source: "Annual Immigration from Mexico to the U.S., 1991–2010, Fig. 2.5, p. 17 in Passel, Jeffrey, Cohn, D'Vera, and Gonzalez-Barrera, Ana. 2013a. "Net Migration from Mexico Falls to Zero—and Perhaps Less." Pew Hispanic Center.

passion: What should be done about unauthorized immigrants? Virtually all of these questions—even those phrased in general, abstract terms—are mainly about the large volume of immigration from Mexico and the porous U.S. southern border.

The federal government continues its attempt to reduce the flow by extending the wall along the border with Mexico and beefing up the Border Patrol, with both increased personnel and more high-tech surveillance technology. Still, as we have seen, communities across the nation—not just in the southern border states—are feeling the impact of Mexican immigration and wondering how to respond. Many citizens support extreme measures to close the borders—bigger, thicker walls and even the use of deadly force—while others ponder ways to absorb the newcomers without disrupting or bankrupting local school systems, medical facilities, or housing markets.

The nation is divided on many of the issues related to immigration. Public opinion polls over the past decade show that about 40% to 50% of all Americans would like to lower the volume of immigration, but an almost equal percentage (30% to 40%) favor keeping present level (Morales, 2010). Figure 7.5 shows that—perhaps surprisingly—there has been persistent support for immigration over the past decade, and the large majority of Americans believe that immigration is a "good thing."

Figure 7.5   Attitudes of U.S. Adults Toward Immigration, 2001–2014

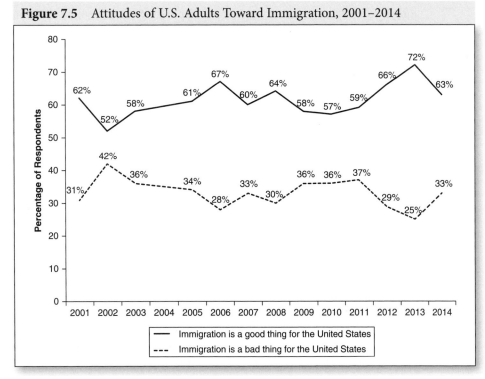

Source: Saad, Lydia. 2013. "Americans More Pro-Immigration Than in the Past." Gallup Polls.

A variety of immigration reforms have been proposed and continue to be debated. One key issue is the treatment of illegal immigrants: Should undocumented people be immediately deported, or should some provision be made for them to legalize their status, as was done in the Immigration Reform and Control Act of 1986? If the latter, should the opportunity to attain legal status be extended to all or only to immigrants who meet certain criteria (e.g., those with steady jobs and clean criminal records)? Many feel that amnesty is unjust because immigrants who entered illegally have broken the law and should be punished. Others point to the economic contributions of these immigrants and the damage to the economy that would result from summary, mass expulsions. Still others worry about the negative impact illegal immigrants may have on the job prospects for the less skilled members of the larger population, including the urban underclass that is disproportionately populated by minority group members. (We address some of these issues later in Chapters 8 and 9.)

Immigration, Colonization, and Intergroup Competition. We focus on three points about Mexican immigration to the United States. First, the flow of population from Mexico was and is stimulated and sustained by powerful political and economic interests in the United States. Systems of recruitment and networks of communication and transportation have been established to routinize the flow of immigrants and to provide a predictable labor source that benefits U.S. employers such as those in agriculture. This movement of people back and forth across the border was well established long before current efforts to regulate it. Depending on U.S. policy, this immigration is sometimes legal and encouraged and sometimes illegal and discouraged. Regardless of the label, it has been steadily flowing for decades in response to opportunities for work in the North (Portes, 1990, pp. 160–163).

Second, Mexican immigrants enter a social system in which the group's colonized status has already been established. The paternalistic traditions and racist systems that were formed in the 19th century shaped the positions that were open to Mexican immigrants in the 20th century. Mexican Americans continued to be treated as a colonized group despite the streams of new arrivals, and the history of the group in the 20th century closely parallels those of African Americans and American Indians. Thus, Mexican Americans might be thought of as a colonized minority group that happens to have a large number of immigrants or, alternatively, as an immigrant group that incorporates a strong tradition of colonization.

Third, this brief review of the twisting history of U.S. policy on Mexican immigration should remind us that prejudice, racism, and discrimination increases as competition and the sense of threat between groups increases. The qualities that make Mexican labor attractive to employers have caused bitter resentment among segments of the Anglo population that feel that "their" jobs and financial security are threatened. Often caught in the middle, Mexican immigrants and Mexican Americans have not had the resources to avoid exploitation by employers or rejection and discrimination by others. The ebb and flow of the efforts to regulate immigration (and sometimes even deport U.S. citizens of Mexican descent) can be understood in terms of competition, differentials in power, and prejudice.

QUESTIONS FOR REFLECTION

1. How do Mexican American and Anglo cultures vary? How have these differences shaped relations between the groups?

2. Why has the volume of immigration from Mexico to the United States fluctuated?

Developments in the United States

As the flow of immigration from Mexico fluctuated with the need for labor, Mexican Americans struggled to improve their status. In the early decades of the 20th century, like other colonized minority groups, they faced a system of repression and control in which they were accorded few rights and had little political power.

Continuing Colonization. Early in the 20th century, Mexican Americans were largely limited to less desirable, low-wage jobs. Split labor markets, in which Mexican Americans are paid less than Anglos for the same jobs, have been common. The workforce often has been further split by gender, with Mexican American women assigned to the worst jobs and receiving the lowest wages in urban and rural areas (Takaki, 1993, pp. 318–319).

Men's jobs often took them away from their families to work in the mines and fields. In 1930, 45% of all Mexican American men worked in agriculture and 28% worked in unskilled nonagricultural jobs (Cortes, 1980, p. 708). Economic necessity often forced women to enter the job market. In 1930, they were concentrated in farm work (21%), unskilled manufacturing jobs (25%), and domestic and other service work (37%) (Amott & Matthaei, 1991, pp. 76–77). They were typically paid less than both Mexican American men and Anglo women. In addition to their job responsibilities, Mexican American women had to maintain their households and raise their children, often facing these tasks without a partner (Baca Zinn & Eitzen, 1990, p. 84).

As the United States industrialized and urbanized during the century, employment patterns became more diversified. Mexican Americans found work in manufacturing, construction, transportation, and other sectors of the economy. Some Mexican Americans, especially those of the third generation or later, moved into middle- and upper-level occupations, and some began to move out of the Southwest. Still, Mexican Americans in all regions (especially recent immigrants) tended to be concentrated at the bottom of the occupational ladder. Women increasingly worked outside the home, but their employment was largely limited to agriculture, domestic service, and the garment industry (Amott & Matthaei, 1991, pp. 76–79; Cortes, 1980, p. 708).

Like African Americans in the segregated South, Mexican Americans were excluded by laws and customs from the institutions of the larger society for much of the 20th century. There were separate (and unequal) school systems for Mexican American children, and in many communities Mexican Americans were disenfranchised and accorded few legal or civil rights. There were "whites only" primary elections modeled after the Jim Crow system, and residential segregation was widespread. The police and the court system generally abetted or ignored the rampant discrimination against the Mexican American community, and discrimination in the criminal justice system and civil rights violations have been continual grievances of Mexican Americans throughout the century.

Protest and Resistance. Like all minority groups, Mexican Americans have attempted to improve their collective position whenever possible. The beginnings of organized resistance and protest stretch back to the original contact period in the 19th century, when protest was usually organized on a local level. Regional and national organizations made their appearance in the 20th century (Cortes, 1980, p. 709).

Like those of African Americans, Mexican Americans' early protest organizations were integrationist and reflected the assimilationist values of the larger society. For example, one of the earlier and more significant groups was the League of United Latin American Citizens (LULAC), founded in Texas in 1929. LULAC promoted Americanization and greater educational opportunities for Mexican Americans and worked to expand civil and political rights for Mexican Americans. LULAC fought numerous court battles against discrimination and racial segregation (Moore, 1970, pp. 143–145).

The workplace has been a particularly conflictual arena for Mexican Americans. Split labor market situations increased anti–Mexican American prejudice; some labor unions tried to exclude Mexican immigrants to the United States, along with immigrants from Asia and southern and eastern Europe (Grebler et al., 1970, pp. 90–93).

At the same time, Mexican Americans played important leadership roles in the labor movement. Since early in the century, Mexican Americans have been involved in union organizing, particularly in agriculture and mining. When excluded by Anglo labor unions, they often formed their own unions to work for the improvement of working conditions. As the 20th century progressed, the number and variety of groups pursuing the Mexican American cause increased. During World War II, Mexican Americans served in the armed forces. As with other minority groups, this experience increased their impatience with the constraints on their freedoms and opportunities in the United States. After the war ended, new Mexican American organizations were founded, including the Community Service Organization in Los Angeles and the American GI Forum in Texas. Compared with older organizations such as LULAC, the new groups were less concerned with assimilation per se, addressed a broad range of community problems, and attempted to increase Mexican American political power (Grebler et al., 1970, pp. 543–545).

Chicanismo. The 1960s were a time of intense activism and militancy for Mexican Americans. A protest movement guided by an ideology called **Chicanismo** began at about the same time as the Black Power and Red Power movements. Chicanismo encompassed a variety of organizations and ideas, united by a heightened militancy and impatience with the racism of the larger society and strongly stated demands for justice, fairness, and equal rights. The movement questioned the value of assimilation and sought to increase awareness of the continuing exploitation of Mexican Americans; it adapted many of the tactics and strategies (marches, rallies, voter registration drives, etc.) of the civil rights movement of the 1960s.

Chicanismo is somewhat similar to the Black Power ideology (see Chapter 5) in that it is partly a reaction to the failure of U.S. society to fulfill the promises of integration and equality. Chicanismo rejected traditional stereotypes of Mexican Americans, proclaimed a powerful and positive group image and heritage, and analyzed the group's past and present situation in American society in terms of victimization, continuing exploitation, and institutional discrimination. The inequalities that separated Mexican Americans from the larger society were seen as the result of deep-rooted, continuing racism and the cumulative effects of decades of exclusion. According to Chicanismo, the solution to these problems lay in group empowerment, increased militancy, and group pride, not in assimilation to a culture that had rationalized and supported the exploitation of Mexican Americans (Acuña, 1988, pp. 307–358; Grebler et al., 1970, p. 544; Moore, 1970, pp. 149–154).

Some of the central thrusts of the 1960s protest movement are captured in the widespread adoption of the term **Chicanos**, which had been a derogatory term, as a group name for Mexican Americans. Other minority groups underwent similar name changes at about the same time. For example, African Americans shifted from *Negro* to *black* as a group designation. These name changes were not merely cosmetic—they marked fundamental shifts in group goals and desired relationships with the larger society. The new names came from the minority groups themselves, not from the dominant group, and they expressed the pluralistic themes of group pride, self-determination, militancy, and increased resistance to exploitation and discrimination.

Organizations and Leaders. The Chicano movement saw the rise of many new groups and leaders; Reies López Tijerina, who formed the Alianza de Mercedes (Alliance of Land Grants) in 1963, was one of the most important. The goal of this group was to correct what Tijerina saw as the unjust, illegal seizure of land from Mexicans during the 19th century. The Alianza was militant and confrontational, and the group seized and occupied federal lands to bring attention to their cause. Tijerina spent several years in jail as a result of his activities, and the movement eventually lost its strength and faded from view in the 1970s.

Another prominent Chicano leader was Rodolfo González, who founded the Crusade for Justice in 1965. The crusade focused on abuses of Mexican American civil and legal rights and worked against discrimination by police and the criminal courts. In a 1969 presentation at a symposium on Chicano liberation, Gonzalez expressed some of the nationalistic themes of Chicanismo and the importance of creating a power base within the group (as opposed to assimilating or integrating):

> Where [whites] have incorporated themselves to keep us from moving into their neighborhoods, we can also incorporate ourselves to keep them from controlling our neighborhoods. We ... have to understand economic revolution. ... We have to understand that liberation comes from self-determination, and to start to use the tools of nationalism to

win over our barrio brothers. . . . We have to understand that we can take over the institutions within our community. We have to create the community of the Mexicano here in order to have any type of power. (Moquin & Van Doren, 1971, pp. 381–382)

A third important leader was José Angel Gutiérrez, organizer of the party La Raza Unida (The People United). La Raza Unida offered alternative candidates and ideas to those of Democrats and Republicans. Its most notable success was in Crystal City, Texas, where, in 1973, it succeeded in electing its entire slate of candidates to local office (Acuña, 1988, pp. 332–451).

Without a doubt, the best-known Chicano leader of the 1960s and 1970s was the late César Chávez, who organized the United Farm Workers, the first union to successfully represent migrant workers. Chávez was as much a labor leader as a leader of the Mexican American community, and he also organized African Americans, Filipinos, and Anglo Americans. Migrant farm workers have few economic or political resources, and the migratory nature of their work isolates them in rural areas and makes them difficult to contact. In the 1960s (and still today), many were undocumented immigrants who spoke little or no English and returned to the cities or to their countries of origin at the end of the season. As a group, farm workers were nearly invisible in the social landscape of the United States in the 1960s, and organizing this group was a demanding task. Chávez's success in this endeavor is one of the more remarkable studies in group protest.

Like Dr. Martin Luther King Jr., Chávez was a disciple of Gandhi and a student of nonviolent direct protest (see Chapter 5). His best-known tactic was the boycott; in 1965, he organized a grape-pickers' strike and a national boycott of grapes. The boycott lasted five years and ended when the growers recognized the United Farm Workers as the legitimate representative of farm workers. Chávez and his organization achieved a major victory, and the agreement provided for significant improvements in the situation of the workers. (For a biography of Chávez, see Levy, 1975.)

Gender and the Chicano Protest Movement. Mexican American women were heavily involved in the Chicano protest movement. Jessie Lopez and Dolores Huerta were central figures in the movement to organize farm workers and worked closely with César Chávez. However, like African American women, Chicano women encountered sexism and gender discrimination within the movement, even as they worked for the benefit of the group as a whole. Activist Sylvia Gonzales described their dilemmas:

Along with her male counterpart, she attended meetings, organized boycotts, did everything asked of her. . . . But, if she [tried to assume leadership roles], she was met with the same questioning of her femininity which the culture dictates when a woman is not self-sacrificing and seeks to fulfill her own needs. . . . The Chicano movement seemed to demand self-actualization for only the male members of the group. (Amott & Matthaei, 1991, p. 83)

Despite these difficulties, Chicano women contributed widely to the movement, for example, by organizing poor communities and working for welfare reform.

Continuing issues include domestic violence, childcare, the criminal victimization of women, and the racial and gender oppression that limits women of all minority groups (Amott & Matthaei, 1991, pp. 82–86; see also Mirandé & Enriquez, 1979, pp. 202–243).

Mexican Americans and Other Minority Groups

Like the Black Power and Red Power movements, Chicanismo began to fade from public view in the 1970s and 1980s. The movement could claim some successes, but perhaps the clearest victory was in raising the awareness of the larger society about the grievances and problems of Mexican Americans. Today, many Chicanos continue to face poverty, powerlessness, and exploitation as a cheap agricultural labor force. The less educated, urbanized segments of the group share the prospect of becoming a permanent urban underclass with other minority groups of color.

Over the course of the 20th century, the ability of Chicanos to pursue their self-interests has been limited by both internal and external forces. Like African Americans, the group has been systematically excluded from the institutions of U.S. society. Continuing immigration from Mexico has increased the size of the group, but these immigrants bring few resources with them that could be directly or immediately translated into economic or political power in the United States.

Unlike immigrants from Europe, who settled in the urban centers of the industrializing East Coast, Mexican Americans tended to work and live in rural areas distant from and marginal to urban centers of industrialization and opportunities for education, skill development, and upward mobility. They were a vitally important source of labor in agriculture and other segments of the economy but only to the extent that they were exploitable and powerless. As Chicanos moved to the cities, they tended to continue their historic role as a colonized, exploited labor force concentrated at the lower end of the stratification system. Thus, the handicaps created by discrimination in the past were reinforced by continuing discrimination and exploitation in the present, perpetuating the cycles of poverty and powerlessness.

At the same time, however, the flow of immigration and the constant movement of people back and forth across the border kept Mexican culture and the Spanish language alive. Unlike African Americans under slavery, Chicanos were not cut off from their homeland and native culture. Mexican American culture was attacked and disparaged, but, unlike African culture, it was not destroyed. Clearly, the traditional model of assimilation—which was based largely on the experiences of European immigrant groups—does not effectively describe the experiences of Mexican Americans. They have experienced less social mobility than European immigrant groups but have maintained their traditional culture and language more completely. Like African Americans, the group is split along lines of social class. Although many Mexican Americans (particularly of the third generation and later) have acculturated and integrated, a large segment of the group continues to fill the same economic role that their ancestors did: an unskilled labor force for the development of the Southwest, augmented with new immigrants at the convenience of U.S. employers. In 2010, more than 16% of employed Mexican Americans—more than double the percentage for non-Hispanic whites—were in the construction and farm sectors of the labor force (U.S. Census Bureau, 2013a). For the less educated and for recent immigrants, cultural and racial differences combine to increase their social visibility, mark them for exploitation, and rationalize their continuing exclusion from the larger society.

QUESTIONS FOR REFLECTION

3. Are Mexican Americans a colonized or immigrant minority group? Both? Neither? Why?

4. Compare Chicanismo with Black Power and Red Power. How and why do these protest movements differ? Describe the key ideas, leaders, and organizations of Mexican American protest.

Puerto Ricans

Puerto Rico became a territory of the United States in 1898 after the defeat of Spain in the Spanish-American War. The island was small and impoverished, and it was difficult for Puerto Ricans to avoid domination by the United States. Thus, the initial contact between Puerto Ricans and U.S. society was made in an atmosphere of war and conquest. By the time Puerto Ricans began to migrate to the mainland in large numbers, their relationship to U.S. society was largely that of a colonized minority group, and they generally retained that status on the mainland.

Migration (Push and Pull) and Employment

At the time of initial contact, the population of Puerto Rico was overwhelmingly rural and supported itself by subsistence farming and by exporting coffee and sugar. As the century wore on, U.S. firms began to invest in and develop the island economy, especially the sugarcane industry. These agricultural endeavors took more and more of the land. Opportunities for economic survival in the rural areas declined, and many people were forced to move into the cities (Portes, 1990, p. 163).

Movement to the mainland began gradually and increased slowly until the 1940s. In 1900, about 2,000 Puerto Ricans lived on the mainland. By World War II, this number had grown to only 70,000, a tiny fraction of the total population. Then, during the 1940s, the number of Puerto Ricans on the mainland increased more than fourfold, to 300,000. During the 1950s, it nearly tripled, to 887,000 (U.S. Commission on Civil Rights, 1976, p. 19).

This massive and sudden population growth was the result of a combination of circumstances. First, Puerto Ricans became citizens of the United States in 1917, so their movements were not impeded by international boundaries or immigration restrictions. Second, unemployment was a major problem on the island. The sugarcane industry continued to displace the rural population, urban unemployment was high, and the population continued to grow. By the 1940s, a considerable number of Puerto

Ricans were available to work off the island and, like Chicanos, could serve as a cheap labor supply for U.S. employers.

Third, Puerto Ricans were pulled to the mainland by the same labor shortages that attracted Mexican immigrants during and after World War II. Whereas the latter responded to job opportunities in the West and Southwest, Puerto Ricans moved to the Northeast. The job profiles of these two groups were similar: both were concentrated in the low-wage, unskilled sector of the job market. However, the Puerto Rican migration began decades after the Mexican migration, at a time when the United States was much more industrialized and urbanized. As a result, Puerto Ricans were more concentrated in urban labor markets than Mexican immigrants (Portes, 1990, p. 164).

In the late 1940s, affordable air travel between San Juan and New York City facilitated movement between the island and the mainland. New York had been the major center of settlement for Puerto Ricans on the mainland even before annexation. A small Puerto Rican community had been established in the city, and, like many other immigrant groups, Puerto Ricans established organizations and networks to ease the transition and help newcomers with housing, jobs, and other issues. Although they eventually dispersed to other regions and cities, Puerto Ricans on the mainland remain centered in New York City. About 53% now reside in the Northeast, with 23% in New York alone (Brown & Patten, 2013d, p. 2).

Economics and jobs were at the heart of the Puerto Rican migration to the mainland that followed the cycle of boom and bust, just as they were for Mexican immigrants. The 1950s, the peak decade for Puerto Rican migration, was a period of rapid U.S. economic growth. Migration was encouraged, and job recruiters traveled to the island to attract workers. By the 1960s, however, the supply of jobs in Puerto Rico expanded appreciably, reducing the average number of migrants from the peak of 41,000 per year in the 1950s to about 20,000 per year. In the 1970s, the U.S. economy faltered, unemployment grew, and the flow of Puerto Rican migration reversed itself, with the number of returnees exceeding the number of migrants in various years (U.S. Commission on Civil Rights, 1976, p. 25). However, movement to the mainland has continued, and in 2011 almost 5 million Puerto Ricans, about 57% of all Puerto Ricans, were living on the mainland (Brown & Patten, 2013d, p. 1).

As the U.S. economy expanded and migration accelerated after World War II, Puerto Ricans moved into a broad range of jobs and locations in society, and the group grew more economically diversified and more regionally dispersed. Still, the bulk of Puerto Ricans remain concentrated in lower-status jobs in the larger cities of the Northeast. Puerto Rican men have often found work as unskilled laborers or in service occupations, particularly in areas where English is not necessary (e.g., janitorial work). The women often have been employed as domestics, hotel maids, or seamstresses for the garment industry in New York City (Portes, 1990, p. 164).

Transitions

Although Puerto Ricans are not "immigrants," the move to the mainland involves a change in culture, including language (Fitzpatrick, 1980, p. 858). Despite nearly a century of political affiliation, Puerto Rican and Anglo cultures differ along many dimensions. Puerto Ricans are overwhelmingly Catholic, but their religious practices and rituals on the mainland are quite different from those on the island. Mainland Catholic parishes often reflect the traditions and practices of other cultures and groups. On the island, "Religious observance reflects the spontaneous and expressive practices of the Spanish and the Italian and not the restrained and well-organized worship of the Irish and Germans" (p. 865). Also, a shortage of Puerto Rican priests and Spanish-speaking clergy exists on the mainland. Although the overwhelming majority of Latinos are Catholic, only about 6% of Catholic priests are Latinos (Olivo & Eldeib, 2013). Thus, members of the group often feel estranged from and poorly served by the Church (Fitzpatrick, 1987, pp. 117–138).

A particularly unsettling cultural difference between the island and the mainland involves skin color and perceptions of race. Puerto Rico has a long history of racial intermarriage. Slavery was less monolithic and total, and the island had no periods of systematic, race-based segregation like the Jim Crow system. Thus, although skin color prejudice still exists in Puerto Rico, it never has been as categorical as on the mainland. On the island, people perceive race as a continuum of possibilities and combinations, not as a simple dichotomy between white and black.

Furthermore, in Puerto Rico, people consider other factors, such as social class, as more important than race as criteria for judging and classifying others. In fact, as we discussed in the Chapter 5 Comparative Focus, social class can affect perceptions of skin color, and people of higher status might be seen as lighter skinned. Coming from this background, Puerto Ricans find the rigid racial thinking of U.S. culture disconcerting and even threatening.

A study of Puerto Rican college students in New York City illustrates this confusion and discomfort. Researchers found dramatic differences between the personal racial identification of the students and their perceptions of how Anglos viewed them. When asked for their racial identification, most students classified themselves as "tan," with one third labeling themselves "white" and only 7% considering themselves "black." When asked how they thought Anglos classified them, none of the students used the "tan" classification. Fifty-eight percent believed they were seen as "white," and 41% believed they were seen as "black" (Rodriguez, 1989, pp. 60–61; see also Rodriguez & Cordero-Guzman, 1992; Vargas-Ramos, 2005).

Another study documented dramatic differences in the terms used by women on the mainland and those in Puerto Rico to express racial identity. The latter identified their racial identities primarily in terms of skin color: black, white, or *trigueña* (a "mixed-race" category with multiple skin tones), while mainland women identified themselves in nonracial terms, such as Hispanic, Latina, Hispanic American, or American. In the view of the researchers, these labels serve to deflect the stigma associated with black racial status on the mainland (Landale & Oropesa, 2002).

In the racially dichotomized U.S. culture, many Puerto Ricans feel they have no clear place. They are genuinely puzzled when they first encounter prejudice and discrimination based on skin color and are uncertain about their own identities and self-image. The racial perceptions of the dominant culture can be threatening to Puerto Ricans to the extent that they are victimized by the same web of discrimination and disadvantage that affects African Americans. There are still clear disadvantages to being classified as black in U.S. society. Institutionalized racial barriers can be extremely formidable, and in the case of Puerto Ricans, they may combine with cultural and linguistic differences to sharply limit opportunities and mobility.

Puerto Ricans and Other Minority Groups

Puerto Ricans arrived in the cities of the Northeast long after the great wave of European immigrants and several decades after African Americans began migrating from the South. They have often competed with other minority groups for housing, jobs, and other resources. In some neighborhoods and occupational areas, a pattern of ethnic succession can be seen in which Puerto Ricans have replaced other groups that have moved out (and sometimes up).

Because of their more recent arrival, Puerto Ricans on the mainland were not subjected to the more repressive paternalistic or rigid competitive systems of race relations such as slavery or Jim Crow. Instead, the subordinate status of the group is manifested in their occupational, residential, and educational profiles and by the institutionalized barriers to upward mobility that they face. Puerto Ricans share many problems with other urban minority groups of color: poverty, failing educational systems, and crime. Like African Americans, Puerto Ricans find their fate to be dependent on the future of the American city, and a large segment of the group is in danger of becoming part of a permanent urban underclass.

Like Mexican Americans, Puerto Ricans on the mainland combine elements of both an immigrant and a colonized minority experience. The movement to the mainland is voluntary in some ways, but in others it is strongly motivated by the transformations in the island economy that resulted from modernization and U.S. domination. Like Chicanos, Puerto Ricans tend to enter the labor force at the bottom of the occupational structure and face similar problems of inequality and marginalization. Also, Puerto Rican culture retains a strong vitality and is continually reinvigorated by the considerable movement back and forth between the island and the mainland.

QUESTIONS FOR REFLECTION

5. Would you say that Puerto Ricans are more an immigrant or colonized minority group? Why or why not?

6. What are some of the key differences between Puerto Rican and Anglo cultures? How have these differences shaped relations between the groups?

Cuban Americans

The contact period for Cuban Americans, as for Puerto Ricans, dates back to the Spanish-American War. At that time, Cuba was a Spanish colony, but it became an independent nation as a result of the war. Despite Cuba's nominal independence, the

United States remained heavily involved in Cuban politics and economics for decades, and U.S. troops actually occupied the island on two different occasions.

The development of a Cuban American minority group bears little resemblance to the experience of either Chicanos or Puerto Ricans. As recently as the 1950s, there had not been much immigration from Cuba to the United States, even during times of labor shortages, and Cuban Americans were a very small group, numbering no more than 50,000 (Perez, 1980, p. 256).

Immigration (Push and Pull)

The conditions for a mass immigration were created in the late 1950s, when a revolution brought Fidel Castro to power in Cuba. Castro's government was decidedly anti-American and began to restructure Cuban society along socialist lines. The middle and upper classes lost political and economic power, and the revolution made it impossible for Cuban capitalists to continue business as usual. Thus, the first Cuban immigrants to the United States tended to come from the more elite classes and included affluent and powerful people who controlled many resources. They were perceived as refugees from Communist persecution (the immigration occurred at the height of the Cold War) and were warmly received by the government and the American public.

The United States was a logical destination for those displaced by the revolution. Cuba is only 90 miles from southern Florida, the climates are similar, and the U.S. government, which was as anti-Castro as Castro was anti-American, welcomed the new arrivals as political refugees fleeing from Communist tyranny.

Prior social, cultural, and business ties also pulled the immigrants in the direction of the United States. Since gaining its independence in 1898, Cuba has been heavily influenced by the U.S. government and by U.S. companies that helped develop the Cuban economy. At the time of Castro's revolution, the Cuban political leadership and the more affluent classes were profoundly Americanized in their attitudes and lifestyles (Portes, 1990, p. 165). Furthermore, many Cuban exiles viewed southern Florida as an ideal spot from which to launch a counterrevolution to oust Castro.

Immigration was considerable for several years. More than 215,000 Cubans arrived between the end of the revolution and 1962, when an escalation of hostile relations resulted in the cutoff of all direct contact between Cuba and the United States. In 1965, an air link was reestablished, and an additional 340,000 Cubans made the journey. When the air connection was terminated in 1973, immigration slowed to a trickle once more.

In 1980, the Cuban government permitted another period of open immigration. Using boats of every shape, size, and degree of seaworthiness, about 124,000 Cubans crossed to Florida. These immigrants are often referred to as the **marielitos**, after the port of Mariel from which many of them departed. This wave of immigrants generated a great deal of controversy in the United States, because the Cuban government used the opportunity to rid itself of a variety of convicted criminals and outcasts. The reception for this group was decidedly less favorable than was the reception for the original wave of Cuban immigrants. Even the established Cuban American community distanced itself from the *marielitos,* who were largely products of the new Cuba, having been born after the revolution, and with whom they lacked kinship or friendship ties (Portes & Shafer, 2006, pp. 16–17).

Regional Concentrations

The overwhelming majority of Cuban immigrants settled in southern Florida, especially in Miami and the surrounding Dade County. Today, Cuban Americans remain one of the most spatially concentrated minority groups in the United States, with 70% of all Cuban Americans residing in Florida (Brown & Patten, 2013b, p. 2). This dense concentration has led to a number of disputes between the Hispanic, Anglo, and African American communities in the area. Issues have centered on language, jobs, and discrimination by the police and other governmental agencies. The conflicts often have been intense, and on more than one occasion have erupted into violence and civil disorder.

Socioeconomic Characteristics

Compared with other streams of immigrants from Latin America, Cubans are, on the average, unusually affluent and well educated. Among the early immigrants of the 1960s were large numbers of professionals, landowners, and businesspeople. In later years, as Cuban society was transformed by the Castro regime, the stream included fewer elites—largely because there were fewer left in Cuba—and more political dissidents and working-class people. Today (as displayed in the figures later in this chapter), Cuban Americans rank higher than other Latino groups on a number of dimensions, a reflection of the educational and economic resources they brought with them from Cuba and the favorable reception they enjoyed in the United States (Portes, 1990, p. 169).

These assets gave Cubans an advantage over Chicanos and Puerto Ricans, but the differences between the three Latino groups run deeper and are more complex than a simple accounting of initial resources would suggest. Cubans adapted to U.S. society in a way that is fundamentally different from the experiences of the other two Latino groups.

The Ethnic Enclave

Most of the minority groups we have discussed to this point have been concentrated in the unskilled, low-wage segments of the economy in which jobs are not secure and not linked to opportunities for upward mobility. Many Cuban Americans have bypassed this sector of the economy and much of the discrimination and limitation associated with it. Like several other groups, such as Jewish Americans, Cuban Americans are an enclave minority (see Chapter 2). An ethnic enclave is a social, economic, and cultural subsociety controlled by the group itself. Located in a specific geographical area or neighborhood inhabited solely or largely by members of the group, the enclave encompasses sufficient economic enterprises and social institutions to permit the group to function as a self-contained entity, largely independent of the surrounding community.

The first wave of Cuban immigrants brought with them considerable human capital and business expertise. Although much of their energy was focused on ousting Castro and returning to Cuba, they generated enough economic activity to sustain restaurants, shops, and other small businesses that catered to the exile community.

As the years passed and the hope of a return to Cuba dimmed, the enclave economy grew. Between 1967 and 1976, the number of Cuban-owned firms in Dade County increased nine-fold, from 919 to about 8,000. Six years later, the number had reached 12,000. Most of these enterprises were small, but some factories employed hundreds of workers (Portes & Rumbaut, 1996, pp. 20–21). By 2001, more than 125,000 Cuban-owned firms existed in the United States and the rate of Cuban-owned firms per 100,000 people was four times greater than the rate for Mexican Americans and 14 times greater than the rate for African Americans (Portes & Shafer, 2006, p. 14).

Cuban-owned firms have become integrated within local economies and increasingly competitive with other firms involved in construction, manufacturing, finance, insurance, real estate, and an array of other activities in the larger society. The growth of economic enterprises has been paralleled by a growth in the number of other types of groups and organizations and in the number and quality of services available (schools, law firms, medical care, funeral parlors, etc.). The enclave has become a largely autonomous community capable of providing for its members from cradle to grave (Logan, Alba, & McNulty, 1994; Peterson, 1995; Portes & Bach, 1985, p. 59).

That the enclave economy is controlled by the group itself is crucial; it separates the ethnic enclave from "the ghetto," or neighborhoods that are impoverished and segregated. In ghettos, members of other groups typically control the local economy; the profits, rents, and other resources flow out of the neighborhood. In the enclave, profits are reinvested in the neighborhood. Group members can avoid the discrimination and limitations imposed by the larger society, and can apply their skills, education, and talents in an atmosphere free from language barriers and prejudice. Those who might wish to venture into business for themselves can use the networks of cooperation and mutual aid for advice, credit, and other forms of assistance. Thus, the ethnic enclave provides a platform from which Cuban Americans can pursue economic success independent of their degree of acculturation or English language ability.

The effectiveness of the ethnic enclave as a pathway for adaptation is illustrated by a study of Cuban and Mexican immigrants, all of whom entered the United States in 1973. At the time of entry, the groups were comparable in levels of skills, education, and English language ability. The groups were interviewed on several different occasions, and although they remained comparable on many variables, there were dramatic differences between the groups that reflected their different positions in the labor market. The majority of the Mexican immigrants were employed in the low-wage job sector. Less than 20% were self-employed or employed by someone of Mexican descent. Conversely, 57% of the Cuban immigrants were self-employed or employed by other Cubans (i.e., in the enclave economy). Among the subjects in the study, self-employed Cubans reported the highest monthly incomes ($1,495), and Cubans otherwise employed in the enclave earned the second-highest monthly incomes ($1,111). The lowest monthly incomes ($880) were earned by Mexican immigrants employed in small, nonenclave firms; many of them worked as unskilled laborers in seasonal, temporary, or otherwise insecure jobs (Portes, 1990, p. 173; see also Portes & Bach, 1985).

A more recent study confirms the advantages that accrue from forming an enclave. Using 2000 census data, Portes and Shafer (2006) compared the incomes of several groups in the Miami–Fort Lauderdale metropolitan area, including the original Cuban immigrants (who founded the enclave), their children (the second generation), Cuban immigrants who arrived after 1980 (the *marielitos* and others), and several other groups. Some of the results of the study for men are presented in Figure 7.6.

The founders and primary beneficiaries of the Cuban enclave are the self-employed, pre-1980 Cuban immigrants (far-left bar). The income for this group is higher than for all other Cuban groups included in the graph, and only slightly less

Figure 7.6 Family Incomes for Self-Employed and Wage Salaried Men From Three Cuban-American Groups, 2000

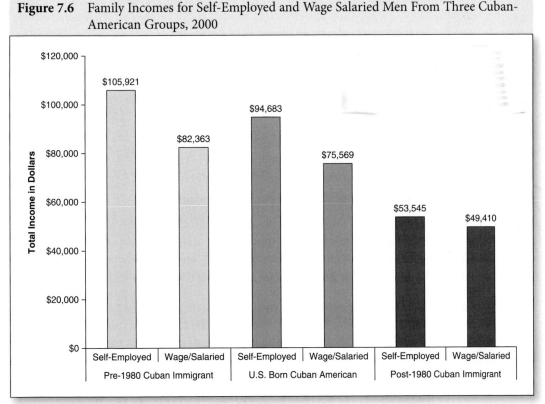

Source: Portes & Shafer (2006, p. 42).

than for non-Hispanic whites (not shown). The sons of the founding generation (U.S.-born Cuban Americans) also enjoy a substantial benefit, both directly (through working in the enclave firms started by their fathers) and indirectly (by translating the resources of their families into human capital, including education, for themselves). The incomes of post-1980 Cuban immigrants are the lowest on the graph and, in fact, are comparable to incomes for non-Hispanic blacks (not shown).

The ability of most Hispanic (and other) immigrants to rise in the class system and compete for place and position is constrained by discrimination and their own lack of economic and political power. Cuban immigrants in the enclave do not need to expose themselves to American prejudices or to rely on the job market of the larger society. They constructed networks of mutual assistance and support and linked themselves to opportunities more consistent with their ambitions and their qualifications.

The link between the enclave and economic equality (an aspect of secondary structural integration) challenges the predictions of some traditional assimilation theories and the understandings of many Americans. The pattern long has been recognized by some leaders of other groups, however, and is voiced in many of the themes of Black Power, Red Power, and Chicanismo that emphasize self-help, self-determination, nationalism, and separation.

However, ethnic enclaves cannot be a panacea for all immigrant or other minority groups. They develop only under certain limited conditions—namely, when business and financial expertise and reliable sources of capital are combined with a disciplined labor force willing to work for low wages in exchange for on-the-job training, future assistance and loans, or other delayed benefits. Enclave enterprises usually start on a small scale and cater only to other ethnic people. Thus, the early economic returns are small, and prosperity follows only after years of hard work, if at all. Most important, eventual success and expansion beyond the boundaries of the enclave depend on the persistence of strong ties of loyalty, kinship, and solidarity. The pressure to assimilate might easily weaken these networks and the strength of group cohesion (Portes & Manning, 1986, pp. 61–66).

Cuban Americans and Other Minority Groups

The adaptation of Cuban Americans contrasts sharply with the experiences of colonized minority groups and with the common understanding of how immigrants are "supposed" to acculturate and integrate. Cuban Americans are neither the first nor the only group to develop an ethnic enclave, and their success has generated prejudice and resentment from the dominant group and from other minority groups. Whereas Puerto Ricans and Chicanos have been the victims of stereotypes labeling them "inferior," higher-status Cuban Americans have been stereotyped as "too successful," "too clannish," and "too ambitious." The former stereotype commonly emerges to rationalize exploitative relationships; the latter expresses disparagement and rejection of groups that are more successful in the struggle to acquire resources. Nonetheless, the stereotype of Cubans is an exaggeration and a misperception that obscures the fact that poverty and unemployment are major problems for many members of this group, especially for the post-1980 immigrants (see the figures at the end of this chapter).

QUESTIONS FOR REFLECTION

7. Would you say that Cuban Americans are more an immigrant or colonized minority group? Why?

8. Are Cuban Americans an enclave minority? What are the most important advantages enjoyed by enclave minority groups? Are there any disadvantages?

COMPARATIVE FOCUS:
Immigration to Europe Versus
Immigration to the United States

The volume of immigration in the world today is at record levels. As we pointed out in Chapter 1 ("Focus on Contemporary Issues: Immigration and Globalization"), just over 3% of the world's population live outside their countries of birth, and there is hardly a nation or region that has not been affected (United Nations, 2012).

The United States may be the most popular destination for immigrants, but there are many others, and the issues of immigration and assimilation we debate so fervently echo across the globe.

The advanced industrial nations of Western Europe are prime destinations for immigrants. Like the United States, they have high standards of living and offer opportunities for economic survival, though the price may be to live at the margins of society or to take jobs scorned by the native-born. Also, most Western European nations have very low birthrates, and in some cases (e.g., Germany and Italy), their populations are projected to decline in coming decades (Population Reference Bureau, 2014, p. 11). This decline will create labor force shortages, attracting immigrants to Western Europe for decades to come.

The immigrant stream to Western Europe is varied and includes people from all walks of life, from highly educated professionals to peasant laborers. The most prominent flows are from Turkey to Germany, from Africa to Spain and Italy, and from many former British colonies (Jamaica, India, Nigeria, etc.) to the United Kingdom. This immigration is primarily an economic phenomenon motivated by the search for jobs and survival, but the stream also includes refugees and asylum seekers spurred by civil war, genocide, and political unrest.

In terms of numbers, the volume of immigration to Western Europe is smaller than the flow to the United States, but its proportional impact is comparable. About 13% of the U.S. population is foreign-born. Many Western European nations (including Belgium, Germany, and Sweden) have a similar profile (Dumont

(Continued)

(Continued)

& LeMaitre, 2011). Thus, in both cases immigration has generated major concerns and debates about how to handle newcomers and manage a pluralistic society, including national language policy, the limits of religious freedom, and the criteria for citizenship.

For example, Germany has the largest immigrant community of any Western European nation and has been dealing with a large foreign-born population for decades. Germany began to allow large numbers of immigrants to enter as temporary workers or "guest workers" (*Gastarbeiter*) to help staff its expanding economy beginning in the 1960s. Most of these immigrants came from Turkey, and Germans saw them as temporary workers only; that is, people who would return to their homeland when they were no longer needed. Thus, Germany saw no particular need to encourage immigrants to acculturate and integrate.

Contrary to this expectation, many immigrants stayed and settled permanently, and many of their millions of descendants today speak only German and have no knowledge of or experience with their "homeland." Although acculturated, they are not fully integrated. In fact—in contrast with the United States—they were denied the opportunity for citizenship until recently.

In recent years, discontent and protests about immigrants have been common across Western Europe, especially with the growth of Muslim communities. Many Europeans see Islamic immigrants as unassimilable, too foreign or exotic to ever fit in to the mainstream of their society. In France, Germany, the Netherlands, and other countries, violence has punctuated these conflicts.

Struggles over the essential meaning of national identity are increasingly common throughout the developed world. Across Europe, just as in the United States (and Canada), nations wrestle with issues of inclusion and diversity: What should it mean to be German, or French, or British, or Dutch, or American? How much diversity can be accepted before national cohesion is threatened? What is the best balance between assimilation and pluralism?

QUESTIONS FOR REFLECTION

9. What similarities and differences between the United States and Western Europe can you cite in terms of immigration?

10. Do you think the United States is more or less successful in dealing with immigrants than the nations of Western Europe? Why?

Prejudice and Discrimination

The American tradition of prejudice against Latinos was born in the 19th century conflicts that created minority group status for Mexican Americans. The themes of the original anti-Mexican stereotypes and attitudes were consistent with the nature of the contact situation: as Mexicans were conquered and subordinated, they were characterized as inferior, lazy, irresponsible, low in intelligence, and dangerously criminal (McWilliams, 1961, pp. 212–214). Prejudice and racism, supplemented with the echoes of the racist ideas and beliefs brought to the Southwest by many Anglos, helped justify and rationalize the colonized, exploited status of the Chicanos.

These prejudices were incorporated into the dominant culture and transferred to Puerto Ricans when they began to arrive on the mainland. However, this stereotype does not fit the situation of Cuban Americans very well. Instead, their affluence has been exaggerated and perceived as undeserved or achieved by unfair or "un-American" means, a characterization similar to the traditional stereotype of Jews and just as prejudiced as perceptions of Latino inferiority.

Some evidence suggests that the level of prejudice against Latinos has been affected by the decline of explicit American racism discussed in Chapters 1 and 5. For example, social distance scales show a decrease in the scores for Mexicans (not shown in the table), although their relative ranking remains fairly stable.

On the other hand, anti-Latino prejudice and racism tend to increase during times of high immigration. In particular, considerable though largely anecdotal evidence suggests that the surge of immigration that began in the 1990s sparked high levels of anti-Latino prejudice in the "borderlands," or the areas along the U.S.–Mexican border. Extreme, racist rhetoric was common, and media prominently featured hate group activities. Many observers see racism in Arizona's state-mandated ban on ethnic studies programs in public schools and in its widely debated State Bill 1070 which, in part, allows police to check anyone for proof of citizenship. In 2012, the Supreme Court upheld this component of the bill but struck down three other provisions, and in 2014, a federal judge rejected additional provisions. At any rate, the level of immigrant bashing and anti-Latino sentiment along the border and in other parts of the United States demonstrates that American prejudice, although sometimes disguised as a subtle modern racism, is alive and well.

In Chapter 4, we mentioned that audit studies have documented the persistence of discrimination against blacks in the housing and job markets; many of the same studies also demonstrate anti-Hispanic biases (see Quillian, 2006, for a review). Discrimination of all kinds, institutional as well as individual, against Latino groups has been common, but it has not been as rigid or as total as the systems that controlled African American labor under slavery and segregation. However, discrimination against Latinos persists across the United States. Because of their longer tenure in the United States and their original status as a rural labor force, Mexican Americans probably have been more victimized by the institutionalized forms of discrimination than have other Latino groups.

Assimilation and Pluralism

As in previous chapters, we will use the central concepts of this text to review the status of Latinos in the United States. When relevant, we'll make comparisons between the major Latino groups and the minority groups discussed in previous chapters.

Acculturation

Latinos are highly variable in their extent of acculturation but are often seen as "slow" to change, learn English, and adopt Anglo customs. Contrary to this perception, research shows that Hispanics follow many of the same patterns of assimilation as European groups. Their rates of acculturation increase with length of residence and are higher for the native-born (Espinosa & Massey, 1997; Goldstein & Suro, 2000; Valentine & Mosley, 2000).

The dominant trend for Hispanic groups, as for immigrants from Europe in the past (see Chapter 2) is that language acculturation increases over the generations, as the length of residence in the United States increases, and as education increases. A 2007 study of more than 14,000 respondents from six different surveys since 2000 (Hakimzadeh & Cohn, 2007) illustrates these points (see Figures 7.7 and 7.8).

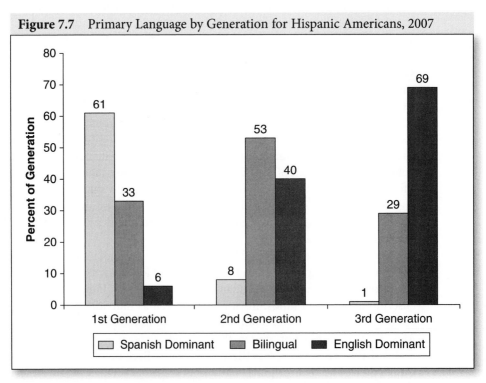

Figure 7.7   Primary Language by Generation for Hispanic Americans, 2007

Source: Taylor, Paul, Lopez, Hugo, Martinez, Jessica, and Velasco, Gabriel, 2012. "When Labels Don't Fit: Hispanics and their Views of Identity" http://www.pewhispanic.org/2012/04/04/when-labels-dont-fit-hispanics-and-their-views-of-identity/.

Figure 7.8   Percentage of Hispanic Americans Who Speak English "Very Well" by Years of Residence and Levels of Education, 2007

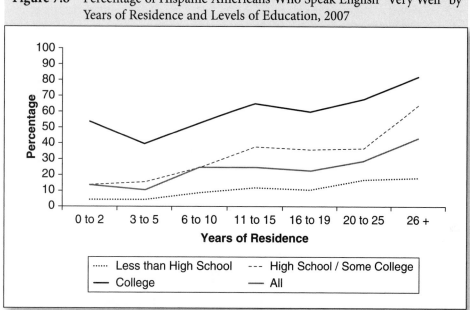

Source: Hakimzadeh, Shirin, & Cohn, D'Vera. 2007. "English Language Usage Among Hispanics in the United States." Pew Hispanic Center. http://pewhispanic.org/files/reports/82.pdf.

An earlier study (Pew Hispanic Center, 2004) found that Anglo and Latino values become virtually identical as length of residence increases, generations pass, and English language ability increases. It found that most Latinos who speak predominantly Spanish (72%) are first generation. The second generation is most likely to be bilingual. Those who speak predominantly English (78%) are third generation. The values of predominantly Spanish speakers are distinctly different from those of non-Latinos, especially on a survey item that measures support for the statement, "Children should live with their parents until they are married." Virtually all the predominantly Spanish speakers supported the statement, but English-speaking Latinos showed the more individualistic values of Anglos. A similar acculturation to American values occurred for the other three items that researchers studied.

Even while acculturation continues, however, immigration revitalizes Hispanic culture and the Spanish language. By its nature, assimilation is a slow process that can require decades or generations to complete. In contrast, immigration can be fast, often accomplished in less than a day. Thus, even as Hispanic Americans acculturate and integrate, Hispanic culture and language are sustained and strengthened. What is perceived to be slow acculturation for these groups is mostly the result of fast and continuous immigration.

Furthermore, colonized minority groups such as Chicanos and Puerto Ricans were not encouraged to assimilate in the past. Valued primarily for the cheap labor they supplied, they were seen as inferior, undesirable, and unfit for integration. For

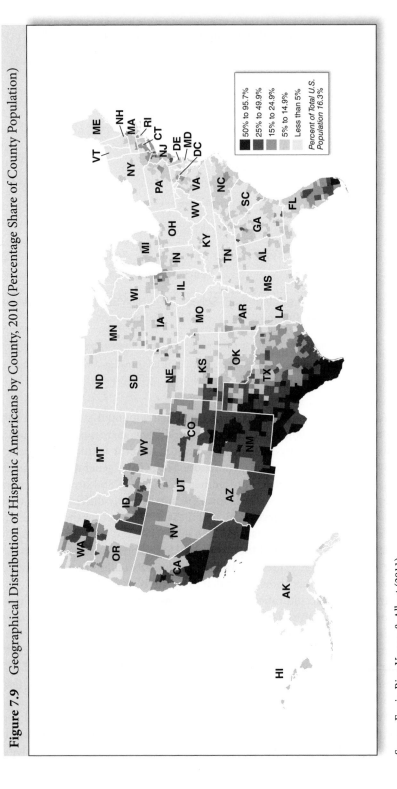

Figure 7.9 Geographical Distribution of Hispanic Americans by County, 2010 (Percentage Share of County Population)

50% to 95.7%
25% to 49.9%
15% to 24.9%
5% to 14.9%
Less than 5%

Percent of Total U.S. Population 16.3%

Source: Ennis, Rios-Vargas, & Albert (2011).

much of the 20th century, Latinos were excluded from the institutions and experiences (e.g., school) that could have led to greater equality and higher rates of acculturation. Prejudice, racism, and discrimination combined to keep most Latino groups away from the centers of modernization and change and away from opportunities to improve their situation.

Finally, for Cubans, Dominicans, Salvadorans, and other groups, cultural differences reflect that they are largely recent immigrants. Their first generations are alive and well. As is typical for immigrant groups, they keep their language and traditions alive.

Secondary Structural Assimilation

In this section, we survey the situation of Latinos in the public areas and institutions of American society, following the same format as the previous two chapters. We begin with where people live.

Residence. Figure 7.9 shows the geographic concentrations of Latinos in 2010. The legacies of the varied patterns of entry and settlement for the largest groups are evident. The higher concentrations in the Southwest reflect the presence of Mexican Americans; those in Florida are the result of the Cuban immigration, and those in the Northeast display the settlement patterns of Puerto Ricans.

Figure 7.10 highlights the areas of the nation where the Latino population is growing fastest. A quick glance at the map reveals that many of the high-growth areas are distant from the traditional points of entry for these groups. In particular, the Hispanic American population is growing rapidly in parts of the New England, the South, the upper Midwest, the Northwest, and even Alaska. This population movement is a response to (among many other forces) the availability of jobs in factories, mills, chicken-processing plants and slaughterhouses, farms, construction, and other low-skilled areas of the economy.

Within each of these regions, Latino groups are highly urbanized, as shown in Figure 7.11. With the exception of Mexican Americans, more than 90% of each of the 10 largest Hispanic American groups live in urban areas, and this percentage approaches 100% for some groups. Mexican Americans are more rural than the other groups, but the percentage of the group living in rural areas is tiny today, in sharp contrast to their historical role as an agrarian workforce.

The extent of residential segregation for Hispanic Americans was displayed in Figure 5.9 (see Chapter 5), using the dissimilarity index for each of the last four census years. Residential segregation is much lower for Hispanics than for blacks: None of the scores for Hispanics in Figure 5.9 approach the "extreme" segregation denoted by a dissimilarity index of 60 or more.

Note that, contrary to the decreasing levels of black–white segregation, Hispanic–white residential segregation has held steady, with minor increases or decreases. Among other factors, this is a reflection of high rates of immigration and "chain" patterns of settlement, which concentrate newcomers in ethnic neighborhoods. In other words, levels of residential segregation for Hispanics remain relatively steady because weakening barriers to integration in the larger society are counteracted by the continuing arrival of newcomers, who tend to settle in predominantly Hispanic neighborhoods.

Figure 7.17 Poverty Rates for Non-Hispanic Whites, All Hispanic Americans, and 10 Largest Hispanic American Groups, 2012

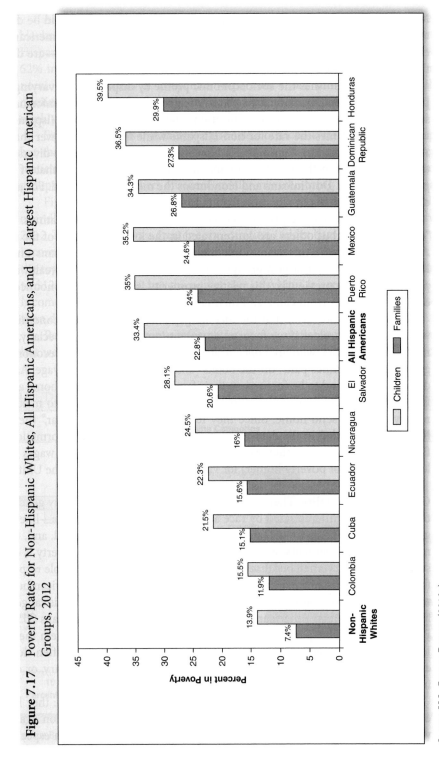

Source: U.S. Census Bureau (2013a).

rate of poverty. Whereas 24% of non-Hispanic white, woman-headed households fall below the poverty line, the percentage is about 41% for Hispanic households headed by women (U.S. Census Bureau, 2013a).

Summary. The socioeconomic situation of Latinos is complex, diversified, and segmented. Many Latinos have successfully entered the mainstream economy, but others face poverty and exclusion. Highly concentrated in deteriorated urban areas (or barrios), segments of these groups, like other minority groups of color, face the possibility of permanent poverty and economic marginality.

Primary Structural Assimilation

Overall, the extent of intimate contact between Hispanic Americans and the dominant group probably has been higher than for either African Americans or Native Americans (e.g., see Quillian & Campbell, 2003; Rosenfield, 2002). This pattern may reflect the fact that Latinos are partly ethnic minority groups and partly racial minority groups. Some studies report that contact is greater for the more affluent social classes, in the cities, and for the younger generations (who are presumably more Americanized) (Fitzpatrick, 1976; Grebler et al., 1970, p. 397; Rodriguez, 1989, pp. 70–72). On the other hand, the extent of contact probably has been decreased by the rapid increase in immigration and the tendency of the first generation to socialize more with coethnics.

Rates of intermarriage are higher for Latinos than for African Americans, but neither is a very high percentage of all marriages. Black and white interracial couples make up less than 1% of all marriages, and the comparable figure for Latinos is 4% of all marriages (U.S. Census Bureau, 2012c, p. 54).

Table 7.3 shows that rates of in-marriage for Hispanics are lower than those for whites. This is partly a function of simple arithmetic: The larger group (white Americans) is more likely to find partners within the group. However, note that the rate of Latino in-marriage is also lower than that of blacks (see Table 5.1), a group of

Table 7.3   Percentages of Whites and Latinos Married to a Person of the Same Group, 1980 and 2008

	Whites		Latinos			
			Men		Women	
Year	Men	Women	Foreign-Born	U.S.-Born	Foreign-Born	U.S.-Born
1980	96%	95%	80%	67%	84%	70%
2008	93%	92%	83%	58%	83%	59%

Source: Qian & Lichter (2011, p. 1072). Copyright © 2011 National Council on Family Relations. Reprinted with permission.

about the same size. This pattern may reflect the tenacity of racial (vs. ethnic) barriers to integration in this institutional area.

Also, note that rates of in-marriage for Latinos are affected by nativity. In both years, the foreign-born were more likely to marry within the group than were the U.S.-born. This pattern, like so many others, reflects the high rates of immigration and the tendency of recent immigrants to socialize within the ethnic subcommunity. For both years, Hispanics who married outside their group were most likely to marry whites.

QUESTIONS FOR REFLECTION

11. This section examined a variety of dimensions of acculturation and integration for Hispanic Americans. Which is most important? Why?

12. Which Hispanic groups have been more successful in U.S. society and why? Do you agree with the definitions of *success* used in this section? What other definitions might be useful, and how might these change your ideas about which group is most successful?

Assimilation and Hispanic Americans

As test cases for what we have called the traditional view of American assimilation, Latinos fare poorly. Almost two centuries after the original contact period, Mexican Americans tend to be concentrated in the low-wage sector of the labor market, a source of cheap labor for the dominant group's economy. Puerto Ricans, who are more recent arrivals, occupy a similar profile and position.

The fundamental reality faced by both groups, in their histories and in their present situations, is their colonized status in U.S. society. Even while many Mexican Americans and Puerto Ricans have risen in the social class and occupational structure of the larger society, others share many problems with other urban minority groups of color.

Traditional views of the nature of assimilation, likewise, fail to describe the experiences of Cuban Americans. They are more prosperous, on the average, than either Mexican Americans or Puerto Ricans, but they became successful by remaining separate and by developing an enclave in South Florida.

There is no single Hispanic American experience or pattern of adjustment to the larger society. We have focused mainly on three of the many Latino groups in the United States, and the diversity of their experiences suggests the variety and complexity of what it means to be a minority group in U.S. society. Additionally, their experiences illustrate some of the fundamental forces that shape minority group experiences: the split labor market and the U.S. appetite for cheap labor, the impact of industrialization, the dangers of a permanent urban underclass, the relationships between competition and levels of prejudice and rejection, and the persistence of race as a primary dividing line between people and groups.

FOCUS ON CONTEMPORARY ISSUES:
Hispanic Americans and the Evolution of the American Racial Order[1]

The United States has, virtually since its birth, been organized into two communities: black and white, separate and unequal. This structural relationship has been reinforced and solidified by the traditional perception that there are *only* two races. What will happen to this tradition as groups that are neither black nor white—Latinos, Asian Americans, and others—continue to grow in numbers and significance in the everyday life of U.S. society?

One possibility, which we will call the whitening thesis, hypothesizes that Latinos (and Asian Americans) eventually will be accepted as white, while African Americans remain relegated to the perpetual black. An opposing position, called the browning thesis, predicts that all "peoples of color" will band together and threaten the dominance of whites. We consider each of these views below, as well as a third possible future for the racial order of the United States.

Whitening. In this model, Latinos and Asian Americans will become part of the white American racial group while blacks will remain disproportionately unequal, powerless, and marginalized. The racial identities of Latinos and Asians will become "thinner," declining in salience for them as they increasingly access the privileges of whiteness, much like the Irish and Italians before them. As they assimilate, the "white" racial identity will grow more prominent and their sense of ethnicity will become largely symbolic.

This prediction is consistent with Gordon's assimilation model and the notion that immigrants move through a series of stages and become more incorporated into the dominant society in a relatively linear fashion. Once a group has completed acculturation, integration, and intermarriage, they will begin to racially identify with the dominant group.

George Yancey (2003) has tested the whitening thesis on a nationally representative data set, and his analysis places Latinos and Asian Americans in the middle stages of assimilation, because their residential patterns, marital patterns, and several key political beliefs align more closely with those of white Americans than they do with those of black Americans. If Gordon's model holds true, these groups will come to identify as white over the next several generations.

Another research project (Murguia & Foreman, 2003) focused on Mexican Americans and found that they tend to prefer spouses, neighbors, coworkers, and friends who are either Puerto Rican or white, not black. The researchers also found that Mexican Americans tend to endorse modern racism (see Chapters 1 and 5): the belief that racism is not much of a barrier to success and that people of color are largely responsible for

(Continued)

(Continued)

their own hardships. This consistency with the ideology of the dominant group also positions Mexican Americans on the path to whiteness.

Finally, note that an important part of the whitening process is to distance oneself from the perpetually stigmatized black group. To the extent that a whitening process occurs for Latino and Asian Americans, these groups will tend to use both traditional and modern anti-black racism to emphasize their differences and align themselves more with the attitudinal and cultural perspectives of the dominant group. We discussed this type of dynamic in our coverage of the racial identity of Puerto Ricans who come to the mainland.

Browning. The browning thesis argues that whites will gradually lose their dominant status as Latino and Asian American groups grow in numbers. The balance of power will tip toward the nonwhite groups, who will use their greater numbers to challenge whites for position in the society.

Some theorists see the loss of white dominance as very negative, a threat to the integrity of Anglo American culture. This version of the browning thesis has been presented by political scientist Samuel Huntington (2004), among many others. Some proponents of this perspective argue that Latinos are "unassimilable" due to their alleged unwillingness to learn English and absorb other aspects of U.S. culture, a view based largely on nativism, ethnocentrism, and prejudice, and refuted by much of the evidence presented in this chapter (e.g., see Figures 7.8 and 7.9). Nevertheless, this version of the browning thesis has gained momentum in popular culture and on some talk radio and cable TV shows. It also manifests itself in the political arena in debates over immigration policy and in the movement to make English the "official" language of the nation (see Chapter 2).

A different version of the browning thesis has taken hold among some sociologists. For example, Feagin and O'Brien (2004) put a positive spin on the idea of the declining white numerical majority. They believe that as nonwhite groups grow in size, whites will be forced to share power in a more democratic, egalitarian, and inclusive fashion. This shift will be more likely to the extent that minority groups can forge alliances with one another. These combinations may be foreshadowed by studies of generational differences in the racial attitudes of immigrants, some of which show that native-born or second-generation Latinos and Asian Americans are more likely to express solidarity with African Americans than are the foreign-born and recently arrived members of their group (Murguia & Foreman, 2003). In contrast to the whitening thesis, this view of the browning thesis expects Latinos and Asian Americans to embrace a more color-conscious worldview and find ways to leverage their growing numbers, in alliance with African Americans, to improve their status in American society.

This version of the browning thesis also adopts a more global perspective. It recognizes that the world is occupied by many more "people of color" than by whites of European descent and that the growing numbers of nonwhites in the United States can be an important resource in the global marketplace. For example, people around the world commonly speak several languages on a daily basis, but Americans are almost entirely monolingual; this places them at a disadvantage in a global marketplace that values linguistic diversity. The United States might improve its position if it encourages the "fluent bilingualism" of its Latino and Asian American citizens, rather than insisting on "English Only" (see Chapter 2).

Something Else? Still another group of scholars challenges both the browning and the whitening theses and foresees a three-way racial dynamic. These scholars focus on the tremendous diversity within the Latino and Asian American communities in the United States in terms of relative wealth, skin color and other "racial" characteristics, religion, and national origins. This diversity leads them to conclude that only some Latino and Asian Americans will "whiten."

For example, Eduardo Bonilla-Silva (2003) sketches out a future racial trichotomy: whites, honorary whites, and the collective black. In this schema, well-off and light-skinned Latinos and Asians would not "become white" but, rather, would occupy an intermediary "honorary whites" status. This status would afford them much of the privilege and esteem not widely accorded to people of color, but it would still be a conditional status, which potentially could be revoked in times of economic crisis or at any other time when those in power found it necessary. Bonilla-Silva predicts that groups such as Chinese Americans and lighter-skinned Latinos would fit into the honorary white category, while darker-skinned Latinos and Asians would fit into the collective black category, along with, of course, American blacks.

Murguia and Foreman (2003) provide some findings from their study of Mexican Americans that can be used to illustrate this process. They point out that skin color and educational level make a difference in whether or not Latinos ally with blacks. Mexican Americans with darker skin and higher educational levels and those born in the United States are less likely to buy into the anti-black stereotypes of the larger culture and more likely to recognize the significance of racism in their own lives. Attitudes such as these may form the basis of future alliances among some (but not all) Latinos, Asian Americans, and African Americans.

How Will the Racial Order Evolve? Will the United States grow browner or whiter? In the face of high levels of immigration and the growing importance of groups that are in the "racial middle"—those that are neither black nor white—it seems certain that the traditional, dichotomous black–white racial order cannot persist. What will replace it? Whichever thesis proves correct, it seems certain that new understandings of race and new relationships among racial groups will emerge in the coming decades.

Note

1. This section based on O'Brien (2008).

Main Points

- Hispanic Americans are a diverse and growing part of U.S. society, including distinct groups; the three largest are Mexican Americans, Puerto Ricans, and Cuban Americans. These groups tend to not think of themselves as a single entity.
- Hispanic Americans have some characteristics of colonized groups and some of immigrant groups. Similarly, these groups are racial minorities in some ways and ethnic minorities in others.
- Since the beginning of the 20th century, Mexico has served as a reserve labor force for the development of the U.S. economy. Immigrants from Mexico entered a social system in which the colonized status of the group was already established. Mexican Americans have been a colonized minority group despite the large numbers of immigrants in the group and have been systematically excluded from opportunities for upward mobility by institutional discrimination and segregation.
- A Mexican American protest movement has been continuously seeking to improve the status of the group. In the 1960s, a more intense and militant movement emerged, guided by the ideology of Chicanismo.
- Puerto Ricans began to move to the mainland in large numbers only in the 1940s and 1950s. The group is concentrated in the urban Northeast, in the low-wage sector of the job market.
- Cubans began immigrating after Castro's revolution in the late 1950s. They settled primarily in southern Florida, where they created an ethnic enclave.
- Anti-Hispanic prejudice and discrimination seem to have declined, mirroring the general decline in explicit, overt racism in American society. Recent high levels of immigration seem to have increased anti-Hispanic prejudice and discrimination, however, especially in the borderlands and other areas with large numbers of immigrants.
- Levels of acculturation are highly variable from group to group and generation to generation. Acculturation increases with length of residence but the vitality of Latino cultures has been sustained by recent immigration.
- Secondary structural assimilation varies from group to group. Poverty, unemployment, lower levels of educational attainment, and other forms of inequality continue to be major problems for Hispanic groups, even the relatively successful Cuban Americans.
- Primary structural assimilation with the dominant group is greater for Hispanic Americans than for African Americans.

APPLYING CONCEPTS

In a classic article, anthropologist Jane Hill (1995) analyzed "mock Spanish"—phrases such as "no problemo," "hasty banana," and "buenos nachos." Mock Spanish is distinct from the blending of Spanish and English ("Spanglish") common in the borderlands of the Southwest among people who speak both languages, in that it is used by mono-English speakers and intended to be a form of humorous, light-hearted banter.

Hill (1995) argues that this seemingly innocent butchering of Spanish is a form of racism that relies on negative stereotypes of Hispanics (particularly Mexicans) for its humor. For example, calling something "el cheapo" will conjure in the minds of many Anglos images of lazy, lower-class Mexicans.

Furthermore, an analysis of mock Spanish reveals a linguistic double standard: Spanish speakers are disparaged or ridiculed for using incorrect English, but English speakers abuse and misuse Spanish with impunity.

Mock Spanish is common in everyday language and in media. Some examples are listed below. Can you identify the source and the speaker?*

1. "Hasta la vista, baby."
2. "You got a lot of 'splainin' to do."
3. "Nurse Espinosa and her nursitas want more dinero."
4. "I need a lift in el trucko to el towno."
5. "I'm promoting myself to 'El Tigre Numero Uno.'"

*Many of these examples are based on materials presented on the website Teaching Resources: Teaching Linguistic Anthropology, at teach.linguisticanthropology.org/tag/mock-Spanish.

FIND THE ANSWERS AT THE END OF THIS SECTION

Review Questions

1. At the beginning of this chapter, you learned that Hispanic Americans "combine elements of the polar extremes [immigrant and colonized] of Blauner's typology of minority groups" and that they are "partly an ethnic minority group and partly a racial minority group." Explain these statements in terms of the rest of the material presented in the chapter.

2. What important cultural differences between Mexican Americans and the dominant society shaped the relationships between the two groups?

3. How does the history of Mexican immigration demonstrate the usefulness of Noel's concepts of differentials in power and competition?

4. Compare and contrast the protest movements of Mexican Americans, Native Americans, and African Americans. What similarities and differences existed in Chicanismo, Red Power, and Black Power? How do the differences reflect the unique experiences of each group?

5. In what ways are the experiences of Puerto Ricans and Cuban Americans unique compared with those of other minority groups? How do these differences reflect other differences, such as differences in contact situation?

6. The Cuban American enclave has resulted in a variety of benefits for the group. Why don't other minority groups follow this strategy? Describe the situation of the major Hispanic American groups in terms of acculturation and integration. Which groups are closest to equality? What factors or experiences might account for the differences between groups? In what ways might the statement "Hispanic Americans are remaining pluralistic even while they assimilate" be true?

Internet Activities

1. How well do you think you understand modern immigration issues? Take the Immigration Quiz at http://www.pbs.org/independentlens/blog/immigration-quiz-2. Which questions/answers surprised you the most and why? Identify at least two online sources that provide answers to the questions that this quiz raised for you. How does what you learned relate to ideas in this chapter?

2. First listen to and analyze one of these two songs by Rage Against the Machine (RATM):

   - "People of the Sun" at https://www.youtube.com/watch?v=C_YtCpC12Kg. (You can find the lyrics here: http://www.ratm.net/lyrics/peo.html.) What is the song about (and what lines tell you)? How does the band characterize the Spaniards' takeover in Central America in 1516? How does this song relate to more contemporary colonization efforts, including those by the U.S. government? (You may wish to note the line, "Blood drenched get offensive like Tet" as a reference to Vietnam.) What do you make of the line, "whip snapped ya back/Ya spine cracked for tobacco"? How does RATM describe Los Angeles ("city of angels"?) in terms of "ethnic cleansing"? (Some suggest this line is a reference to California's Proposition 187. If you are unfamiliar with that proposition, use a search engine to find out more.) Identify at least two concepts from this book that relate to the song and explain the connection.
   - "Maria" at https://www.youtube.com/watch?v=U0pPqNAkBYo. What is RATM's perspective regarding illegal border crossings, sweatshops/maquiladoras, and other issues facing immigrants from Mexico? How do you interpret the line, "He whips her/Her soul chained to his will/My job is to kill if you forget to take your pill"? How does this relate to the idea of intersectionality? Identify at least two other concepts from this book that apply to this song. How do you see those ideas in the lyrics? Then, identify other musicians concerned with Hispanic-related issues, such as Cuban-American rapper Pitbull. (To learn more, listen to this short interview with him at http://www.npr.org/templates/story/story.php?storyId=6428732&ps=rs.) Who are they? What do they write about? How does what they write relate to at least two concepts from this chapter?

3. Investigate the debate over English Only legislation that's happening in your community or state, or in the United States more broadly. Identify two organizations working on different sides of this issue. Summarize their arguments; then, evaluate their evidence. For example, what are the sources of their information? Is their language "loaded" or biased? What issues do they overlook? Which arguments hold the most weight for you and why? How do these debates compare with those in other countries such as France and Germany? Be sure to note the sources of your information.

4. Investigate recent deaths of those attempting to cross into the United States from Mexico. What are the most frequent causes of crossing deaths? What role do border smugglers, or "coyotes," play in illegal immigration? What are the official (i.e., government) and unofficial responses to these deaths in both Mexico and the United States? Identify two organizations working to help people cross the border and/or stop people from crossing the border. Identify each organization's mission, rationale, and evidence.

5. Read or watch at least one of the following pieces related to migrant labor:

   - The four-part series *Product of Mexico*, including the short companion videos at http://graphics.latimes.com/product-of-mexico-camps/.
   - *Children of the Fields* (11min) at https://www.youtube.com/watch?v=wRKmR-qtIjg.

- *Rape in the Fields*, a *Frontline* documentary about a significant problem facing migrant women: http://www.pbs.org/wgbh/pages/frontline/rape-in-the-fields/. (You may wish to note some of the supplementary links such as those that explain what's being done to stop the problem.)

First, explain how your choice relates to at least two ideas from this book. Next, identify new information that you didn't know before and explain how it is useful or relevant. Lastly, what do you want to know now based on what you've learned?

6. Watch the student-made video, "Invisible America: The Migrant Story" at https://www.youtube.com/watch?v=l5QFm0qeAlk. What do you make of people's responses to the question, "Do you know what a migrant camp is?" and "Do you know where most of your fruits and vegetables come from?" Ask five of your friends those same questions and note their responses. How do their answers compare with those in the video? What do you make of that? Then, investigate the Coalition of Imokalee Workers at *http://ciw-online.org/* or Comité de Apoyo a los Trabajadores Agrícolas (CATA—Farmworkers Support Committee) at http://www.cata-farmworkers.org/english%20pages/Resources.htm. If someone were to ask you about migrants and where your food comes from, what would you say now?

7. Explore one of the resources at Ithaca College's Latino Experience, Issues, and Resources page at http://www.ithaca.edu/wise/latino/. How does the link you explored build on what you've learned in this chapter?

8. Watch this short video about how the Census has created racial categories from 1790 to today at https://www.youtube.com/watch?feature=player_embedded&v=55ZCzRGV6jY. Note, in particular, the discussion of the League of United Latin American Citizens (LULAC) and racial categories. What do you make of the debate regarding whether or not Mexicans should be listed as a separate racial category? How does that relate to ideas of power and privilege? Investigate LULAC at http://lulac.org/.

9. Investigate current debates over Puerto Rican statehood such as those found at http://www.debate.org/opinions/should-puerto-rico-seek-american-statehood and http://lulac.org/news/pr/pr_debate/. What do you think and why?

ANSWERS TO APPLYING CONCEPTS

1. This was one of Hill's examples of mock Spanish and comes from the movie *Terminator 2: Judgment Day*. The line was spoken by actor (and later California governor) Arnold Schwarzenegger.

2. This line has its origins in the 1950s sitcom *I Love Lucy* but has been used in everyday language, TV shows, movies, and other situations since, including by U.S. Senator Tom Coburn (R-OK) during the confirmation hearing of Justice Sonia Sotomayor for an appointment to the U.S. Supreme Court (see www.youtube.com/watch?v=a7On14l6wgc).

3. This is from an episode of the TV sitcom *Scrubs* (see www.youtube.com/watch?v=fPhU6FvgrUw).

4. This line was delivered by Brad Pitt in the movie *The Mexican*. You can watch the trailer for the movie at www.youtube.com/watch?v=_30eb3aRmZ0.

5. This line was spoken by Hobbes in the comic strip *Calvin and Hobbes* (see language-culture.binghamton.edu/symposia/2/slides/07.jpg).

Can you cite some examples of mock Spanish from your own experiences? Do you agree that mock Spanish is racist? Who is actually harmed by these idioms? What is at stake here?

⑤SAGE edge™

edge.sagepub.com/healeyds5e

SAGE edge offers a robust online environment featuring an impressive array of free tools and resources for review, study, and further exploration, keeping both instructors and students on the cutting edge of teaching and learning.

SAGE edge for Students provides a personalized approach to help you accomplish your course-work goals in an easy-to-use learning environment.

Asian Americans: Model Minorities?

I had flown from San Francisco . . . and was riding a taxi to my hotel to attend a conference on multiculturalism. My driver and I chatted about the weather and the tourists. The rearview mirror reflected a white man in his forties. "How long have you been in this country?" he asked. "All my life," I replied, wincing. "I was born in the United States." With a strong Southern drawl, he remarked: "I was wondering because your English is excellent!". . . . I explained: "My grandfather came here from Japan in the 1880s. My family has been here for over a hundred years." He glanced at me in the mirror. Somehow, I did not look "American" to him; my eyes and complexion looked foreign.

—Ronald Takaki (1993, p. 2)

These few seconds of conversation speak deeply to U.S. perceptions of Asian Americans (and other minority groups). The taxi driver certainly meant no insult, but his casual question revealed his view, widely shared, that the United States is a white European society. At the time of the conversation, Professor Takaki was a distinguished professor at a prestigious West Coast university, a highly respected teacher, and an internationally renowned expert in his area. Very possibly, his family had been in the United States longer than the taxi driver's family; yet the driver automatically assumed he was an outsider.

Asian Americans, like other peoples of color, continually find themselves set apart, excluded, and stigmatized—whether during the 19th century anti-Chinese campaign in California, after the 1922 Supreme Court decision (*Takao Ozawa v. United States*) that declared Asians

Figure 8.1 Ten Largest Asian American Groups, 2012

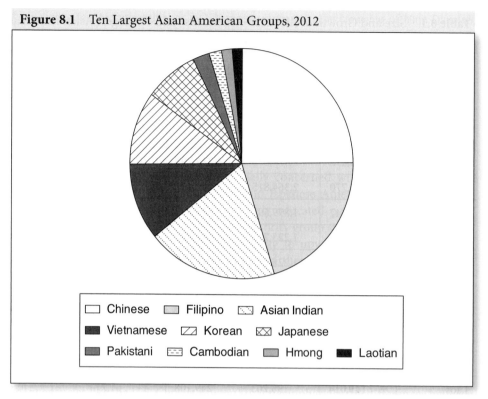

Legend:
☐ Chinese ▨ Filipino ⊡ Asian Indian
■ Vietnamese ▨ Korean ⊠ Japanese
■ Pakistani ⊟ Cambodian ▨ Hmong ■ Laotian

Source: U.S. Census Bureau (2013a).

Origins and Cultures

Asian Americans bring a wealth of traditions to the United States. They speak many different languages and practice religions as diverse as Buddhism, Confucianism, Islam, Hinduism, and Christianity. Asian cultures predate the founding of the United States by centuries. Although no two of these cultures are the same, they share some general similarities. These cultural traits have shaped the behavior of Asian Americans, as well as the perceptions of members of the dominant group, and compose part of the foundation on which Asian American experiences have been built.

Asian cultures tend to stress group membership over individual self-interest. For example, Confucianism, which was the dominant ethical and moral system in traditional China and had a powerful influence on many other Asian cultures, counsels people to see themselves as elements in larger social systems and status hierarchies. Confucianism emphasizes loyalty to the group, conformity to societal expectations, and respect for one's superiors.

In traditional China, as in other Asian societies, the business of everyday life was organized around kinship relations, and most interpersonal relations were with family members and other relatives (Lyman, 1974, p. 9). The family or the clan often owned the

Figure 8.2 Percentage Foreign-Born for Total Population, All Asian Americans, and Ten Largest Asian American Groups, 2012

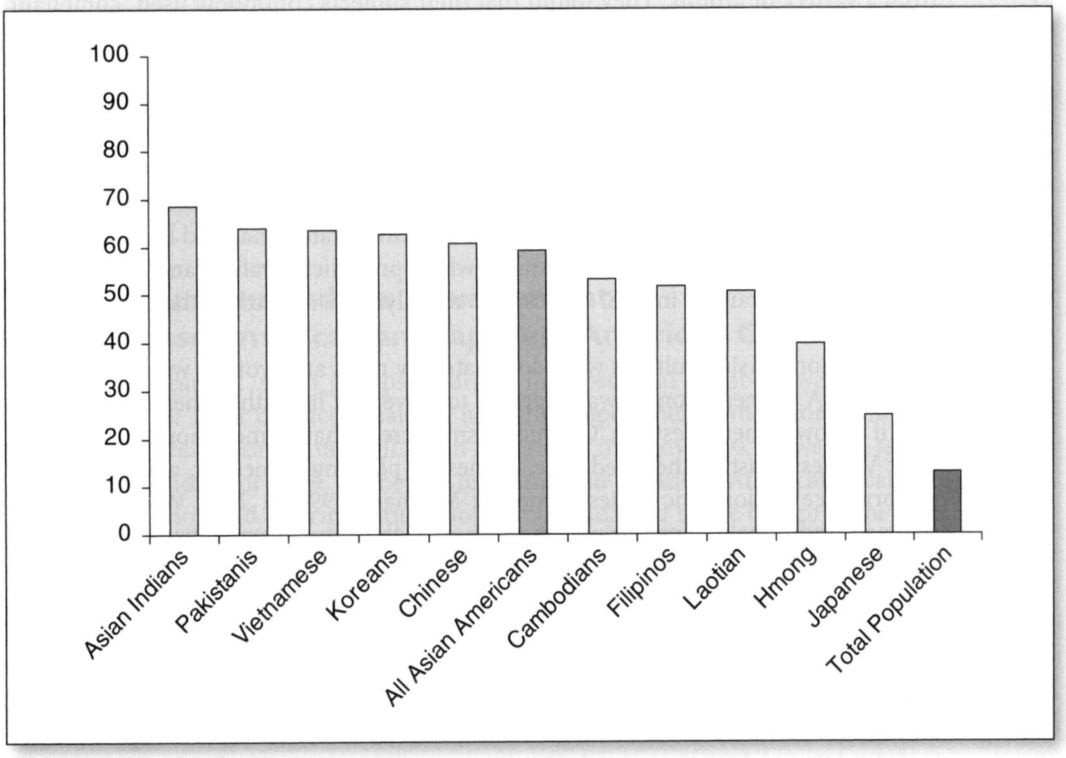

Source: U.S. Census Bureau (2013a).

land on which all depended for survival, and kinship ties determined inheritance patterns. The clan also performed a number of crucial social functions, including arranging marriages, settling disputes between individuals, and organizing festivals and holidays.

Asian cultures stress sensitivity to the opinions and judgments of others and the importance of avoiding public embarrassment and not giving offense. Especially when discussing Japanese culture, these cultural tendencies are often contrasted with Western practices in terms of "guilt versus shame" and the nature of personal morality (Benedict, 1946). In Western cultures, individuals are encouraged to develop and abide by a conscience, or an inner moral voice, and behavior is guided by one's personal sense of guilt. In contrast, Asian cultures stress the importance of maintaining the respect and good opinion of others and avoiding shame and public humiliation. Group harmony, or *wa* in Japanese, is a central concern, and displays of individualism are discouraged. These characteristics are reflected in the Japanese proverb, "The nail that sticks up must be hammered down" (Whiting, 1990, p. 70). Asian cultures emphasize proper behavior, conformity to convention and the judgments of others, and avoiding embarrassment and personal confrontations ("saving face").

Before long, however, the economic boom slowed and the supply of jobs began to dry up. The Gold Rush petered out, and the transcontinental railroad, which thousands of Chinese workers had helped build, was completed in 1869. The migration of Anglo Americans from the East continued, and competition for jobs and other resources increased. An anti-Chinese campaign of harassment, discrimination, and violent attacks began. In 1871, in Los Angeles, a mob of "several hundred whites shot, hanged, and stabbed 19 Chinese to death" (Tsai, 1986, p. 67). Other attacks against the Chinese occurred in Denver, Seattle, Tacoma, and Rock Springs, Wyoming (Lyman, 1974, p. 77).

As the West Coast economy changed, the Chinese came to be seen as a threat, and elements of the dominant group tried to limit competition. The Chinese were a small group—there were only about 100,000 in the entire country in 1870—and by law, they were not permitted to become citizens. Hence, they controlled few power resources with which to withstand these attacks. During the 1870s, Chinese workers were forced out of most sectors of the mainstream economy, and in 1882, the anti-Chinese campaign experienced its ultimate triumph when the U.S. Congress passed the **Chinese Exclusion Act**, banning virtually all immigration from China. The act was one of the first restrictive immigration laws and was aimed solely at the Chinese. It established a rigid competitive relationship between the groups (see Chapter 4) and eliminated the threat presented by Chinese labor by excluding the Chinese people from American society.

Consistent with the predictions of split labor market theory (see Chapter 3), the primary antagonists of Chinese immigrants were native-born workers and organized labor. White owners of small businesses, feeling threatened by Chinese-owned businesses, also supported passage of the Chinese Exclusion Act (Boswell, 1986). Other social classes, such as the capitalists who owned larger factories, might actually have benefited from the continued supply of cheaper labor created by immigration from China. Conflicts such as the anti-Chinese campaign could be especially intense because they confounded racial and ethnic antagonisms with disputes between different social classes.

The ban on immigration from China remained in effect until World War II, when China was awarded a yearly quota of 105 immigrants in recognition of its wartime alliance with the United States. Large-scale immigration from China did not resume until federal policy was revised in 1965.

Population Trends and the "Delayed" Second Generation. Following the Chinese Exclusion Act, the number of Chinese in the United States actually declined (see Figure 8.3), as some immigrants passed away or returned to China and were not replaced by newcomers. The huge majority of Chinese immigrants in the 19th century had been young adult men sojourners who intended to work hard, save money, and return to their home villages in China (Chan, 1990, p. 66). After 1882, it was difficult for anyone from China, men or women, to enter the United States, and the Chinese community in the United States remained dominated by men for many decades. At the end of the 19th century, for example, men outnumbered women by more than 25 to 1, and the gender ratio did not approach parity for decades (Wong, 1995, p. 64; see also Ling, 2000). The scarcity of Chinese women in the United States delayed the second generation (the first generation born in the United States). It wasn't until the 1920s, 80 years after immigration began, that as many as one third of all Chinese in the United States were native-born (Wong, 1995, p. 64).

The delayed second generation may have reinforced the exclusion of the Chinese American community, which began as a reaction to the overt discrimination of the dominant group (Chan, 1990, p. 66). The children of immigrants are usually much more acculturated, and their language facility and greater familiarity with the larger society often permit them to represent the group and speak for it more effectively. In the case of Chinese Americans (and other Asian groups), members of the second generation were citizens of the United States by birth, a status from which the immigrants were barred, and they had legal and political rights not available to their parents. Thus, the decades-long absence of a more Americanized, English-speaking generation increased the isolation of Chinese Americans.

The Ethnic Enclave. The Chinese became increasingly urbanized as the anti-Chinese campaign and rising racism took their toll. Forced out of towns and smaller cities, they settled in larger urban areas, especially San Francisco, which offered the safety of urban anonymity as well as ethnic neighborhoods where the old ways could be practiced and contact with Anglo society minimized. Chinatowns had existed since the start of the

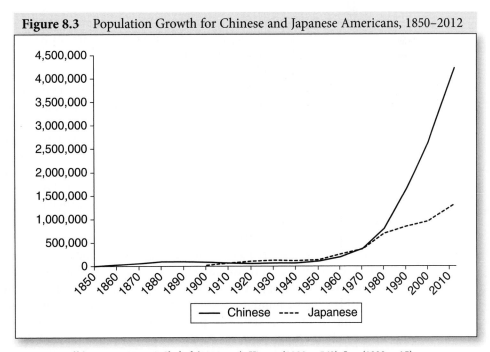

Figure 8.3   Population Growth for Chinese and Japanese Americans, 1850–2012

Sources: Hoeffel, Rastogi, Kim, & Shahid (2012, p.4); Kitano (1980, p.562); Lee (1998, p.15)

immigration, and they now took on added significance as safe havens from the storm of anti-Chinese venom. The Chinese withdrew to these neighborhoods and became an "invisible minority" (Tsai, 1986, p. 67).

These early Chinatowns were ethnic enclaves like those founded by Jews on the East Coast and the more recently founded Cuban community in Miami, and a similar process formed them. The earliest urban Chinese included merchants and skilled artisans who, like the early wave of Cuban immigrants, were experienced in commerce (Chan, 1990, p. 44). They established businesses and retail stores that were typically small in scope and modest in profits. As the number of urban Chinese increased, the market for these enterprises became larger and more spatially concentrated. New services were required, the size of the cheap labor pool available to Chinese merchants and entrepreneurs increased, and the Chinatowns became the economic, cultural, and social centers of the community.

Within the Chinatowns, elaborate social structures developed that mirrored traditional China in many ways. The enforced segregation of the Chinese in America helped preserve much of the traditional food, dress, language, values, and religions of their homeland from the pressures of Americanization. The social structure was based on a variety of types of organizations, including family and clan groups and *huiguan*, or associations based on the region or district in China from which the immigrant had come. These organizations performed various, often overlapping, social and welfare services, including settling disputes, aiding new arrivals from their regions, and facilitating the development of mutual aid networks (Lai, 1980, p. 221; Lyman, 1974, pp. 32–37,116–118).

Life was not always peaceful in Chinatown, and there were numerous disputes over control of resources and the organizational infrastructure. In particular, secret societies called *tongs* contested the control and leadership of the merchant-led *huiguan* and the clan associations. These sometimes bloody conflicts were sensationalized in the American press as "Tong Wars," and they contributed to the popular stereotypes of Asians as exotic, mysterious, and dangerous (Lai, 1980, p. 222; Lyman, 1974, pp. 37–50).

Despite these internal conflicts, American Chinatowns evolved into highly organized, largely self-contained communities, complete with their own leadership and decision-making structures. The internal "city government" of Chinatown was the Chinese Consolidated Benevolent Association (CCBA). Dominated by the larger *huiguan* and clans, the CCBA coordinated and supplemented the activities of the various organizations and represented the interests of the community to the larger society.

The local CCBAs, along with other organizations, also attempted to combat the anti-Chinese campaign, speaking out against racial discrimination and filing numerous lawsuits to contest racist legislation (Lai, 1980, p. 223). The effectiveness of the protest efforts was handicapped by the lack of resources in the Chinese community and the fact that Chinese immigrants could not become citizens. Attempts were made to mobilize international pressure to protest the treatment of the Chinese in the United States. At the time, however, China was itself colonized and dominated by other nations (including the United States). The country was further weakened by internal turmoil and could mount no effective assistance for its citizens in the United States (Chan, 1990, p. 62).

Survival and Development. The Chinese American community survived despite the widespread poverty, discrimination, and pressures created by the unbalanced sex ratio. Members of the group began to seek opportunities in other regions, and Chinatowns appeared and grew in New York, Boston, Chicago, Philadelphia, and many other cities.

The patterns of exclusion and discrimination that began during the 19th-century anti-Chinese campaign were common throughout the nation and continued well into the 20th century. Chinese Americans responded by finding economic opportunity in areas where dominant group competition for jobs was weak, continuing their tendency to be an "invisible" minority group. Very often, they started small businesses that either served other members of their own group (e.g., restaurants) or relied on the patronage of the general public (e.g., laundries). The jobs provided by these small businesses were the economic lifeblood of the community but were limited in the amount of income and wealth they could generate. Until recent decades, for example, most restaurants served primarily other Chinese, especially single men. Since their primary clientele was poor, the profit potential of these businesses was sharply limited. Laundries served the more affluent dominant group, but the returns from this enterprise declined as washers and dryers became increasingly present in homes throughout the nation. The population of Chinatown was generally too small to sustain more than these two primary commercial enterprises (Zhou, 1992, pp. 92–94).

As the decades passed, the enclave economy and the complex subsociety of Chinatown evolved. However, discrimination, combined with defensive self-segregation, ensured the continuation of poverty, limited job opportunities, and substandard housing. Relatively hidden from general view, Chinatown became the world in which the second generation grew to adulthood.

The Second Generation. Whereas the immigrant generation generally retained its native language and customs, the second generation was much more influenced by the dominant culture. The institutional and organizational structures of Chinatown were created to serve the older, mostly male immigrant generation, but younger Chinese Americans tended to look beyond the enclave to fill their needs. They came in contact with the larger society through schools, churches, and voluntary organizations such as the YMCA and YWCA.

They abandoned many traditional customs and were less loyal to and interested in the clan and regional associations that the immigrant generation had constructed. They founded organizations of their own that were more compatible with their Americanized lifestyles (Lai, 1980, p. 225).

As it was for other minority groups, World War II was an important watershed for Chinese Americans. During the war, job opportunities outside the enclave increased, and after the war, many of the 8,000 Chinese Americans who had served in the armed forces were able to take advantage of the GI Bill to further their education (Lai, 1980, p. 226). In the 1940s and 1950s, many second-generation Chinese Americans moved out of the enclave, away from the traditional neighborhoods, and pursued careers in the larger society. This group was mobile and "Americanized," and with educational credentials comparable to those of the general population, they were prepared to seek success outside Chinatown.

In another departure from tradition, the women of the second generation pursued education, also. As early as 1960, median years of schooling for Chinese American women were slightly higher than for Chinese American men (Kitano & Daniels, 1995, p. 48). Additionally, Chinese American women became more diverse in their occupational profile as the century progressed. In 1900, three quarters of all employed Chinese American women worked in manufacturing (usually in garment industry sweatshops or in canning factories) or in domestic work. By 1960, less than 2% were in domestic work, 32% were in clerical occupations, and 18% held professional jobs, often as teachers (Amott & Matthaei, 1991, pp. 209–211).

The men and women of the second generation achieved considerable educational and occupational success, and helped establish the idea that Chinese Americans are a "model minority." A closer examination reveals, however, that the old traditions of anti-Chinese discrimination and prejudice continued to limit the life chances of even the best-educated members of this generation. Second-generation Chinese Americans earned less, on the average, and had less-favorable occupational profiles than did comparably educated white Americans, a gap between qualifications and rewards that reflects persistent discrimination. Kitano and Daniels (1995, p. 50) conclude, for example, that although well-educated Chinese Americans could find good jobs in the mainstream economy, the highest, most lucrative positions—and those that required direct supervision of whites—were still closed to them (see also Hirschman & Wong, 1984).

Furthermore, many Chinese Americans, including many of those who stayed in the Chinatowns to operate the enclave economy and the immigrants who began arriving after 1965, do not fit the image of success at all. A large percentage of these Chinese Americans face many of the same problems as do members of colonized, excluded, exploited minority groups of color. For survival, they rely on low-wage jobs in the garment industry, the service sector, and the small businesses of the enclave economy, and they are beset by poverty and powerlessness, much like the urban underclass segments of other groups.

Thus, Chinese Americans can be found at both ends of the spectrum of success and affluence, and the group is often said to be "bipolar" in its occupational structure (see Barringer, Takeuchi, & Levin, 1995; Min, 2006; Takaki, 1993, pp. 415–416; Wong, 1995, pp. 77–78; Zhou & Logan, 1989). Although a high percentage of Chinese Americans are found in more desirable occupations—sustaining the idea of Asian success—others, less visible, are concentrated at the lowest levels of society. Later in this chapter, we will again consider the socioeconomic status of Chinese Americans and the accuracy of the image of success and affluence.

Japanese Americans

Immigration from Japan began to increase shortly after the Chinese Exclusion Act of 1882 took effect, in part, to fill the gap in the labor supply created by the restrictive legislation (Kitano, 1980). The 1880 census counted only a few hundred Japanese in the United States, but the group increased rapidly over the next few decades. By 1910, the Japanese in the United States outnumbered the Chinese, and they remained the larger of the two groups until large-scale immigration resumed in the 1960s (see Figure 8.3).

The Anti-Japanese Campaign. The contact situation for Japanese immigrants resembled that of the Chinese. They immigrated to the same West Coast regions as the Chinese, entered the labor force in a similar position, and were a small group with few power resources. Predictably, the feelings and emotions generated by the anti-Chinese campaign transferred to them. By the early 1900s, an anti-Japanese campaign to limit competition was in full swing. Efforts were being made to establish a rigid competitive system of group relations and to exclude Japanese immigrants in the same way the Chinese had been barred (Kitano, 1980, p. 563; Kitano & Daniels, 1995, pp. 59–60; Petersen, 1971, pp. 30–55).

Japanese immigration was partly curtailed in 1907 when a "gentlemen's agreement" was signed between Japan and the United States limiting the number of laborers Japan would allow to immigrate (Kitano & Daniels, 1995, p. 59). This policy remained in effect until the United States changed its immigration policy in the 1920s and barred immigration from Japan completely. The end of Japanese immigration is largely responsible for the slow growth of the Japanese American population displayed in Figure 8.3.

Most Japanese immigrants, like the Chinese, were young men laborers who planned to return eventually to their homeland or bring their wives after they were established in their new country (Duleep, 1988, p. 24). The agreement of 1907 curtailed the immigration of men, but because of a loophole, women were able to continue immigrating until the 1920s. Thus, Japanese Americans were able to maintain a relatively balanced gender ratio, marry, and begin families, and a second generation of Japanese Americans began to appear without much delay. Native-born Japanese Americans numbered about half of the group by 1930 and were a majority of 63% on the eve of World War II (Kitano & Daniels, 1995, p. 59).

The anti-Japanese movement also attempted to dislodge the group from agriculture. Many Japanese immigrants were skilled agriculturists, and farming proved to be their most promising avenue for advancement (Kitano, 1980, p. 563). In 1910, between 30% and 40% of all Japanese in California were engaged in agriculture; from 1900 to 1909, the number of independent Japanese farmers increased from fewer than 50 to about 6,000 (Jibou, 1988, p. 358).

Most of these immigrant farmers owned small plots of land, and they made up only a minuscule percentage of West Coast farmers (Jibou, 1988, pp. 357–358). Nonetheless, their presence and relative success did not go unnoticed and eventually stimulated discriminatory legislation, most notably the **Alien Land Act**, passed by the California legislature in 1913 (Kitano, 1980, p. 563). This bill made aliens who were ineligible for citizenship (essentially only immigrants from Asia) also ineligible to own land. The Act did not achieve its goal of dislodging the Japanese from the rural economy. They were able to dodge the discriminatory legislation through various devices, mostly by putting titles of land in the names of their American-born children, who were citizens by law (Jibou, 1988, p. 359).

The Alien Land Act was one part of a sustained campaign against the Japanese in the United States. In the early decades of this century, the Japanese were politically disenfranchised and segregated from dominant group institutions in schools and residential areas. They were discriminated against in movie houses, swimming pools, and other public facilities (Kitano & Daniels, 1988, p. 56). The Japanese were excluded from the mainstream economy and confined to a limited range of poorly paid occupations (see Yamato, 1994). Thus, there were strong elements of systematic discrimination, exclusion, and colonization in their overall relationship with the larger society.

The Ethnic Enclave. Spurned and disparaged by the larger society, the Japanese, like the Chinese, constructed a separate subsociety. The immigrant generation, called Issei (from the Japanese word ichi, meaning "one"), established an enclave in agriculture and related enterprises, a rural counterpart of the urban enclaves constructed by other groups we have examined.

By World War II, the Issei had come to dominate a narrow but important segment of agriculture on the West Coast, especially in California. Although the Issei were never more than 2% of the total population of California, Japanese American–owned farms produced as much as 30% to 40% of various fruits and vegetables grown in that state. As late as 1940, more than 40% of the Japanese American population was involved directly in farming, and many more were dependent on the economic activity stimulated by agriculture, including the marketing of their produce (Jibou, 1988, pp. 359–360). Other Issei lived in urban areas, where they were concentrated in a narrow range of businesses and services, such as domestic service and gardening, some of which catered to other Issei and some of which served the dominant group (Jibou, 1988, p. 362).

Japanese Americans in both the rural and urban sectors maximized their economic clout by doing business with other Japanese–owned firms as often as possible. Gardeners and farmers purchased supplies at Japanese–owned firms, farmers used other members of the group to haul their produce to market, and businesspeople relied on one another and mutual credit associations, rather than dominant group banks, for financial services. These networks helped the enclave economy to grow and also permitted the Japanese to avoid the hostility and racism of the larger society. However, these very same patterns helped sustain the stereotypes that depicted the Japanese as clannish and unassimilable. In the years before World War II, the Japanese American community was largely dependent for survival on their networks of cooperation and mutual assistance, not on Americanization and integration.

The Second Generation (Nisei). In the 1920s and 1930s, anti-Asian feelings continued to run high, and Japanese Americans continued to be excluded and discriminated against despite (or perhaps because of) their relative success. Unable to find acceptance in Anglo society, the second generation, called Nisei, established clubs, athletic leagues, churches, and a multitude of other social and recreational organizations within their own communities (Kitano & Daniels, 1995, p. 63). These organizations reflected the high levels of Americanization of the Nisei and expressed values and interests quite compatible with those of the dominant culture. For example, the most influential Nisei organization was the Japanese American Citizens League, whose creed expressed an ardent patriotism that was to be sorely tested: "I am proud that I am an American citizen. . . . I believe in [American] institutions, ideas and traditions; I glory in her heritage; I boast of her history, I trust in her future" (Kitano & Daniels, 1995, p. 64).

Although the Nisei enjoyed high levels of success in school, the intense discrimination and racism of the 1930s prevented most of them from translating their educational achievements into better jobs and higher salaries. Many occupations in the mainstream economy were closed to even the best-educated Japanese Americans, and anti-Asian prejudice and discrimination did not diminish during the hard times and high unemployment of the Great Depression in the 1930s. Many Nisei were forced to remain within the enclave, and in many cases jobs in the produce stands and retail shops of their parents were all they could find. Their demoralization and anger over their exclusion were eventually swamped by the larger events of World War II.

The Relocation Camps. On December 7, 1941, Japan attacked Pearl Harbor, killing almost 2,500 Americans. President Franklin D. Roosevelt asked Congress for a declaration of war the next day. The preparations for war stirred up a wide range of fears and anxieties among the American public, including concerns about the loyalty of Japanese Americans. Decades of exclusion and anti-Japanese prejudice had conditioned members of the dominant society to see Japanese Americans as sinister, clannish, cruel, unalterably foreign, and racially inferior. Fueled by the ferocity of the war itself and fears about a Japanese invasion of the mainland, the tradition of anti-Japanese racism laid the groundwork for a massive violation of civil rights.

Two months after the attack on Pearl Harbor, President Roosevelt signed Executive Order 9066, which led to the relocation of Japanese Americans living on the West Coast. By the late summer of 1942, more than 110,000 Japanese Americans, young and old, men and women—virtually the entire West Coast population—had been forcibly transported to **relocation camps**, where they were imprisoned behind barbed-wire fences patrolled by armed guards. The majority of these people were American citizens, yet no attempt was made to distinguish between the citizens and the noncitizens. No trials were held, and no one was given the opportunity to refute the implicit charge of disloyalty.

The U.S. government gave families little notice to prepare for evacuation and secure their homes, businesses, and belongings. They were allowed to bring only what they could carry, and had to abandon many of their possessions. Businesspeople sold their establishments and farmers sold their land at panic sale prices. Others locked up their stores and houses and walked away, hoping that the evacuation would be short-lived and their possessions undisturbed.

The internment lasted for nearly three and half years, nearly the entire war. At first, Japanese Americans were not permitted to serve in the armed forces, but eventually more than 25,000 escaped the camps by volunteering for military service. Nearly all of them served in segregated units or doing intelligence work with combat units in the Pacific Ocean. Two all-Japanese American combat units served in Europe and became the most decorated units in American military history (Kitano, 1980, p. 567). Other Japanese Americans were able to get out of the camps by different means. Some, for example, agreed to move to militarily nonsensitive areas far away from the West Coast (and their former homes). Still, about half of the original internees remained when the camps closed at the end of the war (Kitano & Daniels, 1988, p. 64).

The strain of living in the camps affected Japanese Americans in a variety of ways. Lack of activities and privacy, overcrowding, boredom, and monotony were all common complaints. The camps disrupted the traditional forms of family life, as people had to adapt to living in crowded barracks and dining in mess halls. Conflicts flared between people who counseled caution or temperate reactions to their incarceration and those who wanted to protest in more vigorous ways. Many of those who advised moderation were Nisei intent on proving their loyalty by cooperating with the camp administration.

Despite the injustice and dislocations of the incarceration, the camps did reduce the extent to which women were relegated to a subordinate role. Like Chinese women, Japanese women were expected to devote themselves to the care of the men of their family. In Japan, for example, education for women was not intended to challenge their intellect so much as to make them better wives and mothers. In the camps, however, pay for the few jobs available was the same for both men and women, and the mess halls and small living quarters freed women from some of the burden of housework. Many took advantage of the free time to take classes to learn more English and other skills. The younger women were able to meet young men on their own, weakening the tradition of family controlled, arranged marriages (Amott & Matthaei, 1991, pp. 225–229).

Some Japanese Americans protested the incarceration from the start and brought lawsuits to end the relocation program. Finally, in 1944 the Supreme Court ruled that detention was unconstitutional. As the camps closed, some Japanese American individuals and organizations began to seek compensation and redress for the economic losses the group had suffered. In 1948, Congress passed legislation to authorize compensation to Japanese Americans. About 26,500 people filed claims under this legislation. These claims were eventually settled for a total of about $38 million—less than one-tenth of the actual economic losses. Demand for meaningful redress and compensation continued, and in 1988 Congress passed a bill granting reparations of about $20,000 in cash to each of the 60,000 living survivors of the camps. The law also acknowledged that the relocation program had been a grave injustice to Japanese Americans (Biskupic, 1989, p. 2879).

The World War II relocation devastated the Japanese American community and left it with few material resources. The emotional and psychological damage inflicted by this experience is incalculable. The fact that today, only seven decades later, the performance of Japanese Americans is equal or superior to national averages on measures of educational achievement, occupational prestige, and income is one of the more dramatic transformations in minority group history.

Japanese Americans After World War II. In 1945, Japanese Americans faced a world very different from the one they had left in 1942. To escape the camps, nearly half the group had scattered throughout the country and lived everywhere but on the West Coast. As Japanese Americans attempted to move back to their former homes, they found their fields untended, their stores vandalized, their possessions lost or stolen, and their lives shattered. In some cases, there was simply no Japanese neighborhood to return to; the Little Tokyo area of San Francisco, for example, was now inhabited by African Americans who had moved to the West Coast to take jobs in the defense industry (Amott & Matthaei, 1991, p. 231).

Japanese Americans themselves had changed as well. In the camps, the Issei had lost power to the Nisei. The English-speaking second generation had dealt with the camp administrators and held the leadership positions. Many Nisei had left the camps to serve in the armed forces or to find work in other areas of the country. For virtually every American minority group, the war brought new experiences and a broader sense of themselves, the nation, and the world. A similar transformation occurred for the Nisei. When the war ended, they were unwilling to rebuild the Japanese community as it had been before.

Like second-generation Chinese Americans, the Nisei had a strong record of success in school, and they also took advantage of the GI Bill to further their education. When anti-Asian prejudice began to decline in the 1950s and the job market began to open, the Nisei were educationally prepared to take advantage of the resultant opportunities (Kitano, 1980, p. 567).

The Issei-dominated enclave economy did not reappear after the war. One indicator of the shift away from an enclave economy was the fact that the percentage of Japanese American women in California who worked as unpaid family laborers (i.e., worked in family-run businesses for no salary) declined from 21% in 1940 to 7% in 1950 (Amott & Matthaei, 1991, p. 231). Also, between 1940 and 1990, the percentage of the group employed in agriculture declined from about 50% to 3%, and the percentage employed in personal services fell from 25% to 5% (Nishi, 1995, p. 116).

By 1960, Japanese Americans had an occupational profile very similar to that of whites except that they were actually overrepresented among professionals. Many were employed in the primary economy, not in the ethnic enclave, but there was a tendency to choose "safe" careers (e.g., in engineering, optometry, pharmacy, and accounting) that did not require extensive contact with the public or supervision by whites (Kitano & Daniels, 1988, p. 70).

Within these limitations, the Nisei, their children (**Sansei**), and their grandchildren (**Yonsei**) have enjoyed relatively high status, and their upward mobility and prosperity have contributed to the perception that Asian Americans are a "model minority group." An additional factor contributing to the high status of Japanese Americans (and to the disappearance of Little Tokyos) is that unlike the Chinese American community, the Japanese American community has had few new immigrants, and the community has not had to devote many resources to newcomers. Furthermore, recent immigrants from Japan tend to be highly educated professionals whose socioeconomic characteristics add to the perception of success and affluence.

The Sansei and Yonsei are highly integrated into the occupational structure of the larger society. Compared with their parents, their connections with their ethnic past are more tenuous, and in their values, beliefs, and personal goals, they resemble dominant group members of similar age and social class (Kitano & Daniels, 1995, pp. 79–81; also see Spickard, 1996).

COMPARATIVE FOCUS:
Japan's "Invisible" Minority

By the definition stated in Chapter 1, two of the most important characteristics of minority groups are that they (1) are the objects of a pattern of disadvantage and (2) are easily identifiable, either culturally or physically. These two traits work in tandem: Members of the dominant group must be able to determine a person's group membership quickly and easily so the discrimination that is the hallmark of minority-group status can be practiced.

Visibility is such an obvious precondition for discrimination that it almost seems unnecessary to state it. However, every generalization seems to have an exception, and the members of at least one minority group, the Burakumin of Japan, have been victimized by discrimination and prejudice for hundreds of years but are virtually indistinguishable from the general population. How could such an "invisible" minority come into being? How could the disadvantaged status be maintained through time?

The Burakumin were created centuries ago, when Japan was organized into a caste system (see Chapter 3) based on occupation. The ancestors of today's Burakumin did work that brought them into contact with death (e.g., as gravediggers) or required them to handle meat products (e.g., as butchers). These occupations were regarded as very low in status, "unclean," or polluted.

The Burakumin were required to live in separate villages and to wear identifying leather patches (thus raising their social visibility). They were forbidden to marry outside their caste, and any member of the general population who touched a member of the Burakumin had to be ritually purified or cleansed of pollution (Lamont-Brown, 1993, p. 137).

The caste system was officially abolished in the 19th century, at about the time Japan began to industrialize, and most observers today agree that the overall situation of the Burakumin has improved (Ball, 2009). But the Burakumin maintain their minority status, and prejudice against them continues (Neary, 2003, p. 288).

The Burakumin are a small group, about 2% or 3% of Japan's population. About 1 million still live in traditional villages, and another 2 million or so live in non-Burakumin areas, mostly in larger cities. They continue to be seen as "filthy," "not very bright," and "untrustworthy"—stereotypical traits often associated with minority groups mired in subordinate and unequal positions. Also, as is the case for many American minority groups, the Burakumin have a number of protest organizations—including the Buraku Liberation League (www.bll.gr.jp/eng.html)—that are dedicated to improving conditions.

The situation of the Burakumin might seem puzzling. If the group is indistinguishable from the general population, why don't the Burakumin simply blend in and disappear? What keeps them attached to their group?

Some Burakumin are proud of their heritage and refuse to surrender to the dominant culture. They have no intention of trading their identity for acceptance or opportunity. For others, even those attempting to pass, the tie to the group and a subtle form of social visibility are maintained by the ancient system of residential segregation. The identity of the traditional Burakumin areas of residence are well known, and this information—not race or culture—is what establishes the boundaries of the group and forms the ultimate barrier to Burakumin assimilation.

There are reports that Japanese firms use lists of local Burakumin addresses to screen out potential employees. Also, the telltale information may be revealed when applying to rent an apartment (some landlords refuse to rent rooms to Burakumin because of their alleged "filthiness") or purchase a home (banks may be reluctant to provide loans to members of a group that is widely regarded as "untrustworthy").

Another line of resistance can arise with marriage. It is common for Japanese parents to research the family history of a child's fiancé, a process which is sure to unearth any secret Burakumin connections. Thus, members of the Burakumin who pass undetected at work and in their neighborhood are likely to be "outed" if they attempt to marry outside the group.

This link to the traditional Burakumin residential areas means that this group is not really invisible: There is a way to determine group membership, a mark or sign of who belongs and who doesn't. Consistent with our definition, this "birthmark" is the basis for a socially constructed boundary that differentiates "us" from "them," and for the discrimination and prejudice associated with minority-group status.

QUESTIONS FOR REFLECTION

3. Are the Burakumin unique? What other minority groups are similarly "invisible"?

4. Are the Burakumin advocacy groups justified in attempting to preserve the group's heritage? Should they be working for greater assimilation? Explain.

5. What do you suppose the future holds for the Burakumin? Will they disappear and assimilate into the larger society? Explain.

Figure 8.5 Relative Size of Immigrant Groups From Asia, 1950–2013

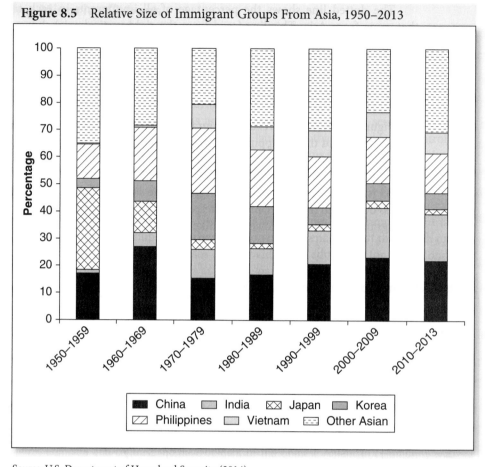

Source: U.S. Department of Homeland Security (2014).

stream also includes a large contingent of highly educated professionals seeking opportunities to practice their careers and expand their skills.

These more elite immigrants contribute to the image of "Asian success," but many Asian immigrants are less skilled and educated, and often undocumented. Thus, this stream of immigrants includes a healthy representation of people from both the top and the bottom of the occupational and educational hierarchies.

Of course, other factors besides economics attract these immigrants. The United States has maintained military bases throughout the region (including South Korea, Japan, and the Philippines) since the end of World War II, and many Asian immigrants are the spouses of American military personnel.

Also, U.S. involvement in the war in Southeast Asia in the 1960s and 1970s created interpersonal ties and governmental programs that drew refugees from Vietnam, Cambodia, and Laos, many of whom lived in camps and relocation centers for years before immigrating to the United States. Because of the conditions of their escape from their homelands, they typically bring little in the way of human or material capital.

Among the refugee groups are the Hmong, hill people from Laos and other Southeast Asian nations who fought with the American forces in the Vietnam War. They are relatively small in number (see Table 8.1) and face some unique challenges in their adjustment to U.S. society. Their culture is very traditional and, in many ways, far removed from the modernized, Western world in which they find themselves.

Prior to the Vietnam War, the Hmong were at the hunter-gatherer level of subsistence technology and brought very little social and cultural capital with them. Anthropologist Anne Fadiman illustrates the complex challenges the Hmong face in acculturating to the United States in her 1998 account of an epileptic Hmong girl, Lia Lee. According to traditional Hmong cultural understandings, illness is caused by spirits and needs to be treated in the time-honored way, by traditional healers or shamans. The girl's loving parents found it difficult to understand and accept the instructions of Lia's Californian doctors that attempted to treat her with medicine and pills, in part because of linguistic barriers but mainly because of cultural differences. The resultant tragedy illustrates the challenges of acculturation for this group (Fadiman, 1998). Contrary to the stereotypical image of Asian American success, the Hmong generally display a socioeconomic profile more consistent with America's colonized minority groups.

Another striking contrast is between immigrants from India, many of whom are highly educated and skilled, and Vietnamese Americans, who have a socioeconomic profile that more resembles those of non-Asian racial minorities in the United States. Part of the difference between these two groups relates to their contact situations and can be illuminated by applying the Blauner hypothesis. Immigrants from India are at the "immigrant" end of Blauner's continuum. They tend to bring strong educational credentials and to be well equipped to compete for favorable positions in the occupational hierarchy.

The Vietnamese, in contrast, began their American experience as a refugee group fleeing the turmoil of war. Although they do not fit Blauner's "conquered or colonized" category, most Vietnamese Americans had to adapt to American society with few resources and few contacts with an established immigrant community. The consequences of these vastly different contact situations are suggested by the data presented in the figures throughout this chapter. We will address some of these groups in more detail in Chapter 9, too.

QUESTIONS FOR REFLECTION

9. Identify the major groups of recent immigrants from Asia. How do they differ from Chinese and Japanese Americans?

10. How did the motivation for immigration vary for the different Asian groups? How have these differences affected their relationship with U.S. society?

11. Are these groups colonized or immigrant groups? Why or why not?

Prejudice and Discrimination

American prejudice against Asians first became prominent during the anti-Chinese movement of the 19th century. The Chinese were believed to be racially inferior, docile, and subservient, but also cruel and crafty, despotic, and threatening (Lai, 1980, p. 220; Lyman, 1974, pp. 55–58). The Chinese Exclusion Act of 1882 was justified by the idea that the Chinese could never fully assimilate into U.S. society. The Chinese were seen as a threat to the working class, to American democracy, and to other American institutions. Many of these stereotypes and fears transferred to the Japanese later in the 19th century and then to other groups as they, in turn, arrived in the United States.

The social distance scores presented in Table 1.2 provide the only long-term record of anti-Asian prejudice in the society as a whole. In 1926, the five Asian groups included in the study ranked in the bottom third of the scale, along with other racial and colonized minority groups. Twenty years later, in 1946, the Japanese had fallen to the bottom of the rankings, and the Chinese had risen seven positions, changes that reflect America's World War II conflict with Japan and alliance with China. This suggests that anti-Chinese prejudice may have softened during the war as distinctions were made between "good" and "bad" Asians. For example, an item published in a December 22, 1941, issue of *Time* magazine, "How to Tell Your Friends From the Japs," provided some tips for identifying "good" Asians: "The Chinese expression is likely to be more placid, kindly, open; the Japanese more positive, dogmatic, arrogant. . . . Japanese are nervous in conversation, laugh loudly at the wrong time."

In more recent decades, the average social distance scores of Asian groups have fallen even though the ranking of the groups has remained relatively stable. The falling scores probably reflect the society-wide increase in tolerance and the shift from blatant prejudice to modern racism that we have discussed previously. However, the relative position of Asians in the American hierarchy of group preferences has remained remarkably consistent since the 1920s. This stability may reflect the cultural or traditional nature of much of the anti-Asian prejudice in America.

Numerous reports document violent attacks and other forms of harassment against Asian Americans, especially recent immigrants. High school and middle school students of Asian descent report that they are stereotyped as "high achieving students who rarely fight back," making them excellent candidates for bullying and scapegoating by other groups (Associated Press, 2005). Harassment at one high school in New York rose to such severe levels that the U.S. Department of Justice intervened at the request of school officials (Associated Press, 2005). Incidents such as these suggest that the tradition of anti-Asian prejudice is close to the surface and could be reactivated under the right combination of competition and threat.

On the other hand, a recent survey suggests that discrimination and prejudice are not perceived as major problems by most Asian Americans. According to the survey, which was administered to a representative sample, only 13% of the Asian Americans interviewed said that discrimination was a "major problem," with results ranging from 24% for Korean Americans to only 8% for Japanese Americans (Pew Research Center, 2013, p. 110). Also, only about 20% said they had personally experienced discrimination because of their Asian origin, and only 10% said they had been called offensive names (p. 114). These levels are far below those of African Americans and Hispanic Americans when asked similar questions. For example, 43% of a representative sample of African Americans said there was "a lot" of discrimination against their group, and 61% of Hispanic Americans said discrimination was a "major problem" for them (p. 115).

What might account for these differences? One possibility is that Asian Americans are downplaying the extent of their negative experiences, in conformity with the cultural tendency to avoid confrontation and stress harmony.

Another possibility is that these reports are accurate and Asian Americans truly experience less discrimination than do other racial minorities. As we discussed in Chapter 7, some analysts argue that Asian Americans (along with lighter-skinned, more affluent Latinos) will become "honorary whites," positioned between whites and blacks (and darker-skinned, less affluent Latinos) in the American racial order. If society is actually evolving in this direction, we would expect Asian Americans to feel somewhat less victimized than blacks and some Hispanic Americans.

A final possibility, closely related to the second, is that Asian Americans benefit from "positive" stereotypes and are seen in a more favorable light than other racial minorities. The perception of Asian Americans as a "model minority"—polite, successful, and deferential—could explain their lower levels of discrimination. As we shall see, the "model minority" image is a stereotype, exaggerated and overstated. For some Asian American groups, the image is simply false. The label has been applied to these groups by the media, politicians, and others. It is not an identity the Asian American groups themselves have developed or advocated—in fact, many virulently oppose it because it obscures many of the problems that exist in Asian American communities. As you might suspect, people who apply this label to Asian Americans have a variety of hidden moral and political agendas, and we will explore these dynamics later in this chapter.

Assimilation and Pluralism

In this section, we continue to assess the situation of Asian Americans today using the same conceptual framework used in the previous three chapters.

Acculturation

The extent of acculturation of Asian Americans is highly variable from group to group. Japanese Americans represent one extreme. They have been a part of American society for more than a century, and the current generations are highly acculturated. Immigration from Japan has been low and has not revitalized the traditional culture or language. As a result, Japanese Americans are the most acculturated of the Asian American groups, as illustrated in Figure 8.6, and have the lowest percentage of members who speak English "less than very well."

Filipino and Indian Americans also have low percentages of members who are not competent English speakers, but for different reasons. The Philippines has had a strong American presence since the Spanish-American War of 1898, whereas India is a former British colony in which English remains an important language for higher education and of the educated elite.

Chinese Americans, in contrast, are highly variable in their extent of acculturation. Many are members of families who have been American for generations and are highly acculturated. Others, including many recent undocumented immigrants, are newcomers who have little knowledge of English or of Anglo culture. On this dimension, as in occupations, Chinese Americans are "bipolar." This great variability within the group makes it difficult to characterize their overall degree of acculturation.

Also, note that the groups who are refugees from the 1960s and 1970s wars in Southeast Asia (Vietnamese, Cambodians, Hmong, and Laotians) are less acculturated. They, along with the Chinese and Koreans, have many foreign-born members (see Figure 8.2) and are still largely in their first generation.

Gender and Physical Acculturation: The Anglo Ideal. Anglo-conformity can happen on levels other than the cultural. A number of studies document the feelings of inadequacy and negative self-images that often result when minority group members—especially women—compare themselves with the Anglo standards of attractiveness and beauty that dominate U.S. culture.

Figure 8.6   Percentage Who Speak English Less Than "Very Well" for Total Population, All Asian Americans, and Ten Largest Asian American Groups, 2012

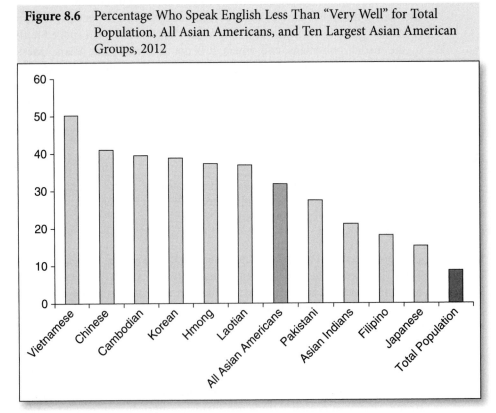

Source: U. S. Census Bureau, 2013g.

Some of the studies in this tradition are classics of the social science literature, including the "doll studies" conducted by social psychologists Kenneth and Mamie Clark in the 1930s and 1940s (Clark & Clark, 1940, 1950). The Clarks showed pairs of white and black dolls to a sample of young African American children and asked them a series of questions, including "Which doll is pretty?" "Which doll is nice?" "Which doll would you like to play with?" and "Which doll is ugly?"

They documented a preference for the white doll, which they interpreted as evidence that the children had internalized white standards of beauty and developed negative self-images as a consequence. Contemporary projects inspired by the Clark doll study include a YouTube video entitled "A Girl Like Me" (2005) by then 17-year-old Kiri Davis[1], and a documentary by comedian Chris Rock entitled *Good Hair* (2009).

Asian American women, like most women in modern U.S. society, are pressured by the cultural message that physical beauty should be among their most important concerns. As racial minorities, they are also subjected to the additional message that they are inadequate by Anglo standards and that some of their most characteristic physical traits (e.g., "slanted" eyes and flat noses) are devalued—indeed ridiculed—in the larger society (Kaw, 1997).

These messages generate pressures for minority women to conform not only culturally but also physically. For example, African Americans spend millions of dollars on hair straightening and skin bleaching. For Asian American women, the attempt to comply with Anglo standards of beauty may include cosmetic surgery to sculpt their noses or to "open" their eyes.

Eugenia Kaw (1997) studied these issues by conducting in-depth interviews with medical practitioners and with a small sample of Asian American women, most of whom had had surgery on their eyelids or noses. The women tended to see their surgeries as simply their personal choice, not unlike putting on make-up. However, Kaw found that they consistently described their presurgical features in negative terms. They uniformly said "that 'small, slanty' eyes and a 'flat' nose" suggest a person who is dull and passive "and a mind that is 'closed.'" For example, one subject said that she considered eyelid surgery while in high school to "'avoid the stereotype of the Oriental bookworm' who is 'dull and doesn't know how to have fun.'" Kaw concludes that the decision of Asian American women to change the shape of their eyes and noses is greatly influenced by racist stereotypes and patriarchal norms: an attempt—common among all racial minority groups—to acculturate on a physical as well as a cultural level.

Secondary Structural Assimilation

We will cover this topic in the order followed in previous chapters.

Residence. Figure 8.7 shows the regional concentrations of all Asian Americans in 2010. The tendency to reside on either coast and around Los Angeles, San Francisco, and New York City stands out clearly. Note also the sizable concentrations in a variety of metropolitan areas, including Chicago, Atlanta, Miami, Denver, and Houston.

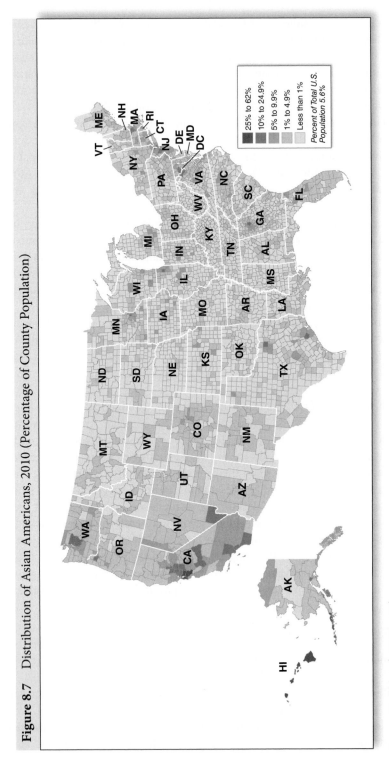

Figure 8.7 Distribution of Asian Americans, 2010 (Percentage of County Population)

Legend:
- 25% to 62%
- 10% to 24.9%
- 5% to 9.9%
- 1% to 4.9%
- Less than 1%

Percent of Total U.S. Population 5.6%

Source: Hoeffel et al. (2012, p.10).

The various Asian American groups are concentrated in different regions, with the huge majority of Filipino and Japanese Americans residing in the West, along with about half of Chinese and Vietnamese Americans. Asian Indians have the highest percentage living in the Northeast (30%), and Vietnamese Americans have the highest percentage in the South (32%), mostly concentrated in the fishing industry on the Texas and Louisiana coasts. The Hmong, alone among Asian American groups, are concentrated in the upper Midwest, especially in Wisconsin and Minnesota (Hoeffel et al., 2012, pp. 18–20).

Figure 8.8 shows that Asian Americans, like Hispanic Americans, are moving away from their "traditional" places of residence into new regions. Between 2000 and 2010, the Asian American population increased especially rapidly along the East and West Coasts, in Arizona, and in some areas of the upper Midwest.

Between 2000 and 2010, the Asian population increased more than 50% in 30 of the 50 states, with 8 more closely approaching the 50% mark. In seven states (including Arizona, Nevada, Delaware, and North Carolina) the Asian population increased by more than 75% (Hoeffel et al., 2012, p. 7).

Asian Americans in general are highly urbanized, a reflection of the entry conditions of recent immigrants as well as the appeal of ethnic neighborhoods, such as Chinatowns, with long histories and continuing vitality. As Figure 8.9 shows, all but 2 of the 10 largest Asian American groups were more than 90% urbanized in 2000, and several approach the 100% mark.

As we saw in Figure 5.9 in Chapter 5, Asian Americans are much less residentially segregated than either African Americans or Hispanic Americans. The levels of residential segregation for Asian Americans have been well below "high" (dissimilarity scores greater than 60) but tend to be slightly higher in cities with more concentrated Asian populations. The level of residential segregation is holding steady, a reflection of high rates of immigration and the tendency of newcomers to settle close to other members of their group. Also, these lower scores may reflect the more favored position for Asian Americans—as opposed to blacks and darker-skinned Hispanic Americans—which we noted earlier when discussing their lower levels of reported discrimination.

Asian Americans are also moving away from their traditional neighborhoods and enclaves and into the suburbs of metropolitan areas, most notably in the areas surrounding Los Angeles, San Francisco, New York, and other cities where the groups are highly concentrated. For example, Asian Americans have been moving in large numbers to the San Gabriel Valley, just east of downtown Los Angeles. Once a bastion of white, middle-class suburbanites, these areas have taken on a distinctly Asian flavor in recent years. Monterey Park, once virtually all white, is now majority Chinese American and is often referred to as "America's first suburban Chinatown" or the "Chinese Beverly Hills" (Fong, 2002, p. 49; see also Chowkwanyun & Segall, 2012).

Education. Asian American children experience less school segregation than Hispanic and Black American children (Fry, 2007), although the extent of segregation for this population may have increased in recent years because of high rates of immigration and residential concentration, particularly in larger cities.

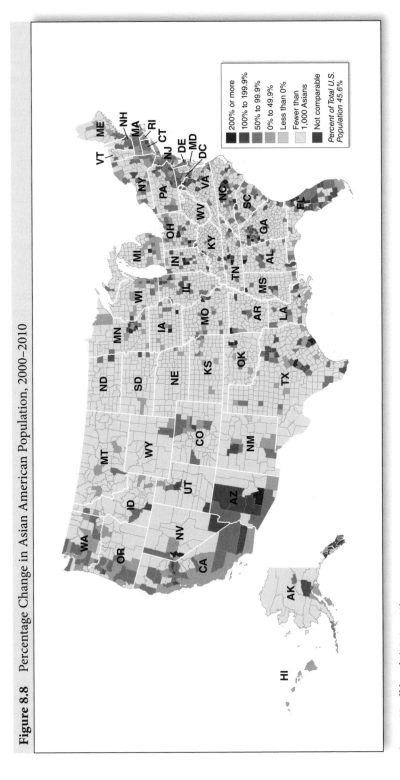

Figure 8.8 Percentage Change in Asian American Population, 2000–2010

Legend:
- 200% or more
- 100% to 199.9%
- 50% to 99.9%
- 0% to 49.9%
- Less than 0%
- Fewer than 1,000 Asians
- Not comparable

Percent of Total U.S. Population 45.6%

Source: Hoeffel et al. (2012, p 11).

Figure 8.9   Urbanization of Ten Largest Asian American Groups, All Asian Americans, and Total Population, 2000

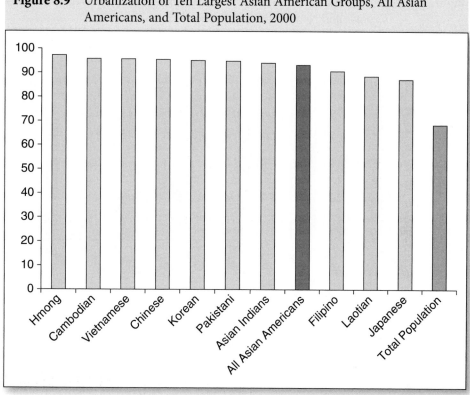

Source: U.S. Census Bureau (2000a).

The extent of schooling for Asian Americans is very different from that for other U.S. racial minority groups, at least at first glance. Asian Americans as a whole compare favorably with society-wide standards for educational achievement, and they perform above those standards on many measures. Figure 8.10 shows that 3 of the 10 Asian American groups rank higher than non-Hispanic whites in completing high school, and 6 of 10 rank higher in completing college degrees, a pattern that has been reinforced by the high levels of education of many recent Asian immigrants.

A quick glance at Figure 8.10 might sustain the image of Asian American success, but note that several groups are relatively low in educational attainment. Asian Americans display a full range of achievement: While it is true that some groups (or at least some elements of some groups) are quite successful, others have profiles that are closer to those of colonized racial minority groups.

This more balanced view of Asian Americans is further explored in Figures 8.11 and 8.12. The former shows the percentage of each group with *less than* a high school education and includes Hispanic Americans, African Americans, American Indians, and non-Hispanic whites for comparison. As we saw in Chapter 7, recent Hispanic immigrants tend to bring modest educational credentials, and the same point can be

Figure 8.10 Educational Attainment for All Asian Americans, Ten Largest Asian American Groups, and Non-Hispanic Whites, 2012

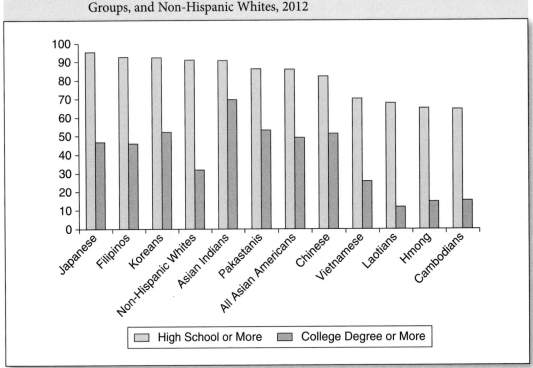

Source: U.S. Census Bureau (2013a).

made for several of the Asian American groups, all of which have a high percentage of foreign-born members and include many refugees from the wars in Southeast Asia. On this measure of educational attainment, the Southeast Asian groups actually fare worse than African Americans and American Indians, both colonized racial minorities. Information such as this presents a serious challenge to glib characterizations of Asian Americans as successful "model minorities."

Figure 8.12 further challenges the "model-minority" image by comparing the educational attainment of Chinese Americans and non-Hispanic whites. More than 50% of Chinese Americans hold college and graduate degrees, far outnumbering whites (31%) at this level. Note, however, that Chinese Americans are also disproportionately concentrated at the lowest level of educational achievement. About 18% of the group has less than a high school diploma, as opposed to a little less than 10% of non-Hispanic whites. Many of these less educated Chinese Americans are recent immigrants (many undocumented), and they supply the unskilled labor force—in retail shops, restaurants, and garment industry "sweatshops"—that staffs the lowest levels of the Chinatown economy.

Assessments of Asian American success must also differentiate between the native-born and the foreign-born members of the groups. The native-born are generally better

Figure 8.11 Percentage With Less Than a High School Education

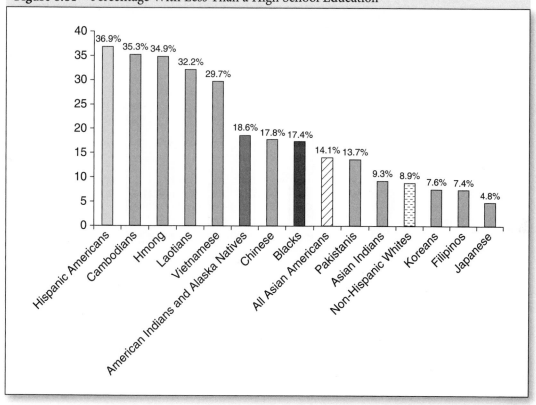

Source: U.S. Census Bureau (2013a).

educated, and the foreign-born are split between highly educated professionals and those who bring lower levels of human capital. For example, according to a recent survey, almost all (98%) native-born Chinese Americans were high school graduates and 73% had college degrees. In contrast, only 77% of foreign-born Chinese Americans had finished high school and only 41% had earned a college degree (computed from Pew Research Center, 2013).

As illustrated by these examples, the image of success for Asian Americans needs to be balanced with the recognition that there is a full range of achievement in the group and average levels of educational attainment are inflated for some groups by recent immigrants who are highly educated, skilled professionals.

Political Power. The ability of Asian Americans to pursue their group interests has been sharply limited by a number of factors, including the relatively small size of the population, institutionalized discrimination, and the same kinds of racist practices that have limited the power resources of other minority groups of color. However, and contrary to the perception that Asian Americans are a "quiet" minority, the group has

Figure 8.12 Educational Levels for Non-Hispanic Whites and Chinese Americans, 2012

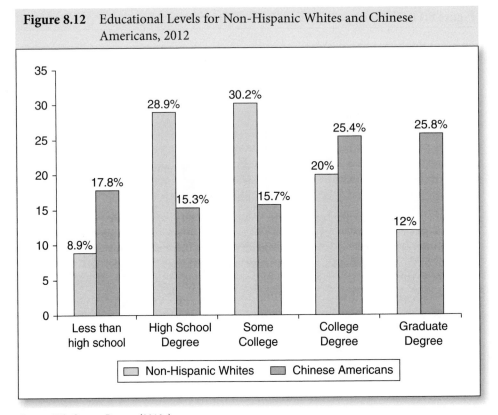

Source: U.S. Census Bureau (2013a).

a long history of political action, including a civil rights movement in the 1960s and 1970s (Fong, 2002, pp. 273–281).

The political power of Asian Americans today is also limited by their high percentage of foreign-born members and, for some groups, lack of facility in English. Rates of political participation for the group (e.g., voting in presidential elections) are considerably lower than national norms. For example, as was the case with Hispanic Americans, less than half (47%) of Asian Americans voted in the 2012 presidential election (vs. about two thirds of non-Hispanic whites and blacks). This level of participation was about the same as in the 2008 presidential election, although slightly higher than in earlier presidential elections (File, 2013, pp. 3–5). Like Hispanic Americans, the impact of this group on national politics will likely increase as more members Americanize, learn English, and become citizens.

There are signs of the group's growing power, especially in areas where they are most residentially concentrated. Of course, Asian Americans have been prominent in Hawaiian politics for decades, but they are increasingly involved in West Coast political life as well. At present, 12 Asian and Pacific Islanders serve in the U.S. House of Representatives (about 2% of the membership) and one in the Senate, Senator Mazie

Hirono of Hawaii, the first Asian American woman to serve in the Senate (Manning, 2013, p. 8).

Jobs and Income. The economic situation of Asian Americans is mixed and complex, as it is for Hispanic Americans. On some measures, Asian Americans as a whole exceed national norms, a reflection of the high levels of academic achievement combined with the impressive educational credentials of many new arrivals. However, overall comparisons can be misleading, and we must also recognize the economic diversity within the group "Asian Americans."

Starting with occupational profiles, the image of success is again sustained. Both men and women are overrepresented in the highest occupational categories, a reflection of the high levels of educational attainment for the group. Asian American men are underrepresented among manual laborers, but, otherwise, the group's occupational profiles are in rough proportion to the society as a whole (U.S. Census Bureau, 2013a).

Figure 8.13 shows median household incomes for Asian Americans and non-Hispanic whites for the past 25 years and reveals that Asian Americans have *higher*

Figure 8.13 Median Household Income for Non-Hispanic Whites and All Asian Americans, 1987–2012

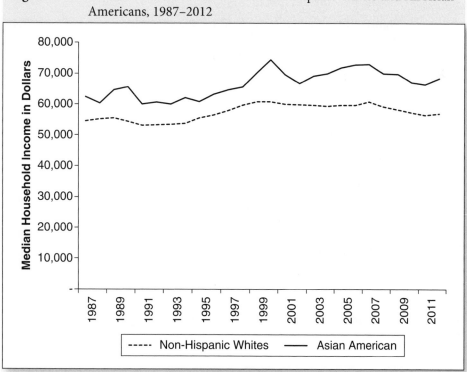

Source: U.S. Census Bureau (2013c).

median household incomes, a picture of general affluence that is in dramatic contrast to the other racial minority groups we have examined in this text. The gap fluctuates, but Asian Americans' median household income is generally 115% of whites'.

This image of success, glittering at first glance, becomes more complicated and nuanced when we look at the separate subgroups within the Asian American community. Figure 8.14 displays median household incomes for all non-Hispanic whites, all Asian Americans, and the 10 largest subgroups. We can see immediately that economic success is not universally shared: half of the Asian American groups are below the average income for non-Hispanic whites.

A still more telling picture emerges when we consider income per capita (or per person) as opposed to median incomes for entire households. This is an important comparison because the apparent prosperity of so many Asian American families is linked to their ownership of small businesses in the enclave. These enterprises typically employ the entire family for many long hours each day, with children adding their labor after school and on weekends and other relatives (many of them new immigrants, a percentage of which are undocumented) contributing as well. The household unit may post a high income as a result of these collective efforts, but, when spread across many family members, the glow of "success" is muted.

Figure 8.14   Median Household Incomes for All Asian Americans, Ten Largest Asian Americans Groups, and Non-Hispanic Whites, 2012

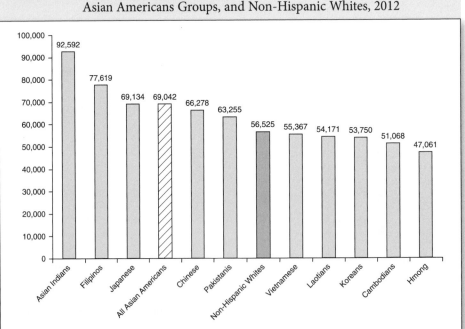

Source: U.S. Census Bureau (2013a).

Figure 8.15 shows that, on per capita income, only two Asian American groups exceed non-Hispanic whites. The other eight groups (including Chinese and Korean Americans, the groups most dependent on small business ownership) enjoy much lower levels of relative prosperity. In particular, the Southeast Asian groups with high percentages of refugees from the Vietnam War (especially the Hmong) are below national norms on this measure.

Figure 8.16 provides additional evidence that the image of a "model minority"—uniformly prosperous and successful—is greatly exaggerated. Asian Americans, unlike other racial minority groups, are overrepresented in the three highest income categories: 24% of all Asian Americans are in these categories compared with only 16% of non-Hispanic whites. However, note that Asian Americans are also overrepresented in the lowest income category, a reflection of the "bipolar" distribution of Chinese Americans and some other groups.

Figures 8.17 and 8.18 finish the economic portrait of Asian Americans and reinforce the picture of complexity and diversity. While the poverty levels of all Asian Americans, considered as a single group, are comparable to those of non-Hispanic whites, several of the groups have much higher rates of poverty, especially for children. As we have seen in other figures, Japanese Americans, Filipino Americans, and Asian

Figure 8.15   Per Capita Income for All Asian Americans, Ten Largest Asian American Groups, and Non-Hispanic Whites, 2012

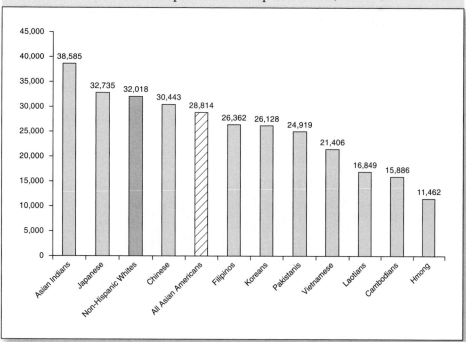

Source: U.S. Census Bureau (2013a).

Figure 8.16 Distribution of Household Income for Non-Hispanic Whites and Asian Americans, 2013

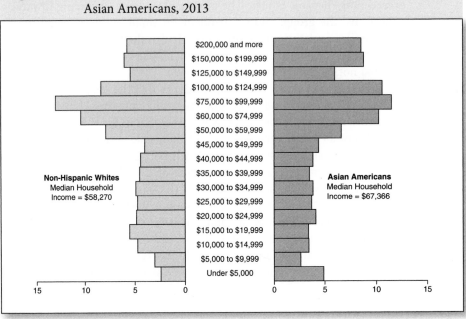

Source: U.S. Census Bureau (2013e).

Figure 8.17 Percentage of Families and Children in Poverty for All Asian Americans, Ten Largest Asian American Groups, and Non-Hispanic Whites, 2012

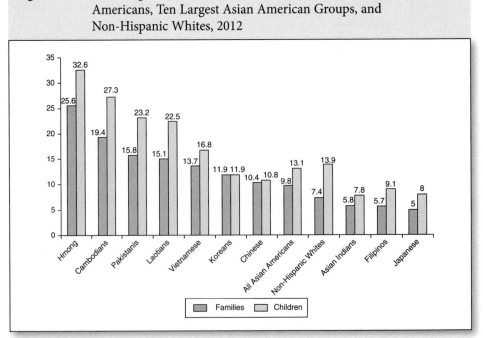

Source: U.S. Census Bureau (2013a).

Figure 8.18 Percentage of Selected Native-Born and Foreign-Born Asian American Groups and Non-Hispanic Whites With Incomes Less Than $30,000

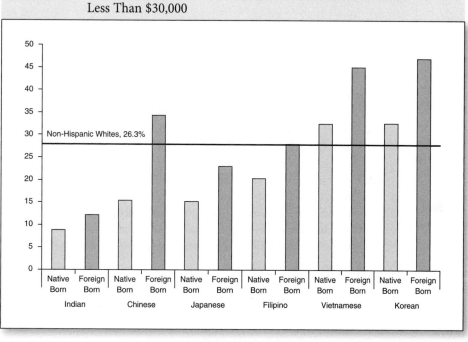

Source: Compiled from Pew Research Center (2013c).

Indian Americans are "successful" on this indicator, but other groups have poverty levels comparable to those of colonized racial minority groups.

Figure 8.18 examines the situation of several Asian Americans in terms of their nativity. Once again, we see the great diversity from group to group, with foreign-born Vietnamese Americans (largely refugees) and Korean Americans exhibiting the highest percentage of members earning less than $30,000. For all six groups, in fact, the native-born have much lower percentages of members with low incomes, and in some cases (e.g., for Chinese Americans) the difference is quite dramatic.

These socioeconomic profiles reflect the diversity of Asian American groups. Some are indeed prosperous and successful, and their financial wealth exceeds national norms, sometimes by a considerable margin. Other groups resemble other American racial minority groups. Japanese and Chinese Americans have the longest histories in the United States and generally rank at the top in measures of wealth and prosperity. Other groups—particularly those that include large numbers of refugees from Southeast Asia—have not fared as well and present pictures of poverty and economic distress. Some "bipolar" groups, such as Chinese Americans, fit in both categories. Additionally, we should note that the picture of economic distress for these groups would be much greater if we focused on undocumented immigrants, who are numerous in the community and concentrated in the informal, irregular economy.

Primary Structural Assimilation

Levels of integration at the primary level for Asian Americans, are, once again, highly variable from group to group. Japanese Americans tend to be the most integrated on this dimension. One study found that, of the six Asian American groups studied, Japanese Americans were the most likely to have friends outside their group and to marry across group lines (Pew Research Center, 2013, pp. 32, 98). The same study found that, as would be expected, integration at the primary level was lower for the foreign-born and those with less English language ability.

Generally, rates of primary integration tend to be higher than for other groups but are declining as the number of Asian Americans grows and the percentage of foreign-born increases (Passel, Wang, & Taylor, 2010, p. 17). This pattern reflects the tendency of newcomers to marry within their group.

Table 8.2 compares in-marriage trends in 1980 and 2008 following the same format used in previous chapters. Asian Americans have much lower rates of in-marriage than do African Americans and Hispanic Americans, although they have somewhat higher rates than Native Americans. Again, this is partly a function of the relative sizes of these groups but also reflects the more favored position of Asian Americans in the dominant group's perceptions.

Also note that the percentage of foreign-born Asian Americans marrying within the group increased for both men and women. This is consistent with high rates of immigration in recent years and the idea that the first generation tends to socialize more with coethnics.

Table 8.2 Percentage of Whites and Asian Americans Married to a Person of the Same Group, 1980 and 2008

	Whites		Asian Americans			
			Men		Women	
Year	Men	Women	Foreign-Born	U.S.-Born	Foreign-Born	U.S.-Born
1980	96%	95%	58%	57%	45%	51%
2008	93%	92%	77%	53%	55%	52%

Source: Qian and Lichter (2011, p. 1072). Copyright © 2011 National Council on Family Relations. Reprinted with permission.

QUESTIONS FOR REFLECTION

12. In this section, we examined a variety of dimensions of acculturation and integration for Asian Americans. Which is most important? Why?

13. What evidence is presented to support the idea that Asian Americans are a "model minority"? What evidence is presented against this characterization? Which argument is more convincing? Why?

FOCUS ON CONTEMPORARY ISSUES:
How Successful Are Asian Americans?
At What Price?

The materials presented in this chapter should make it clear that the view of Asian Americans as "model minorities" is exaggerated and stereotypical. It is true that, as a whole, the group compares favorably to national statistical norms in terms of education and income. However, when we look closer and especially when we take account of the separate subgroups, we find that some Asian American groups are "bipolar" and that others have profiles that closely resemble those of colonized racial minority groups.

Some further qualifications on the stereotypical view of Asian American success should be noted. First, the group is concentrated in cities where the cost of living is very high. For example, the cities with the largest Asian American populations (e.g., New York, Honolulu, Los Angeles, and San Francisco) are commonly ranked as the most expensive places to live (e.g., see Browne, 2011). Thus, the higher average incomes buy less in the way of housing, food, and other necessities.

Second, as illustrated in Figure 8.15, per capita income for Asian Americans is *lower* than the national average, so the higher average incomes have to be shared across a larger number of people.

Third, researchers commonly find that Asian Americans—especially the foreign-born—get lower income returns for their years of schooling and earn less than whites of the same educational level (see Min, 2006, pp. 82–84 for a review). Also, like other racial minority groups, Asian Americans face a glass ceiling that limits their access to the highest and most lucrative positions in the U.S. status hierarchy, and the group is underrepresented on the boards of Fortune 500 companies (Chou & Feagin, 2008, p. 13).

Finally, while it might seem that the "model minority" stereotype is benign and positive, it can have serious negative consequences. The image can create pressure for members of the group, especially children and students, and the resultant stress can impact mental health and result in depression and even suicide. Chou and Feagin (2008) point out the "lose-lose" dilemma faced by many Asian Americans: if they live up to the "model minority" stereotype, they are labeled as "geeks" and

(Continued)

(Continued)

"nerds," and if they fail—or enjoy only moderate success in school or work—they can be seen as inferior.

The "model minority" stereotype not only distorts the situation of Asian American groups, but it also can lead to oversimplified and negative views of other minority groups. So-called modern racists sometimes attribute the success of Asian Americans solely to their cultural values, such as a strong work ethic or a traditional respect for education, an argument that implies that other minority groups are less successful because they lack these values, deemphasizing or ignoring the role of structural barriers and past-in-present discrimination. Thus, in the ever-evolving interplay of American group relations, the supposed success of Asian Americans can be used as a way of scolding other minority groups of color, particularly black Americans.

Comparing Minority Groups: Explaining Asian American Success

To conclude this chapter, let's return to a question raised in the opening pages: How can we explain the apparent success of some Asian American groups? Relative affluence and high status are not characteristic of the other racial minority groups we have examined, and, at least at first glance, there seems to be little in our theories and concepts to help us understand the situation of Asian Americans. Of course, as we have noted on several occasions, we need to recognize that the "success" label is simplistic and even incorrect for some groups, especially for Southeast Asian groups with a high percentage of refugees, who have profiles that resemble those of colonized racial minority groups. To better focus this discussion, we will concentrate on the groups with the longest histories in the United States: Chinese and Japanese Americans. We present several different views on the nature and causes of "success" for these groups. In this section, we compare Chinese and Japanese Americans with European immigrant groups and colonized minority groups. What crucial factors differentiate the experiences of these groups? Can we understand these differences in terms of the framework provided by the Blauner and Noel hypotheses and the other concepts developed in this text?

The debate over the causes of Asian American success often breaks down into two different viewpoints. One view offers a cultural explanation, which accepts the evidence of Asian American success at face value and attributes it to the "good values" of traditional Asian cultures that we briefly explored at the beginning of this chapter. These values—including respect for elders and for authority figures, hard work and thriftiness, and conformity and politeness—are highly compatible with U.S. middle-class Protestant value systems and consistent with traditional assimilation theory and human capital theory.

The second point of view stresses the ways in which Chinese Americans and Japanese Americans entered American society and their reactions to the barriers of racism and exclusion they faced. This approach could be called a "structural explanation," and it emphasizes contact situations, modes of incorporation, enclave economies, group cohesion, position in the labor market, and institutionalized discrimination, rather than cultural values.

Also, this approach questions the notion that Asian Americans are "successful" and stresses the realities of Asian American poverty and the continuing patterns of racism and exclusion. The structural approach is more compatible with the theories and concepts used throughout this text, and it identifies several of the important pieces needed to solve the puzzle of Asian "success" and put it in perspective. However, this is not to suggest that the cultural approach is wrong or irrelevant. The issues we raise are complex and will probably require many approaches and perspectives before they are fully resolved.

Asian Americans and White Ethnics

Chinese and Japanese immigrants arrived in America at about the same time as immigrants from Southern and Eastern Europe (see Chapter 2). Both groups consisted mainly of sojourning young men who were largely unskilled, from rural backgrounds, and not highly educated. Immigrants from Europe, like those from Asia, encountered massive discrimination and rejection and were also victims of restrictive legislation. Yet the barriers to upward mobility for European immigrants (or at least for their descendants) fell away more rapidly than the barriers for immigrants from Asia. Why?

Some important differences between the two immigrant experiences are clear, the most obvious being the greater racial visibility of Asian Americans. Whereas the cultural and linguistic markers that identified Eastern and Southern Europeans faded with each passing generation, the racial characteristics of the Asian groups continued to separate them from the larger society.

Thus, Asian Americans are not "pure immigrant" groups (see Blauner, 1972, p. 55). For most of the 20th century, Chinese Americans and Japanese Americans remained in a less favorable position than did European immigrants and their descendants, excluded by their physical appearance from the mainstream economy until the decades following World War II.

Another important difference relates to position in the labor market. Immigrants from Southern and Eastern Europe entered the industrializing East Coast economy, where they took industrial and manufacturing jobs. Although such jobs were poorly paid and insecure, this location in the labor force gave European immigrants and their descendants the potential for upward mobility in the mainstream economy. At the very least, these urban industrial and manufacturing jobs put the children and grandchildren of European immigrants in positions from which skilled, well-paid, unionized jobs were reachable, as were managerial and professional careers.

In contrast, Chinese and Japanese immigrants on the West Coast were forced into ethnic enclaves and came to rely on jobs in the small business and service sector, and, in the case of the Japanese, in the rural economy. By their nature, these jobs did not link Chinese and Japanese immigrants or their descendants to the industrial sector or to better-paid, more secure, unionized jobs. Furthermore, their exclusion from the mainstream economy was reinforced by overt, racially based discrimination from both employers and labor unions (see Fong & Markham, 1991).

Asian Americans and Colonized Racial Minority Groups

Comparisons between Asian Americans and African Americans, American Indians, and Hispanic Americans have generated a level of controversy and a degree of heat and passion that may be surprising at first. An examination of the issues and their implications, however, reveals that the debate involves some thinly disguised political and moral agendas and evokes sharply clashing views on the nature of U.S. society. What might appear on the surface to be merely an academic comparison of different minority groups turns out to be an argument about the quality of American justice and fairness and the very essence of the U.S. value system.

What is not in dispute in this debate is that some Asian groups (e.g., Japanese Americans) rank far above other racial minority groups on all the commonly used measures of secondary structural integration and equality. What is disputed is how to interpret these comparisons and assess their meanings. Of course, gross comparisons between entire groups can be misleading. If we confine our attention to averages (mean levels of education or median income), the picture of Asian American success is sustained. However, if we also observe the full range of differences within each group (e.g., the "bipolar" nature of occupations among Chinese Americans), we see that the images of success have been exaggerated and need to be placed in a proper context.

Even with these qualifications, however, discussion often slides on to more ideological ground, and political and moral issues begin to cloud the debate. Asian American success is often taken as proof that American society is truly the land of opportunity and that people who work hard and obey the rules will get ahead: in America, all people can be anything they want as long as they work hard enough.

When we discussed modern racism in Chapters 1 and 5, we pointed out that a belief in the openness and fairness of the United States can be a way of blaming the victim and placing the responsibility for change on the minority groups rather than on the structure of society or on past-in-present or institutionalized discrimination. Asian success is sometimes taken as a "proof" of the validity of this ideology. The none-too-subtle implication is that other groups (African Americans, Hispanic Americans, American Indians) could achieve the same success as Asian Americans but, for various reasons, "choose" not to. Thus, the relative success of Chinese Americans and Japanese Americans has become a device for criticizing other minority groups. A more structural approach to investigating Asian American success begins with a comparison of the history of the various racial minority groups and their modes of incorporation into the larger society. When Chinese Americans and Japanese Americans were building their enclave economies in the early part of the 20th century, African Americans and Mexican Americans were concentrated in unskilled agricultural occupations.

American Indians were isolated from the larger society on their reservations, and Puerto Ricans had not yet begun to arrive on the mainland. It follows, then, that social class differences between these groups today flow from their respective situations in the past.

Many of the occupational and financial advances made by Chinese and Japanese Americans have been due to the high levels of education achieved by the second generations. Although education is traditionally valued in Asian cultures, the decision to invest limited resources in schooling is also quite consistent with the economic niche occupied by these immigrants. Education is one obvious, relatively low-cost strategy to upgrade the productivity and profit of a small-business economy and improve the economic status of the group as a whole. Educated, English-speaking second-generation Chinese and Japanese Americans could act as intermediaries with the larger society and bring expertise and business acumen to the family enterprises and lead them to higher levels of performance. Education might also be the means by which the second generation could enter professional careers. This strategy may have been especially attractive to an immigrant generation that was itself relatively uneducated and barred from citizenship (Hirschman & Wong, 1986, p. 23; see also Bonacich & Modell, 1980, p. 152; Sanchirico, 1991).

The efforts to educate the next generation were largely successful. Chinese Americans and Japanese Americans achieved educational parity with the larger society as early as the 1920s. One study found that for men and women born after 1915, the median years of schooling completed were actually higher for Chinese Americans and Japanese Americans than they were for whites (Hirschman & Wong, 1986, p. 11).

Before World War II, both Asian groups were barred from the mainstream economy and from better jobs. When anti-Asian prejudice and discrimination declined in the 1950s, however, the Chinese and Japanese second generations had the educational background necessary to take advantage of the increased opportunities.

Thus, there was a crucial divergence in the development of Chinese and Japanese Americans and the colonized minority groups. At the time when native-born Chinese Americans and Japanese Americans reached educational parity with whites, the vast majority of African Americans, American Indians, and Mexican Americans were still victimized by Jim Crow laws and legalized segregation and excluded from opportunities for anything but rudimentary education. The Supreme Court decision in *Brown v. Board of Education of Topeka* (1954) was decades in the future, and most American Indian schoolchildren were still being subjected to intense Americanization in the guise of a legitimate curriculum.

Today, these other racial minority groups have not completely escaped from the disadvantages imposed by centuries of institutionalized discrimination. African Americans have approached educational parity with white Americans only in recent years (see Chapter 5), and the educational achievements of American Indians and Mexican Americans remain far below national averages (see Chapters 6 and 7, respectively).

The structural explanation argues that the recent upward mobility of Chinese and Japanese Americans is the result of the methods by which they incorporated themselves into American society, not so much their values and traditions. The logic of their enclave economy led the immigrant generation to invest in the education of their children, who would then be better prepared to develop their businesses and seek opportunities in the larger society.

As a final point, note that the structural explanation is not consistent with traditional views of the assimilation process. The immigrant generation of Chinese Americans and Japanese Americans responded to the massive discrimination they faced by withdrawing, developing ethnic enclaves, and becoming "invisible" to the larger society. Like Jewish Americans and Cuban Americans, Chinese Americans and Japanese Americans used their traditional cultures and patterns of social life to create and build their own subcommunities, from which they launched the next generation. Contrary to traditional ideas about how assimilation is "supposed" to happen, we see again that integration can precede acculturation and that the smoothest route to integration may be the creation of a separate subsociety independent of the surrounding community.

Note

1. See YouTube: http://www.youtube.com/watch?v=5f71JW2zJTU.

Main Points

- Asian Americans and Pacific Islanders are diverse and have brought many different cultural and linguistic traditions to the United States. These groups are growing rapidly but are still only a tiny fraction of the total population. Like Hispanic Americans, Asian Americans have a high percentage of first-generation members and are growing more rapidly than the population as a whole.

- Chinese immigrants were the victims of a massive campaign of discrimination and exclusion and responded by constructing enclaves. Chinatowns became highly organized communities, largely run by the local CCBAs and other associations. The second generation faced many barriers to employment in the dominant society, although opportunities increased after World War II.

- Japanese immigration began in the 1890s and stimulated a campaign that attempted to oust the group from agriculture and curtail immigration from Japan. The Issei formed an enclave, but during World War II Japanese Americans were forced into relocation camps, and this experience devastated the group economically and psychologically.

- Recent immigration from Asia is diverse in terms of national origins, contact situation, levels of human capital, and mode of incorporation into U.S. society. Some immigrants are highly educated professionals, while others more closely resemble the "peasant laborers" who have come from Mexico in recent decades and from Italy, Ireland, Poland, and scores of other nations in the past.

- Overall levels of anti-Asian prejudice and discrimination have probably declined in recent years but remain widespread. A recent survey suggests that people perceive prejudice and discrimination as being less of a problem for Asian Americans than for other racial minority groups. This might reflect "positive" stereotypes of Asian Americans and/or the movement of the group toward "honorary" whiteness.

- Levels of acculturation and secondary structural assimilation are variable. Members of these groups whose families have been in the United States longer tend to be highly acculturated and integrated.

Recent immigrants from China, however, are "bipolar." Many are highly educated and skilled, but a sizable number are "immigrant laborers" who bring modest educational credentials and are likely to be living in poverty.

- The notion that Asian Americans are a "model minority" is exaggerated, but comparisons with European immigrants and colonized minority groups suggest some of the reasons for the relative "success" of these groups.

APPLYING CONCEPTS

Do Asian Americans and Anglo Americans behave differently because of their cultural differences? Do these different reactions lead to misunderstandings and problems for Asian Americans?

Below is a series of statements you might hear on a college campus. Although any of them might be spoken by a student of any background, which are more likely to be said by an Asian American student? Which are more reflective of Anglo culture?

Statement	Asian	Anglo
"I really love the social life on this campus—I really enjoy chatting with all different kinds of people, making small talk, and trading gossip."		
"It's really important to show respect to our professors and the college administrators."		
"I was so proud to be recognized in front of everyone—the entire class—for my research project."		
"I don't like to talk in class when I am directly called on."		
"I don't think that people should bottle their emotions—let it all hang out!"		

Review Questions

1. Describe the cultural characteristics of Asian American groups. How did these characteristics shape relationships with the larger society? Did they contribute to the perception of Asian Americans as "successful"? How?

2. Compare and contrast the contact situation for Chinese Americans, Japanese Americans, and Cuban Americans (in Chapter 7). What common characteristics led to the construction of ethnic enclaves for all three groups? How and why did these enclaves vary from one another?

3. In what sense was the second generation of Chinese Americans "delayed"? How did this affect the relationship of the group with the larger society?

4. Compare and contrast the campaigns that arose in opposition to the immigration of Chinese and Japanese people. Do the concepts of the Noel hypothesis help to explain the differences? Do you see any similarities with the changing federal policy toward Mexican immigrants across the 20th century? Explain.

5. Compare and contrast the Japanese relocation camps with Indian reservations in terms of paternalism and coerced acculturation. What impact did this experience have on the Japanese Americans economically? How were Japanese Americans compensated for their losses? Does the compensation paid to Japanese Americans provide a precedent for similar payments (reparations) to African Americans for their losses under slavery? Why or why not?

6. How do the Burakumin in Japan illustrate "visibility" as a defining characteristic of minority group status? How is the minority status of this group maintained?

7. What gender differences characterize Asian American groups? What are some of the important ways in which women's and men's experiences vary?

8. Describe the situation of the Chinese Americans and Japanese Americans in terms of prejudice and discrimination, acculturation, and integration. Are these groups truly "success stories"? How? What factors or experiences might account for this "success"? Are all Asian American groups equally successful? Describe the important variations from group to group. Compare the integration and level of equality of these groups with other American racial minorities. How would you explain the differences? Are the concepts of the Noel and Blauner hypotheses helpful? Why or why not?

ANSWERS TO APPLYING CONCEPTS

Statement	Asian	Anglo
"I really love the social life on this campus—I really enjoy chatting with all different kinds of people, making small talk, and trading gossip."		X
Asian American values place less emphasis on spontaneity, sociability, and flexibility, and more on self-control and discipline.		
"It's really important to show respect to our professors and college administrators."	X	
Asian Americans are more likely to stress obedience to authority, while Anglos are more likely to stress questioning authority.		
"I was so proud to be recognized in front of everyone—the entire class—for my research project."		X
Asian American values prize humility, cooperation with others, and shared responsibility, not individual achievement.		
"I don't like to talk in class when I am directly called on."	X	

Statement	Asian	Anglo
In Anglo culture, individual visibility is acceptable, even encouraged. Asian American culture places more value on the collective.		
"I don't think that people should bottle their emotions—let it all hang out!"		X
Anglo culture places more stress on "telling it like it is" and openly expressing all emotions.		

Could these differences in values be a problem for Asian American students? How about in situations where students are graded for their contributions to class discussion or expected to speak out and express their ideas? More broadly, might there be issues in situations where students face racism, must make contact across ethnic or racial lines, or desire to date someone from another group? How?

Note: This exercise is largely based on Japanese American Citizens League (2009).

Internet Activities

1. Watch the short interview with Professor Heather Fryer about her book, *Perimeters of Democracy: Inverse Utopias and the Wartime Social Landscape in the American West* at http://www.c-span.org/video/?326502-1/book-discussion-perimeters-democracy. How does it add to your awareness of the Japanese-American internment camps during World War II? What connections does she make to earlier kinds of government internment such as Native American reservations? Based on your reading, what connections do you see between the two?

2. On May 10, 2014, 500 people took images of the Asian Pacific American experience around the world for the first crowdsourced exhibit of its kind. Visit http://smithsonianapa.org/life2014/, look at 10 of the photos, and consider what story they tell about Asian American diversity. Does anything surprise you? What does this exhibit add to your understanding? How does it relate to this chapter (or prior chapters)?

3. Explore the online exhibit, "A More Perfect Union: Japanese Americans and the U.S. Constitution," which documents the history of Japanese American internment camps in the U.S. during World War II. Go to http://amhistory.si.edu/perfectunion/experience/index.html and explore at least two of the six main sections (e.g., "Immigration to Justice"). After reading the summary for the section you choose, click on the photo on the left. Then, use the slider bar at the bottom to scroll through each subsection. For example, the "Immigration" section has subsections on the "Issei," "Hawaii," "U.S. Mainland," and "Legalizing Racism." When you see a photograph that interests you, you can click on it to reveal the date and description. Don't forget to listen to the sound files. What new information is relevant or important?

4. Explore the website of Densho at http://www.densho.org/. Densho is a group devoted to "preserv[ing] the testimonies of Japanese Americans who were unjustly incarcerated during World War II before their memories are extinguished." Start with the "Core Story" link and watch at least two of the videos, making sure to read the summaries. Note the live links embedded in the text that take you to the

Densho encyclopedia. Explore at least two entries. What's most important or relevant to you and why? What was most interesting or surprising? Why is it important to preserve these testimonies?

5. Watch the viral video, "Asians in The Library Ching Ching Ling Long Ting Tong" at https://www.you tube.com/watch?v=AQQr3hUepZM. What do you think about what Alexandra says? For example, what does her language (e.g., "hordes, "ching chong," "our school") suggest? Is it racist or problematic? Why or why not? How does it illustrate at least two concepts you've learned so far? Next, find at least one critique of her video (for example, http://www.colorlines.com/articles/alexandra-wallace-says-sorry-asians-library-youtube-rant) and consider its argument. What points are most important? Then, watch this reinterpretation by spoken word artist Beau Sia at https://www.youtube.com/watch?v=F84NWh8 Uzok. Which points seem most relevant or useful? What critiques might you offer? How do these pieces relate to other pop culture issues about race such as Sia's video response to Rosie O'Donnell at https://www.youtube.com/watch?v=VJCkHu3trKc?

6. Visit the Japan Sociology blog http://japansociology.com by Robert Moorehead and his students at Ritsumeikan University. Read at least two of the posts and note what they add to your understanding of issues of race, ethnicity, class, and gender. See the website's subject tags such as "discrimination," "beauty," and "gender roles."

7. Visit the "Ethnic Groups" tab of Asian Nation at http://www.asian-nation.org/index.shtml to learn more about one other Asian American ethnic group that interests you (or that you don't know much about) such as Cambodian Americans, Laotian Americans, and Korean Americans. Then, click on "Issues" or "Links" and find a topic of interest. Also, note the "Assimilation & Ethnic Identity" and "Multi-Racial/ Hapa" links under the "Culture" section. What was most interesting or relevant to you? How does what you read build on what you've learned in the book so far?

8. Watch the video featuring Professor Jennifer Lee at https://www.youtube.com/watch?t=117&v=-VG4H4298vU. What do you make of her statement, "Not only do positive stereotypes place extraordinary pressure on Asian American students to excel, but they can make students feel like abject failures when they don't stand out and place them at a disadvantage in competing for spots at top universities." What, if anything, might be problematic in her broader argument? Also, what connections do you see between this video and the "Asians in the Library" video noted above?

9. Watch satire on stereotyping at "What Kind of Asian Are You?" at https://www.youtube.com/watch?v=DWynJkN5HbQ. Do you think its approach is effective? What do you think about the questions he asks her? What about her response? Identify at least two problematic statements from each actor. Would you consider them racist, rude, ill-informed, or something else? Why? Next, watch the actors read selected comments posted by viewers at https://www.youtube.com/watch?v=S0QeIq6xt1U. What comments are useful? Which are off the mark?

10. Read the "I Want the Wide American" e-comic from an exhibit of the same name at http://smithsoni anapa.org/earth=0-, which explores topics such as the Chinese Exclusion Act and Asian Pacific American history. How effective is the method for conveying information? If you were drawing a comic about what you've learned in this chapter, what would you say and how would you illustrate it?

11. Read the article on "ethnic plastic surgery" at http://nymag.com/thecut/2014/07/ethnic-plastic-surgery .html. What do you think? How is getting this kind of surgery not just an individual choice but a reflection of social forces? How might it reflect tensions between Anglo and Asian cultures? How does it reflect ideas about gender? What else is important to take away from this article?

Learning Resources on the Web

⑤SAGE edge™

edge.sagepub.com/healeyds5e

SAGE edge offers a robust online environment featuring an impressive array of free tools and resources for review, study, and further exploration, keeping both instructors and students on the cutting edge of teaching and learning.

SAGE edge for Students provides a personalized approach to help you accomplish your coursework goals in an easy-to-use learning environment.

PART 4

Challenges for the Present and the Future

Chapter 9 New Americans, Assimilation, and Old Challenges

Chapter 10 Minority Groups and U.S. Society: Themes, Patterns, and the Future

In this section, we analyze the new immigration, continuing issues of assimilation, and equality, inclusion, and racism. Many of these issues relate to what it means to be an American and have been discussed and debated throughout our history. In the final chapter, we summarize the major themes of this text, bring our analysis to a close, and speculate about the future of race and ethnic relations in the United States.

New Americans, Assimilation, and Old Challenges

❖

Sade and four of his twenty-something friends are at a hookah cafe almost underneath the Verrazano Narrows Bridge in Brooklyn. It's late, but the summer heat is strong and hangs in the air. They sit on the sidewalk in a circle, water pipes bubbling between their white plastic chairs.

Sade is upset. He recently found out that his close friend of almost four years was an undercover police detective sent to spy on him, his friends, and his community. Even the guy's name... was fake, which particularly irked the 24-year-old Palestinian American....

"I was very hurt," he says. "Was it friendship, or was he doing his job?" He takes a puff from his water pipe. "I felt betrayed." The smoke comes out thick and smells like apples....He shakes his head....

Informants and spies are regular conversation topics [among Arab Americans] in the age of terror, a time when friendships are tested, trust disappears, and tragedy becomes comedy. If questioning friendship isn't enough, Sade has also had other problems to deal with. Sacked from his Wall Street job, he is convinced that the termination stemmed from his Jerusalem birthplace. Anti-Arab and anti-Muslim invectives were routinely slung at him there, and he's happier now in a technology firm owned and staffed by other hyphenated Americans. But the last several years have taken their toll. I ask him about life after September 11 for Arab Americans. "We're the new blacks," he says. "You know that, right?"

—Moustafa Bayoumi (2008, pp. 1–2)

Sade's comparison between Arab Americans and blacks may be overstated, but there is no question that America finds itself in a new era of group relations today. The "traditional" minority groups—black Americans, Mexican Americans, and others—have been joined by new groups from places that most Americans could not find on a map: Armenia, Zimbabwe, Bhutan, Guyana, and Indonesia to name but a few.

What do these newcomers bring? What do they contribute, and what do they cost? How are they changing the United States? What will the country look like in 50 years? We asked at the beginning of this text: "What does it mean to be an American?" How will that question be answered in the future?

The world is on the move as never before, and migration connects even the remotest villages of every continent in a global network of population ebb and flow. As we have seen, people are moving everywhere, but the United States remains the single most popular destination. Migrants will pay huge amounts of money—thousands of dollars—veritable fortunes in economies where people survive on dollars a day—and undergo considerable hardship for the chance to work in the United States.

What motivates this population movement? How does it differ from migrations of the past? What impact will the newcomers have on U.S. society? Will they absorb American culture? What parts? Will they integrate into American society? Which segments?

We have been asking questions like these throughout the text. In this chapter, we focus specifically on current immigrants and the myriad issues stimulated by their presence. We mentioned some groups of new Americans in Chapters 7 and 8. In this chapter, we begin by addressing recent immigration in general terms and then consider some additional groups of new Americans, including Hispanic, Caribbean, and Asian groups; Arabs and Middle Easterners, and immigrants from sub-Saharan Africa. A consideration of these groups will broaden your understanding of the wide cultural variations, motivations, and human capital of the current immigration stream to the United States.

We will next address the most important and controversial immigration issues facing U. S. society and conclude with a brief return to the "traditional" minority groups: African Americans, Native American, and other peoples of color who continue to face issues of equality and full integration and must now pursue their long-standing grievances in an atmosphere where public attention and political energy are focused on other groups and newer issues.

Current Immigration

As you know, the United States has experienced three different waves of mass immigration. In Chapter 2, we discussed the first two waves (see Figure 2.2). As you recall, the first wave lasted from the 1820s to the 1880s and consisted of mostly Northern and

Western European immigrants. The second, from the 1880s to the 1920s, brought primarily Southern and Eastern European immigrants. During these two periods, more than 37 million people immigrated to the United States, an average rate of about 370,000 per year. These waves of newcomers transformed American society on every level: its cities, its neighborhoods and parishes, its popular culture, its accents and dialects, its religion, its cuisine, and so much more.

The third wave of mass immigration promises to be equally transformative. This wave began after the 1965 change in U.S. immigration policy and includes people from every corner of the globe. Since the mid-1960s, over 30 million newcomers have arrived (not counting undocumented immigrants). This rate of more than 600,000 people per year is much higher than the earlier period although the rate is lower as a percentage of the total population. Figure 9.1 shows that the number of legal immigrants per year has generally increased over this period, at least until the U.S. economy turned sour in recent years.

The official record for most immigrants in a year was set in 1907, when almost 1.3 million people arrived in the United States. That number was almost equaled in 2006 and, if undocumented immigrants had been included in the count, the 1907 record would have been eclipsed several times since the 1960s.

The more recent wave of immigration is much more diverse than the first two. In 2012 alone, immigrants arrived from more than 200 separate nations—from

Figure 9.1 Number of Legal Immigrants to the United States, 1960–2013

Source: U.S. Department of Homeland Security (2013b).

Afghanistan and Albania to Zambia and Zimbabwe. Only about 8% of the newcomers were from Europe, about a third were from North America (mostly Mexico), and 40% were from Asia. Figure 9.2 lists the numbers for the top 25 sending nations for 2012. Note that the number of Mexican immigrants is almost double the number from China, the next-highest sending nation. Also, note the variety of nations and regions of origin. Immigration to the United States is truly a global phenomenon!

How will this new wave of immigration transform the United States? How will these new immigrants be transformed by the United States? What do they contribute? What do they cost? Will they adopt the ways of the dominant society? What are the implications if they don't?

We begin by reviewing several case studies of new Americans, focusing on information and statistics comparable to those used in Chapters 5 through 8. Each of the groups covered in this chapter has had some members in the United States for decades, some for more than a century. However, in all cases the groups were quite small until the latter part of the 20th century. Although they are growing rapidly now, all remain relatively small, and none composes more than 1% of the population. Nonetheless, some will have a greater impact on American culture and society in the future, and

Figure 9.2   Number of Legal Immigrants for the Top 25 Sending Nations, 2013

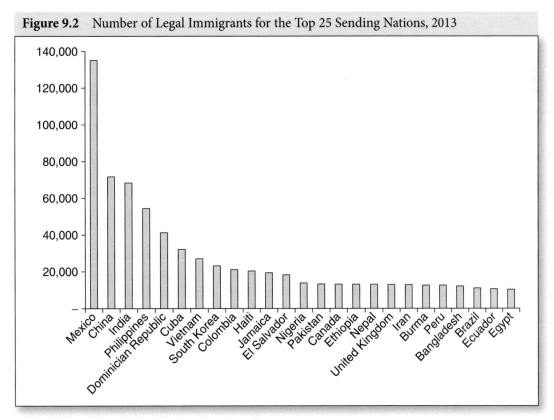

Source: U.S. Department of Homeland Security (2013d).

some groups—Muslims and Arab and Middle Easterner Americans—have already become a focus of concern and controversy because of the events of September 11 and the ensuing war on terrorism.

QUESTIONS FOR REFLECTION

1. What are some of the key differences between the first two waves of mass immigration from the 1820s to the 1920s and the current, post-1965 wave?

2. Why is the current wave of immigration so diverse? What are the implications of this diversity for the future of American society?

New Hispanic Groups: Immigrants From the Dominican Republic, El Salvador, and Colombia

Immigration from Latin America, the Caribbean, and South America has been considerable, even excluding Mexico. As with other sending nations, the volume of immigration from these regions increased after 1965 and has averaged about 200,000 per year. Generally, Latino immigrants—not counting those from Mexico—have composed about 25% of all immigrants since the 1960s (U.S. Department of Homeland Security, 2012).

The sending nations for these immigrants are economically less developed, and most have long-standing relations with the United States. In Chapter 7, we discussed the roles that Mexico and Puerto Rico have played as sources of cheap labor and the ties that led Cubans to immigrate to the United States. Each of the other sending nations has been similarly linked to the United States, the dominant economic and political power in the region.

Although the majority of these immigrants bring educational and occupational qualifications that are modest by U.S. standards, they tend to be more educated, more urbanized, and more skilled than the average citizens of the nations from which they come. Contrary to widely held beliefs, these immigrants do not represent the poorest of the poor, the "wretched refuse" of their homelands. They tend to be rather ambitious, as evidenced by their willingness to attempt to succeed in a society that has not been notably hospitable to Latinos or people of color in the past. Most of these immigrants are not only fleeing poverty or joblessness but also are attempting to pursue their ambitions and seek opportunities for advancement that are generally not available in their countries of origin (Feliciano, 2006; Portes & Rumbaut, 1996, pp. 10–11).

This characterization applies to legal and unauthorized immigrants alike. In fact, the latter may illustrate the point more dramatically, because the cost of illegally entering the United States can be considerable, much higher than the cost of a legal entry. The venture may require years of saving or the combined resources of a large kinship group. Forged papers and other costs of being smuggled into the country can easily amount to many thousands of dollars, a considerable sum in nations in which the usual wage is a tiny fraction of the U.S. average. Also, the passage can be extremely dangerous and can require a level of courage (or desperation) that many Americans do not often associate with undocumented immigrants.

Rather than attempting to cover all South and Central American groups, we have selected three of the largest to serve as case studies: those from the Dominican Republic, El Salvador, and Colombia. In recent years, these three groups have made up 7% to 8% of all immigrants and about 30% of the immigrants from Central and South America and the Caribbean. These groups had few members in the United States before the 1960s, and all have had high rates of immigration over the past four decades. However, the motivation of the immigrants and the immigration experience has varied from group to group, as we shall see.

Three Case Studies

Table 9.1 presents some basic information about these three groups that we explored in Chapter 7. We're reviewing it here to provide a common frame of reference for the groups covered in this chapter.

Each of these groups has a high percentage of foreign-born members, and, predictably with so many members in the first generation, proficiency in English is an important issue. Although Colombian Americans approach national norms in education, the other two groups have relatively low levels of human capital (education). They are well below national norms for income; thus, they have higher rates of poverty.

Although these groups share some characteristics, there exhibit important differences. They differ in their "racial" characteristics, with Dominicans being more

Table 9.1 Selected Characteristics of Three Hispanic American Groups and Non-Hispanic Whites, 2012

Group	Size	Percentage With Less Than High School Diploma	Percentage With College Degree or More	Percentage Foreign-Born	Percentage Who Speak English Less Than "Very Well"	Median Household Income	Percentage of Families in Poverty
Non-Hispanic whites	—	8.9	31.9	3.9	1.7	$56,525	7.4
Dominicans	1,568,168	34.0	15.5	46.6	44.0	$33,900	27.3
Salvadorans	1,937,369	51.4	7.7	60.9	52.3	$43,487	20.6
Colombians	1,000,125	14.2	31.5	63.9	39.0	$50,102	11.9

Source: U.S. Census Bureau (2013a).

African in appearance, Colombians more European, and Salvadorans more Indian. The groups tend to settle in different places. Colombians are clustered in the South (49%), particularly in Florida, and the Northeast (33%), mostly in New York and New Jersey (Brown & Patten, 2013a, p. 2). Dominicans are concentrated in the Northeast (78%), with almost half living in New York alone (Brown & Patten, 2013c, p. 2). In contrast, Salvadorans tend to reside in the West (40%), mostly in California, and the South, mostly in Texas (Brown & Patten, 2013e, p. 2).

Finally, the groups differ in the conditions of their entry or contact situations—a difference that, as we have seen, is consequential. Salvadorans are more likely to be political refugees who fled a brutal civil war and political repression, while Dominicans and Colombians are more likely to be motivated by economics and the employment possibilities offered in the United States. Let's consider each of these groups briefly and further explore some of their differences.

Dominicans. The Dominican Republic shares the Caribbean island of Hispaniola with Haiti. The island economy is still largely agricultural, although the tourist industry has grown in recent years. Unemployment and poverty are major problems, and Dominicans average about five years of education (NationMaster, 2014). Dominican immigrants, like those from Mexico, are motivated largely by economics, and they compete for jobs with Puerto Ricans, other immigrant groups, and native-born workers with lower levels of education and jobs skills.

Although Dominicans are limited in their job options by the language barrier, they are somewhat advantaged by their willingness to work for lower wages. They are concentrated in the service sector, as day laborers (men) or domestics (women). Dominican immigrants maintain strong ties with home and are a major source of income and support for the families left behind.

In terms of acculturation and integration, Dominicans are roughly similar to Mexican Americans and Puerto Ricans, although some studies suggest that they are possibly the most impoverished immigrant group (e.g., Table 9.1 and Figures 7.15 and 7.17). A high percentage of Dominicans are undocumented, and many spend a great deal of money and take considerable risks to get to the United States. If these less visible members of the community were included in the official, government-generated statistics used in the figures presented later in this chapter, the portrait of poverty and low levels of education and jobs skills likely would be even more dramatic.

Salvadorans. El Salvador, like the Dominican Republic, is a relatively poor nation, with a high percentage of the population relying on subsistence agriculture for survival. Approximately 36% of the population lives below the poverty level (Central Intelligence Agency, 2013) due to major problems with unemployment and underemployment. About 80% of the population is literate, and the average number of years of school completed is a little more than five (NationMaster, 2014).

El Salvador, like many sending nations, has a difficult time providing sufficient employment opportunities for its population, and much of the pressure to migrate is economic. However, El Salvador also suffered through a brutal civil war in the 1980s, and many of the Salvadorans in the United States today are actually political refugees. The United States, under the administration of President Ronald Reagan, refused to grant political refugee status to Salvadorans, and returned many of them to El Salvador. This federal policy resulted in high numbers of undocumented immigrants and also stimulated a sanctuary movement, led by American clergy, to help Salvadoran immigrants, both undocumented and legal, stay in the United States. As is the case with Dominicans, if the undocumented immigrants from El Salvador were included in official government statistics, the picture of poverty would become more extreme.

Colombians. Colombia is somewhat more developed than most other Central and South American nations but has suffered from more than 40 years of internal turmoil, civil war, and government corruption. It is a major center for the production and distribution of drugs to the world in general and the United States in particular, and the drug industry and profits are complexly intertwined with domestic strife.

Colombian Americans are closer to U.S. norms of education and income than are other Latino groups (see Table 9.1, as well as Figures 7.13, 7.15, and 7.17). Recent immigrants are a mixture of less-skilled laborers and well-educated professionals seeking to further their careers. Colombians are residentially concentrated in urban areas, especially in Florida and the Northeast, and often settle in areas close to other Latino neighborhoods. Of course, the huge majority of Colombian Americans are law abiding and not connected with the drug trade, but still they must deal with the pervasive stereotype that portrays Colombians as gangsters and drug smugglers (not unlike the Mafia stereotype about Italian Americans).

Non-Hispanic Immigrants From the Caribbean

Immigrants from the western hemisphere bring a variety of traditions to the United States other than Hispanic ones. Two of the largest non-Latino groups come from Haiti and Jamaica in the Caribbean. Both nations are much less developed than the United States, and this is reflected in the educational and occupational characteristics of their immigrants. A statistical profile of both groups is presented in Table 9.2, along with statistics for non-Hispanic whites for purposes of comparison.

Two Case Studies

Haitians. Haiti is the poorest country in the western hemisphere, and most of the population relies on small-scale subsistence agriculture for survival. An estimated 80% of the population lives below the poverty line, and less than one third of adults hold formal jobs (Central Intelligence Agency, 2013). Less than half the population is literate, and Haitians average less than three years of formal education (NationMaster, 2014). A massive earthquake in January 2010 intensified the difficult conditions in Haiti; it will take years for the tiny nation to recover fully.

Haitian migration was virtually nonexistent until the 1970s and 1980s, when thousands began to flee the brutal repression of the Duvalier dictatorship, which—counting

Figure 9.3 Regional Distribution of Arab Americans, 2000

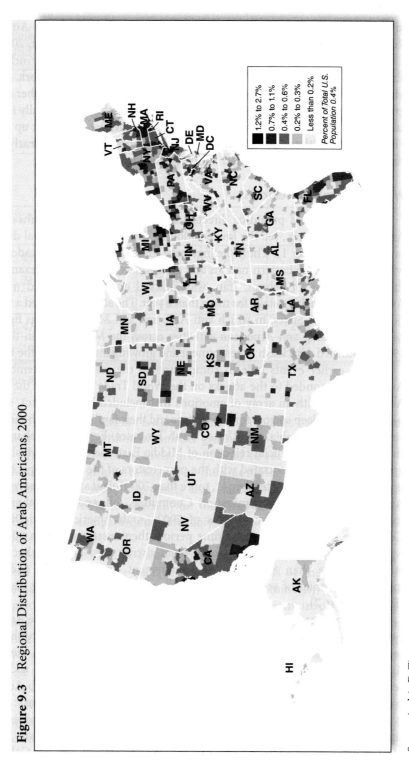

Source: Andria D. Timmer.

Italians, they are victimized by a strong stereotype that is often applied uncritically. A recent survey of Muslim Americans, a category that includes the huge majority of Arab and Middle Eastern Americans, finds them to be "middle class and mostly mainstream." They have a positive view of U.S. society and espouse distinctly American values. At the same time, they are very concerned about becoming scapegoats in the war on terror, and a majority (53%) say that it became more difficult to be a Muslim in the United States after 9/11 (Pew Research Center, 2007).

Relations between Arab Americans and the larger society are certainly among the most tense and problematic of any minority group, and given the U.S. invasions of Iraq and Afghanistan and the threat of further terrorist attacks, they will not ease anytime soon.

FOCUS ON CONTEMPORARY ISSUES:

Detroit's Arab American Community

Dr. Steven Gold

The greater Detroit area has long been a center of Arab American life. It continues to display vitality, with growing numbers of businesses, continued arrivals from the Middle East, and the creation of communal institutions such as the Arab American National Museum and the Islamic Center of America, the nation's largest Muslim house of worship. The population, which traces its local presence back 100 years, is large and continues to grow. However, due to recent arrivals, difficulties in enumeration, and the effects of intermarriage, estimates of the population are subject to debate. While the 2000 U.S. Census counted some 130,000 people of Arab origin in the tri-county Detroit area, the Zogby Worldwide polling firm pegs the community at more than 400,000.

Major nationality groups making up the Arab American population include Lebanese, Iraqi, Palestinian, and Yemeni. In addition, these groups reflect considerable religious diversity associated with several traditions, including Chaldean, Melkite, Maronite, and Roman Catholics; Protestants and Orthodox Christians; as well as Sunni and Shi'a Muslims. Local enclaves based on nationality and religion can be found throughout Metro Detroit's three counties, revealing significant diversity in housing, class membership, and way of life.

Detroit's Arab Americans have created a broad array of organizations that address the population's social service, cultural, religious, health, educational, political, and economic needs. Among the most well-known is ACCESS (Arab Community Center for Economic and Social Services). Established in the early 1970s, ACCESS is the largest Arab American human services nonprofit in the United States. With eight locations and more than 100 programs, it caters to a diverse population. Ismael Ahamed, the organization's founder,

(Continued)

(Continued)

has gone on to serve as the director of the Michigan Department of Human Services—the state government's second-largest agency—and is currently associate provost of the University of Michigan at Dearborn. While inclusive and large-scale organizations such as ACCESS maintain a communitywide focus, others reflect particular concerns associated with the population's varied subgroups.

Arab Detroit is noted for its extensive self-employment. The population is estimated to own some 5,000 enterprises—with Chaldeans (Iraqi Catholics) and Lebanese having especially high rates of entrepreneurship. The growth of Arab American businesses is most evident in Dearborn, where thousands of Arabic signs advertise a whole range of goods and services to local customers. At the same time, Arab-owned shops, restaurants, car dealerships, gas stations, and professionals serve consumer needs throughout the region in neighborhoods ranging from the inner city to affluent suburbs.

Business success is enabled by a wide range of resources, including familial and communal ties and personal experience with self-employment. In addition, the population's generally high levels of education and intact families are known to facilitate proprietorship. Indeed, Middle Eastern–origin groups have long revealed a propensity toward self-employment in the United States. In 1911, the Dillingham Commission of the U.S. Congress found that more than 75% of Syrian immigrant men (who would now be classified as Lebanese) in New York were self-employed. Recent evidence suggests that the trend endures. According to the 1990 U.S. Census, 6 of the 10 nationality groups with the highest rates of self-employment in the United States were from the Middle East.

Finally, a variety of ethnic organizations, including the Arab American Chamber of Commerce, Chaldean Federation of America, Arab American Women's Business Council, Chaldean American Chamber of Commerce, Chaldean American Bar Association, Chaldean American Association for Health Professionals, and Lebanese American Chamber of Commerce, provide services and contacts for Arab American entrepreneurs in Southeast Michigan.

Despite the community's size, wealth, and influence, a number of activists and observers contend that the population suffers from significant hostility and discrimination. This includes both racial profiling and surveillance conducted by U.S. government agencies since September 11, 2001, as well as discrimination and violence from members of the American public. The net impact of these trends causes Arab Americans to feel unsafe in their own homes, deprecated for their national and religious origins, pressured to apologize for acts they had nothing to do with, and compelled to cooperate with intrusive surveillance activities.

Based on decisions made by federal agencies, South Asians and Middle Easterners in the United States are treated as a special population. In the years following the September 11 attacks, more than 1,200 persons—who were neither named nor charged with crimes—were detained, with about half being deported. At the same time, numerous ethnic and religious organizations representing the same nationalities have been accused of assisting terrorists—generally with little or no evidence—an action that permits the freezing of their assets and the criminalization of their members.

In addition to dealing with criminal justice and migration officials, Arab Americans also confront various forms of hostility, including insults, vandalism, and violence, as they go about their daily lives. This is evidenced by the cancellation of the Dearborn Arab International Festival in 2013, an event that for the previous 18 years brought together hundreds of thousands of people from throughout the United States and the world to enjoy Middle Eastern food and culture and family-friendly entertainment.

The festival was targeted by fundamentalist Christian groups as a setting where they could confront Arabs and Muslims. These missionaries—who included Florida Pastor Terry Jones, best known for the public burning of a Quran (the Muslim holy book)—brought with them a pig's head and signs insulting Islam's prophet. When the fundamentalist protestors won a 2010 lawsuit protecting their First Amendment rights, the city of Dearborn withdrew its support of the festival. Instead, officials encouraged the festival's organizers to hold it in a park where public order could be more easily maintained.

Representatives of the Arab American community rejected this option because they favored the event's previous location, adjacent to numerous Arab businesses that have been vital to improving the city's (and region's) economic and cultural vitality. With too little time to make alternative arrangements, the popular and highly successful event had to be cancelled.

In sum, Detroit's Arab community continues to grow and prosper, bringing vitality and development to a location more commonly associated with economic decline and population loss. Yet, even as its members seek to celebrate their successful participation in American life, the circumstances of their religion, heritage, and regional origins often result in their being denied access to opportunities that groups with different origins might take for granted.

Source: From Gold, S. (2002). *The Arab American Community in Detroit, Michigan.* Reprinted with permission of the University of California Press.

Immigrants From Africa

Our final group of new Americans consists of immigrants from Africa. Immigration from Africa has been quite low over the past 50 years. However, there was the usual increase after the 1960s, and Africans were about 5% of all immigrants after 1960 and have been almost 10% since 2000.

Table 9.5 shows the total number of sub-Saharan Africans in the United States in 2010, along with the two largest national groups. The number of native Africans in the United States has more than doubled since 1990. This rapid growth suggests that these groups may have a greater impact on U.S. society in the future.

The category "sub-Saharan African" is extremely broad and encompasses people as diverse as destitute black refugees from African civil wars and relatively affluent white South Africans. In the remainder of this section, we will focus on Nigerians and Ethiopians rather than on this very broad category.

Although their numbers may be growing, Nigerians and Ethiopians are tiny minorities: neither group is as much as 0.1% of the total population. They are recent immigrants and have a high representation of first-generation members. Nigerian and Ethiopian immigrants tend to be highly skilled and educated, and they bring valuable abilities and advanced educational credentials to the United States. Both compare favorably to national norms for education; thus, they provide another example of a "brain drain" from their countries of origin. Like some other groups, many of the immigrants from Nigeria and Ethiopia are motivated by a search for work, and they compete for more desirable positions in the U.S. job structure.

Nigeria is a former British colony, so the relatively high level of English fluency among its immigrants is not surprising. Table 9.5 shows that, on average, members of the group have been able to translate their relatively high levels of human capital and English fluency into a favorable position in the U.S. economy. They compare quite favorably with national norms in their income levels.

Compared with Nigerians, Ethiopians rank lower in their English fluency and are more mixed in their backgrounds. They include refugees from domestic unrest along with the educated elite (see Table 9.5). Although Ethiopians compare favorably with national norms in education, they have much lower levels of income and, therefore, much higher rates of poverty. These contrasts suggest that Ethiopians are less able to translate their educational credentials into higher-ranked occupations in the United States.

Modes of Incorporation

As the case studies included in this chapter (and those in Chapters 7 and 8) demonstrate, recent immigrant groups occupy a wide array of different positions in U.S. society. One way to address this diversity is to look at the contact situation, especially the characteristics the groups bring with them (e.g., their race and religion, the human capital with which they arrive) and the reaction of the larger society. There are three main modes of incorporation for immigrants in the United States: entrance through the primary labor market, the secondary labor markets (see Chapter 4), or the ethnic enclave. We will consider each pathway separately and relate them to the groups discussed in this chapter.

Immigrants and the Primary Labor Market

The primary labor market consists of more desirable jobs with greater security, higher pay, and more benefits, and the immigrants entering this sector tend to be highly educated, skilled professionals and businesspeople. Members of this group are generally fluent in English, and many were educated at U.S. universities. They are highly integrated into the global urban-industrial economy, and, in many cases, they

Table 9.5   Selected Characteristics of Sub-Saharan African Groups and Non-Hispanic Whites, 2012.

Group	Size	Percentage With Less Than High School Diploma	Percentage With College Degree or More	Percentage Foreign-Born	Percentage Who Speak English Less Than "Very Well"	Median Household Income	Percentage of Families in Poverty
Non-Hispanic whites	—	8.9	31.9	3.9	1.7	$56,525	7.4
All sub-Saharan Africans	2,908,097	13.3	31.2	41.4	13.5	$41,213	20.9
Ethiopians	209,816	15.8	25.9	72.3	34.4	$41,547	18.0
Nigerians	265,782	3.4	61.8	60.4	9.6	$58,534	10.8

Source: U.S. Census Bureau (2013a).

are employees of multinational corporations transferred here by their companies. These immigrants are affluent, urbane, and dramatically different from the peasant laborers so common in the past (e.g., from Ireland and Italy) and in the present (e.g., from the Dominican Republic and Mexico). The groups with high percentages of members entering the primary labor market include Indian, Egyptian, Iranian, and Nigerian immigrants.

Because they tend to be affluent, immigrants with professional backgrounds tend to attract less notice and fewer racist reactions than their more unskilled counterparts. Although they come closer to Blauner's pure immigrant group than most other minority groups we have considered, racism can still complicate their assimilation. In addition, Arab American Islamic group members must confront discrimination and prejudice based on their religious affiliation.

Immigrants and the Secondary Labor Market

This mode of incorporation is more typical for immigrants with lower levels of education and fewer job skills. Jobs in this sector are less desirable and offer lower pay, little security, and few benefits and are often seasonal or in the underground or informal economy. This labor market includes jobs in construction or the garment industry, in which workers are paid "off the books," and working conditions are unregulated by government authorities or labor unions; domestic work; and some forms of criminal or deviant activity, such as drug sales and sex work. The employers who control these jobs often prefer to hire undocumented immigrants because they are easier to control and less likely to complain to the authorities about abuse and mistreatment. The groups with high percentages of members in the secondary labor market include Dominicans, Haitians, and the less-skilled and less-educated kinfolk of the higher-status immigrants.

Immigrants and Ethnic Enclaves

As we have seen, some immigrant groups—especially those that can bring financial capital and business experience—have established ethnic enclaves. Some members of these groups enter U.S. society as entrepreneurs and become owners of small retail shops and other businesses; their less-skilled and less-educated coethnics serve as a source of cheap labor to staff the ethnic enterprises. The enclave provides contacts, financial and other services, and social support for the new immigrants of all social classes. Korean Americans and Arab Americans, like Cuban Americans and Jewish Americans in the past, have been particularly likely to follow this path.

Summary

This classification suggests some of the variety of relationships between the new Americans and the larger society. The contemporary stream of immigrants entering the United States is extremely diverse and includes people from the most sophisticated and urbane to the most desperate and despairing. The variety can be seen in a list of occupations in which recent immigrants are overrepresented. For men, the list includes biologists and other natural scientists, taxi drivers, farm laborers, and waiters. For women, the list includes chemists, statisticians, produce packers, laundry workers, and domestics (Kritz & Girak, 2004).

QUESTIONS FOR REFLECTION

3. List and describe the characteristics of the largest groups of immigrants from Central America, the Caribbean, Asia, the Middle East, and Africa.

4. Which of these groups is most likely to assimilate into the primary labor market? Why? Which group is most likely to be incorporated into the secondary labor market? Why? Which is most likely to be an enclave minority? Why?

COMPARATIVE FOCUS:
The Roma: Europe's "True Minority"

Professor Andria D. Timmer studies the Roma of Europe and, especially, of Hungary. She lived and worked in Roma communities in Hungary for several years while conducting research.

Dr. Andria D. Timmer

Figure 9.4   Roma Population in Europe, 2009

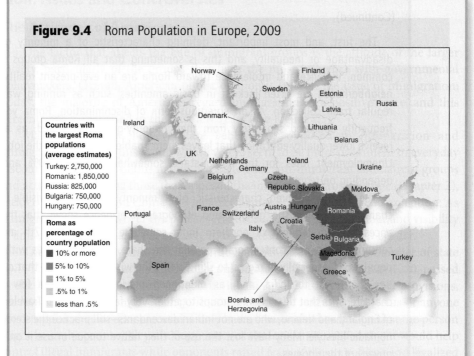

Countries with
the largest Roma
populations
(average estimates)
Turkey: 2,750,000
Romania: 1,850,000
Russia: 825,000
Bulgaria: 750,000
Hungary: 750,000

Roma as
percentage of
country population
■ 10% or more
■ 5% to 10%
■ 1% to 5%
■ .5% to 1%
■ less than .5%

The Roma (often called "Gypsies") live throughout the world, but they are most populous in Europe. They can be found in every European nation, and their geographic distribution is depicted in Figure 9.4. According to many historical documents, the Roma have been part of central and eastern European society since at least the 14th century, when they arrived in several migratory waves from India. Despite the fact that they have lived in Europe for more than half a millennium, they are still treated as recent immigrants in many respects. Thus, the Roma illustrate the point made by Gordon (see Chapter 2) and many others that length of residence in a country is not necessarily related to a group's ability to assimilate and gain acceptance.

The Roma do not form one singular group but comprise several different ethnic enclaves. In most cases, members of these groups have little in common and are more similar to the majority members of the country in which they reside than to one another. However, from a pan-European perspective, they are often considered a single group. To understand how these different peoples get grouped together, it is necessary to return to the definition of *minority group* provided in Chapter 1 of this text. We will use the first two elements of the definition to help us examine the situation of the Roma in Europe.

(Continued)

vulnerable Americans and those who feel most threatened by the increase in immigration over the past several decades (e.g., see Wallace & Figueroa, 2012).

On the other hand, some research projects (Hainmueller & Hiscox, 2010; Reyna, Dobria, & Wetherell, 2013) do not support the idea that prejudice and group competition are closely related. These projects found little correlation between a person's anti-immigrant feelings and personal economic situation. Rather, they found that both high- and low-status respondents were less concerned with their own pocketbooks and more focused on the potential costs of low-skill immigrants—for schooling, health care, and other services—and their impact on the U.S. economy in general.

Of course, "competition" can be much broader than fights over jobs and votes. Many opponents to immigration in the United States (and Europe) seem to be motivated by a collective sense of threat, the idea that the newcomers will compromise the way of life and cultural integrity of the host nation. These defensive forms of prejudice can stimulate powerful emotions, as we have seen repeatedly throughout this text.

Finally, we have seen that prejudice and negative feelings toward other groups can be motivated by a variety of factors, not just competition. Anti-immigrant attitudes are highly correlated with other forms of prejudice and are caused by the same processes we examined in Chapter 1—for example, exposure to racist cultural norms and values during childhood, and low levels of education (Pettigrew, Wagner, & Christ, 2007).

Is everyone who has reservations and questions about immigration a racist? Absolutely not. While anti-immigrant feelings, prejudice, and a sense of threat seem to be linked, this does not mean that all who oppose immigration are bigots or that all proposals to decrease the flow of immigrants are racist. These are serious and complex issues, and it is not helpful simply to label people as bigots or dismiss their concerns as prejudiced.

On the other hand, we need to clearly recognize that anti-immigrant feelings—particularly the most extreme—are linked to some of the worst, most negative strains of traditional American culture: the same racist and prejudicial views that helped justify slavery and the near genocide of Native Americans. In popular culture, on some talk radio and cable TV "news" shows, in letters to the editor, and so forth, these views are regularly used to demonize immigrants, blame them for an array of social problems, and stoke irrational fears and rumors, such as the idea that Latino immigrants are aiming to return parts of the Southwest to Mexico. At any rate, when American traditions of prejudice and racism are linked to feelings of group threat and individual insecurity, the possibilities for extreme reactions, hate crimes, and poorly designed policy and law become formidable.

The Immigrants

One survey of immigration issues (National Public Radio, 2004) included a nationally representative sample of immigrant respondents. Not surprisingly, the researchers found that the immigrants' attitudes and views differed sharply from those of native-born respondents on a number of dimensions. For example, immigrant respondents were more likely to see immigration as a positive force for the larger society and more likely to say that immigrants work hard and pay their fair share of taxes. The survey also showed that immigrants are grateful for the economic opportunities available in the United States, with 84% agreeing that there are more opportunities to get ahead here than in their countries of origin.

A more recent survey (Taylor, Cohn, Livingston, Funk, & Morin, 2013) documents the willingness of immigrants to take advantage of opportunities through a commitment to hard work. Large majorities of both Hispanic (78%) and Asian (68%) immigrants supported the idea that hard work results in success, an endorsement of the Protestant ethic that exceeds that of the general public (58%) (p. 85). On the other hand, the survey also showed that immigrants are ambivalent about U.S. culture and values. For example, only 32% of Hispanic immigrants and 14% of Asian immigrants believed that the family is stronger in the United States than in their homelands, and less than half (44% of Hispanic and 36% of Asian immigrants) said that moral values are better in the United States (p. 77).

Another helpful report (Motel & Patten, 2013) used census data to compile a statistical portrait of the 40 million Americans—about 13% of the total population—who are foreign-born or first-generation immigrants. As you would expect, Mexicans are the single largest segment of this group (29%), with Asian immigrants being the second largest (25%). Almost 40% of the foreign-born immigrated before 1990 (this category includes the surviving members of the last great wave of European immigrants), but an almost equal percentage (36%) are true newcomers, having arrived since 2000.

Most (58%) of the foreign-born are married (vs. 47% of the native-born), and they have a higher fertility rate than the general population. As we have seen, facility with English is an important issue for immigrants: Only about one third of immigrants speak English "very well." As we have also seen, there is a great deal of diversity among the foreign-born in terms of education. Overall, 16% of the foreign-born (vs. 18% of the native-born) are college educated, but this percentage varies from about 4% for immigrant Mexican Americans to almost 30% for immigrants from Asia. Occupation, income, and poverty are also highly variable from group to group.

What can we conclude? Synthesizing the information in this and previous chapters, we can say that the immigrant stream is highly diversified and that the United States is growing more diverse as a result. The "typical immigrant" is from Mexico, China, or another Asian or Central American nation, and is motivated primarily by economics and the absence of viable opportunities at home. Those who come from less-developed nations bring little human capital, education, or job skills, but others bring glowing educational and professional credentials.

As is typical of the first generation, they are often more oriented to their homes than to the United States. Many, especially the "low-skilled" immigrants, don't have the time, energy, or opportunity to absorb much of Anglo culture or the English language, while others—the more skilled and educated—move easily between their native cultures and American lifestyles. Like past waves of immigrants, even the least skilled and educated are determined to find a better way of life for themselves and their children, even if the cost of doing so is living on the margins of the larger society.

Costs and Benefits

Many Americans believe that immigration is a huge drain on the economic resources of the nation. Common concerns include the ideas that immigrants take jobs from native-born workers, strain societal institutions including schools, housing markets, and medical facilities, and do not pay taxes. These issues are complex and hotly debated at all levels of U.S. society—so much so that passion and intensity of feeling on all sides often compromises the objective analysis of data.

The debate is further complicated because conclusions about these economic issues can vary depending on the type of immigrants being discussed and the level of the analysis being used. For example, conclusions about costs and benefits can be very different depending on whether we focus on less-skilled or undocumented immigrants or on the highly educated professional immigrants entering the primary market. Immigrants in their 20s and 30s are more likely to make a net contribution (especially if they have no children) than those who are over 65 and out of the workforce. Also, national studies might lead to different conclusions than studies of local communities, since the former spreads the costs of immigrants over the entire population while the latter concentrates those costs in a specific locality.

Contrary to widespread beliefs, many studies, especially those done at the national level, find that immigrants to the United States are not a particular burden. For one thing, most immigrants are ineligible for most publically funded services (such as Medicaid and food stamps), and undocumented immigrants are ineligible for virtually all such services. The exceptions are the children of immigrants, who are eligible for many programs targeted at children, and schools—U.S. schools must educate all children regardless of legal status (West, 2011, pp. 433–434).

Various studies (e.g., Smith & Edmonston, 1997) find that immigrants are a positive addition to the economy. They add to the labor supply in areas as disparate as the garment industry, agriculture, domestic work, and higher education. Other researchers find that low-skilled immigrants tend to find jobs in areas of the economy in which few U.S. citizens work or in the enclave economies of their own groups, taking jobs that would not have existed without the economic activity of their coethnics (Heer, 1996, pp. 190–194; Smith & Edmonston, 1997), and thus do not have a negative effect on the employment of native-born workers (Kochhar, 2006; Meissner, 2010). One important recent study of the economic impact of immigrants concluded that there is a relatively small effect on the wages and employment of native workers, although there may be negative consequences for earlier immigrants and for less-skilled African American workers (Bean & Stevens, 2003).

Another concern is the strain immigrants place on taxes and services such as schools and welfare programs. Again, these issues are complex and far from settled, but many research studies show that immigrants generally "pay their own way." Taxes are automatically deducted from their paychecks (unless, of course, they are being paid "under the table"), and their use of public services is actually lower than their proportional contributions. This is particularly true for undocumented immigrants, whose use of services is sharply limited by their vulnerable legal status (Marcelli & Heer, 1998; Simon, 1989). Bean and Stevens (2003, pp. 66–93) found that immigrants are not overrepresented on the welfare rolls. Rather, the key determinant of government aid use is refugee status. Groups such as Haitians, Salvadorans, and Vietnamese—who arrive without resources and, by definition, are in need of assistance on all levels—are the most likely to be its recipients.

In general, immigrants—undocumented as well as legal—pay local, state, and federal taxes and make proportional contributions to Social Security and Medicare. The undocumented are the most likely to be paid "off the books" and receive their wages tax-free, but estimates are that the vast majority (50% to 75%, depending on the study) pay federal and state taxes through payroll deduction (White House, 2005). Also, *all* immigrants pay sales taxes and other consumption taxes (e.g., on gas, cigarettes, and alcohol).

Some evidence suggests that immigrants play a crucial role in keeping the Social Security system solvent. This source of retirement income is being severely strained by the "baby boomers"—the large number of Americans born between 1945 and 1960 who are now retiring. This group is living longer than previous generations and, since the U.S. birth rate has stayed low over the past four decades, there are relatively fewer native-born workers to support them and replace the funds they withdraw as Social Security and Medicare benefits. Immigrants may supply the much-needed workers to take up the slack in the system and keep it solvent. In particular, most undocumented immigrants pay into the system but (probably) will never draw any money out, because of their illegal status. They thus provide a tidy surplus—perhaps as much as $7 billion a year or more—to help subsidize the retirements of the baby boomers and keep the system functioning (Porter, 2005; see also Dewan, 2013).

Final conclusions about the impact and costs of immigration must await the findings of ongoing research, and there is no question that many local communities experience distress as they try to deal with the influx of newcomers in their housing markets, schools, and health care facilities. Concerns about the economic impact of immigrants are not unfounded, but they may be exaggerated by prejudice and racism directed at newcomers and strangers. The current opposition to immigration may be a reaction to "who" as much as to "how many" or "how expensive."

Finally, we can repeat the finding of many studies (e.g., Bean & Stevens, 2003), that immigration is generally a positive force in the economy. As they have for decades, immigrants—legal and undocumented—continue to find work and niches in American society in which they can survive. The highly skilled immigrants fill gaps in the primary labor market and in schools and universities, corporations, hospitals, and hundreds of other sectors of the economy. Less-skilled immigrants provide cheap labor for the low-wage secondary job market; frequently, the primary beneficiaries of this long-established system are not the immigrants (although they are often grateful for the opportunities), but employers, who benefit from a cheaper, more easily exploited workforce, and American consumers, who benefit from lower prices in the marketplace and reap the benefits virtually every time they go shopping, have a meal in a restaurant, pay for home repairs or maintenance, or place a loved one in a nursing home (for an overview, see Griswold, 2012).

Undocumented Immigrants

Americans are particularly concerned with undocumented immigrants but, again, are split in their attitudes. A recent poll (Saad, 2010) asked about people's concerns regarding undocumented immigrants and found that 61% of respondents were concerned with the burden on schools, hospitals, and government services, 55% were concerned that "illegal immigrants might be encouraging others to move here illegally," and 53% were concerned that undocumented immigrants are lowering wages for native-born workers. At the same time, 64% of respondents proclaimed themselves to be "very" or "somewhat" sympathetic toward undocumented immigrants. Only 17% said they were "very unsympathetic."

The high level of concern is certainly understandable because the volume of illegal immigration has been huge over the past few decades. As displayed in Figure 9.5, the estimated number of undocumented immigrants increased from 8.4 million in 2000 to a high of 12 million in 2007, an increase of more than 40%. The number has declined during the recession and is now 10.7 million. About 55% of all unauthorized immigrants are from Mexico (Passel, Cohn, & Gonzalez-Barrera, 2013).

Some undocumented immigrants enter the country on tourist, temporary worker, or student visas and simply remain in the nation when their visas expire. In 2012 alone, the Department of Homeland Security processed more than 165 million tourists, businesspeople, temporary workers, and foreign students entering the United States (Monger, 2012). These numbers suggest how difficult it is to keep tabs on this source of illegal immigration. Others cross the border illegally in the hopes of evading the Border Patrol and finding their way into some niche in the American economy. The fact that people keep coming suggests that most succeed.

One of the reasons the supply of unauthorized immigrants is so high is the continuing demand for cheap labor in the U.S. economy. As we have noted on several occasions, the Global South—and Mexico in particular—has functioned as a reserve labor force for the U.S. economy for decades. Even in 2010, after several years of economic recession, undocumented immigrants provided a sizeable percentage of the workforce in many states and were as much as 10% of the workers in several (see Figure 9.6).

Figure 9.5   Estimated Total and Mexican Undocumented Immigrants, 1990–2012

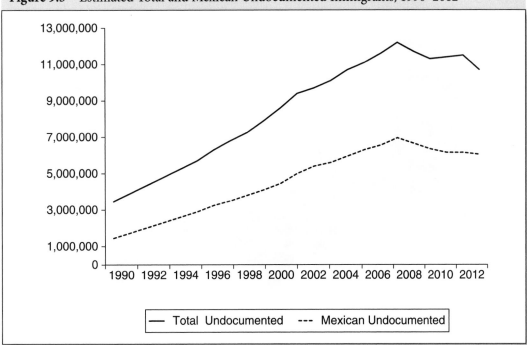

Source: Passel et al. (2013).

The demand for cheap (undocumented) labor varies by the sector of the economy, and one of the biggest users has been the agricultural sector. Arturo Rodriguez (2011), president of the United Farm Workers of America (the union founded by César Chávez and mentioned in Chapter 7), estimates that as much as 70% of the 2 million agricultural workers in the United States—the people who pick the crops and prepare them to be shipped to market—are undocumented immigrants. U.S. agriculture and the food supply would collapse without the contributions of undocumented workers.

A variety of efforts continue to be made to curtail and control the flow of illegal immigrants. Various states have attempted to lower the appeal of the United States by limiting benefits and opportunities. Other than the aforementioned State Bill 1070 in Arizona, one of the best known of these attempts occurred in 1994, when California voters passed Proposition 187, which would have denied educational, health, and other services to illegal immigrants. The policy was declared unconstitutional, however, and never implemented.

Other efforts to decrease the flow of illegal immigration have included proposals to limit welfare benefits for immigrants, denial of in-state college tuition to the children of illegal immigrants, increases in the size of the Border Patrol, and the construction of taller and wider walls along the border with Mexico. Over the past decade,

Figure 9.6 Unauthorized Immigrants as Share of Labor Force by State, 2010

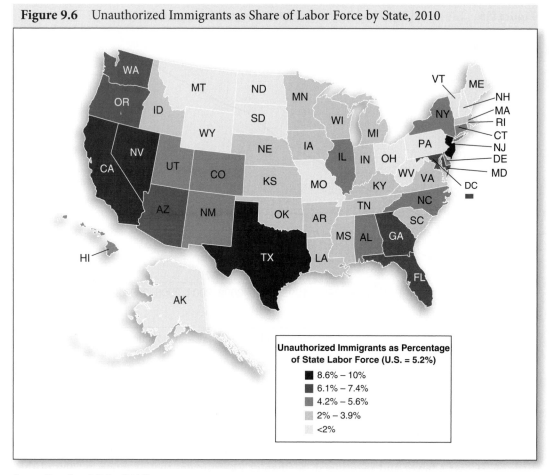

Source: Passel and Cohn (2011).

a variety of proposals to reform the national immigration policy have been hotly debated at the highest levels of government, but none has been passed.

Although Americans will continue to be concerned about this problem, many people wonder if much can be done (within the framework of a democratic, humane society) to curtail the flow of people. The social networks that deliver immigrants—legal as well as illegal—are too well established, and the demand for cheap labor in the United States is simply insatiable. In fact, denying services, as envisioned in Proposition 187, may make illegal immigrants *more* attractive as a source of labor by reducing their ability to resist exploitation. For example, if the children of illegal immigrants were not permitted to attend school, they would become more likely to join the army of cheap labor on which some employers depend. Who would benefit from barring access to public schools or denying in-state college tuition for the children of illegal immigrants?

DREAMers

In 2001, the U.S. Senate considered the Development, Relief, and Education for Alien Minors (DREAM) Act. This act, like so many attempts to address immigration issues, stalled and was never passed, but it did give a name (DREAMers) to a population that has increased in size since that time and remains a continuing concern: the children of undocumented immigrants who were brought to the United States as young children.

DREAMers are in the United States illegally but not because of any choice of their own. They are not citizens of the United States (unlike the children born to undocumented immigrants in the United States), and, in many ways, they are not citizens of their "native" land either. Many have never visited their "homeland" and are unfamiliar with its customs or even its language.

They are caught in the middle—residents of the United States but not citizens, strangers to the homelands of their parents. They live in fear of deportation, and their illegal status can prevent them from competing for jobs in the primary labor market, getting a driver's license, attending college, or receiving unemployment benefits or food stamps. Where do the roughly two million DREAMers (most of them Mexican) belong?

Attempts to revive the 2001 bill have failed, as have various alternative measures. Because of the political gridlock at the highest levels of government, many members of the group feared that their situation would never be reasonably addressed, let alone resolved.

Then, in June 2012, the Obama administration enacted a program under which the children of undocumented immigrants can apply to stay in the United States without threat of deportation. Those who meet the conditions of the program (e.g., they must be high school graduates with no significant criminal violations) can get driver's licenses, get work permits, and attend college. More than 500,000 people have applied to and been approved for the program.

The program grants a two-year, renewable reprieve from deportation for the DREAMers (but not for their parents and other relatives). It does not offer permanent legal status or a pathway to citizenship. More permanent and comprehensive immigration programs continue to be proposed in the U.S. Congress.

QUESTIONS FOR REFLECTION

10. Do immigrants cost more than they contribute? What are some of the factors that have to be taken into account in dealing with this issue?

11. Has the number of undocumented immigrants grown in recent years? What factors affect the size of this population? Will it continue to grow in the future?

12. Who are the DREAMers? What should be done to resolve their situation, if anything?

FOCUS ON CONTEMPORARY ISSUES:
Birthright Citizenship

Who should be granted American citizenship? Among advanced industrial nations, the United States and Canada alone automatically confer citizenship on any baby born within their borders, including babies born to undocumented immigrants. This policy is based on the Fourteenth Amendment to the U.S. Constitution, which was passed shortly after the Civil War to guarantee the citizenship rights of ex-slaves. The amendment has been interpreted ever since as guaranteeing citizenship for anyone born on American soil.

Birthright citizenship is one of many hotly debated immigration issues. Does this policy make sense and what are the costs of maintaining it? Is it too broad a definition of who should be an American? What message would be sent by changing it? What are people really saying when they speak about issues like this?

Let's begin with some facts. In 2010 about 4.5 million children (about 6% of all children) born in the United States had at least one parent who was an unauthorized immigrant. That's more than double the number (2.1 million) born in 2000. An additional 300,000 to 400,000 babies are born to undocumented immigrants each year (Passel & Cohn, 2011, p 12). These numbers document the scope of this issue: birthright citizenship impacts hospital delivery rooms and school systems.

What are the arguments for and against birthright citizenship? We cannot present all relevant points in these few paragraphs but let's consider some of the common arguments.

Arguments for ending birthright citizenship commonly cite the costs to taxpayers (see Federation for American Immigration Reform, 2010). Undocumented immigrants are, as we have seen, poor, and the costs of delivery and care for newborns amounts to millions of dollars per year. These costs are passed on to taxpayers and strain local, state, and national treasuries.

On the other hand, ending birthright citizenship would have other costs. If citizenship were granted at birth only to children of U.S. citizens, the government would have to establish some procedure to check parental status. This would come at some expense to taxpayers. The total costs might be difficult to estimate but a program that limited citizenship would not be free.

Another common argument for eliminating birthright citizenship is that it would reduce the incentive for people to enter illegally. This argument might make sense on its face, but if the primary incentive for immigration is work and job opportunities, ending this policy would have little impact on population flows. No European nation grants birthright citizenship, yet they have a sizeable population of unauthorized immigrants.

Furthermore, some research (Van Hook, 2010) argues that repeal of birthright citizenship would increase the size of the unauthorized immigrant population and create a large, permanent class of marginalized people, alien to both the United States and to the native country of their ancestors. In effect, this group would be stateless, without full citizenship rights anywhere, making them easily exploited.

These points just scratch the surface of a complex legal, political, economic, and social issue. Birthright citizenship will probably be a prominent issue in American politics for some time. As you consider evidence and opinions, remember to exercise your critical faculties: Are claims supported by evidence from verifiable sources? Do the arguments come from advocacy or special interest groups that are known to favor or oppose immigration reform? Is the issue being used to frighten voters or demonize immigrants? Is the language needlessly inflammatory or vague? It is easy to get swept up in the emotions of the moment, but remember that this issue affects the lives of—literally—millions, and that there is a lot at stake here, both for the migrants and for the United States.

Is Contemporary Assimilation Segmented?

In Chapter 2, we reviewed the patterns of acculturation and integration that typified the adjustment of Europeans who immigrated to the United States before the 1930s. Although their process of adjustment was not smooth or simple, these groups eventually acculturated and achieved levels of education and affluence comparable to national norms.

Will contemporary immigrants experience similar success? Will their children and grandchildren rise in the occupational structure to positions similar to those of the dominant group? Will their cultures and languages fade and disappear?

Final answers to these questions must await future developments. In the meantime, there is considerable debate on these issues. Some analysts argue that the success story of the white ethnic groups will not be repeated and that assimilation for contemporary immigrants will be segmented: some will enjoy success and rise to middle-class prosperity, but others will become mired in the urban underclass, beset by crime, drugs, school failure, and marginal, low-paid menial jobs (Haller, Portes, & Lynch, 2011, p. 737).

Other analysts find that the traditional perspective on assimilation—particularly Milton Gordon's model of assimilation—continues to provide a useful framework for describing the experience of contemporary immigrants. They argue that these groups will be successful like earlier immigrants. Next, we will review the most important and influential arguments from each side of this debate. Finally, we will attempt to come to some conclusions about the future of assimilation.

The Case for Segmented Assimilation

This thesis has many advocates, including some of the most important researchers in this area of the social sciences. Here, we will focus on two of the most important works. The first presents an overview and the second is based on an important, continuing research project on the second generation, the children of contemporary immigrants.

Assimilation Now Versus Then. Sociologist Douglas Massey (1995) argued that there are three crucial differences between past (before the 1930s) and contemporary (after the mid-1960s) assimilation experiences. Each calls the traditional perspective into question.

First, the flow of immigrants from Europe to the United States slowed to a mere trickle after the 1920s because of restrictive legislation, the worldwide depression of the 1930s, and World War II (see Figure 2.2). Immigration in the 1930s, for example, was less than 10% of the flow of the early 1920s. Thus, as the children and grandchildren of the European immigrants Americanized and grew to adulthood in the 1930s and 1940s, few new immigrants fresh from the old country replaced them in the ethnic neighborhoods. European cultural traditions and languages weakened rapidly with the passing of the first generation and the Americanization of their descendants.

It is unlikely, Massey argues, that a similar hiatus will interrupt contemporary immigration. For example, as we saw in Figure 9.6, the number of undocumented immigrants remained even after the economic recession that began in 2007. Massey argues that immigration has become continuous, and as some immigrants (or their descendants) Americanize and rise to success and affluence, new immigrants will replace them and revitalize ethnic cultures and languages.

Second, the speed and ease of modern transportation and communication will maintain cultural and linguistic diversity. A century ago, immigrants from Europe could maintain contact with the old country only by mail, and many had no realistic expectation of ever returning. Modern immigrants, in contrast, can return to their homes in a day or less and can use telephones, television, e-mail, and the Internet to stay in intimate contact with the families and friends they left behind. Thus, the cultures of modern immigrants can be kept vital and whole in ways that were not available (or even imagined) 100 years ago.

Third, and perhaps most important, contemporary immigrants face an economy and a labor market that are vastly different from those faced by European immigrants of the 19th and early 20th centuries. The latter group generally rose in the class system as the economy shifted from manufacturing to service. Today, rates of upward mobility have decreased, and the children of contemporary immigrants—especially those whose parents are undocumented—face myriad challenges in securing access to a quality education.

For the immigrants from Europe a century ago, assimilation meant a gradual rise to middle-class status and suburban comfort, a process often accomplished in three generations. Massey fears that assimilation today is segmented, and that a large percentage of the descendants of contemporary immigrants—especially many of the "peasant immigrants," such as some Hispanic groups, Haitians, and other peoples of color—face permanent membership in a growing underclass population and continuing marginalization and powerlessness.

The Second Generation. An analysis of the second generation of recent immigrant groups (Haller et al., 2011) also found support for the segmented assimilation model. The researchers interviewed the children of immigrants in the Miami and San Diego areas at three different times—in the early 1990s (when they were at an average age of 14), 3 years later, and 10 years later, when the respondents were at an average age of 24. The sample was large (more than 5,000 respondents at the beginning) and representative of the second generation in the two metropolitan areas where the study was conducted. This is an important study because its longitudinal design permits the researchers to track these children of immigrants in precise detail.

The researchers argue, consistent with Massey (1995) and with many of the points made previously in this text, that contemporary immigrants face a number of barriers to successful adaptation, including racial prejudice (since the huge majority are non-white), a labor market sharply split between a primary sector that requires high levels of education and a secondary sector that is low paid and insecure, and a widespread criminal subculture, based on gangs and drug sales, that provides a sometimes attractive alternative to the conventional pursuit of success through education.

Whether immigrants and their descendants can overcome these obstacles depends decisively on three factors (listed at the far left of Figure 9.7). Figure 9.7 also depicts several different projected pathways for mobility across the generations. Immigrants who arrive with high levels of human capital enter the primary labor market, and their descendants generally have entered the economic and social mainstream by the third generation (see the top row of Figure 9.7). The descendants of immigrants with lower levels of human capital can succeed if they benefit from strong families and strong coethnic communities that reinforce parental discipline. This pathway, depicted in the

Figure 9.7 Paths of Immigrant Mobility Across Generations

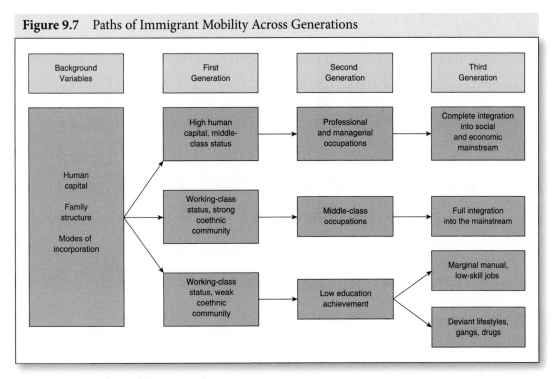

Source: Based on Haller et al. (2011, p. 738).

middle row of Figure 9.7, also results in full acculturation and integration in the economic mainstream by the third generation.

The bottom row of the figure outlines a very different pathway for a large percentage of some contemporary immigrant groups. The mode of incorporation for these immigrants does not place them in a strong coethnic community. Further, they may experience weaker family structures, sometimes because of their undocumented status or because the family is split between the United States and their home country. The result is lower educational achievement, economic marginalization, and, potentially, assimilation into gangs, the drug subculture, and other deviant lifestyles.

The researchers present a variety of evidence to support segmented assimilation theory. For example, the second generations of different groups have different experiences in school, different income levels, and different interactions with the criminal justice system. Figure 9.8 illustrates the large variations in the percentage

Figure 9.8 Percentage of Second Generation Who Are High School Graduates or Less

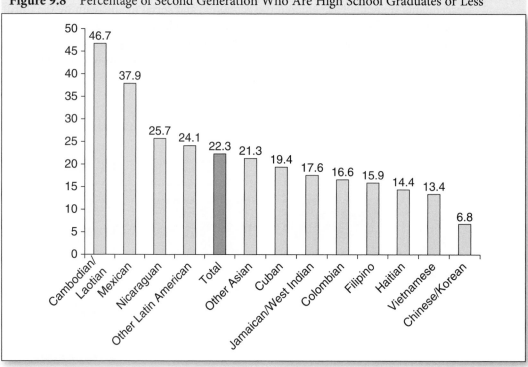

Source: Based on Haller, Portes, and Lynch (2011, p. 742).

Notes:

Chinese and Korean Americans were combined, as were Cambodian and Laotian Americans, because of similar patterns and in order to create groups large enough for statistical analysis.

"Other Latin" consists mostly of Salvadoran and Guatemalan Americans.

"Other Asian" is a diverse group that includes many nationalities.

of second generation individuals (by ethnic group) who do not pursue education beyond high school. Figure 9.9 shows patterns of incarceration by group.

These patterns are not random. Rather they reflect large differences in the human capital of the immigrant generation and variations in modes of incorporation (especially in terms of legal status and racial prejudice). They show that large percentages of the second (and third and later) generations of some groups are likely to assimilate into low-status, marginalized, or deviant sectors of American society, in direct contradiction to the patterns predicted by some versions of traditional assimilation theory.

Another important recent study reinforces some of these points. Sociologists Telles and Ortiz (2008) studied a sample of Mexican Americans who were interviewed in 1965 and again in 2000. They found evidence of strong movements toward acculturation and integration on some dimensions (e.g., language) but not on others. Even

Figure 9.9 Percentage of Second Generation Men Incarcerated

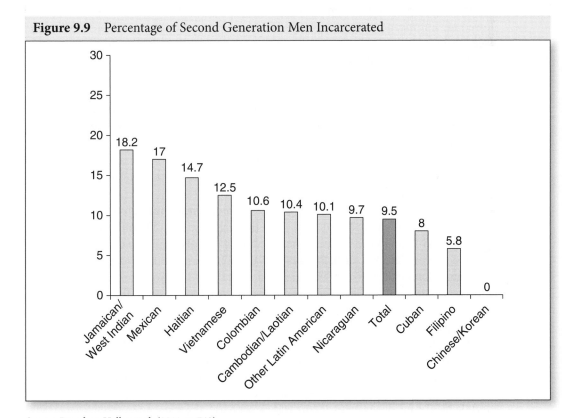

Source: Based on Haller et al. (2011, p. 742).

Notes:

Chinese and Korean Americans were combined, as were Cambodian and Laotian Americans, because of similar patterns and in order to create groups large enough for statistical analysis.

"Other Latin" consists mostly of Salvadoran and Guatemalan Americans.

"Other Asian" is a diverse group that includes many nationalities.

fourth-generation members of their sample continued to live in "the barrio" and marry within the group, and did not reach economic parity with Anglos. The authors single out institutional discrimination (e.g., underfunding of public schools that serve Mexican American neighborhoods) as a primary cause of the continuing separation, a point consistent with Massey's (1995) conclusion regarding the decreasing rates of upward mobility in American society.

The Case for "Traditional" Assimilation Theory

Other recent studies come to a different conclusion regarding the second generation: they are generally rising relative to their parents. This contradicts the segmented assimilation thesis and supports traditional assimilation theories. These studies (e.g., Alba & Nee, 2003; Bean & Stevens, 2003; Kasinitz et al., 2008; White & Glick, 2009) argue that contemporary assimilation will ultimately follow the same course that it followed for European immigrant groups 100 years ago, as described in Gordon's theory (see Chapter 2).

For example, two studies (Alba & Nee, 2003; Bean & Stevens, 2003) find that most contemporary immigrant groups are acculturating and integrating at the "normal" three-generation pace. Those groups that appear to be lagging behind this pace (notably Mexicans) may take as many as four to five generations, but their descendants will eventually find their way into the primary job market and the cultural mainstream.

Studies of acculturation show that immigrants' values become Americanized and that English language proficiency grows with time of residence and generation (Bean & Stevens, 2003, p. 168). We discussed some of these patterns in Chapter 7 (see Figures 7.7 and 7.8).

In terms of structural integration, contemporary immigrant groups may be narrowing the income gap over time, although many groups (e.g., Dominicans, Mexicans, Haitians, and Vietnamese) are disadvantaged by low levels of human capital at the start (Bean & Stevens, 2003, p. 142). Figures 9.10 and 9.11 illustrate this process with respect to wage differentials between Mexican and white non-Hispanic men and women of various generations and levels of education. (As you look at these figures, remember that complete income equality with non-Hispanic whites would be indicated if the bar touched the 100% line at the top of the graph.)

Looking first at all men workers (the leftmost bars in Figure 9.10), it is evident that recent Mexican immigrants earned a little less than half of what white men earned. The difference in income is smaller for earlier immigrants and even smaller for second and third generations of Mexicans. Separating out men with high school diplomas (the middle bars) and college degrees (the rightmost bars), the wage differential is generally lower for the more educated members of each generation. In other words, income equality tends to increase over the generations and as education increases.

On the other hand, note that third-generation men do not rise relative to their parents' generation. This contradicts the view that assimilation will proceed in a linear, stepwise fashion across the generations and is reminiscent of the findings of Telles and Ortiz (2008) noted earlier. For women, the wage differential also shrinks as the generations pass and level of education increases. Note that for third-generation,

Figure 9.10 Wage Differential of Mexican Workers Relative to Whites, Men

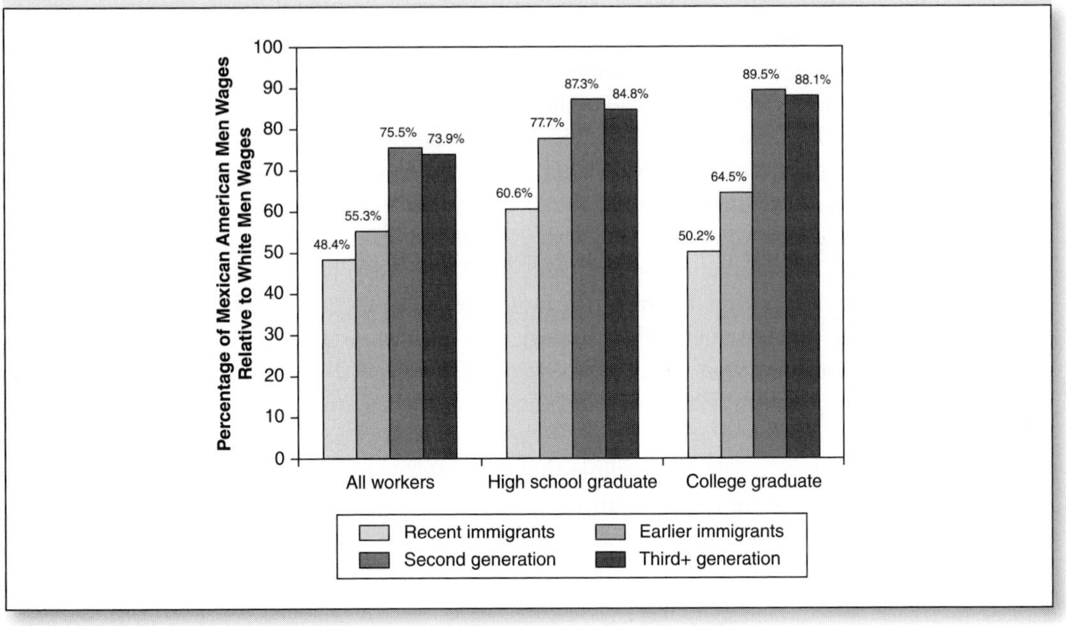

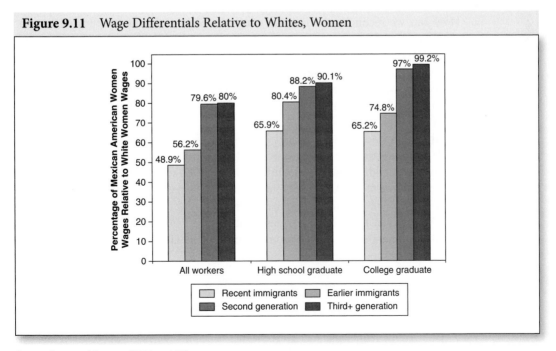

Source: Bean and Stevens (2003, p. 139).

Figure 9.11 Wage Differentials Relative to Whites, Women

Source: Bean and Stevens (2003, p. 139).

college-educated women, the wage differential shrinks virtually to zero, indicating integration on this variable (at least compared with dominant group women).

Another study (Taylor et al., 2013) used census data to compare immigrants and their children, and generally found that the latter rose in the society relative to the former. The second generation had higher incomes and levels of education, and lower levels of poverty. For example, for Hispanics, median household income rose from $34,600 for the immigrant generation to $48,400 for the second generation. Levels of education showed a similar upgrade: Almost half the immigrant generation had less than a high school education compared with only 17% of the second generation. The study found similar but less dramatic improvements for Asians, largely because of the high levels of human capital brought by the immigrant generation (e.g., 50% had college degrees).

These patterns generally support the traditional perspective on assimilation. Income and education tend to improve by generation, even though the pattern is not linear or complete. The second and third generations, on average, seem to be moving toward the economic mainstream, even though they do not close the gap completely. Bean and Stevens (2003) conclude that the patterns in Figures 9.10 and 9.11 are substantially consistent with the "three-generation model." The assimilation trajectory of Mexican Americans and other recent immigrant groups is not toward the urban poor, the underclass, or the disenfranchised, disconnected, and marginalized. Assimilation is not segmented, but is substantially repeating the experiences of the European groups on which Gordon (1964) based his theory.

Summary

How can we reconcile the directly contradictory conclusions supported by the segmented and traditional perspectives on assimilation? In large part, this debate concerns the type of evidence and judgments about how much weight to give various facts and trends. On one hand, Massey's (1995) points about the importance of the postindustrial economy, declining opportunities for less-educated workers, and the neglect that seems typical of inner-city schools are well taken. Other studies provide evidence to support the segmented assimilation thesis.

On the other hand, it seems that even the least-educated immigrant groups have been able to find economic niches in which they and their families can manage long enough for their children and grandchildren to rise in the social structure, a pattern that has been at the core of the American immigrant experience for almost two centuries.

This debate will continue, and new evidence and interpretations will appear. Ultimately, however, these disputes may continue until immigration stops (which is very unlikely to happen, as Massey points out) and the fate of the descendants of the last immigrant groups is measured.

QUESTIONS FOR REFLECTION

13. What are the arguments and evidence for the segmented assimilation model and for traditional assimilation theory.

14. Which of these perspectives is more convincing? Why? What questions would have to be answered before one of them could be discarded?

Recent Immigration in Historical and Global Context

The current wave of immigration to the United States is part of a centuries-old process that spans the globe. Underlying this immense and complex population movement are the powerful forces of continuing industrialization, economic development, and globalization. The United States and other advanced industrial nations are the centers of growth in the global economy, and immigrants flow to the areas of greater opportunity. In the 19th century, population moved largely from Europe to the western hemisphere. Over the past 50 years, the movement has been from the Global South to the Global North. This pattern reflects the simple geography of industrialization and opportunity and the fact that the more-developed nations are in the northern hemisphere.

The United States has been the world's dominant economic, political, and cultural power for much of the past 100 years, and the preferred destination of most immigrants. Newcomers from around the globe continue the collective, social nature of past population movements (see Chapter 2). The direction of their travels reflects contemporary global inequalities: labor continues to flow from the less-developed nations to the more-developed nations. The direction of this flow is not accidental or coincidental. It is determined by the differential rates of industrialization and modernization across the globe. Immigration contributes to the wealth and affluence of the more-developed societies and particularly to the dominant groups and elite classes of those societies.

The immigrant flow is also a response to the dynamics of globalization, particularly since the 1980s (Sen & Mamdouh, 2008). The current era of globalization has been guided by the doctrine of neoliberalism, or free trade, which urges nations to eliminate barriers to the movement of goods and capital. The North American Free Trade Agreement (NAFTA), mentioned on several occasions in this book, is an example of a neoliberal policy. These policies open less-developed nations such as Mexico to consumer goods manufactured and controlled by large, transnational corporations. These corporations often undersell goods made in those countries, which often drives small-scale local farmers and manufacturers out of business.

In addition, the international agencies such as the International Monetary Fund (IMF) that regulate the global economy pressure nations to reduce the size of their governmental sector. This often means that a country's budget for health and education is slashed and that services once controlled and subsidized by the government (e.g., water, electricity) are sold to private businesses, which then raise prices beyond what many people can afford. The combined result of these global forces is an increasingly vulnerable group of people in less-developed nations, unable to provide for themselves, educate their children, or afford the simplest of daily necessities such as food and water.

Americans tend to see immigrants as individuals acting of their own free will and, often, illegally. ("They chose to come to the United States and break the law.") However, that picture changes when we see immigration as the result of powerful, global economic and political forces. While domestic economies and social systems crumble, the victims of neoliberal globalization are left with few choices: they cross borders into the United States and to other advanced industrial nations. They do so illegally, if they have to, because "it is the best choice to achieve a dignified life—if not for themselves, then for their children" (Sen & Mamdouh, 2008, p. 7).

When viewed through the lens of globalization, it is clear that this population movement will continue because immigrants simply have no choice. It is unlikely that they can be stopped by further militarization of the border or by building bigger and taller walls. Immigrants come to the United States in such numbers, as they did in the past, because the alternatives in their home countries are unacceptable or nonexistent.

This perspective suggests that the tendency to reject, demonize, and criminalize immigrants is self-defeating. Punitive, militaristic policies will not stem the flow of people from the Global South to the Global North. Globalization, in its neoliberal form, is incomplete: It allows for the movement of goods and capital but not of people. It benefits transnational corporations and the mega-businesses that produce consumer goods but victimizes the vulnerable citizens of the less-developed nations. As long as these forms of globalization hold, the population pressure from South to North will continue.

New Immigrants and Old Issues

In this chapter, we focused on some of the issues raised by high levels of immigration since the 1960s. As we discuss, debate, and consider these issues, we need to remember a fundamental fact about modern American society: The issues of the "traditional" minority groups—African Americans and American Indians, for example—have not been resolved. As we saw in earlier chapters, these groups have been a part of American society from the beginning, but they remain, in many ways, distant from achieving complete equality and integration.

Many of the current issues facing these groups involve class and race. The urban underclass is disproportionately made up of peoples of color and continues to have marginal access to education and job opportunities, decent housing, and good health care when compared with the dominant Anglo society. While it is probably true that the United States is more open and tolerant than ever before, we must not mistake a decline in blatant racism or a reduction in overt discrimination with its demise. As we have seen, abundant evidence shows that racism and discrimination have not declined, but have merely changed form, and that the patterns of exclusion and deprivation sustained in the past continue in the present.

Similarly, gender issues and sexism remain on the national agenda. Blatant sexism and overt discrimination against women are probably at historic lows, but, again, we cannot mistake change for disappearance. Most important, minority women remain the victims of a double jeopardy and are among the most vulnerable and exploited segments of our society. Many women members of the new immigrant groups find themselves in similarly vulnerable positions.

Some societal trends exacerbate these problems of exclusion and continuing prejudice and sexism. For example, the continuing shift in subsistence technology away from manufacturing to the service sector privileges groups that, in the past as well as today, have had access to education. The urban underclass consists disproportionately of groups that have been excluded from education in the past and have unequal access in the present.

New immigrant groups have abundant problems of their own and need to find ways to pursue their self-interests in their new society. Some segments of these groups—the well-educated professionals seeking to advance their careers in the world's most advanced economy—will be much more likely to find ways to avoid the harshest forms of American rejection and exclusion. Similarly, the members of the "traditional" minority groups that have gained access to education and middle-class status will enjoy more opportunities than previous generations could have imagined. (As we have seen, however, their middle-class position will be more precarious than that of their dominant group counterparts.)

Will we become a society in which ethnic and racial groups are permanently segmented by class, with the more favored members enjoying a higher, if partial, level of acceptance while other members of their groups languish in permanent exclusion and segmentation? What does it mean to be an American? What *should* it mean?

Main Points

- Since the mid-1960s, immigrants have been coming to the United States at nearly record rates. Most of these immigrant groups have coethnics who have been in the United States for years, but others are "new Americans."

- Recent immigrant groups include Hispanic immigrants, non-Hispanic Caribbean immigrants, Asian, Arab and Middle Eastern, and African immigrants. Some are driven by economic needs, others are political refugees, and some are highly educated. All face multiple issues including racism, institutionalized discrimination, and a changing U.S. economy. Arab Americans remain a special target for hate crimes and for security concerns.

- Contemporary immigrants experience three different modes of incorporation: the primary labor market, the secondary labor market, and the enclave. The pathway of each group is strongly influenced by the amount of human capital they bring, their race, the attitude of the larger society, and many other factors.

- Relations between immigrants and the larger society are animated by a number of issues, including the relative costs and benefits of immigration, concerns about undocumented immigrants, and the speed of assimilation. One important issue currently being debated by social scientists is whether assimilation for new Americans will be segmented or will ultimately follow the pathway established by immigrant groups from Europe in the 19th and 20th centuries.

- Segmented assimilation theory, in contrast to traditional assimilation theory, predicts that not all immigrants will rise to the middle class and that some will become part of a permanent, marginalized underclass. At present, evidence supports both theories.

- Prominent immigration issues include relative costs and benefits, the fate of undocumented immigrants, and the situation of DREAMers. Immigration is thought to be a generally positive force in the economy.

DREAMers are illegal immigrants who were brought to the United States as children. An executive order in 2012 allows DREAMers who meet certain criteria to stay in the United States for a renewable two-year term, without fear of deportation.

APPLYING CONCEPTS

Listed below are five nations, the number of immigrants each sent to the United States in 2012, and the level of literacy for each. How familiar are you with these new Americans? Can you identify the geographical region from which each group comes and the most common religious affiliation in its homeland? Also, what's your best guess as to whether immigrants from each group are above or below national averages for education, income, and poverty levels?

Nation of Origin	Number of Immigrants, 2012	Percentage Literate, Home Nation	Region of the World	Most Common Religion	Percentage With College Degree or More	Median Household Income	Percentage of Families in Poverty
Nepal	10,198	57			__ Above __ Below	__ Above __ Below	__ Above __ Below
Ghana	10,592	72			__ Above __ Below	__ Above __ Below	__ Above __ Below
Guyana	5,683	92			__ Above __ Below	__ Above __ Below	__ Above __ Below
Peru	12,609	90			__ Above __ Below	__ Above __ Below	__ Above __ Below
Ukraine	7,642	100			__ Above __ Below	__ Above __ Below	__ Above __ Below

SEE THE END OF THIS SECTION FOR THE ANSWERS.

Review Questions

1. What differences exist among these new Americans in terms of their motivations for coming to the United States? What are the implications of these various "push" factors for their reception and adjustment to the United States?

2. Compare and contrast the Hispanic and Asian immigrant groups discussed in this chapter. What important differences and similarities can you identify in terms of modes of incorporation and human capital? What are the implications of these differences for the experiences of these groups?

3. Compare Arab and Middle Eastern immigrant groups with those from the Caribbean. Which group is more diverse? What differences exist in their patterns of adjustment and assimilation? Why do these patterns exist?

4. Compare and contrast African immigrants with immigrants from the other groups. How do they differ? What are the implications of these differences for their adjustment to the larger society?

5. What, in your opinion, are the most important issues facing the United States in terms of immigration and assimilation? How are these issues playing out in your community? What are the implications of these issues for the future of the United States?

6. Will assimilation for contemporary immigrants be segmented? After examining the evidence and arguments presented by both sides, and using information from this and previous chapters, which side of the debate seems more credible? Why? What are the implications of this debate? What will the United States look like in the future if assimilation is segmented? How will the future change if assimilation follows the "traditional" pathway? Which of these scenarios is more desirable for immigrant groups? For society as a whole? For various segments of U.S. society (e.g., employers, labor unions, African Americans, consumers, the college educated, the urban underclass)?

ANSWERS TO APPLYING CONCEPTS

Nation of Origin	Number of Immigrants, 2012	Percentage Literate, Home Nation	Region of the World	Most Common Religion	Percentage With College Degree or More	Median Household Income	Percentage of Families in Poverty
Nepal	10,198	57	South Asia	Hindu (81%)	X Above / Below	Above / X Below	X Above / Below
Ghana	10,592	72	Western Africa	Christian (71%)	X Above / Below	Above / X Below*	X Above / Below
Guyana	5,683	92	Northern South America	Christian (56%), Hindu (28%)	Above / X Below	X Above / Below	Equal
Peru	12,609	90	Western South America	Catholic (81%)	Above / X Below**	Above / X Below	X Above / Below
Ukraine	7,642	100	Eastern Europe	Eastern Orthodox (77%)	X Above / Below	X Above / Below	Above / X Below

Sources: Number of immigrants, U.S. Department of Homeland Security (2012); percentage literate and dominant religion, Central Intelligence Agency (2013); education, income, and poverty, U.S. Census Bureau (2013a).

*The Ghanaian median household income is only $40 less than the national average.

**The difference is less than 1%.

ⓈSAGE edge™

edge.sagepub.com/healeyds5e

SAGE edge offers a robust online environment featuring an impressive array of free tools and resources for review, study, and further exploration, keeping both instructors and students on the cutting edge of teaching and learning.

SAGE edge for Students provides a personalized approach to help you accomplish your coursework goals in an easy-to-use learning environment.

10

Minority Groups and U.S. Society: Themes, Patterns, and the Future

Throughout the previous nine chapters, we have analyzed ideas and theories about dominant–minority relations, examined the historical and contemporary situations of minority groups in U.S. society, and surveyed a variety of dominant–minority situations around the globe. Now it is time to reexamine our major themes and concepts and determine what conclusions can be derived from our analysis.

In this final chapter, we restate the general themes of this text, draw conclusions from the material we have covered, and speculate about the future. As we look backward to the past and forward to the future, it seems appropriate to paraphrase the words of the historian Oscar Handlin (1951): "Once I thought to write a history of the minority groups in America. Then, I discovered that the minority groups *were* American history" (p. 3).

We should remember that our understandings are limited by who we are, where we come from, and what we have experienced. Our ability to imagine the realities faced by others is never perfect, and what we can see of the world depends very much on where we are situated in the social structure.

If we are to understand the forces that have created dominant–minority relationships in the United States and around the globe, we must find ways to surpass the limitations of our personal experiences and honestly confront the often ugly realities of the past and present. We believe that the information and ideas developed in this text can help liberate our sociological imaginations from the narrow confines of our own experiences and perspectives.

The Importance of Subsistence Technology

One of the most important sociological ideas we have developed is that dominant–minority relations are shaped by large social, political, and economic forces and they change as these broad characteristics change. To understand the evolution of America's minority groups is to understand the history of the United States, from the earliest colonial settlement to the modern megalopolis. As we have seen throughout the text, these same broad forces have left their imprint on many societies around the globe.

Subsistence technology is the most basic force shaping a society and the relationships between dominant and minority groups in that society. In the colonial United States, minority relations were bent to the demands of a land-hungry, labor-intensive agrarian technology, and the early relationships between Africans, Europeans, and American Indians flowed from the colonists' desire to control both land and labor. By the mid-1800s, two centuries after Jamestown was founded, the same dynamics that had enslaved African Americans and nearly annihilated American Indians made a minority group out of Mexican Americans.

The agrarian era came to an end in the 19th century as the new technologies of the Industrial Revolution increased the productivity of the economy and eventually changed every aspect of life in the United States. The paternalistic, oppressive systems used to control the labor of minority groups in the agrarian era gave way to competitive systems of group relations. These newer systems evolved from more rigid forms to more fluid forms as industrialization and urbanization progressed.

As the United States grew and developed, new minority groups were created, and old minority groups, including women and lesbian, gay, bisexual, and transgender (LGBT) people, were transformed. Rapid industrialization, combined with the opportunities available on the frontier, made the United States an attractive destination for immigrants from Europe, Asia, Latin America, and other parts of the world. Immigrants helped farm the Great Plains, mine the riches of the West, and, above all, supply the armies of labor required by industrialization.

The descendants of the immigrants from Europe benefited from the continuing industrialization of the economy, rising slowly in the social class structure as the economy grew and matured. Immigrants from Asia and Latin America were not so fortunate. Chinese and Japanese Americans survived in ethnic enclaves on the fringes of the mainstream society, and Mexican Americans and Puerto Ricans supplied low-paid manual labor for both the rural and the urban economy. For much of the 20th century, both Asian and Hispanic Americans were barred from access to dominant group institutions and higher-paid jobs.

The racial minority groups, particularly African Americans, Mexican Americans, and Puerto Ricans, began to enter the urban working class after European American ethnic groups had started to move up in the occupational structure, at a time when the supply of manual, unskilled jobs was starting to dwindle. Thus, the processes that allowed upward mobility for European Americans failed to work for the racial minority groups, who confronted urban poverty and bankrupt cities in addition to the continuing barriers of racial prejudice and institutional discrimination.

Immigration to the United States has been quite high for the past several decades and has delivered highly educated professionals to help staff the postindustrial economy, along with large numbers of undocumented immigrants to supply workers for the secondary labor market and the irregular economy. This stream has evoked the usual American nativism and racism, along with intense debates—in the social sciences as well as in the general public—about the cost and benefits of the immigrants and their ultimate places in the social structure.

We can only speculate about what the future holds, but the emerging information-based, high-tech society is unlikely to offer many opportunities to people with lower levels of education and few occupational skills. It seems highly likely that, at least for the foreseeable future, a substantial percentage of racial and colonized minority groups and some recent immigrant groups will be participating in the mainstream economy at lower levels than will the dominant group, the descendants of the European immigrants, and the more advantaged recent immigrant groups. This outcome would be consistent with the segmented assimilation thesis, as discussed in Chapter 9. Upgraded urban educational systems, job-training programs, and other community development programs might alter the grim scenario of continuing exclusion, but current public opinion on matters of race and discrimination makes creation of such programs unlikely.

The perpetuation of the status quo will bar a large percentage of the population from the emerging mainstream economy. Those segments of the African, Hispanic, and Asian American communities currently mired in the urban underclass will continue to compete with some of the newer immigrants for jobs in the low-wage, secondary labor market or in alternative opportunity structures, including crime.

Shifts in subsistence technology also helped transform gender roles and the situation of women. In the postindustrial era, women are heavily involved in the paid labor force and, because of the concerted, long-term efforts of the feminist movements, enjoy greater opportunities and more choices than ever before. However, as we have documented, women also face gender gaps in wages, glass ceilings, sexual harassment, and a variety of other issues and limitations. Women today are less constrained by institutional barriers, stereotypes, and presumptions of inferiority; yet what we have called the "invisible privileges" of masculinity continue to operate across society, from intimate family relations to corporate boardrooms. Across the globe, the status of women continues to depend heavily on subsistence technology, and women in more agrarian societies face especially formidable barriers to gender equality.

As with other minority groups, LGBT people have benefited from the greater tolerance and openness associated with more educated, more advanced industrial societies. The anonymity of urban spaces provided opportunities for them to find one another and begin to develop associations and form organizations, even when the labels of mental illness and stigmas of deviance and criminality were strongest. In recent decades, after considerable struggle and hard work, gay and lesbian Americans have reduced their marginalization and experienced a number of triumphs, including the growing acceptance of same-sex marriage among the general public and its legitimation by the U.S. Supreme Court in the summer of 2015. However, much work

tended to take the least-desirable, lowest-status positions available in the economy, often while trying to raise children and attend to other family needs. Others have expected them to provide support for family members, kinship groups, and communities, often sacrificing their own self-interests for the welfare of others. At the other end of the continuum, white, Anglo, heterosexual, affluent, Protestant men have enjoyed—and continue to enjoy—a system of privilege and advantage so pervasive that it is invisible to its beneficiaries.

Finally, understanding the complexities of inequality requires the recognition of the multiple roles we all occupy. For example, a heterosexual woman of color and a white lesbian have different goals in life, despite the fact that both are women. One must deal with modern racism, while the other confronts the pervasive (although perhaps lessening) rejection of homosexuality: neither faces the world as a woman only. Likewise, a working class man of color and an upper class Anglo man may have similarities based on their gender, but their experiences are shaped differently by class and race. Similar comparisons and contrasts can be made for virtually any pair of Americans, and they outline the difference and diversity in society and the need to recognize the multiple realities that define each of us.

Assimilation and Pluralism

It seems fair to conclude that the diversity and complexity of minority group experiences in the United States are not well characterized by some of the traditional, or "melting pot," views of assimilation. For example, the idea that assimilation is a linear, inevitable process has little support. Immigrants from Europe probably fit that model better than other groups, but as the ethnic revival of the 1960s demonstrated, assimilation and ethnic identity can take surprising turns.

Also without support is the notion that there is always a simple, ordered relationship among the various stages of assimilation: acculturation, integration into public institutions, integration into the private sector, and so forth. We have seen that some groups integrated before they acculturated, others have become more committed to their ethnic or racial identity over the generations, and still others have been acculturated for generations but are no closer to full integration. New expressions of ethnicity come and go, and minority groups emerge, combine, and recombine in unexpected and seemingly unpredictable ways. The 1960s saw a reassertion of ethnicity and loyalty to old identities among some groups, even as other groups developed new coalitions and invented new ethnic identities (e.g., pan-tribalism among Native Americans). No simple or linear view of assimilation can begin to make sense of the array of minority group experiences.

Indeed, the very desirability of assimilation has been subject to debate. Since the 1960s, many minority spokespersons have questioned the wisdom of becoming a part of a sociocultural structure that was constructed by the systematic exploitation of minority groups. Pluralistic themes increased in prominence as the commitment of the larger society to racial equality faltered. Virtually every minority group, including women and people who are LGBT, proclaimed the authenticity of its own experiences, its own culture, and its own version of history, separate from but as valid as that of the dominant groups. From what might have seemed like a nation on the verge of integration in the 1950s (at least for white ethnic groups), America evolved into what might have seemed like a Tower of Babel in the 1960s. The consensus that assimilation was the best solution and the most sensible goal for all of America's groups was shattered (if it ever really existed at all).

Let's review the state of acculturation and integration in the United States on a group-by-group basis:

- African Americans are highly acculturated. Despite the many unique cultural traits forged in America and those that survive from Africa, black Americans share language, values and beliefs, and most other aspects of culture with white Americans of similar class and educational background. In terms of integration, in contrast, African Americans present a mixed picture. For middle-class, more-educated members of the group, American society offers more opportunities for upward mobility and success than ever before. Without denying the prejudice, discrimination, and racism that remain, this segment of the group is in a favorable position to achieve higher levels of affluence and power for their children and grandchildren. At the same time, a large percentage of African Americans remain mired in urban poverty, and for them, affluence, security, and power are just as distant as they were a generation ago (perhaps even more so). Considering the group as a whole, African Americans are still highly segregated in their residential and school attendance patterns, and unemployment and poverty remain serious problems, perhaps even more serious than they were a generation ago.

- Native Americans are less acculturated than African Americans, and some tribes and organizations are trying to preserve American Indian cultures and languages. Overall, however, the strength and vitality of these traditions is probably decreasing. On measures of integration, there is some indication of improvement, but many American Indians are among the most isolated and impoverished minority group members in the United States. One possible bright spot for some reservations lies in the further development of the gambling industry and the investment of profits in the tribal infrastructure to upgrade schools, health clinics, job training centers, and so forth.

- Members of the largest Hispanic American groups are also generally less acculturated than African Americans. Hispanic traditions and the Spanish language have been sustained by the exclusion and isolation of these groups within the United States and have been continually renewed and revitalized by immigration. Cubans have moved closer to equality than Mexican Americans and Puerto Ricans. They did so by resisting assimilation and building an ethnic enclave economy. Mexican Americans and Puerto Ricans share many of the problems of urban poverty that confront African Americans, and they are below national norms on measures of equality and integration.

The smaller Hispanic groups consist mostly of new immigrants who are just beginning the assimilation process. Many members of these groups, along with

Mexican Americans and Puerto Ricans, are less educated and have few occupational skills, and they face the dangers of blending into a permanent urban underclass. Nonetheless, some evidence suggests that these groups (or, more accurately, their descendants) may eventually find their way into the American mainstream (recall the debate over segmented assimilation in Chapter 9).

- As with Hispanic Americans, the extent of assimilation among Asian Americans is highly variable. Some groups (e.g., third- and fourth-generation Japanese Americans and Chinese Americans) have virtually completed the assimilation process and compare favorably to national norms in terms of integration and equality, at least in terms of group averages. Some Asian American groups (the more elite immigrants from India and the Philippines) seem to be finding a place in the American mainstream. Other groups consist largely of newer immigrants with occupational and educational profiles that often resemble those of colonized minority groups, and these groups face the same dangers of permanent marginalization and exclusion. Still other Asian American groups (e.g., Korean Americans) have constructed ethnic enclaves and pursue economic equality by resisting acculturation.

- Only European American ethnic groups, covered in Chapter 2, seem to approximate the traditional model of assimilation. The development even of these groups, however, has taken unexpected twists and turns, and the pluralism of the 1960s and 1970s suggests that ethnic traditions and ethnic identity, in some form, may withstand the pressures of assimilation for generations to come. Culturally and racially, these groups are the closest to the dominant group. If they still retain a sense of ethnicity, even if merely symbolic, after generations of acculturation and integration, what is the likelihood that the sense of group membership will fade in racially stigmatized minority groups?

- Different gendered expectations continue to shape the socialization experiences of women and men throughout the life cycle and, in that sense, "acculturation" has not been accomplished. Women are equal to men on some measures of equality (e.g., education), but large gaps in other areas (e.g., income) persist. The gaps vary from group to group, but women in general continue to be disproportionately concentrated in less well-paid occupations and continue to confront glass ceilings and other limits to their social mobility.

For racial and ethnic minority groups, assimilation is far from accomplished. The group divisions that remain are real and consequential; they cannot be willed away by pretending we are all "just American." Group membership continues to be important because it continues to be linked to fundamental patterns of exclusion and inequality. The realities of pluralism, inequality, and ethnic and racial identity persist to the extent that the American promise of a truly open opportunity structure continues to fail. The group divisions forged in the past and perpetuated over the decades by racism and discrimination will remain to the extent that racial and ethnic group membership continues to be correlated with inequality and position in the social class structure.

Along with economic and political pressures, other forces help to sustain the pluralistic group divisions. Some argue that ethnicity is rooted in biology and can never be fully eradicated (e.g., see van den Berghe, 1981). Although this may be an extreme position, many people find their own ancestries to be a matter of great interest. Some (perhaps most) of the impetus behind the preservation of ethnic and racial identity may be a result of the most vicious and destructive intergroup competition. In other ways, though, ethnicity can be a positive force that helps people locate themselves in time and space and understand their position in the contemporary world. Ethnicity remains an important aspect of self-identity and pride for many Americans from every group and tradition. It seems unlikely that this sense of a personal link to particular groups and heritages within U.S. society will soon fade.

Can we survive as a pluralistic, culturally and linguistically fragmented, racially and ethnically unequal society? What will save us from this division and inequality? Given our history of colonization and racism, can U.S. society move closer to the relatively harmonious models of race relations found in places such as Hawaii?

As we deal with these questions, we need to remember that in and of itself, diversity is no more "bad" than unity is "good." Our society has grown to a position of global preeminence despite, or perhaps because of, our diversity. In fact, many have argued that our diversity is a fundamental and essential characteristic of U.S. society and a great strength to be cherished and encouraged. Sociologist Ronald Takaki (1993) ended his history of multicultural America, *A Different Mirror*, with an eloquent endorsement of our diversity and pluralism:

> As Americans, we originally came from many different shores and our diversity has been at the center of the making of America. While our stories contain the memories of different communities, together they inscribe a larger narrative. Filled with what Walt Whitman celebrated as the "varied carols" of America, our history generously gives all of us our "mystic chords of memory."
>
> Throughout our past of oppressions and struggles for equality, Americans of different races and ethnicities have been "singing with open mouths their strong melodious songs" in the textile mills of Lowell, the cotton fields of Mississippi, on the Indian reservations of South Dakota, the railroad tracks high in the Sierras of California, in the garment factories of the Lower East Side, the cane fields of Hawaii, and a thousand other places across the country. Our denied history "bursts with telling." As we hear America singing, we find ourselves invited to bring our cultural diversity [into the open], to accept ourselves. (p. 428)

To this heady mix of diversity in race, ethnicity, language, and culture, we must add the dimensions of gender and sexual orientation, and their infinite intersections and combinations with group membership. The "varied carols" of American life are voiced by a complex, diversified chorus: The tune will not be the same for heterosexual, middle-class African Americans as for lesbian, Hispanic immigrants with low levels of human capital. How can we sort out this complexity? How can we answer the question we raised at the beginning of this text: What does it mean to be an American?

The question for our future might not be so much, "Unity or diversity?" as "What blend of pluralism and assimilation will serve us best in the 21st century?" How can American society prosper without repressing our diversity? How can we increase the degree of openness, fairness, and justice without threatening group loyalties? The one-way, Anglo-conformity mode of assimilation of the past is too narrow and destructive to be a blueprint for the future, but the more extreme forms of minority group pluralism and separatism might be equally dangerous.

How much unity do we need? How much diversity can we support? These are questions you must answer for yourself, and they are questions you will face in a thousand different ways over the course of your life. The ideas presented in this text cannot fully resolve them. As long as immigrants and minority groups are a part of the United States, as long as prejudice and discrimination and inequality persist, the debates will continue and new issues will arise as old ones are resolved.

As U.S. society attempts to deal with new immigrants and unresolved minority grievances, we should recognize that it is not diversity per se that threatens stability but, rather, the realities of exclusion and marginalization, split labor markets, racial and ethnic stratification, urban poverty, and institutionalized discrimination. We need to focus on the issues that confront us with an honest recognition of the past and the economic, political, and social forces that have shaped us. As the United States continues to remake itself, an informed sense of where we have been will help us decide where we should go next.

Photo 10.2   These world flags reflect the diversity of America.

Minority Group Progress and the Ideology of American Individualism

There is so much sadness, misery, and unfairness in the history of minority groups that evidence of progress sometimes goes unnoticed. Lest we be guilty of ignoring the good news in favor of the bad, let us note some ways in which the situations of American minority groups are better today than they were in the past. Evidence of progress is easy to find for some groups; we need look only to the relative economic, educational, and income equality of European American ethnic groups and some Asian American groups, or recall the two elections of President Barack Obama. The United States has become more tolerant and open, and minority group members can be found at the highest levels of success, affluence, and prestige. Women, in large numbers, are entering occupations traditionally held by men, and American society has become increasingly inclusive of sexual-orientation minorities.

One of the most obvious changes is the decline of traditional racism and prejudice, sexism, and homophobia. The strong racial and ethnic sentiments and stereotypes of the past are no longer the primary vocabulary for discussing race relations among dominant group members, although prejudice in all its forms unquestionably still exists.

The demise of blatant bigotry is, without doubt, a positive change. However, negative intergroup feelings and stereotypes have not so much disappeared as changed form. The old racist feelings are now being expressed in other forms, specifically in what has been called "modern" or "symbolic" racism: the view that holds that opportunity channels and routes of upward mobility of American society are opened to all.

This individualistic view of social mobility is consistent with the human capital perspective and the traditional, melting-pot view of assimilation. Taken together, these ideologies present a powerful and widely shared perspective on the nature of minority group problems in modern American society. Proponents of these views tend to be unsympathetic to the plight of minorities and to programs, such as affirmative action, intended to ameliorate these problems. The overt bigotry of the past has been replaced by an indifference more difficult to define and harder to measure than old-fashioned racism, yet it still reflects resistance to racial change.

We have argued that the most serious problems facing contemporary minority groups, however, are structural and institutional, not individual or personal. For example, the scarcity of jobs and high rates of unemployment in the inner cities are the result of economic and political forces beyond the control not only of the minority communities, but also of local and state governments. The marginalization of the minority group labor force is a reflection of the essence of modern American capitalism. National and multinational corporations control mainstream, higher-paying, blue-collar jobs available to people with modest educational credentials. These corporations maximize profits by automating production and moving the remaining jobs to areas, often outside the United States, with abundant supplies of cheaper labor.

We have also seen that some of the more effective strategies for pursuing equality require strong in-group cohesion and networks of cooperation, not heroic individual

Hanson, Jeffery, and Linda Rouse. 1987. Dimensions of Native American Stereotyping. *American Indian Culture and Research Journal* 11:33–58.

Harjo, Suzan. 1996. Now and Then: Native Peoples in the United States. *Dissent* 43:58–60.

Hawkins, Hugh. 1962. *Booker T. Washington and His Critics: The Problem of Negro Leadership.* Boston: D. C. Heath.

Heartland Geopolitical Maps. 2009. European Immigration to the United States. http://temi .repubblica.it/limes-heartland/european-immigration-to-the-united-states-2/867.

Heer, David M. 1996. *Immigration in America's Future.* Boulder, CO: Westview.

Herberg, Will. 1960. *Protestant–Catholic–Jew: An Essay in American Religious Sociology.* New York: Anchor.

Higham, John. 1963. *Strangers in the Land: Patterns of American Nativism, 1860–1925.* New York: Atheneum.

Hill, Jane. 1995. Mock Spanish: A Site for the Indexical Reproduction of Racism in American English. *Language and Culture: Symposium 2.* http://language-culture.binghamton.edu/ symposia/2/part1/.

Hirschman, Charles. 1983. America's Melting Pot Reconsidered. *Annual Review of Sociology* 9:397–423.

Hirschman, Charles, and Morrison Wong. 1984. Socioeconomic Gains of Asian Americans, Blacks, and Hispanics: 1960–1976. *American Journal of Sociology* 90:584–607.

———. 1986. The Extraordinary Educational Attainment of Asian-Americans: A Search for Historical Evidence and Explanations. *Social Forces* 65:1–27.

His Horse Is Thunder, Deborah, Nate Anderson, and Darlene Miller. 2013. *Building the Foundation for Success: Case Studies of Breaking Through Tribal Colleges and Universities.* Boston: Jobs for the Future. http://www.jff.org/sites/default/files/publications/ BuildingFoundationSuccess_ExSumm_040813.pdf.

Hochschild, Arlie. 1979. Emotion Work, Feeling Rules, and Social Structure. *American Journal of Sociology* 85:551– 575.

Hoeffel, Elizabeth, Sonya Rastogi, Myoung Ouk Kim, and Hasan Shahid. 2012. *The Asian Population: 2010.* Washington, DC: U.S. Census Bureau. http://www.census.gov/prod/ cen2010/briefs/c2010br-11.pdf.

Hopcroft, Rosemary. 2009. Gender Inequality in Interaction: An Evolutionary Account. *Social Forces* 87:1845–1872.

Hostetler, John. 1980. *Amish Society.* Baltimore, MD: Johns Hopkins University Press.

How to Tell Your Friends From the Japs. 1941. *Time,* October–December, p. 33.

Hoxie, Frederick. 1984. *A Final Promise: The Campaign to Assimilate the Indian, 1880–1920.* Lincoln: University of Nebraska Press.

Hraba, Joseph. 1994. *American Ethnicity* (2nd ed.). Itasca, IL: F. E. Peacock.

Huber, Joan. 2007. *On the Origins of Gender Inequality.* Colorado Springs, CO; Paradigm.

Hughes, Michael, and Melvin Thomas. 1998. The Continuing Significance of Race Revisited: A Study of Race, Class, and Quality of Life in America, 1972 to 1996. *American Sociological Review* 63:785–803.

Huntington, Samuel. 2004. *Who Are We? The Challenges to America's National Identity.* New York: Simon & Schuster.

Hurh, Won Moo. 1998. *The Korean Americans.* Westport, CT: Greenwood.

Hyman, Herbert, and Paul Sheatsley. 1964. Attitudes Toward Desegregation. *Scientific American* 211:16–23.

Ibish, Hussein (Ed.). 2003. *Report on Hate Crimes and Discrimination Against Arab Americans: The Post–September 11 Backlash.* Washington, DC: American-Arab Anti-Discrimination Committee. http://www.adc.org/hatecrimes/pdf/2003_report_web.pdf.

Iceland, John, Donald Weinberg, and Erika Steinmetz. 2002. *Racial and Ethnic Residential Segregation in the United States: 1980-2000* (U.S. Census Bureau, Series CENSR-3).

Washington, DC: U.S. Government Printing Office. http://www.census.gov/prod/2002pubs/censr-3.pdf.

Ifill, G. 2009. *The Breakthrough: Politics and Race in the Age of Obama.* New York: Doubleday.

Illegal Immigrant Deaths, by Border Patrol Sector. 2010. *Arizona Daily Star,* August 22. http://tucson.com/online/pdf/pdf_731dc548-ada5-11df-9449-001cc4c03286.html.

Jackson, Beverly. 2000. *Splendid Slippers: A Thousand Years of an Erotic Tradition.* Berkeley, CA: Ten Speed Press.

Jacobs, David, and Katherine Wood. 1999. Interracial Conflict and Interracial Homicide: Do Political and Economic Rivalries Explain White Killings of Blacks or Black Killings of Whites? *American Journal of Sociology* 105:157–180.

Japanese American Citizens League. 2009. *Myths and Mirrors: Real Challenges Facing Asian American Students.* San Francisco, CA: Author. http://www.jacl.org/leadership/documents/MythsandMirrorsFinal.pdf.

Jibou, Robert M. 1988. Ethnic Hegemony and the Japanese of California. *American Sociological Review* 53:353–367.

Joe, Jennie, and Dorothy Miller. 1994. Cultural Survival and Contemporary American Indian Women in the City. In Maxine Zinn and Bonnie T. Dill (Eds.), *Women of Color in U.S. Society* (pp. 185–202). Philadelphia, PA: Temple University Press.

Jones, N., and J. Bullock. 2012. *The Two or More Races Population: 2010.* http://www.census.gov/prod/cen2010/briefs/c2010br-13.pdf.

Jordan, Winthrop. 1968. *White Over Black: American Attitudes Towards the Negro: 1550–1812.* Chapel Hill: University of North Carolina Press.

Josephy, Alvin M. 1968. *The Indian Heritage of America.* New York: Knopf.

Kallen, Horace M. 1915a. Democracy Versus the Melting Pot. *Nation* 100(February 18): 190–194.

———. 1915b. Democracy Versus the Melting Pot. *Nation* 100(February 25): 217–222.

Kasarda, John D. 1989. Urban Industrial Transition and the Underclass. *Annals of the American Academy of Political Science* 501:26–47.

Kasindorf, Martin. 2012. Racial Tensions Are Simmering in Hawaii's Melting Pot. *USA Today,* March 6. http://usatoday30.usatoday.com/news/nation/2007-03-06-hawaii-cover_N.htm.

Kasinitz, Philip, John H. Mollenkopf, Mary C. Waters, and Jennifer Holdaway. 2008. *Inheriting the City: The Children of Immigrants Come of Age.* New York: Russell Sage Foundation.

Katz, Michael B., and Mark J. Stern. 2008. *One Nation Divisible: What America Was and What It Is Becoming.* New York: Russell Sage Foundation.

Katz, Phyllis. 1976. The Acquisition of Racial Attitudes in Children. In Phyllis Katz (Ed.), *Towards the Elimination of Racism* (pp. 125–154). New York: Pergamon.

———. 2003. Racists or Tolerant Multiculturalists? How Do They Begin? *American Psychologist* 58:897–909.

Katznelson, Ira. 2005. *When Affirmative Action Was White: An Untold History of Racial Inequality in Twentieth-Century America.* New York: Norton.

Kaw, Eugenia. 1997. Opening Faces: The Politics of Cosmetic Surgery and Asian American Women. In M. Crawford and R. Under (Eds.), *In Our Own Words: Readings on the Psychology of Women and Gender* (pp. 55–73). New York: McGraw-Hill.

Kaye, Jeffrey. 2010. *Moving Millions: How Coyote Capitalism Fuels Global Immigration.* Hoboken, NJ: Wiley.

Kennedy, Randall. 2001. Racial Trends in the Administration of Criminal Justice. In N. Smelser, W. Wilson, and F. Mitchell (Eds.), *America Becoming: Racial Trends and Their Consequences* (Vol. 2, pp. 1–20). Washington, DC: National Academy Press.

Kennedy, Ruby Jo. 1944. Single or Triple Melting Pot? Intermarriage Trends in New Haven, 1870–1940. *American Journal of Sociology* 49:331–339.

———. 1952. Single or Triple Melting Pot? Intermarriage in New Haven, 1870–1950. *American Journal of Sociology* 58:56–59.

Kephart, William, and William Zellner. 1994. *Extraordinary Groups.* New York: St. Martin's Press.

Killian, Lewis. 1975. *The Impossible Revolution, Phase 2: Black Power and the American Dream.* New York: Random House.

Kinder, Donald R., and David O. Sears. 1981. Prejudice and Politics: Symbolic Racism Versus Racial Threats to the Good Life. *Journal of Personality and Social Psychology* 40:414–431.

King, Martin Luther, Jr. 1958. *Stride Toward Freedom: The Montgomery Story.* New York: Harper & Row.

———. 1963. *Why We Can't Wait.* New York: Mentor.

———. 1968. *Where Do We Go From Here: Chaos or Community?* New York: Harper & Row.

Kitano, Harry H. L. 1980. Japanese. In Stephan Thernstrom, Ann Orlov, and Oscar Handlin (Eds.), *Harvard Encyclopedia of American Ethnic Groups* (pp. 561–571). Cambridge, MA: Harvard University Press.

Kitano, Harry, and Roger Daniels. 1988. *Asian Americans: Emerging Minorities.* Englewood Cliffs, NJ: Prentice Hall.

———. 1995. *Asian Americans: Emerging Minorities* (2nd ed.). Englewood Cliffs, NJ: Prentice Hall.

———. 2001. *Asian Americans: Emerging Minorities* (3rd ed.). Upper Saddle River, NJ: Prentice Hall.

Kluegel, James R., and Eliot R. Smith. 1982. Whites' Beliefs About Blacks' Opportunities. *American Sociological Review* 47:518–532.

Kochhar, Rakesh. 2004. *The Wealth of Hispanic Households: 1996 to 2002.* Washington, DC: Pew Hispanic Center. http://pewhispanic.org/files/reports/34.pdf.

———. 2006. *Growth in the Foreign-Born Workforce and Employment of the Native Born.* Washington, DC: Pew Hispanic Center. http://pewhispanic.org/files/reports/69.pdf.

Kochhar, Rakesh, Richard Fry, and Paul Taylor. 2011. *Wealth Gap Rises to Record Highs Between Whites, Blacks, and Hispanics.* Washington, DC: Pew Research Center. http://www.pewsocialtrends.org/files/2011/07/SDT-Wealth -Report_7-26-11_FINAL.pdf.

Krauss, Michael. 1996. Status of Native American Language Endangerment. In G. Cantoni (Ed.), *Stabilizing Indigenous Languages.* Flagstaff: Center for Excellence in Education, Northern Arizona University.

Kraybill, Donald B., and Carl F. Bowman. 2001. *On the Backroad to Heaven: Old Order Hutterites, Mennonites, Amish, and Brethren.* Baltimore, MD: Johns Hopkins University Press.

Kristofic, Jim. 2011. *Navajos Wear Nikes: A Reservation Life.* Albuquerque: University of New Mexico Press.

Kritz, Mary, and Douglas Girak. 2004. *The American People: Immigration and a Changing America.* New York: Russell Sage Foundation.

Krysan, Maria, and Reynolds Farley. 2002. The Residential Preferences of Blacks: Do They Explain Persistent Segregation? *Social Forces* 80:937–981.

Kuperman, Diane. 2001. Stuck at the Gates of Paradise. *UNESCO Courier,* September, pp. 24–26.

Lacy, Dan. 1972. *The White Use of Blacks in America.* New York: McGraw-Hill.

Lai, H. M. 1980. Chinese. In Stephan Thernstrom, Ann Orlov, and Oscar Handlin (Eds.), *Harvard Encyclopedia of American Ethnic Groups* (pp. 217–234). Cambridge, MA: Harvard University Press.

Lamont-Brown, Raymond. 1993. The Burakumin: Japan's Underclass. *Contemporary Review* 263:136–140.

Landale, Nancy, and R. S. Oropesa. 2002. White, Black, or Puerto Rican? Racial Self-Identification Among Mainland and Island Puerto Ricans. *Social Forces* 81:231–254.

Lee, Sharon. 1998. Asian Americans: Diverse and Growing. *Population Bulletin* 53(2): 1–40.

Lenski, Gerhard, Patrick Nolan, and Jean Lenski. 1995. *Human Societies: An Introduction to Macrosociology* (7th ed.). New York: McGraw-Hill.

Levine, Lawrence. 1977. *Black Culture and Black Consciousness.* New York: Oxford University Press.

Levy, Jacques. 1975. *César Chávez: Autobiography of La Causa.* New York: Norton.

Lewis, John (with Michael D'Orso). 1999. *Walking with the Wind: A Memoir of the Movement.* New York: Harvest Books.

Lewis, Oscar. 1959. *Five Families: Mexican Case Studies in the Culture of Poverty.* New York: Basic Books.

———. 1965. *La Vida: A Puerto Rican Family in the Culture of Poverty.* New York: Random House.

———. 1966. The Culture of Poverty. *Scientific American* (October): 19–25.

Lewis, Valerie, Michael Emerson, and Stephen Klineberg. 2011. Who We'll Live With: Neighborhood Composition Preferences of Whites, Blacks, and Latinos. *Social Forces* 89:1385–1408.

Lewy, G. 2004. Were American Indians the Victims of Genocide? *Commentary* 118:55–63.

Lieberson, R. 1998. *Shifting the Color Line: Race and the American Welfare System.* Cambridge, MA: Harvard University Press.

Lieberson, Stanley. 1980. *A Piece of the Pie: Blacks and White Immigrants Since 1880.* Berkeley: University of California Press.

Lieberson, Stanley, and Mary C. Waters. 1988. *From Many Strands.* New York: Russell Sage Foundation.

Light, Ivan, and Edna Bonacich. 1988. *Immigrant Entrepreneurs: Koreans in Los Angeles, 1965–1982.* Berkeley: University of California Press.

Lincoln, C. Eric. 1961. *The Black Muslims in America.* Boston: Beacon.

Ling, Huping. 2000. Family and Marriage of Late-Nineteenth and Early-Twentieth Century Chinese Immigrant Women. *Journal of American Ethnic History* 9:43–65.

Liptak, Adam. 2013. Supreme Court Invalidates Key Part of the Voting Rights Act. *New York Times*, June 25. http://www.nytimes.com/2013/06/26/us/supreme -court-ruling.html.

Locust, Carol. 1990. Wounding the Spirit: Discrimination and Traditional American Indian Belief Systems. In Gail Thomas (Ed.), *U.S. Race Relations in the 1980s and 1990s: Challenges and Alternatives* (pp. 219–232). New York: Hemisphere.

Loewen, James. 2005. *Sundown Towns: A Hidden Dimension of American Racism.* New York: Simon & Schuster.

Logan, John, Richard Alba, and Thomas McNulty. 1994. Ethnic Economies in Metropolitan Regions: Miami and Beyond. *Social Forces* 72:691–724.

Logan, John, and Brian Stults. 2011. *The Persistence of Segregation in the Metropolis: New Findings From the 2010 Census.* http://www.s4.brown.edu/us2010/Data/Report/report2 .pdf.

Lopata, Helena Znaniecki. 1976. *Polish Americans.* Englewood Cliffs, NJ: Prentice Hall.

Lurie, Nancy Oestrich. 1982. The American Indian: Historical Background. In Norman Yetman and C. Hoy Steele (Eds.), *Majority and Minority* (3rd ed., pp. 131–144). Boston: Allyn & Bacon.

Lyman, Stanford. 1974. *Chinese Americans.* New York: Random House.

Malcolm X. 1964. *The Autobiography of Malcolm X.* New York: Grove.

Mann, Charles. 2011. *1491: New Revelations of the Americas Before Columbus.* New York: Vintage Books.

Manning Jennifer. 2013. Membership of the 133th Congress: A Profile. Congressional Research Service http://www.senate.gov/CRSReports/crs-publish.cfm?pid=%260BL%2BR%5CC%3F%0A.

Mannix, Daniel P. 1962. *Black Cargoes: A History of the Atlantic Slave Trade.* New York: Viking.

Marable, Manning. 2011. *Malcolm X: A Life of Reinvention.* New York: Penguin.

Marcelli, Enrico, and David Heer. 1998. The Unauthorized Mexican Immigrant Population and Welfare in Los Angeles County: A Comparative Statistical Analysis. *Sociological Perspectives* 41:279–303.

Marteleto, Leticia. 2012. Educational Inequality by Race in Brazil, 1982–2007: Structural Changes and Shifts in Racial Classification. *Demography* 49:337–358.

Martin, Philip, and Elizabeth Midgley. 1999. Immigration to the United States. *Population Bulletin* 54(2): 1–44. Washington, DC: Population Reference Bureau.

Marx, Karl, and Friedrich Engels. 1967. *The Communist Manifesto.* Baltimore: Penguin. (Original work published 1848)

Massarik, Fred, and Alvin Chenkin. 1973. United States National Jewish Population Study: A First Report. In *American Jewish Committee, American Jewish Year Book, 1973* (pp. 264–306). New York: American Jewish Committee.

Massey, Douglas. 1995. The New Immigration and Ethnicity in the United States. *Population and Development Review* 21:631–652.

———. 2000. Housing Discrimination 101. *Population Today* 28:1, 4.

———. 2007. *Categorically Unequal: The American Stratification System.* New York: Russell Sage Foundation.

Massey, Douglas, and Nancy Denton. 1993. *American Apartheid.* Cambridge, MA: Harvard University Press.

Mauer, Marc. 2011. Addressing Racial Disparities in Incarceration. *The Prison Journal* 91:875–1015.

McConahy, John B. 1986. Modern Racism, Ambivalence, and the Modern Racism Scale. In John F. Dovidio and Samuel Gartner (Eds.), *Prejudice, Discrimination, and Racism* (pp. 91–125). Orlando, FL: Academic Press.

McDowell, Amber. 2004. Cracker Barrel Settles Lawsuit; Black Customers, Workers Reported Discrimination. *Washington Post,* September 10, p. E1.

McLemore, S. Dale. 1973. The Origins of Mexican American Subordination in Texas. *Social Science Quarterly* 53:656–679.

McNickle, D'Arcy. 1973. *Native American Tribalism: Indian Survivals and Renewals.* New York: Oxford University Press.

McPherson, Miller, Lynn Smith-Lovin, and Matthew Brashears. 2006. Social Isolation in America: Changes in Core Discussion Networks Over Two Decades. *Social Forces* 71:353–375.

McWilliams, Carey. 1961. *North From Mexico: The Spanish-Speaking People of the United States.* New York: Monthly Review Press.

Medoff, Marshall. 1999. Allocation of Time and Hateful Behavior: A Theoretical and Positive Analysis of Hate and Hate Crimes. *American Journal of Economics and Sociology* 58:959–973.

Meek, Barbara. 2006. And the Indian Goes "How!": Representations of American Indian English in White Public Space. *Language in Society* 35:93–128.

Meissner, Doris. 2010. 5 Myths about Immigration. *Washington Post,* May 2, p. B2.

Mikulak, M. 2011. The Symbolic Power of Color: Construction of Race, Skin-Color, and Identity in Brazil. *Humanity and Society* 35:62–99.

Min, Pyong Gap (Ed.). 1995. *Asian Americans: Contemporary Trends and Issues.* Thousand Oaks, CA: Sage.

———. 2006. *Asian Americans: Contemporary Trends and Issues* (2nd ed.). Thousand Oaks, CA: Sage.

Mirandé, Alfredo. 1985. *The Chicano Experience: An Alternative Perspective.* Notre Dame, IN: University of Notre Dame Press.

Mirandé, Alfredo, and Evangelina Enríquez. 1979. *La Chicana: The Mexican-American Woman.* Chicago: University of Chicago Press.

Mississippi Band of Choctaw Indians. 2011. *Tribal Profile.* Choctaw, MS: Office of the Tribal Miko. http://www.choctaw.org/aboutMBCI/tribalProfile.pdf.

Monger, Randall. 2012. *Nonimmigrant Admissions to the United States: 2012.* Washington, DC: U.S. Department of Homeland Security. https://www.dhs.gov/sites/default/files/publications/ois_ni_fr_2012.pdf.

Moore, Joan W. 1970. *Mexican Americans.* Englewood Cliffs, NJ: Prentice Hall.

Moore, Joan W., and Harry Pachon. 1985. *Hispanics in the United States.* Englewood Cliffs, NJ: Prentice Hall.

Moore, Joan, and Raquel Pinderhughes. 1993. *In the Barrios: Latinos and the Underclass Debate.* New York: Russell Sage Foundation.

Moquin, Wayne, and Charles Van Doren (Eds.). 1971. *A Documentary History of Mexican Americans.* New York: Bantam.

Morales, Lyman. 2010. Amid Immigration Debate, Americans' Views Ease Slightly. Gallup Politics. http://www.gallup.com/poll/141560/Amid -Immigration-Debate -Americans-Views-Ease -Slightly.aspx.

Morawska, Ewa. 1990. The Sociology and Historiography of Immigration. In Virginia Yans-McLaughlin (Ed.), *Immigration Reconsidered: History, Sociology, and Politics* (pp. 187–238). New York: Oxford University Press.

Morgan, Edmund. 1975. *American Slavery, American Freedom.* New York: Norton.

Morris, Aldon D. 1984. *The Origins of the Civil Rights Movement.* New York: Free Press.

Motel, Seth, and Eileen Patten. 2013. *Statistical Portrait of the Foreign-Born Population in the United States, 2011.* Washington, DC: Pew Hispanic Center. http://www.pewhispanic .org/2013/01/29/statistical -portrait-of-the-foreign-born -population-in-the-united -states-2011.

Moynihan, Daniel. 1965. *The Negro Family: The Case for National Action.* Washington, DC: U.S. Department of Labor.

Murguia, Edward, and Tyrone Foreman. 2003. Shades of Whiteness: The Mexican American Experience in Relation to Anglos and Blacks. In Ashley Doane and Eduardo Bonilla-Silva (Eds.), *White Out: The Continuing Significance of Racism* (pp. 63–72). New York: Routledge.

Muslim West Facts Project. 2009. *Muslim Americans: A National Portrait.* Washington, DC: Gallup. http://www.gallup.com/strategicconsulting/153572/report-muslim-americans -national-portrait.aspx.

Myrdal, Gunnar. 1962. *An American Dilemma: The Negro Problem and Modern Democracy.* New York: Harper & Row. (Original work published 1944)

Nabakov, Peter (Ed.). 1999. *Native American Testimony* (Rev. ed.). New York: Penguin.

National Advisory Commission. 1968. *Report of the National Advisory Commission on Civil Disorders.* New York: Bantam Books.

National Council on Crime and Delinquency. 2007. *And Justice for Some: Differential Treatment of Youth of Color in the Justice System.* http://www.nccdglobal.org/sites/default/files/publication_pdf/justice-for-some.pdf.

National Indian Gaming Commission. 2011. NIGC Tribal Gaming Revenues. http://www.nigc .gov/LinkClick.aspx?fileticket=1k4B6r6dr-U%3d&tabid=67.

National Indian Gaming Commission. 2014. Indian Gaming Revenues Increased by 0.5%. http://www.nigc.gov/linkclick.aspx?fileticket=E3BeULzk1cA%3d&tabid=1006.

National Indian Gaming Commission. 2015. Growth in Indian Gaming. http://www.nigc.gov/commission/gaming-revenue-reports.

National Opinion Research Council. 1972–2014. *General Social Survey.* Chicago: Author. http://www.norc.org/Research/Projects/Pages/general-social-survey.aspx.

National Origins Act, Pub. L. 139, Chapter 190, § 43 Stat. 153 (1924).

National Park Service. 2014. Indian Reservations in the Continental United States. U.S. Department of the Interior. http://www.nps.gov/nagpra/DOCUMENTS/ResMAP.HTM

National Public Radio. 2004. Immigration in America: Survey Overview. http://www.npr.org/templates/story/story.php?storyId=4062605.

NationMaster. 2014. Education—Average Years of Schooling of Adults: Countries Compared. http://www.nationmaster.com/graph/edu_ave_yea_of_sch_of_adu-education-average -years-schooling-adults.

Neary, Ian. 2003. Burakumin at the End of History. *Social Research* 70:269–294.

Nelli, Humbert S. 1980. Italians. In Stephan Thernstrom, Ann Orlov, and Oscar Handlin (Eds.), *Harvard Encyclopedia of American Ethnic Groups* (pp. 545–560). Cambridge, MA: Harvard University Press.

Newport, Frank. 2013a. Gulf Grows in Black-White Views of the U.S. Justice System Bias. http://www.gallup.com/poll/163610/gulf-grows -black-white-views-justice-system-bias .aspx.

———. 2013b. In U.S., 24% of Young Black Men Say Police Dealings Unfair. http://www.gallup .com/poll/163523/one-four-young-black-men-say-police-dealings-unfair.aspx?version=print.

Nishi, Setsuko. 1995. Japanese Americans. In Pyong Gap Min (Ed.), *Asian Americans: Contemporary Trends and Issues* (pp. 95–133). Thousand Oaks, CA: Sage.

Noel, Donald. 1968. A Theory of the Origin of Ethnic Stratification. *Social Problems* 16:157–172.

Nolan, Patrick, and Gerhard Lenski. 2004. *Human Societies.* Boulder, CO: Paradigm.

Norris, Tina, Paul Vines, and Elizabeth Hoeffel. 2012. The American Indian and Alaska Native Population: 2010. *2010 Census Briefs.* Washington, DC: U.S. Census Bureau. http://www .census.gov/prod/cen2010/briefs/c2010br-10.pdf.

Novak, Michael. 1973. *The Rise of the Unmeltable Ethnics: Politics and Culture in the 1970s.* New York: Collier.

Obama, Barack. 2008. Barack Obama's Speech on Race. *New York Times,* March 18. http://www .nytimes.com/2008/03/18/us/politics/18text-obama.html?pagewanted=all

Ogunwole, Stella. 2006. *We the People: American Indians and Alaska Natives in the United States.* Washington, DC: U.S. Census Bureau. http://www.census.gov/prod/2006pubs/censr-28.pdf.

Oldenburg, Ann. 2013. Miss America Nina Davulari Brushes Off Racist Remarks. *USA Today,* September 16. http://www.usatoday.com/story/life/people/2013/09/16/miss-america -nina-davuluri-brushes-off -racist-remarks/2819533.

Oliver, Melvin, and Thomas Shapiro. 2006. *Black Wealth, White Wealth* (2nd ed.). New York: Taylor & Francis.

———. 2008. Sub-Prime as a Black Catastrophe. *American Prospect* (October): A9–A11.

Olivo, Antonio, and Duaa Eldeib. 2013. Catholic Church Works to Keep Up With Growing Latino Membership. *Chicago Tribune,* March 17. http://articles.chicagotribune.com/2013- 03-17/news/ct-met-chicago-latino -catholics-20130317_1_latino-appointments-latino -candidates-priests.

Olson, James, and R. Wilson. 1984. *Native Americans in the Twentieth Century.* Provo, UT: Brigham Young University Press.

Omi, Michael, and Howard Winant. 1986. *Racial Formation in the United States From the 1960s to the 1980s.* New York: Routledge & Kegan Paul.

Orfield, Gary, and Chungmei Lee. 2007. *Historic Reversals, Accelerating Resegregation, and the Need for New Integration Strategies.* Los Angeles: Civil Rights Project, UCLA. http://www .eric.ed.gov/PDFS/ED500611.pdf.

Orfield, Gary, John Kuesera, and Genevieve Siegel-Hawley. 2012. E Pluribus . . . Segregation: Deepening Double Segregation for More Students. *The Civil Rights Project, UCLA*. http://civilrightsproject.ucla.edu/research/k-12-education/integration-and-diversity/mlk-national/e-pluribus. . .separation-deepening-double-segregation-for-more-students.

Oswalt, Wendell, and Sharlotte Neely. 1996. *This Land Was Theirs*. Mountain View, CA: Mayfield.

Pager, Devah, and Hana Shepherd. 2008. The Sociology of Discrimination: Racial Discrimination in Employment, Housing, Credit, and Consumer Markets. *Annual Review of Sociology* 34:181–209.

Parish, Peter J. 1989. *Slavery: History and Historians*. New York: Harper & Row.

Park, Robert E., and Ernest W. Burgess. 1924. *Introduction to the Science of Society*. Chicago: University of Chicago Press.

Parke, Ross, and Raymond Buriel. 2002. Socialization Concerns in African American, American Indian, Asian American, and Latino Families. In Nijole Benokraitis (Ed.), *Contemporary Ethnic Families in the United States* (pp. 211–218). Upper Saddle River, NJ: Prentice Hall.

Parrillo, Vincent, and Christopher Donoghue. 2013. The National Social Distance Study: Ten Years Later. *Sociological Forum* 28:597–614.

Passel, Jeffrey, and D'Vera Cohn, 2011. *Unauthorized Immigrant Population: National and State Trends, 2010*. Washington, DC: Pew Hispanic Center. http://pewhispanic.org/files/reports/133.pdf.

Passel, Jeffrey, D'Vera Cohn, and Ana Gonzalez-Barrera. 2012. *Net Migration From Mexico Falls to Zero—and Perhaps Less*. Washington, DC: Pew Hispanic Center. http://www.pewhispanic.org/files/2012/04/Mexican -migrants-report_final.pdf.

———. 2013. *Population Decline of Unauthorized Immigrants Stalls, May Have Reversed*. Washington, DC: Pew Research Center. http://www.pewhispanic.org/2013/09/23/population -decline-of-unauthorized -immigrants-stalls-may -have-reversed.

Passel, Jeffrey, Wendy Wang, and Paul Taylor. 2010. *Marrying Out: One-in-Seven New U.S. Marriages Is Interracial or Interethnic*. Washington, DC: Pew Research Center. http://www.pewsocialtrends.org/2010/06/04/marrying -out/.

Pego, David. 1998. To Educate a Nation: Native American Tribe Hopes to Bring Higher Education to an Arizona Reservation. *Black Issues in Higher Education* 15:60–63.

Perez, Lisandro. 1980. Cubans. In Stephan Thernstrom, Ann Orlov, and Oscar Handlin (Eds.), *Harvard Encyclopedia of American Ethnic Groups* (pp. 256–261). Cambridge, MA: Harvard University Press.

Petersen, Williams. 1971. *Japanese Americans*. New York: Random House.

Peterson, Mark. 1995. Leading Cuban-American Entrepreneurs: The Process of Developing Motives, Abilities, and Resources. *Human Relations* 48:1193–1216.

Pettigrew, Thomas. 1958. Personality and Sociocultural Factors in Intergroup Attitudes: A Cross-National Comparison. *Journal of Conflict Resolution* 2:29–42.

———. 1971. *Racially Separate or Together?* New York: McGraw-Hill.

Pettigrew, Thomas, Ulrich Wagner, and Oliver Christ. 2007. Who Opposes Immigration? Comparing German and North American Findings. *Du Bois Review* 4:19–39.

Pettit, Becky, and Bruce Western. 2004. Mass Imprisonment and the Life Course: Race and Class Inequality in U.S. Incarceration. *American Sociological Review* 69:151–169.

Pew Charitable Trust. 2008. *One in 100: Behind Bars in America 2008*. http://www.pewtrusts.org/uploadedFiles/wwwpewtrustsorg/Reports/sentencing_and_corrections/one_in_100.pdf.

Pew Hispanic Center. 2004. *Survey Brief: Assimilation and Language*. Washington, DC: Author. http://pewhispanic.org/files/factsheets/11.pdf.

———. 2005. *Hispanics: A People in Motion.* Washington, DC: Author. http://pewhispanic.org/files/reports/40.pdf.

———. 2013. *A Nation of Immigrants: A Portrait of the 40 Million, Including 11 Million Unauthorized.* Washington, DC: Author. http://www.pewhispanic.org/files/2013/01/statistical_portrait_final_jan_29.pdf.

Pew Research Center. 2007. *Muslim Americans: Middle Class and Mostly Mainstream.* Washington, DC: Author. http://pewresearch.org/assets/pdf/muslim-americans.pdf.

———. 2011. *Muslim Americans: No Signs of Growth in Alienation or Support for Extremism.* Washington, DC: Author. http://www.people-press.org/files/legacy-pdf/Muslim%20American%20Report%2010-02-12%20fix.pdf.

———. 2013. *The Rise of Asian Americans.* Washington, DC: Author. http://www.pewsocialtrends.org/2012/06/19/the-rise-of -asian-americans.

Phillips, Ulrich B. 1918. *American Negro Slavery.* New York: Appleton.

Pitt, Leonard. 1970. *The Decline of the Californios: A Social History of the Spanish-Speaking Californians, 1846–1890.* Berkeley: University of California Press.

Plessy v. Ferguson, 163 U.S. 537 (1896).

Pollard, Kelvin, and William O'Hare. 1999. America's Racial and Ethnic Minorities. *Population Bulletin* 54(3): 29–39.

Population Reference Bureau. 2014. *2014* World Population Data Sheet. Washington, DC: Author. http://www.prb.org/Publications/Datasheets/2014/2014-world-population-data-sheet/data-sheet.aspx.

Porter, Eduardo. 2005. Illegal Immigrants Are Bolstering Social Security With Billions. *New York Times,* April 5, p. A1.

Portes, Alejandro. 1990. From South of the Border: Hispanic Minorities in the United States. In Virginia Yans-McLaughlin (Ed.), *Immigration Reconsidered* (pp. 160–184). New York: Oxford University Press.

Portes, Alejandro, and Robert L. Bach. 1985. *Latin Journey: Cuban and Mexican Immigrants in the United States.* Berkeley: University of California Press.

Portes, Alejandro, and Robert Manning. 1986. The Immigrant Enclave: Theory and Empirical Examples. In Susan Olzak and Joanne Nagel (Eds.), *Competitive Ethnic Relations* (pp. 47–68). New York: Academic Press.

Portes, Alejandro, and Rubén Rumbaut. 1996. *Immigrant America: A Portrait* (2nd ed.). Berkeley: University of California Press.

———. 2001. *Legacies: The Story of the Immigrant Second Generation.* New York: Russell Sage Foundation.

Portes, Alejandro, and Steven Shafer. 2006. *Revisiting the Enclave Hypothesis: Miami Twenty-Five Years Later* (Working Paper No. 06-10). Princeton, NJ: Center for Migration and Development, Princeton University. https://www.princeton.edu/cmd/working-papers/papers/wp0610.pdf.

Posadas, Barbara. 1999. *The Filipino Americans.* Westport, CT: Greenwood.

Potok, Mark. 2013. The Year in Hate and Extremism. Southern Poverty Law Center. http://www.splcenter.org/home/2013/spring/the-year-in-hate-and-extremism.

Potter, George. 1973. *To the Golden Door: The Story of the Irish in Ireland and America.* Westport, CT: Greenwood.

Powlishta, K., L. Serbin, A. Doyle, and D. White. 1994. Gender, Ethnic, and Body-Type Biases: The Generality of Prejudice in Childhood. *Developmental Psychology* 30:526–537.

Qian, Zhenchao, and Daniel Lichter. 2011. Changing Patterns of Interracial Marriage in a Multiracial Society. *Journal of Marriage and Family,* 75:1065–1084.

Quillian, Lincoln. 2006. New Approaches to Understanding Racial Prejudice and Discrimination. *Annual Review of Sociology* 32:299–328.

Quillian, Lincoln, and Mary Campbell. 2003. Beyond Black and White: The Present and Future of Multiracial Friendship Segregation. *American Sociological Review* 68:540–567.

Rader, Benjamin G. 1983. *American Sports: From the Age of Folk Games to the Age of Spectators.* Englewood Cliffs, NJ: Prentice Hall.

Rastogi, Sonya, Tallese Johnson, Elizabeth Hoeffel, and Malcolm Drewery. 2011. *The Black Population, 2010.* Washington, DC: U.S. Census Bureau. http://www.census.gov/prod/cen2010/briefs/c2010br-06.pdf.

Raymer, Patricia. 1974. Wisconsin's Menominees: Indians on a Seesaw. *National Geographic* 146:228–251.

Read, Jen'nan Ghazal. 2004. Cultural Influences on Immigrant Women's Labor Force Participation: The Arab-American Case. *International Migration Review* 38:52–77.

Reyna, Christine, Ovidiu Dobria, and Geoffrey Wetherell. 2013. The Complexity and Ambivalence of Immigration Attitudes: Ambivalent Stereotypes Predict Conflicting Attitudes Toward Immigration Policies. *Cultural Diversity and Ethnic Minority Psychology* 19:342–356.

Ricci v. DeStefano, 557 U.S. (2009).

Ridgeway, Cecilia. 2011. *Framed by Gender: How Gender Inequality Persists in the Modern World.* New York: Oxford University Press.

Rifkin, Jeremy. 1996. *The End of Work: The Decline of the Global Labor Force and the Dawn of the Post-Market Era.* New York: Putnam.

Robertson, Claire. 1996. Africa and the Americas? Slavery and Women, the Family, and the Gender Division of Labor. In David Gaspar and Darlene Hine (Eds.), *More Than Chattel: Black Women and Slavery in the Americas* (pp. 4–40). Bloomington: Indiana University Press.

Rock, Chris (Producer). 2009. *Good Hair.* HBO Films.

Rockquemore, Kerry Ann, and David Brunsma. 2008. *Beyond Black: Biracial Identity in America* (2nd ed.). Lanham, MD: Rowman & Littlefield.

Rodriguez, Arturo. 2011. UFW Written Statement on House Judiciary Subcommittee on Immigration Policy and Enforcement Hearing on "The H-2A Visa Program—Meeting the Growing Needs of American Agriculture?" http://ufwfoundation.org/_ cms.php? mode=view&b_code=00300200000 0000&b_no=8777& page=14&field=..&key=& n=717.

Rodriguez, Clara. 1989. *Puerto Ricans: Born in the USA.* Boston: Unwin-Hyman.

Rodriguez, Clara, and Hector Cordero-Guzman. 1992. Placing Race in Context. *Ethnic and Racial Studies* 15:523–542.

Rosenblum, Karen E., and Toni-Michelle C. Travis. 2002. *The Meaning of Difference: American Constructions of Race, Sex and Social Class, and Sexual Orientation* (3rd ed.). New York: McGraw-Hill.

Rosenfield, Michael. 2002. Measures of Assimilation in the Marriage Market: Mexican Americans 1970–1990. *Journal of Marriage and the Family* 64:152–163.

Rosich, Katherine. 2007. *Race, Ethnicity, and the Criminal Justice System.* Washington, DC: American Sociological Association. http://www.asanet.org/images/press/docs/pdf/ASARaceCrime.pdf.

Rouse, Linda, and Jeffery Hanson. 1991. American Indian Stereotyping, Resource Competition, and Status-Based Prejudice. *American Indian Culture and Research Journal* 15:1–17.

Royster, Deirdre. 2003. *Race and the Invisible Hand: How White Networks Exclude Black Men From Blue-Collar Jobs.* Berkeley: University of California Press.

Rumbaut, Rubén. 1991. Passage to America: Perspectives on the New Immigration. In Alan Wolfe (Ed.), *America at Century's End* (pp. 208–244). Berkeley: University of California Press.

Russell, James W. 1994. *After the Fifth Sun: Class and Race in North America*. Englewood Cliffs, NJ: Prentice Hall.

Saad, Lydia. 2010. Americans Value Both Aspects of Immigration Reform. http://www.gallup .com/poll/127649/Americans-Value-Aspects -Immigration-Reform.aspx.

Saenz, Rogelio. 2005. The Social and Economic Isolation of Urban African Americans. Washington, DC: Population Reference Bureau. http://www.prb.org/Articles/2005/ TheSocialandEconomicIsolationofUrbanAfrican Americans.aspx.

Sanchirico, Andrew. 1991. The Importance of Small Business Ownership in Chinese American Educational Achievement. *Sociology of Education* 64:293–304.

Santiago, Esmeralda. 1993. *When I Was Puerto Rican*. Cambridge, MA: De Capo Press.

Satter, Beryl. 2009. *Family Properties: Race, Real Estate, and the Exploitation of Black Urban America*. New York: Henry Holt.

Schafer, John, and Joe Navarro. 2004. The Seven-Stage Hate Model: The Psychopathology of Hate Groups. *The FBI Law Enforcement Bulletin* 72:1–9.

Schlesinger, Arthur M., Jr. 1992. *The Disuniting of America: Reflections on a Multicultural Society*. New York: Norton.

Schmid, Carol. 2001. *The Politics of Language: Conflict, Identity, and Cultural Pluralism in Comparative Perspective*. New York: Oxford University Press.

Schoener, Allon. 1967. *Portal to America: The Lower East Side, 1870–1925*. New York: Holt, Rinehart, & Winston.

Schuette v. BAMN, 572 U.S. 12-682 (2014).

Sears, David. 1988. Symbolic Racism. In Phyllis Katz and Dalmas Taylor (Eds.), *Eliminating Racism: Profiles in Controversy* (pp. 53–84). New York: Plenum.

Sears, David, and P. J. Henry. 2003. The Origins of Modern Racism. *Journal of Personality and Social Psychology* 85:259–275.

See, Katherine O'Sullivan, and William J. 1988. Race and Ethnicity. In Neil Smelser (Ed.), *Handbook of Sociology* (pp. 223–242). Newbury Park, CA: Sage.

Selzer, Michael. 1972. *"Kike": Anti-Semitism in America*. New York: Meridian.

Sen, Rinku, and Fekkah Mamdouh. 2008. *The Accidental American: Immigration and Citizenship in the Age of Globalization*. San Francisco, CA: Berrett-Koehler.

Shannon, William V. 1964. *The American Irish*. New York: Macmillan.

Shapiro, Thomas, Tatjana Meschede, and Sam Osoro. 2013. *The Roots of the Widening Racial Wealth Gap: Explaining the Black-White Economic Divide*. Waltham, MA: Institute on Assets and Social Policy, Brandeis University. http://iasp.brandeis.edu/pdfs/Author/ shapiro-thomas-m/racialwealthgapbrief.pdf.

Sheet Metal Workers v. EEOC, 478 U.S. 421 (1986).

Sherif, Muzafer, O. J. Harvey, B. Jack White, William Hood, and Carolyn Sherif. 1961. *Intergroup Conflict and Cooperation: The Robber's Cave Experiment*. Norman, OK: University Book Exchange.

Sheth, Manju. 1995. Asian Indian Americans. In Pyong Gap Min (Ed.), *Asian American: Contemporary Issues and Trends* (pp. 168–198). Thousand Oaks, CA: Sage.

Simon, Julian. 1989. *The Economic Consequences of Immigration*. Cambridge, MA: Blackwell.

Simpson, George, and Milton Yinger. 1985. *Racial and Cultural Minorities: An Analysis of Prejudice and Discrimination*. New York: Plenum.

Skinner, Benjamin. 2008. A World Enslaved. *Foreign Policy* 165:62–68.

Sklare, Marshall. 1971. *America's Jews*. New York: Random House.

Small, Mario Luis, David J. Harding, and Michèle Lamont. 2010. Reconsidering Culture and Poverty. *Annals of the American Academy of Political and Social Science* 629:6. http://ann .sagepub.com/content/629/1/6.

Smedley, Audrey. 2007. *Race in North America: Origin and Evolution of a Worldview* (3rd ed.). Boulder, CO: Westview.

Smith, James, and Barry Edmonston (Eds.). 1997. *The New Americans: Economic, Demographic, and Fiscal Effects of Immigration.* Washington, DC: National Academy Press.

Smith, Tom, and Glenn Dempsey. 1983. The Polls: Ethnic Social Distance and Prejudice. *Public Opinion Quarterly* 47:584–600.

Snipp, C. Matthew. 1989. *American Indians: The First of This Land.* New York: Russell Sage Foundation.

———. 1992. Sociological Perspectives on American Indians. *Annual Review of Sociology* 18:351–371.

———. 1996. The First Americans: American Indians. In S. Pedraza and R. G. Rumbaut (Eds.), *Origins and Destinies: Immigration, Race, and Ethnicity in America* (pp. 390–403). Belmont, CA: Wadsworth.

Social Science Data Analysis Network. n.d. Segregation: Dissimilarity Indices. *CensusScope.* Retrieved September 25, 2015, from http://www.censusscope.org/us/s40/p75000/chart_dissimilarity.html.

Spicer, Edward H. 1980. American Indians. In Stephan Thernstrom, Ann Orlov, and Oscar Handlin (Eds.), *Harvard Encyclopedia of American Ethnic Groups* (pp. 58–122). Cambridge, MA: Harvard University Press.

Spickard, Paul. 1996. *Japanese Americans: The Formation and Transformations of an Ethnic Group.* New York: Twayne.

Spilde, Kate. 2001. The Economic Development Journey of Indian Nations. http://www.indiangaming.org/library/articles/the -economic-development -journey.shtml.

Stainback, Kevin, and Donald Tomaskovic-Devey. 2012. *Documenting Desegregation: Racial and Gender Segregation in Private-Sector Employment Since the Civil Rights Act.* New York: Russell Sage.

Stampp, Kenneth. 1956. *The Peculiar Institution: Slavery in the Antebellum South.* New York: Random House.

Stannard, David E. (1992). *American Holocaust.* New York: Oxford University Press.

Staples, Brent A. 1986. Black Men and Public Space. *Harper's Magazine* (December). http://harpers.org/archive/1986/12/black -men-and-public-space/.

Staples, Robert. 1988. The Black American Family. In Charles Mindel, Robert Habenstein, and Roosevelt Wright (Eds.), *Ethnic Families in America* (3rd ed., pp. 303–324). New York: Elsevier.

Steinberg, Stephen. 1981. *The Ethnic Myth: Race, Ethnicity, and Class in America.* New York: Atheneum.

———. 2011. Poor Reason: Culture Still Doesn't Explain Poverty. *Boston Review,* January 13. http://www.bostonreview.net/steinberg.php.

Stepick, Alex, Carol Dutton Stepick, Emmanuel Eugene, Deborah Teed, and Yves Labissiere. 2001. Shifting Identities and Intergenerational Conflict: Growing Up Haitian in Miami. In Rubén Rumbaut and Alejandro Portes (Eds.), *Ethnicities: Children of Immigrants in America* (pp. 229–266). Berkeley: University of California Press.

Stoddard, Ellwyn. 1973. *Mexican Americans.* New York: Random House.

Stoll, Michael. 2004. *African Americans and the Color Line.* New York: Russell Sage Foundation.

Stuckey, Sterling. 1987. *Slave Culture: Nationalist Theory and the Foundations of Black America.* New York: Harper & Row.

Takaki, Ronald. 1993. *A Different Mirror: A History of Multicultural America.* Boston: Little, Brown.

Takao Ozawa v. United States, 260 U.S. 178 (1922).

Taylor, Jonathan, and Joseph Kalt. 2005. *American Indians on Reservations: A Databook of Socioeconomic Change Between the 1990 and 2000 Censuses.* Cambridge, MA: The Harvard Project on American Indian Economic Development. http://www.hks.harvard.edu/hpaied/pubs/documents/AmericanIndianson ReservationsADatabookof Socioeconomic Change.pdf.

Taylor, Paul, D'Vera Cohn, Gretchen Livingston, Cary Funk, and Rick Morin. 2013. *Second Generation Americans: A Portrait of Adult Children of Immigrants.* Washington, DC: Pew Research Center. http://www.pewsocialtrends.org/files/2013/02/FINAL_immigrant_generations_report_2-7-13.pdf.

Taylor, Paul, Mark Lopez, Jessica Martinez, and Gabriel Velasco. 2012. *When Labels Don't Fit: Hispanics and Their Views of Identity.* Washington, DC: Pew Hispanic Center. http://www.pewhispanic.org/2012/04/04/when-labels-dont-fit-hispanics-and-their-views-of-identity/.

Telles, Edward. 2004. *Race in Another America: The Significance of Skin Color in Brazil.* Princeton, NJ: Princeton University Press.

Telles, Edward, and Vilma Ortiz. 2008. *Generations of Exclusion: Mexican Americans, Assimilation, and Race.* New York: Russell Sage Foundation.

Thornton, Russel. 2001. Trends Among Indians in the United States. In N. Smelser, W. Wilson, and F. Mitchell (Eds.), *American Becoming: Racial Trends and Their Consequences* (Vol. 1, pp. 125–169). Washington, DC: National Academy Press.

Tilly, Charles. 1990. Transplanted Networks. In Virginia Yans-McLaughlin (Ed.), *Immigration Reconsidered: History, Sociology, and Politics* (pp. 79–95). New York: Oxford University Press.

Treuer, Anton. 2012. *Everything You Wanted to Know About Indians But Were Afraid to Ask.* St. Paul, MN: Borealis Books.

Treuer, David. 2012. *Rez Life: An Indian's Journey Through Reservation Life.* New York: Atlantic Monthly Press.

Tsai, Shih-Shan Henry. 1986. *The Chinese Experience in America.* Bloomington: Indiana University Press.

Udry, Richard. 2000. Biological Limits of Gender Construction. *American Sociological Review* 65:443–457.

United Nations. 1948. New York: Author. Convention on the Prevention and Punishment of the Crime of Genocide. http://www.hrweb.org/legal/genocide.html.

United Nations. 2012. International Migrant Stock. http://esa.un.org/migration/

United Nations Department of Economic and Social Affairs, Population Division. 2013. *Population Facts* (No. 2013/2). http://esa.un.org/unmigration/documents/The_number_of_international_migrants.pdf.

United Nations Development Programme. 2013. *Mexico: Human Development Indicators.* New York: Author. http://hdr.undp.org/en/countries/profiles/MEX.

United Steelworkers of America, AFL-CIO-CLC v. Weber, 443 U.S. 193 (1979).

U.S. Bureau of Labor Statistics. 2013. *Employment Status of the Civilian Non-Institutional Population by Race, Hispanic or Latino Ethnicity, Sex, and Age, Seasonally Adjusted.* http://www.bls.gov/web/empsit/cpseea04.pdf.

U.S. Bureau of Labor Statistics. 2015. *Labor Force Characteristics by Race and Ethnicity, 2013.* http://www.bls.gov/opub/reports/cps/race_ethnicity_2013.pdf

U.S. Census Bureau. 1978. *Statistical Abstract of the United States, 1977.* Washington, DC: Author.

——. 1990. Summary File 3. http://factfinder2.census.gov/faces/nav/jsf/pages/index.xhtml.

——. 1993. *Statistical Abstract of the United States, 1992.* Washington, DC: Government Printing Office.

———. 1997. *Statistical Abstract of the United States, 1996.* Washington, DC: Government Printing Office.

———. 2000a. Summary File 1. *Census 2000.* https://www.census.gov/census2000/sumfile1 .html.

———. 2000b. Summary File 4. *Census 2000.* https://www.census.gov/census2000/SF4.html.

———. 2002. *Statistical Abstract of the United States, 2001.* Washington, DC: Author.

———. 2004a. Ancestry. In *Census Atlas of the United States* (pp. 138–155). http://www.census. gov/population/www/cen2000/censusatlas/pdf/9_Ancestry.pdf.

———. 2004b. *Population by Region, Sex, and Hispanic Origin Type, With Percent Distribution by Hispanic Origin Type, 2004.* http://www.census.gov/population/socdemo/hispanic/ ASEC2004/2004CPS_tab19.2.pdf.

———. 2005. *Statistical Abstract of the United States, 2005.* Washington, DC: Author.

———. 2007. *Statistical Abstract of the United States, 2007.* Washington, DC: Author. http://www .census.gov/compendia/statab/past_years.html.

———. 2008. 1990 Summary Tape File 3. http://factfinder.census.gov/servlet/ DatasetMainPageServlet?_program=DEC&_tabId=DEC2&_submenuId=datasets_1&_ lang=en&_ts=222966 429406.

———. 2010. *Statistical Abstract of the United States: 2010.* Washington, DC: Author. http://www .census.gov/compendia/statab/2010/2010edition.html.

———. 2011. *Statistical Abstract of the United States, 2011.* Washington, DC: Author.

———. 2012a. Most Children Younger Than Age 1 Are Minorities, Census Bureau Reports. News release. http://www.census.gov/newsroom/releases/archives/population/cb12-90 .html.

———. 2012b. *National Population Projections: Summary Tables.* http://www.census.gov/ population/projections/data/national/2012/summarytables.html.

———. 2012c. *Statistical Abstract of the United States, 2012.* Washington, DC: Government Printing Office. http://www.census.gov/compendia/statab/2012edition.html.

———. 2012d. *2010 Census American Indian and Native Alaska Summary File.* http://factfinder2 .census.gov/faces/nav/jsf/pages/index.xhtml.

———. 2013a. *American Community Survey 3-Year Estimates, 2010–2012.* http://factfinder2 .census.gov/faces/tableservices/jsf/pages/productview.xhtml?pid=ACS_sumfile_2010 _2012&prod Type=document.

———. 2013b. Educational Attainment—People 25 Years Old and Over, by Total Money Earnings in 2012, Work Experience in 2012, Age, Race, Hispanic Origin, and Sex (Table PINC-03). *Current Population Survey.* http://www.census.gov/hhes/www/cpstables/032013/ perinc/pinc03_000.htm.

———. 2013c. Historical Income Tables: Household. *Current Population Survey.* http://www .census.gov/hhes/www/income/data/historical/household.

———. 2013d. Historical Poverty Tables. *Current Population Survey.* http://www.census.gov/ hhes/www/poverty/data/historical/index.html.

———. 2013e. Household Income Tables. *Current Population Survey.* http://www.census.gov/ hhes/www/cpstables/032013/hhinc/hinc01_000.htm.

———. 2013f. Selected Characteristics of People 15 Years and Over, by Total Money Income in 2012, Work Experience in 2012, Race, Hispanic Origin, and Sex (Table PINC-01). *Current Population Survey.* http://www.census.gov/hhes/www/cpstables/032013/perinc/ pinc01_000.htm.

———. 2013g. Selected Economic Characteristics (Table DP03). *American Community Survey, 2006–2012.* http://factfinder2.census.gov/faces/tableservices/jsf/pages/productview.xhtml? pid= ACS_10_SF4_DP03&prod Type=table.

———. 2014. Historical Income Tables: People. *Current Population Survey.* Table P-36 http://www.census.gov/hhes/www/income/data/historical/people/.

———.2015a. Age of Householder - Households, by Total Money Income in 2013, Type of Household, Race and Hispanic Origin of Householder (Table HINC-02). http://www/cpstables/032014/hhinc/hinc02_000.htm.

———. 2015b. Households by Type and Tenure of Householders for Selected Characteristics (Table H 1). http://www.census.gov/hhes/families/data/cps2014H.html

———. 2015c. "Languages Spoken at Home." *American Community Survey, 2009–2013.*

———. 2015d. Percent of People 25 Years and Over Who Have Completed High School or College, by Race, Hispanic

U.S. Commission on Civil Rights. 1976. *Puerto Ricans in the Continental United States: An Uncertain Future.* Washington, DC: Government Printing Office.

U.S. Department of Homeland Security. 2012. *Yearbook of Immigration Statistics, 2012.* http://www.dhs.gov/yearbook-immigration -statistics-2012-legal -permanent-residents.

———. 2013a. Table 2: Persons Obtaining Legal Permanent Resident Status by Region and Selected Country of Last Residence, 1820–2013. Yearbook of Immigration Statistics, 2013. http://www.dhs.gov/yearbook-immigration-statistics-2013-lawful-permanent-residents.

———. 2013b. *Yearbook of Immigration Statistics 2013.* Table 1. Persons Obtaining Lawful Permanent Resident Status: Fiscal Years 1820 to 2013. http://www.dhs.gov/sites/default/files/publications/ois_yb_2013_0.pdf.

———. 2013c. Yearbook of Immigration Statistics 2013. Table 2. Persons Obtaining Lawful Permanent Resident Status by Region and Selected Country of Last Residence: Fiscal Years 1820 to 2013. http://www.dhs.gov/yearbook-immigration-statistics-2013-lawful-permanent-residents.

———. 2013d. *Yearbook of Immigration Statistics 2013.* Table 3. Persons Obtaining Lawful Permanent Resident Status By Region and Country of Birth: Fiscal Years 2004 to 2013. http://www.dhs.gov/sites/default/files/publications/ois_yb_2013_0.pdf.

———. 2014. *Yearbook of Immigration Statistics, 2013.* Table 2 Persons Obtaining Lawful Permanent Resident Status by Region and Selected Country of Last Residence: Fiscal Years 1820 to 2013. http://www.dhs.gov/sites/default/files/publications/ois_yb_2013_0.pdf.

U.S. Immigration and Naturalization Service. 1993. *Statistical Yearbook of the Immigration and Naturalization Service, 1992.* Washington, DC: Author.

U.S. Office of Juvenile Justice and Delinquency Prevention. 2015. Juvenile Arrest Rate Trends. http://www.ojjdp.gov/ojstatbb/crime/JAR_Display.asp?ID=qa05274.

Utah Supreme Court Rules That Non-Indian Members of Native American Church Can Use Peyote in Church Ceremonies. 2004. *New York Times,* June 23, p. A20.

Valentine, Sean, and Gordon Mosley. 2000. Acculturation and Sex-Role Attitudes Among Mexican Americans: A Longitudinal Analysis. *Hispanic Journal of Behavioral Sciences* 22:104–204.

Van Ausdale, Debra, and Joe Feagin. 2001. *The First R: How Children Learn Race and Racism.* Lanham, MD: Rowman & Littlefield.

van den Berghe, Pierre L. 1967. *Race and Racism: A Comparative Perspective.* New York: Wiley.

———. 1981. *The Ethnic Phenomenon.* New York: Elsevier.

Van Hook, J. 2010. *The Demographic Impacts of Repealing Birthright Citizenship.* http://www.migrationpolicy.org/pubs/BirthrightInsight-2010.pdf.

Vargas-Ramos, Carlos. 2005. Black, Trigueño, White . . . ? Shifting Racial Identification Among Puerto Ricans. *Du Bois Review* 2:267–285.

Vincent, Theodore G. 1976. *Black Power and the Garvey Movement.* San Francisco: Ramparts.

Vinje, David. 1996. Native American Economic Development on Selected Reservations: A Comparative Analysis. *American Journal of Economics and Sociology* 55:427–442.

Vock, Daniel. 2013. With Little Choice, Alabama Backs Down on Immigration Law. *Stateline,* October 30. Pew Charitable Trusts. http://www.pewstates.org/projects/stateline/headlines/with -little-choice-alabama -backs-down-on-immigration -law-85899516441.

Voting Rights Act, 42 U.S.C. § 1971 (1965).

Wagley, Charles, and Marvin Harris.1958. *Minorities in the New World: Six Case Studies.* New York: Columbia University Press.

Wallace, Michael, and Rodrigo Figueroa. 2012. Determinants of Perceived Immigrant Job Threat in the American States. *Sociological Perspectives* 55:583–612.

Wang, Wendy. 2012. *The Rise of Intermarriage: Rates, Characteristics Vary by Race and Gender.* Washington, DC: Pew Research Center. http://www.pewsocialtrends.org/2012/02/16/the-rise-of -intermarriage.

Washington, Booker T. 1965. *Up From Slavery.* New York: Dell.

Waters, Mary. 1990. *Ethnic Options.* Berkeley: University of California Press.

Waters, M., and T. Jimenez, 2005. Assessing Immigrant Assimilation: New Empirical and Theoretical Challenges. *American Review of Sociology* 31:105–125.

Wax, Murray. 1971. *Indian Americans: Unity and Diversity.* Englewood Cliffs, NJ: Prentice-Hall.

Weeks, Philip. 1988. *The American Indian Experience.* Arlington Heights, IL: Forum.

Wellner, Alison. 2007. *U.S. Attitudes Toward Interracial Dating Are Liberalizing.* Washington, DC: Population Reference Bureau. http://www.prb.org/Publications/Articles/2005/USAttitudes TowardInterracialDating AreLiberalizing.aspx.

West, Darrel. 2011. The Costs and Benefits of Immigration. *Political Science Quarterly* 126: 427–443.

White, Deborah Gray. 1985. *Ar'n't I a Woman? Female Slaves in the Plantation South.* New York: Norton.

White, Michael, and Jennifer Glick. 2009. *Achieving Anew: How New Immigrants Do in American Schools, Jobs, and Neighborhoods.* New York: Russell Sage Foundation.

White House. 2005. *Economic Report of the President.* Washington, DC: Author. http://www .gpoaccess.gov/eop/2005/2005_erp.pdf.

Whiting, Robert. 1990. *You Gotta Have Wa.* New York: Macmillan.

Wilkens, Roger. 1992. L.A.: Images in the Flames; Looking Back in Anger: 27 Years After Watts, Our Nation Remains Divided by Racism. *Washington Post,* May 3, p. C1.

Williams, Gregory. 1995. *Life on the Color Line.* New York: Dutton.

Wilson, William J. 1973. *Power, Racism, and Privilege: Race Relations in Theoretical and Sociohistorical Perspectives.* New York: Free Press.

———. 1987. *The Truly Disadvantaged: The Inner City, the Underclass, and Public Policy.* Chicago, IL: University of Chicago Press.

———. 1996. *When Work Disappears.* New York: Knopf.

———. 2009. *More Than Just Race.* New York: W. W. Norton.

Wingfield, A., and J. Feagin. 2010. *Yes We Can? White Racial Framing and the 2008 Presidential Campaign.* New York: Routledge.

Wirth, Louis. 1945. The Problem of Minority Groups. In Ralph Linton (Ed.), *The Science of Man in the World* (pp. 347–372). New York: Columbia University Press.

Wogan, J. B. 2013. Alabama's Anti-Immigration Law Gutted. *Governing,* November 13. http://www.governing.com/news/headlines/gov-alabamas-anti-immigration-law-dies-amid-hunger-for-reform.html.

Wolfenstein, Eugene V. 1993. *The Victims of Democracy: Malcolm X.* New York: Guilford Press.

Wong, Morrison. 1995. Chinese Americans. In Pyong Gap Min (Ed.), *Asian Americans: Contemporary Trends and Issues* (pp. 58–94). Thousand Oaks, CA: Sage.

Woodward, C. Vann. 1974. *The Strange Career of Jim Crow* (3rd ed.). New York: Oxford University Press.

World Bank. 2013. Data: Mexico. http://data.worldbank.org/country/mexico.

Worsnop, Richard. 1992. Native Americans. *CQ Researcher,* May 8, pp. 387–407.

Wyman, Mark. 1993. *Round Trip to America.* Ithaca, NY: Cornell University Press.

Yamato, Alexander. 1994. Racial Antagonism and the Formation of Segmented Labor Markets: Japanese Americans and Their Exclusion From the Workforce. *Humboldt Journal of Social Relations* 20:31–63.

Yancey, George. 2003. *Who Is White? Latinos, Asians, and the New Black/Non-Black Divide.* Boulder, CO: Lynne Rienner.

Yinger, J. Milton. 1985. Ethnicity. *Annual Review of Sociology* 11:151–180.

Zhou, Min. 1992. *Chinatown.* Philadelphia: Temple University Press.

Zhou, Min, and John R. Logan. 1989. Returns on Human Capital in Ethnic Enclaves: New York City's Chinatown. *American Sociological Review* 54:809–820.

Glossary

abolitionism: The movement to abolish slavery.

acculturation: The process by which one group (generally a minority or immigrant group) learns the culture of another group (generally the dominant group); also called **cultural assimilation.**

affective prejudice: The emotional or "feeling" dimension of individual prejudice. The prejudiced individual attaches negative emotions to members of other groups.

affirmative action: Programs designed to reduce the effects of past institutional discrimination or increase diversity in workplaces and schools.

Alien Land Act: Bill passed by the California legislature in 1913 declaring that aliens who were ineligible for citizenship (effectively meaning only immigrants from Asia) were also ineligible to own land.

Americanization: The model of assimilation in which groups are pressured to conform to Anglo-American culture (same as **Anglo-conformity**).

Anglo-conformity: The model of assimilation in which groups are pressured to conform to Anglo-American culture (same as **Americanization**).

anti-Semitism: Prejudice or ideological racism directed specifically toward Jews.

apartheid: The policy of extreme racial segregation formerly followed in South Africa.

ascribed status: A position in society that is assigned to the individual, usually at birth. Examples of ascribed status include positions based on ethnicity, race, and gender.

assimilation: The process by which formerly distinct and separate groups come to share a common culture and merge together socially.

Black Power movement: A coalition of African American groups that rose to prominence in the 1960s. Some central themes of the movement were Black Nationalism, autonomy for African American communities, and pride in race and African heritage.

Black protest movement: *See* **Civil rights movement.**

Blauner hypothesis: Minority groups created by colonization will experience more intense prejudice, racism, and discrimination than those created by immigration. The disadvantaged status of colonized groups will persist longer and be more difficult to overcome than the disadvantaged status faced by groups created by immigration.

bourgeoisie: The elite or ruling class in an industrial society that owns or controls the means of production.

Bracero: A Mexican laborer in the United States, especially in relation to the Bracero Program.

Bureau of Indian Affairs: The agency of the U.S. government that has primary responsibility for the administration of American Indian reservations.

capital-intensive: Capital-intensive technology replaces hand labor with machine labor. Large amounts of capital are required to develop, purchase, and maintain the machines.

caste system: A closed system of stratification with no mobility between positions. A person's class at birth is permanent and unchangeable.

chattel: An item of personal property. In a system of chattel slavery, slaves were defined by law not as persons but as the personal property of their owners.

Chicanismo: A militant ideology of the Mexican American protest movement that appeared in the 1960s. The ideology took a critical view of U.S. society, made strong demands for justice and an end to racism, expressed a positive image for the group, and incorporated other pluralistic themes.

Chicanos: A group name for Mexican Americans associated with the ideology of Chicanismo, which emerged in the 1960s.

Chinese Exclusion Act: Passed in 1882 by the U.S. Congress, banned virtually all immigration from China.

civil rights movement: The effort of African Americans and their allies in the 1950s and 1960s to end de jure segregation in the South.

cognitive prejudice: The "thinking" dimension of individual prejudice. The prejudiced individual thinks about members of other groups in terms of stereotypes.

colonized minority groups: Groups whose initial contact with the dominant group was through conquest or colonization.

competition: A situation in which two or more parties struggle for control of some scarce resource.

cultural assimilation: *See* **acculturation.**

cultural pluralism: A situation in which groups have not acculturated or integrated and each maintains a distinct identity.

culture: All aspects of the way of life associated with a group of people. Culture includes language, beliefs, norms, values, customs, technology, and many other components.

culture of poverty theory: A theory asserting that poverty causes certain personality traits—such as the need for instant gratification—which, in turn, perpetuate poverty.

de facto segregation: A system of racial separation and inequality that appears to result from voluntary choices about where to live, work, and so forth. Often, this form of segregation is really de jure segregation in thin disguise.

de jure segregation: Racial segregation that is institutionalized in local and state law.

deindustrialization: The shift from a manufacturing economy to a service-oriented, information-processing economy.

differential in power: Any difference between two or more groups in their ability to achieve their goals.

discrimination: The unequal or unfair treatment of a person or persons based on their group membership.

dissimilarity index: A measure of residential segregation. The higher the score, the greater the segregation, and scores above 60 are considered to indicate extreme segregation.

dominant group: The group that benefits from and, typically, tries to sustain minority-group subordination.

enclave minority group: A group that establishes its own neighborhood and relies on a set of interconnected businesses, each of which is usually small in scope, for its economic survival.

ethclass: The group formed by the intersection of social class and racial or ethnic groups.

ethnic minority groups: Minority groups identified primarily by cultural characteristics, such as language or religion.

ethnic revival: The movement toward increased salience for ethnic identity, which began for European Americans in the 1960s.

ethnic succession: The process by which white ethnic groups affected one another's positions in the social class structure.

ethnocentrism: Judging other groups, societies, or cultures by the standards of one's own.

extractive (or primary) occupations: Those that produce raw materials, such as food and agricultural products, minerals, and lumber; often involve unskilled manual labor, require little formal education, and are generally low paying

fatalism: The view that one's fate is beyond one's control.

fluid competitive systems: Systems of group relations in which minority group members are freer to compete for jobs and other scarce resources; associated with advanced industrialization.

gender: Social characteristics typically associated with women or men. Gender is a social status or position in the social structure. People typically assume a gender identity that is normative and congruent with their biology (e.g., one born male typically identifies with being a boy or man).

gender roles: Societal expectations regarding the behavior, attitudes, and personality traits of women and men.

genocide: The deliberate attempt to exterminate an entire group.

*huiguan***:** Associations in Chinese American society based on the region of China from which an individual or his or her family came. The *huiguan* performed a number of social and welfare functions.

human capital theory: Consistent with the traditional view of assimilation, this theory considers success to be a direct result of individual efforts, personal values and skills, and education.

ideological racism: A belief system asserting that a particular group is inferior. Although individuals may subscribe to racist beliefs, the ideology itself is incorporated into the culture of the society and passed on from generation to generation.

immigrant minority groups: Groups whose initial contact with the dominant group was through immigration.

indentured servants: Contract laborers who are obligated to serve a particular master for a specified length of time.

Indian Reorganization Act: Federal legislation passed in 1934 that was intended to give Native American tribes more autonomy.

Industrial Revolution: The shift in subsistence technology from labor-intensive agriculture to capital-intensive manufacturing.

institutional discrimination: A pattern of unequal treatment based on group membership that is built into the daily operations of society.

integration: The process by which a minority group enters the social structure of the dominant society; also called **structural assimilation.**

intermarriage: Marriage between members of different groups; same as **marital assimilation.**

intersectionality: A theoretical perspective in sociology that stresses the cross-cutting, linked nature of inequality and the multiplicity of statuses all people occupy.

Issei: First-generation immigrants from Japan.

Jim Crow system: The system of rigid competitive race relations that followed Reconstruction in the South. The system lasted from the 1880s until the 1960s and was characterized by laws mandating racial separation and inequality.

labor-intensive: A form of production in which the bulk of the effort is provided by human beings working by hand. Machines and other labor-saving devices are rare or absent.

level of development: The stage of societal evolution. The stages discussed in this text are agrarian, industrial, and postindustrial.

machismo: A cultural value stressing men's dominance, virility, and honor.

manufacturing (or secondary) occupations: Occupations involving the transformation of raw materials into finished products ready for the marketplace. An example is an assembly line worker in an automobile plant.

marielitos: Refugees from Cuba who arrived in the United States in 1980.

marital assimilation: Marriage between members of different groups; same as **intermarriage.**

means of production: The materials, resources, and social relations by which the society produces and distributes goods and services.

melting pot: A type of assimilation in which all groups contribute in roughly equal amounts to the creation of a new culture and society.

middleman minority groups: Groups that rely on interconnected businesses, dispersed throughout a community, for economic survival.

minority group: A group that experiences a pattern of disadvantage or inequality, has a visible identifying trait, and is a self-conscious social unit. Membership is usually determined at birth, and group members tend to form intimate relations within the group.

miscegenation: Marriage or sexual relations between members of different racial groups.

modern institutional discrimination: A more subtle and covert form of institutional discrimination that is often unintentional and unconscious.

modern racism: A subtle and indirect form of prejudice that incorporates negative feelings about minority groups but not the traditional stereotypes. Also known as color-blind racism and symbolic racism.

multiculturalism: A general term for some versions of pluralism in the United States. Generally, multiculturalism stresses mutual respect for all groups and celebrates the multiplicity of heritages that have contributed to the development of the United States.

New Immigration: Immigration from Southern and Eastern Europe to the United States between the 1880s and the 1920s.

Nisei: Second-generation Japanese Americans.

Noel hypothesis: A theory about the creation of minority groups that asserts that if two or more groups come together in a contact situation characterized by ethnocentrism, competition, and a differential in power, some form of racial or ethnic stratification will result.

nonviolent direct action: The central tactic used during the civil rights movement in the South to defeat de jure segregation.

Old Immigration: Immigration from Northern and Western Europe to the United States between the 1820s and the 1880s.

Operation Wetback: A government program developed in the 1950s to deport illegal immigrants from Mexico.

past-in-present institutional discrimination: Patterns of inequality or unequal treatment in the present that are caused by some pattern of discrimination in the past.

paternalism: A form of dominant–minority relations often associated with plantation-based, labor-intensive, agrarian technology. In paternalistic relations, minority groups are extremely unequal and highly controlled. Rates of overt conflict are low.

patriarchy: Men's dominance. In a patriarchal society, men tend to monopolize power and decision making.

plantation system: A labor-intensive form of agriculture that requires large tracts of land and a large, cheap labor force. This was the dominant form of agricultural production in the American South before the Civil War.

pluralism: A situation in which groups maintain separate identities, cultures, and organizational structures.

postindustrial society: A society dominated by service work, information processing, and high technology.

power: The ability to affect the decision-making process of a social system.

prejudice: The tendency of individuals to think and feel negatively toward others.

prestige: The amount of honor or respect accorded a particular person or group.

primary labor market: The segment of the labor market that encompasses better-paying, higher-status, more-secure jobs, usually in large bureaucracies.

primary sector: Relationships and groups that are intimate and personal. Groups in the primary sector are small.

principle of third-generation interest: The notion that the grandchildren of immigrants will stress their ethnicity much more than the second generation will.

proletariat: The workers in an industrial society.

pull factors: Factors that cause population movement out of an area.

push factors: Factors that cause population movement into an area.

race relations cycle: A concept associated with Robert Park, who believed that relations between different groups would go through predictable cycles, from conflict to eventual assimilation.

racial minority groups: Minority groups identified primarily by physical characteristics such as skin color (e.g., Asian Americans).

Reconstruction: The period of Southern race relations following the Civil War. Reconstruction lasted from 1865 until the 1880s and witnessed many racial reforms, all of which were reversed during de jure segregation, or the Jim Crow era.

relocation camps: The camps in which Japanese Americans were held during World War II.

repatriation: A government campaign begun during the Great Depression of the 1930s to deport illegal immigrants back to Mexico. The campaign also caused some legal immigrants and native-born Mexican Americans to leave the United States.

revolution: A minority-group goal. A revolutionary group wishes to change places with the dominant group or create a new social order, perhaps in alliance with other groups.

rigid competitive group system: A system of group relations in which the dominant group seeks to exclude minority groups or limit their ability to compete for scarce resources such as jobs.

Sansei: Third-generation Japanese Americans.

secondary labor market: The segment of the labor market that includes low-paying, low-skilled, insecure jobs.

secondary sector: Relationships and organizations that are public, task oriented, and impersonal. Organizations in the secondary sector can be large.

segmented assimilation: The idea that assimilation can have a number of outcomes, in addition to eventual entry into mainstream society. Some groups may enter the middle class, but others may be permanently excluded, marginalized, and impoverished.

selective perception: The tendency to see only what one expects to see; associated with stereotyping in individual prejudice.

separatism: A minority-group goal. A separatist group wishes to sever all ties with the dominant group.

service (or tertiary) occupations: Jobs that involve providing services. Examples include retail clerk, janitor, and schoolteacher.

sexism: Belief systems that label women as inferior to men and rationalize their lower social status.

sharecropping: A system of farming often used in the South during de jure segregation. The sharecropper (often black), or tenant, worked the land, which was actually owned by someone else (usually white), in return for a share of the profits at harvest time. The landowner supplied a place to live and credit for food and clothing.

social classes: Groups of people who command similar amounts of valued goods and services, such as income, property, and education.

social constructions: Perceptions shared by a group. These perceptions become real to the people who share them.

social distance: The degree of intimacy a person is willing to accept with members of other groups.

social mobility: Movement up and down the stratification system.

social structure: The networks of social relationships, groups, organizations, communities, and institutions that organize the work of a society and connect individuals to one another and to the larger society.

socialization: The process of physical, psychological, and social development by which a person learns his or her culture.

sojourners: Immigrants who intend to return to their countries of origin.

stereotypes: Overgeneralizations that are thought to apply to all members of a group.

stratification: The unequal distribution of valued goods and services (e.g., income, job opportunities, prestige and fame, education, health care) in society; the social class system.

structural assimilation: *See* **integration.**

structural mobility: Rising occupational and social class standing that is the result of changes in the overall structure of the economy and labor market, as opposed to individual efforts.

structural pluralism: A situation in which a group has acculturated but is not integrated.

subsistence technology: The means by which a society satisfies basic needs. An agrarian society relies on labor-intensive agriculture, whereas an industrial society relies on machines and inanimate fuel supplies.

symbolic ethnicity: A sense of ethnicity that is superficial, voluntary, and changeable.

termination: A policy by which all special relationships between the federal government and American Indians would be abolished.

tongs: Secret societies in Chinatowns that sometimes fought with each other and with other organizations over control of resources.

triple melting pot: The idea that structural assimilation for white ethnic immigrants took place within the context of the three major American religions.

urban underclass: The urban lower classes, consisting largely of African Americans and other minority groups of color, which have been more or less permanently barred from the mainstream economy and the primary labor market.

vicious cycle (of prejudice): A process in which a condition (e.g., minority-group inferiority) is assumed to be true, and forces are then set in motion to create and perpetuate that condition.

Yonsei: Fourth-generation Japanese Americans.

Index

About the Authors

Joseph F. Healey is professor emeritus of sociology at Christopher Newport University in Virginia. He received his PhD in sociology and anthropology from the University of Virginia. An innovative and experienced teacher of numerous race and ethnicity courses, he has written articles on minority groups, the sociology of sport, social movements, and violence, and he is also the author of *Statistics: A Tool for Social Research* (10th ed., Cengage, 2015).

Andi Stepnick is a professor of sociology at Belmont University in Tennessee. She earned her PhD from Florida State University. In addition to other publications, she coedited *Disrupting the Culture of Silence: Confronting Gender Inequality and Making Change in Higher Education* with Kris De Welde (Stylus, 2014). She earned Belmont University's 2004 Presidential Faculty Achievement Award for significant contributions to students' intellectual, personal, and professional needs and was named its 2015 Simmons Distinguished Lecturer for excellence in teaching and scholarship.